KU-732-118

BLOOMSBURY GUIDES TO ENGLISH LITERATURE

The Twentieth Century

The Bloomsbury Guides to English Literature

General Editor: Marion Wynne-Davies

Guide to English Renaissance Literature
Marion Wynne-Davies

Guide to Restoration and Augustan Literature
Eva Simmonds

Guide to Romantic Literature
Geoff Ward

Guide to the Novel
Andrew Roberts

BLOOMSBURY GUIDES TO ENGLISH LITERATURE

The Twentieth Century

A Guide to Literature from 1900 to the Present Day

Edited by Linda R. Williams

BLOOMSBURY

This edition published in 1994 by
Bloomsbury Publishing Plc
2 Soho Square, London W1V 6HB

This hardback edition produced
exclusively for The Folio Society

A copy of the CIP entry for this book is available from the British Library.

ISBN 0 7475 2055 0

Typeset by Hewer Text Composition Services, Edinburgh
Printed in England by Clays Ltd, St Ives plc

Contents

Acknowledgements vi

General Editor's Preface vii

Editor's Note viii

Editor's Preface ix

Essay Section

1. Introduction: Writing from modernism to postmodernism 1
   Linda R. Williams
2. Contemporary Approaches to Literature 15
   John Drakakis
3. Culture and Consciousness in the Twentieth-century English Novel 31
   Andrew Roberts
4. Developments in Modern Drama: The Slow Road to Change 53
   Andrew Piasecki
5. 'Rule and Energy in View': The Poetry of Modernity 65
   Linda R. Williams

Reference Section 89

Chronology 327

Acknowledgements

General Editor

Marion Wynne-Davies

Editor

Linda R. Williams

Originator

Christopher Gillie

Contributors

Catherine Byron (Irish Literature) Loughborough College of Art and Design
Edmund Campion (Australian Literature) St Patrick's College, Manly, NSW, Australia
John Drakakis (Critical Theory) University of Stirling
David Jarrett (Science Fiction) Polytechnic of North London
Mark Kermode (Horror Fiction) Journalist
John O'Brien (French Literature) University of Liverpool
Val Pedlar (Context of Literature) University of Liverpool
Andrew Piasecki (Modern Drama) University of London
Andrew Roberts (Modern Novel) University of London
Mercer Simpson (Welsh Literature)
John Thieme (Commonwealth Literatures) University of Hull
Linda R. Williams (Poetry) University of Liverpool

Editorial

Editorial Director Kathy Rooney
Project Editor Tracey Smith

General Editor's Preface

The Bloomsbury guides to English literature derive directly from *The Bloomsbury Guide to English Literature* (1989), and are intended for those readers who wish to look at a specific period or genre, rather than at the wide-ranging material offered in the original text. As such, the guides include material from the larger and earlier work, but they have been updated and supplemented in order to answer the requirements of their particular fields. Each individual editor has selected, edited and authored as the need arose. The acknowledgements appropriate for the individual volumes have been made in the respective editors' prefaces. As general editor I should like to thank all those who have been involved in the project, from its initial conception through to the innovative and scholarly volumes presented in this series.

Marion Wynne-Davies

Editor's Note

Cross references

A liberal use of cross references has been made. In both the essays and the reference entries, names, titles and topics are frequently marked with an arrow (▷) to guide the reader to the appropriate entry in the reference section for a more detailed explanation. Cross-reference arrows appear both in the text and at the end of entries.

Dates

Dates after the names of people indicate their life spans, except when they follow the names of monarchs when they show the length of the reign.

Editor's Preface

This book offers the interested reader a variety of positions on the major genres, forms and influences on 20th-century literature written in English. It is a book with several points of entry and many conclusions. It will, I hope, offer readers with a variety of desires and questions about the literature of the period some satisfaction in itself, and a framework within which to develop further interests and reading. It contains four distinct essays on literary theory, poetry, drama and prose fiction, and a wide range of reference entries giving more specific details of individual authors and works, as well as a number of background pieces on major writers and movements in pre-20th-century periods. The reference entry section, which was compiled by a diverse collection of scholars, stands as a body of information in its own right, enabling each entry to be read as interesting on its own terms, and as a range of contexts within which to situate the essays.

It has been important for me in editing this book to show that 20th-century literature did not come into being in a cultural vacuum, nor did it burst as if from nowhere at the turn of the century. Consequently along with information on the most obvious 20th-century writers, I have included entries on key pre-20th-century writers and thinkers whose influence requires that they be included as necessary to an understanding of work in this century, as well as on writers, works and movements emerging from other cultures than that of the British mainland. Of those who write or wrote in English, some have been included because their work is characterized as part of the vast body of 'Commonwealth literatures', writing produced in cultures which, having undergone the transition from colonial rule by Britain to independence, have nevertheless remained English-speaking. Many of these writers are to some extent concerned with the legacy of imperialism their countries are working through.

However, this book does not pretend to cover exhaustively all literatures in English, and in particular it is not concerned with American writing. I have included references to American authors when either their influence on certain aspects of British writing has been particularly strong, or when much of their work has focused on European culture. The more obvious examples of classic modernist writers whose original American identity became fully submerged into British culture or even British citizenship – the cases of, say, Henry James, Ezra Pound, H.D., or T.S. Eliot – obviously need no explanation. These figures emphasize the shrinking of the pond which has accompanied modern writing. Other choices were more difficult and therefore necessarily more subjective: both Djuna Barnes and Henry Miller, for instance, focused important writing energy on Paris bohemianism, both rejected a narrow image of cultural identity, both drew on European Surrealism, and both returned to America after living and writing for a long time in Europe. Barnes has, for various reasons, been a more difficult figure for students to find out about than the ubiquitous Miller, and she seems to me to be one of the best illustrations of Virginia Woolf's dictum: 'as a woman I have no country . . . As a woman my country is the whole world', and hence I have claimed her for this book, whilst leaving the better-known Miller out, along with a large range of his contemporaries.

On the other hand, I was also keen to include new work on less 'respectable' genres, such as science fiction and popular romance, which are often excluded from other more canon-oriented reference books. This book aims to redress several balances, in that it includes writers whose work has been excluded from the canon in a number of ways. There are many ways of justifying marginalization of a writer or a work, and I have tried to represent voices here which have been hitherto silenced in texts such as this for a variety of reasons. New writings in English from post-colonial countries, sometimes referred to here as 'Commonwealth literatures', are included as much as space would allow. Little-known women writers, or writers working in 'unrespectable' genres or dealing with transgressive issues are discussed. There are entries on some popular romantic novelists, background entries on detective writing, horror and science fiction, and some more informative individual entries on major writers working in these genres whose work has exercised a profound influence on British writers even though they themselves are not British. American horror writer Stephen King, New Zealand detective writer Ngaio Marsh, or Canadian novelist Margaret Atwood are all examples of writers who are included for specific reasons, whilst other, perhaps more famous, non-British writers have been left out. Whilst their nationality should exclude them, their influence in Britain in recent years on writers working in new genres needs to be accounted for. As with all texts of this type, finally choices are personal and anomalies remain, although I have tried to be consistent and clear.

Extra entries for this edition were supplied by Mark Kermode, Andrew Roberts and myself. I would like to thank Dr Kermode for his help in the production of this book as well as Marion Wynne-Davies and Tracey Smith at Bloomsbury for their rigorous and sympathetic editing.

This book is dedicated to Irene, George and Derrick Williams.

Essay section

Introduction: Writing from modernism to postmodernism

1

Linda R. Williams
University of Liverpool

> They last a second, a minute, they come and go like a moving winking light; but they have impressed their mark, deposited some kind of sensation before they vanished . . . Secret stirrings that go unnoticed in the remote parts of the mind, the incalculable chaos of impressions, the delicate life of the imagination seen under the magnifying glass; the random progress of these thoughts and feelings; untrodden, trackless journeying of brain and heart, strange workings of the nerves, the whisper of the blood, the entreaty of the bone, all the unconscious life of the mind . . .

Who speaks here, in this quotation written in 1890? Is this the statement of a peculiarly poetic psychologist, outlining the territory with which an embryonic psychoanalysis is to concern itself? Are these the ravings of an eloquent madman, the patient or subject of the analysis itself? It may seem strange to begin a book on 20th-century writing in English with a statement in translation, written by a Norwegian writer (Knut Hamsun, in 'From the Unconscious Life of the Mind') in the late 19th century. Curiouser and curiouser, it doesn't appear to be a particularly 'literary' passage at all, but rather an ephemeral account of a mind subject to (what French poet Arthur Rimbaud embraced as) 'the systematic disordering of the senses', quoted perhaps as evidence in a psychoanalytic case history written up to demonstrate the processes of derangement.

If this does not seem to be a fitting subject for literature to encounter, then the image and interpretation of 20th-century writing which this book offers should challenge that notion, along with the idea that a century's writing begins with the beginning of a century. As this book will also show, with modern writing things seldom begin when or where they're supposed to begin; moreover the very notion of beginnings and endings becomes questionable with some of the century's most radical works (as ▷ D.H. Lawrence writes, 'In the beginning – there never was any beginning'), which might loop back into themselves, Finnegan-like, beginning again in defiance of any final full stop. Indeed, ▷ James Joyce's ▷ *Finnegans Wake* actually does 'end' like this, the opening sentence being the completion of the final one, the final sentence thus turning the reader back to the start of the work again. With such challenging material in its scope, this book must offer an alternative set of boundaries and definitions which also show the origins of the century's important work in cultures and aesthetic centres quite other than that of mainland Britain, beginning, it seems, at any moment other than the turning of the year – 1900. For many, 20th-century literature begins in the mid- to late 19th century, particularly with the influence of French ▷ Symbolism; for others, like ▷ Virginia Woolf, 'in or about December

1910, human character changed', and with it forms of writing, and what is written, changed too.

This change – the 'shock of the new' – emphasized most starkly the power of *difference*, both in the sense of the mark of difference gouged into literary history by many of the writings discussed below (the difference of an innovative 'now' from a conventional 'then'), and in the sense of difference*s* within texts and subjects explored and opened up by a range of modern visions: the *self*-divisions of the painfully alienated or exuberantly 'post-impressionist' subject (like Hamsun), or the *sexual* differences of new literary voices deliberately challenging taboos concerning what can be written or who it can be written by. The former is the 'private' division within, of a self which betrays its own self-differences, which displays in language the ways in which it is divided or different from itself; using the perception of this inner division creatively, modern writers thus set about making the 'self' into the intricate object of its own scrutiny. The latter realm of difference – we might call it the 'public' differences of 20th-century writing from previous periods – made possible most strikingly by modern writing might be, respectively, transgressive writers who were keen to challenge sexual censorship laws (like D.H. Lawrence), or women writers who seized upon ▷ modernism as a formally revolutionary movement in writing. The space opened up for writers by the sense that now, artistically speaking, there is 'no map' (in the words of poet ▷ H.D., quoted in my essay on poetry below) promoted forms of women's writing which fitted closer to women's different experiences. In Virginia Woolf's phrase (writing about novelist ▷ Dorothy Richardson), what could (and should) at last be written was 'the psychological sentence of the feminine gender'. Less specifically, the writing project set out so energetically by novelists and critics such as Woolf shows modern writing to be driven by a democratic desire to listen to, use, and give voice to a variety of inner and outer selves and influences. Marking the difference between 'Modern Fiction' (the title of the essay from which this quotation comes) and older forms, she writes,

> . . . there is no limit to the horizon, and . . . nothing – no 'methods', no experiment, even of the wildest – is forbidden, but only falsity and pretense. 'The proper stuff of fiction' does not exist; everything is the proper stuff of fiction, every feeling, every thought; every quality of brain and spirit is drawn upon; no perception comes amiss. And if we could imagine the art of fiction come alive and standing in our midst, she would undoubtedly bid us break her and bully her, as well as honour and love her, for so her youth is renewed and her sovereignty assured.

This sense of use and abuse, of working with, whilst radically subverting and overthrowing, the power of traditions – the working material one has inherited – characterizes the image of 20th-century writing which this book conveys. It will be the work of this introduction to trace some of these innovative 'differences', by identifying in brief the clearest hallmarks of early and 'classic' modernism, before outlining the importance of ▷ postmodernism as the primary late 20th-century movement, in order to give readers a simple frame upon which they can map their own readings of individual writers and texts, and a way into the specific discussions of ▷ genre and theory which take place in the essays below.

Earlier in 'Modern Fiction' Woolf offers what is possibly a more familiar (because English) image of the modern obsession with the intricacies of the mind than Knut Hamsun's epigraph to this introduction. Whilst the essay is a response to James Joyce's ▷ *Ulysses*, one of the most striking things a reader of modernist work who is used to the conventions of classic realist characterizations will notice is that modern characters constantly contradict themselves; they are guided more by irrational betrayals than by rational purposefulness, through plots in which nothing very much happens. Woolf celebrates this:

> Look within and life, it seems, is very far from being 'like this'. Examine for a moment an ordinary mind on an ordinary day. The mind receives a myriad of impressions – trivial, fantastic, evanescent, or engraved with the sharpness of steel. From all sides they come, an incessant shower of innumerable atoms; and as they fall, as they shape themselves into the life of Monday or Tuesday, the accent falls differently from of old; the moment of importance came not here but there . . . Life is not a series of gig lamps symmetrically arranged; life is a luminous halo, a semi-transparent envelope surrounding us from the beginning of consciousness to the end.

It is this sense of the plenitude of possible images and experiences which any moment of life has the power to offer, a kaleidoscope of contradictions revealed by simply looking in a new way, which modernism most obviously explores. Woolf is careful to show that this complex, impressionistic, endlessly rewarding subject (the *human* subject) is there for everyone to explore, and find: the grand passions, cosmic paradoxes and psychological intricacies, which in previous literary eras were seen to be the preserve of the heroes of individualism, become democratized with modernism: 'the ordinary mind on an ordinary day' is precisely the proper subject of writing – and this is, indeed, exactly what *Ulysses* presents, one day in the life of Leopold Bloom, ordinary, if exemplary, Dublin citizen.

In his essay below, Andrew Roberts emphasizes the diverse roots of the modernist novel by situating 20th-century developments in the context of the influences of the mid-19th-century novel. What Woolf characterizes as the 'old' form, the 'symmetrically arranged' dictates of a ▷ realism in which 'the accent falls differently', had to be challenged, and it is this challenge which characterizes other innovative forms of modern writing (not just the novel). In prose, the realist tradition – deploying an omniscient narrator, forms of characterization which gloss over 'myriad impressions' in favour of more coherent behaviour patterns, and a sequential narrative structure which orders and forces chaotic reality into a neat chronology – was subverted by radical novelistic techniques which allowed and encouraged other forms of representation, or eschewed the notion of fiction as representation altogether.

With modernism, narrators cease to be reliable, let alone all-seeing; but what they do choose to see they look at with a microscopic vision and a sense of relativity. As the essays in this book will show, the literature of this century is almost by definition recalcitrant, refusing rules of subject, coherence and accessibility in an incessant project of experimentation. Even the literature which *doesn't* do this, preferring to stick with the givens and known qualities of, say, classic realism in the novel or strict poetic versification, is paradoxically perverse in that it is forced in its conformity to older literary models to react against innovations. Rebellion is the rule, even if you want to be conventional.

Perhaps the 20th century is a century of black sheep, with the very few white ones becoming the odd ones out. Literary criticism often likes to portray the history of writing rather like a family tree, with paths of influence traced like paths of generational lineage, so that disagreements of subject matter or style, or formal rebellions against established modes of writing, are consequently read as family feuds or children's challenges to parental authority. If this is so, then in this century the family has become heterogeneous, obsessed with forging new paths in what is writable, formally (as with, say, *Finnegans Wake*) and morally (as with, say, D.H. Lawrence's sexually explicit ▷ *Lady Chatterley's Lover*), thus losing sight of literary 'normality'. In an attenuated moment which modernism traces to the mid to late 19th century, high Victorian writing (classic realism in the novel, conventionally versified or narrative poetry, both issuing a general sense that writing is and should represent a shared social, material and spiritual reality) mutated into something quite other than itself. Modernist writing – formally self-referential, difficult, often obscure, obsessed with looking at itself in the mirror of itself – is in a sense the abnormal child of a literary parentage more wholesomely concerned with accessible 'content' – conventional linear plot structures and characters who, as D.H. Lawrence puts it, behave 'according to a pattern'. For Lawrence, the 'dead' novel of the past needs to be revived with a shot of spontaneity; characters need the injection of change, and changeability, and it is this which past work was seen as unable to incorporate. Characters, then, are like lovers:

> If the one I love remains unchanged and unchanging, I shall cease to love her. It is only because she changes and startles me and defies my inertia, and is herself staggered in her inertia by my changing, that I can continue to love her. If she stayed put, I might as well love the pepper-pot.
>
> ('Why the Novel Matters')

Thus Lawrence and his diverse contemporaries set about wresting the novel from the inertia he describes, by producing characters who 'change and startle' their readers, who do not, as he famously wrote in a letter to Edward Garnett, conform to 'the old stable ego . . . of the character', thus representing a more dynamic sense of subjectivity. Literature embraced the world of relativity and defied a literary past too firmly gripped by 'absolutes':

> Once and for ever, let us have done with the ugly imperialism of any absolute.

> There is no absolute good, there is nothing absolutely right. All things flow and change, and even change is not absolute. The whole is a strange assembly of apparently incongruous parts, slipping past one another.
>
> ('Why the Novel Matters')

Although one strategy employed by many of the arguments and observations in this book is the setting up of modern writing against and in contrast to its past, the writers here do not presume to suggest that these images of the past – of realist fiction, or of Victorian poetry – are in fact right or accurate. It is not the aim of this present book to suggest that modernism's image of Victorianism is a true reflection of the previous century at all, but rather that many of the familiar images of Victorian writing which we might unthinkingly work with were set up for a variety of interesting reasons by modernist writers, deliberately through written polemics (such as ▷ Ezra Pound's 'A Few Don'ts by an Imagiste'; ▷ Imagism, discussed in my essay on poetry below) or used unconsciously and by implication, as necessary points of opposition. Victorian writing *needed* to be characterized as accessible, realist and psychologically coherent, so that disparate modernist writers interested in doing something quite different could have a firm point of disagreement with a past set up as a springboard into the future. I am not concerned here with challenging the early 20th-century image of the 19th century – it would be the job of one introducing readers to the complexities, the playfulness, the psychological paradoxes of Victorian writing to show how in reality it contradicts cherished modern illusions about Victorian certainty and coherence – although it is true that any discussion of modern writing may gesture toward this implied image of the previous period. However, whatever can be demonstrated as the properties of modernism's ancestry, it is nevertheless true that the avant-garde, the experimental, the transgressive have dominated this century's important works, and consequently the 'family line' has become rather twisted. To both use and subvert the traditional language of literary inheritance, it could be said that 20th-century writing is the mutant child of the 19th century. Following the path of exemplary black sheep ▷ Oscar Wilde, modernism and postmodernism have celebrated a freedom from the need to represent morally a shared image of reality:

> The final revelation is that lying, the telling of beautiful untrue things, is the proper aim of art.
>
> (*The Decay of Lying*)

The powerful perversity of this is important (and Wilde is a writer who takes perversity seriously): what is being heralded is the disruption of the realist relationship between a thing in the world and its literary representation. There need be no direct link between literature and life; indeed, the more that literature fantasizes, and cuts itself adrift from 'real events', the more 'literary' its final effect will be.

The impact of this active project to free writing from the need to represent a shared, ideal image of the world has been profound. Wilde's outrageous celebration of 'beautiful untrue things' sets the tone for a century in which what has decayed is not the art of fantasy but the more characteristically 'past' literary values which produced accessible stories, recognizable images of 'normal' reality and rational and integrated characters who move through a linear narrative with a sense of moral purpose. It's not just that there are no more happy endings, but that the endgame is often a preface, or a novel might end with a question which looks like a beginning, and so endings and beginnings cannot be found where you expect them to be, and nor can they be trusted to sit neatly in place. The reader of modern writing may often feel that she or he is being seduced into playing a game for which the rules are being written as the game proceeds. Novels can be plotless, plays can be written in which nothing happens, narrative poetry gives way to introspective or plainly nonsensical lyric poetry or 'free verse'. As Lawrence, again, has written, 'Never trust the artist, trust the tale. / As for the artist, he's usually a dribbling liar'. And since the writer here is himself an artist, this must be read as a literary version of that pop-philosophy paradox, the statement 'I am lying'. Who, in this century of perverse nonsense-speakers and rule-breakers, can we trust?

Perhaps all this at least accounts for some of the difficulty which many readers find in getting to grips with modern writing, but it also accounts for modern writing's playfulness and exuberant sense of fun. With Joyce's wordplays, ▷ Beckett's puns, ▷ Surrealism's uncanny juxtapositions of images which betray playful and sick humour by turns, ▷ Djuna Barnes's parodic, tragicomic jibes at sexual roles, the reader who braves the initial inaccessibility is offered the rewards of pleasure. It is also unfortunately true, however, that this century has seen a decline in popularity for many writing forms, and this is particularly the case with poetry, the avant-garde tendencies of modernism alienating the formerly large poetry-reading public. As John Drakakis outlines below in his essay on critical theory, dramatist ▷ Bertolt Brecht (arguably the century's dramatic mentor) celebrates the estranging powers of literature on similar lines to those marked out by the critical school of Russian ▷ Formalism, but the effect of this on readers and audiences has not been popular. 'Literariness', however, was not invented by the modernists, and modernism's consolidation or celebration of this formal self-consciousness has been famously traced back to the writings of many of this century's more eccentric, or else more untimely, literary ancestors. For instance, when Laurence Sterne draws a series of lines on the pages of *Tristram Shandy* (1760–67) as a comic visual representation of its narrative journey, one of the things that he is doing is making his readers conscious of the fact that they are reading a fiction, not a transparent or unmediated representation of a series of real events. The novel is a twisted and elaborate narrative of things which never existed, and Sterne's comic self-consciousness draws attention to the fact that the text *is a text*, a work of playful fiction which we should be prevented from 'losing ourselves' in. Amongst other things, modernism is the moment in literary history when this tendency becomes dominant. To put it crudely but clearly, form is all: as Beckett wrote about Joyce, 'His writing is not about something, it is that something itself'.

John Drakakis develops this below by showing how Brecht's *Verfremdungseffekt* (▷ alienation effect) is akin to this, in that it overtly portrays on the stage the fact that the play being performed is a work of artifice, rather than a simple representation of reality to which the audience can sacrifice its critical faculties. Brecht wanted to keep his audience sharp, self-aware and conscious of the processes through which the play is being constructed before its very eyes. This self-consciousness – also one of the hallmarks of modernist *fiction* – may have produced challenging works of invention, but it has not necessarily produced a pleasurable spectacle or read. Where the art of lying has perhaps stayed alive most obviously is in the popular forms of ▷ science fiction, fantasy and ▷ horror, in which a carnivalesque 'world turned upside down' is elaborated in a plenitude of directions. In a contemporary confirmation of Lawrence's point, horror writer ▷ Stephen King alchemically turns lying back into truth again when he argues that 'the primary duty of literature' is 'to tell us the truth about ourselves by telling us lies about people who never existed' (*Danse Macabre*).

If one thing is clear so far, it is that modern literature is knotted with paradoxes, with counter-intuitive 'truths'. This is the case even when we attempt to understand its provenance and first principles. However, this book is to some extent a work of literary history, and it is our job to trace a map of the century's literature, to give a fairly coherent range of intellectual co-ordinates as a rough guide to the literary century. The beginning of a century is not necessarily the century's *literary* beginning. It could, for instance, be argued that modernist writing actually began well into the century itself, and was engendered, was given its first breath, by war: English modernism emerged in its clearest form during the vast conflict of World War I, which gave the first kick to literary and artistic forms self-consciously characterizing themselves as 'modern' rather than 'Victorian'. It is strange that world-scale death can be understood as giving life to the creative arts. It is also strange that whilst the world was being torn in two by the divisive allegiances of the war, so modernism was becoming a cosmopolitan literary and artistic form, with its centres across Europe (and to some extent in America) staked out in defiance of enemy lines. This is not, however, to say that the arts propounded a spirit of creative harmony in a crazed world. For D.H. Lawrence, World War I intensified what Frank Kermode has called his 'apocalyptic vision'; though married to a German and physically prevented from travelling to Germany, Lawrence would at least applaud the conflict from the sidelines, not patriotically but because for him the war had the potential to sweep away the cobwebs of old worlds: 'We ought to be grateful to Germany that she still has the power to burst the bound hide of the cabbage' (*Study of Thomas Hardy*). On a different note, as philosopher and film theorist Paul Virilio has persuasively argued (in *War and Cinema*), the rise of cinema – this century's major new art form, which has had a profound and fascinating inter-relationship with literature – is intimately bound up with the development of military technology.

Another problem with definitions of this century's work in English lies in our understanding of the word 'English' itself. This book reflects the cosmopolitanism of early modernism and the multiculturalism of postmodernism in its liberal range of reference entries on writers and influences from other countries and languages. The essays also show how the century's key works were part of a wider philosophy of boundary-challenging, which has caused critics such as ▷ Marxist writer Georg Lukács to describe (particularly in *Theory of the Novel*) the modern sensibility as 'metaphysically homeless' or 'nomadic'. With the advent of modernism, literature written in English ceased to be anchored to the English landscape: Paris, Berlin, Munich, all were centres of English culture equal to London and Dublin. The battle *against* the primacy of an English literature rooted in a wholesome and parochial English landscape was *not* fought on the playing-fields of Eton, but in Berlin bars and Paris studios. This book aims to give readers a framework within which they can enjoy and understand writing this century, writing which the essays below align with the dominant but loose movements of modernism and postmodernism, and the recalcitrant writings which actively refuse to be categorized. Recent literature has had to work in a world of increased secularization and mass communications, and this too has contributed to a challenging of boundaries, both in terms of how we label (or value) works, and in terms of where those works originally situated themselves. If modernist 'wandering' promoted an inter-cultural sensibility which deployed the voices of a variety of disciplines and cultures, postmodernism radicalizes this in a rampant disregard for the integrity of the original forms it draws upon.

Late modernism and postmodernism

The initial sense of fragmentation produced by the modernistic challenge to the idea that literature written in a particular language had to be bound to a particular land or range of cultural givens was only the first step in a century-long movement. The rise of radical nationalist movements in Britain's colonial dependencies did much to change the literary map. The consequent decline of Britain's colonial hold over other parts of the world, the freer movement of people between cultures and particularly the explosion of mass communications have all made the world a smaller place. Air travel, even space travel, radio and satellite technology, computer languages – all have promoted contact between cultures and have subverted our previous sense of a specific cultural identity deriving from nationality. It is fitting that this technology should be the result of warfare; just as in military terms wars have raged in defence of national boundaries, so the two world wars have produced the means to subvert cultural boundaries.

It is the resultant sense of cultural collage which characterizes both modernism and postmodernism. If World War I prompted writers to range across the world, embracing Lukács's sense of cultural nomadism just as individual nations were closing down borders, so World War II signalled the further explosion of mass communications and the dawn of the nuclear age, and post-war literature responds to and works necessarily in the context of the resulting world-historic anxiety. What is now known as postmodernism, however, has emerged more recently for different historical and artistic reasons. The term 'postmodernism' covers a variety of disparate and often contradictory literary and cultural movements and impulses. The term itself suggests a reaction against modernism. This is only partially true, however; for many critics there are few differences between modern and postmodern writers, so much so that for some readers certain classic modernist texts exemplify, perhaps more than many postmodern ones, the postmodernist way of operating. ▷ T.S. Eliot's ▷ *The Waste Land*, for instance, deploys quotation and references from a vast collage of other texts, and one of its more unsettling qualities is the way that voices within it are at times subjectively unclear: it's hard to tell when one 'self' finishes speaking and another begins. This sense that boundaries are being constantly subverted in the poem, as subjects flow into each other or are uneasily juxtaposed, is a key postmodern motif, as well as a modern one.

However, there is a sense in which the fragmentary bits of the poem finally 'add up' to an organic conclusion, a final moment of unity and peace which causes the poem to turn back on itself, so that its early fragments are reworked and homogenized into the final whole. Postmodernism emerged at a chaotic but exhilarating time in history – the 1960s – to challenge this process of *homogenization*. By the 1960s, the radical impulses of modernism which I outlined above, which fought *against* the self-satisfaction of high Victorianism, had been appropriated by the established system, its fragmented possibilities assimilated into a great tradition of 'artistic genius' by the growing forces of Leavisite criticism (▷ F.R. Leavis) and ▷ New Criticism. Crucially, the period from about 1930 onwards not only signalled the end of the most intensive modernist production, it was also the period in which English literature began to be studied more widely in its own right in the universities of Britain. The literature which had so excited the new young critics – who from the early 1930s onwards were establishing the terms of academic literary criticism – was to become fossilized as the final moment of cultural production worthy of study. T.S. Eliot was both one of the key poets to figure on the new syllabuses as eminently respectable, and also one of the critics who was writing the rules of the game. D.H. Lawrence had been a notorious figure for his radical and explicit descriptions of sexuality, but as a favourite of F.R. Leavis his work soon found a place as a key prop to the Leavisite canon which was to dominate the study of literature at both secondary and degree levels. In the 1960s, a new generation of writers and students reacted against the sanitization of the previously shocking forms of modernism, and sought other creative forms which were strong or bizarre enough to resist actively any re-evaluation in the wholesome, unifying terms of Leavis. *The Waste Land* may pass through an agonizing, disparate struggle, shoring fragments 'against my ruins', but it seems to conclude with all the loose ends neatly tied. Against this, in Marxist critic Fredric Jameson's terms, a composer such as John Cage offers a disharmony which cannot resolve itself into harmony. Cage's 'disconnection and fragmentation' is, for Jameson, 'related to the way we describe a text today as the production of discontinuous sentences without any larger unifying forms'. Thus *The Waste Land*, upon which critics have spent an inordinate amount of time demonstrating how its 'larger unifying forms' gather together its 'discontinuous sentences', is modernist, and that which deliberately sets out to disrupt or disavow those unities is postmodernist. Postmodernism thus takes the modernist rejection of sequential plots and develops an aesthetics of the instantaneous, of the unoriginal, of the plagiarized.

Like modernism, which had its manifesto, as I have indicated, in Pound's 'A Few Don'ts . . .', postmodernism is often defined in negative terms: as Jameson again says, 'it isn't this, it isn't that, it isn't a whole series of things that modernism was'. Reaction against the previous moment has characterized its progress, but like modernism it also has positive qualities. Critics disagree on what these are exactly, however. For instance, the postmodern technique of showing how a thing works before you show what it is – display one's formal heart on one's sleeve, as it were – is for some also evident in modernist writing. As with modernism, postmodernism is an interdisciplinary form: it is a movement in art, sculpture, music, film and architecture just as much as in writing. Indeed, in as much as postmodernism is concerned with breaking down the boundaries between disciplines, an extreme postmodernist would disregard these distinguishing generic terms. Some modernist texts play out and play with the collapse of traditional distinctions between high and low culture in a way which has been seen to be politically radical: for instance, James Joyce's novels actively incorporate speech idioms from working-class life in Dublin, or credit dream-imagery and irrational motifs with as much value as rational representation and discourse. For postmodernism, this collapse is taken to be an absolute, so that even the distinction between high and low culture becomes meaningless. As Andrew Ross, quoting Dirk Hebdige, has written:

> . . . postmodern can be used today to refer to:
> the decor of a room, the design of a building, the diegesis of a film, the construction of a record, or a 'scratch' video, a TV commercial, or an arts documentary, or the 'intertextual' relations between them, the layout of a page in a fashion magazine or a critical journal . . . the attack on the 'metaphysics of presence' . . . the collective chagrin and morbid projections of a post-War generation of Baby Boomers confronting disillusioned middle age . . . a proliferation of surfaces, a new phase in commodity fetishism, a fascination for 'images', codes and styles . . . the 'implosion of meaning', the collapse of cultural hierarchies, the dread engendered by the threat of nuclear self-destruction, the decline of the University . . .
>
> (*Universal Abandon*)

At its most extreme, postmodern writing is populated with a variety of voices, quoted or plagiarized from 'intertextual' sources to give a sense of difference and disruption, a deliberate disturbance of organic, unified representations of world or psyche, or a wider patchwork of borrowings from different genres and discourses. Postmodernism is parody and pastiche; if modernism actively makes links between disciplines, encouraging a cosmopolitanism of subject, a borrowing and connecting of ideas across an interdisciplinary network, then postmodernism transgresses this too, often flagrantly plagiarizing rather than playfully quoting and borrowing. Eliot may produce a careful collage of borrowed writings which are respectfully acknowledged, but for 1980s writer Kathy Acker past texts are there to be plundered wholesale, to the extent of copying out passages from Dickens and turning favourite authors into fictional characters to be manipulated by the whims of the plot.

However, it would be extremely misleading to offer an image of 20th-century writing as conforming to a single set of points or qualities, just as using the umbrella terms 'modernism' and 'postmodernism' to characterize all the significant works and literary movements of this century would be unhelpfully exclusive. ▷ Doris Lessing's *The Golden Notebook* is a good example of many of these techniques, although argument about where to situate it continues. It constantly draws attention to itself as a text; the heroine, Anna, is a novelist, and struggles with herself as creator in the production of five disparate notebooks which claim to 'represent' herself in various ways, but which also display themselves as material texts, and show the process of the construction of the novel as a whole. When we read each of the notebooks, which trace different aspects of Anna's past and present (such as her life in Africa or her involvement with the Commmunist Party or the 'life' of one of her characters, Ella), we are also simultaneously aware of the notebook as a material object, which has rested on a desk as the other narratives in the book have been played out. One of the notebooks disintegrates as Anna's psyche does under analysis, changing from a personal diary form to a 'diary' composed of newspaper cuttings which tell the story of national events, on a large and a trivial scale. The reader is invited to connect the historical narrative which this produces with the subjective narrative which Anna cannot speak, but the words themselves are just snippets and fragments, which display the processes through which they were edited and chosen.

The Golden Notebook does also, however, place itself within a realist tradition, because the five notebooks – black, red, yellow, blue and golden – are punctuated by sections (entitled 'Free Women') dealing much more conventionally with the events of Anna's life in the 'present' of the novel. This technique is also characteristic of the resurgence of accessible, realist post-war writing, which developed in parallel with the more popular poetry and drama of the period, discussed by myself and by Andrew Piasecki in the essays below. In fact, *The Golden Notebook* as a whole is best known as 'the Bible of the ▷ Women's Movement', a proto-feminist novel and one of the major post-war texts to represent actively its heroine's personal struggle as a political one, and vice versa, thus working through the feminist dictum coined sometime later, 'The Personal is the Political'. However, this motto in itself – which was taken up by many women in the 1960s and the 1970s as a call to consciousness-raising – is in many ways a postmodernist statement. When the boundary between 'inside' and 'outside' breaks down, or when the interconnection of subjective state and material conditions is recognized in art in a particular way, the methods of postmodernism come into play.

As is clear from this brief survey, the word 'play' used in this and in many other senses continues to be operative. Many of the texts discussed in this book are characterized more by the aesthetic *tendencies* of modernism or postmodernism than by genuine allegiance to an '-ism': they play with categories, using or ignoring them. Few could be called fully paid-up members of either 'movement'. Indeed, a polemical attempt at resisting general or totalizing categories has often been at the heart of the works and movements discussed here. It might, for instance, be helpful in one way to erect a signpost and call James Joyce's *Finnegans Wake* a modernist novel, but doing so simultaneously creates a smokescreen which might prevent us from looking creatively at the ways in which it *isn't* a 'novel' in the conventional sense, or at the ways in which *as* a novel it actively challenges and breaks open the novel form. The obvious fact that *Finnegans Wake* largely resists categories – including the category 'modernist' – is one of the things which paradoxically makes it a modernist work. The same could be said of any work we might label modernist or postmodernist: to do either is to ignore or repress the ways that literary works do as much to disrupt creatively the categories critics want to fit them into as they do to sit still in those boxes. It is one of the qualities of both modernism and postmodernism to challenge totalizing labels *per se*.

The essays: interpretation and literary movements

Literary history, like family history, is a question of how you tell it. Modern perspectives on literature counter the traditional notion that critical judgements are made through an ideal process of evaluation and emotional response, both ostensibly disregarding the processes of power; as John Drakakis writes below, 'the history of literary criticism offers many varied ways of reading: . . . how you interpret texts depends upon who is "master".' *Who* decides the patterns of literary history, and *what* has made them decide that, are questions that need to be opened up by anyone hoping to set out a fresh image of the developments of 20th-century writing.

This book offers such an image in composite through its genre essays and references, but it does not claim to escape the responsibilities which come with offering another map of modern literature. All of the essays here are more or less chronological, and all to some extent stress the violence done across this century when new writers seek to overthrow the aesthetic priorities of the old, in ways which some critics have seen as analogous to family history. My essay on the chain of poetic movements, sparked off by the initial modernist revolt against Victorianism and ▷ Georgianism, perpetuates this sense that writers often work with a strong desire to rebel against prior movements. Just as relationships between the members of families are made real by the stories that people weave around themselves and each other, so critics narrate the links and lines between writers, and turn a disparate mass of texts written across a range of historical periods into an ostensibly coherent network of relationships. Whoever tells the story is thus able to privilege certain moments, to single out 'significant' texts, to create relationships persuasively as patterns. Criticism fills in the gaps, forges the links between writers and makes connections across the writing generations, connections which look like family relationships; it traces who has influenced whom, which writings echo, repeat, or defy past works, which texts 'behave' according to the current conventions, which texts 'misbehave' and become the celebrated black sheep. Pointing out resemblances, literary criticism remembers and explains the arguments, how new generations of writing come into being, and it looks at the need for texts to argue and fall out with each other, the necessity of disagreement, refutation and contradiction between texts of different periods, differences which make new writings possible.

This position is most famously articulated by Harold Bloom in *The Anxiety of Influence*, although his is perhaps most importantly a consolidation of a multitude of positions taken across literary history. When F.R. Leavis traces a 'Great Tradition' of English novelists, he is claiming them as part of an authentic literary lineage – an elite descendancy of influence. ▷ Raymond Williams countered the Leavis lineage with his own alternative Marxist tradition, whilst feminist critics Sandra Gilbert and Susan Gubar followed both Bloom and Virginia Woolf in tracing a tradition of women writers who 'think back through their literary mothers' (after Woolf's statement 'We think back through our mothers if we are women'). Criticism has thus organized literary history metaphorically. Because Western-style family structures in a sense prototypically mark out relationships between individuals with common characteristics, or who, from shared assumptions and influences, strive to individuate themselves from their origins, these family structures have become the dominant pattern critics have imposed upon our literary heritage. It is perhaps unfortunate that even the most radical critics still represent literary movements in terms of familial metaphors. Feminists who otherwise advocate a politics which would open to question all patriarchal structures, including that of the traditional family unit, have nevertheless created an alternative literary lineage which sees patterns of influence as running between older generations of writing 'mothers' and younger women writers who become literary 'daughters'. Whilst most feminist critics seem to want to stress the non-violent continuity of this matrilineage, male critics working since Harold Bloom sometimes use a Freudian model to stress the violence of development. Distinct movements are seen as rejections of and reactions against the past, so that all innovations are deemed to be the reactions of literary adolescence, the efforts of younger writers keen to move on to something new.

All this is to say that more recent writings, as the essays below demonstrate, freely deploy techniques from a wide range of cultures and genres in their urge to inscribe differences. But marking differences has worked in tandem with the apparently contrary action of breaking down boundaries. As John Drakakis discusses in his essay on critical theory below, interpretations are powerfully determined by material factors which will prioritize different issues for different readers. Drakakis's account of the main movements of critical theory this century is included here not simply to supplement the genre-based essays, but as an account in its own right of a body of 20th-century writing which has an increasingly high profile on English syllabuses, as part of the wider discipline of English studies. Indeed, it is becoming increasingly difficult to distinguish between critically 'knowing' fictional texts and new forms of theory which are self-consciously 'literary'.

This tendency to challenge boundaries has been expressed in different forms in different genres. Andrew Roberts highlights, for instance, the importance of the ▷ stream of consciousness technique which enabled novelists to explore a more intense psychological 'realism' such as that suggested in my epigraphs by Woolf and by Hamsun. Modernism in this form disrupts the conventional discrepancy between inside and outside, in which a more or less coherent interior monologue is finally distinguishable from the 'externals' of social and material reality 'out there'. As I have begun to suggest here, and as Roberts develops below, modern writers show how in the psychological reality of character and narrator, subject and object are interrelated or, at extreme moments, indistinguishable. This sense of the interdependence of subject and object is also a primary concern for modern poets, which I discuss also in my essay on poetry. And, as Roberts argues, the rise of other powerful genres such as science fiction and fantasy writing has also problematized the notion of literature as directly representational. More recently, horror fiction, a late 20th-century version of the Gothic novel, has embraced the fantastic and the macabre possibilities of English prose, if not the linguistic pyrotechnics explored by modernists. In drama, a history of spectacular artistic and political experiment has unfolded despite the material circumstances of shameful underfunding, a factor which underpins Andrew Piasecki's history of the developments of British theatre. Experiment, and the forward-movement which embraces differences in a variety of ways, clearly drive many of the literary forms with which this book concerns itself. In a century of work which is marked by a reluctance to stay still, even nostalgia or the counter-modernism of, say, the ▷ Movement poets of the 1950s, has, ironically, been 'progressive'. Looking back in anger or in pastiche or assimilation of the past, writers have deployed nostalgia for lost forms in a way which has seldom been debilitating.

Contemporary Approaches to Literature 2

John Drakakis
University of Stirling

Introduction

'I don't know what you mean by "glory",' Alice said.

Humpty Dumpty smiled contemptuously. 'Of course you don't – till I tell you. I meant "there's a nice knock-down argument for you!"'

'But "glory" doesn't mean a "nice knock-down argument",' Alice objected.

'When I *use a word,' Humpty Dumpty said in rather a scornful tone, 'it means just what I choose it to mean – neither more nor less.'*

'The question is,' said Alice, 'whether you can *make words mean different things.'*

'The question is,' said Humpty Dumpty, 'which is to be master – that's all.'

(*Through the Looking-Glass and What Alice Found There*, Lewis Carroll)

The contemporary reader entering the field of critical theory for the first time must often feel a little like Alice passing through the looking-glass. Up until this point he or she has, with few questions, accepted that words have fixed meanings and that language is a simple and accurate reflection of reality. But Humpty's total disregard for commonly accepted practices and his anarchic and subjective use of words present us with a text so bizarre that we cannot relate it to our own experience. The first thing we must learn, like Alice, is that language cannot mirror reality. As the story continues, Humpty goes on to teach Alice that, contrary to her expectations, language itself can construct meaning. He does this by trying to make sense of the poem 'Jabberwocky' and, at first, his efforts are founded on logical criteria: '"*Brillig*" means four o'clock in the afternoon – the time when you begin *broiling* things for dinner.' It's not long, however, before the words appear almost to provoke their own interpretations:

'And "the wabe" *is the grass plot round a sun-dial, I suppose?' said Alice, surprised at her own ingenuity.*

'Of course it is. It's called "wabe", *you know, because it goes a long way before it, and a long way behind it –'*

'And a long way beyond it on each side,' Alice added.

'Wabe', a word hitherto without meaning in the text, generates a surprisingly vivid image which simultaneously expands its physical size and solidity of interpretation so as to intrude into Alice's, and the reader's perception of reality. A word has produced a concept rather than the other way about.

The negotiation between the real world and that of the looking-glass, which is produced when Alice undertakes her adventures, is a metaphor for the reader's experience of literary texts. The mirror at first appears to reflect passively and accurately Alice's own drawing room, just as words seem to have fixed and true meanings. But the world behind the glass, like a literary text, destabilizes that certainty, for the language of *Through the Looking-Glass* constructs our world, rather than reflecting it. Much of modern critical theory enacts the same function: to make the reader self-consciously aware that meaning is not passive and universal but produced through the language and contextualization of literary texts. This essay sets out to explore those relationships between literature, criticism, author and reader from different theoretical positions: in other words, it offers an invitation to step through the looking-glass.

F.R. Leavis and evaluation

The history of literary criticism offers many varied ways of reading: as Humpty implies, how you interpret texts depends upon who is 'master'. A productive point at which to start understanding the development of 20th-century literary theory is with the work of ▷ F. R. Leavis. Although Leavis's ideas have long since been rejected by the critics and schools discussed later in this essay, his importance as one of the first 'masters' remains unchallenged.

In a sometimes acrimonious exchange with the editor of ▷ *Essays in Criticism* whose declared policy was to rival the literary critical review ▷ *Scrutiny* – his own journal – F. R. Leavis asserted that the competent critic's primary concern was with questions of evaluation, that is to discover the universal truth behind the language of the text. Critical judgement was to be clearly distinguished from social processes, since it was founded upon an unexplainable intelligence and sensitivity. Yet, at the same time, Leavis did not wish to concede that literature and criticism had no relevance to life. This problem serves to focus for us a range of questions which are of a deeply theoretical nature and which move beyond the literature–history debate enacted by the journals *Scrutiny* and *Essays in Criticism* in the early 1950s.

The questions, which will be addressed throughout this essay, concern the ways in which literature and criticism are produced, the values which readers bring to the texts and the freedoms and constraints under which both writers and readers operate. We must also ask about theories of language, the concept of authority, the idea of the individual or human subject and his or her relationship to literature. Finally, we will also need to ask whether literary language may be equated with 'essence' or with 'process', an idea which was explained at the beginning of this essay. Placed within the framework of an idealist criticism, such as Leavis's, the answers can differ radically from when they are located in a materialist, that is, social, set of concerns.

For example, the separation of an essential 'idea' from the way in which language produces meaning can be observed in the approach of another *Scrutiny* critic, L. C. Knights (b 1906). He explains that a Shakespearean tragedy such as *Macbeth* can be understood in terms of an essential theme which determines the critical response: 'I have called *Macbeth* a statement of evil; but it is a statement not of a philosophy but of ordered emotion' (*Explorations*; 1946). This theme is the structural motif, which underlies an emotionally charged language, through whose clouded surface the sensitive and intelligent reader may just glimpse the universal idea. This formula also demands the presence of an author whose discriminating consciousness has articulated these ideas and who allows us to see the true meaning. This way of reading and understanding literature is informed by a philosophical position which can be traced back through English literature to Plato and Aristotle, and which has accompanied the development of ▷ humanism.

Still, as we have discovered with the aid of Humpty Dumpty, text and context, literature and society, words and meaning are not divorceable oppositions, but mutually determining forces which are caught up in the same process of production. As such, questions of 'mastery' as well as questions about the relationships between author, text, reader and society require radical revision. This revision takes the discussion beyond the boundaries of what has traditionally been thought of as literary history. Today literary criticism is no longer concerned exclusively with either essence or with background, but with the way different histories can interlock to generate ideas, with different reading communities, and most importantly with the complex conditions which determine the reception of individual texts.

Saussure and Structuralism

In the sphere of literary criticism the response to particular texts has usually been built on recognizing that the text is an object of enquiry which has its origin in the writer's creative power. Where matters of history are involved then they are relegated to the category of background. For example, in *A Theory of Literature* (1963) René Wellek and Austin Warren define literature as 'creative, an art', whereas literary study is 'not precisely a science', but is nonetheless, 'a species of knowledge or learning'. The framework within which such statements are possible remains unexamined and, to some extent, not receptive to theory. One of the most influential theorists of the 1980s, the late ▷ Paul de Man, observed that,

> *Literary theory can be said to come into being when the approach to literary texts is no longer based on non-linguistic, that is to say historical and aesthetic considerations.*
>
> (*The Resistance to Theory*; 1986)

He went on to argue that 'resistance to theory is a resistance to the use of language about language'.

A fuller understanding of the problem that de Man identifies may be yielded by the analysis of language undertaken in ▷ Ferdinand de Saussure's *Course in General Linguistics* (published posthumously in 1915), which is at the root of the resurgence of literary theory since the late 1960s. Saussure's work covers a vast area but some of his most influential writing focuses upon the linguistic ▷ sign which he defines as 'not a link between a thing and a name, but between a concept and a sound pattern.' The connection between the signifier (sound pattern) and the signified (its conceptual meaning) is an *arbitrary* one. Saussure's example explains this idea:

> *There is no internal connection, for example, between the idea 'sister' and the French sequence of sounds* s-o-r *which acts as its signal. The same idea might be represented by any other sequence of sounds.*
>
> (*Course in General Linguistics*)

Saussure suggests then that the signifier and signified are joined or 'cohere' like the recto and verso sides of a sheet of paper:

> *Thought is one side of the sheet and sound the reverse side. Just as it is impossible to take a pair of scissors and cut one side of the paper without at the same time cutting the other, so it is impossible in a language to isolate thought from sound or sound from thought.*
>
> (*Course in General Linguistics*)

If thought, language and social process are mutually interdependent, then meaning itself cannot be unchanging and simple. It therefore follows that the mechanisms used in the construction of utterances and the choices involved in the selectivity of reading determine the ways in which a particular community makes sense of the world. In other words, the means of establishing a hierarchy of values at the conceptual level correspond to those at the material level. A final, essential and enormously influential element of Saussure's investigations is his recognition that each sign is made up of a fixed number of units which are easily distinguished from one another. This leads him directly to the radical observation that in 'language itself, there are only differences'. The importance of ▷ 'difference' to the interpretation of texts is explored more fully later on in this essay, but a simplistic and graphic example would be the drawing of a letter with white chalk on a black surface – the difference of colour produces a meaning. If the same letter had been written with a black crayon, no such interpretation could have taken place.

In practical terms the model proposed by Saussure opened up a form of structural analysis which gave rise to the theory of ▷ Structuralism. Structuralist critics concentrate on the various sets of binary oppositions which 'structure' a text, on the systems which link it to other texts, and thence to the process of cultural production of which both are a part. For example, ▷ Roman Jakobson's formalistic analysis of a ▷ Shakespeare ▷ sonnet, 'Shakespeare's Verbal Art in "Th'Expence of Spirit"' (1970) deals with the differences in the poem, such as the tension between centres and margins or couplets and quatrains. Here the structuring of meaning is shown to depend upon a detailed series of 'differences' in the Saussurean sense of the term, which come into play in this particular sonnet, as well as in the sonnet as a poetic form.

What Jakobson calls 'the poetic function' is determined by the activities of selection and combination, that is the establishment of contiguities and similarities respectively. This ▷ dialectic ultimately leads to the preference for either 'metaphoric' or 'metonymic' poles of language and hence to a distinction between poetry and prose. Saussure contended that all systems of signification were structured in accordance with the differential mode of language through which reality is mediated and represented. Thus, beneath each sign system there lies a deep structural affinity with language, thereby rendering them open to structural(ist) analysis. What unites the otherwise disparate group of theoretical writings loosely classified as structuralist – such as the social anthropology of Claude Lévi-Strauss (b 1908) and the 'mythological' investigations of ▷ Roland Barthes – is a commitment to the Saussurean precept that analysis will uncover a series of structural and nonvariable laws. Further, these laws are the basis for the social, political and artistic institutions which sustain cultural values. It is here that both the strengths and weaknesses of Structuralism lie. On the one hand, it reveals the interdependence of all institutions and so brings literature firmly into the social sphere, but on the other, its strict idea of rules denies variation and limits change.

Formalism and Bakhtin

The identification of 'difference' as the principal mechanism in the production of meaning is one that has appealed to a range of theoretical schools. One of the earliest of these was Russian ▷ Formalism which began in 1915–16 with the foundation of the Moscow Linguistic Circle and the Society for the Investigation of Poetic Language (Opoiaz), which included scholars such as Roman Jakobson (1896–1982) and ▷ Mikhail Bakhtin. Briefly, Russian Formalism was dedicated to the investigation of the 'literariness' of literary language, and to understanding the ways in which it could be distinguished from other forms of linguistic usage. They were particularly interested in poetry because they observed that it subverted 'ordinary speech' with its emphasis on multiple meanings. Secondly, literature was said to distance itself from reality in such a way as to expose the exact manner in which experience could be represented in language. It was this process of 'making strange' that the dramatist ▷ Bertolt Brecht was to use in his development of the ▷ 'alienation effect' (*Verfremdungseffekt*) in his plays.

The Russian Formalists also concerned themselves with larger questions of literary history, seeking to establish the 'literary' nature of certain texts, not as universal and timeless, but in relation to other texts which shared a common body of rhetorical devices. The consequent blurring of the division between the literary canon and other forms of writing has had a long-term effect. Today ▷ genres regarded as 'popular', such as ▷ science fiction, are admitted into the canon, and literature as a field of academic study is often integrated into the broader framework of 'Cultural Studies'.

One of Russian Formalism's early founders, and one of its most stringent critics, was Mikhail Bakhtin who argued that, although the 'formalist(s) led the captive word out of prison' (*The Formal Method in Literary Scholarship*,

1928), they sacrificed history for novelty, and thus reduced art to a 'device'. Under the pseudonym of V. N. Volosinov, Bakhtin published a critique of Saussurean Structuralism, *Marxism and the Philosophy of Language* in 1930. Where Saussure had been concerned with the mechanisms which produce meaning within an invariant system, Bakhtin sought to establish a connection between the differential aspects of language and the framework which produces social and political order. Thus language and ▷ ideology – that is a series of beliefs through which people perceive and state their versions of reality – are firmly linked. Consequently, if signs are constructed out of differences then the production of meaning must also involve some measure of social conflict. Moreover, it is through this conflict that a dominant interest group constructs a hierarchy of representations in order to assert its political supremacy.

Another influential and controversial aspect of Bakhtin's legacy is the insistence upon the plurality of voices contained in any one text, which has contributed to the concepts of 'textual polyphony' and ▷ 'intertextuality'. In *Rabelais and His World* (1965) he chronicled the nature of these opposing voices. In fact, in recent literary theory the whole concept of 'voice' with its implied privileging of speech over writing, has been supplanted by the more precise term, ▷ 'discourse'. A discourse is a particular way of talking, writing or thinking which is founded on shared beliefs, for example the discourse of socialism or the discourse of architecture. Also in relation to Rabelais' *Gargantua and Pantagruel* (1532–4), he proposed the category of the 'carnivalesque' (▷ Carnival) as a form of festive language which threatens disruption and celebrates the materialist impulse for change in the social order. Bakhtin writes:

> *Carnival was the true feast of time, the feast of becoming, change and renewal. It was hostile to all that was immortalized and completed.*
>
> (*Rabelais and His World*)

Two contradictory propositions follow from the idea of carnivalesque: firstly, that by identifying class antagonisms it is able to subvert them, and secondly, that by highlighting the distinction between its own and official discourses it can be contained and defused like licensed misrule. Whether a reactionary or radical reading of Bakhtin is preferred, the view that a literary text is structured according to a hierarchy of social differences is one that has had far-reaching effects for literary theory. For example, in the 1960s French theorists, such as the semioticians (▷ Semiotics), developed along diverse lines many of the ideas put forward by Saussure and the Russian Formalists, so that their critiques encompassed cultural anthropology, psychoanalysis and ▷ feminism, as well as literary criticism. Probably the most outstanding of this school, gathered around the journal ▷ *Tel Quel*, was Roland Barthes whose penetrating investigations of contemporary mythologies, such as the face of Garbo or advertisements for soap powder reveal that what appear to be given truths about a society are instead constructed ideologies through which they sustain their hierarchical systems. However, the most persistent strain of influence was to be seen in ▷ Marxist criticism and its fascinating mutations.

Marxism to materialism: Althusser, Macherey and Foucault

The foregrounding of the relationship between literature and ideology occurs in the work of the French theorist ▷ Louis Althusser. By drawing upon Marxism, psychoanalysis and Structuralism, Althusser was able to propose not only a model for social relations within ▷ capitalism, but also a series of mechanisms whereby individuals or 'subjects' were positioned within the social formation. Althusser's model of society as a series of relatively autonomous structures, each with its own internal contradictions – determined only finally by economic factors – was a controversial departure. He believed that a revolutionary situation would not be brought about by one dominant set of social contradictions, but that each autonomous structure contains and contributes to a diversity of potentially explosive forces. Together with this idea, Althusser developed the concept of a 'destabilized' social formation in which perpetual division and fragmentation were possible. It was within this web of autonomous structures that the individual identity or 'subject' was produced, whose actions, attitudes and feelings were articulated through ideology. In this context, ideology is not a body of consciously held ideas, but the representation of discontinuous and contradictory human relations in terms of an imaginary unity. Althusser defined ideology as a representation of 'the imaginary relationship of individuals to their real conditions of existence' (*Lenin and Philosophy*; 1971). This system of representations supplements, at the personal and psychological level, the system of freedoms and constraints produced by the dominant structure within the social formation at any one historical moment. The privileging of 'ideology' had far-reaching consequences for the study of literature and artistic production in general. Althusser suggests that art offers us a

> *form of* 'seeing', 'perceiving', *and* 'feeling' (*which is not the form of knowing*) . . . *the* ideology *from which it is born, in which it bathes, from which it detaches itself as art, and to which it* alludes.
>
> (*A Letter on Art*)

Thus art is a specific category which is deeply implicated in ideology, but which is, at its best, able to distance itself from it. Following on from a similar argument by the French critic Pierre Macherey in his *Theory of Literary Production* (1978), Althusser argues that the novels of Balzac and Solzhenitsyn presuppose,

> *a* retreat, *an internal* distantiation *from the very ideology from which their novels emerged. They make us 'perceive' [but not know] in some sense* from the inside, *by an* internal distance, *the very ideology in which they are held.*
>
> (*A Letter on Art*)

Althusser's *A Letter on Art* is contentious in that he did not really address issues important to literary critics, such as the question of authorial intention and whether the institution of literature is itself an ideological category. It was

Pierre Macherey who, to some extent, followed through the ideas initiated by Althusser. For Macherey the literary text is constructed in difference, and the conflict of which he speaks,

> *is not the sign of an imperfection; it reveals the inscription of an* otherness *in the work, through which it maintains a relationship with that which it is not, that which happens at its margins.*
>
> *(A Theory of Literary Production)*

Consequently the literary text is complex and decentred, and therefore a challenge to ideologically motivated forms of reading which would give more importance to concepts such as 'harmony' and 'centre'.

A Theory of Literary Production is concerned primarily with the historical conditions of the production of literary texts, and the extent to which those conditions are inscribed. Since then, Macherey has turned his attention to the issue of the ideological *effects* which texts produce when they are read. The result of this move is to problematize both the status of the text, and the historical process of its reception, and to raise fundamental questions about the category of 'literature' itself. Here ideology is shown to enter into the dialectical transaction between reader and text so as to shatter the divisions which have traditionally kept the categories of 'literature' and 'history' apart, or preserved their relationship as one of foreground and background.

Althusser and Macherey focused attention, away from the traditional Marxist notion of society as single unit, on to the the range of social practices and discourses through which ideology operates. This is part of a larger post-structuralist (▷ Post-structuralism) challenge to the metaphysical notion of 'authority', and as such has considerable implications for the literary question of authorship.

In the work of Roland Barthes, and more particularly in the writings of ▷ Michel Foucault, the 'author', traditionally regarded as the origin of meaning, is given a place in language at the point where a range of discourses converge. The writer does not, therefore, occupy a transcendent position, but rather manipulates, and is manipulated by, those discourses which are available at that particular historical moment. Thus questions of the meaning of Sir Philip Sidney's *An Apologie for Poetrie*, or Coleridge's *Biographia Literaria*, or Matthew Arnold's *Culture and Anarchy*, become secondary to the enquiry into the ways in which these texts intersect with history, the assumptions they make, what they include, what they omit, and the manner in which reality is represented in their language.

Although aware of context, Foucault acknowledges no notion of a continuous or a progressive 'history', but only a series of discourses which determine forms of intellectual enquiry and linguistic representation. Foucault states that his aim,

> *. . . is most decidedly not to use the categories of cultural totalities (whether world-views, ideal types, the particular spirit of an age) in order to impose on history, despite itself, the forms of structural analysis. The series described, the limits*

> *fixed, the comparisons and correlations made are based not on the old philosophies of history, but are intended to question teleologies and totalizations.*
>
> (*The Archaeology of Knowledge*; 1972)

Within this framework 'authority' is shown to be related to power and to desire. Together these insights undermine the traditional grounding of history, and Foucault's emphases on fragmentation, discontinuity and the questions of discourse, knowledge and power, have been eagerly endorsed by more recent criticism. A movement in North America known as ▷ 'new historicism', its British counterpart 'cultural materialism' (▷ materialism), and its feminist manifestation 'materialist feminism' have enthusiastically developed Foucault's premises. However, while most critics have responded positively to the focusing on the power of discourse, there remains a concern that what is missing from Foucault's analysis is an emphasis upon the *political* nature of those social conflicts, antagonisms and contradictions which can be found in different discourses.

Lacan and psychoanalytic criticism

▷ Psychoanalytic criticism may at first appear to occupy different territory from that already mapped out by this essay, but there is a significant overlapping of interest. For example, let us take the importation of Saussure on linguistics into psychoanalysis through such writings as those of Emile Benveniste. Benveniste draws a useful distinction between the Saussurean identification of arbitrariness in the linguistic sign, the manner in which it is perceived by its users, and the way in which a system of linguistic values is constructed; he argues that:

> *For the speaker there is a complete equivalence between language and reality ... [but that] ... all values are values of opposition and are defined only by their difference. Opposed to each other, they maintain themselves in a mutual relationship of necessity.*
>
> (*Problems in General Linguistics*; 1971)

These two aspects of linguistic theory accord perfectly with what the influential theorist and psychoanalytic critic ▷ Jacques Lacan designates as the 'imaginary' and the 'symbolic' spheres. The imaginary rests on the fantasy (not that it is perceived as such) of a direct relationship between language and reality, in which the latter as 'absence' can be recalled in its entirety by the former. As Lacan puts it, 'It is the world of words that creates the world of things' (*Ecrits*; 1977). On the other hand, the symbolic designates a differentially derived value structure through which the human subject or individual enters into the social order.

The consequences for the human subject are examined by Benveniste who writes that language is 'so organized that it permits each speaker to *appropriate to himself* an entire language by designating himself "*I*"'. For this 'I' there is an equivalence between language and reality, but for the symbolic self, 'I' is part of a social and material process. The first is the site of the imaginary where the subject is centred, while the second directs attention to *difference* and hence to the decentred nature of the subject. It is to this decentring process that Lacan addresses himself in his analysis of the relationship between the conscious and the unconscious.

Lacan's insistence that, 'the unconscious is structured like a language' (*The Four Fundamental Concepts of Psychoanalysis*; 1977) directs attention to the space between the 'signifier' and 'signified'. This is not an unreasonable claim, since neither the subject nor the unconscious exist in some pre-linguistic realm, but are brought into being through the differential mechanisms which may be said to structure language. This analysis emerges from Lacan's rereading of the works of the founder of psychoanalysis, ▷ Sigmund Freud. For Freud the unconscious is the primal scene of an Oedipal drama (▷ Oedipus complex) whose stages correspond to the growth of the human subject from infancy to maturity, but whose effects must be repressed and redirected in order for successful socialization to occur. If, as Lacan says, the unconscious is structured linguistically then what is repressed must actually be a *representation*. This functions as the 'other' of language, that is a system of desires which language perpetually seeks to recover, but never fully satisfies. The human subject learns to manage this potentially disruptive otherness or system of representations in two ways. Firstly, he or she must learn to recognize himself or herself and to construct an imaginary 'unity' (this is Lacan's famous 'mirror stage'), and secondly he or she must enter the symbolic order where the demands of the other are encountered through the regulating context of ideology. Thus Lacan develops a materialist theory of subjectivity which marks the point at which ideology enters into the subject's consciousness. The result is a direct challenge to any notion of a transcendent relationship between subject and language:

> *it is not only man who speaks, but that in man and through man* it *speaks* (ça parle), *that his nature is woven by effects in which is to be found the structure of language, of which he becomes the material, and that therefore there resounds in him, beyond what could be conceived of by a psychology of ideas, the relation of speech.*
>
> *(Ecrits)*

What 'resounds in him' is the representation of the unconscious where the unstable elements of language, prior to their formation as a fantasy of coherence, reside. The effect is a continuous double play of ▷ condensation and ▷ displacement in the production of the signified. This is the process of 'splitting' which is the price paid at the level of the unconscious for the subject's emergence into the symbolic order of language. It is for this reason that the notion of subjectivity as wholeness is regarded as a fantasy created from the repression of the unstable elements out of which the unconscious is constituted.

For Lacan the unconscious functions as a text whose repetitions, condensations and displacements trace its emergence into the symbolic order, and the process of reading serves to implicate the reader as the one who is analysed (that is, the analysand), rather than the analyst. To this extent the literary text functions as a mirror reflecting back an imaginary order whose images position the reader as 'the subject who is supposed to know', but whose claims to certainty are constantly undercut.

Feminist criticism

An extraordinarily productive area of critical theory which has appropriated Lacanian methods is psychoanalytic feminist criticism. Nevertheless, in *Feminine Sexuality* the critic Jaqueline Rose demonstrates how Lacan reveals his own phallocentrism through his argument that the phallus is the signifier about which the symbolic order is constructed, and that this symbolic order actually generates 'femininity' as its opposite or other. This echoes concerns expressed by some feminist critics that ▷ gender identity can only ever be produced within patriarchal symbolic structures and that 'woman' is the mirror in which masculinity views itself positively as the power of the law, while at the same time identifying her as lack, repression or the space of the unconscious. Entry into the symbolic order, and hence into language, grammar and signifying practices means, as feminist critic Toril Moi points out, 'to accept the phallus as the representation of the law of the father' (*Sexual/Textual Politics*; 1985). Thus the way in which theory tends to construct the gendered subject is precisely that which feminism as a political movement, as well as feminist literary theory, seeks to contest.

There is a contradiction inherent in the aligning of feminist literary criticism with any theoretical position since, in certain manifestations, feminism would resist theory as a form of mastery of knowledge, which articulates those very patriarchal structures from which it seeks emancipation. Indeed, in their pioneering study of the woman writer in the 19th century, *The Madwoman in the Attic* (1979), Sandra Gilbert and Susan Gubar take the view that the act of writing itself is a patriarchal gesture. They suggest that in western culture,

> *the text's author is a father, a progenitor, a procreator, an aesthetic patriarch whose pen is an instrument of generative power like his penis.*
>
> (*The Madwoman in the Attic*)

They identify the pen(is) as a metaphor for power, especially political and spiritual control. But they go on to make claims for a distinctly female imagination which seeks to challenge masculine insistence upon the universality of its knowledge and its allegedly neutral value judgements.

Can there be, then, distinctive areas of feminine experience and styles of writing? The French theorist, ▷ Hélène Cixous insists that female experience, hitherto repressed, is very different from that of men, and must therefore require a different style of articulation:

> *Time and again, I, too, have felt so full of luminous torrents that I could burst – burst with forms much more beautiful than those which are put up in frames and sold for a stinking fortune. And I, too, said nothing, showed nothing: I didn't open*

> *my mouth, I didn't repaint my half of the world. I was ashamed. I was afraid, and I swallowed my shame and my fear. I said to myself: You are mad!*
> (*New French Feminisms*; 1980)

Cixous's celebration of the female body and female desire represents an attempt to re-state in material terms the positive value of what, in masculine terms, is described negatively as 'other'. She also re-examines the entry of the gendered human subject into the symbolic order of language and discourse, in order to reclaim the ground that Lacan has designated simply as a 'lack'. Cixous asks ironically, 'What's a desire originating in a lack? A pretty meagre desire.' Instead she tries to free feminine language through a new form of writing drawn from the unconscious (▷ Écriture féminine).

In focusing upon female energy and its repression by the patriarchy, Cixous shares certain concerns with the influential French critic ▷ Julia Kristeva. Cixous registers her dissatisfaction with the subject position and feelings accorded to her by the phallocentric order, but Kristeva takes the issue further. First, she appropriates Bakhtin's association of the pre-Oedipal phase with the 'feminine', and then goes on to examine exactly how the gendered subject enters into the symbolic order, becoming positioned socially, linguistically and psychologically. She describes entry into the signifying process as the 'thetic phase', by which she means a process which begins when subject and object are recognized as different. This process is completed in the gendered subject through the discovery of castration which, in turn,

> *detaches the subject from his dependence on the mother, and the perception of this lack* (manque) *makes the phallic function a symbolic function* – the *symbolic function.*
> (*A Kristeva Reader*; 1986)

However, prior to and still residing beneath that symbolic order is the 'semiotic'. For Kristeva this means a mobile and amorphous feminine force which can distort the masculine chain of signification, and she lays claim to poetic language as especially close to the semiotic. Poetry thus becomes a form of linguistic ▷ subversion that continually threatens those meanings established by the symbolic order. If, at the psychological level, we were to submit fully to these disruptions they would produce 'illness' – hallucination and psychosis. But by incorporating these subversive energies into language we are able to produce artistic creations, and therefore writing ceases to be an authoritarian process. Rather, for Kristeva, writing is dialectical, incorporating both subversion and production into its structures.

The reversal of the values which masculine discourse ascribes to binary oppositions is both philosophical and politically strategic. But some feminists have expressed concern that to situate women's writing in the body and to celebrate the unconscious, as opposed to the masculine symbolic order, risks complicity with the very structures from which women wish to escape. In other words, imprisoned within the dialectic of *difference*, the political and linguistic gains might well be limited. It is true that, at a theoretical level, the critique of a symbolic order has resulted in the interrogation of traditional categories of knowledge, especially those concerned with masculine representations of femininity. But as Toril Moi has argued, the major consequence of feminism as a form of analysis is pre-eminently political, and feminists

> *find themselves in a position roughly similar to that of other radical critics: speaking from their marginalized positions on the outskirts of the academic establishments, they strive to make* explicit *the politics of the so-called 'neutral' or 'objective' works of their colleagues, as well as to act as cultural* critics *in the widest sense of the word.*
>
> *(Sexual/Textual Politics)*

In other words, in addition to producing analyses of female writing or the masculine representations of women in male-authored texts, feminism must undertake a critique of the mechanisms used by these works in order to transform social and personal relations.

This political programme receives different emphases in different historical situations. The female retreat into 'gyno-criticism' – that is, the study of texts written by women, feminine literary creativity, and the development and form of a female tradition of writing – and the challenge to accepted masculine formulations of subjectivity/subjection, has served to emphasize the personal as the primary area of feminist concern. Clearly though, the logic of its arguments suggest that materialist feminist criticism will have to form a theory of subjectivity which takes into account more fully the political connection between social relations and personal behaviour. A feminism which pursues the personal at the expense of the political is in danger of removing the gendered human subject from history altogether. In her perceptive review of the French '*écriture féminine*' Ann Rosalind Jones identifies the danger in pursuing one at the expense of the other:

> *Without making deprecatory psychoanalytic diagnoses feminists may still doubt the efficacy of privileging changes in subjectivity over changes in economic and political systems; is this not dangling the semiotic carrot in front of the mare still harnessed into phallocentric social practices?*
>
> *(Making the Difference)*

Materialist feminist critics who focus on the political and social formations seek to explore the ideological implications for the female subject within 'difference', but proceed from the assumption that subjectivity is a political space to be contested. The critic Catherine Belsey in *Feminist Criticism and Social Change* (1985) argues that those literary forms which capitalism has sanctioned depend upon the presence of the author as 'authority' and position of the reader as 'subject'. A classic example of this would be the realist novel, which proposes an exact correspondence between itself and reality. Her argument is that the grammatical formulation of mimetic representation enacts the very hierarchical conditions of the symbolic order itself. In this way classic realism may be seen to be founded in an ideology which treats its readers as subjects who are placed in positions of subjection and subjectivity. What Belsey, like both Cixous and Kristeva, focuses on are the ways in which gendered subjects are drawn into a complicity with liberal humanism which superficially admits differences, only to transform itself into a non-contradictory 'truth', under whose masculine image they are invited voluntarily to live in subjection.

Derrida and deconstruction

If feminism is the most politically challenging of current theoretical innovations, then ▷ deconstruction represents the greatest methodological challenge to traditional knowledge systems. Deconstruction, as advocated by ▷ Jacques Derrida, presents a radical challenge to the entire western tradition of philosophy, from Plato onwards. As a theory it has developed out of Structuralism, drawing also upon the philosophical scepticism of ▷ Friedrich Nietzsche. The objective of deconstruction is to demystify language's claimed ability to refer outside itself; this is achieved through the disclosure of the rhetorical figures underpinning all systems of thought. However, Derrida does accept that it is not possible to escape metaphysical meaning entirely: a more practicable deconstruction is defined as

> *a simultaneous* marking *and* loosening *of the limits of the system in which the concept was born and began to serve, and thereby [it]* also represents, to a certain *extent, an uprooting of the sign from its own soil.*
>
> *(Positions)*

We may recall Saussure's insistence that in language there are no positive terms, only 'differences', and that particular combinations of sounds or letters (signifiers) produced particular meanings (signifieds). In addition, the rules governing each instance of language (▷ *parole*) are those of a larger and invariant structure (▷ *langue*) to which each 'instance' ultimately refers. Derrida challenges Saussure's signifier/signified principle because it privileges sound, and therefore implies that the voice is synonymous with consciousness itself. Moreover, Derrida rejects the assumption that a linguistic sign constitutes a static unit of reality, derived from a larger structure or system. Rather, he suggests that the sign's construction through difference can never truly recall the totalizing system of which it was a part, and the totality is never available to the reader, who is left instead with a constant 'play' of differences. Derrida explains further that if

> *totalization no longer has any meaning, it is not because the infiniteness of a field cannot be covered by a finite glance or a finite discourse, but because the nature of the field – that is, language and a finite language – excludes totalization. This field is in effect that of* play, *that is to say, a field of infinite substitutions only because it is finite, that is to say, because instead of being an inexhaustible field, as in the classical hypothesis, instead of being too large, there is something missing from it: a centre which arrests and grounds the play of substitutions.*
>
> *(Writing and Difference*; 1978)

The status of the centre cannot be fixed any more than the 'play' of the signs about it, for the basic concept of a 'centre' issues from a process of signification which can be shown to be figural and divided, always already in motion, a series of endless substitutions. Clearly, Derrida regards this notion of infinite 'play' as a Nietzschean form of liberation, since he insists notoriously that the loss of the centre should not lead to nostalgia, negativity and guilt, but to a joyous and anarchic 'play', where interpretation is never-ending.

Derrida also develops Saussure's idea of 'difference' through a provocative punning in French: a vowel substitution into *différance* combines the sense of *différence* as substitution with the principle of 'deferral' in time. *Différance* then, is the movement of play which produces differences and as such is the originator of an infinite deferral of meaning. This has repercussions for the notion of subjectivity, for if, as Derrida argues, nothing precedes *différance*, then there can be no uniquely self-founded authorship or mastery and even the human subject itself must become an *effect* of *différance*. The challenge to traditional concepts of metaphysical presence inevitably draws attention to the linguistic mechanisms which allow that challenge. This decentring of the subject has been explained with different emphases by different theoretical positions, but Derridean *différance* directs us to the problems and dangers of attempting to halt a play of substitutions about a supposedly fixed centre.

It is not difficult to see how Derridean deconstruction involves forms of analyses common to all of the theoretical positions described so far in this essay. Marxism, feminism and psychoanalysis are all concerned with human subjects who are in some sense 'alienated' or divided, and all show how this decentring is articulated in language. But deconstruction foregrounds the unending postponement of a point of 'presence', a point which must, of necessity, exist outside the play of *différance*. But Derrida asserts that '*Il n'y a pas de hors-texte*' (there is nothing outside the text) and that any move outside language is a misplaced gesture in the direction of an unattainable transcendence.

As had already been suggested, Derrida attacked Saussure's privileging of speech and the voice, which relegates writing to a subsidiary role. What he locates at the heart of Saussure's language is that very same impulse to organic wholeness and the 'naturalness' of writing which may be seen – transformed into a critique of industrial society – in the work of F. R. Leavis. What Derrida is attacking is the metaphysics of 'presence' and the whole concept of a referential language. He argues that, if we accept the principle of *différance*, then speech must be implicated in the process of writing and bear traces of that involvement. Indeed, he proposes the inversion of the customary hierarchy, that speaking precedes writing, by suggesting that speech could not have existed without being differentially produced by writing. It is this 'arch writing' that Derrida proposes as the basis for his ▷ 'grammatology', that is his investigation of the units of signification produced through *différance*.

It is not difficult to see the implications of this process for traditional literary concepts such as 'mimesis' or 'realism', although the effects reach far more deeply into critical practices than those of genre or style. The charge that

Derrida lays against all writing is that its own rhetoricity predicates a deadlock – 'aporia' – at the heart of linguistic activity. This deadlock is detectable both in the representational quality of the text and in the language of criticism. The only way to resolve it would be through an appeal beyond language to some transcendent meaning which, as we have seen, for Derrida has the status of 'prejudice'.

Derrida's challenging theoretical approach appeared on the literary scene at the very moment when American ▷ new criticism and, in Britain, Leavisite practical criticism seemed to reach the point of bankruptcy. Subsequently, the deconstruction of 'master-narratives' and the questioning of boundaries, exclusions, suppressions, and displacements, have been of value to feminists, psychoanalytic critics and Marxists alike. In America it has come as a timely successor to new criticism and has been taken up by the ludic exuberances of the Yale School critics, such as J. Hillis Miller and Geoffrey Hartman. Also at Yale, the more sceptical rigour of Paul de Man's writing gained added impetus from the dialogue with the work of Derrida. This adoption of deconstruction for pedagogic purposes has meant that in America the radical free play of meaning and unsettling consequences of semantic indeterminacy have been denuded of their political implications.

Conclusions

Although this essay has dealt with various schools and critics in a formal order, it would be misleading to think of 'literary theory' in simple chronological terms. The concept of a linear progression cannot encompass the shifts backwards and forwards that have taken place over the last half-century. Perhaps Foucault's notion of 'genealogy' best describes both the complex web of relationships, and the constant debates, between different theoretical positions. Our whole understanding of 'literature' and 'literary criticism' has been unsettled by this unceasing discussion and disruption of traditional boundaries. It seems as if it is no longer enough simply to look at the literary text, nor even to bring a particular theory to bear on that text. Today we are faced with an arresting display of theories, for example we must distinguish between Marxism and feminism and between feminism and psychoanalysis. Moreover, the language used is often difficult for us to understand, although more and more critical terms become current in our everyday speech, 'ideology' for example. But while this is intimidating, it is also exhilarating. No longer do we need to turn to a 'master' author, critic or particular theory, nor do we need to remain constrained by a single interpretation. Rather our practice of literary criticism can become

> *the joyous affirmation of the play of the world and of the innocence of becoming, the affirmation of a world of signs without fault, without truth, and without origin which is offered to an active interpretation.*
>
> (*Writing and Difference*, Jacques Derrida)

Culture and Consciousness in the Twentieth-century English Novel 3

Andrew Roberts
University of London

PART I – 1900 to 1930

Between 1900 and 1930 revolutionary developments took place in the English novel. These developments involved new subject matter, style and technique, and led ultimately to a radical rethinking of the relationship between fiction and reality. This era in the history of the novel, like the corresponding periods in the history of drama, poetry and other arts, is now widely known as ▷ modernism. The roots of modernism are exceptionally diverse, because it was a result of cross-fertilization between cultures, between art forms and between disciplines.

Culture and reality: James and Conrad

▷ Joseph Conrad (1857–1924) and ▷ Henry James (1843–1916), both of whom first published in the 19th century, are the earliest of the great modernist novelists writing in English. One form of cross-fertilization is evident at once, in that James was born an American and Conrad a Pole. Each chose to settle in England and to become an English subject and for each the collision of different cultures was an important theme. The relation of America to Europe is a central concern of James's fiction: in major novels such as ▷ *The Portrait of a Lady* (1881) and ▷ *The Wings of the Dove* (1902), as well as ▷ novellas such as ▷ *Daisy Miller* (1879), the moral consequences of the meeting of American innocence and enthusiasm with a sophisticated but corrupt European culture are explored by means of irony, a sustained attention to the nuances of individual consciousness, and a prose style of increasing subtlety and complexity. It was not only in theme that James was cosmopolitan; influences on his work include Jane Austen, George Eliot, Nathaniel Hawthorne, Balzac and Turgenev.

Conrad's life as a merchant seaman, and his upbringing in Poland and Russia, brought him into contact with a wide range of cultures. His prose style owes much to the influences of the 19th-century French writers Maupassant and Flaubert, and in a number of his works he explores what was to become a major concern of the 20th-century English novel: the experience of the European in Asia, Africa or South America. In ▷ *Heart of Darkness* (1902) a supposedly enlightened colonial programme is revealed as ruthless commercial exploitation and a journey up the Congo becomes symbolic of an exploration of the darkness within man, the atrocities of history, the powerful forces of the unconscious, the mystery of evil. This work epitomizes many features of modernist fiction: the need to confront violence, nihilism and despair; the fascination with, but fear of, the unconscious; the centrality of a dramatized narrator who is not omniscient but rather himself searching for understanding; a symbolic richness which invites multiple interpretations. The last two of these features reflect the influence on modernism of the French Symbolist (▷ Symbolism) movement of the 19th century, one of whose exponents, Rémy de Gourmont, defined the writer's purpose as being 'to unveil to others the kind of world which he beholds in his own personal mirror'. Conrad's critique of the ideology of Empire also foreshadows the many later works of fiction which use colonial or post-colonial settings to explore the European mind through its contact with what is alien and with what is shared in other cultures, while protesting against bigotry and exploitation. Examples include ▷ E. M. Forster's ▷ *A Passage to India* (1924), ▷ George Orwell's *Burmese Days* (1934), ▷ Graham Greene's *The Heart of the Matter* (1948), and, more recently, the Indian novels of ▷ Ruth Prawer Jhabvala.

But it is in their technique that James and Conrad are most revolutionary. While novelists such as ▷ Arnold Bennett (1867–1931) and ▷ John Galsworthy (1867–1933) continued to write in the accepted realist mode, using an omniscient narrator, a chronologically sequential narrative and the accumulation of details of social and public life, modernist novelists sought radical redefinitions of the real. One such redefinition is based on the view that, since the individual always perceives reality through his or her own consciousness, the contents and structure of consciousness represent the only accessible reality. A number of philosophical influences are relevant here. William James, the brother of Henry James, was an American psychologist and philosopher. In *Essays in Radical Empiricism* (1912) he elaborated the notion of a world of 'pure experience', all reality being described in terms of subjective human experience. (James is also the originator of the term ▷ 'stream of consciousness'.) ▷ Sigmund Freud (1856–1939), whose work began to be known in Britain around 1912, has had an enormous influence on modern literature, though less through direct application of his ideas than as a result of his contribution to the assumptions and preoccupations of modern Western society. One of his most potent ideas is also one of the simplest: that all mental phenomena have meaning. This assumption helped to validate new ways of structuring narrative based on dreams, fantasies, and chains of association. ▷ Henri Bergson (1859–1941), the French philosopher of evolution, distinguished between scientific time (a mathematical, abstract, homogeneous medium) and 'real duration' (our direct experience of time as a flowing, irreversible succession of heterogeneous and concrete states). The former, he claimed, is essentially an illusion; it is our subjective experience of time which is 'real'.

The novel was a particularly suitable form for the exploration of such perceptions, because of the possibility of manipulating the reader's experience of time by means of disruption of narrative chronology, and the possibility of representing the nature of consciousness by describing events through the awareness of one or more characters.

In the opening chapters of Conrad's ▷ *Lord Jim* (1900) a sense of foreboding is created so that the reader's expectation and interest are engaged, but at precisely the point of crisis, when an accident occurs to the ship on which Jim is first mate, the narrative jumps forward to the subsequent inquiry. Conrad thus deliberately frustrates the desire for plot satisfaction, diverting our interest from what happens to the moral and philosophical significance of events. The narrative is structured as an investigation; an attempt, largely on the part of Marlow, who befriends Jim, to understand Jim's life. However, Marlow himself obtains much of his information at second hand, through accounts of events given to him by other characters, so that the effect is one of an enigmatic reality seen through a series of consciousnesses.

But it was Henry James above all who, in practice in his novels and in theory in his prefaces, developed the use of an observing consciousness whose viewpoint shapes the narrative. Here we need to distinguish between the narrator (the narrating 'voice' which, if it refers to itself, must do so in the first person) and the focal character or 'reflector' (the character whose point of view orients the narrative perspective). In Conrad's *Heart of Darkness* Marlow is both narrator and focal character, but the two are not identical since they represent Marlow at different points in his life. One of the subtle pleasures of the story is our sense of Marlow the narrator (middle-aged, sitting on a boat on the Thames) reflecting on and reassessing the experience of Marlow the focal character (younger, more idealistic, in the Congo). James's most favoured device is the restriction of the narrative focalization to a reflector who is not the narrator but is referred to in the third person, a prime example being Strether in ▷ *The Ambassadors* (1903). Associated Jamesian techniques include a dominance of 'scene' (the highly detailed account of particular occasions) and long accounts of the nuances of the reflector's sense of events. These reflectors become centres of interest themselves. Viewing events through their eyes, we share the limitations of their knowledge and the distortions of their viewpoint, and this is realistic in the sense that our actual experience of life is always limited in this way; we do not have all the facts, nor access to the thoughts of others. We share in the progressive illumination of Marlow and Strether. Conrad and James inaugurated a form of realism which ▷ Malcolm Bradbury (b 1932) has aptly described as 'not so much a substantiation of reality as a questing for it'.

These various manipulations of narrator and reflector are fruitful sources of irony, a primary characteristic of much modern fiction. Irony can be generated when the reader perceives more, or understands better, than the narrator and/or reflector, and can occur even when our perspective is technically limited to that of this character. James's novella *The Aspern Papers* (1888) is entirely first-person narration, but we gradually realize, through his own words and thoughts, the moral and emotional limitations of the narrator. A different form of irony is developed by Conrad in ▷ *The Secret Agent* (1907) and ▷ *Under Western Eyes* (1911): a pervasive irony of tone and event. The former is produced by a portrayal of human activity as largely futile and human nature as inherently given to self-deception and illusory beliefs. The latter occurs as characters' actions consistently go awry and produce the opposite effect to that intended.

The result is a blend of black comedy with a satirical and tragic view of humanity, its pretensions, and its ideals.

A special case of the dramatized central consciousness is the unreliable narrator or reflector. One of the most fascinating examples of the unreliable narrator is Dowell in ▷ Ford Madox Ford's novel *The Good Soldier* (1915). Our initial tendency to accept a first-person narrator as an accurate source of information is exploited so that the cruelty, deception and insanity lurking beneath the genteel surface of the lives of two couples emerges with a greater sense of shock. Dowell also reflects on the nature of story-telling and its relation to truth ('I don't know how it is best to put this thing down . . .') and this novel thus anticipates two recurrent features of the 20th-century novel. The first is the use of narrators or reflectors who are unbalanced, malevolent, of limited understanding or otherwise in an abnormal state of mind. Examples include *The Collector* (1963) by ▷ John Fowles (parts 1 and 3), and *The Spire* (1964) by ▷ William Golding. The second feature is reflexive narrative, in which the nature and purpose of writing becomes a constant secondary theme, or even the primary interest of the work. Examples include ▷ Doris Lessing's *The Golden Notebook* (1962) and William Golding's *Rites of Passage* (1980).

History and art: Lawrence and Woolf

The relationship of history and the novel may be formulated in two ways. On the one hand, we may regard history as an objective series of public events, and the novel as an art form which may represent, ignore or fictionalize them. On the other hand, we may regard history itself as a narrative, and its relation with the novel as more reciprocal, our sense of the nature and significance of narrative influencing our sense of historical pattern and meaning and vice versa. Modernism is sometimes accused of ignoring historical and social realities. But the sense of living in a period of historical crisis is an important aspect of much modernist fiction. The apocalyptic world view which the critic Frank Kermode has identified in the work of ▷ D. H. Lawrence (1885–1930) is at once a reaction to accelerating social change and an expression of a mystical or prophetic view of the role of the artist, influenced by the Bible, and especially the Book of Revelation. ▷ *The Rainbow* (1915) describes the life of three generations of the Brangwen family in the English Midlands, and ▷ *Women in Love* (1921) (originally planned as part of the same work), continues the story of the third generation. In neither novel is there extensive reference to historical events in the conventional sense, though the effect on rural life of progressive industrialization is powerfully felt. Rather, what Lawrence writes is a history of the development of human consciousness and the unconscious life, in which the individual's relation with partner, family, work and the natural and man-made environment reflects large-scale cultural changes. The harmony achieved by Tom and Lydia, the first-generation couple living at Marsh Farm, is symbolized by the biblical image of the rainbow; by the end of *The Rainbow*, when Ursula, the modern woman, rejects marriage with Skrebensky, the representative of the mechanistic modern society, the rainbow can be only a tentative hope for a future regeneration. Just as James's novels seem to take place in a theatre of consciousness which is his unique discovery, so a considerable part of Lawrence's achievement is his development of a wholly new way of writing about human experience. The aspect of life to which he attends does not fit any of our normal categories; it cannot be summarized as the realm of the instinctual, nor of the unconscious, not of the physical, nor of the emotional, though it touches all of these. It reflects Lawrence's radically new sense of the nature of the self and his rejection of what he called 'the old stable ego of the character', and is realized by techniques of ▷ symbolism, the repetition of imagery, and the use of sustained passages of highly poetic yet often abstract language to describe the development of the individual. In *Women in Love* contemporary society is unequivocally rejected as mechanistic and destructive, and regeneration is located in personal relations of mystical intensity.

In its apocalyptic view Lawrence's work may be said to subordinate the contingency of history to a typological pattern: that is to say, a pattern of 'types' (events or persons), analogous to, and in many cases based upon, the events and persons of the Old Testament which foreshadow the dispensation of the New Testament. It is a feature of modernist narratives to order their material by symbol, pattern or metaphor rather than by the linear sequence of history. If the patterns to which history conforms are for Lawrence apocalyptic and typological, for ▷ Virginia Woolf (1882–1941) they are the patterns of art and of human sensibility. ▷ *To The Lighthouse* (1927) was described by Leonard Woolf as a 'psychological poem', and this reflects the privileging of consciousness and the work of art as a made object over the chronological sequence of conventional fiction. The novel is in three sections, of which the first and third describe the life of a family in their holiday home in Scotland on two days, one before and one after World War I. These sections use the stream of consciousness technique developed in the English novel by Woolf, ▷ James Joyce (1882–1941) and ▷ Dorothy Richardson (1873–1957). So *To The Lighthouse* represents the thought sequences of the Ramsay family and their guests, moving freely in time and space. The middle section of the novel, entitled 'Time Passes', is concerned with the non-human, with change, with history and the ravages of time (the war takes place and several of the characters die; the house decays). An opposition is set up in the novel between, on the one hand, the destructive effect of history and of impersonal nature, and on the other the ordering power of art (represented by the painter, Lily Briscoe) and of human consciousness as a builder of social relationships (represented by Mrs Ramsay's drawing together of family and friends). The novel ends with Lily finishing her painting, completing a pattern in which the past and the dead are not lost, but reconciled in memory and in art. In so far as this painting is an analogue for the novel itself, history is mastered by art.

In Woolf's work the stream of consciousness technique moves towards a radical view of the nature of the self, which is of particular importance for ▷ feminist writing. In ▷ *The Waves* (1931) the lives of six characters are represented, and the close interaction of their consciousnesses is symbolically associated with a pattern of waves on the sea, separate yet part of a greater whole. From her first novel, *The Voyage Out* (1915), Woolf expressed a sense of the fluid nature of the self, its interdependence with the selves of others, and its relation to ▷ gender and class-based power structures. Feminists have increasingly seen the self as socially and politically constructed and have drawn inspiration from Woolf's moves towards ▷ deconstruction of the idea of immutable gender identity. Her interest in androgyny, her sense of the social protest which madness can represent and her satire on repressive psychiatric practices in ▷ *Mrs Dalloway* (1925) have also remained points of reference for feminist writers, although there is disagreement as to how far she tended to withdraw from political issues.

Phases of modernism: Forster and Joyce

It is possible to distinguish an early phase of modernism, ending around the beginning of World War I. In the first decade of the century James's three last great novels appeared, together with most of Conrad's major fiction and the first two novels of E. M. Forster (1879–1970), whose work is frequently regarded as containing both modernist and Victorian elements. In Forster's novel ▷ *Howards End* (1910) English society is seen as divided between the business world of action and the refined world of culture and the emotions, and a symbolic reconciliation is suggested by the marriage of the chief representatives of each group, and the inheritance of a house (the Howards End of the title), which stands for a threatened continuity in English life. The sense of threat and change is distinctively modernist, as is the location of renewal and reconciliation in the realm of the symbolic and the imagination. But Forster's social comedy, his narrative technique and his ▷ humanism associate him with more traditional strains in the English novel.

A Passage To India is at once more symbolic and less schematic than *Howards End*, and, appearing in 1924, belongs to the later post-war phase of modernism. While its satire on the arrogance and narrow-mindedness of British officials in India reflects the same belief in tolerance and liberalism as Forster's earlier work, the novel also explores at a deeper level the philosophical issues arising from the meeting of cultures. This is achieved in part through a symbolic evocation of the Indian landscape, and in particular the mysterious Marabar Caves, which call into question the identity and beliefs of several of the characters by their immitigable otherness. The novel ends with the voice of the landscape itself, on a note of ambivalent hope. While Forster made a contribution to both phases of modernism, the main figures of this post-war phase are Lawrence, Joyce and Woolf. Joyce's ▷ *Dubliners* (1914) is a seminal influence on the modern ▷ short story in English. He described his intention as that of writing 'a chapter in the moral history of my culture', using 'a style of scrupulous meanness'. Drawing on French influences, Joyce does indeed inaugurate in English the oblique, laconic short story, later developed by American writer Ernest Hemingway (1899–1961) and *The New Yorker* ▷ magazine. But the use of symbol, Joyce's miming of the diction and speech patterns of his Dublin characters, and his idea of the epiphany – a sudden spiritual manifestation in the ordinary – point to a more poetic and symbolic strain which culminates in the powerful yet ironic romanticism of the last story in the collection, 'The Dead'.

▷ *A Portrait of the Artist as a Young Man* (1916) is comparable to Lawrence's ▷ *Sons and Lovers* (1913) in its semi-autobiographical nature. In each the primary interest is in the psychological and intellectual development of a young man, with great concentration on the protagonist. This is most obvious in the *Portrait*, where the other characters remain shadowy and the language and structure of the novel seeks to render the contents of Stephen's mind, but it is important that in *Sons and Lovers* much of what we learn about the other characters is essentially their roles in Paul Morel's psychological economy. The protagonists of both novels seek independence, but whereas in Lawrence's work this is primarily emotional independence, in that of Joyce it is predominantly cultural and intellectual, involving Stephen's escape from the restrictions of Irish society and the Catholic Church.

Joyce's ▷ *Ulysses* (1922) is a central text of modernism. A novel of over 600 pages concerned with one day in Dublin, it has an amazing richness of texture, combining mythical and literary allusions, parody and pastiche, punning and humour, with a powerful sense of the infinite complexity and subtlety of the individual's emotional and intellectual life. It is structured around a loose correspondence to the episodes of Homer's *Odyssey*, so that the juxtaposition of the ordinary with the heroic generates irony and wit while at the same time drawing on an archetypal level of experience comparable to that which the Swiss psychoanalyst ▷ Carl Jung located in a collective unconscious. The symbolist aspiration to imitate musical form is evident in the use of repeated words, phrases and images as forms of *leitmotif*. The novel encountered virulent opposition at the time of publication, being banned in England until 1936 on grounds of obscenity. Its acceptance into the canon of major works of English literature, together with the successful defence of D. H. Lawrence's ▷ *Lady Chatterley's Lover* at a 1960 obscenity trial, signalled the public endorsement of the principle that all areas of human experience could be valid subjects for the serious artist. It is in part for its combination of mundane details with a vast inclusiveness of reference that *Ulysses* is valued so highly.

The realist tradition: Bennett, Galsworthy, Wells

Despite the genuinely innovative and radical nature of modernist fiction, we should be wary of too schematic an opposition between modernists and traditionalists. We are inheritors of a distinction made by writers such as Woolf and Lawrence in order to define their artistic identity and literary programme. As Frank Kermode has pointed out, modernist programmes have the habit of claiming that they have to 'get out from under something', and Arnold Bennett, John Galsworthy and ▷ H. G. Wells (1866–1946) were cast in the role of that 'something'. Wells himself participated in this process in his well-known comment in a letter to Henry James (8 July 1915): 'To you literature like painting is an end, to me literature is a means, it has a use . . . I had rather be called a journalist than an artist'. Nevertheless, there are some affinities between the realists and the modernists in terms of influences and subject matter: Bennett was influenced by French and Russian novelists, and Wells, in his scientific romances, shows a strong sense of the apocalyptic and of the impact of war and technology on 20th-century society. These writers are also part of important continuities in English fiction. Wells's emphasis on ideas is continued by ▷ Aldous Huxley (1894–1963) and ▷ George Orwell (1903–50) in the 1930s and 40s, while Bennett's regional settings in the Potteries district connect him with the regional realists of the 1950s. Wells, in works such as *The War of the Worlds* (1898) and *The First Men in the Moon* (1901), was also a pioneer of ▷ science fiction, one of the most fruitful of the popular genres in the 20th-century novel.

Bennett's best work, such as *The Old Wives Tale* (1908) and *Riceyman Steps* (1923), contains telling studies of ordinary lives, with a strong sense of the rich detail of society, and of the passing of time. The limitations of his style include a liability to give information too directly, to 'telling' rather than 'showing'. Like Bennett, Galsworthy was extremely popular and successful during his lifetime, with works such as ▷ *The Forsyte Saga* (1906–21) which are primarily concerned with upper-class society. The most general criticism of his work is that his satire is often lacking in focus and rigour. Wells was an extremely versatile writer of fiction and journalism; his fiction included Dickensian social comedy such as *The History of Mr Polly* (1910) and studies of contemporary social issues such as *Ann Veronica* (1909), as well as his science fiction or scientific romances. George Orwell, who considered Wells's thinking to be outmoded by the 1940s, nevertheless asserted of his own generation that 'the minds of us all, and therefore the physical world, would be perceptibly different if Wells had never existed.'

1920s satire: Lewis, Huxley and Waugh

Alongside the modernist experimentation of the 1920s a vein of tragicomic satire emerged in the English novel in the work of Aldous Huxley, ▷ Wyndham Lewis (1882–1957) and ▷ Evelyn Waugh (1903–66). These authors shared a sense of the absurdity of modern society, and one form which this takes in their novels is that of dehumanization and the dissolution of the self. Wyndham Lewis, an artist, philosopher and editor as well as a novelist, was a leading spirit of Vorticism, an anti-realist movement in art, based on jagged, rhythmical, mechanistic forms. Such principles are also reflected in the portrayal of character in Lewis's novels, such as *Tarr* (1918); he described men as comic because they were 'things, or physical bodies, behaving as persons'. Aldous Huxley's *Crome Yellow* (1921) is primarily a novel of ideas, similar in form to the novels of Thomas Love Peacock (1785–1866), in which characters carry on debates in the setting of a country house. It is based on a somewhat schematic antithesis between men of thought and men of action.

The protagonist, Dennis Stone, an example of the former who wants to be the latter, is a characteristic satirical anti-hero of the period, weak and ineffectual, but both types are portrayed as inadequate. The hero of Evelyn Waugh's first novel, *Decline and Fall* (1928) is described as a shadow; passively enduring a series of outrageous injustices and misfortunes, he ends up precisely where he started. The book describes itself as 'an account of the mysterious disappearance of Paul Pennyfeather'. Paul's adventures, however, bring him up against a large number of eccentrics, so that his shadowiness only serves to emphasize the egregious personalities which surround him.

These works contain images of the modern world as manic, mechanized and incomprehensible; they are essentially about the problem of how to live in a society which seems meaningless. The stance of the implied author (the author as he is manifest in the text) varies: Huxley tends to include some equivalent for himself in the novel, thereby making his own intellectual approach part of the object of his satire; Waugh is detached and invisible; Lewis is outraged, polemical and assertive. Drawing on the tradition of such European writers as Voltaire, Gogol and Swift, they represent a powerful alternative vision of the modern condition.

PART II – 1930 to 1950

In the 1930s and 40s political events were felt in English prose writing with a particular directness. The impact of World War I and the associated social changes on the modernist novel tended to take place primarily at the level of the author's general world view, and to filter through into the content of the novel transformed by some principle of artistic shaping. From around 1930, however, there arose in many writers a sense that historical events were of such overwhelming importance in their implications for society that they demanded forms of writing which would attempt to represent, with as much immediacy as possible, the feel of contemporary experience, while also explicitly taking sides in a political or moral debate. In general terms, then, the period was one in which social or documentary realism reasserted itself; that form of realism which is concerned with an outward fidelity to the experience of the mass of individuals and an engagement with public issues. Such a generalization is, however, necessarily an oversimplification. Individual authors continued or commenced their literary careers, responding in a variety of ways to their own experiences, influences and interests as well as to the temper of the times. New works by Joyce and Woolf were still appearing during the early part of the period; Woolf's last novel was *Between The Acts* (1941) while Joyce's final work, ▷ *Finnegans Wake*, was published in 1939. ▷ Ivy Compton-Burnett (1884–1969), whose first novel had appeared as early as 1911, elaborated further her vision of power, pain and obsession in wealthy families of late Victorian and early Edwardian England, rendered almost entirely through dialogue. Evelyn Waugh's novels of the 1930s, including the hilarious *Scoop* (1938), continued and developed the satirical vein begun with *Decline and Fall*. ▷ Elizabeth Bowen (1899–1973), in novels such as *The Heat of the Day* (1949) and short stories such as 'Mysterious Kôr' (from *The Demon Lover*, 1945), combined an evocation of the atmosphere of wartime London with a Jamesian attention to the nuances of personal relations. ▷ Samuel Beckett's unique exploration of man as an isolated being confronting existential despair began with his first novel, *Murphy*, in 1938, which had been preceded by a collection of Joycean stories, *More Pricks than Kicks* (1934).

The approach of war: Orwell and Isherwood

In the public sphere the 1930s were dominated by two factors. The first was the economic depression which, from the collapse of the Wall Street Stock Market in 1929, began to cause widespread unemployment and poverty. The second was the rise of ▷ fascism in Europe: Hitler seized power in Germany in 1933; in Italy Mussolini had ruled since 1922; in 1932 Sir Oswald Mosley founded the British Union of Fascists. The most coherent ideological response to both these developments came from the left wing, so that during the 1930s a considerable number of British writers and intellectuals became socialists or communists. The Left Book Club, founded in 1936, provided a focus for this tendency. It is primarily from a left-wing perspective that modernism has been rejected or criticized, both in the 1930s and since. George Orwell, a socialist, though a very independent one, described the 1920s as 'a period of irresponsibility such as the world has never before seen'. Georg Lukács, the Hungarian Marxist critic (▷ Marx, Karl), writing in 1955 from a more dogmatic perspective, attacked modernism on the grounds that it treated man as a solitary and asocial being, thus denying the reality of history.

Orwell's own writings seek to bring home to readers the human consequences of the economic and political situation: the soul-destroying nature of poverty in *Down and Out in London and Paris* (1933) and *The Road to Wigan Pier* (1937), the miseries of war and the distortions of the press in *Homage to Catalonia* (1938) and the oppressions of British imperialism in *Burmese Days* (1934). The first three of these works blend reportage and autobiography with an element of the fictional, and in each many facts are given, ranging from the minute details of daily life in the trenches of the Spanish Civil War to the income and itemized expenditure of a Yorkshire miner in 1935. This might be seen as a return to the 'materialism' which Woolf objected to in the work of Galsworthy and Bennett, but it gains new force both from Orwell's passionate indignation, and from his imaginative realization of the influence of material conditions on human consciousness and society. However, his individualism and his sometimes sentimental portrayal of the working classes have been criticized by socialist thinkers such as ▷ Raymond Williams.

Orwell's novel *Coming Up For Air* was published in 1939, on the eve of World War II, in the same year as a work by another writer of left-wing views, ▷ Christopher Isherwood's *Goodbye to Berlin*. In each there is a powerful sense of foreboding, of European civilization slipping into violence and chaos. The contrast of narrative techniques illustrates the range of 1930s realism. *Goodbye to Berlin* is a series of linked short episodes set in the decadent atmosphere of

Berlin during the Nazi rise to power. The detached quality of the first-person narrator is defined on the first page: 'I am a camera with its shutter open, quite passive, recording, not thinking'; he says relatively little of his own feelings as he moves among a cast of largely manipulative, destructive or self-destructive characters. The narrator's very passivity and neutrality of stance comes to epitomize the failure of the European mind to confront the rise of fascism. Orwell's narrator is George Bowling, a disillusioned insurance salesman approaching middle age who returns to the village of his childhood in an attempt to recapture something of what now seems to him to have been an idyllic Edwardian age. He is an egregiously personal dramatized narrator, who addresses the reader throughout in a conversational tone, masking a highly skilful rhetoric which persuades us to share his vision of an England of petty, narrow lives, a civilization of rubbish dumps and synthetic food, a people with fascist violence hanging over them, 'so terrified of the future that we're jumping straight into it like a rabbit diving down a boa constrictor's throat'. George's anticipation of 'the coloured shirts, the barbed wire, the rubber truncheons', looks forward to Orwell's post-war vision of totalitarianism *1984* (1949) and his political allegory *Animal Farm* (1945).

These post-war works reflect a general disillusionment with communism, resulting from the revelation of the Stalinist show trials, and the Nazi-Soviet pact of 1941. But during the 1930s many writers and intellectuals had become Marxists, and a considerable number fought for the Republicans in the Spanish Civil War. Many novels of the 1930s reflect this commitment, including ▷ Rex Warner's allegory *The Wild Goose Chase* (1937), and Edward Upward's *Journey to the Border* (1938). Both these novels have propagandist Marxist conclusions; in *Journey to the Border* the protagonist's hallucinations and fantasies are associated with a decadent society, and at the end of the novel he decides to regain reality by joining the workers' movement. Thus by the end of the 1930s 'reality' has become for many a politically defined concept, a matter of class commitment rather than of the nuances of consciousness. The experience of working-class life is perhaps most powerfully expressed in the work of writers who grew up in working-class regional communities. ▷ Lewis Grassic Gibbon in *A Scot's Quair* (1932–34) and Walter Greenwood in *Love on the Dole* (1933) use dialect to convey social cohesion and social deprivation in north-east Scotland and northern England respectively. Gibbon's trilogy is especially remarkable for its sense of community, history and the impact of the Scottish landscape on the consciousness of the characters.

The inner and outer worlds: Greene and Lowry

The dangers of oversimplification inherent in an antithesis between a modernist concentration on the individual inner world, and a politically committed attention to social relations becomes evident when we consider the work of ▷ Graham Greene (1904–91). His early work of the 1930s, such as *It's a Battlefield* (1934) and *Brighton Rock* (1938) has a sense of the oppressive squalor of areas of modern urban life, a sense which is later translated into the more exotic settings of late colonialism; visions of seediness and corruption in such settings as Africa (*The Heart of the Matter*; 1948), Vietnam (*The Quiet American*; 1955) and South America (*The Honorary Consul*; 1973). He had a long-standing, if moderate, left-wing commitment, evident not only in his novels, with their critique of the Western role in the Third World, but also in his active friendship and support for those resisting the right-wing dictatorships of Central America, recounted in his memoir *Getting to Know the General* (1984). Yet characters such as the whisky priest of *The Power and the Glory* (1940) confront their moral choices in a condition of existential isolation and Greene himself associated his use of journeys (he was an inveterate traveller) with the methods of psychoanalysis (▷ Psychoanalytical criticism); in the introduction to *Journey Without Maps* (1936) he explains that he sought to give general significance to his travels in Liberia by using 'memories, dreams and word-associations' to suggest a parallel, inner journey. From the time of *Brighton Rock* his ▷ Catholicism became more apparent. Though he did not regard himself as a 'Catholic novelist', his work is informed by a powerful sense of good and evil, and of the sinfulness of human nature, combined with a somewhat determinist tragic irony. In these respects, as well as in his use of extreme situations which test human morality and endurance, he has links to Conrad and Dostoievski as precursors, and to the post-war English novelist ▷ William Golding (b 1911) as a successor. Many of Greene's novels are narrated in the third person in a detached, unemotive style which serves to highlight violence, tragedy, the sordid and the grotesque. This style has affinities with American writers of the 1920s such as Ernest Hemingway and John Dos Passos.

▷ Malcolm Lowry's *Under the Volcano* (1947), like Greene's best work, endows a tragic story of human failure with metaphysical overtones. Set in Mexico, where the presence of fascist elements anticipates the approaching world war, the story of the alcoholic British Consul Geoffrey Firmin achieves a wide resonance by means of symbol, an intricate metaphorical structure and a stream of consciousness technique in which the beautiful but sinister Mexican landscape becomes an equivalent for inner turmoil. This novel belongs to the high modernist tradition in its formal experimentation and literary allusiveness, as well as in its somewhat Laurentian apocalyptic vision of political and cultural crisis. D. H. Lawrence had also previously engaged with a revolutionary Mexico in his much earlier novel *The Plumed Serpent* (1923), in his short stories, and in his travel essays, *Mornings in Mexico*. In *Under the Volcano*, however, Firmin's story is associated with that of Doctor Faustus, who sold his soul to the devil, while Mexico is presented as an archetype both of paradise and of hell. Firmin's inebriation, self-destructiveness and guilt are attributed to contemporary civilization as a whole. The novel, intended as part of a trilogy which was never completed, owes much to Joyce's *Ulysses* in its shifts of consciousness, its concentration on one day, with extended flashbacks, and its intricate, allusive structure.

The complex interplay of modernist experiment and the impulse towards social realism and political commitment was to contribute to a remarkable diversity of modes in fiction of the post-war era.

PART III – 1950 to the present

There has been a tendency among critics to see the post-war English novel as lacking in power and scope compared to the great age of modernism, and essays on the subject frequently begin by acknowledging the lack of either a great genius of the novelist's art or a single dominant movement with techniques and themes which are felt as central to contemporary culture. Gilbert Phelps, for example, in his essay 'The Post-War English Novel' (*New Pelican Guide to English Literature*, 1983), asserts that 'the trend of the English novel since the war has, on the whole, been ... a turning aside from the mainstream of European literature and a tendency to retreat into parochialism and defeatism'. Several points need to be made about such a view. There is the obvious but important fact that both greatness and cultural significance are more readily detected in retrospect. Furthermore, contemporary critical theory has made us increasingly aware that this retrospective detecting involves an element of construction. A sense of literary history, of the significance of particular works and authors, and of the existence of a canon of recognized major or serious works is necessarily a matter of a subjective, value-loaded and culturally specific process of consensus. This is not to say that such judgements are arbitrary, but only that they represent a characteristically human activity of creating patterns of meaning. Such a conception of cultural process is a powerful aspect of contemporary thought, and it may therefore be claimed that the diversity of contemporary fiction, by encouraging the reader to select from a huge range of available modes and styles, itself characterizes the prevailing *Zeitgeist* more effectively than could any dominant individual or group. Theories of cultural ▷ postmodernism emphasize the transformation of culture into a commodity and the simultaneous availability of many forms, including imitation and pastiche, of those of the past. More specifically in terms of the novel, the modernist claim to centrality depended, as we have seen, on a doctrine of experimentation and radical newness, according to which changes in novel technique accompanied changes in the nature of human experience. Works such as Joyce's *Finnegans Wake* (1939) pushed innovation along modernist lines close to the point where the coherence of the novel as a genre seemed in doubt. We have observed one form of reaction against modernism in the politically committed writings of the 1930s. Experimentation did not die out, but it increasingly came to seem one option among many, rather than an essential expression of the times. Furthermore, the shock to the idea of western civilization administered by World War II, the death camps and the atomic bomb rendered the very idea of cultural centrality a dubious one. On the other hand, fictionality itself seemed an increasingly appropriate focus of attention in a culture where clear standards of truth and significance were felt as elusive.

The awareness of fictionality

Samuel Beckett (1906–89) continued the Joycean line of experimentation, combining a fascination with words with an acute awareness of their limitations, and with a rich vein of parody, irony, imitation and pastiche. His vision is, however, a darker one, although humour is an essential aspect of it. In his trilogy of the 1950s, *Molloy* (1956), *Malone Dies* (1956) and *The Unnamable* (1959), isolated, aged and decrepit social outcasts of obscure identity narrate their own stories with a mixture of black humour and remorseless grimness. They are aware of themselves as story-tellers, making reference to the futility of this activity, yet continuing with the story in order to pass the time, as an act of defiance, or as an obsessive compulsion. As in Beckett's plays, there is a progressive minimalism, in which life is reduced to language, mundane and sordid physical details and the isolated human consciousness. In this respect his novels represent the ultimate breakdown of the classic realist novel, in which character is portrayed in a rich social context. In drawing attention to their own fictionality, and in playing games with language (including the game of teasing the critics by laying false clues) Beckett's narrators anticipate the contemporary fascination with the idea of fiction and of narration. Such concerns are not, of course, the prerogative of the 20th century, being prominent in, for example, Laurence Sterne's *Tristram Shandy* (1759–67) and Cervantes' *Don Quixote* (1605–15). However, the current interest in this area reflects ▷ structuralist and ▷ post-structuralist scepticism about the ability of language to refer to a non-linguistic reality, and the sense that fictionality is an attribute of forms of discourse other than fiction, such as history and the social sciences. This has generated an increasing interest in narrative as a model for the structuring both of culture and of individual experience.

Contemporary novelists who explore this model include ▷ John Fowles (b 1926), whose book *The French Lieutenant's Woman* (1969) combines a pastiche of a Victorian novel with passages of social history and statistics about Victorian sexual habits. The author addresses the reader, discussing his own techniques and the reader's likely response, and later, appearing as a minor character, decides to abrogate his authorial power over his characters by providing two alternative endings, even going to the length of tossing a coin to decide their order. The effect is that of an intriguing, if scarcely subtle, consideration of issues of free will, determinism, power and meaning.

Other experimental works which test the limits and nature of fiction include ▷ B. S. Johnson's 1969 novel, *The Unfortunates*, which has twenty-seven loose-leaf sections of which twenty-five may be read in any order, the randomness of the resulting structure serving as a metaphor for the circling and shifting of the mind. Johnson saw 'truth' and 'fiction' as antithetical terms, and his last work, *See the Old Lady Decently* (1975), employs documents and photographs in an attempt to create a non-fictional novel. This aspiration is paralleled in the documentary style of Alan Burns (b 1929), some of whose novels are structured around news items or press-cuttings. There are therefore two contrary but complementary impulses detectable in the experimental novel: one towards documentary objectivity, and the other towards the recognition of perspectivism. ▷ Lawrence Durrell (1912–90), in his sequence *The Alexandria Quartet* (1957–60) provides multiple perspectives on an intricate series of relationships in a community by means of a diversity of narratives, including third-person and first-person narratives, letters, journals and parts of an inset novel by a character. The reader's understanding of both character and event is subject to revision in the light of new information and perspectives, making the work what has been described as 'a game of mirrors'.

In a sense, experimental novels are particularly dependent upon the traditional qualities of a good novel, such as plot interest and imaginative power in the realization of social context. In the absence of such qualities the reader is unlikely to overcome the difficulties of coming to terms with an unfamiliar form. A novelist who combines imaginative power with a wittily expressed examination of the nature of the fictional is ▷ Dan Jacobson (b 1929). *The Rape of Tamar* (1970) is set in the time of the Old Testament King David, and narrated by Yonadab, who is intensely aware of the philosophical and moral dilemmas of his role as narrator. He has knowledge of our own time as well as that of the story, and shares with us his reflections on the resulting ironies. Thus the act of narrating is a source of interest throughout, generating insights into such issues as hypocrisy, self-deception, voyeurism, the function of art, the pleasures and vicissitudes of speaking, and the culturally specific nature of modes of interpretation. But these sophisticated intellectual concerns are matched and sustained by a powerful poetic evocation of the physical and cultural context, and above all by the sheer vitality of Yonadab's personality as he addresses us with engaging frankness in what he terms 'the simulacrum of time in which you and I have managed to meet'. Self-conscious narrative, which by various means draws attention to its own fictionality, serves to question the nature of reality, and of our understanding of it, and to highlight issues of freedom and control. It has therefore held a strong appeal for writers influenced by French ▷ existentialist thought, including ▷ Christine Brooke-Rose (b 1926) and ▷ David Caute (b 1936). In the postmodernist anti-novel, practised by writers such as ▷ Gabriel Josipovici (b 1940), structures based around repeated scenes or interwoven narratives create a radical uncertainty, and the world evoked by the text disintegrates in order to fulfil the author's aim of, in his own words, 'insisting that his book is a book and not the world' (from *The World and the Book, a Study of Modern Fiction*; 1971).

Morality and art

A feature of the work of several considerable post-war novelists is a renewed attempt to present a vision of the world as a battleground of forces of good and evil. William Golding has had outstanding success in the construction of moral fables, shaped by Christian archetypes of sin, guilt, purgation and the tentative but precious hope of redemption. His novels, of which the first was *Lord of the Flies* (1954), show a powerful interest in the primitive and the physical, particularly in the examination of extreme conditions or states of consciousness in which human experience is stripped to moral and physical essentials. This description does not, however, do justice to the range of his settings and techniques. *The Inheritors* (1955) attempts to realize the mind and culture of Neanderthal man. This relatively idyllic and innocent culture is used to make us see our own nature (as represented by the arrival of *homo sapiens*) in a new and largely unflattering light; a technique which owes much to Conrad's comparable use of non-European cultures. *The Spire* (1964) renders the tormented consciousness of a fanatical medieval cleric, while *Rites of Passage* (1980) uses pastiche and the ironies arising from a self-confident but mistaken narrator to portray the moral awakening of a gentleman traveller in the early 19th century. The limitation of Golding's work is its explicitness. The thrust of his moral vision and his mythic patterning can sometimes seem overbearing, though many readers will feel that this is a small price to pay for its power and authority.

In contrast to Golding's historical and cultural range, most of the novels of ▷ Iris Murdoch (b 1919) are set in contemporary English middle-class society, but are informed by a range of philosophical concerns centring on moral responsibility, individual freedom, the nature of love, and the possibility of actively pursuing goodness. They combine a serious, and at times tragic, exploration of these concerns with exciting plots, and elements of the comic, supernatural, and fantastic. These features have been sustained through a prolific career since the appearance of her first novel, *Under the Net* in 1954. Doubts about her work focus on a sense that characters are excessively manipulated in the interest of illustrating abstract ideas, and a dissatisfaction with her use of violence and accident as a plot device. Of her early novels, *The Bell* (1958) is notable for its complex symbolic structure. The moral significance of the lives of a group of characters, brought together in a rather bizarre religious community, is examined by a pattern of interaction centred around the symbol of a convent bell, but using also animal and water symbolism. *The Sea, The Sea* (1978), a Booker Prize winner, and one of the most acclaimed of her works, is a typically dark comedy about obsession, guilt and egotism, but is remarkable for the richness of its symbols and characters. ▷ A. S. Byatt (b 1936) shows the influence of Murdoch in her use of symbolic structures and her portrayal of the inter-relations of a large group of central characters. The latter feature is particularly evident in the opening books of a projected tetralogy: *The Virgin in the Garden* (1979) and *Still Life* (1985). Moral concerns are evident, but less explicit than in Murdoch's work, more attention being given to correspondences between experience and mythic or aesthetic patterns, and to the process of cultural change. Byatt's most recent and successful work, the Booker Prize-winning *Possession*, is a cleverly interwoven pastiche of Victorian poetry, the lives of its writers, and the lives of a network of 20th-century literary critics. The inter-relations of characters is thus wittily carried out across time, as the lives of Victorian poets intersect with those of their modern readers.

In the work of ▷ Muriel Spark (b 1918), manipulation is less a risk for the author than an explicit theme and, as in Ford Madox Ford's *The Good Soldier* (1915), the manipulative aspects of the narrating activity are exploited as a source of irony in the rendering of patterns of social and psychological control. Thus in the ▷ novella *The Driver's Seat* (1970) the use of the present tense, and an entirely external focalization on one character (the narrative recounting events from her point of view, but with almost no revelation of her feelings, thoughts or intentions) creates a grim and enigmatic vision of a woman with a psychological compulsion and a violent destiny which seem fixed and unchangeable, yet not understood either by author or reader. In *The Prime of Miss Jean Brodie* (1961) humour is more in evidence, but dark shadows of fascism and personal betrayal, evoked particularly through prolepses (jumps forward to later events), lurk around the story of a teacher's charismatic influence on a group of pupils. Spark's Catholic sensibility emerges in her portrayal of diabolic figures, such as the charming, egregiously manipulative Dougal Douglas of *The Ballad of Peckham Rye* (1960).

While Spark is a convert to Catholicism, ▷ Anthony Burgess (b 1917) has a Catholic background, and though not a practising member of the Church, acknowledges the importance of Catholic modes of thought in his work. *A Clockwork Orange* (1962) is concerned with the relation of evil and free-will. The protagonist makes a deliberate choice of a life of horrifying violence and sadistic cruelty, and attempts by a futuristic authoritarian society to reform him by brainwashing can only destroy his human identity. The novel is notable for its use of an invented teenage patois, Nadsat, reflecting Burgess's enthusiasm for Joycean linguistic multiplicity and invention. Burgess has stated that he sees the duality of good and evil as the ultimate reality, and in *Earthly Powers* (1980) the history of the 20th century is portrayed in terms of such a moral struggle, seen through the memories of the narrator, a homosexual writer. As in Murdoch's work, a strong sense of moral patterning underlies and unifies a complexity of events. In the novels of ▷ Margaret Drabble (b 1939) moral concern is focused on social justice and the individual quest for identity, particularly on the part of women. Works such as *The Ice Age* (1977) reflect her admiration for Arnold Bennett in their realist portrayal of the state of contemporary British society.

Feminist writing

The question of what constitutes 'feminist' writing is a contentious issue, but what is certain is that novels concerned with women's experience represent a significant section of the contemporary fiction market, and make rich use of innovations in narrative technique and of a range of styles and genres. An important divide among feminist critics is between those, such as Elaine Showalter, who see the role of contemporary female writing as that of self-discovery, articulating the nature of women's personal experience within society and revealing structures of oppression, and those such as Toril Moi, who advocate rather the deconstruction of the idea of the unitary self, and the rejection of the male/female dichotomy in favour of some ideal of androgyny.

The project of articulating women's experience includes the rediscovery of the unrecorded, of what has been omitted from the conventional histories and novels. Thus ▷ Eva Figes (b 1932), in *The Seven Ages* (1986), writes a fictional chronicle of the lives of seven generations of women, from pre-history up to the present, concentrating on their struggles with poverty and violence, and their experience of childbirth and child-rearing. An associative, free-floating narrative style suggests a collective female consciousness, transcending the individual self and linking women to natural forces of generation. ▷ Zoe Fairbairns's *Stand We At Last* (1983) also recounts the lives of successive generations of women, though with closer attention to the detailed historical context, while the Manawaka series of novels and stories by the Canadian writer ▷ Margaret Laurence (1926–87) are narrated by women of various ages and generations in such a way as to simultaneously explore the social history of Canada and the dilemmas and achievements of women in the context of a prairie town. ▷ Jean Rhys (1894–1979), in *Wide Sargasso Sea* (1966), writes a feminist complement to Charlotte Brontë's *Jane Eyre*, recounting the early life of the mad first Mrs Rochester, from her childhood in the West Indies. Rhys gives consciousness to the character who, in the original novel, is an inarticulate symbolic location for a rejected violence of feeling. Madness is a recurrent theme of feminist writing, because, considered as a refusal to conform to an imposed social identity, it can become a potent symbol of revolt against oppression. ▷ Doris Lessing (b 1919) does not see herself as primarily a feminist writer, but her novel *The Golden Notebook* (1962) has become a seminal feminist text. It is built out of a skeleton narrative, entitled 'Free Women', plus four notebooks kept by Anna, one of the characters of 'Free Women'. This fragmentation reflects her fear of breakdown as she confronts political, literary and sexual problems as an independent woman, but in the fifth and final 'Golden Notebook', a new unity is achieved through a mental breakdown shared with a man, during which the collapse of divisions leads to 'formlessness with the end of fragmentation'.

A number of writers, without adopting an overtly feminist standpoint, attend particularly to women's experience of isolation, betrayal, loss or guilt within the limitations imposed on their lives by social convention or male attitudes and behaviour. They include ▷ Edna O'Brien (b 1932), whose popular and entertaining novels are concerned particularly with the vicissitudes of sexuality and passion, and ▷ Anita Brookner (b 1928), who portrays the disillusionment of her sensitive female characters with an elegant, detached attention to the nuances of human relationships. In one sense these writers are the opposite of feminist, since their work could be held to accept as a premise the view that women seek self-fulfilment largely through relations with men. Yet in representing the tragedy or frustration which may result from such dependence, their novels raise crucial feminist issues, and are part of the context for the debate about the fictional portrayal of women.

▷ Fay Weldon (b 1931) recounts the lives of her women characters with a sort of desperate black humour. In works such as *Down Among the Women* (1971) and *Praxis* (1978), a constant shifting of relationships and roles suggests a terrifying instability of identity; both men and women move between the role of victim and victimizer, but the women are consistently the more disadvantaged, both socially and biologically. Both novels end by suggesting that a new breed of emancipated woman is emerging, but offer little convincing evidence for this hope, and Weldon's work has gradually tended towards disillusion, with an element of biological determinism. Women's sexuality, and sexual politics, have been central feminist concerns. In contrast to Weldon's cynical realism, ▷ Angela Carter (1940–92) approached these issues through fantasy, myth and fairy-tale. Fantasy and dream can serve as forms of experience emancipated from rational modes of thought which are seen as essentially male, and ▷ Emma Tennant (b 1937), in *The Bad Sister* (1978), employs a split between realist and fantasy modes to develop this opposition. Radical perspectives on sexual relations are also a feature of the work of ▷ Maureen Duffy (b 1933), who explores particularly working-class and lesbian experience.

Realism, satire, social comedy

There is a continuing strain in the English novel which is concerned with the analysis of contemporary English culture by means of satire, humour, or irony, primarily within realistic modes. The satirical strain, building on the earlier work of writers such as Waugh and Huxley, includes ▷ Angus Wilson (1913–91), whose novel, *Anglo-Saxon Attitudes* (1956), set in the late 1940s, is a portrait of academic and London life and the egotism and self-deception of a range of characters. These concerns, however, take on a broader historical and social resonance because of the novel's examination of the effect of the past on the present via the troubled personal life of an historian and the confusion arising out of an historical fraud committed in 1912. *The Old Men at the Zoo* (1961) continues the vein of satirical analysis, but moves into fantasy and allegory in its bizarre tale of the administration of the London Zoo during another war. Wilson is also a writer of short stories, which combine a sharp satirical edge with a considerable emotional charge in their exposure of cruelty, snobbishness and pretension.

During the 1950s a group of writers emerged whose work combined a realist portrayal of provincial communities with a strong sense of social injustice. Some of these writers became known by the label ▷ 'angry young men'; they include ▷ Alan Sillitoe (b 1928), ▷ Stan Barstow (b 1928), ▷ John Wain (b 1925), ▷ John Braine (b 1922) and ▷ David Storey (b 1933), and in their early novels the heroes are working class, or in revolt against the demands of a middle-class background. Novels such as John Braine's *Room at the Top* (1957), John Wain's *Hurry on Down* (1953), Stan Barstow's *A Kind of Loving* (1960) and Alan Sillitoe's *Saturday Night and Sunday Morning* (1958) seemed to epitomize a post-war sense of futility, discontent and rebellion. Their subsequent careers have developed in various ways, as, for example, towards narrative innovation in the case of Storey, or to a reaction against radicalism in the case of Braine. They were brought up outside London, coming in most cases from working-class backgrounds, and their work continued the tradition of working-class regional writing found earlier in the novels of Walter Greenwood and Lewis Grassic Gibbon.

Of those originally seen as 'angry young men', it is perhaps ▷ Kingsley Amis (b 1922) who has most successfully sustained his popular appeal over the succeeding decades. Unlike Angus Wilson, who, influenced by Virginia Woolf, used a range of interior monologues in his sixth novel *No Laughing Matter* (1967), Amis eschews modernist experiment, though working with a number of sub-genres, such as the ghost-story (*The Green Man*; 1969) and the fantasy of an alternative world (*The Alteration*; 1976). His novels are characterized by sharp wit, inventiveness, and a considerable animus against whatever Amis sees as bogus or blameworthy. *Lucky Jim* (1954), his very entertaining first novel, inaugurated the genre of the humorous campus novel, since developed by ▷ Malcolm Bradbury (b 1932) in *Stepping Westward* (1965) and *The History Man* (1975), and ▷ David Lodge (b 1935) in *Changing Places* (1975) and *Small World* (1984). Amis specializes in dislikeable characters, with objectionable attitudes, such as the xenophobia of the protagonists of *I Like It Here* (1958) and *One Fat Englishman* (1963), or the misogyny of Stanley in *Stanley and the Women* (1984). While these attitudes are subjected to a degree of satirical censure, they are not altogether repudiated. Amis's position is now a conservative one, marked by a distrust of the cosmopolitan and the experimental.

The influence of Jane Austen is apparent in the work of ▷ Barbara Pym (1913–80), which enjoyed a revival in the late 1970s, and consists of subtle and ironical studies of middle-class life, combining a shrewd humour with an uncompromising sense of the commonness of frustration, isolation and ennui. The delicacy of her work might be contrasted with the satirical shock-tactics of ▷ Martin Amis (b 1949) who employs black humour to portray human fears, obsessions and desires. Surprisingly, Amis (who is Kingsley Amis's son), claims to be influenced by Jane Austen too; he shares with Pym the use of humour of some sort to reveal human weakness, but they stand at opposite ends of a spectrum stretching from gentle irony to vigorous satire.

Commonwealth writers

This essay started by referring to the cross-fertilization of cultures as essential to the modernist movement at the beginning of the century. Since that time Britain's political and cultural relations with the rest of the world have changed radically. The British Empire has ended; two world wars have brought enormous social changes; technological developments have transformed the world economic system, and therefore the manner in which cultural artefacts are circulated. The diversity and plurality which have been noted as aspects of postmodern society have a particular value insofar as they promote an attention to the radical otherness of different cultures. There is thus a new, postmodern form of cross-fertilization taking place. The difference between the two forms might be epitomized by the difference between reading E. M. Forster's *A Passage to India*, the reaction of a sensitive and perceptive Englishman to Indian society, and reading the novels of ▷ R. K. Narayan (b 1906) which, though using the English language, are written by an Indian who knows that society from within. The availability of works in translation is also a part of this openness; since the 1970s the English novel-reading public has been less likely to read English works which somehow attempt to incorporate world culture, and more likely to read works in translation, such as the Latin American novels of Jorge Luis Borges (1899–1987), Gabriel García Márquez (b 1928), Carlos Fuentes (b 1928) or Mario Vargas Llosa (b 1936) and the Eastern European novels of Alexander Solzhenitsyn (b 1918) or Milan Kundera (b 1929). But a very considerable contribution to the development of the novel written in English has been made by Commonwealth writers (▷ Commonwealth literatures). The term is not satisfactory, being increasingly politically outdated, but there is not as yet a suitable alternative term for those countries, once part of the Empire, where English provides a common literary language.

The novels of ▷ Chinua Achebe (b 1930) articulate the impact on Nigerian culture of white colonialism and its aftermath, from 1920s tribal life, the setting of *Arrow of God* (1964), to Lagos in the 1960s in *A Man of the People* (1966). But the interest of his work is by no means limited to its political implications. Writing in English, Achebe incorporates African proverbs and idioms in such a way as to make the cultural context vivid and compelling for both African and English readers, and characters such as Okonkwo, the village leader who is the principal character of Achebe's first novel, *Things Fall Apart* (1958), achieve psychological complexity, and a considerable tragic status. The continuing oppression of white rule in South Africa dominates the novels of ▷ Nadine Gordimer (b 1932), but is addressed obliquely through its impact on private experience. Writing primarily about the white middle classes, she traces the decay resulting from their involvement in a brutal and segregated social system.

▷ Patrick White (1912–90) was one of the most accomplished Australian novelists of the late twentieth century. His work draws on the stark polarities of Australian life: the polite social milieu of suburban Sydney, satirized by White with a dry wit, and the starkly primitive outback, which in *Voss* (1957) becomes a spiritual testing ground. The eponymous hero of this novel is a dedicated German explorer, with a compulsive though enigmatic sense of his own destiny, who leads an expedition into the Australian interior. In the early part of the novel the narrative shifts freely between realistic observation of social mores and poetic evocation of characters' inner worlds of memory, anticipation and desire. This blend is characteristic of White's idiosyncratic style, which startles by its immediacy and tonal range. Voss's journey, like those of Graham Greene's characters, is also an inner journey, and, as in the work of Joseph Conrad, the confrontation with a harsh and alien landscape is endowed with philosophical and spiritual resonance through the questioning of personal identity; external and internal landscapes function as mutual metaphors. Central to *Voss* is the duality of the physical world and the human imagination; the latter becomes concentrated in the intense and mystical relationship between Voss and a woman he has met in Sydney, a relationship carried on in their thoughts and letters. White is both a social satirist and a visionary and the authority of his work was recognized by the award of the Nobel Prize for Literature in 1973. More recently another Australian novelist, ▷ Peter Carey (b 1943), has achieved considerable popular success with highly inventive works including *Illywhacker* (1985) and *Oscar and Lucinda* (1988).

In both New Zealand and Canada strong traditions of women's writing have grown up. The analysis of New Zealand society by Edith Searle Grossman at the start of the 20th century, and by ▷ Katherine Mansfield (1888–1923) and Jane Mander in the 1920s has continued since 1950 in the work of writers such as ▷ Janet Frame (b 1924). In Canada, Margaret Laurence and ▷ Margaret Atwood (b 1939) have represented social change and individual quests for identity with a strong sense of the physical and historical context of Canadian life. Just as Laurence uses her fictional prairie town of Manawaka to chart Canadian social history, so R. K. Narayan has built his work around the fictional South Indian town of Malgudi (based on Mysore), as an epitome of Indian culture, while the work of his fellow countryman ▷ Salman Rushdie (b 1947) employs postmodernist strategies and the techniques of ▷ magical realism.

Barbadian ▷ George Lamming (b 1927) is notable for his direct treatment of the legacy of colonialism, and in particular of slavery. Some of his works, such as *Water with Berries* (1971), deal with these issues in a British setting: Lamming has lived in England since 1950, contributing to a strong movement of black writing in Britain, along with others such as ▷ Samuel Selvan, who came to England from Trinidad at the same time, and the Kenyan Ngugi Wa Thiong'o. Among West Indian writers it is ▷ V. S. Naipaul (b 1932) who has met with the greatest popular success and critical acclaim. His early novels, such as *The Mystic Masseur* (1957) evoke the life of Trinidad with an elegant clarity which emphasizes both its sordid aspects and its vitality. His best-known work, *A House for Mr Biswas* (1961) deals with the hero's search for independence combined with the capacity to love and accept responsibility. This search is articulated by the metaphor of the building of a house, a focus of self-respect and growth in the face of the displacement which is the aftermath of colonialism. *A House for Mr Biswas* is a work of considerable scope in the comic realist tradition. As such it exemplifies the role of Commonwealth authors in rediscovering a vitality and power in the existing forms of the English novel, while developing a style and technique appropriate to their distinctive concerns and cultures.

Conclusion

The field of contemporary fiction is large and expanding. This essay attempts to provide an introduction to 20th-century fiction by examining some perspectives on the major work of the first half of the century, and by suggesting something of the range and variety of writing since 1950, in the hope that the reader will be encouraged to explore further. Traditional features of the novel, such as satire, the pleasure of narrative, the excitement of plot and the rendering of moral distinctions still find new and original exponents. Narrative experiment and the awareness of fictionality provide powerful means for exploring the particular philosophical preoccupations of our age, while genres such as science fiction, ▷ horror and the fantasy novel offer popular alternative modes of writing. At the same time both the language and the techniques of the novel are successfully adapted to various and changing cultures. The diversity of the contemporary English novel is a sign of the vitality of the form and of the continuing ability of fiction to engage at many levels with both intellectual issues and cultural processes.

Developments in Modern Drama: The Slow Road to Change

4

Andrew Piasecki
University of London

Early experiments

▷ Henry James lamented the feebleness of English dramatic writing towards the end of the 19th century. Whether or not we agree with his judgement the fact is that the theatre itself was thriving, at least in London, the inevitable focus of this survey. For the more popular market there were melodramas, music hall shows and variety entertainments. Meanwhile, the middle classes, the fashionable and the leisured, were being lured back to the theatre by more self-consciously respectable forms of drama. These ranged from the Savoy operas of Gilbert and Sullivan to the farces and more serious 'problem plays' of Sir Arthur Wing Pinero and Henry Arthur Jones to the pictorially spectacular productions of ▷ Shakespeare by the great actor-managers of the period, Sir Henry Irving and Sir Herbert Beerbohm Tree. Apart from historical English insularity, the cultivation of respectability explains the slowness of the English theatre to respond to new developments in drama on the continent. The new drama of playwrights like ▷ Ibsen and ▷ Strindberg was critical of complacent bourgeois values and easily identified as politically subversive. Theatre managers, in a competitive commercial business, were hardly likely to promote this kind of dramatic material. After all, English polite society did not go to the theatre to see its moral values attacked. Given the conditions of the English theatre at this time, it is not surprising that it took a long time for Ibsen, Strindberg and ▷ Chekhov to make any serious impact on the English stage.

The new European playwrights initially appealed to a relatively small circle of intellectuals rather than the general theatre-going public. In 1891 ▷ Jack Thomas Grein formed the Independent Theatre Society in an attempt to encourage a native drama comparable to that of France and Scandinavia. The first production was Ibsen's *Ghosts*, which predictably aroused a storm of abuse for openly referring to venereal disease. Unfortunately the Independent Theatre produced little of Ibsen's work thereafter. ▷ George Bernard Shaw (1856–1950) was another campaigner for the new Ibsenite drama and in 1890 he gave a series of lectures on the subject for the ▷ Fabian Society, later published as *The Quintessence of Ibsenism*. This was followed up with a practical project, an experiment in a repertory system at the Court Theatre, between 1904 and 1907, run by the director ▷ Harley Granville Barker and the manager John Eugene Vedrenne. The success of Shaw's plays there enabled the theatre to present Ibsen's *Hedda Gabler* and *The Wild Duck*. Even then there was only a handful of performances, since this new and unfamiliar drama was financially risky. In retrospect it is no surprise that plays at least superficially resembling the drawing-room dramas of Jones and Pinero were favoured above Ibsen's more poetical works like *Brand* and *Peer Gynt*, which made much more challenging demands in performance terms. So long as the theatre was run on commercial principles this was bound to be the case. To Fabians like Barker and Shaw it was part of the business of good government to promote the national culture, and of good plays to educate the audience. They yearned for a national subsidized theatre where a new serious drama might be nurtured. Barker actually produced a detailed scheme for such a theatre with the critic William Archer, entitled *The National Theatre: A Scheme and Estimates* (1903). They suggested a policy for encouraging new writers, and provided detailed samples of possible repertory, focusing on world classics; they even laid down principles for actors' training. Unfortunately, such ideas did not impress a government which believed firmly in the principles of free enterprise. Perhaps Henry James should have considered that the dearth of original playwrights was related to the way in which the theatre was financially organized.

Although Shaw claimed to imitate Ibsen, he was shrewd enough not to ignore popular native forms of drama. As he put it, 'my stage tricks and suspenses and thrills and jests are the ones in vogue when I was a boy'. To reject outright the English tradition was to consign oneself to obscurity. This was clearly understood by the other major Irish (▷ Irish literature in English) dramatist of the period, ▷ Oscar Wilde (1856–1900). Wilde openly exploited the devices of melodrama, the implausible plots of farce and the tried and tested theme of 'a woman with a past'. What he added was his own unique wit which gives his plays their distinctive charm and flavour. His most famous play, *The Importance of Being Earnest* (1895), is essentially a light-hearted mockery of aristocratic manners, and derivative of Gilbert's *Engaged*. In his other comedies, such as *Lady Windermere's Fan* (1892) and *A Woman of No Importance* (1893), he used his wit more savagely, particularly to expose the hypocrisy of male double standards. He was himself a victim of the Victorian intolerance he had satirized when his career was ruined by prosecution and imprisonment for homosexuality.

The establishment was just as quick to label Shaw a subversive. In one of his earliest works, *Mrs Warren's Profession*, written in 1893, he adapted the theme of 'a woman with a past' to deal with another taboo subject, prostitution. The reward for his candour was to have the play banned from public performance for thirty years. Though he gained a reputation as a champion of radical causes in the 1890s, it was actually in the Edwardian period that he established his popularity with the British public. The Court Theatre seasons which gave a modest platform to Ibsen helped Shaw gain a reputation as the leading intellectual playwright in the English theatre of the early 20th century. Eleven of his plays were produced at the Court, including *Man and Superman* (1903), *You Never Can Tell* (1899), *John Bull's Other Island* (1904) and *Major Barbara* (1905). Shaw's plays were by far the most popular in the Court repertory and thereafter his success continued right up until 1939, with his last memorable full-length play, *In Good King Charles's Golden Days*. His plays depend heavily on witty argument and this idiosyncratic style of propagandist humour has acquired its own term, Shavian. In Shaw's best works, such as the popular *Saint Joan*, first performed in 1924, argument and dramatic action are wholly integrated to produce drama which is both entertaining and thought-provoking.

The longer runs of Shaw's plays at the Court helped to subsidize the work of new writers like ▷ W. B. Yeats, ▷ John Galsworthy, ▷ J. M. Barrie and Harley Granville Barker. Apart from Ibsen a small sample of the work of the more experimental European authors, ▷ Maeterlinck, Hauptmann and Schnitzler was presented. Though not exclusively so, there was an Ibsenite emphasis on plays which addressed social issues. Galsworthy's *The Silver Box* (1906) and Elizabeth Robins's *Votes for Women* (1907) explored the themes of class discrimination and female emancipation in a style combining both innovative and highly conventional features. Thus, *Votes for Women* includes an unusual crowd scene of a mass women's suffrage rally in Trafalgar Square, but elsewhere relies heavily on the conventions of late 19th-century Society drama, as does Granville Barker's *The Voysey Inheritance* (1905), which explores that great Victorian totem, the family. In his play, family wealth and respectability are shown to be based on fraud and deception. He also dealt with corruption and exploitation in his other two major plays from this period, *Waste* (1907) and *The Madras House* (1910). *Waste* was heavily censored for openly dealing with extra-marital sex and laying the blame for an abortion on a senior politician and aspiring prime minister.

Harley Granville Barker (1877–1946) was one of the first true directors in the English theatre, in the sense that he saw the director's role as entirely separate from that of the actor. Between 1912 and 1914 he directed distinguished and highly influential productions of Shakespeare's *Twelfth Night*, *The Winter's Tale* and *A Midsummer Night's Dream* at the Savoy Theatre. Characteristic of these productions were a careful consideration of original performance conditions, an emphasis on ensemble acting and the development of a new aesthetic in theatre design. Inevitably though, there were financial difficulties and shortly after World War I Granville Barker distanced himself from the London theatre scene, disillusioned with its philistinism. He applied his creative talent to the more academic pursuits of translating plays and writing his famous *Prefaces to Shakespeare*. He was less of a pragmatist than Shaw and was ultimately unwilling to compromise his idealism in order to survive the pressures of the commercial market.

At almost the same time as the Court venture, W. B. Yeats (1865–1939) launched his campaign to promote a national Irish culture through drama with the creation of the Irish National Theatre. With the support of like-minded nationalists, notably the benefactress and playwright ▷ Lady Gregory, Yeats established the ▷ Abbey Theatre in Dublin as one of the most experimental European theatres of its time. Its attempt to further the cause of Irish independence by promoting a national cultural identity based on a revival of Celtic mythology was a rather idealistic mission; nonetheless, whatever one might think of the political purpose of Yeats's plays, they were certainly significant experiments in verse dramas. Though they are sometimes criticized for being unstageable, almost all of his plays from *The Countess Cathleen* (1892) to *Purgatory* (1939) were performed. The Abbey Theatre also provided an audience for the work of ▷ J. M. Synge (1871–1909). Synge preferred a more earthy, if poetic, prose style to the grander mystical verse drama favoured by Yeats. With the exception of *Deirdre of the Sorrows* (published in 1910), based on Celtic legend, he also tended to eschew the Yeatsian spiritual dimension and restricted his subject matter to the lives of the ordinary Irish people. One of his most famous plays ▷ *The Playboy of the Western World* (1907) provides a gentle satirical view of romance and fantasy in a remote Irish community. Its light-hearted and mildly cynical wit was too much for the Abbey Theatre audience which rioted after interpreting the play as an attack on Irish values and the integrity of Irish womanhood. In his short life Synge wrote only six plays, but with these he established himself as an important, if controversial, figure in the Irish dramatic revival. The Abbey continued to flourish under the watchful eye of Yeats long after Synge's untimely death in 1909, and from 1924, shortly after Irish independence, it was granted financial aid by the government, thus making it one of the first subsidized English-speaking theatres.

These attempts to develop a serious intellectual drama on both sides of the Irish Sea made little immediate impact on London's West End. The dominant view of the theatre was summed up by one of the most successful of the Edwardian playwrights, ▷ William Somerset Maugham (1874–1965), when he said that 'its purpose is to afford delight. I do not think it can usefully concern itself with the welfare of humanity or the saving of civilization'. Evidently he did provide delight, for in 1908 he had four plays running simultaneously. He saw himself as an exponent of the comedy of manners, writing in a tradition dating back to the Restoration period and to Goldsmith and Sheridan. His cynical and artificial comedies sometimes shocked and even scandalized, but never really gave serious offence. Maugham's popularity lasted right up until the 1930s, when he decided that he was losing touch with the public and retired.

By the end of World War I the English theatre was as insular as ever. The old actor-manager system was replaced by a few multiple managements which sought quick profits and promoted light musical entertainment as the staple of West End entertainment. Few writers of 'serious' drama found an outlet on the stage. In fact, serious writers were much more likely to turn to the forms of the novel and poetry than drama. The farces of ▷ Ben Travers (1886–1980), written for a popular group of comic actors at the Aldwych Theatre, were a typical product of the 1920s, years of gaiety and frivolity for the affluent in society. Though some of the humour would now appear to be dated, his meandering but well-constructed plots based on implausible coincidence have proved to be surprisingly durable, as a revival of *Plunder* at the National Theatre in 1976 demonstrated. He was a pioneer of the English sex farce, a form which is still dominant in the West End.

The sense of gay abandonment and impending crisis associated with the 1920s and 30s is often captured in the plays of ▷ Noël Coward (1899–1973), who was adept at exploiting the new formulae for commercial success. Coward followed in the tradition of Wilde, often balancing wit with sentiment and probing beyond the English veneer of respectability. Although his unconventional treatment of sex and social manners did arouse controversy, he was generally a good judge of English tolerance and his knowledge of the theatre from boyhood gave him the experience to know what he could get away with. Admittedly his first staged play, *The Vortex* (1924), gave him a reputation as a radical, despite his adherence to the framework of the old drawing-room drama of Jones and Pinero, and *Sirocco* (1927) was greeted with a first-night riot. However, the six comedies written between 1923 and 1942, *Fallen Angels, Hay Fever, Private Lives, Design for Living, Bitter Sweet* and *Present Laughter* did much to establish him as a successful mainstream playwright rather than a critic on the theatrical fringe. Coward was one of those curious English figures who manage to play the role of the rebel whilst being accepted as part of the establishment. The satirical impulse in his plays is generally tempered by his shrewd commercial sense.

In the years just before and just after Irish independence in 1921, Dublin had little in common with fashionable London. The difference could not be better illustrated than by the three early plays of ▷ Sean O'Casey (1880–1964), *The Shadow of a Gunman* (1923), *Juno and the Paycock* (1924) and *The Plough and the Stars* (1926), which were first performed at the Abbey Theatre during the 1920s. Here the violence of colonialism and misery of poverty is portrayed from the viewpoint of the working-class slum tenement dweller. Bleak as this world may be, it is not devoid of humour. The characters are given a poetic, often flamboyant style of speech, which is frequently used to expose their desire for escapism into a world of fantasy and romance. O'Casey found a means of expression for the lives of the urban Irish, as Synge had done for the Irish peasant communities. The influences for this kind of drama, which extended tragedy to the lives of ordinary people, came from continental political playwrights like the German Gerhart Hauptmann (1862–1946), as well as from the popular native melodrama. It was also to the continent, and Germany in particular, that O'Casey turned for inspiration for his next play, *The Silver Tassie*, in 1928. In this he experimented with the theatrical devices of ▷ expressionism which had been pioneered by German playwrights around the time of World War I. The play's avant-garde mixture of styles and bitter satire of religion and war made it unacceptable for production at the Abbey. Thereafter O'Casey continued his non-naturalistic experiments in exile. Much of his later work from the autobiographical *Red Roses for Me* (1943) to *Cock-a-Doodle-Dandy* (1949) and *The Bishop's Bonfire* (1955) is only just beginning to be given the recognition it deserves.

Commercial consolidation

During the 1930s, years of the Depression and the growing international threat of fascism, the more interesting experiments in a socially committed and serious drama continued to take place outside the West End, on the theatrical fringe as it were. Again, economic factors contributed to the conservatism of mainstream theatre, as competition from the new forms of radio and film reversed the boom of the early 1920s and discouraged managements from taking financial risks. In London the ▷ Unity Theatre was formed, an amateur company which pursued a policy of dramatizing topical issues, such as the Spanish Civil War and the popular front against ▷ fascism, from a left-wing point of view. This was the first theatre to present ▷ Brecht in English with *Senora Carrar's Rifles* in 1938. The Group Theatre, a private society based at the Westminster Theatre, produced three experimental verse plays by ▷ W. H. Auden and ▷ Christopher Isherwood, *The Dog Beneath the Skin* (1936), *The Ascent of F6* (1937) and *On the Frontier* (1938). ▷ T. S. Eliot's fragmentary and innovatory verse drama *Sweeney Agonistes*, was also produced here in 1935. Admittedly this was drama for minority audiences, but such activity did provide a welcome alternative to the complacency of the theatrical establishment, and at a time when it was certainly needed. Eliot's contribution in reintroducing verse drama on to the stage is of major significance, although he never quite forced the revolutionary break from prose drama he had hoped for. To him the prosaic was anathema to art; in *The Family Reunion* (1939) and, later, *The Cocktail Party* (1950), he used the conventional drawing-room stage scenario as a starting point to show how 'our own sordid, dreary world would be suddenly illuminated and transfigured' with the power of verse. It was not the traditional English blank verse that he employed, but his own contemporary idiom, sometimes difficult to distinguish from prose. His most assured success was the historical religious play about the martyrdom of Thomas à Becket, *Murder in the Cathedral* (1935). Here the ritualistic style of expression is perfectly suited to the subject matter and the location of Canterbury Cathedral, where it was first performed.

Two new serious, if less unconventional, playwrights, ▷ James Bridie (1888–1951) and ▷ J. B. Priestley (1894–1984), also helped to keep the theatre vital and challenging at a time when it was threatened by frivolity, complacency and commercialism. Both were prolific writers who never quite lived up to early expectations. Bridie was dubbed a second Shaw for his interest in an intellectual drama of ideas. He was by profession a doctor, which perhaps helps to explain the slightly detached concern with the welfare of the world, characteristic of his plays. He also had a tendency to lose inspiration by the final act, for which he had the perfect excuse, 'Only God can write third acts, and He seldom does.' By contrast Priestley is a recognized master of well-constructed plays. His career was long and varied, beginning with *Dangerous Corner*, in 1932, the first of a series of so-called 'time' plays, and continuing up to 1968 with the television script, *Anyone for Tennis?* He described his prosaic style of dialogue somewhat dismissively as a 'familiar flat thin idiom'. Nonetheless, it was used to good effect to explore major issues, such as the moral nature of mankind and human destiny, subjects which are now accepted as relevant matters for modern dramatists to deal with but at the time were laudably daring.

The 1930s also saw important developments in Shakespeare productions, particularly at the ▷ Old Vic in London and the Memorial Theatre in Stratford. Here were the beginnings of the modern ▷ National Theatre and the ▷ Royal Shakespeare Company. The insistence of Granville Barker and ▷ William Poel on a scholarly re-examination of Elizabethan stage conditions was clearly influential on new directors like Tyrone Guthrie, ▷ John Gielgud and ▷ William Bridges-Adams. ▷ Laurence Olivier, Charles Laughton, Ralph Richardson, Edith Evans, Peggy Ashcroft and Sybil Thorndike were all part of a new generation of actors who combined the role of star performer with that of ensemble player. There was inevitably, though, a tension for these actors between the attraction of working for a dedicated but poorly paid company and the financial appeal of the West End and the film industry.

During World War II the Council for the Encouragement of Music and Arts (▷ C.E.M.A.) was formed to provide morale-boosting entertainment on the home front. This was to prove highly significant, for it later evolved into the ▷ Arts Council of Great Britain, which was founded in 1946 and which aimed 'to develop a greater knowledge, understanding, and practice of the Fine Arts, to increase their accessibility to the public, and to improve their standard of execution'. Once the principle of government subsidy for the theatre was established, the likelihood of a development of serious drama increased. This did not happen at once; the initial subsidies were small and the immediate post-war years were times of hardship and struggle. The new welfare state era began to make its impact on the theatre in the 1950s and 60s. In the meantime, with little new material available, Shakespeare, the old national stalwart, continued to attract audiences in London and Stratford-on-Avon, as did a profusion of revivals and imports.

▷ Christopher Fry (b 1907) enjoyed an unexpectedly brief period of fame with the success of his verse dramas, *A Phoenix Too Frequent* (1946) and *The Lady's Not For Burning* (1948). His attempts to develop a poet's theatre as pioneered by Yeats and Eliot was considerably helped by the strength of actors like Laurence Olivier, John Gielgud and Edith Evans, who took leading roles in his plays. He seemed to have broken the mould of the commercial theatre but the interest in verse plays was short-lived. Fry was in and out of fashion all too quickly and by the mid 1950s he was already falling out of favour. Typical of the period were the lighter entertainments of ▷ Terence Rattigan (1911–77). In his more serious work *The Winslow Boy* (1946), the story of a father's fight to clear his son of a charge of theft, he offered a sophisticated version of the old drawing-room problem play. This won the award for the best play of the year in London. Despite his popularity with the Aunt Ednas, as he called his audiences, his plays hardly qualify as landmarks in English drama. Perhaps had he not been writing at a time when homosexuality could not be openly discussed on stage, this sublimated theme in his work might have been developed into something more interesting. Amongst the others writing at this time only ▷ John Whiting (1917–63) and Peter Ustinov (b 1921) stand out. Whiting died tragically young and Ustinov never developed into the dramatist he was expected to become.

1956 and all that

Nineteen fifty-six is often suggested as a starting date for modern political drama in Britain. This was the year of the first visit of Bertolt Brecht's company, the Berliner Ensemble, to London; it was also the year of ▷ John

Osborne's success at the Royal Court with ▷ *Look Back in Anger*, in which the central character, the ▷ angry young man Jimmy Porter, seemed to represent a whole generation of disaffected youth. Like all such apparently seminal dates it can be misleading. One should not overlook the activities of organizations like the Unity Theatre and Group Theatre during the 1930s and the work of ▷ Joan Littlewood and Theatre Workshop which began as early as 1943 (though wider recognition came much later with productions of ▷ Brendan Behan's *The Hostage* in 1958 and Joan Littlewood's improvised piece *Oh, What a Lovely War* in 1963). Still, it is undeniable that from the late 1950s there was an explosion of dramatic activity which has given rise to the most exciting period in British drama since the Elizabethan and Jacobean age. A growing interest in international theatre, increased government subsidies and the building of many regional repertory theatres, and changes in the social structure of Britain all contributed to this.

Brecht died in 1956 before the Berliner Ensemble's London visit; but the work of the company which he had set up in East Berlin after World War II exemplified his approach to the theatre. Part of its initial attraction was that it received sufficient subsidy to rehearse at length and develop a genuine ensemble style of performance. Brecht's desire to use the theatre to communicate the need for social change to the working class also had, and still has, its appeal, although it cannot be claimed that theatre-going is a working-class activity. Nonetheless, his style of writing and theories of performance assisted a development in the British theatre away from the predominant mode of ▷ naturalism. He trained actors in a method of performing which discourages the audience from suspending disbelief and imagining that what they see on stage is real life. Actors were not to encourage empathy but were to create a critical distance between themselves as performers and the roles they played. The world, and its representation on stage, was to be made available for scrutiny by a technique of 'estrangement', of making the familiar seem strange and the strange seem familiar. Typical 'estrangement' devices were the introduction of songs to interrupt the dramatic action; the juxtaposition of scenes with unexpected shifts of location or viewpoint; and the introduction of scenes with placards explaining the action about to follow. Brecht's was a theatre of reason and political commitment. This did not mean that emotion was banned from the stage but that the ultimate aim was to encourage the audience to think, to look at the world in new ways and understand how it might be changed. As Brecht was a ▷ Marxist it was to be expected that he presented the world and its social relations from a Marxist perspective. Since many of the new British playwrights in the post-war period were themselves politically committed and of the left, it was no surprise that they found in Brecht a model for a new kind of drama, both in terms of subject matter and of form.

Other European influences such as the ▷ Theatre of Cruelty and the ▷ Theatre of the Absurd helped dramatists, directors and actors to explore non-naturalistic techniques. The Theatre of Cruelty conceived by ▷ Antonin Artaud (1896–1948) aimed to communicate with the audience at a primitive, subconscious level by means of symbols, gesture, movement and sound. His most significant impact in the British theatre has been on the director ▷ Peter Brook. The greatest exponent of Absurdist theatre on the English stage has been ▷ Samuel Beckett (1906–89), an Irishman who lived in France, was heavily influenced by French ▷ existentialist philosophy and who wrote many of his plays in French. His rejection of conventional plots and refusal to supply pat explanations of his plays' meanings established him at once as an avant-garde figure. In 1955 ▷ *Waiting for Godot* was performed in London at the Arts Theatre. In this play Beckett created a novel situation in which two tramps in a sparse and inhospitable landscape wait hopefully for help which never comes. The harsh view of life's essential pointlessness is typical of his plays; and his great achievement as a dramatist has been to create sharp and often humorous theatrical images to portray such a bleak philosophy of life. The process of absorbing all these new influences was assisted by one theatre in particular, the ▷ Royal Court. Under the general direction of George Devine, the Royal Court consistently promoted the work of new writers who were given the opportunity to explore a range of theatrical forms of expression which had not been available to preceding generations. Admittedly Brecht's influence on John Osborne was fairly superficial, limited to a few technical devices, but it was certainly profound in the case of ▷ John Arden (b 1930), another product of the Royal Court and one of the most innovatory of the young British dramatists of the 1950s. For Arden, Brecht was one of several models who could help bring back to the theatre the 'noise, disorder, drunkenness, lasciviousness, nudity, generosity, corruption, fertility and ease' which he thought the playwright should provide. It was refreshing for Arden and his contemporaries to be able to experiment with a variety of theatrical techniques, whether they derived from Brecht, Beckett, Artaud or whoever else. Suddenly the days of a theatre characterized by English parochialism and genteel respectability seemed to be over.

Categories such as Theatre of the Absurd and Theatre of Cruelty are useful as rough generalizations about different styles of drama but they do not necessarily say much about the particular qualities of individual authors whose plays fall into these categories. Both ▷ N. F. Simpson (b 1919) and ▷ Harold Pinter (b 1930) could be said to be influenced by the Theatre of the Absurd yet their plays are very different. Much of Simpson's drama, like the commercially successful *One Way Pendulum* (1959), is characterized by a slightly quirky farcical style, very much in an English tradition; Pinter made his reputation via the commercial stage with *The Birthday Party* (1958), originally a stage failure but revived by television, and *The Caretaker* (1960). His plays are certainly less whimsical and more menacing in their portrayal of a hostile and insecure world. Like Beckett, he does not attempt to provide explicit meanings. As he has said, there are 'no hard distinctions between what is real and what is unreal, nor between what is true and what is false. The thing is not necessarily either true or false.' His freedom with dramatic form and precision with language, again characteristic of Beckett, enables him to pinpoint human repressions, anxieties, guilt, struggles for power, primitive desires and behaviour, in a far bolder, more startling manner than was possible within the traditional dramatic conventions. From his earliest plays there was, in effect, a full-scale assault on the decorous drawing-room-style drama which rarely probed beyond the surface of English reserve, awkwardness and embarrassment.

The first wave of new writers also included ▷ Ann Jellicoe, ▷ Arnold Wesker and ▷ Shelagh Delaney. As a group they no longer seem as rebellious as they once did and none of them could now be described as shocking. But they all helped in the development of an alternative drama which could be challenging, provocative and socially critical; and they paved the way for dramatists like ▷ Edward Bond, ▷ Joe Orton, ▷ Trevor Griffiths and ▷ Howard Brenton who became known for their radical or iconoclastic tendencies in the late 1960s and early 1970s. A vital quality of the work of these writers and many of their contemporaries is their strong anti-establishment stance. Usually their perspective is political and left-wing; though in the case of Orton the impulse is more anarchic and gleefully outrageous. Orton and Bond both fell foul of ▷ censorship laws during the 1960s; Bond's *Saved* (1965) was heavily censored for its realistic street language and relatively explicit sex scenes, and his later play *Early Morning* (1968) was banned for its apparently scurrilous treatment of Queen Victoria. The resulting furore revealed all too clearly just how much the law was out of touch with the times and in 1968 stage censorship was finally abolished. Since then Bond has remained a controversial and outspoken figure; and is now recognized by many as one of Britain's leading political playwrights.

1968, a date which brings to mind student unrest and political agitation, was also the year in which ▷ Jerzy Grotowski's *The Poor Theatre* was published in English. Grotowski evolved a detailed training programme for the actor, intended to develop both his or her physical and mental powers; and he also challenged the formal division in the theatre between actor and audience. The emphasis on the adaptability of almost any space for performance and the rejection of the costly paraphernalia of standard theatre was of enormous appeal to those who sought an alternative kind of drama. Again the director Peter Brook was notably receptive to continental developments and applied some of Grotowski's theories to his productions for the Royal Shakespeare Company. By the 1970s the Royal Shakespeare Company was offering more than the traditional large-stage productions by setting up its own low-budget touring group which regularly performed in schools and community centres around the country.

However, many of the new radicals active in the theatre rejected outright the idea of working for such established and relatively well-subsidized theatre companies. They were critical of a policy of capital investment in buildings like the Royal Shakespeare Theatre and the new National Theatre, finally completed in 1976. A plethora of new companies appeared, often with no permanent theatre base, and these attempted to provide entertainment at alternative venues (sometimes quite simply the street or a city square) for alternative audiences. Some companies were overtly political, embracing specific causes like issues of race, gender or class; others concentrated more on experimental avant-garde theatre or performance art. What they all tended to share was the desire to democratize the theatrical process itself and provide an alternative to the standard repertory theatre which had been promoted by the Arts Council since World War II.

Although there is nothing unusual historically about women writing plays it is only really since the late 1960s that female playwrights began to be taken seriously. ▷ Caryl Churchill, Sarah Daniels, ▷ Pam Gems, Susan Todd and Michelene Wandor are just a few of the women writers who have contributed in a major way to a widening of dramatic and cultural horizons beyond those traditionally recognized by a male-dominated theatre establishment. Today around fifteen per cent of British playwrights are women, though this figure is certainly not represented in terms of publishing and performance.

Many of the successful playwrights from the post-1956 period, such as John Mortimer, ▷ Robert Bolt, ▷ Tom Stoppard, ▷ Alan Ayckbourn, ▷ Peter Shaffer and Peter Nichols were relatively unaffected by these developments and are not obviously products of an era of radicalism at all. Others like Howard Brenton, ▷ David Edgar, ▷ David Hare, Caryl Churchill and Susan Todd wrote regularly for companies which were very much part of this political ▷ fringe movement challenging the values of mainstream theatre. In recent years dramatists have shifted freely between the two camps and transfers from the fringe to the mainstream theatre have been common. An obvious problem for writers and actors working for small touring companies has been the lack of money and the annual fight for government subsidy. It is no surprise, therefore, to find both Brenton and Hare now working for the National Theatre and to see plays by feminist writers like Caryl Churchill appearing in the West End. For some, there is still an ideological resistance to the perpetuation of London as the focus of cultural life. ▷ John McGrath, for example, founder of the highly successful touring company 7:84, has resolutely avoided the prestigious London theatres. There has also been an ideological debate about the advantages and disadvantages of writing for television. Trevor Griffiths, who has written for both stage and television, has welcomed the opportunity to reach a mass audience unattainable in the theatre; David Edgar has argued against working for television on the grounds that the writer has little control over his or her product and the form is too heavily dominated by naturalistic conventions. Television is certainly a superior form for providing an imitation of real life and this has had its appeal. One might also argue that this has encouraged the theatre to be more experimental in its use of non-naturalistic forms; since it cannot hope to compete with television it has had to avoid being seen as a poor imitation.

Much has happened in the last thirty years, yet, on the whole, the changes and developments have not been revolutionary. Many influences have been reformed and absorbed by the established theatre in a characteristically British manner, much in the way that the old Fabians Shaw and Granville Barker might have approved of. The general trend has been progressive and liberating although recent events are more ominous. Legislation against the 'promotion' of homosexuality in the theatre heralds the return of direct stage censorship.

If the 1960s and 70s were the years of radical experiments, since the 1980s, the theatre has suffered from a sense of stagnation and decline, following recession and cutbacks in public subsidies. Funding for theatre companies is severely limited and the emphasis is now on self-sufficiency and private sponsorship rather than public support. The effect of this has been most severe on fringe companies which have always had to survive on extremely low budgets. Without the challenges and provocations of its 'alternative' and experimental practitioners the theatre is always in danger of slipping back into a state of complacency which Peter Brook has so appositely termed 'deadly theatre'.

'Rule and Energy in View': The Poetry of Modernity 5

Linda R. Willams
University of Liverpool

'Less is more': Pound and Imagism

To mark the turn of the century as also a turning point in literature is a rather arbitrary gesture. English ▷ modernism established itself slowly, well behind the French precedent, and the first decade of the 20th century was dominated by the popular conservatism of ▷ Georgian poetry. People read and enjoyed the poetry of ▷ A. E. Housman, ▷ Rudyard Kipling and ▷ Thomas Hardy, and eagerly bought the Georgian anthologies as they appeared from 1912 onwards. Georgianism perhaps epitomizes the popular notion of English poetry – parochial, solid and unironic, celebrating English rural life, particularly the home counties variety. Its importance lies in the way it fed into the poetry of World War I – many Georgians are better known as ▷ War poets – which sharpened nostalgia into something that could 'draw blood', especially in the later years as the full horror became apparent.

In order to emphasize how shocking modernist poetry was after the technical familiarity of writing up to 1910, I want to focus upon the Imagist (▷ Imagism) movement which, whilst not offering the most powerful or famous texts of the modernist period, certainly exemplifies much of what modernist verse was trying to achieve against Victorianism. '(T)he first heave' of modernism was, in poet ▷ Ezra Pound's words, 'to break the pentameter' ('Canto 81'). Pound was a great polemicist against what he called 'the crepuscular spirit in modern poetry' ('Revolt'). Certainly, much poetry of the late Victorian period was supremely 'crepuscular', languid, pale and dreamy, and in his early so-called ▷ 'Celtic Twilight' period ▷ W. B. Yeats was rather prone to this. He had begun his writing career as a writer of the Victorian *fin de siècle*, and ended it as a key figure of modernist anti-decadence. His early poems are infused with an elegiac quality and peopled with mythological and heroic figures from an 'old Ireland' of ephemeral, supernatural beauty. There is a haunting sense of the inaccessible, characteristic of much Nineties poetry, which rejected earlier Victorians' building of 'brick and mortar inside the covers of a book' (Yeats, 'The Symbolism of Poetry'; 1900). This is Yeats the 'last romantic'.

But Yeats is also arguably the first modernist of poetry, his feeling of alienation from his time strengthening his later apocalyptic poems, which 'sing amid our uncertainty' ('Per Amica Silentia Lunae'; 1917). The cultural crisis of the early 20th century turned the task of re-thinking the limits and drives of language into one of almost world-historic importance for many poets, impatient that the untenable realist notion of a shared common experience between writer and reader be exposed. If Yeats's early work is marked by a bygone aesthetic, and is metrically and syntactically conventional, his later work – particularly that written from *The Wild Swans at Coole* (1919) until his death in 1939 – would strongly assert his modernity, and was undoubtedly urged towards this point by Pound's influence.

The movement which exploded on to the poetry scene in 1912, of which Pound was initially a key member, sought to counter sloppy diction and to free verse from too much emotion. Later in the war years Imagism developed into the multi-art form movement ▷ Vorticism, publishing two polemical texts edited by poet and painter ▷ Percy Wyndham Lewis, *Blast* (1914 and 1915). Vorticism was a movement which brought writing and visual art together in a futuristic celebration of energy and speed. The anti-romantic figures of the 'Great English Vortex' included Wyndham Lewis and Ezra Pound, plus artists David Bomberg (1890–1957), Henri Gaudier-Brzeska (1891–1915) and Jacob Epstein (1880–1959). Imagism in its purest form most aggressively countered Victorian versification, producing 'poetry that is hard and clear, never blurred or indefinite' (Preface to *Some Imagist Poets 1915*). Modernist poetry in this form intensifies and condenses; the poetry of modernity is written most strongly in the lyric form, rather than as narrative poems or epic novel-poems favoured by the Victorians. Imagism takes the emphasis on brevity to an extreme, its definitions being heavily reactive (just as its founders were politically reactionary), prescribing the new poetry negatively; in Pound's words modern poetry should be: 'Objective – no slither; direct – no excessive use of adjectives, no metaphors that won't permit examination . . . straight as the Greek!'

Imagism, then, rejected the use of loose simile and, like ▷ Hopkins in a different sense, strove to evoke the 'isness' of things: to present reality in a naïvely unmediated sense, avoiding flaccid re-presentation. For the Imagist, brevity is the soul of poetry: 'less is more'. Condensation counters verbiage, and so lyric poetry is put on a strict diet; in Pound's words, it is 'de-suetized'.

Whirl up, sea –
Whirl your pointed pines,
Splash your great pines
On our rocks,
Hurl your green over us,
Cover us with pools of fir.
('Oread', H. D.)

This is a poem by ▷ H. D. in its entirety; indeed, 'Oread' (1915) is often tendered as the exemplary Imagist poem, with the complex of sea, pines and nymph fusing as image. Pound had defined the image as 'that which presents an intellectual and emotional complex in an instant of time'; H. D.'s text pares down superfluity to a series of discrete, sparse phrases. What the poem 'is' is the relation between these phrases, how they build up into an image which does not come from individual key words or vague feelings but from the ways in which the component elements of the poem *relate*.

This can be clarified by looking at an even shorter Imagist poem of Pound's, 'In a Station of the Metro':

The apparition of these faces in the crowd;
Petals on a wet, black bough.

It is perhaps hard today to recapture the feelings of shock which hit the first readers of these poems. It is no wonder that at this point in literary history poetry began to become perhaps the most unpopular of art forms. The difficulty of this text lies in its requirement that we simply *accept* it on its own terms, which brings it close to the oriental form of the *haiku*, much admired by Pound.

This text is also exemplary in its peculiar atmosphere and influences. In an effort to achieve delicate clarity, Imagist poetry deployed Japanese motifs, petals, hyacinth and lotus blossoms, and clear contours, and allowed itself to become emotional only in the dexterity with which these evoke feelings. Pound's 'Fan-piece, for her Imperial Lord' (1914) is as much about loss as any Victorian elegy, but is delicately rinsed free of heavy sentiment:

O fan of white silk,
clear as frost on the grass-blade,
You also are laid aside.

Understated, it is also impersonal, a key word at this point and reinforced by ▷ T. S. Eliot's notion, in 'Tradition and the Individual Talent' (1919), that: 'Poetry is not a turning loose of emotion, but an escape from emotion; it is not the expression of personality, but an escape from personality.' Thus an Imagist poem may be poignantly posed, but it should not slide into agonized self-reflections or sentiment.

Language speaking: Eliot and the linguistic crisis

Modernist poetry not only demanded intensity, however; crucially it challenged the prevalent philosophy of language with which it was traditionally assumed 19th-century verse worked. This philosophy posited language as a transparent medium through which an unproblematic and undistorted 'reality' is represented. For the modernist poet language is emphasized and foregrounded to such an extent that it becomes the most important 'point' of the poem. Poetry scrutinizes the form, the contours, the material of the mask of language. As ▷ Samuel Beckett said of ▷ James Joyce, 'His writing is not *about* something; *it is that something itself.*'

Modernist writing is agonizingly self-conscious, probing its own limits and restrictions, foregrounding itself as text, as the interface of many texts. The process of poetry-writing becomes the object of poetry, so that the way a text is constructed, *how* it connotes many possibilities of meaning and many voices, becomes that which the poem is *about*. We can, perhaps, see why Browning was read with interest by many early 20th-century poets. Modernism foregrounds form over content, or rather, it opens up for questioning the whole economy of language through which form and content are established as distinct and separate textual dimensions. Pound's later work, especially his long sequence of ▷ the *Cantos*, continually emphasizes its own materiality – the silken-folded mask betrays its own material construction. Alongside their other project of historical synthesis, the *Cantos* expose language as dirty, desirous splashes of ink; echoes of other languages intrude, typographical errors aren't edited out. Sometimes words are 'chosen' not for reasons of sense or meaning but because of the pattern they make on the page, how they sound, or how other words have suggested them. Chinese characters are included, asserting to the uncomprehending eye language's typographic existence. Pound's occasional rantings can seem more like the operation of a multi-lingual machine than a rational mind, reading rather like one enormous ▷ Freudian slip. As with many of Gertrude Stein's (1874–1946) texts and ▷ Surrealist automatic writing, words seem to suggest other words because of unconscious drives which are operating on the poem.

All of this has a profound bearing on how the role of the poet and of the reader is understood. A form of writing in which writing itself is so prioritized has also to re-write our understanding of who is 'responsible for' poetry – of who ultimately can guarantee its meaning. Despite the authoritarian postures adopted by particular modernist writers, poetry may be read as acknowledging that the position of both writer and reader is relative, non-omniscient, constructed by the forces of language. Furthermore, this sense of fragmentation has permeated the possibilities of writing to such an extent that the resultant feeling is that *all* possibilities of unity have been lost. Modernist poetry, to use the words of Lewis Carroll's *The Hunting of the Snark* (1876), spurned 'merely conventional signs', navigating itself by a map which was: 'A perfect and absolute blank!' It thus affirms – against the desires of its writers, whose quest is still towards the lost home of stable selfhood and meaning – a problematization of the individual subject somewhat analogous to that enacted by Freudian ▷ psychoanalysis and ▷ Marxist political theory.

What these breaks in poetic consciousness and linguistic coherence were signalling was the chasm in personal and national identity which World War I brought to crisis point. The War poets, particularly ▷ Siegfried Sassoon, ▷ Wilfred Owen and ▷ Isaac Rosenberg, represented this breakdown thematically, but through pre-war structures of versification and diction. Modernist poetry was more like a linguistic acting-out of the destruction of innocence which took place in the trenches.

Modernism is also identifiable as the point at which writing acknowledges that it doesn't originate purely within the soul of the author; the modernist text plagiarizes shamelessly, building itself up out of a patchwork of unacknowledged quotations from a variety of international cultural sources, fragments 'shored against my ruins' ('What the Thunder Said', from T. S. Eliot's ▷ *The Waste*

Land). This is its cosmopolitanism. *The Waste Land*, to the frustration of many an undergraduate reader, straddles eastern and western cultural history in a dazzling and maddening parade of name-dropping and references, which build up into a polemical lament for fallen culture. Geographically, modernism wasn't centred on one cultural-Imperial capital, but danced from London to Paris to Vienna to Berlin to New York to Dublin and back again. It cannot be situated, and this cultural uncertainty is, in *The Waste Land* at least, a symptom of decay:

What is the city over the mountains
Cracks and reforms and bursts in the violet air
Falling towers
Jerusalem Athens Alexandria
Vienna London
Unreal

(*The Waste Land*, ll. 371–6)

Texts jump from 'home' to 'home', emphasizing how they are written 'intertextually' by a wide range of influences, and are a point at which an extraordinarily wide cultural memory is unlocked. Again, the *Cantos* are an extreme example of this in English poetry, as James Joyce's ▷ *Ulysses* is in the modern novel. The wandering poet has become poet-as-exile.

Ezra Pound was an energetic figure, tirelessly championing the modern and collaborating with T. S. Eliot in the preparation of *The Waste Land*, which is dedicated to Pound. Eliot's work is painfully aware of this crisis of the self, and its challenge to 19th-century writing is enormous. For Eliot, the lyric poem is 'the voice of the poet talking to himself, or to nobody'. But the manner of his 'talking' is quite bizarre, and shocking to our 'realist' expectations. Eliot's verse plays with and parodies traditional structures, the same poem oscillating in its versification and rhythms. Sometimes it comes near to solidity and fixity of form, only to dissolve into a much more fluid formal structure deploying, in his own words, a 'contrast between fixity and flux', and 'unperceived evasion of monotony'. *The Waste Land* exemplifies this, being an extreme example of formal eclecticism and teasing, a startling series of lyric fragments which jump schizophrenically from the sublimity of dream language to the ridiculousness of pub language and interrogate each through the other.

The problem of who writes is, then, accentuated by Pound's collaboration in the final editorial processing of *The Waste Land*, which caused Eliot to write 'I am never sure that I can call my verse my own'. So just who or what the poet's 'I' is at this stage in literary history is a painful problem, and Eliot's verse highlights this in several aspects. Thematically it often evokes disturbed mental states; in 'Rhapsody on a Windy Night' (1917), for instance, clear perception is distorted, objective reality is twisted to the point of frightening hallucination. A street-lamp tells the 'hero' about women's eyes, twisted 'like a crooked pin', and 'A crowd of twisted things' closes in. When he eventually reaches home, its safety turns out to be 'The last twist of the knife'. The figure of modernity characteristically has no home, wandering nomadically in a world stripped of values, in a shifting reality which confounds fixity in mental states. Many of Eliot's early poems seem close to the knife-edge of madness. 'Morning at the Window' (1917) consists of only two stanzas, the second an ugly, twisted re-writing of the relatively rational first, in which 'I' sits at a window looking on the street. This then becomes an experience subject to 'brown waves of fog' which toss twisted faces and tear smiles from passers-by. The 'brown fog of a winter dawn' returns as the climactic condition of *The Waste Land*'s 'Unreal City'.

For Eliot the problem of poetry feeds into the problem of culture and its role in (Christian) society. In 'The Use of Poetry' (1933) he asserts that poetry must be able to account for the sordid and the horrific, the thought that (from Pound's 'Hugh Selwyn Mauberley') 'Caliban casts out Ariel':

> *. . . the essential advantage for a poet is not to have a beautiful world with which to deal: it is to be able to see beneath both beauty and ugliness; to see the boredom, and the horror, and the glory.*

The Waste Land scrutinizes the grand dualism of beauty and ugliness and finds, in the critic and poet ▷ I. A. Richards's words, modernity's 'persistent concern with sex', which is then used as the lens through which history is seen as the history of progressive wastage. Just as 'Mauberley' reads the heroes of Victorian culture as the path to modernity's crisis, so *The Waste Land* re-reads history as a sordid parade, witnessed by the bisexual Tiresias who shuffles across its stage, and which climaxes in a series of sordid liaisons. Tiresias, an 'old man with wrinkled dugs', witnesses and foretells the sterility of a heterosexual love. The double edges of Victorian discourse on sex indelibly mark and open up modernist writing. Indeed, pleasure occupies a very warped position in Eliot's corpus, a symptom of the need for a kind of communication and communion which he perceived was no longer possible. The desperate desire for, and the impossibility of, communication, is both a 'truth' of sexual relations and of modernist writing.

However unpalatably, Eliot foregrounded a politicization of writing which aestheticism had repressed in marking out Art for Art's sake against the political engagement of High Victorian writing. His statement, 'I am sojourning amongst the termites', in a letter to ▷ Lytton Strachey, speaks eloquently of both the actual immersion of modern poetry in the most sordid aspects of social life, and the depth of his right-wing repulsion. Eliot's treatment of human beings in his poetry can be obsessively cruel and vindictive. Indeed, the extremely reactionary politics of Yeats, Pound and Eliot are problematic, and often make their work painful reading for reasons other than 'difficulty'. Yeats's advocacy of an integrated poetry as 'blood, imagination, intellect, running together' ('Discoveries'; 1906) was undoubtedly informed by the intolerant social pressures which also produced ▷ D. H. Lawrence's 'blood conscious' reactionary politics, but it is equally symptomatic of a climate which made possible the more positive politicization of writing in the 1930s. As the 1920s closed, Eliot turned to high-church Anglicanism, and the emphasis in critical theory and poetic practice became that of unity rather than disintegration. For the Eliot of 'The Metaphysical Poets', modern poetry needed to heal the 'dissociation of sensibility' which occurred at the end of the 17th century, so that it could 'devour' the plethora of modern experience. In the 1930s this was interpreted as the need for a poetry which countered obscurity and unpopularity with the addressing of relevant social issues, or what ▷ George Orwell called 'the invasion of literature by politics'.

And not before time: as the Western world spiralled towards economic breakdown, as unemployment rocketed, as Germany and Italy lurched into ▷ fascism, poets recognized that lack of commitment was tantamount to support of the right. ▷ W. H. Auden's poems of the very late 1920s are concerned with psychic landscapes, but in the 1930s his poetry became explicitly politicized and sought again to bridge the gap between theory and praxis in the pursuit of relevance, donning once more the mantle of moral guide. 'Thirties poetry' generally refers to the more politically engaged poetry of Auden, ▷ Stephen Spender, ▷ Louis MacNeice and ▷ C. Day-Lewis, the group of left-wing, psychoanalytically informed poets who met in the early 1930s at Oxford. The work of this 'school' is characterized by three collections, all edited by Michael Roberts: *New Signatures* (1932), *New Country* (1933) and the 1936 *Faber Book of Modern Verse*. Through these texts poetry can be seen to become more explicitly concerned not only with diagnosing the world historic disease, but with prescribing a cure. If modernist poetry is antihumanist, showing the human subject as already subverted by desire, the poets of the 1930s re-humanized the subject, as an effective agent of political action.

Poetry since World War II

Lay the coin on my tongue and I will sing
of what the others never set eyes on.
('Desert Flowers', Keith Douglas; 1943)

H.D. and Douglas: seer and soldier

Although H.D. had begun publishing her intense verses when she was part of the Imagist group, her most important work was written during and after World War II. She wrote *Trilogy* (1944) whilst living through the London Blitz. The war had come home; never had British people been so subjected to its extremities of violence and terror as was the urban population in the Blitz. The poets of World War I were fighters at the front; those of World War II didn't have to go to war because the war came to them, and its violence marked texts as different as ▷ Roy Fuller's *A Lost Season* (1944),

T. S. Eliot's *Four Quartets (*1935–42) and ▷ Edith Sitwell's 'Still Falls the Rain' (1940). H.D.'s *Trilogy* opens with a ruined London laid out like a sacrifice, but its tone is positive. Only barriers, boundaries, proprieties are destroyed:

there, as here, ruin opens
the tomb, the temple; enter,
there as here, there are no doors . . .

ruin everywhere, yet as the fallen roof
leaves the sealed room
open to the air,

so, through our desolation,
thoughts stir, inspiration stalks us
through gloom . . .

The *Trilogy* poems, like many of H.D.'s texts, draw on a wealth of female mythological and historic/heroic figures to spin together a text of new possibilities. H.D. turns destruction into a positive value: the last section of *The Walls Do Not Fall* describes the physical effects of the bombing, but turns debilitating doubt into a clear horizon of possibilities:

we know no rule
of procedure,

we are voyagers, discoverers
of the not-known

the unrecorded;
we have no map;

possibly we will reach haven,
heaven.

Pessimistic texts have abounded since 1942 when this was written, but H.D. chooses to turn doubt into a possibility of affirmation, to stress the fact that negatives have been blasted away. Indeed, this last quotation could also be a statement about women's writing, which, in its marginalization from the canon and the difficulties of its being written at all, also knows no rule, is unrecorded, and has no map. Many post-war women poets have actively used their exclusion from the English poetic tradition as a fresh breathing space.

One of the most famous poets of World War II is undoubtedly ▷ Keith Douglas (1920–44) who was killed in Normandy, his corpus cut down but his influence disturbing writers in the post-war years. Anxious to make the right mark before it's too late, his perception is fired by the possibility of its termination, and in a clear, precise way is almost extra-sensory. On 'each side of the door of sleep' he finds a nightmare-scape in which sexual desire and unspeakable violence are inextricable. Sexuality comes into Douglas's poetry with cold images of death, corruption and violence. Rather like H.D.'s astonishment that the walls do *not* fall, Douglas finds an intensely positive desire in the midst of blasted desert and mindless military discipline. The murderer has 'a lover's face', and he is one of the

> *kindly visitors who meant*
> *so well all winter but at last fell*
> *unaccountably to killing in the spring.*
> ('These grasses, ancient enemies'; 1941)

The poetry is in the chilling, clear, simple diction. Words themselves are militarized; poetry has always been in various guises the object of poetry, but in Douglas's case it is viewed as the soldier views his victim. In 'Words' (1943) it is scrutinized, as if (in George MacBeth's words) seen 'through the sights of a rifle':

> *. . . I lie in wait*
> *for them. In what the hour or the minute invents,*
> *in a web formally meshed or inchoate*
> *these fritillaries are come upon, trapped . . .*
> *The catch and the ways of catching are diverse.*

Words are trapped by macabre war-scapes and dead faces:

> *. . . the pockmarked house . . .*
> *whose insides war has dried out like gourds*
> *attract words*

Trap and attraction are interchangeable words for Douglas; an image has already trapped its written description and all it needs is for the poet to close in for the kill.

Dylan Thomas and the Apocalypse

Certainly World War II was a watershed in British life, and in ▷ Charles Causley's words, 'The signature of murder' (in 'I Saw a Shot Down Angel') is scrawled across the history of writing since the war. If certain experiences, cold and macabre for Douglas, actively *attract* words, we need to ask what manner of themes and experiences have words 'found desirable' in the post-war period.

Perhaps the most famous 'forties poet', Dylan Thomas, had produced much of his most interesting and characteristic work before 1940, yet his verve and style exemplify that of the so-called 'New Apocalypse', which was carried through into the dry, sardonic 1950s by Thomas's disciple, ▷ W. S. Graham. 'Apocalypse' writing was unbridled, gloriously undisciplined and heavily emotional. In consequence one can see this moment in poetic history as pitted against Eliot's impersonality, H.D.'s spartan, hard verse, or the political engagement of 1930s poetry. It is important to acknowledge the power of this poetic movement before we can really understand the significance of the philosophies of the more famous and self-conscious movements of the 1950s and the 1960s, which were very much, in turn, established in reaction to the Apocalyptics. Thomas's verse is famous for its exuberance and verbal excesses. Like the later poet ▷ Thom Gunn, Thomas often deploys syllabics to convey his sense of the natural world and himself in it rolling out of control. *Fern Hill* (1945) is perhaps typical; just as the 'I' who speaks it recalls roving and falling 'Down the rivers of the windfall light', the poem itself runs its 'heedless ways, / [Its] wishes raced through the house-high hay'; it seems to be driven, polemically and self-consciously, against the repression of formal disciplines, even though Thomas himself was in fact a meticulous and formally tight writer.

The apocalyptic poet would ostensibly free the riches, the thickness, of language from the boundaries of rationality. Thomas himself deploys bizarre juxtapositions to this end in his effort to conjure up unconscious powers; his incessant repetition connotes the power of unconscious rhythmicality when it doesn't simply irritate. In this he can perhaps be compared with Surrealist poets such as ▷ David Gascoyne or the American poet Robert Bly (b 1926), Gascoyne being a figure who continues to represent a certain disturbing undercurrent in English poetry, whose writing analyses the relationship between language and the unconscious against the empirical grain of 1930s or 1950s poetry. Indeed, it could be said that Gascoyne *is* the unconscious of the English poetic establishment, repressed and marginalized for peculiar obsessions and failure to fit neatly into the ironic moulds of the 1950s, or the passionate egotism of the 1940s and 1960s. In asserting, in a way different from the modernists, that there is nothing commonsensical about reality, he remains resolutely anti-empirical.

In Surrealism obscurity takes on new powers. Dylan Thomas is nothing if not repetitive and obscure, but the Surrealist project is rather different in emphasis from his. Surrealism resists rational explanation; images are peculiarly juxtaposed so as to disrupt common-sense understandings and analogies. Gascoyne's 'Very Image' (1936) gathers a strange exhibition of surreal juxtapositions together:

And all these images
and many others
are arranged like waxworks
in model bird-cages
about six inches high.

Why? Empiricism can do nothing with such incongruity; reading this requires not only a suspension of disbelief but a suspension of rationality – indeed, in 1936 the Surrealist poet Hugh Sykes Davies (b 1909) supplemented the word 'surreal' with the word 'surrational'. Working through every possible permutation of a statement, rearranging its order so as to unhinge sense and cause meaning to self-deconstruct is something which we also encounter constantly in, say, Samuel Beckett's novel *Watt* (1953). This technique is frequently used to explore the outer reaches of paranoia, and the disturbing meeting of mental illness and political repression, at which point, writes Hugh Sykes Davies, 'ANYTHING YOU SEE WILL BE USED AGAINST YOU' ('Poem'; 1938).

To return to Dylan Thomas; his repetitiveness is of a different order, and his relationship with language is both more wilfully erratic than that of Surrealist poetry, and more superficial. If Douglas renders his words corpses with his rifle-pen and his sniper's eye, Thomas consciously throws himself into them as into a fierce alien element. He wants words to seduce him; he wants to be possessed. In 'Especially When the October Wind' (1934) the fact that language has already inhabited the 'I' is particularly clear: his heart sheds 'syllabic blood' on hearing the raven speak; stick-trees and 'The wordy shapes of women' have a typographical significance; the 'rows' of children are 'star-gestured'. Beeches are 'vowelled', oaks have voices, the water speaks. From this plenitude of verbal nature and life-signs – 'The signal grass', 'the meadow's signs', 'the dark-vowelled birds' – Thomas reads his poem and re-writes it. Indeed, in reading he is also trying to liberate: poetic excess and sexual freedom are inextricable. Thus the incantatory element in Thomas is linked to an attempt to allow words to bleed into a plurality of significance, meanings and connotations, spinning off of their own volition. In the 1950s this verbal free-fall was denigrated as adolescent self-indulgence, and, indeed, on its own terms, there is something inescapably restrictive about Thomas's habit of repetition.

We can, perhaps, clarify one of the positions of 1940s poetry through a statement Thomas made about his attitude to the image, in comparison with Pound's notion that an Imagist image is 'an intellectual and emotional complex in an instant of time':

> *I let . . . an image be 'made' emotionally in me and then apply to it what intellectual and critical forces I possess – let it breed another, let that image contradict the first, make, of the third image bred out of the other two together, a fourth contradictory image, and let them all, within my imposed formal limits, conflict . . .*
>
> (*Fifty Modern British Poets*, Michael Schmidt)

Such an errant fecundity had to end somewhere, and one ending was a fresh return to the hardness of a confined, complex Poundian image. The re-working of modernism, especially in its American form is, then, one important strand of contemporary poetry. But immediately on Thomas's heels came the ironic self-discipline of the ▷ Movement.

'No Renaissances, please': the Movement and the 1950s

... the minipoet is basically safe.
not well equipped for (but who would think of)
leaving the highway, he is attuned
to the temporary surface, balanced,
reliable, yes, we have few regret
for the archpoet, who either would not start
or starting stopped; was temperamental
wanted to show off, steamed up, was punctured ...
('minipoet', Miles Burrows; 1966)

The poetry of the Movement was, *par excellence*, that of post-war Anglo-Saxon rationalism. Like the famous car of the late 1950s, small but perfectly formed, the Movement poet was repulsed by grand gestures and took on the mask of a 'minipoet', 'slim, inexpensive, easy to discard/nippy rather than resonant, unpretentious' (Miles Burrows). Introducing the Movement anthology of 1956, *New Lines*, Robert Conquest (b 1917) wrote: 'It ... like modern philosophy – is empirical in its attitude to all that comes'. Movement poetry resists 'agglomeration of unconscious commands'; banished at a stroke to the soupy Romantic past are, it seems, all poetic forms which credit unconscious selves with the power to undermine conscious, common-sense control. It has often, then, been seen as the logical reaction to 1940s excesses. Movement poetry met excess with the wisdom of tradition. But which tradition? Certainly the work of 'the Georgians cultivating their gardens' (Stephen Spender); a stable tradition of homely, pre-modernist English writers such as Thomas Hardy and Wilfred Owen, whose descendants would include ▷ John Betjeman. Conquest, again, celebrates 'rational structure and comprehensible language' in his choice of verse, as does ▷ D. J. Enright both in his own humanistic, dry, anti-Romantic verse and in the poems he collected in the equally important Movement anthology of 1955, *Poets of the 1950s*. The Bible of the Movement was ▷ Donald Davie's critical work of 1952, *Purity of Diction in English Verse*, which supported stylistic discipline and verbal austerity; words should be rationed and undue extravagance curbed. In Davie's work the obvious parallels between the 1950s and the 18th century become concrete, his role being that of the spokesperson of the anti-Bohemian poetic age when he wrote:

> *... there is no necessary connection between the poetic vocation on the one hand, and on the other exhibitionism, egoism, and licence.*
>
> *(Purity of Diction in English Verse)*

With the Movement English poetry again scaled itself down, and, clad in the hues of post-war Ealing movies, sardonically stated the primacy of the parochial and the provincial over the eclectic internationalism of modernism. ▷ Philip Larkin exemplifies Movement poetry, in his deflationary, perfectly formed phrases, and in his almost xenophobic stance against other cultures and cultural forms:

> *... to me the whole of the ancient world, the whole of biblical and classical mythology means very little, and I think that using them today not only fills poems full of dead spots but dodges the writer's duty to be original.*
>
> ('Four Conversations', *The London Magazine*)

Larkin's provincialism was adamantly rooted in his life in Hull, and his resistance to London's literary elite. The south-east's imperialization of other British cultures has since the 1960s found more energetic and positive forms in the growing importance of various regional poetic groups, from Northern Ireland, Newcastle, Scotland and Liverpool in particular. But the adamant Englishness of Larkin in the 1950s is another matter, and is itself beautifully deflated by the poet and critic ▷ Charles Tomlinson:

> *Larkin's narrowness suits the English perfectly. They recognize their own abysmal urban landscapes, skilfully caught with just a whiff of English films c. 1950. The stepped-down vision of human possibilities (no Renaissances, please), the joke that hesitates just this side of nihilism, are national vices.*

If these are vices, Larkin is an exemplary sinner, melancholically resigning himself to monochrome rather than confront the abyss. His poetic departure from the dominant romantic image of daring and heroism is beautifully epitomized by his poem 'Poetry of Departures' (1955). The 'audacious, purifying, / Elemental' movements of romantic action are parodied in implicit praise of safety, order and domestic banality which are for Larkin at least genuine:

So to hear it said

He walked out on the whole crowd
Leaves me flushed and stirred,
Like Then she undid her dress
Or Take that you bastard;
Surely I can, if he did?
And that helps me stay
Sober and industrious.
But I'd go today

Yes, swagger the nut-strewn roads,
Crouch the fo'c'sle
Stubbly with goodness, if
It weren't so artificial...

Larkin, then, is an ironic conformist; his poetry seems to be always already middle-aged. In 'Church Going' (1955) he responds to the divine by taking off his cycle-clips. Even in his passion for jazz music – he was an important jazz critic as well as poet – his stance is resolutely anti-40s, preferring traditional jazz – his patience ends where the fast pyrotechnics of be-bop begin. Sexual magic is regarded dispassionately:

. . . Why be out here?
But then, why be in there? Sex, yes, but what
Is sex? Surely, to think the lion's share
Of happiness is found by couples – sheer
Inaccuracy, as far as I'm concerned.
('Reasons for Attendance'; 1955)

Other sides of nihilism: Gunn, Hughes, Plath

He tells you in the sombrest notes,
If poets want to get their oats
The first step is to slit their throats.
The way to divide
The sheep of poetry from the goats
Is suicide.
(James Fenton)

Post-Movement writers strove to break the 'minipoet' mould by formulating a poetics of irrationality and violence, reacting against genteel statements of common-sense experience. This reaction took various forms, particularly towards confessional writing, expressionism, and a further working through of the modernist techniques and internationalism which had been abandoned by the Movement. Georgian moderation was scorned, in favour of more primal passions.

Poetry has had to meet the abysmal possibilities of violence opened up after 1945 in some form or other, one way being an overt thematic acknowledgement of the exponential accumulation of military hardware and the lengthening nuclear shadow of the Cold War years. The Movement had responded by consolidating safe images of a humane England for which the violations of tradition by modernists were simply interruptions or moments of forgetting. However, writing 'death of god' poetry becomes a new and darker practice after the Holocaust, Dresden and Hiroshima, events which necessarily violated the pre-war idyll of a safe and sunny England. A. Alvarez, in his seminal introduction to the anthology of 1962, *The New Poetry*, echoes the title of Freud's pathbreaking text on the theory of the death drive (published just after World War I), *Beyond the Pleasure Principle*, when he writes that the new poetry of the early 1960s goes 'Beyond the Gentility Principle'. Alvarez collected together writing which partly reacted against the sobriety of the Movement, took more risks, was more confessional, and again explored pathological states of mind. Poet-as-man-next-door had become poet-as-victim. Alvarez's prescription was taken up particularly in the intense and grotesque work of ▷ Ted Hughes, ▷ Sylvia Plath, ▷ Peter Redgrove, and American expressionists Robert Lowell (1917–77) and John Berryman (1914–72). Both Freud and Alvarez are observing modern forces of disintegration in developing their theories of psychic and poetic development. Alvarez writes:

> *Theologians would call these forces evil, psychologists, perhaps, libido. Either way, they are the forces of disintegration which destroy the old standards of civilization. Their public faces are those of two world wars, of the concentration camps, of genocide, and the threat of nuclear war.*
>
> (*The New Poetry*)

In the 1960s British poetry begins to affirm more strongly these disturbing aspects of the human psyche and its 20th-century productions.

Given the clear rational tone of much Movement work, and the at times passionate violence of much post-Movement poetry, one is tempted to superimpose the reaction from Movement to post-Movement on to the old Enlightenment/Romantic polarity, especially since Davie's overt championing of Augustan (▷ Augustanism) values. However, the simplicity of such an opposition would be challenged by the work of someone like ▷ Thom Gunn, who uses elements from both poetic worlds. He is something of a bridging figure between the Movement poets, particularly Larkin, and the early 1960s poets, particularly Ted Hughes. On the surface, and from the point of view of his work in the 1960s, Gunn could not be further from Larkin, especially when he celebrates the heroes of rock and roll, the Hemingwayesque swaggerers, 'stubbly with goodness'. When Gunn's poetry crosses the Atlantic it goes on the road – 'On the Move' (1957), with an epigram from Marlon Brando and signed just 'California', is typical – and formally Gunn's work in the 1960s, lavish and energetic, took him towards more fluid forms and free verse. But in a couplet from his poem of 1955, 'To Yvor Winters', he anticipates this move from 'Rule' to 'Energy', and unfolds a Blakean umbrella across his corpus to cover both 1950s reason and 1960s passion – at its most effective, a 20th-century marriage of rational heaven and energetic hell:

> *You keep both Rule and Energy in view,*
> *Much power in each, most in the balanced two.*

What, then, of Energy? Ted Hughes is a writer known for his Romanticism, his evocations of violence and vitalistic cruelty. He is often a very disturbing writer, showing how the idyll of England reinvoked in the 1950s is already subverted or betrayed from within by the 'stirrings beyond sense' which ghost control and self-possession. 'Esther's tomcat' sleeps by day on the mat but by night 'Walks upon sleep . . . over the round world of men'; thrushes aren't safely part of an English country garden but are 'more coiled steel than living'; a skylark is 'shot through the crested head / With the command, Not die'. Hughes's verse draws strongly on mythological motifs and can seem over-written; breaking with the parochialism of the Movement, it unearths as well as savagery the sinister and harrowing visions of a volume such as *Crow* (1970).

Hughes's work serves as relief for several comparisons which could be made at this point. Conceptually it owes much to Freud and Lawrence, who meet at the point in his verse where it becomes clear that violence and human repression are inextricably part of the same mechanism, civilization engendering a more insidious violence bred of repression itself. But he is quite starkly not a liberationist writer like Dylan Thomas or Lawrence, as he bleakly emphasizes the closure or inevitability of this mechanism. Other authorial personae exist, of course, in his children's poetry, his critical essays, even in his efforts as Poet Laureate, where Hughes the painfully private poet becomes public property. As part of a new wave in poetry – confessional, naked, anguished – which looked back in anger at 1950s self-satisfaction, Hughes exemplified the impolite twist which Alvarez celebrates, and in this is often compared with the work of Sylvia Plath, primarily because they were married until 1962 and worked closely together. Hughes was also a strong champion of Keith Douglas, and marks of disintegration brought to consciousness by the war are foregrounded by their poetic relation. Finally, in his Romantic extravagance Hughes's work can be contrasted with that of those poets who picked up the loose ends of modernism.

These links coalesce at the point at which the 'I' of the poem or poet needs to be discussed. Again questions of the poet's identity and of his or her relationship to the text and its context, to writing as public or private are brought to the fore. One way into this problem is to look briefly at the work of Charles Tomlinson, whose resistance to the influences of Thomas in the late 1940s made him turn to the precision of American modernism; he wrote 'here was a clear way of going to work, so that you could cut through this Freudian swamp and say something clearly'. The image of Pound and Eliot cutting through the Georgian 'swamp' and returning to the intellectual hardness of the Metaphysical poets has an uncanny echo in Tomlinson's practice; his 'I' is a problematic entity, rather like Eliot's. It is marginalized but, since something of a process of self-conscious depersonalization is being enacted, it takes centre-stage in its impersonality. His attempt to objectify the image, resisting Thomas's emotionalism and surreal obscurity, echoes the austerity of the Imagist project: in his own words he wants to give his images 'The hardness of crystals, the facets of cut glass'. The title of his 1960 volume *Seeing is Believing* emphasizes his attempt to bring together Movement empiricism with Imagism's valuation of visual clarity.

Compare, for instance, Tomlinson's 'Fox' with Hughes's 'Thought-Fox'. Tomlinson's animal is dead in the snow, it has a sharp correctness but in the shifting romantic blizzard gives up its own existence and becomes an image of the hill itself. Tomlinson has to work hard against the drive of his poem to slide into a chaos of white and crosswinds with his mind at the confused centre:

> *... the drift still mocked*
> *my mind as if the whole*
> *fox-infested hill were the skull of a fox ...*

The image of hill-as-skull crystalizes from the blinding blizzard of this text. Hughes's poem begins, however, with fox-as-text; where Tomlinson's fox-skull and hill are 'out there' and the poet's job is to respect and accord them this objective autonomy, Hughes's fox finds his quickness only inside the interior of the poem, the writing of which depends upon a poetic incorporation of the natural world. For Hughes there is no critical distance which gives the image outline; the fox is already inside the self, actually entering the human skull ('the dark hole of the head'), becoming subject to the desire of writing, so that the page can be printed. Similarly, Tomlinson's hawk in 'How still the Hawk' hangs purely 'out there', innocent in its distance from human interpretation, whereas Hughes's 'Hawk Roosting' famously signifies the sinister, cold egotism of the totalitarian personality – Hughes's hawk has a subjective existence, so that it speaks the poems from the point of view of a post-war 'I'. The stillness of the hawk's image is for Tomlinson, then, a challenge to objectivism, for Hughes a point of aberrant control in the maelstrom of modern cruelty, whilst for Dylan Thomas in 'Over Sir John's Hill' it was a moment of emotionally intense poise:

Over Sir John's Hill
The hawk on fire hangs still;
In a hoisted cloud, at drop of dusk, he pulls to his claws.

The dialogue between these poems, then, serves to illustrate the familiar modern dichotomy in British poetry, that of the privileging of inside or outside. Is poetic writing an attempt to clarify as succinctly as possible the autonomous and the objective, or is it an act of poetic individuation and self-definition? The Romantic question – Coleridge's notion that poet and poem are indistinguishable – often recurs at this moment in poetic history as the dilemma between confessional, violent, personal writing and a post-war form of Imagism, like Tomlinson's, or like the precise and abrupt decompositional writing of ▷ Christopher Middleton. Who, then, is the poet? Is he or she now dead, like other authors in the ▷ post-structuralist world? And how does the fresh political engagement of the 1980s affect this question? The problem of the self and its relations to writing is intensified as personal subjectivity is viewed increasingly suspiciously in recent times. The question of objectivity, of the subjectivity of the poet and the status of his or her images, which clearly Tomlinson is engaging with, became a sharper problem in the 1980s with the increased politicization of radical poetic writing, and, in another form, with the distorted perceptions of 'Martian eye' (▷ Martian poetry) writing. I shall return to this shortly.

Sylvia Plath is, like Keith Douglas, another untimely poet, who wrote four brilliant and disturbing slim volumes of poetry in the early 1960s, three of which were published well after her suicide in 1963. It is hard to read Plath's verse outside the enormous interest in her private life which has burgeoned since her death; in modern mythology she exemplifies the self-consciously tragic poetic genius-figure. The nature of her death also evokes a more disturbing myth, that of the woman writer wracked by neurosis and too weak in body to contain her talent. Whoever Plath was, there is no doubt that her work relentlessly pursues the question of the 'I', of poetry and madness, with all Douglas's desire of words for words. The 'late mouths' of 'Poppies in October' which 'cry open / In a forest of frost' cause her to ask 'O my God, what am I?'; to whom do the poppies come, like a macabre gift, suggesting bleeding in ambulances? There is warfare in her work, a sharp killer's eye and a grotesque but erotic drive. A bleeding, fizzing cut across her thumb is the result of an Indian scalping, a sabotage, a Kamikaze act, a symptom of masochism. The image of blood as the running of 'A million soldiers . . ., / Redcoats, every one' ('Cut') is typically acute, almost humorous, but bites with paranoia as she then asks, 'Whose side are they on?' The sinister possibility that one's own flowing blood could be one's enemy speaks the psychological complexity of Plath's work, which never rests in the notion of anguish as 'authentic'. Cruel humour and ruthless self-suspicion undermine sincerity; arrogance and tragic self-glorification are deflated in 'Lady Lazarus', as suicide is paraded with the grotesque props of concentration camps:

Dying
Is an art, like everything else.
I do it exceptionally well.
I do it so it feels like hell.
I do it so it feels real.
I guess you could say I've a call.

Plath's 'reality' is not that of the every-day Movement, but that is not to say that her work can be marginalized as a depoliticized expression of private agonies; she was acutely aware of the political nature of writing for a woman, and insists on drawing parallels between her experience and disturbing political and historical reality. If she is a personal writer it is because, in the phrase coined by 1960s feminism, 'the personal is the political': 'Daddy' is as much about the powers of horror, opened up by post-war images of death camps and fascist obsession, as it is a text working through a daughter's ambivalent relationship with her father. As Plath said in an interview just before she died, poetry 'should be generally relevant, to such things as Hiroshima and Dachau'. Plath gazes straight at taboo, where a writer like ▷ Peter Porter, in 'Annotations of Auschwitz' for instance, looks satirically sideways at it. Porter's 'Your Attention Please' casts a black-comic nuclear shadow, whilst reminding us of something we meet constantly in Plath's work: 'Death is the least we have to fear'. 'Lady Lazarus' comes back,

Out of the ash
I rise with my red hair
And I eat men like air.

'A dangerous weapon': contemporary poetry

I am neither internee nor informer;
An inner émigré, grown long-haired
And thoughtful; a wood-kerne

Escaped from the massacre.
('Exposure', Seamus Heaney)

The crisis of writing and identity which is traced here as infecting British poetry has recently reached fever pitch. The problems of what constitutes a poem and of who the poet is have more recently become politicized into questions about what constitutes the *British* in 'British poetry'. Poets now, be they black, female or Irish, have felt themselves to be 'inner émigrés': as Guyanan-born poet John Agard (b 1949) writes 'I didn't graduate / I immigrate', ('Listen Mr Oxford Don', 1985). The phrase 'poetry in English' is compromised by other voices from Ireland, Scotland, regions of England, and the Commonwealth (▷ Commonwealth literatures). From a traditional point of view it seems that English poetry is slowly undergoing an undignified death-process, that the incorporation of other voices into 'Eng. Lit.' constitutes the blowing into oblivion of a much-cherished friend. More energetically and optimistically we could say, rather, that what is gaining prominence is a kind of 'multiverse', a plurality of accents and experiences breaking open the poised egocentric tradition. From going 'Beyond the Gentility Principle' we reach the late 1980s with poet and critic Eric Mottram's assertion that the modern avant-garde constitutes 'A Treacherous Assault on British Poetry' (*The New British Poetry*; 1988). The critic Colin MacCabe writes, 'It is perhaps no longer appropriate to talk of English literature but of a literature in broken English':

> *If the members of the United Kingdom are all nominally British, it is instructive to recall that English as a language has been imposed, often by force, throughout the British Isles. And the peoples of those islands find that along with the imposed language they have acquired a literature to which their relationship is profoundly ambiguous – one need only think of Joyce or MacDiarmid to realise exactly how ambiguous.*
>
> (McCabe, 'Broken English', *Futures for English*, 1988)

This realization began to find some purchase in British poetry in the mid-1960s, although it is true that in a different way internationalist strains in modernist writing had already undermined the notion of a truly English culture. From the regional focus which constituted much poetic activity during the 1960s, to the broad cultural base of much radical poetry today, British writing now can be defined only as a space within which its vital differences are affirmed. It has many homes: Trinidad-born poet John Lyons now resides in Britain but has left a nomadic trail leading back to his 'Island Muse':

I come long years with my pen
and island hauntings
from where my navel string tree
still grows.

Thus poetry split its focus into a thriving network of regional groups, in the Mordern Tower poets of Newcastle, who found their mentor in the rediscovered ▷ Basil Bunting, and the new renaissance of poetry from Northern Ireland which has emerged as contemporaneous with the troubles, from poets such as ▷ Seamus Heaney, ▷ Paul Muldoon and ▷ Derek Mahon. The emphasis was resolutely anti-London and the cultural imperialism of the south-east. The famous 'Liverpool poets' of the early and mid-1960s – Adrian Henri (b 1932), Henry Graham (b 1930), Roger McGough (b 1937) and Brian Patten (b 1946), collected in the anthologies *The Mersey Sound* (1967) and *New Volume* (1983) – were a British version of American Beat poetry. All four had strong links with the world of pop music, and emphasized poetry as live performance, thus opening up their writing to a wide young audience. Like pop art, Mersey poetry uses the familiar images of throwaway culture in its quick-fire surreal humour, but the effect is ultimately naughty rather than revolutionary. Pop art and pop music found their way into poetry at this time as never before, and the link between rock and writing was kept bubbling underground in the late 1960s largely due to the ministrations of the poet and publisher Michael Horovitz (b 1935) – his magazine *New Departures*, founded in 1959, had long been the organ of the poetic underground, and his anthology *Children of Albion* (1969) exemplifies a late 1960s celebration of liberation politics and poetics, taking William Blake as mentor. Whilst it is true that much avant-garde writing in the 1960s and 1970s displays the preoccupations of the economically privileged young British middle classes, it also eventually encouraged a certain disrespect – against the gentility principle once more – which opened a space for the more multi-racial and working-class forms of punk, dub, reggae poetry, and New Wave performance in the late 1970s.

The regionalist movement was roughly contemporary with the establishment of a large number of small presses, through which more experimental and avant-garde work found a space outside the mainstream monolithic publishing houses, just as the high street bookshop's failure to sell marginalized writing urged poets into using local live outlets for their work. The small presses, often set up by poets themselves, have effectively countered the overwhelming influence of the major houses like Chatto & Windus and Faber & Faber – Faber in particular has long dominated poetry publication and in effect established the official canon of post-war and contemporary verse. Aesthetic valuation has seldom walked so nakedly in the profit margins. So the small presses have been vital in countering profitable orthodoxies: names such as Gael Turnbull's Migrant Press, Peterloo Poets, Stuart Montgomery's Fulcrum, Andrew Crozier's Ferry, Desmond Johnson's Akira and Ian Hamilton Finlay's Wild Hawthorn, in conjunction with small magazines like *Stand, Poetry Information* and *Agenda*, have over the years given younger and more experimental writers a space within which to work and have access to publishing facilities. In 1971 the champion of experimental and post-modernist work Eric Mottram was made editor of the Poetry Society's *Poetry Review*, an unprecedented move, as a result of which other forms of writing found a voice through the National Poetry Centre, until the scandalous dissolution of the editorial board by the ▷ Arts Council in 1977.

It must be said, however, that these energies remain fired partly by the task of countering the familiar conservatism of the poetic establishment. Two of the larger publishing houses, Anvil Press and Carcanet Press, are indeed open to more obscure and challenging types of modern writing, but Carcanet's statement of its aesthetic policy when it was established in 1969 displays a continued cherishing of bourgeois 'reasonable' traditions. Something of this survived in the compilation of the much criticized 1982 anthology, *The Penguin Book of Contemporary Poetry*, edited by ▷ Blake Morrison (b 1950) and ▷ Andrew Motion (b 1952), which collected together a chic, sophisticated body of modern verse, challenging nothing, and punctuated for bizarre effect only by sideways glances from the 'Martian eyes' of ▷ Craig Raine and Christopher Reid.

The modernist question of homelessness has recently been rearticulated by women poets as a problem of one's tradition and one's literary home; women's writing continues to disrupt the smooth contours of the traditional mask. As a woman writer, where does one come from? ▷ Denise Levertov's verse is unsettling in its sense of exile, echoing ▷ Virginia Woolf's '. . . as a woman I have no country'. Ruth Fainlight's work also knows no fixed identity; a multitude of feminine voices insinuate threats or coaxings from between its lines. Her poems are populated by female 'others' – Sibyls, forgotten sisters, 'Stone-Age' selves, Medusas, 'Sophia, Anima, Kali', 'Gloria', 'Lilith' or the faces in the mirror. They speak to free the texts 'from whomsoever's definition: / Jew, poet, woman'.

Levertov's verse protests strongly against the stench of war and her adoptive America's aggression. Like Douglas, it exults in moments lived as if at 'the last minute', intensified by the consciousness of ending. Death breathes across the still, awestruck poems, 'Living', 'Passage', '. . . That Passeth All Understanding', a finitude which concentrates; if her poetry is spiritual it is so because it exists in the shadow of oblivion:

The fire in leaf and grass
so green it seems
each summer the last summer
('Living')

a day of spring, a needle's eye
space and time are passing through like a swathe of silk
('Passage')

The intense interest in women's writing since the 1960s has, then, been important both to the ▷ women's movement and in opening up literature to a variety of other voices. Indeed, opening up the canon of contemporary poetry has occurred from inside poetry itself. Modernism's amalgamating energies, which brought many other languages and voices forth from the crevices and underbelly of the canon – its otherwise repressed voices – have been realized in a less authoritarian form since the 1960s. Almost as soon as a new contemporary canon could gather itself, it was eroded by a wave of work penned by black writers, women writers – a self-consciously politicized alternative. Canon challenging has, then, recently been more than an academic exercise, especially since poetry now is written from an acute awareness of the possibilities of academic incorporation and judgement.

MacCabe's punning phrase 'Broken English' suggests both a body terminally injured and broken open, ready for new growth – we are back, perhaps, with H.D.'s celebration of the destruction of restrictive models, which for John Agard again can be achieved armed only 'wit mih human breath / but human breath / is a dangerous weapon'. If the impetus of 1960s poetry was an urge to harmony, that of the 1980s is an affirmation of difference, as the teeming voices of other cultural forms (the language of reggae, for instance) breaks out from the broken body of 'Eng. Lit.':

I dont need no axe
to split/ up yu syntax
I dont need no hammer
to mash/ up yu grammar
('Listen Mr Oxford Don', John Agard; 1985)

'Tradition' continues to be a problem, but one which contemporary poetry encounters through a strategy of incorporation. Two recent anthologies illustrate this extremely well. Denise Riley's *Poets on Writing* (1992) places poems by new young poets alongside short prose responses and observations concerning their writing history, their influences and motivations. The collection shows the diversity of poetic 'climates' which breathe in and out of the texts included (as Riley puts it, 'what there was in the air'). The anxiety about tradition which has engendered the violent reactions of the 20th century movements I have described here has to some extent been replaced by a writing spirit which casts the net of influence culturally wider and with a greater sense of critical scepticism regarding the question of influence *per se*. Thus poet and critic Geoffrey Ward (b 1954), citing a range of elements and images (such as the Fun House at Southport, early Auden, or the whole poetic climate of his early student life) which form some of the 'troubled' origins of a poem, writes,

Writing only ever takes place at some juncture; in relation, Poetry articulates the coincidence and/or contradiction where what's heard on the radio meets what happens in the street, where what you are reading questions what you are read as doing.

('Objects That Come Alive at Night', *Poets on Writing*, ed. Denise Riley, Macmillan 1992)

Similarly, Carol Rumens's *New Women Poets* (1991) stresses the eclecticism of her writers, their variety of dialects and enthusiastic formal innovation. Citing the poetry of Briar Wood (b 1958) and Jackie Kay (b 1951), Rumens writes:

> *What is new is the emergence of a kind of late twentieth-century urban dialect, a montage that reverberates with the noise, colour, slanginess, jargonizing and information-glut of daily life.*

In presenting this final collage, I do not wish to suggest that the project of modern poetry is a return to representation, albeit the representation of a *new* range of cultural phenomena or experiences. But perhaps modern poetry, informed by the 'climate' of popular music, films or images, and theoretical perspectives on influence, is better able to articulate its response to a wider range of materials. In this sense modern poetry comes close to ▷ postmodernism, although the term is more commonly used in relation to a range of other forms. The strategy of incorporation which I have described has, however, more clearly been deployed as a response to marginalization. Modern poetry uses its marginalization and the elements of literary crisis to form something which has not only a future but many futures, as many futures as there are cultural forms and languages to be incorporated. What is being affirmed, then, is a process of innoculation; the crisis passes as new forms of writing learn how to grow from that which formerly threatened and marginalized. The canon is being opened from within; to paraphrase Nietzsche, what doesn't kill poetry makes it stronger.

Reference section

A

Aaron
In the ▷ Bible, the founder of the Jewish priesthood; he assisted Moses in leading the Jews out of Egypt to the frontiers of Canaan, the 'Promised Land'. His rod was a sacred emblem which Moses and he held up above the battle when the Jews were fighting the Amalekites (*Exodus* 17). The novel *Aaron's Rod* (1922) by ▷ D. H. Lawrence, is about a coal-miner who transforms his life with the aid of his flute.

Abbey Theatre, Dublin
The home of the Irish National Theatre Society from 1904 until a fire destroyed the building in 1951. The Society, usually known by the name of its theatre, grew from a fusion of the Irish National Dramatic Company, led by the actor W. G. Fay, and the Irish Literary Theatre founded by the poet ▷ W. B. Yeats, his friend ▷ Lady Gregory and others. The time was propitious: there was an intense national feeling in Ireland and an accompanying literary revival; Europe was undergoing the awakening influences of ▷ Ibsen and ▷ Strindberg; Yeats was a major poet with strong interest in the drama. Consequently the Abbey Theatre was a focus for creative energies which made it a unique institution in the history of the English-speaking theatre. However, the movement was neither the mere mouthpiece of Irish patriotism, nor just a vehicle for European fashions. Though Ibsen was a stimulus and dominated at least one of the Irish dramatists (Edward Martyn), its most outstanding contributor, ▷ J. M. Synge, was in reaction against Ibsen, as was Yeats himself. Neither of them tolerated the prejudices of the more radical nationalists. Synge's masterpiece, ▷ *The Playboy of the Western World*, caused a riot in the theatre when it was produced there in 1907. Yeats used verse of increasing vigour and austerity in a renewal of poetic drama that ranked the Abbey with the most interesting experimental theatres of the time in Europe – the Théâtre Libre in Paris and the Freie Bühne in Berlin. The heroic period of the Abbey Theatre ended with Synge's death and Yeats's retirement from its management in 1909; but under Lennox Robinson the Abbey remained a theatre of distinction. Its most notable playwright after that time was ▷ Sean O'Casey.

▷ Irish literature in English.

Abse, Dannie (b 1923)
Poet. Abse was born in Cardiff, and trained as a doctor in Cardiff and London. His volumes of verse include: *After Every Green Thing* (1949); *Tenants of the House* (1957); *A Small Desperation* (1968); *Selected Poems* (1970); *Way Out in the Centre* (1981); *Collected Poems, 1948–1976* (1977). He has also written novels and plays, and has published two volumes of his ▷ autobiography.

Absurd, Theatre of the
▷ Theatre of the Absurd.

Achebe, Chinua (b 1930)
Nigerian novelist, poet and ▷ short-story writer. Born Albert Chinualumogu in Ogidi, East Central State, his mother tongue is Ibo, but he studied English from an early age and in 1953 graduated in English Literature from University College, Ibadan. He has worked in radio, publishing, journalism and as an academic, visiting universities in the U.S.A. In his five novels he has successfully incorporated African idioms and patterns of thought in a lucid English prose style. *Things Fall Apart* (1958), with its title drawn from ▷ W. B. Yeats's poem 'The Second Coming', explores a principal African dilemma: the destruction of the indigenous culture by European influence. It concerns Okonkwo, a village leader whose inflexible adherence to tradition cannot withstand the influence of white missionaries. *No Longer At Ease* (1960) continues the theme of the conflict of African and European values, but in the urban context of Lagos in the 1950s. *Arrow of God* (1964) returns to tribal society, but at an earlier stage of colonialism, in the 1920s, while *A Man of the People* (1966) is again set in Lagos, with direct reference to the turbulent political events following Nigerian independence in 1960. His most recent novel, *Anthills of the Savannah*, was published in 1987. He has published two volumes of short stories, *The Sacrificial Egg* (1962) and *Girls at War* (1972) and two volumes of poetry: *Beware Soul-Brother and Other Poems* (1971) and *Christmas in Biafra and Other Poems* (1973). He also writes children's stories.
Bib: Lindfors, B., and Innes, C. L. (ed.), *Achebe*.

Ackroyd, Peter (b 1949)
Novelist, poet and critic. Born in London and educated at Cambridge University, he has been literary editor of the *Spectator* and a reviewer of books, television and cinema for ▷ *The Times* and the *Sunday Times*. His first novel was *The Great Fire of London* (1982), followed by *The Last Testament of Oscar Wilde* (1983), which took the form of the fictional

diaries of ▷ Wilde during his tragic last years in Paris, and won the Somerset Maugham award. *Hawksmoor* (1985) interweaves a police investigation in contemporary East London with a narrative set during the great plague of the 17th century, in which the architects Hawksmoor and Wren appear; the novel won both the Guardian Fiction Award and the Whitbread Prize for the best novel. *Chatterton* (1987) is in part literary ▷ detective story (in which it resembles ▷ A. S. Byatt's *Possession*) and combines historical pastiche (also a notable feature of *Hawksmoor*) with black comedy and elements of the sentimental and grotesque. *First Light* (1989) stages a confrontation between science and magic through the story of an archaeological dig in Dorset. Ackroyd has published three volumes of poetry: *London Lickpenny* (1973); *Country Life* (1978) and *The Diversions of Purley* (1987). His non-fiction includes: *Notes for a New Culture: An Essay on Modernism* (1976); *Dressing Up: Transvestism and Drag: The History of an Obsession* (1979); *Ezra Pound and his World* (1980); *T.S. Eliot* (1984) (which won the Whitbread Prize for ▷ biography); *Dickens* (1990).

Act

In drama: a division of a play; acts are sometimes subdivided into scenes. The ancient Greeks did not use divisions into acts; the practice was started by the Romans, and the poet-critic Horace (1st century BC) in his *Ars Poetica* laid down the principle that the number of acts should be five. Since the renaissance of classical learning in the 16th century, most dramatists have used act divisions, and many have obeyed Horace's precepts.

Acting, The profession of

Acting began to achieve recognition as a profession in the reign of Elizabeth I. The important date is the building of The Theatre – the first theatre in England – by James Burbage in 1576. It was followed by many others in London, and theatres soon became big business. Previously, actors had performed where they could, especially in inn yards and the halls of palaces, mansions, and colleges. They continued to do so, but the existence of theatres gave them a base and (though they still required an official licence) independence such as they badly needed in order to win social recognition.

Until the mid-16th century acting was practised by many kinds of people: ordinary townsmen at festivals, wandering entertainers, boys and men from the choirs of the great churches, and members of the staffs of royal or aristocratic households. It was from these last that the professional actors emerged. They still wore the liveries – uniforms and badges – of the great households, but the connection was now loose (good performers could transfer from one household to another) and was chiefly a means of procuring a licence to perform. This licence was essential because the City of London, around which dramatic activity concentrated, feared the theatre as providing centres of infection for the recurrent plague epidemics (which from time to time sent the companies away on tour) and disliked acting as a morally harmful and anomalous way of life. Moreover, the royal court, which favoured the stage, was nonetheless on guard against it as a potential source of sedition. Censorship and licensing, however, had the advantage of helping to distinguish the serious performers from the vulgar entertainers.

By the time of Elizabeth's death two great companies were dominant: the Lord Chamberlain's Men, for whom ▷ Shakespeare wrote, and the Lord Admiral's Men, headed by the leading actor of the day, Edward Alleyn. Women did not perform; their parts were taken by boys who enlisted as apprentices. Companies of boy actors from the choirs of St Paul's and the Chapels Royal also had prestige (see *Hamlet* II.2), especially in the 1570s. The establishment of the profession owed most to the dramatists, but much to the energy of actor-managers and theatre proprietors such as Philip Henslowe, Edward Alleyn, James Burbage, and his son Richard.

Actresses were allowed to perform after the Restoration of the monarchy (1660). The status of the profession continued to rise, aided by the theatre's ceasing to be the entertainment of all classes and becoming a fashionable pleasure of the London West End. In the 18th century the genius and culture of David Garrick greatly enhanced the prestige of the profession. From his time on, there is a long roll of great acting names; the drama, however, declined until the end of the 19th century, partly because the intrinsic value of plays came to be considered secondary to the merit of their performance. Radical theatrical developments in the 20th century have challenged the traditional relationship between an actor and the audience, and the growth of improvised theatre has widened the actor's performance skills. ▷ Antonin Artaud's ▷ Theatre of Cruelty and ▷ Bertolt Brecht's practice of *Verfremdungseffekt* (▷ alienation effect) have had a profound impact on the

acting profession this century. More recently, actors have been seriously affected by the more material conditions of decline in public funding for theatres.
▷ Theatres; R.S.C.; Littlewood, Joan; Olivier, Laurence.

Adcock, Fleur (b 1934)
Poet and translator. Born and educated in New Zealand, Adcock has lived in Britain since 1963. Her volumes of poetry include: *The Eye of the Hurricane* (1964); *Tigers* (1967); *High Tide in the Garden* (1971); *The Scenic Route* (1974) and *The Inner Harbour* (1970). In 1982 she edited the *Oxford Book of Contemporary New Zealand Poetry* and the *Faber Book of 20th Century Women's Poetry*, and more recent works include *The Incident Book* (1986) and *Time-Zones* (1991). A volume of her *Selected Poems* appeared in 1983. She has also translated medieval Latin poetry and Greek poetry.

Adult education
The scope of adult education has widened and its emphasis changed in recent years. Late educational opportunities, places for mature students at university, evening classes and residential courses of various kinds used to be promoted as desirable for the development of the person as an end in itself. The 1970s and 1980s have seen a more pragmatic approach in the interests of creating a more efficient workforce. Tasks with specific aims have been embraced, such as supplementing an inadequate initial schooling for the illiterate and innumerate, and the updating of workers in their own fields by in-service training. The ▷ Open University's Continuing Education Programme, devoted to vocational updating for community workers, teachers and managers, has received a new emphasis. This shift is matched by the government's investment in PICKUP (1982), a Professional, Industrial and Commercial Updating Programme designed to direct institutions of higher education to provide courses to broaden the skills of white-collar workers in mid-career. REPLAN, for the adult employed, was launched in 1984 and in 1987 the first courses of the Open College were begun, providing vocational education and training below degree level. There is provision for mature students at conventional universities, though funding may present problems. Courses, mostly part-time, are also held by a variety of bodies, including further education colleges, extra-mural departments of universities and the Workers Educational Association, the largest of the voluntary bodies.
▷ Williams, Raymond.

Aeschylus 525–456 BC
With Sophocles and Euripides, one of the three great tragic poets of ancient Greece. Only seven of his 70 plays survive; of these the best known are *Agamemnon*, *Choephori* and *Eumenides*, making up the *Oresteia* trilogy. Aeschylus is the great starting point of all European tragedy; ▷ T. S. Eliot used the Oresteia myth for his verse drama *The Family Reunion* (1939).

Aestheticism
A movement of the late 19th century, influenced by the Pre-Raphaelites and John Ruskin, but its immediate inspiration was the writings of the Oxford don Walter Pater. His two most influential books were *Studies in the History of the Renaissance* (1873) and *Marius the Epicurean* (1885). These show him as a ritualistic moralist, laying emphasis on the value of ecstatic experience. Apart from Pater and his predecessors, the aesthetes owed much to the current French doctrine of *'L'Art pour l'Art'* (Art for Art's Sake) but they retained, if sometimes not obviously, a typically English concern with moral values and issues. The outstanding aesthete was ▷ Oscar Wilde (1865–1900), and a characteristic aesthetic product was his novel *The Picture of Dorian Gray* (1891). As the movement lacked a programme, writers of very different characters were influenced by it: the naturalistic novelist ▷ George Moore; the poet Lionel Johnson who was a Catholic convert; Swinburne, a main channel for the art for art's sake doctrine; ▷ W. B. Yeats, the Celtic revivalist. A characteristic aestheticist periodical was ▷ *The Yellow Book* (1894–7), so called because French novels, conventionally considered 'daring', were printed on yellow paper. Its main illustrator was ▷ Aubrey Beardsley, whose line drawings were notorious for their sensuality. The excesses and affectations of the movement's adherents were much ridiculed in ▷ *Punch*.
Bib: Aldington, R. (ed.), *The Religion of Beauty: Selections from the Aesthetes*; Jackson, H., *The 1890s*.

Agnosticism
The term was invented by the biologist Thomas Huxley in 1869 to express towards religious faith the attitude which is neither of belief nor of disbelief (▷ atheism). In his own words, 'I neither affirm nor deny

the immortality of man. I see no reason for believing it, but on the other hand I have no means of disproving it.' Agnosticism was widespread among writers between 1850 and 1914; it arose from the scientific thought of the time, especially that of Huxley himself, and that of another biologist, Charles Darwin.

Albion
The most ancient name for Britain, used in Greek by Ptolemy and in Latin by Pliny. The word possibly derived from Celtic, but it was associated by the Romans with the Latin *albus* = white, referring to the white cliffs of Dover. From the ▷ Middle Ages on it has often been used poetically to stand for Britain, notably by William Blake, one of the main influences on Michael Horowitz's key poetry anthology, *Children of Albion* (1970).

Aldiss, Brian (b 1925)
▷ Science Fiction.

Alienation effect
Term, '*Verfremdungseffekt*', developed by the German dramatist ▷ Bertolt Brecht in his theatrical and theoretical writings. He demanded that his audiences should realize that they were not watching 'life' but a representation, and he urged that actor and audience alike should preserve a critical 'distance' from events on the stage.
▷ Defamiliarization.

Allegory
From the Greek, meaning 'speaking in other terms'. A way of representing thought and experience through images, by means of which (1) complex ideas may be simplified, or (2) abstract, spiritual, or mysterious ideas and experiences may be made immediate (but not necessarily simpler) by dramatization in fiction.

In both uses, allegory was most usual and natural as a medium of expression in the ▷ Middle Ages. ▷ Catholic doctrine prevailed as deeply as it did widely; even the physical structures of the universe and of man seemed to be living images of spiritual truth. The morality plays, notably *Everyman* (15th century), were practical applications of this doctrine to ordinary experience. But the tendency to see experience in allegorical terms extended to secular literature, for example the romances of sexual love, such as *The Romance of the Rose* (14th century) in part translated from the French by ▷ Chaucer. When Chaucer wrote a romance in which there was no overt allegory, *eg Troilus and Criseyde*, the allegorical spirit was still implicit within it (see ▷ C. S. Lewis, *Allegory of Love*). Such implicit allegory extended into much Renaissance drama, *eg* ▷ Shakespeare's *Henry IV, Parts I and II*.

In the ▷ Renaissance, however, explicit allegory, though still pervasive, was greatly complicated by the break-up of the dominant Catholic framework; various Christian doctrines competed with one another and with non-Christian ones such as ▷ neo-Platonism, and also with political theories. Thus in a work like Spenser's *Faerie Queene* religious, political and Platonic allegories are all employed, but intermittently and not with artistic coherence.

Since the 17th century deliberate and consistent allegory has continued to decline; yet the greatest of all English allegories, *The Pilgrim's Progress* by John Bunyan, is a 17th-century work. The paradox is explained by Bunyan's contact with the literature of the village sermon, which apparently continued to be conducted by a simple allegorical method with very little influence from the Reformation. Moreover allegory has continued into modern times, partly as an indispensable habit of explanation, partly in a suppressed form (*eg* the names of characters in Dickens's novels), and partly as a resource in the expression of mysterious psychological experience incommunicable in direct terms; here allegory merges with ▷ symbolism, from which, however, it needs to be distinguished. ▷ George Orwell's dystopian novel *Animal Farm* is an allegory of totalitarian society, and there has been a lively debate concerning the role of allegory centring on the work of ▷ Paul de Man, who wrote *Allegories of Reading* (1979) and *Blindness and Insight* (1983) in discussion of the subject.
▷ Fable.

Allingham Margery (1904–66)
Writer of ▷ detective fiction. One of the foremost women detective writers of the 20th century, Allingham's work is characteristic of the inter-war 'golden age' of detective fiction, along with the work of ▷ Agatha Christie, ▷ Ngaio Marsh and ▷ Dorothy L. Sayers. Like Christie's Poirot or Miss Marple, or Sayer's Lord Peter Wimsey, Allingham has a chief detective, Albert Campion (said to be modelled on Wimsey), who is however a rather enigmatic, mysterious character, working in a London full of atmosphere and populated by eccentrics. She began writing in the 1920s and continued until her death in 1966; her many novels include: *The Crime at*

Black Dudley (1929); *Look to the Lady* (1931); *Police at the Funeral* (1931); *Sweet Danger* (1933); *Dancers in Mourning* (1937); *The Fashion in Shrouds* (1938); *The Case Book of Mr Campion* (1947); *The Tiger in the Smoke* (1952); *The Mind Readers* (1965).

Althusser, Louis (1918–90)
One of the most influential French ▷ Marxist philosophers of the 1960s, whose work began to appear in English translation from 1965 onwards: *For Marx* (1965), *Reading Capital* (with Etienne Balibar; 1968), and *Lenin and Philosophy* (1971). Althusser's ideas have been influential in the area of cultural studies, where his particular brand of structural Marxism has led to a radical rethinking of all social institutions, and the place of the human subject within their structures. His essay 'Ideology and Ideological State Apparatuses' (*Lenin and Philosophy*) laid the foundation for a reconsideration of literature and its relationship to ▷ ideology, and has had far-reaching effects also in the area of media studies.

***Ambassadors, The* (1903)**
A novel by ▷ Henry James. It belongs to his last period, during which he returned to his earlier theme of the interaction of the European and American character.

Lambert Strether, a conscientious, middle-aged American, is engaged to the rich American widow, Mrs Newsome. She sends him over to Paris to bring back her son Chad to run the family business. He arrives to find Chad immersed in Parisian culture, and absorbed in a love affair with the Comtesse de Vionnet, a relationship which Strether mistakenly assumes to be virtuous. Strether, instead of persuading Chad to return, finds his sensibilities released by the freedom and richness of Parisian life, and delays his own return. Chad's sister, Mrs Pocock, and her husband, Jim, are now sent over by Mrs Newsome. Strether urges upon Chad the duty of loyalty to the Comtesse, and Mrs Newsome breaks off her engagement to Strether. After discovering the true nature of Chad's relations with the Comtesse, Strether decides to go back, abandoning his friendship with the intelligent and sympathetic Maria Gostrey, an American expatriate. Chad, however, remains.

Mrs Newsome is an authoritarian American matron, full of rectitude and prejudice. Strether has the highly developed New England conscience (it is his conscience that forces him to return) and a hitherto starved imagination. He is the focal character of the narrative throughout, so that his progressive understanding and development is a rich source of interest and irony. The Pococks stand for American philistinism, without imagination or sensibility. Together with ▷ *The Golden Bowl* (1904) and ▷ *The Wings of the Dove* (1902), the novel shows James's art at its most highly wrought and difficult stage.

Amis, Kingsley (b 1922)
Novelist and poet. Associated at first with the ▷ 'angry young men' of the 1950s for his novels, and with the ▷ Movement for his poetry, he has long outgrown such labelling, achieving considerable popular success with a series of sharp, ironic novels notable for entertaining incident, vivid caricatures and the comic demolition of pretension. *Lucky Jim* (1954; filmed 1957) is a hugely enjoyable novel about a young English lecturer in a provincial university and his battles against the academic establishment and a range of comically infuriating characters. It is not really a subversive work; it ends with the hero being given a good job in London by a wealthy man as well as winning the best girl. Amis's later novels tend to be less good humoured; the protagonist of *One Fat Englishman* (1963) retains some of Jim's methods, but is fully as unpleasant as his enemies. Although Amis has remained within the format of a well-crafted plot and largely conventional modes of narration, he has employed a wide range of genres such as the ▷ detective story (*The Riverside Villas Murder*; 1973), the spy-story (*The Anti Death League*; 1966) and the ghost-story (*The Green Man*; 1969). *The Alteration* (1976), one of his most inventive works, imagines a 20th-century society dominated by the Catholic Church. The publication of his *Memoirs* (1991) caused a brief flurry in the literary world with its personal revelations about fellow authors, such as ▷ Philip Larkin and ▷ Anthony Burgess.

Amis's other novels are: *That Uncertain Feeling* (1955); *I Like It Here* (1958); *Take A Girl Like You* (1960); *The Egyptologists* (1965); *I Want It Now* (1968); *Colonel Sun* (as Robert Markham; 1968); *Girl, 20* (1971); *Ending Up* (1974); *The Alteration* (1976); *Jake's Thing* (1978); *Russian Hide and Seek* (1980); *Stanley and the Women* (1984); *The Old Devils* (1986); *Difficulties With Girls* (1988). Story collections include: *My Enemy's Enemy* (1962); *Dear Illusion* (1972); *The Darkwater Hall Mystery* (1978); *Collected Short Stories* (1980). Poetry: *Bright November* (1947); *A Frame of Mind* (1953); *A Case of Samples* (1956); *The Evans Country* (1962); *A Look Around the Estate:*

Poems 1957–1967 (1967); *Collected Poems 1944–1979* (1979). Essays and criticism include: *New Maps of Hell* (on ▷ science fiction; 1960); *The James Bond Dossier* (1965); *What Became of Jane Austen?* (1975); *Rudyard Kipling and His World* (1975).
Bib: Salwak, D., *Kingsley Amis, A Reference Guide*.

Amis, Martin (b 1949)
Novelist. Son of ▷ Kingsley Amis, he was educated at schools in Britain, Spain and the U.S.A., and at Oxford University. He has worked for the *Times Literary Supplement*, the *New Statesman* (as literary editor) and the *Observer*. His novels are characterized by black humour, concern with the sordid, violent and absurd, and a apparent misogyny, features which he defends as satire. *The Rachel Papers* (1973) is an account of adolescence through flashback and memories; *Dead Babies* (1975) (paperback as *Dark Secrets*) is a tale of decadence and sadism; *Success* (1978) is closer to the hilarity of *The Rachel Papers*, while *Other People* (1981) is an experiment in ambiguity. Other works: *Money* (novel; 1984); *The Moronic Inferno* (essays; 1986); *Einstein's Monsters* (stories; 1987); *London Fields* (1989); *Time's Arrow* (1991) was shortlisted for the 1991 Booker Prize.

***Androcles and the Lion* (1912)**
A comedy by ▷ George Bernard Shaw based on a tale by a 2nd-century Latin writer, Aulus Gellius. The lion has a wounded paw which Androcles, a runaway slave, heals; subsequently the lion meets Androcles in an arena combat, and spares his life.

Anglican
From medieval Latin, *anglicanus* = English. The Catholic Church of medieval Christendom divided Europe into provinces for administrative purposes; England was the 'Anglican' province. Since the separation of the Church of England from Rome in the 16th century, 'Anglican' has been used adjectivally for the Churches in Britain, the U.S.A. and the Commonwealth which are in communion with the Church of England, as well as for that Church itself. The Anglican Church of England has come to be closely associated with the maintenance of establishment values and traditional power relations between classes and between the sexes. Recent moves, particularly towards the ordination of women, may cause this stereotype to be modified. Anglicanism = doctrine and practices of the Church of England and kindred Churches.

Angry young men
A term which was loosely applied to novelists and dramatists of the 1950s who expressed a sense of dissatisfaction and revolt against established social mores. ▷ John Osborne's play *Look Back In Anger* (1956) epitomized the mood. Other authors of whom the term was used include ▷ John Braine, ▷ John Wain, ▷ Alan Sillitoe, and ▷ Kingsley Amis.
▷ Realism.
Bib: Allsop, K., *The Angry Decade*.

Anthology
A collection of short works in verse or prose, or selected passages from longer works, by various authors. Some anthologies lay claim to authority as representing the best written in a given period, *eg* the Oxford Books (of Sixteenth Century Verse, etc.) and others are standard examples of taste at the time of compiling, *eg* Palgrave's *The Golden Treasury of the Best Songs and Lyrical Poems in the English Language* (1861). Others have had an important influence on taste, or on later literary development. Some examples of the most important poetry anthologies of the 20th century which have given shape to movements are the ▷ Georgian poetry anthologies which appeared between 1912 and 1922, A. Alvarez's *The New Poetry* (1962) and ▷ D. J. Enright's ▷ Movement collection, *Poets of the 1950s*.

Anti-industrialism
A tradition of writing identified initially by the work of ▷ Raymond Williams in *Culture and Society*. 19th-century observers, the foremost of whom was Thomas Carlyle, identified a number of threats to what they saw as constructive social living brought by industrialism. When the industrial system was being imposed it could be seen how its pressures obliged the workforce into working in mechanical unison and consequently altered their sense of themselves. The emphasis it brought on material production and material acquisition changed the conditions of life and sapped the individual's powers of resistance. ▷ D. H. Lawrence was its most impassioned 20th-century opponent, and his work influenced the Romantic anti-industrialism of ▷ F. R. Leavis.
▷ Further education; Capitalism.

Aphasia
Generally used to designate language disorder. However, in literary criticism it has been given a more specific definition by the linguistician and supporter of the Russian

▷ Formalist movement, ▷ Roman Jakobson. Jakobson begins with the observation that language functions through the *selection* and *combination* of its elements into units such as words and sentences. *Combination* is a term used to designate the process whereby a linguistic ▷ sign can generate meaning only through its relationship with other signs which provide a context for it. *Selection* permits the substitution of one element for another from the total number of elements that make up the linguistic code as a whole, and which both speaker (addresser) and listener (addressee) share. The addresser encodes a particular message, and the addressee decodes or interprets it. Any interference with either the selection or combination of linguistic units which form an utterance, such as an unusual use in a literary work, is designated as aphasia, and this disordering serves, by contrast, to reveal the ways in which language operates normally.

Aphorism, apophthegm
A terse sentence, weighted with sense; with more weight of wisdom than an ▷ epigram need have, but less elegance.

Apocalypse
From Greek 'disclosure'. A kind of visionary literature, especially *Revelation* in the ▷ Bible. The essence of such literature, for instance, the visionary poetry of William Blake and ▷ W. B. Yeats, is that it expresses in symbolic terms truths and events which surpass the ordinary reach of the human mind. The strongest poetic movement of the 1940s was known as the 'New Apocalypse', a neo-Romantic celebration of passion and emotion, whose key figures were ▷ Dylan Thomas and ▷ W. S. Graham. Modern ▷ science-fiction writing, produced in the ▷ nuclear age, is often referred to as 'apocalyptic'.

Archaeology
This term is commonly used to describe the scientific study of the remains of past times. However, in the 20th century the French philosopher ▷ Michel Foucault has sought to redefine it in such a way that the focus of attention becomes not objects, or documents, but the very ▷ discourses through which they come to have meaning. In other words, 'archaeology' does not designate the process of returning to some sort of 'origin' or basis which has an existence outside or beyond language (*ie* the bottom layer of a 'dig'); rather it concerns itself with what Foucault himself describes as 'the systematic description of a discourse-object' (*The Archaeology of Knowledge*; 1972). Foucault contends that knowledge is produced within social contexts where questions of power, politics, economics and morality intersect. It is the purpose of archaeology to rediscover discursive formations in all their complexity as indices of the ways in which society is organized. Archaeology is therefore interdisciplinary in its historical concerns. This form of analysis is to be distinguished from a more traditional 'history of ideas' which privileges evolution and development.
Bib: Foucault, M., *The Archaeology of Knowledge* (1969; translated into English, 1972).

Arden, John (b 1930)
Dramatist. First play: *All Fall Down* (1955). In 1956 he won a B.B.C. drama prize with *The Life of Man*. This brought him to London's best-known theatre for serious modern drama, the ▷ Royal Court Theatre, where his next three plays were produced: *The Waters of Babylon* (1957); *Live Like Pigs* (1958), and *Sergeant Musgrave's Dance* (1959). The last attracted much attention among critics, though it was not a popular success. It is a play about an army sergeant who deserts with three soldiers from his unit which is stationed in a colonial territory. They come to a mining town in the north of England with the mission to inspire the people with a hatred of war; they seek alliance with the miners who are in conflict with the mine-owners. The multiple conflict that arises from this situation is used to propound complex ideas about the nature of conflict and its resolution; but the play ends in tragedy without a solution to the problems. No dramatist in England since ▷ Shaw had used the theatre for such thorough exploration of political and social ideas, but whereas Shaw made the ideas central to his dramas and the characters merely instrumental to them, Arden makes his characters central, presenting them through a dialogue which sometimes achieves poetic intensity without sacrificing truth to the northern idiom. This play is one of the most substantial achievements of the dramatic revival which most distinguishes English literature in recent years. The most important shaping influence on this and others of Arden's plays seems to be that of the German dramatist ▷ Bertolt Brecht, most noticeably in the simple energy of the dialogue and the dramatic use of lyrics. Arden's later plays are: *Soldier Soldier* (1960); *The Happy Haven* (1960); *The Business of Good Government* (1960); *Wet Fish* (1962); *The Workhouse*

Donkey (1963); *Ironhand* (1963); *Ars Longa Vita Brevis* (with Margaretta D'Arcy; 1964); *Armstrong's Last Goodnight* (1964); *Left-handed Liberty* (1965); *Friday's Hiding* (1966); *The Royal Pardon* (1966); *The Hero Rises Up* (1968); *Island of the Mighty* (1972); *The Ballygombeen Bequest* (1972); *The Island of the Mighty* (1972); *The Non-Stop Connolly Show* (1975); *Vandaleur's Folly* (1978); *The Little Gray Home in the West* (1978); *The Manchester Enthusiasts* (1984).

▷ Beckett, Samuel; Osborne, John; Pinter, Harold.

Bib: Hunt, A., *Arden: A Study of His Plays*; Gray, F., *John Arden*.

***Arms and the Man* (1894)**

An early play by ▷ George Bernard Shaw with the theme that the glamour of war and of military heroism is essentially a civilian fiction. The hero, Bluntschli, is a Swiss mercenary soldier and unheroic 'anti-hero' such as was to become common in 20th-century literature, but, with his ironic intelligence, was a type special to Shaw.

Artaud, Antonin (1896–1948)

French actor, director and poet, associated with the Surrealist theatre and founder of the Théâtre Alfred Jarry. He developed an approach to theatre which he named ▷ 'Theatre of Cruelty'. In this he downgraded the written text in favour of a theatrical language based on ritualistic gesture, movement and sound. His aim was to release in the actor and spectator the primitive human forces ordinarily suppressed by social morality and convention. His theories are explained in his collection of essays entitled *Le théâtre et son double*. He has been a strong influence on French authors, particularly Camus and Genet, and on the English director ▷ Peter Brook.

Bib: Esslin, M., *Artaud*; Hayman, R., *Artaud and After*.

Arts Council of Great Britain

This body began as the Council for the Encouragement of Music and Art in 1940, to promote theatrical and musical entertainment during World War II. It now provides funding for a great variety of arts projects, including regional and national theatres and touring companies, throughout Britain. Its purpose is 'to develop a greater knowledge, understanding, and practice of the Fine Arts, to increase their accessibility to the public, and to improve their standard of execution'. Although its distribution of funds has often been contentious, its existence has helped the proliferation of theatre companies during the last two decades.

▷ C.E.M.A.

Ash Wednesday

1 The first day of the religious season of Lent, a day of penitence when, in the Catholic Church, the penitents had their foreheads marked with ash.

2 *Ash-Wednesday* is the title of a sequence of poems (1930) by ▷ T. S. Eliot (1888–1965), marking poetically the conversion of the poet to Christianity.

***Aspects of the Novel* (1927)**

A critical work on the novel by ▷ E. M. Forster, based on his Clark Lectures delivered at the University of Cambridge. Well known for its engaging conversational style, the book anticipates aspects of ▷ narratology in its consideration of point of view and ▷ flat and round characters, but is sharply distinguished from later narratology, as well as from the more earnest and prescriptive approach of ▷ Henry James's Prefaces, by Forster's jaunty scepticism about any pretensions to abstract rigour.

Atheism

Disbelief in God. In the ▷ Middle Ages and the 16th and 17th centuries, atheism was abhorrent; it was equivalent to a denial of conscience. There were some who adopted this position and effectively challenged the power of organized religion. ▷ Renaissance dramatist Christopher Marlowe was charged with it in 1593. Nevertheless atheism at this period was different from the systematic belief that man's reason suffices for his welfare. This belief grew in the 18th century and emerged in the ▷ French Revolution, influencing such English intellectuals as William Godwin and through him P. B. Shelley, whose atheism caused him to be expelled from Oxford, and for whom ▷ Platonism sufficed. Different, but still 18th century in its sources, was the atheism of Utilitarians such as James Mill (1773–1836) and John Stuart Mill, who were less naïve about Reason than Godwin but, as practical men, saw religion as unnecessary in their scheme for human betterment. The scientific ideas of the ▷ Victorian period, especially those of Charles Darwin and Thomas Huxley, were more productive of ▷ agnosticism than of atheism. Modern atheism is exemplified by the Rationalist Press, but it remains a minority attitude among writers, in contrast to agnosticism, which is rather commoner than professed faith.

Atwood, Margaret (b 1939)
Canadian novelist, poet and ▷ short-story writer. Born in Ottawa, she spent part of her early years in the wilds of northern Quebec, and her poetry makes considerable metaphorical use of the wilderness and its animals. Her first two novels are poetic accounts of the heroines' search for self-realization, and each has a dominant central metaphor: emotional cannibalism in *The Edible Woman* (1969) and drowning and surfacing in *Surfacing* (1972). *Lady Oracle* (1976) is a more comic and satirical work, portraying the limitations of middle-class Canadian life. Her poetry, which is unrhymed, shares many themes with her novels; *The Journals of Susanna Moodie: Poems* (1970) employs pioneering as a metaphor for contemporary feminist questioning of gender roles. Her recent novels have broader social themes: *Bodily Harm* (1981) is a political satire set on a Caribbean island, while *The Handmaid's Tale* (1986) is a vision of a futuristic dystopia, influenced by ▷ George Orwell's *1984*. It focuses on the exploitation of women in a state ruled by religious fundamentalism, and the ambivalent, ironic conclusion promotes a complex sense of the novel's relevance to our own times. Her last two works, the novel *Cat's Eye* (1989) and the collection of short stories *Wilderness Tips* (1991), return to her Canadian background, evoking with acute irony the middle-class Canada of the 1950s, 1960s and 1970s. Atwood's interest in Canadian nationalism and in feminism have made her an important figure in contemporary Canadian culture.

Other novels: *Life Before Man* (1979). Story collections: *Dancing Girls* (1977); *Murder in the Dark* (1984); *Bluebeard's Egg* (1986). Volumes of poetry include: *Selected Poems* (1976); *Marsh, Hawk* (1977); *Two Headed Poems* (1978); *True Stories* (1981); *Notes Towards a Poem That Can Never Be Written* (1981); *Snake Poems* (1983); *Interlunar* (1984). Criticism: *Second Words: Selected Critical Prose* (1982).

▷ Commonwealth literature.

Bib: Rigney, B. H., *Margaret Atwood*.

Auden, W. H. (Wystan Hugh) (1907–73)
Poet and dramatist. Born in York, Auden spent much of his childhood in Birmingham, but was educated at Gresham's School, Norfolk, a ▷ public school with liberal ideas about education, and at Oxford University. The landscape of the industrial Midlands influenced his work throughout his life. Auden began writing poetry at 15, and twice edited the journal *Oxford Poetry* when he went up to Oxford in 1925. As a student he became the central figure in the 1930s group of left-wing intellectuals, which included ▷ Stephen Spender (who printed Auden's first collection of poems on a hand press), ▷ Cecil Day-Lewis, ▷ Louis MacNeice and ▷ Christopher Isherwood. His background was a middle-class intellectual one, which produced a sense of social responsibility and a strong didactic tendency in his poetry. He became a teacher and worked both in an English school and in English and American universities. He married Erika Mann, Thomas Mann's daughter and an anti-Nazi, in 1938, so that she could obtain British citizenship, although Auden was himself a homosexual. He emigrated to the U.S.A. in 1939, becoming an American citizen in 1946. In 1956 he became professor of poetry at Oxford, and died in Austria in 1973.

His first book, *Poems* (1930), was published during the great economic crisis which originated in the U.S.A. in 1929. This was followed by *The Orators* (1932), the 'charade' *The Dance of Death* (1933), *Look, Stranger!* (1936), *Letters from Iceland* (with MacNeice, 1937), *Journey to a War* (with Isherwood, 1939) and *Another Time* (1940). He also wrote plays, often with Isherwood: *The Dog Beneath the Skin* (with Isherwood; 1935); *The Ascent of F6* (with Isherwood; 1936); *On the Frontier* (with Isherwood; 1938).

His verse is full of topical reference to the social and international crises of the time; it gives direct expression to the anxieties of the contemporary intelligentsia as perhaps no other writing has done. Auden was interested in verse technique, and influenced by an extensive range of writing, extending from the alliterative styles of Old and Middle English to ▷ T. S. Eliot and the late work of ▷ W. B. Yeats. Throughout his life he was interested in ▷ Freud and ▷ psychoanalytic theory, and also absorbed ▷ Marxism, the work of Danish philosopher Søren Kierkegaard, and the 20th-century German-American theologian Niebuhr. After 1940 he became increasingly committed to Anglo-Catholic Christianity.

After his emigration to America, Auden published a wide range of poetry in different forms: *New Year Letter* (1941), *For the Time Being* (1945), *The Age of Anxiety* (1948), *Nones* (1952), *The Shield of Achilles* (1955), *Homage to Clio* (1960). He also wrote criticism (*The Enchafèd Flood* (1951), *The Dyer's Hand* (1963)), libretti for operas, and he edited a number of ▷ anthologies. Towards the end of his life he became an isolated figure, in marked contrast with the first decade of his writing when he had seemed to be the voice of a generation – although perhaps, in reality, only the generation of the younger middle class. Later works and editions include: *About the House* (1966); *City Without Walls* (1969); *Epistle to a Godson* (1972); *Thank You Fog; Last Poems* (1974); *Collected Poems* (ed. Mendelson; 1976); *The English Auden* (ed. Mendelson; 1977); *Collected Poems* (1990), *Plays and Other Dramatic Writings 1928–1938* (with Christopher Isherwood) (1989).

Bib: Hoggart, R., *Introductory Essay*; Muir, E. and Daiches, D., *The Present Age*; Drew, E., *Directions in Modern Poetry*; Beach, J. W., *The Making of the Auden Canon*; Spears, M. K., *The Poetry of W. H. Auden*; Everett, B., *Auden* in the Writers and Critics Series; Hynes, S., *The Auden Generation*; Mendelson, E., *Early Auden*.

Augustanism

There are two aspects to 'Augustanism', one political, the other more strictly literary.

1 *Political Augustanism* In the decades following the Restoration a more or less fanciful parallel between recent English history and that of early imperial Rome was developed, following similar gestures by Ben Jonson earlier in the century. Both the Emperor Augustus (27 BC–AD 14) and King Charles II could be felt to have restored order to the state as legitimate successors to rulers who had been assassinated by Republicans (Julius Caesar, Charles I). Both preserved the forms of constitutionality, and kept at least the appearance of a balance of power between Senate or Parliament and the head of state. Both rulers, and their successors, presided over an expansion of imperial power which extended their own civilization over other cultures by means of military power – the army in the case of Rome, the navy in the case of Britain. Where there had previously been the *Pax Romana* there would now be a *Pax Britannica*. Political Augustanism was concerned essentially with society and with public issues, and was optimistic about British civilization and its role in the world as imperial power. It is detectable in such diverse works as Daniel Defoe's *Robinson Crusoe* and James Thomson's *Castle of Indolence*.

2 *Literary Augustanism* The reign of Augustus coincided with the golden age of Roman culture and literature, and Roman writers of the time, such as Horace and Virgil, explicitly celebrate the Roman imperial destiny. During the period of stability and growing prosperity following the Restoration, the somewhat naïve adulation of the classics found in such Tudor writers as George Chapman and Ben Jonson is replaced by a growing understanding of, and sense of equality with, the great Latin writers, evident in a self-conscious theoretical confidence, technical sophistication and diversity of genre and metrical form. The foundation of the ▷ Poet Laureateship as a regular court office was a sign of this new confidence. In his essays John Dryden (1631–1700) constantly parallels the achievements of modern English writers with their classical ancestors. The young Alexander Pope picked up the spirit of the age very young and was promoted by his friends as an English Virgil. The true poet, it was vaguely felt, would follow Virgil in writing first ▷ pastorals then would move on to Georgics, or longer discursive compositions, and would crown his life's work with an ▷ epic. With a little licence this pattern could be read into the careers of the earlier English writers, Edmund Spenser and John Milton, who were achieving classic status at this time. Ornamental, courtly forms, such as the ▷ sonnet and Spenserian stanza, were now despised as childishly 'gothic', or employed with a conscious sense of their quaint primitiveness. The 'heroic' ▷ couplet emerged as the most dignified ▷ metre of which English verse was felt to be capable. Alongside the cultivation of the couplet a doctrine of 'kinds' grew up which prescribed specific 'high' or noble vocabulary for epic writing, and specific vocabularies for the other genres. This notion, which reflects the class consciousness of the new bourgeoisie, as much as any purely literary doctrine, is seen at its most rigid in Thomas Parnell's *Essay on the Different Stiles of Poetry* (1713).

It is important to stress that such Augustanism is, like ▷ Romanticism, the artificial construction of literary historians, and never constituted a systematic programme or manifesto for poetry. The summary above lends it a coherence and exactitude which it never achieved in the work of any poet. Like most literary movements Augustanism was only defined after it was virtually over. Oliver Goldsmith seems to have been the first to use the adjective 'Augustan' in regard to English literature, applying it in *The Bee* (1759) to the reigns of William III and Queen Anne. The noun Augustanism seems not to have come into use until the early 20th century. In 1904 Theodore Watts-Dunton accused Thomas Gray of being 'a slave to "Augustanism"', a judgement that Gray himself would have found quite bewildering. In the later 19th and early 20th centuries all 18th-century poetry tended to be characterized as overformal and emotionless, and the terms 'Augustan', 'Augustanism' and 'The Augustan Age', frequently served to obscure rather than illuminate the poetry of the period.

Bib: Ford, B. (ed.), *New Pelican Guide to English Literature, Vol. 4: From Dryden to Johnson*; Rogers, P., *The Augustan Vision*; Rogers, P., *Hacks and Dunces: Pope, Swift and Grub Street*; Novak, M., *Eighteenth-Century English Literature*; Sambrook, J., *The Eighteenth Century*; Doody, M. A., *The Daring Muse: Augustan Poetry Reconsidered.*

Authorized Version of the Bible
▷ Bible in England.

Autobiography
The word came into English at the very end of the 18th century. In the 19th and 20th centuries the writing of the story of one's own life has become a common literary activity. However, the practice already had an ancient history, and English autobiography may be divided into three overlapping historical segments: 1 the spiritual confession; 2 the memoir; 3 the autobiographical novel.

1 The spiritual confession has as its basic type the Confessions of St Augustine of Hippo (345–430) who described his conversion to Christianity. The great age for them was the 17th century, when the Puritans, depending on the Word of God in the Bible and the inner light of their own consciences, made a practice of intensive self-examination. By far the best known of these records is John Bunyan's *Grace Abounding to the Chief of Sinners* (1666). It is characteristic of such works that they contain detailed accounts of the emotional life, but little factual description of events.

2 The memoir, on the other hand, of French derivation, originates largely in the 17th century and owes much to the practice of extensive letter-writing which then developed. An example from 18th-century England is the fragmentary *Memoirs* (pub 1796) by the historian Edward Gibbon. But the objective memoir and the subjective confessions came together in the *Confessions* of the French-Swiss Jean-Jacques Rousseau, and this is the most prevalent form of the outstanding English autobiographies of the 19th century. The varieties of this form are extensive: they may be a record of emotional struggles and experiences. They may be essentially a history of the growth of ideas, convictions, and the strengthening of vocation, in the life of the writer, *eg, My Apprenticeship* (1926) by ▷ Beatrice Webb. In any case, an autobiographical element becomes prominent in works which are not strictly autobiographies from the early 19th century on. It may be said that from 1800 on it becomes the instinct of writers of many kinds to use autobiographical material, or to adopt from time to time an autobiographical standpoint.

3 Thus we come to the autobiographical novel: this begins with the novels of Charlotte Brontë (*Jane Eyre*, 1847, and *Villette*, 1853), and Charles Dickens's *David Copperfield* (1849–50). This method of writing a novel really came into its own, however, with ▷ Samuel Butler's ▷ *Way of all Flesh* (1903), which led to many successors in the 20th century, notably ▷ James Joyce's ▷ *Portrait of the Artist as a Young Man* (1916), and ▷ D. H. Lawrence's ▷ *Sons and Lovers* (1913), both autobiographical discussions of the development of the artist. More recent examples are ▷ Margaret Atwood's *Cat's Eye*, (1989), ▷ Sylvia Plath's *The Bell Jar* (1963), American writer Alice Walker's *The Color Purple* and ▷ Jeanette Winterson's *Oranges are Not the Only Fruit.*

***Awkward Age, The* (1899)**
A novel by ▷ Henry James. Nanda Brookenham is a young girl brought up in a smart but corrupt section of London society; her mother and her mother's circle are willing to carry on immoral intrigues so long as respectable appearances are scrupulously protected. Nanda is in love with Vanderbank, who, as she learns later, is her mother's lover, and she feels some affection for Mitchett, a young man of less charm than Vanderbank, but with an attractive simplicity of heart. Unlike the other members of her mother's circle, she is free and candid in her feelings and open in her conduct; this alarms Vanderbank and inhibits him from declaring his love for her. Her elderly friend, Mr Longdon, an admirer of her dead grandmother, gives Nanda a dowry to attract Vanderbank, but this only increases the latter's fastidious reluctance to declare himself. Meanwhile, the Duchess, Mrs Brookenham's friend and rival, conspires to capture Mitchett for her own daughter, Aggie, whose appearance of immaculate innocence immediately breaks down when it has served its purpose of qualifying her for the marriage market. Vanderbank's mixture of scrupulousness and timidity remains a

permanent barrier between himself and Nanda. Mr Longdon adopts her, and they remain together in their love of truthful feeling, isolated from the sophisticated but essentially trivial society which has hitherto constituted Nanda's environment.

The novel is an example of James's interest in the survival of integrity in a materialistic society blinded by its own carefully cultivated artificiality.

Ayckbourn, Alan (b 1939)
Until recently an underestimated dramatist whose plays have often been dismissed (or presented) as light entertainment for unthinking bourgeois audiences. He often writes about the middle classes in order to explore serious issues of modern life. Recent plays such as *A Small Family Business* (1987) have illustrated his inclination to use farce as a weapon of moral force. He has been commercially very successful and after a long period at the Stephen Joseph Theatre in Scarborough he was, until recently, a resident writer and director at the National Theatre. His other plays include: *Relatively Speaking* (1967); *Absurd Person Singular* (1972); *The Norman Conquests* (1973); *Bedroom Farce* (1975); *Season's Greetings* (1982); *Way Upstream* (1982); *A Chorus of Disapproval* (1984); *Henceforward* (1988).
Bib: Billington, M., *Alan Ayckbourn*.

Bainbridge, Beryl (b 1933)
Novelist. Brought up near Liverpool, she worked as an actress before writing her first novel (though not the first to be published), *Harriet Said* (1972), which concerns two girls involved in a murder. Initially seen as a writer of macabre thrillers, she has gained an increasing following and has gradually attracted more serious critical attention. Her novels are characterized by black humour, economy of style and portraits of lower-middle-class manners with a strong element of the ▷ Gothic and grotesque. *The Bottle Factory Outing* (1974) centres on the relationship of two women on an increasingly sinister works outing which leads to the death of one of them. Confused and sordid lives are observed in a detached and ironic manner. *A Quiet Life* (1976) is a partly ▷ autobiographical tale of family eccentricities and the tragic precariousness of love, while *Winter Garden* (1980) draws on a visit Bainbridge made to the Soviet Union to create a chilling though comic account of confusion and intrigue on a tour of that country. Other novels are: *A Weekend with Claude* (1967); *Another Part of the Wood* (1968); *The Dressmaker* (1973); *Sweet William* (1975); *Injury Time* (1977); *Young Adolf* (1978); *Watson's Apology* (1984); *Filthy Lucre* (1986); *An Awfully Big Adventure* (1989); *The Birthday Boys* (1991).

Bakhtin, Mikhail (1895–1975)
Bakhtin's first major work was *Problems in Dostoevsky's Poetics* (1929), but his most famous work, *Rabelais and His World*, did not appear until 1965. Two books, *Freudianism: a Marxist Critique* (1927), and *Marxism and the Philosophy of Language* (1930) were published under the name of V. N. Volosinov, and a third, *The Formal Method in Literary Scholarship* (1928) appeared under the name of his colleague P. N. Medvedev. Bakhtin's concern throughout is to show how ▷ ideology functions in the process of the production of the linguistic ▷ sign and to develop and identify the concept of 'dialogism' as it operates in literary texts. In Bakhtin's words 'In dialogue a person not only shows himself outwardly, but he becomes for the first time that which he is, not only for others but himself as well. To be means to communicate dialogically.' His work has in recent years enjoyed a revival, particularly among critics. Especially important is the way in which he theorizes and politicizes the concept of festivity and ▷ carnival. Also one of his concerns is to identify the dialectical relationship between those various 'texts' of which any one literary work is comprised. This notion of ▷ 'intertextuality' is currently used within areas such as ▷ feminism and ▷ deconstruction. Much of Bakhtin's work was suppressed during his life-time and not published until after his death.
Bib: Lodge, D. *After Bakhtin: Essays on Fiction and Criticism.*

Ballad
Traditionally the ballad has been considered a folkloric verse narrative which has strong associations with communal dancing, and support for that link has been found in the derivation of the word 'ballad' itself (from the late Latin verb *ballare* – to dance). More recently scholars have viewed the association between ballads and dance forms rather more sceptically. Generally, the term is used of a narrative poem which uses an elliptical and highly stylized mode of narration, in which the technique of repetition with variation may play an important part. Often ballads contain repeated choral refrains but this is not a universal feature. Twentieth-century ballads include *Miss Gee* and *Victor* by ▷ W. H. Auden, and works by ▷ Louis MacNeice and ▷ Rudyard Kipling. Arguably the clearest form in which the ballad has survived is in the work of the musicians and lyricists of the folk revival of the 1950s and 1960s; many of Bob Dylan's songs are ballads.

Ballard, J. G. (James Graham) (b 1930)
Novelist and short-story writer. Ballard is closely identified with the ▷ science fiction genre, primarily because his more widely read novels and short stories, though essentially uncategorizable, fit most readily into the sci-fi/fantasy bracket. However, whilst his obsessions with mental decay, violence and its imagery, and the fragmentation of contemporary culture are filtered through the landscapes of more conventional fantasy writing, his allegiance with mainstream fantasy or science fiction is uneasy, and his later writing, particularly the Booker Prize shortlisted *Empire of the Sun* (1984), has moved nearer to realism, drawing upon Ballard's own childhood experiences. His works include: *The Drowned World* (1962); *The Terminal Beach* (1964); *The Drought* (1965); *The Crystal World* (1966); *The Atrocity Exhibition* (1970); *Crash* (1973); *The Unlimited Dream Company* (1979); *The Day of Creation* (1987); *The Kindness of Women* (1991).

Barker, Clive (b 1952)
Novelist, playwright, painter, screenwriter

and director. Born, raised and educated in Liverpool, Barker wrote a number of plays (*The Magician*, *The History of the Devil*) before achieving fame as a leading light of Britain's 'new wave' of horror writers (▷ horror fiction). In 1987, *Hellraiser* established Barker as a maverick directorial talent; he currently lives in Hollywood where he continues to write and direct. Barker's early short stories (collected in *The Books of Blood* Volumes 1 to 6, 1984–5) celebrate cultural multiplicity and sexual perversity, inverting the traditional conservatism of the horror genre. Describing himself as 'a proselytizer on behalf of horror', Barker has sought both on the page and screen to subvert concepts of 'monstrousness'. Most ambitiously, his lengthy novel *Cabal* (1988, filmed as *Nightbreed* 1990) posits a tribe of variegated shape-shifters in whose bizarre disfigurement the reader is encouraged to delight. Barker's later works (*Weaveworld* 1987, *Imajica* 1991) have eschewed the visceral revelry which characterized his short stories and explored the worlds of mythology and fantasy. Despite his huge success as a writer/film-maker, Barker maintains that painting is his first love.
Bib: Jones, S. (ed.), *Shadows in Eden*.

Barker, George Granville (1913–91)
Poet. His first collection, *Thirty Preliminary Poems*, was published in 1933, along with a novel, *Alanna Autumnal*. After that he kept up a steady output of visionary and ▷ autobiographical verse that includes *Calamiterror* (1937), *Lament and Triumph* (1940) and the two parts of *The True Confession of George Barker* (1950 and 1964). His most celebrated later volume is *Anno Domini* (1983).
Bib: Fraser, R. (ed.), *Collected Poems*.

Barker, Howard (b 1946)
Modern political dramatist known particularly for the shocking power of his language and imagery. His plays deal frequently with madness, lust, corruption, and despair, so that although he claims to be a socialist and presents capitalism as a barbaric and destructive system there is generally little hope in his view of contemporary life. He is a prolific writer and many of his plays have been produced by the ▷ Royal Shakespeare Company and the ▷ Royal Court. These include: *Stripwell* (1975); *Fair Slaughter* (1977); *The Hang of the Gaol* (1978); *The Loud Boy's Life* (1980); *Crimes in Hot Countries* (1983); an adaptation of Thomas Middleton's *Women Beware Women* (1985); *Last Supper* (1988) and *Bite of the Night* (1988). *The Poor Man's Friend* (1981), an account of a hanging in a rope-making town, was produced in response to an invitation by ▷ Ann Jellicoe to write a community play for a cast of nearly a hundred. He has also written a number of plays for television, some of which have never been transmitted due to censorship.
Bib: Chambers, C. and Prior, M., *Playwright's Progress*; Craig, S. (ed.), *Dreams and Deconstructions*.

Barrie, Sir James Matthew (1869–1937)
A Scots dramatist, nowadays chiefly famous for his creation of ▷ *Peter Pan* (1904). Early in this century he was extremely popular for the theatrical skill and the humour and sentimentality of his plays, which sometimes carried penetrating satire, *eg The Admirable Crichton* (1902).
Bib: Darton, F. J. Harvey, *Barrie*; Hammerton, J. A., *Barrie, the Story of a Genius*; Mackail, D., *The Story of J.M.B.*; Rose, J., *The Case of Peter Pan, or, the Impossibility of Children's Fiction*.

Barstow, Stan (b 1928)
Novelist and short-story writer. His best-known work is his first novel, *A Kind of Loving* (1960), a first-person, present-tense narrative of a young man forced to marry his pregnant girlfriend. Barstow came to prominence as one of a group of novelists from northern, working-class backgrounds, including ▷ John Braine, ▷ Alan Sillitoe and Keith Waterhouse. He has retained his commitment to the realist novel (▷ realism) with a regional setting and his suspicion of metropolitan and international culture. *The Watcher on the Shore* (1966) and *The True Right End* (1976) form a trilogy with *A Kind of Loving*. Other novels are: *Ask Me Tomorrow* (1962); *Joby* (1964); *A Raging Calm* (1968); *A Brother's Tale* (1980); *Just You Wait and See* (1986); *B Movie* (1987). Story collections include: *The Desperadoes* (1961); *A Season with Eros* (1971); *A Casual Acquaintance* (1976); *The Glad Eye* (1984).

Barnes, Djuna (1892–1982)
Novelist, poet and playwright, who was influential, but until recently little read. Barnes was born in America but lived, like many ▷ modernist artists, in the European 'cities of modernism'. Her best-known and most reprinted work *Nightwood* (1936), a poetic novel championed by ▷ T. S. Eliot (who wrote the introduction to the Faber edition), is a dark, at times surrealist and deeply evocative account of decadence and

transgression in Bohemian and expatriate circles in inter-war Paris and Berlin. Barnes wrote eloquently about lesbianism, both in this novel and in her other essays (particularly the Virago collection, *I could never be lonely without a husband*), and in her works of fiction. *Ladies' Almanack* celebrates lesbian sexuality in the form of a parody of a medieval calendar. Barnes also experimented in her drama, the earliest works being *Three from the Earth, An Irish Triangle* and *Kurtzy from the Sea* (1928); her last significant work was *The Antiphon* (1958), a surreal play in blank verse. Her first collection of poems was *The Book of Repulsive Women* (1915), and her first novel was *Ryder* (1929).
Bib: Hanscombe, G. and Smyers, V., *Writing for their Lives: The Modernist Women 1910–1940*.

Barnes, Julian (b 1946)
Novelist. Born in Leicester and educated in London and Oxford, Barnes has worked as a lexicographer on the O.E.D. Supplement (1969–72), and in journalism, writing for the *New Statesman*, the *Sunday Times*, *The Observer*, and as the notorious gossip columnist 'Edward Pygge' in the journal of modern literature, the *New Review*, which ran from 1974 to 1979 under poet and critic Ian Hamilton's editorship. Greatly influenced by French 19th-century novelist Gustave Flaubert (the ostensible subject of the playful and very successful 1984 novel *Flaubert's Parrot*), Barnes's work is witty and parodic. Novels include: *Metroland* (1981); *Before She Met Me* (1982); *Flaubert's Parrot* (1984) – which was shortlisted for the 1985 Booker Prize and won the Geoffrey Faber Memorial prize; *Staring at the Sun* (1986) and *Talking It Over* (1991). Barnes also writes crime fiction, and under the pseudonym Dan Kavanagh published *Duffy* (1980); *Fiddle City* (1983) and *Putting the Boot In* (1985). In 1986 he won the E. M. Forster Award from the American Academy of Arts and Letters.

Barthes, Roland (1915–80)
Probably the best known and most influential of all the ▷ structuralist and ▷ post-structuralist critics. In books such as *Writing Degree Zero* (1953), *Mythologies* (1957), and *S/Z* (1970), Barthes undertook to expose how language functioned, and its relationship with ▷ ideology. Moreover, he was also concerned to uncover the distinctions between literary texts which operated on the basis of a stable relationship between ▷ signifier and ▷ signified, and those for whom the act of signification (establishing meaning) itself was of primary importance. The terms he uses to distinguish between the two types of text are 'readerly' (*lisible*) and 'writerly' (*scriptible*). In later works, such as *The Pleasure of the Text* (1975), he went on to investigate the sources of pleasure which the text affords to the reader, and distinguished between 'the text of pleasure' which does not challenge the cultural assumptions of the reader and which is therefore comforting, and 'the text of bliss' where the reader experiences a '*jouissance*' from the unsettling effect elicited from the text's representation of the crisis of language. In addition to offering penetrating analyses of literary texts, Barthes concerned himself with the structural analysis of all cultural representations, including topics such as advertising, film, photography, music and wrestling.

Baudelaire, Charles (1821–67)
French poet. His best-known work, *Les Fleurs du mal* (1857), points the way out of ▷ Romanticism towards ▷ modernism. Formally, it draws on the tradition of ▷ sonnet and song which Baudelaire inherited from the ▷ Renaissance. Conceptually, it springs from the perception of 'two simultaneous feelings: the horror of life and the ecstasy of life', periods of heightened sensitivity and sensibility alternating with the monotony of existence without meaning. The book's five sections explore these twin conditions, in art and love (*Spleen et Idéal*), in city life (*Tableaux Parisiens*), in stimulants (*Le Vin*), in perversity (*Fleurs du mal*) and in metaphysical rebellion (*La Révolte*), ending (in the poem 'Le Voyage') with man's yearning unsatisfied but finding in death a new journey of discovery.

Baudelaire also wrote fine music and art criticism (he championed Wagner and Delacroix); his translations of Edgar Allan Poe (1809–49) helped confirm, in France, interest in tales of the fantastic; and he was the first to investigate extensively the new genre of prose poetry. In England, his influence has been constant, though at the outset it raised moral controversy. Reviewing *Les Fleurs du mal* in the *Spectator* of 1862, Swinburne responded to the sensualism of Baudelaire, and this version of Baudelaire was handed on to the late 19th-century 'decadent' poets. ▷ T. S. Eliot 'rescued' Baudelaire and identified the French poet's sense of sin with 'Sin in the permanent Christian sense', even though Baudelaire himself in a letter to Swinburne warned against easy moral readings of his work.

Bawden, Nina (b 1925)
Novelist, reviewer and writer for children. Nina Bawden is best known for her award-winning novels for children, particularly *Carrie's War* (1973) and *The Peppermint Pig* (1975). For Bawden, childhood and adolescence are times of frustration, difficulty and excitement, and her writing is both ▷ realist (*ie* not fantasy writing for children) and realistic – stories of children's perceptions of adult situations. Bawden also writes novels for adults, notably *A Woman of My Age* (1967), *Familiar Passions* (1979) and *The Ice-House* (1983).

Beardsley, Aubrey (1872–98)
An artist and poet famous in the 1890s for his black and white illustrations to writers such as ▷ Oscar Wilde and Ernest Dowson (▷ Nineties Poets). He contributed to the periodicals ▷ *The Yellow Book* (the first four covers of which he designed) and *The Savoy* (including his tale, *Under the Hill*), which were regarded as organs of the aesthetic movement. The flowing lines and sumptuous compositions of his illustrations expressed what was considered most bold and most daring in the movement, but Beardsley's work itself was considered pornographic and scandalous. It has, however, had a profound influence on twentieth-century design and erotica.
Bib: Zatlin, L. G., *Aubrey Beardsley and Victorian Sexual Politics*.

Beckett, Samuel (1906–89)
Dramatist and novelist. Born in Dublin, he was educated at Trinity College. He became a lecturer in English at the École Normale Supérieure in Paris (1928–30) and was then a lecturer in French at Trinity College. From 1932 he lived chiefly in France, and wrote in both French and English. In Paris he became the friend and associate of the expatriate Irish novelist ▷ James Joyce (1882–1941), whose ▷ 'stream of consciousness' subjective method of narrative strongly influenced Beckett's own novels; another important influence upon him was the French novelist ▷ Marcel Proust (1871–1922).

Poems include: *Whoroscope* (1930); *Echo's Bones* (1935).

Novels and stories include: *More Pricks than Kicks* (1934); *Murphy* (1938); *Watt* (1944); *Molloy* (1951; English, 1956); *Malone Meurt* (1952; trans. *Malone Dies*, 1956); *L'Innommable* (1953; trans. *The Unnamable*, 1960); *Comment C'est* (1961; English, 1964); *Imagination Dead Imagine* (1966, from French); *Nouvelles et textes pour rien* (1955); *Le Depeupleur* (1971; trans. *The Lost Ones*, 1972); *First Love* (1973); *Mercier et Camier* (1974).

Plays include: *En attendant Godot* (1952; trans. ▷ Waiting for Godot, 1954); *Fin de partie (*1957; trans. *Endgame*, 1958); *Krapp's Last Tape* (1959); *Happy Days* (1961); *Play* (1963); *Eh Joe* (1966); *Breath and Other Short Plays* (1972); *Not I* (1973); *That Time* (1976); *Footfalls* (1976); *Ghost Trio* (1976); *. . . But the Clouds . . .* (1977); *Rockaby* (1980); *Ohio Impromptu* (1981); *Quad* (1982); *Catastrophe* (1982); *Nacht und Träume* (1983); *What Where* (1983). Plays for radio include: *All that Fall* (1957); *Embers* (1959); *Cascando* (1964).

Beckett is one of the most singular and original writers to appear in English, or possibly in French, since 1945. Like Joyce an Irish expatriate, he belongs to both Ireland and to Europe; his characters are commonly Irish, and his background the desolation of European culture. In both narrative and drama (it is in the second that his achievement is perhaps the more remarkable) his method was to create art out of increasingly simplified material, reducing his images of humanity to the sparest elements. His particular view of life's absurdity is often expressed through striking theatrical images which reveal a vision of life which is both bleak and grotesquely comic. Thus, in *Happy Days* Winnie appears on stage buried up to her waist in a mound of earth; in *Not I* the audience sees only a mouth on stage struggling to deliver a monologue of reminiscences; and in *Endgame* two elderly characters, Nagg and Nell, are placed in dustbins throughout the play. In so far as he is related to an English literary tradition, it is to the generation between the wars of 1914–18 and 1939–45 when, most notably in the work of James Joyce, communication with an audience was often secondary to experiments in the medium of language. His novels have accordingly had little influence on English fiction. His plays, on the other hand, especially *Waiting for Godot* and the plays for radio, have shown new possibilities in the handling of dialogue, by which speech is used less for communication than for the expression of minds that feel themselves in isolation, or on the point of sinking into it. Such use of dialogue perhaps had its beginnings in the late 19th-century dramatists, the Russian ▷ Chekhov and the Belgian Maeterlinck, and has superficial parallels with the work of the contemporary English dramatist, ▷ Harold Pinter.

▷ Irish literature in English.
Bib: Kenner, H., *Samuel Beckett, a Critical Study*; Jacobsen, J. and Mueller, W.R., *The Testament of Beckett*; Esslin, M. in *Theatre of the Absurd*; Bair, D., *Beckett: A Biography*.

Bedlam
A famous lunatic asylum. Originally it was a priory, founded in 1247, for members of the religious order of the Star of Bethlehem. Lunatics were admitted to it in the 14th century, and in 1547, after the dissolution of the monasteries, it was handed over to the City of London as a hospital for lunatics. ▷ Antonia White's novel, *Beyond the Glass* (1954) gives an account of being ill there and of the primitive treatment used in this century for women in a state of breakdown. The name became shortened to Bedlam, and a Bedlamite, Tom o'Bedlam, Bess o'Bedlam, became synonymous for lunatics; Bedlam itself a synonym for lunatic asylum. In modern English, 'bedlam' is a scene of uproar and confusion.
Bib: Showalter, E., *The Female Malady*.

Beer, Patricia (b 1924)
Poet. Beer was educated at Exeter and Oxford universities, has been a university teacher, and now writes full-time – she is also a novelist and critic. She grew up in Devon and her work draws strongly on West Country images. Her volumes of poetry include: *The Loss of Magyar* (1959); *The Survivors* (1963); *The Estuary* (1971); *Driving West* (1975); *Selected Poems* (1979); *The Lie of the Land* (1983).

Beerbohm, Max (1872–1956)
Essayist, cartoonist, writer of fiction. When he began his career Beerbohm belonged to the so-called 'decadent' generation of the aesthetic school in the 1890s; this included ▷ W. B. Yeats in his ▷ Celtic Twilight phase, ▷ Oscar Wilde, ▷ Aubrey Beardsley, and the poets Lionel Johnson and Ernest Dowson. He showed his affiliation to this school by the playful fastidiousness of his wit, especially in his cartoons and parodies. *A Christmas Garland* (1912) contains parodies of contemporary writers including ▷ H. G. Wells, ▷ Arnold Bennett, and ▷ Joseph Conrad. But it is in his cartoons that his satirical wit is displayed with most pungency and originality, *eg Caricature of Twenty-five Gentlemen* (1896), *The Poet's Corner* (1904), *Rossetti and his Circle* (1922). As a writer he was above all an essayist; he entitled his first slim volume with humorous impertinence *The Works of Max Beerbaum* (1896), to which he added *More* (1899), *Yet Again* (1909), *And Even Now* (1920). He also wrote stories (*Seven Men*; 1919), and he is probably now most read for his burlesque romance *Zuleika Dobson* (1911), about the visit of a dazzling beauty to the University of Oxford where she is responsible for a mass suicide among the students.

Beerbohm was educated at Charterhouse and Merton College Oxford. He contributed to the ▷ *Yellow Book*, and in 1898 succeeded ▷ George Bernard Shaw as dramatic critic on the *Saturday Review*. From 1910 he lived in Italy, except during the two world wars. He was knighted in 1939. His personal and literary fastidiousness caused him to be known as 'the Incomparable Max', and as such ▷ Ezra Pound commemorates him as 'Brennbaum the Impeccable' in section 8 of *Hugh Selwyn Mauberley*.

Behan, Brendan (1923–64)
Irish dramatist. His first play, *The Quare Fellow*, was staged in Dublin in 1954, but made its impact after it was adapted by ▷ Joan Littlewood's company, Theatre Workshop, in 1956. Behan spent time in borstal, and in prison as a political prisoner, and this influenced his play about a British soldier captured by the I.R.A., *The Hostage* (1958). His last play, *Richard's Cork Leg*, was unfinished. Many of his dramatic techniques drawing on popular traditions of entertainment, such as the use of song and dance and direct addresses to the audience, are typical of the style developed by Joan Littlewood's Theatre Workshop company.
Bib: O'Connor, U., *Behan*.

Belloc, Hilaire (1870–1953)
A versatile writer (novelist, poet, essayist, biographer, historian) now especially remembered for his association with ▷ G. K. Chesterton in Roman Catholic propaganda. The most important phase of his career was before 1914, when he was one of a generation of popular, vivid, witty propagandists; ▷ George Bernard Shaw, ▷ H. G. Wells, and Chesterton were his equals, and the first two (as agnostic socialists) his opponents. With Chesterton, he maintained the doctrine of Distributism – an alternative scheme to socialism for equalizing property ownership. Among his best works is his earliest: *The Path to Rome* (1902), a discursive account of a journey through France, Switzerland and Northern Italy. He is now chiefly read for his light verse, *eg Cautionary Tales* (1907), *A Bad Child's Book of Beasts* (1896).

▷ Catholicism in English literature; Children's books.
Bib: Hamilton, R., *Belloc: An Introduction to his Spirit and Work*; Speaight, R., *The Life of Hilaire Belloc.*

Bennett, Arnold (1867–1931)
Novelist. His principal novels are: ▷ *The Old Wives' Tale* (1908); the Clayhanger trilogy – ▷ *Clayhanger* (1910); *Hilda Lessways* (1911), and *These Twain* (1916) – all three reprinted as *The Clayhanger Family* (1925); *Riceyman Steps* (1923); *The Grand Babylon Hotel* (1902). His distinctive characteristics as a novelist are his regionalism and his ▷ naturalism. His books mainly concern life in the industrial Five Towns of the north-west Midlands (the Potteries), the particular characteristics of which differentiate his fiction considered as an image of English society. He was strongly influenced by the naturalism of French fiction-writers such as Zola and Maupassant. This led him to emphasize the influence of environment on character, and to build his artistic wholes by means of a pattern of mundane details. This importance that he attached to environment caused a reaction against his artistic methods on the part of novelists like ▷ Virginia Woolf (see her essay 'Modern Fiction' in *The Common Reader, First Series*; 1925) and ▷ D. H. Lawrence, who found Bennett too rigid in his notions of form and too passive in the face of environmental influence. Nonetheless, Bennett lacked the ruthlessness of the French naturalists, and softened his determinism with a sentimentality that recalls Charles Dickens (1812–70).
Bib: Drabble, M., *Arnold Bennett, a Biography*; Hepburn, J., *The Art of Arnold Bennett*; Lucas, J., *Arnold Bennett: A Study of His Fiction.*

Bentley, E. C. (Edmund Clerihew) (1875–1956)
Journalist and writer of detective fiction and light verse. E. C. Bentley's famous detective novel *Trent's Last Case* (1903), dedicated to his friend ▷ G. K. Chesterton, was originally written as an 'exposure of detective stories', but it was soon received as a classic of the genre (▷ detective fiction). In the same spirit, he published a brilliant parody of ▷ Dorothy L. Sayers, 'Greedy Night', in 1939. Bentley is also known as the originator of the humorous, aphoristic verse form, ▷ 'clerihew' (from his middle name), which aims to capture the subject of the poem in two rhyming couplets, a well-known example being,

The art of Biography
Is different from Geography
Geography is about maps,
But Biography is about chaps.

Bentley worked as a journalist for *The Daily News* and *The Daily Telegraph*, and his other books include *Trent's Own Case* (1936), *Trent Intervenes* (1938) and *Elephant's Work: An Enigma* (1950).

Berger, John (b 1926)
Novelist, painter and art critic. His novels reflect both his Marxism (▷ Marx, Karl), in their attention to the oppressive structures of society, and his painting, in their vivid realization of sensual detail. *A Painter of Our Time* (1958), through the story of an émigré Hungarian painter, explores the role of the artist in a consumer society and the relationship of art to experience. His best-known work is *G* (1972), in which authorial self-consciousness, open-ended, fragmentary narrative and documentary elements serve to resist the imposition of order on political events.

He has collaborated with the photographer Jean Mohr on a number of works which address political and social issues by combining various media and genres, including photographs, political and social analysis, poems and fictionalized case studies; these are *Ways of Seeing* (1972); *A Fortunate Man* (1967); *A Seventh Man* (1981); *Another Way of Telling* (1982). Berger has also published two volumes of a trilogy entitled *Into Their Labours*; these are *Pig Earth* (1979), which comprises short stories and poems, and *Once in Europa* (1987). Other novels include: *The Foot of Clive* (1962); *Corker's Freedom* (1964). Drama: *A Question of Geography* (1987; with Nella Bielski). Volumes of essays include: *Permanent Red* (1960); *The White Bird* (1985). Art criticism includes: *The Success and Failure of Picasso* (1965).

Henri Bergson (1859–1941)
French philosopher. Bergson's work on time and consciousness had a great influence on 20th-century novelists, particularly modernist writers engaged in so-called ▷ 'stream of consciousness' work such as ▷ James Joyce, ▷ Dorothy Richardson and ▷ Virginia Woolf. His text of 1889, which was published in English in 1910 as *Time and Free Will: An Essay on the Immediate Data of Consciousness*, was particularly important. Bergson is also known as one of the key theorists of vitalism,

the belief that the material progress of the world is not underpinned by determining biological or physical mechanisms but by the movements of living energy; his theory of an essential *élan vital* or *life force*, which animates material progress through its constant process of change and becoming, was taken up by ▷ George Bernard Shaw in his plays. Bergson was awarded the Nobel Prize for literature in 1928, and was married to a cousin of French novelist ▷ Marcel Proust, whose work he also greatly influenced.
Bib: Humphrey, R., *Stream of Consciousness in the Modern Novel*; Sokel, W. H., *The Writer in Extremis*; Hanna, T. (ed.), *The Bergson Heritage*.

Berry, James (b 1924)
Poet. Berry comes from the West Indies, but has lived in Britain since 1948, a prolific writer and great promoter of multi-cultural education. Like that of younger poets ▷ Linton Kwesi Johnson, Edward Kaman Brathwaite and Benjamin Zephaniah, his work draws strongly on West Indian vernacular and reggae rhythms, and his volumes of verse include *Chain of Days* and *Lucy's Letters and Loving* (1982). He has also edited the poetry volumes: *Bluefoot Traveller: An Anthology of West Indian Poets of Britain* (1976); *News From Babylon* (1984); and a collection from the 1983 Brixton festival, *Dance to a Different Drum*. Berry also writes widely for radio and television, short stories and children's books – his children's book, *A Thief in the Village*, won the Grand Prix Prize in 1987. In 1981 he was awarded the National Poetry Prize.
▷ Commonwealth literatures.

Bestiaries
Compilations of descriptions of creatures (natural and fantastic), especially popular in the medieval period, in which a brief account of the habits and appearance of the creature is usually followed by allegorical interpretations of its significance, and the moral lessons it may provide. The most accessible example of a medieval bestiary is the 12th-century Latin bestiary, translated by T. H. White, *A Book of Beasts* (1954).

Best-sellers
A transformation of the means of production in the early years of the 19th century made it possible for a single text to be printed, advertised, distributed and sold in numbers hitherto inconceivable. Charles Dickens's *Pickwick Papers* was the first work of fiction to exploit these new conditions. The financial return on this new mode of production was highly profitable, and a wide market for the commodity was opened up. In our own day the best-seller is associated not only with high sales, however, but also with quick ones. Though there is no agreement on the sales figures which define a text as a best-seller, national newspapers carry weekly charts, showing the titles which are selling most strongly in fiction and non-fiction. This may be seen as a form of advertisement, encouraging further sales of what has been guaranteed as an acceptable product by market success. Writing a best-seller may make a large sum of money for the author and some make it clear (Jeffrey Archer or Shirley Conran for instance) that they gear their fiction to the market with that intention. Recent moves, by publishers as well as authors, to aim writing and publication towards the best-seller lists inevitably threaten to narrow the range of what is published and to discourage publishers from taking chances with new authors and new kinds of writing.
▷ Detective Fiction; Horror Fiction; Science Fiction.

Betjeman, Sir John (1906–84)
Poet and critic of architecture. His poetry is highly nostalgic and written in a style which has given it wide popularity: the 1958 *Collected Poems* was a best-seller. It is largely pastiche and parody, witty and anti-modernist in its form. His works include: *Mount Zion* (1931); *Continual Dew* (1937); *Old Lights in New Chancels* (1940); *New Bats in Old Belfries* (1945); *A Few Late Chrysanthemums* (1954); *Summoned by Bells* (autobiography in verse; 1960); *The Best of Betjeman* (ed. Guest; 1978); *Uncollected Poems* (1982). Betjeman was ▷ Poet Laureate from 1972–84. He was a forceful champion of ▷ Victorian architecture, and editor of the *Shell Guides*. He published some 20 books on architectural subjects.
Bib: Brook, J., *Writers and their Work*, British Council Pamphlet, 153.

Bible in England
The Bible falls into two parts.
1 Old Testament
The first and larger part of the Bible, consisting of the sacred writings of the Jews. It concerns the peculiar, divinely ordained destiny of the Jewish race from earliest times, and it is considered by Christians to expound the divine promise which the New Testament fulfils not merely for the Jews but for the whole of mankind. The Old Testament is divided into books which are

grouped by Jews into three main sections, as follows:

1 The Torah ('Law', otherwise called the Pentateuch), consisting of five books as follows: *Genesis, Exodus, Leviticus, Numbers, Deuteronomy*. They are called 'the five books of Moses'. The first two are narrative and descriptive, and move from the creation of the world to the escape of the Jews from slavery in Egypt. The remainder contain laws and discourses.

2 The Prophets. This section is divided into two in the Hebrew Bible: the 'Former Prophets', consisting of *Joshua, Judges*, the two books of *Samuel* and the two books of *Kings*; and the 'Latter Prophets', consisting of *Isaiah, Jeremiah, Ezekiel*, and the Minor Prophets. The books of the Former Prophets tell the story of the establishment of the Jews in the kingdom of Israel, and their subsequent history. The Latter Prophets contain history together with prophetic discourses.

3 The Sacred Writings, or Hagiographa, which are divided into three sections: (i) the Poetical books, consisting of *Psalms, Proverbs, Job*; (ii) the five 'Rolls', which are read at special seasons in the Jewish year: *Song of Songs, Ruth, Lamentations, Ecclesiastes, Esther* – of these *Esther* and *Ruth* are narratives; the other three are poetic meditations; (iii) *Daniel, Ezra, Nehemiah*, and *Chronicles*, all consisting mainly of historical narrative.

2 New Testament

The second and shorter part of the Bible, containing the sacred books of the Christians. It is divided into books, on the pattern of the Old Testament, and dates as a whole collection from the end of the 2nd century AD. It is customary to divide the books into four groups.

1 The three Synoptic (*ie* 'summary narrative') Gospels of Saints Matthew, Mark and Luke, and the *Acts of the Apostles*. The Gospels are narratives about Jesus Christ, and *Acts* is the narrative of the missionary careers of the apostles (including St Paul) after Christ's death.

2 The Epistles (letters) of St Paul. The four shortest of these are addressed to individuals: two to Timothy, and one each to Titus and Philemon. The remainder are addressed to various early Christian communities. These are the Epistles to the Romans, Galatians, Ephesians, Philippians, Colossians, two to the Corinthians, and two to the Thessalonians. The Epistle to the Hebrews has been ascribed to Paul, but is nowadays considered to be by a disciple of his.

3 The Catholic Epistles, so called because they were directed to Christians generally. Two of these are ascribed to St Peter, and one each to James and Jude.

4 The Johannine writings, ascribed to the Apostle John. These are the Gospel of St John, distinguished from the Synoptic Gospels as probably not intended as a historical narrative, the Epistles of John, and the poetic, visionary narrative called the *Apocalypse*, or *Revelation*.

In the Middle Ages the only version of the Bible authorized by the Church was the Vulgate, *ie* the translation into Latin by St Jerome, completed in 405. Partial translations were made into Old English before the 11th century. From the 14th century translations were made by reformers, who believed that men without Latin should have the means of seeking guidance from divine scripture without dependence on Church authority. The main translators were these: Wycliffe (14th century); Tyndale, and Coverdale (16th century). The last-named was the producer of the Great Bible (also called Cranmer's Bible after the Archbishop of the time), but Henry VIII, concerned for his intermediate position between Catholics and Protestants, ended by restricting its use. Under the Catholic Mary I (1553–8) English reformers produced the Geneva Bible abroad, with annotations suited to Puritan Calvinist opinion; and in 1568 the so-called Bishops' Bible was issued by the restored Anglicans to counteract Puritan influence. Finally, in 1611 the Authorized Version was produced with the approval of James I (1603–25). For three centuries it was to be the only one in general use, and it is still the prevailing version. In the 19th century it was revised (Revised Version) and recently a new translation has been authorized and produced (New Testament 1961; Old Testament 1961; Old Testament Apocrypha 1970). A Catholic translation (the Douai Bible) was issued at about the same time as the Authorized Version.

In spite of various other translations, Catholic and Protestant, in the 19th and 20th centuries the Authorized Version is by far the most important for its literary and social influence. It was based on previous translations, especially that of Tyndale, so that the cast of its prose is characteristically more 16th than early 17th century in style. Nonetheless much of it is of supreme eloquence, *eg* the Book of *Job*, and last 15 chapters of *Isaiah*. It was for many people in the 17th and 18th centuries the only book that was constantly read, and it was familiar to all from its use in church and education. The musical cadence of Authorized Version prose can be often heard in the prose of English writers, whether or not professing Christians. It is conspicuous in John Bunyan's *Pilgrim's Progress* but it can also be heard in the prose of 20th-century novelist ▷ T. F. Powys, *eg Mr Weston's Good Wine* (1927). The *New World Bible* is also a 20th-century translation into modern English vernacular.

▷ Apocalypse.

Bib: Daches, D., *The King James Version of the Bible.*

Bildungsroman

A novel which describes the youthful development of the central character. Prominent examples in English include ▷ James Joyce's ▷ *A Portrait of the Artist as a Young Man* (1916), ▷ Samuel Butler's ▷ *The Way of All Flesh* (1902) and ▷ D. H. Lawrence's ▷ *Sons and Lovers* (1913).

Biography

The chief source of inspiration for English biographers was the Greek Plutarch (1st century AD), whose *Parallel Lives* of Greek and Roman great men was translated into English by Sir Thomas North in 1579 and was widely read. Biography had been practised before in England; there had been the lives of the saints in the Middle Ages, and in the 16th century Cavendish's life of the statesman Cardinal Wolsey had appeared. The regular practice of biography, however, starts with the 17th century, not merely owing to the influence of North's translation of Plutarch, but as part of the outward-turning, increasingly scientific interest in many kinds of people (not merely saints and rulers) which in the 18th century was to give rise to the novel. Biography is a branch of history, and the art of historical writing advanced with biography. In the 18th century the writing of biographies became habitual; and also biography, or autobiography, became a way of disguising pure fiction, *eg* in the novels of Defoe. Samuel Johnson was a master of biography in his *Lives of the Poets* (1779–81), most notable among which is his *Life of Mr Richard Savage*, previously published in 1744. The outstanding biography of the century, however, is the life of Johnson himself by James Boswell, 1791. As an intimate and vivid account of a great man, it was never equalled in the 19th century when so many biographies were written and some classic ones, amongst them and perhaps pre-eminent, Elizabeth Gaskell's life of her friend, Charlotte Brontë (1857). The 19th century was, however, more outstanding for its achievements in the largely new form, ▷ autobiography. The 20th century saw a new approach to the art in the work of ▷ Lytton Strachey (1880–1932). His *Eminent Victorians* (1918) sought for the truth in the lives of its subjects in unexpected details, and instead of expounding their greatness exposed the weakness of their mere humanity. In the last 10 years biography has become one of the biggest growth areas in publishing, Michael Holroyd and Richard Ellman being two of the major biographers of the 1980s.

Bib: Gittings, R., *The Nature of Biography.*

Blatty, William Peter (b 1928)

American novelist, screenwriter and director. The leading contemporary exponent of 'theological thrillers', a reluctant father of modern horror and highly underrated humorist, Blatty uses popularist fictional formats to discuss questions of man's spiritual progress. Although Blatty is an American novelist, his influence on recent British ▷ horror fiction has been immense. Schooled by Jesuits, he became a writer of lightweight screen comedies (*A Shot in the Dark; Darling Lili*) and novels (*John Goldfarb; Please Come Home; I, Billy Shakespeare*) which hinted at a putative satirical talent. In 1969 he attempted unsuccessfully to gain permission to write an account of an exorcism which took place in Mount Rainier in 1949. Thwarted, Blatty used his extensive research as the basis for his multi-million-selling fictional novel *The Exorcist* (1971), which he subsequently adapted for the screen in collaboration with director William Friedkin, garnering an Oscar for Best Screenplay. In 1979, Blatty expanded and rewrote his earlier work *Twinkle, Twinkle, 'Killer' Kane* (1966) under the title *The Ninth Configuration* (1979). Set in an isolated army psychiatric institute, *The Ninth Configuration* posits man's potential for selfless action as proof of the existence of God. A film adaptation followed (written, directed and produced by Blatty), for which the author won The Golden Globe for Best Screenplay. In 1983, Blatty published the best-seller *Legion*, an extraordinary blend of fantasy and philosophy which uses the detective novel format (▷ detective fiction) to present a convoluted discussion of the nature of divinity; *Legion* was filmed in 1990 as *The Exorcist III*. Blatty is currently working on *Dimitri*, a theological thriller whose title alludes to Dostoevski's *The Brothers Karamazov.*

Bloom, Harold (b 1930)
One of the leading members of the so-called Yale school of literary criticism, along with the late ▷ Paul de Man, Geoffrey Hartman, and J. Hillis Miller. In books such as *The Anxiety of Influence* (1973), *A Map of Misreading* (1975), and *Poetry and Repression* (1976) Bloom seeks to offer a revisionary account of poetry, based especially on a ▷ Freudian model of the relationship between the aspiring poet and his literary predecessors. In this way Bloom moves away from the tenets of American ▷ new criticism in his suggestion that all poetry seeks, but fails, to exclude 'precursor' texts, with which it enters into a struggle, both destructive and creative, in order to achieve its particular identity.

Bloomsbury Group, The
An exclusive intellectual circle that centred on the house of the publisher, Leonard Woolf, and his wife, the novelist, ▷ Virginia Woolf, in the district of London round the British Museum, known as Bloomsbury. It flourished notably in the 1920s, and included, besides the Woolfs, the economist Lord Keynes, the biographer ▷ Lytton Strachey, the art critics Roger Fry and Clive Bell, and the painters Vanessa Bell and Duncan Grant, as well as others. The group owed much to the Cambridge philosopher ▷ G. E. Moore and the importance he attached to the value of friendship and aesthetic appreciation. The close relationships which resulted from this, in addition to the fastidiousness which arose from their critical attitude to the prevailing culture of English society, gave them an apparent exclusiveness which made them many enemies. Moore's influence also contributed to their scepticism about religious tradition and social and political conventions; they tended to be moderately left-wing and agnostic. Positively, they were innovators in art and represented an important section of the English avant-garde. Their more constructive opponents attacked them for excessive self-centredness and an aestheticism which was too individualistic and self-regarding to be really creative in social terms.

Blunden, Edmund (1896–1974)
Poet and critic, and author of one of the most famous books about World War I, *Undertones of War* (1928). His lyrical poetry produced during and just after that war is drawn especially from the English countryside, and its sincerity redeemed for many readers what was becoming a hackneyed convention of 'nature poetry'. His poetry was first published in the 1914 ▷ *Georgian Poetry* anthology. His literary studies have been important especially for the 'Romantic' period, *eg Life of Shelley*, *Charles Lamb and his Contemporaries*; and he played a great part in editing and raising the reputation of the nineteenth-century poet John Clare. His best-remembered book now is probably *Cricket Country* (1944).
Bib: Hart-Davies, R., *Edmund Blunden*.

Blyton, Enid (1897–1968)
Writer for children. Blyton is one of the most famous and maligned children's novelists of the 20th century. She was phenomenally prolific, beginning with *The Enid Blyton Book of Fairies* (1924), writing school stories and the Famous Five sequence in the 1940s and 1950s, the Noddy stories in the 1950s and 1960s, as well as adaptations of classical and Uncle Remus stories, and non-fiction for children. Blyton's works are severely chastised by contemporary critics both on educational grounds (her works do not tax their young readers, their vocabulary is limited, their characters thin, and their plots simple-minded) and on political grounds (her writing is sexist, racist and nostalgic for a pre-war middle-class idyll). Despite this her novels continue to sell and most are still in print. Other works include: *Naughty Amelia Jane* (1939); *The Naughtiest Girl in the School* (1940); *Five on a Treasure Island* (1942); *First Term at Malory Towers* (1946); *Noddy and His Car* (1951) and *Noddy in Toyland* (1955).
Bib: Ray, S. G., *The Blyton Phenomenon*; Stoney, B., *Enid Blyton: A Bibliography*.

Bohemian
Applied to artists and those who live a life supposedly dedicated to the spirit of the imaginative arts, it means living freely, refusing to observe social conventions, especially when they depend on mere habit, snobbery or fear of 'seeming different'. It often carries a slightly mocking tone and is rarely used now without irony. Literally, Bohemian means native to Bohemia, now the western part of Czechoslovakia. In the 15th century gipsies were supposed to have come from there; in the 19th century, French students were supposed to live like the gipsies and hence to be 'Bohemian'. The word was then introduced into English with this meaning by the novelist William Makepeace Thackeray. His novel *The Newcomers* is one of the first studies in English of Bohemianism.

Twentieth-century avant-garde movements have often been regarded as loosely 'bohemian' (*eg* ▷ the Bloomsbury Group), and the term is still in currency, used to describe a range of counter-cultural attributes and aspirations.

Bolt, Robert (b 1924)
British dramatist whose first major success was with the ▷ Chekhovian *Flowering Cherry* (1957). This was followed by *A Man for All Seasons* (1960), a play about the life of Sir Thomas More, which has some superficial resemblances to the style of ▷ Brecht, such as the use of a common man figure who plays a variety of roles in the play. However, the audience is not encouraged to maintain a critical distance from the action in the manner of Brecht nor are the particular historical circumstances of More's life explored in any detail. Bolt is primarily concerned with More's conflict between his commitment to himself, to his own sense of integrity, and his commitment to society, a theme which is common in his work. Other plays include: *The Tiger and the Horse* (1960); *Gentle Jack* (1963); *Vivat! Vivat Regina!* (1970); *State of Revolution* (1977). Film scripts: *Lawrence of Arabia* (1962); *Dr Zhivago* (1965); *A Man for All Seasons* (1967); *Ryan's Daughter* (1970); *Lady Caroline Lamb* (1972); *The Bounty* (1984); *The Mission* (1986).
Bib: Hayman, R., *Robert Bolt*.

Bond, Edward (b 1934)
British dramatist and one of the new left-wing writers to establish themselves at the ▷ Royal Court theatre during the 1960s. His plays have often aroused controversy; the early play *Saved* (1965) created a furore for its scene of a baby being stoned to death and *Early Morning* (1968) was banned for depicting Queen Victoria as a lesbian. He has written plays regularly on a wide range of subjects for the past 20 years and is recognized as a leading modern dramatist. Other major works are: *The Pope's Wedding* (1962); *Narrow Road to the Deep North* (1968); *Lear* (1971); *The Sea* (1973); *Bingo* (1974); *The Fool* (1976); *The Bundle* and *The Woman* (both 1978); *Restoration* (1981); *The War Plays* (1985).
Bib: Coult, T., *The Plays of Edward Bond*; Hay, M. and Roberts, P., *Bond: A Study of His Plays*; Hirst, D. L., *Bond*.

Bowen, Elizabeth (1899–1973)
Novelist and short-story writer. Born in Dublin and educated in England, she worked in a Dublin hospital during World War I, and for the Ministry of Information in London during World War II. Her novels are concerned with themes of innocence and sophistication, the effect of guilt and of the past on present relationships, and the damaging consequences of coldness and deceit. Her portrayal of the inner life of female characters and her symbolic use of atmosphere and environment show the influence of ▷ Virginia Woolf, as does the structure of her first novel, *The House in Paris* (1935). Her treatment of childhood and youthful innocence owes something to the work of ▷ Henry James, especially in *The Death of the Heart* (1938), where Bowen narrates the story partly through the consciousness of a young girl. Bowen powerfully conveyed the atmosphere of World War II London during the Blitz, and the emotional dislocation resulting from the war, both in *The Heat of the Day* (1949) and in short stories such as 'In The Square' and 'Mysterious Kôr' (in *The Demon Lover*, 1945). Her other novels are: *The Hotel* (1927); *The Last September* (1929); *A World of Love* (1955); *Eva Trout* (1969). Other story collections include: *The Cat Jumps* (1934); *Look at all those Roses* (1941); *A Day in the Dark* (1965).
Bib: Glendinning, V., *Elizabeth Bowen: Portrait of a Writer*; Craig, P., *Elizabeth Bowen*.

Bradbury, Malcolm (b 1932)
Novelist and critic. His novels are: *Eating People is Wrong* (1959); *Stepping Westward* (1965); *The History Man* (1975); *Rates of Exchange* (1983); *Cuts* (1987). These are witty, satirical portraits of the four decades since 1950; the first three use university settings to epitomize the changing moral and political situation of western liberalism. He is often compared to ▷ Kingsley Amis for his hilarious send-ups of academic habits and pretensions, but Bradbury also has a fascination with the idea of fictionality, which he sees as central to the contemporary understanding of reality. His works are therefore informed by current critical theory (a feature which they share with the novels of ▷ David Lodge). *Rates of Exchange* draws on ▷ structuralist theories, has an eastern European setting, and a somewhat harsher tone than Bradbury's earlier work, in an attempt to register the atmosphere of the 1980s. The title of *Cuts* refers to both cuts in funding and film cutting, and the novel portrays Tory Britain in the mid 1980s through the story of a collision between an academic and a woman television executive. Bradbury teaches on the successful creative writing postgraduate course at the University of East Anglia, which has included among

its graduates ▷ Ian McEwan and ▷ Kazuo Ishiguro.

Bradley, F. H. (Francis Herbert) (1846–1924)
Brother of A. C. Bradley, the literary critic. He was himself an eminent philosopher, author of *Ethical Studies* (1876); *Principles of Logic* (1883); *Appearance and Reality* (1893); and *Essay on Truth and Reality* (1914). His position philosophically was an idealist one, and in this he has been opposed by most British philosophers ever since, beginning with ▷ G. E. Moore. Bradley, however, had a strong influence on ▷ T. S. Eliot, the poet and former philosophy student, whose early thesis on him has now been published.
▷ Idealism; Realism.

Braine, John (b 1922)
Novelist. His most famous novels are *Room at the Top* (1957; filmed 1958) and *Life at the Top* (1962; filmed 1965). Both of these deal with the new kinds of social mobility and anxiety, characteristic of Britain since World War II, and led to him being thought of as one of the ▷ 'angry young men' of the 1950s. Like the heroes of his novels, however, he has become progressively more conservative in his attitudes. Other novels are: *The Vodi* (1959); *The Jealous God* (1964); *The Crying Game* (1968); *Stay with me till Morning* (1970); *The Queen of a Distant Country* (1972); *The Pious Agent* (1975); *Waiting For Sheila* (1976); *The Only Game in Town* (1976); *Finger of Fire* (1977); *One and Last Love* (1981); *The Two of Us* (1984); *These Golden Days* (1985).
▷ Realism.
Bib: Salwak, D., *John Braine and John Wain: A Reference Guide*.

Brathwaite, E. R. (b 1912)
Novelist and autobiographer. Born in Guyana, most of Brathwaite's writing is concerned with his working life in Britain in the 1950s and 1960s. His most successful work (which was turned into a popular film), *To Sir, With Love* (1959), is concerned with his experiences as a black teacher in London, and other semi-autobiographical novels have discussed his social work and time in the RAF. He is the author of: *Paid Servant* (1962); *Reluctant Neighbours* (1972); *A Kind of Homecoming* (1962) and *A Choice of Straws* (1967).

Brecht, Bertolt (1898–1956)
One of the most significant theatre practitioners and theorists of the 20th century. His work has had a major influence on British drama since the late 1950s. Brecht's early plays were written shortly after World War I and were influenced by the Expressionist movement. From the mid-1920s he became interested in applying Marxist (▷ Marx, Karl) ideas to plays and performance and developed his concept of '▷ epic theatre'. The essential characteristic of 'epic', as Brecht used the term, was the creation of a critical distance (*Verfremdungseffekt*) between the audience and the performance on stage (and a similar critical distance between the actor/actress and the role he or she performed). The purpose of this was to prevent empathy and encourage audiences instead to reflect on the relationship between social conditions and human action, in such a way that they would recognize their power and agency in the process of history. Brecht was forced to leave his native Germany during the Nazi era and continued writing in exile in Europe and later America. After World War II he returned to Germany and formed the Berliner Ensemble company in East Berlin, where he directed a number of his plays written in exile. The Berliner Ensemble first visited London in 1956 and performed three of Brecht's plays: *Mother Courage and her Children, Drums and Trumpets* and *The Caucasian Chalk Circle*. Other plays include: *Baal* (1918); *Man is Man* (1926); *The Threepenny Opera* (1928; with music by Kurt Weill); *The Measures Taken* (1930); *St Joan of the Stockyards* (1932); *The Seven Deadly Sins* (1933; with Kurt Weill); *The Resistible Rise of Arturo Ui* (1941); *The Life of Galileo* (1943); *The Good Person of Szechwan* (1943). Brecht's influence on dramatists, directors and actors has been profound and is best understood by referring to the following books: Needle, J. and Thomson, P., *Brecht*; Willett, J., *Brecht in Context*.

Breeze, Jean Binta (b 1957)
Poet. Born in Jamaica, Jean Binta Breeze now lives and works in London, writing and performing live her vibrant form of dub poetry. Her works are collected in *Riddym Ravings and Other Poems* (1988), and in the collection of *the new british poetry* (ed. G. Allnutt et al.). See also Breeze's essay 'Can a Dub Poet be a Woman?' in *Women: A Cultural Review* (April 1990).

Brenton, Howard (b 1942)
British left-wing dramatist, strongly influenced by ▷ Brecht, who has worked with both ▷ fringe and mainstream theatre companies since the late 1960s. His iconoclastic plays have frequently caused controversy,

particularly when they have been staged at major theatres. He began writing for the Combination, at Brighton, and The Portable Theatre, a touring company.

Recently he has worked at the ▷ National Theatre despite his having expressed doubts in the past about the value of such 'establishment' institutions. Major plays are: *Magnificence*, a ▷ Royal Court success in 1973; *Brassneck* (1973), a collaboration with ▷ David Hare; *The Churchill Play* (1974); *Weapons of Happiness* (1974); *Epsom Downs* (1977); *Romans in Britain* (1978); *The Genius* (1983); *Bloody Poetry* (1984); *Pravda* (1985), also a collaboration with David Hare; *Greenland* (1988).
Bib: Bull, J., *New British Political Dramatists*; Chambers, C. and Prior, M., *Playwright's Progress*.

Breton, André (1896–1966)
French poet, founder of ▷ Surrealism, which he launched in 1924 with the first *Surrealist Manifesto*. Prior to this, Breton had met both the poet Guillaume Apollinaire (during 1917–18) and ▷ Sigmund Freud (in 1921), both of whom provided inspiration for the movement. In 1919, he published his first collection of poems, *Mont de piété*, and in the same year he collaborated with Philippe Soupault on his first properly Surrealist text, *Les Champs magnétiques*, which preceded the official launch of Surrealism. Between 1919 and 1921, he participated in the ▷ Dadaist movement, although it was his initiative to hold in Paris the international congress which led to the break-up of Dada. Believing firmly in the radicalism of Surrealism, Breton resisted any attempt to make the movement subservient to an established political creed. In *Légitime Défense* (1926), he rejected any form of control, even Marxist control, of the psychic life and, by contrast with other members of the movement, this was to lead to his break with communism in 1935. After the war, Breton continued to campaign vigorously on behalf of Surrealist radicalism. He opposed Albert Camus's (1913–60) thesis, as expounded in *L'Homme révolté* (1952) that revolt has its limitations, and a year before his death organized a final Surrealist exhibition, *L'Ecart absolu*, which aimed to challenge the consumer society. Breton contributed to Surrealist writing not only by the three manifestoes (1924, 1930, 1934) and other polemical writing, but also by numerous collections of poetry and prose, the original editions of which were usually illustrated by leading artists connected with Surrealism.
Bib: Bozo, D., *André Breton: La beauté convulsive*.

Bridges, Robert Seymour (1844–1930)
Poet and dramatist. He was ▷ Poet Laureate from 1913–30. After medical training and work as a consultant at Great Ormond Street Children's Hospital, Bridges turned his energies fully to poetry in 1882. His first volume of verse was published in 1873, after which he wrote prolifically: his collected *Poetical Works* (1936), excluding eight dramas, are in six volumes. He was a fine classical scholar and in his experiments with classical rhythms, was something of an innovator. His most ambitious work was the long, philosophical *The Testament of Beauty*, which appeared in five parts from 1927 to 1929. Other works include: *Shorter Poems* (1890); *The Spirit of Man* (1916) and *New Verse* (1925). He was the chief correspondent and literary executor of the poet ▷ Gerard Manley Hopkins; the latter developed his poetic theories through their letters. A selection of Bridge's work, *Poetry and Prose*, has been edited by John Sparrow.
Bib: Smith, N. C., *Notes on The Testament of Beauty*; Guerard, A. J., *Bridges: A Study of Traditionalism*; Thompson, E., *Robert Bridges*.

Bridie, James (1888–1951)
Pseudonym of Dr Osborne Henry Mavor. He was a successful playwright during the 1930s and 1940s and part-founder of the Citizen's Theatre in Glasgow. He wrote 42 plays, many of which were performed on the London stage. He is often compared to ▷ George Bernard Shaw for his prolific output and range of subject matter. His best-known plays today are *The Anatomist* and *Tobias and the Angel* (both 1930), *Jonah and the Whale* (1932), *A Sleeping Clergyman* (1933), *Colonel Wotherspoon* (1934), *The Black Eye* (1935), *Storm in a Teacup* (1936), *Mr Bolfry* (1943), *Dr. Angelus* (1947) and *Daphne Laureola* (1949).
Bib: Luybem, H., *Bridie: Clown and Philosopher*.

Brighton
An English seaside resort on the south coast, one of the first to become fashionable when, in the 18th century, sea-bathing was first held to be good for health. Early in the next century the Prince Regent made Brighton his favourite resort and ordered the erection of the oriental-style Pavilion there. Since then, Brighton has remained one of the largest of a line of seaside resorts extending

almost the whole length of the south coast. The underside of Brighton was explored in ▷ Graham Greene's novel, *Brighton Rock* (1938), *The West Pier* (1951) by Patrick Hamilton and *Dirty Weekend* (1991) by Helen Zahavi.

Britain, British, Briton
Britain (Latin: *Britannia*) was the name given by the Romans to the island that includes modern England, Wales and Scotland, though the Roman province of Britain (AD 43–410) only reached the south of Scotland. Speaking of pre-Roman times, we call the island Ancient Britain and we call its mixed people Ancient Britons.

Political, rather than descriptive, the term was revived when King James VI of Scotland became also James I of England (including Wales) in 1603 and called himself King of Great Britain. It was officially adopted by ▷ Parliament when England and Scotland were united in 1707. In 1801 the United Kingdom of Great Britain and Ireland was formed, but most of Ireland became separate again in 1922. Terms now in use are:
British Isles: Great Britain and all Ireland, geographically.
United Kingdom: Great Britain and Northern Ireland.
Great Britain or *Britain*: England, Scotland and Wales, geographically.
British, referring loosely to the U.K. or to Britain.
Briton: a native of the U.K., but the term is rarely used.
Britisher: American name for a Briton.
England and *English*: These are often loosely and wrongly used for Britain and British, simply because England is the largest and most powerful partner and English is the common language.

▷ Irish literature; Scottish literature; Welsh literature.

British Academy
Founded in 1901 it was intended to complement the function of the ▷ Royal Society by representing 'literary science', which was defined as 'the sciences of language, history, philosophy and antiquities, and other subjects the study of which is based on scientific principles but which are not included under the term "natural science"'. It derived its authority from the backing of the Royal Society, the grant of a Royal Charter (1902) and the addition of bye-laws by Order in Council (1903). The British Academy elects its own Fellows, up to a total of 200: candidates have to be nominated by not fewer than three and not more than six existing Fellows. The British Academy publishes its *Proceedings* and certain lectures; research awards are annually made available for competition, and it now controls funding for post-graduate studies at British universities.

British Council
Established in 1934, it receives three-quarters of its funds, amounting to £260 million in 1987–8, from the Foreign and Commonwealth Office. Its brief is to promote an enduring understanding and appreciation of Britain overseas through cultural, technical and educational exchange. The Council has staff in over 80 countries and is responsible for the implementation of more than 30 cultural agreements with other countries. It has 116 libraries world-wide and its activities include the recruitment of teachers for posts overseas, fostering personal contacts between British and overseas academics, and the placing and welfare of overseas students in Britain. It is exceptionally powerful in determining how Britain represents itself abroad in that the Council decides what is to be presented overseas as 'the best of British arts and culture'. ▷ Graham Greene, ▷ Lawrence Durrell and ▷ Olivia Manning in various novels offer a view of the early years of the Council's work.

Brittain, Vera (1893–1970)
Autobiographer, poet, novelist and journalist. Vera Brittain is best known for her autobiographical books, *Testament of Youth* (1933) and *Testament of Experience* (1957), the first detailing with great feeling her life as a nurse in France during World War I, and particularly the loss of her fiancé to the war itself, whilst the second recounts the period from 1925–1950, including an account of the therapeutic experience of writing the first book itself. She is also something of a war poet, offering a perspective on the conflict not represented by those usually characterized as ▷ War poets, in *Poems of the War and After* (1934). Her other novels and non-fiction writing include: *The Dark Tide* (1923); *Account Rendered* (1945); *Born 1925* (1948); *Lady into Woman: A History of Women from Victoria to Elizabeth II* (1953); *The Women at Oxford: A Fragment of History* (1960).

Her friendship with fellow-novelist ▷ Winifred Holtby, whom she had met at Oxford after the war when the two were students, and with whom she set up house

after the two graduated, was an important factor in her early life, and their friendship is represented in *Selected Letters of Winifred Holtby and Vera Brittain* (1960), and in Brittain's *Testament of Friendship* (1940), a memorial to Holtby written on her death. Brittain was also deeply committed to ▷ Labour Party politics (one of her children, Shirley Williams, became a prominent Labour, and then SDP, politician), and she was an important founder-member of ▷ CND, writing in support of the peace movement (see particularly *The Rebel Passion: A Short History of Some Pioneer Peace-Makers* (1964)).
Bib: Bailey, H., *Vera Brittain*.

Brook, Peter (b 1925)
One of the most experimental British theatre directors, renowned for his international outlook and rejection of parochial traditions in the British theatre. By the time he was 20 he was directing at the Birmingham Repertory Theatre and a year later he directed *Love's Labour's Lost* for the ▷ Royal Shakespeare Company at Stratford-on-Avon. His most famous ▷ Shakespeare production was *A Midsummer Night's Dream* in 1970, also at Stratford. This was praised for its imaginative interpretation and liberation of the play from traditional ideas of performance, characteristic of his directorial approach. He has been strongly influenced by the work of ▷ Artaud and ▷ Grotowski. Other major productions are: Weiss's *Marat/Sade* (1966); *Orghast* (1971); *The Ik* (1976); *The Mahabharata* (first staged at the Avignon Festival in 1985). Since 1970 he has worked with his own company in Paris at the International Centre of Theatre Research. Brook's ideas about theatre should be read first hand in his publication *The Empty Space*.
Bib: Brook, P., *The Shifting Point*; Williams, D., *Peter Brook: A Theatrical Casebook*.

Brooke Rupert (1887–1915)
A young poet of exceptional promise, who contributed to the ▷ *Georgian Poetry* volumes, and who died of septicaemia in the Dardanelles during World War I without having taken part in the campaign. His almost legendary physical beauty and the idealistic quality of his work caused him to be represented as the hero of the first phase of the war. 'The Soldier' (1915) and 'The Old Vicarage, Granchester' (1912) are much-anthologized poems. Just as it had been patriotically revered, Brooke's work dramatically declined in public opinion as the horror of war was fully understood, although after World War II his slim and unfinished corpus gained more critical respect.
Bib: Keynes, G. (ed.), *Poems*.

Brooke-Rose, Christine (b 1926)
Novelist and critic. Born in Geneva, of an English father and a Swiss/American mother, she is bilingual, and her best-known works are influenced by the French ▷ *nouveau roman* of Alain Robbe-Grillet and Nathalie Sarraute. *Out* (1964) uses Robbe-Grillet's technique of exhaustive description of inanimate objects. In *Such* (1966) a scientist recalls his past during the three minutes taken to bring him back to consciousness after heart failure, while *Thru* (1975) is a multilingual, playful, Joycean novel, employing typographical patterns and self-referential discussion of its own narrative technique. More recently, *Xorander* (1986) is a work of ▷ science fiction, exploring the possibilities of a computer-dominated society. Brooke-Rose lives in France, where until recently she was a professor at the University of Paris, and her resolute commitment to modernist (▷ Modernism) experimental techniques has led to her relative neglect by English-speaking readers.

Brookner, Anita (b 1928)
Novelist. Since her first novel, *A Start In Life*, was published in 1981 she has rapidly achieved popular success, confirmed by the award of the Booker Prize to her fourth novel, *Hôtel Du Lac* (1984). Her novels have an autobiographical element and somewhat similar heroines; sensitive, intelligent, but not glamorous, their search for love and fulfilment leads to disillusionment and betrayal by attractive but selfish men. Brookner's prose style is careful, elegant, lucid and mannered in a way somewhat reminiscent of ▷ Henry James. She lectures and writes on the subject of art history.

Her other novels are: *Providence* (1982), *Look At Me* (1983); *Family And Friends* (1985); *A Misalliance* (1986); *A Friend From England* (1987); *Latecomers* (1988); *A Closed Eye* (1991).

Brophy, Brigid (b 1929)
Novelist and critic. The daughter of the novelist John Brophy, she won immediate acclaim with her first novel, *Hackenfeller's Ape* (1953), a fable about imprisonment, rationality and the instinctive life. During the 1960s she acquired a reputation as a polemical and aggressive writer, with controversial libertarian views on sex and ▷ marriage. She campaigned for animal rights, defended ▷ pornography,

and, with ▷ Maureen Duffy, set up a writers' action group in the 1970s to campaign for Public Lending Right (the Public Lending Right Bill, which provides payments to authors out of a central fund on the basis of library lending, was passed in 1979). Her novels reflect her adherence to ▷ Freudian ideas, and to the evolutionism of ▷ George Bernard Shaw. *Flesh* (1962) is a detached yet poetic study of sexual awakening; *The Finishing Touch* (1963), described as 'a lesbian fantasy', is stylistically inspired by the work of ▷ Ronald Firbank; *The Snow Ball* (1964) is an artificial, baroque black comedy of seduction; *In Transit* (1969) uses a bizarre combination of styles and characters and is set in an airport. Her works of criticism include psychological studies of creative artists: *Mozart the Dramatist* (1964); *In Black and White: A Portrait of Aubrey Beardsley* (1968); *Prancing Novelist* (on Ronald Firbank; 1973); *Beardsley and his World* (1976). Her other works of non-fiction include: *Black Ship to Hell* (1962), a Freudian account of the nature of hate; *Don't Never Forget* (1966) and *Baroque and Roll* (1987), collections of her journalism on a wide range of subjects. Other novels include: *The King of a Rainy Country* (1956); *Pussy Owl: Super Beast* (1976); *Palace Without Chairs* (1978). *The Adventures of God in His Search for the Black Girl* (1973) is a series of fables. *The Burglar* (1968) is a play.

Bryher (1894–1983)
Novelist. Bryher's historical novels, always published under the single name she legally took on (after one of the Scilly Isles) so as not to be identified with her influential industrialist father, are serious and meticulously researched works on the Greek and Roman Empires (particularly *Roman Wall*, 1954, *Gate to the Sea*, 1958, and *The Coin of Carthage* 1963) and on the connections between early British history and contemporary life (*The Fourteenth of October*, 1951, *The January Tale*, 1966, and *Beowulf*, 1956). Bryher lived with the poet ▷ H. D. for much of her life, and wrote two autobiographies, *The Heart of Artemis* (1962) and *The Days of Mars* (1972). She also wrote literary criticism (a book, in 1918, on the poet Amy Lowell), and on film, setting up the film journal *Close-Up*.
Bib: Hanscombe, G. and Smyers, V. L., *Writing For Their Lives*.

Bunting, Basil (1900–85)
Poet. Bunting's association with the poetry world began in the 1920s, but he did not achieve real recognition until the 1960s – the story of his rediscovery after years of obscurity is one of the legends of contemporary poetry. Bunting had been associated with ▷ Ezra Pound and other ▷ modernists in the 1930s, even to the extent that ▷ W. B. Yeats called him one of Pound's 'savage disciples'. *Redimiculum Matellarum* was published in Milan in 1930, followed by *Attis* (1931), *The Well of Lycopolis* (1935), and, later, *Poems* in 1950, but the text which gave Bunting enormous recognition after many years of neglect in Britain was *Briggflatts* (1966). Undoubtedly Bunting's most important and challenging work, *Briggflats* is a long, intense, mystical synthesis of Northumbrian legend, ▷ autobiography and mythology. Other works include: *Collected Poems* (1968).
Bib: Davie, D., *Under Briggflatts*.

Burgess, Anthony (b 1917)
Novelist and critic. Born John Anthony Burgess Wilson of a Roman Catholic Lancashire family, he was educated at Manchester University. After military service during World War II he worked as a schoolmaster in Oxfordshire, Malaya and Borneo. His experiences in Malaya inspired his *Malayan Trilogy* (1956–9), a rich portrait of the Malayan culture and people, employing words and expressions from Malay, Urdu, Arabic, Tamil and Chinese. A fascination with the textures of language and a ▷ Joycean inventiveness and multilingual playfulness have characterized much of Burgess's work. In 1959 Burgess returned to England with a brain tumour, expecting to survive only a year, yet in that year wrote five novels: *The Doctor is Sick* (1960), *One Hand Clapping* (1961), *The Worm and the Ring* (1961), *The Wanting Seed* (1962) and *Inside Mr Enderby* (1963). During the 1960s he worked as a music and drama critic, and produced plays, T.V. scripts, short stories and numerous book reviews. He has since done a considerable amount of university teaching, and lived in Malta, Rome and Monaco. *A Clockwork Orange* (1962), filmed in 1971 by Stanley Kubrick, is an anti-utopian vision with an appallingly vicious protagonist who deliberately chooses evil, and who is brainwashed by penal techniques based on behaviourist psychology. Its most striking feature is the use of Nadsat, an invented teenage underworld slang largely based on Russian words and English colloquialisms. *Nothing Like the Sun* (1964) is a fictional account of ▷ Shakespeare's love life, told as the parting lecture of a schoolmaster in the Far East, who progressively identifies himself with his subject. An impression of Elizabethan

life is conveyed through descriptive detail and imitation of contemporary idiom. *Earthly Powers* (1980) is a large-scale consideration of the nature of evil, with extensive reference to 20th-century literary and political history. Other novels include *1985* (1978), *The Piano Players* (1986), *Any Old Iron* (1989), *The Devil's Mode* (1989) and *Mozart and the Wolf Gang* (1991). Non-fiction includes: *The Novel Today* (1963); *Language Made Plain* (1964); *Ernest Hemingway and his World* (1978); *Flame into Being: the Life and Work of D. H. Lawrence* (1985).
Bib: Aggeler, G., *Anthony Burgess, the Artist as Novelist*.

Burlesque
A form of satirical comedy (not necessarily dramatic) which arouses laughter through mockery of a form usually dedicated to high seriousness. The word is from the Italian *burla* = 'ridicule'. Burlesque is similar to ▷ parody, but parody depends on subtler and closer imitation of a particular work.
▷ Satire.

Butler, Samuel (1835–1902)
Satirist, scientific writer, author of an ▷ autobiographical novel, *The Way of All Flesh* (1903) in a form which became a model for a number of 20th-century writers. His satires *Erewhon (Nowhere* reversed) and *Erewhon Revisited* (1872 and 1901) are anti-utopias, *ie* instead of exhibiting an imaginary country with ideal customs and institutions in the manner of Sir Thomas More's *Utopia* (1516), Butler describes a country where the faults of his own country are caricatured, in the tradition of Jonathan Swift's Lilliput (in *Gulliver's Travels*). He attacks ecclesiastical and family institutions; in Erewhon, machines have to be abolished because their evolution threatens the human race – a blow at Darwinism.

His scientific work concerned Charles Darwin's theory of evolution, to which he was opposed because he considered that it left no room for mind in the universe; he favoured the theory of Lamarck (1744–1829) with its doctrine of the inheritability of acquired characteristics. His disagreements and his own theories are expounded in *Life and Habit* (1877), *Evolution Old and New* (1879), *Unconscious Memory* (1880) and *Luck or Cunning?* (1886).

The Way of All Flesh attacks the parental tyranny which Butler saw as the constant feature of Victorian family life (despite much evidence to the contrary); so close did he keep to his own experience that he could not bring himself to publish the book in his own lifetime.

▷ George Bernard Shaw admitted a great debt to Butler's evolutionary theories and to Butler's stand against mental muddle, self-deception and false compromise in society. Writers as different from Butler and from each other as ▷ D. H. Lawrence and ▷ James Joyce wrote autobiographical novels after him in which the facts were often as close to their own experience.
Bib: Cole, G. D. H., *Butler and The Way of All Flesh*; Henderson, P., *The Incarnate Bachelor*; Furbank, P. N., *Samuel Butler*; Jeffers, T. L., *Samuel Butler Revalued*; Joad, C. E. M., *Samuel Butler*; Muggeridge, M., *Earnest Atheist*; Pritchett, V. S., 'A Victorian Son' in *The Living Novel*.

Byatt, A. S. (Antonia Susan) (b 1936)
Novelist, critic and reviewer. Born in Sheffield and educated at the universities of Cambridge and Oxford, she has worked as a teacher and lecturer in English. The novelist ▷ Margaret Drabble is her sister. Her novels are influenced by the work of ▷ Proust and of ▷ Iris Murdoch (Byatt has published two books on Murdoch), and combine a realistic portrayal of English manners with symbolic structures and a wide range of reference to history, myth and art. *The Shadow of a Sun* (1964) is a feminist ▷ *Bildungsroman* about a girl seeking to escape from a dominating novelist father, while *The Game* (1967), a story of the tragic rivalry between two sisters, has overtones of the Fall of Man. *The Virgin in the Garden* (1979) and *Still Life* (1985) are the first two volumes of a projected tetralogy, intended to trace the lives of a group of characters from the accession of Queen Elizabeth II in 1952 up to the 1980 Post-Impressionist Exhibition in London. Byatt's later style includes quotation, allusion, narrative prolepses (anticipations of later events) and metafictional reflections on novel writing. Story collection: *Sugar* (1987). Her 1990 novel *Possession*, an academic whodunnit which splices the story of two young scholars' researches on the love between a male and female poet in the 19th century, with the story of the romance itself, was a ▷ best-seller, and won the Booker Prize in 1990.

C

Campbell, Ramsey (b 1946)
Novelist and journalist. Born and raised in Liverpool, Campbell is a leading light of Britain's 'new wave' of horror writers, described by Robert Hadji as 'the finest living exponent of the British weird fiction tradition'. Has published pseudonymously under the names Carl Dreadstone and Jay Ramsay. Campbell was a young devotee of H. P. Lovecraft whose style he mimicked in his early short stories, collected in *The Inhabitant of the Lake and Less Welcome Tenants* (1964). Although his first novel *The Doll Who Ate His Mother* (1976) was a minor success, Campbell came of age with *The Face That Must Die* (1979, revised 1983) which presents a coherently grim portrait of the world through the eyes of a psychotic. His subsequent novels successfully transpose the terrors of writers such as Lovecraft, M. R. James, Robert Aickmen and Arthur Machen into starkly realistic situations of modern urban collapse. A fierce defender of the honourable tradition of horror fiction, Campbell describes himself as 'working against the innate prejudices and conservatisms of the field', using visceral horror to make people look again at things they may have taken for granted. Campbell has also edited a number of horror anthologies and critical works. Works include *Demons by Daylight* (1973); *The Parasite* aka *To Wake The Dead* (1980); *Incarnate* (1983); *Obsession* (1985); *Scared Stiff* (1987); *Ancient Images* (1989); *The Count of Eleven* (1991); and *Waking Nightmares* (1992).

Campbell, Roy (1902–57)
A South African poet, mainly resident in England, and well known in the 1930s for his opposition to the dominant left-wing school of poets led by ▷ Auden, ▷ Spender and ▷ Day Lewis whom he satirized under the composite name of Macspaunday. Much of his best verse was satirical in heroic ▷ couplets, a form otherwise very rare in 20th-century English verse. He also wrote eloquent, clear-cut lyrics. He was vigorous in all he wrote, but not distinctively original. Among his best-known works are: *The Flaming Terrapin* (1924), exalting the instinctive, vital impulses in man; *The Waygoose* (1928), a satire on South African writers; *Adamastor* and *Georgiad*. Amongst his finest works is his translation of the poems of San Juan de la Cruz, *St John of the Cross* (1951). *Collected Poems* in 3 volumes, 1960.

Canto
Used in Italian literature as a division of a long poem, such as might be sung or chanted at one time (*canto* = song). The term has been borrowed for some long poems in English.

▷ Pound, Ezra *Cantos*, The.

***Cantos*, The**
Long poem by ▷ Ezra Pound, unfinished at his death. The latest English collected edition runs to 119 ▷ cantos, and began publication with the first three cantos (later revised) in 1917. Loosely based on the 100 cantos of Dante's *Divine Comedy*, it attempts a panoramic, encyclopaedic survey of both western and oriental history, dwelling in particular on those rulers and thinkers who had exemplary significance for Pound: Confucius, Sigismondo Malatesta, Duke of Rimini, the early American presidents and Mussolini. Its main targets are usurious international finance and armament manufacturers. However, with the collapse of ▷ fascism the later stages of the poem became successively more mystical and self-consciously exploratory, and it meditates on Pound's vision of the ideal rather than on the possibilities of its earthly realization.
Bib: Bush, R., *The Genesis of Ezra Pound's 'Cantos'*; Terrell, C. F., *A Companion to the 'Cantos' of Ezra Pound.*

Capitalism
The system by which the means of production is owned privately. Production is for private profit and productive enterprise is made possible by large-scale loans of money rewarded by the payment of interest.

Before about 1350, in England as in much of the rest of Europe, there was little opportunity for capitalism. On the land, the economic unit was the manor (corresponding approximately to a village) which consumed its own produce and had little left over for sale; the economic relations were feudal, *ie* the landlords provided protection to the peasants in return for economic services, and the peasants were mostly serfs, *ie* they were bound to the land they worked on and were unable to sell their labour freely. The towns were small and manufacture was by master craftsmen, who worked with their own hands, and employed apprentices and journeymen only in small numbers. The masters combined in craft guilds which regulated trade and limited profits to a communally arranged 'just price'. Moreover, commerce, except for the export of wool, was mainly limited to the districts round the towns. Finally, it was difficult to borrow money for capital investment, partly because the Church disapproved of the taking of interest on money loans, since it regarded this as the sin of usury. The economic bond was not, in fact, a money relationship but a personal one, bound up with an elaborate system of rights and duties; these divided society into something more like castes than the modern social classes, which are differentiated chiefly by wealth.

But already by the lifetime of the poet Chaucer capitalism was making beginnings. Towns were growing, and they now contained a substantial middle class, as the *Prologue* to *The Canterbury Tales* illustrates. Master craftsmen were gradually becoming employers of labour rather than workers themselves; this was particularly true in the manufacture of cloth, which required a variety of processes impossible for one man, or even one guild, to undertake alone. The craft guilds were becoming supplemented by the merchant companies, such as the Merchants of the Staple, who had a monopoly of the export of wool to the cloth manufacturers of Flanders, and later (15th and 16th centuries) the Merchant Adventurers, whose export of cloth became even more important than the older commerce of the export of wool. The economic cause of the Hundred Years' War was Edward III's determination to protect the English wool staple towns – *ie* those through which the export of wool was channelled into Flanders – from the threat of France. To sustain the war, Edward III and Henry V had to borrow extensively from foreign bankers, who were finding methods of escaping the Church's prohibition of usury. Meanwhile, on the land the serfs were becoming independent wage-earners, able to sell their labour freely and where they pleased; this was thanks to the shortage of labour that resulted from the ▷ Black Death epidemics (about 1350). Lack of labour caused many landowners to turn their arable land into pasture and to enclose open land with hedges. This process continued in Tudor times for economic reasons, despite a labour surplus. It weakened the landowners' ties with the peasantry and encouraged the 'drift to the towns' which drained the countryside in the 18th–19th centuries.

The rapid growth of capitalism in the 17th and 18th centuries was aided by the Reformation, since certain of the Puritan sects – notably the Calvinist Presbyterians – found that religious individualism gave support to and was supported by economic individualism. The dramatists of the period of English drama 1580–1640 found the Puritans to be against them, and they (*eg* Ben Jonson, Thomas Middleton, Philip Massinger) tended to satirize the money-loving, socially ambitious middle classes, among whom the Puritans had their main strength. By the end of the 17th century, however, Puritanism was losing its ferocity; the traditional non-economic bonds of community were by then gravely weakened, and the novels of Daniel Defoe depict the loneliness of men guided predominantly by economically individualistic motives.

The full triumph of capitalism came only with the fulfilment of the ▷ Industrial Revolution in the 19th century. Workers were, for the first time on a large scale, employed in the mass, in factories. The employers (backed by a number of gifted theorists, such as Adam Smith, Jeremy Bentham, Malthus and Ricardo) developed a ruthless philosophy, according to which their relationship with their workers should be governed entirely by the economic laws of supply and demand, with which the state interfered, in their opinion, only at the cost of wrecking national prosperity, even if the interference were dictated by the need to save the workers from intolerable misery. This stream of opinion among the industrialist employers was, however, progressively opposed by Evangelical Christians among the politicians (*eg* Lord Shaftesbury), by socialists of the school of Robert Owen and by the very popular novelists between 1830 and 1860, such as Elizabeth Gaskell, Benjamin Disraeli and Charles Dickens. The most cogent and revolutionary opposition, however, was formulated in the work of Friedrich Engels, *The Condition of the Working Class in England* (1845) and of ▷ Karl Marx, *Das Kapital* (1867). The two men collaborated, in London, on the *Communist Manifesto* (1848). Gradually industrial capitalism became less inhumane, and in the last 20 years of the 19th century, socialist opinion grew, aided by the leadership of intellectuals such as ▷ George Bernard Shaw and ▷ Beatrice Webb. The principal issue now dividing the main political parties is how much economic activity should be left in private hands and how much freedom this 'free enterprise' should be allowed: the Conservatives support capitalist enterprise and the ▷ Labour Party emphasizes the value of state control. This compromise between capitalism and socialism since the Second World War produced the ▷ Welfare State, within which nobody should starve and nobody is supposed to suffer social injustice, though many still do. One of the projects of the Thatcher administration in Britain from

1979–1990 was the dismantling of Welfare State developments. The Welfare State combined with better education since the war to produce a more articulate working class than has ever been seen in Britain before; one result of this has been a much larger production of novels, plays and films exploring the experience of social mobility, *eg* the plays of ▷ Arnold Wesker and the novels of ▷ Alan Sillitoe.

▷ Further education; Anti-industrialism.

Carey, Peter (b 1943)
Australian novelist and short-story writer. He has published two volumes of short stories: *The Fat Man in History* (1974) (in the U.K. as *Exotic Pleasures*, 1981) and *War Crimes* (1979). His first two novels were: *Bliss* (1981), a bleak black comedy of the Australian suburbs about a man who believes himself to be dead and in Hell; and *Illywhacker* (1985), which combines realist elements with an outrageously ▷ unreliable narrator, who announces on the first page that he is a 'terrible liar'. These were followed by: *Oscar and Lucinda* (1988), which won the Booker Prize, and *The Tax Inspector* (1991), a sinister and violent story about abuse within a family over several generations in a suburb of Sydney. Carey is often described as a fabulist, and has acknowledged the influence on his work of the magic realism of Gabriel García Márquez.

▷ Commonwealth literatures.

Carnival
The literal meaning of this term is the 'saying good-bye' to meat at the start of Lent. Traditionally it was a period of feasting during the Christian calendar which reached its climax on Shrove Tuesday, and included many forms of festive inversion of normal behaviour, often comic and mocking of authority. To this extent it signifies a spontaneous eruption of those social forces shortly to be restrained by Lent. This sense of disruption of the norm has brought the term 'carnival' into the language of contemporary critical theory. ▷ Mikhail Bakhtin first used the term to describe a form of festive language which threatens disruption and challenges the social order. The association of carnival with popular energies highlights the political tension between official ▷ ideology and potentially subversive energies. In contemporary critical theory, the carnivalesque points to the polyphonic nature of literary texts, identifying in them a series of different and frequently opposing 'voices'.

▷ Deconstruction; Discourse.

Bib: Bakhtin, M., *Rabelais and His World.*

Carrington (1893–1932)
Carrington (who did not use her first name) was a central figure in the ▷ Bloomsbury Group, and the live-in companion of ▷ Lytton Strachey (whose homosexuality prevented her passion for him from being expressed in marriage or any sexual connection). She is best known for her letters and diaries (published as *Carrington: Letters and Extracts from her Diaries*, edited by David Garnett (1970)). Carrington studied art at the Slade School with many of the more well-known artists of the day, and was herself a gifted painter.
Bib: Carrington, N., *Carrington: Paintings, Drawings and Decorations.*

Carswell, Catherine (1879–1946)
Novelist and critic. Catherine Carswell was a member of the 'Other Bloomsbury' – the circle centred on ▷ D. H. Lawrence which strove to distinguish itself from ▷ Virginia Woolf's more cerebral and self-consciously bohemian group (▷ Bloomsbury). One of the first favourable critics of Lawrence's ▷ *The Rainbow* (her review of the book lost her her job at the *Glasgow Herald* in 1915), Carswell's famous *The Savage Pilgrimage* (1932) is a vindication of Lawrence against ▷ John Middleton Murry's pseudo-Freudian attack on his former friend, *Son of Woman* (1931). Lawrence encouraged Carswell in her novelistic endeavours, including *Open the Door* (1920), *The Camomile* (1922). Her autobiography appeared posthumously in 1952 as *Lying Awake.*
Bib: Delaney; P. *D. H. Lawrence's Nightmare: The Writer and His Circle in the Years of the Great War.*

Carter, Angela (1940–92)
Novelist and short-story writer. From her first novel, *Shadow Dance* (1966), her work was notable for a strain of ▷ surrealist ▷ Gothic fantasy, a fascination with the erotic and the violent, and a blending of comedy and horror. *The Magic Toyshop* (1967) is a ▷ Freudian fairy-tale seen through the eyes of an orphaned 15-year-old girl, sent, with her brother and baby sister, to live in the claustrophobic and sinister home of her uncle, a sadistic toymaker. Her new family are examples of Carter's ability to create vivid Dickensian caricatures. After *Several Perceptions* (1968) her work became unequivocally Gothic and anti-realist, centring on the reworking of myth and

fairy-tale, and the exploration of aggressive and sexual fantasies. *Heroes and Villains* (1969), *The Infernal Desire Machines of Doctor Hoffman* (1972) and *The Passion of New Eve* (1977) are bizarre and fantastic visions of imaginary worlds, projections of the 'subterranean areas behind everyday experience', with picaresque and pastiche elements. One of her collections of short stories, *The Bloody Chamber* (1979), is a feminist re-working of traditional European fairy-tales; one of these stories, 'The Company of Wolves', was filmed by Neil Jordan in 1984, with screenplay by Angela Carter. Her interest in the politics of sexuality is reflected in her non-fiction work *The Sadeian Woman* (1979), an analysis of the codes of ▷ pornography. Her other novels are: *Love* (1971); *Nights at the Circus* (1984). Story collections are: *Fireworks* (1974); *Black Venus* (1985); *Come Unto These Yellow Sands* (1985) (radio plays). Her last novel was *Wise Children* (1991), a pastiche of family life in theatrical and vaudeville circles, and is perhaps Carter's most comic and accessible text, although overall her powerful work has been categorized as fantasy, ▷ science fiction and anti-realist. *Expletives Deleted: Selected Writings* was published in 1992.

Cartland, Barbara (b 1901)
Romantic novelist. According to the *Guinness Book of Records*, Barbara Cartland holds the record as the most prolific living author. She has written over 300 books, including 27 in 1977 alone, and she has a deeply loyal, overwhelmingly female, readership. Her novels are remarkable for their sheer numbers and similarity of plot and theme: although she has written drama, biography and other non-fiction, she is known to many as the ▷ best-selling author of a conservative brand of romantic fiction which champions the escapist delights of marriage, monogamy and absolute sexual difference. Her heroines are nothing if not feminine, and Cartland's preference for pink is legendary. Whilst she could by no stretch of the imagination be deemed a feminist writer, she has been writing constantly since the 1920s (her first novel was published in 1925), and is something of a figurehead for older women in her fierce commitment to her writing career (despite her obvious wealth and connections to the British aristocracy, and despite the doctrine of her own books which suggests that a woman's identity should be found in her husband rather than in her own work), and in her active attitude to health and fitness (she has recently set up a successful health-food business, and in 1971 published her *Health Food Cookery Book*). Her books include: *Jig-Saw* (1925); *Touch the Stars* (1935); *Love is an Eagle* (1951); *Love Under Fire* (1960); *Men Are Wonderful* (1973); *A Shaft of Sunlight* (1982); *Tempted to Love* (1983); and *A Runaway Star* (1987).
Bib: Cloud, H., *Barbara Cartland: Crusader in Pink*; Radford, J., *The Progress of Romance: The Politics of Popular Fiction*; Anderson, R., *The Purple Heart Throbs*.

Cary, Arthur Joyce Lunel (1888–1957)
Novelist. He was born in Northern Ireland, where there is a strong tradition of Protestantism; he was brought up against a background of devout ▷ Anglicanism, lost his faith, and later constructed an unorthodox but strongly ethical faith of his own along Protestant lines. His first novel, *Aissa Saved*, appeared in 1932. His subsequent works include: *An American Visitor* (1933); *The African Witch* (1936); *Mister Johnson* (1939); *Charley is my Darling* (1940); the trilogy *Herself Surprised* (1941), *To Be a Pilgrim* (1942) and *The Horse's Mouth* (1944); *The Moonlight* (1946); another trilogy, *Prisoner of Grace* (1952); *Except the Lord* (1953), and *Not Honour More* (1955); *The Captive and the Free* (1959). *Spring Song* (1960) is a collection of stories. He also produced three volumes of verse, *Verse* (1908), *Marching Soldier* (1945) and *The Drunken Sailor* (1947), and a number of political tracts – *Power in Men* (1939), *The Case for African Freedom* (1941; revised 1944), *Process of Real Freedom* (1943), and *Britain and West Africa* (1946).

In the first 30 years of the 20th century novelists tended to be open to foreign influences and experimental in expression; Cary was among the first distinguished novelists to return to English traditions and direct narrative, although he here and there uses the ▷ stream of consciousness technique of narration evolved by novelists of the 1920s, notably ▷ James Joyce. He is one of the most eclectic of modern novelists, both in method and in subject. In his comedy and his loose, vigorous narrative he has been compared to the 18th-century novelists – Smollett and Defoe; in his characterization, to Dickens; in his attitude to human nature, to ▷ D. H. Lawrence; in his concern with heroic morality, to ▷ Joseph Conrad; in his endeavour to present experience with immediacy, to ▷ Virginia Woolf and Joyce; in his interlocking of human destiny and social patterns he might be compared with George Eliot. His first three novels and *Mister Johnson*

are products of his African experience; *Charley is my Darling* and *A House of Children* are novels of childhood, and his two trilogies – thought by some to be his major work – are attempts, in his words, to see 'English history, through English eyes, for the last 60 years'.
Bib: Wright, A., *Joyce Cary: a Preface to his Novels*; Mahood, M. M., *Joyce Cary's Africa*; Fisher, B., *Joyce Cary, the Writer and his Theme*.

Catholicism (Roman) in English literature
Until the Act of Supremacy (1534) by which King Henry VIII separated the English Church from Roman authority, and the more violent revolution in ▷ Scotland a little later, both countries had belonged to the European community of Catholic Christendom. In the 16th century this community of cultures broke up, owing not only to the Protestant rebellions but also to the increase of national self-consciousness, the influence of non-Christian currents (especially Platonism), and the gradual release of various fields of activity – political, commercial, philosophical – from religious doctrine. The Counter-Reformation after the Catholic Council of Trent (1545–63), even more than the Reformation, tended to define Roman Catholicism in contrast to Protestantism.Thus, although the dramatists and lyric poets in England from 1560 to 1640 show a plentiful survival of medieval assumptions about the nature of man and his place in the universe, in conflict with newer tendencies of thought and feeling, the Roman Catholic writer in the same period begins to show himself as something distinct from his non-Catholic colleagues. The clearest example in the 17th century is the poet Richard Crashaw. Milton's epic of the creation of the world, *Paradise Lost*, is in many ways highly traditional, but the feeling that inspires it is entirely post-Reformation. By the 18th century, however, religion of all kinds was becoming a mere department of life, no longer dictating ideas and emotions in all fields, even when sincerely believed; it is thus seldom easy to remember that the poet Alexander Pope was a Roman Catholic. By the 19th century, writers of strong religious conviction were increasingly feeling themselves in a minority in an indifferent and even sceptical world. They therefore tended to impress their work once more with their faith, and this was especially true of the few Catholic writers, since Catholic faith was dogmatically so strongly defined, *eg* the poet ▷ Gerard Manley Hopkins. The century also saw a revival of Anglo-Catholicism. From the time of the Reformation there had been a school of opinion which sought to remain as close to Roman Catholicism as ▷ Anglican independence allowed. This wing of the Church was important under Charles I, but lost prestige until it was revived by the Oxford Movement. Since then it has remained important in the strength of its imprint on literature. Thus in the 20th century the Anglo-Catholicism of the poet ▷ T. S. Eliot is as conspicuous as and more profound than the Roman Catholicism of the novelists ▷ Evelyn Waugh and ▷ Graham Greene. Amongst writers later in the 20th century, Catholicism is noticeable in the work of ▷ Anthony Burgess and ▷ David Lodge.

Causley, Charles (b 1917)
Poet. Causley is Cornish by birth, and his writing has been compared to his contemporary ▷ John Betjeman in its usage of traditional forms, and to the Spanish poet he admires, Federico Garcia Lorca (▷ Spanish literature), in its usage of the ballad form. He draws his influences from pre-modernist poets, particularly ▷ Victorian, ▷ Georgian and World War I poets (Causley himself fought in World War II in the Royal Navy). His first publication was *Hands to Dance* (1951); this was followed by *Union Street* (1957); *Underneath the Water* (1967); *Figure of Eight* (1969); *Figgie Hobbin* (1970); *Collected Poems* (1975).

Caute, David (b 1936)
Novelist and dramatist. Caute is one of a group of English writers, including ▷ Andrew Sinclair and Julian Mitchell, interested in formal experiment, self-referential narrative strategies and the blending of ▷ realism with elements of fantasy. He admires the work of ▷ Christine Brooke-Rose, and is strongly influenced by ▷ Jean-Paul Sartre. *The Confrontation* is a trilogy consisting of a play, *The Demonstration* (produced 1969), a critical essay supposedly by one of the characters in the play, *The Illusion* (1970) and a novel, *The Occupation* (1971). The questioning of the borders of fiction with other discourses is sustained by the competing narrators and narrative strategies within *The Occupation*. Caute's works reflect his commitment to Marxism (▷ Marx, Karl) in their analysis of society and history, and his novel *The Decline of the West* (1966) has been criticized as being over-didactic. He has worked as a lecturer, and as literary and arts editor of the ▷ *New Statesman*. Later novels include *News from Nowhere* (1986).

Celtic Twilight, The
Originally *The Celtic Twilight* was a book of short stories by the poet ▷ W. B. Yeats, published in 1893. The book dealt with the widespread beliefs in magic and the supernatural which were current among Irish peasants. Since then, the term Celtic Twilight has been widely used to describe the idea that the Celts, especially in Ireland, preserve a mystical, imaginative, poetic vision which the practical and materialistic Anglo-Saxons (both in England and in southern Scotland) have lost. At the end of the 19th century and beginning of the 20th century Yeats and other Irish poets used this conception of the Celtic character as a weapon in the cause of Irish nationalism, and they cultivated ancient Irish legends about heroes such as ▷ Cuchulain and heroines such as Queen Deirdre so as to build up a distinctively Irish literary consciousness to replace the dominant English culture.

▷ Irish literature in English.

C.E.M.A.
The Council for the Encouragement of Music and the Arts was founded in 1939, and financed by the Pilgrim Trust and the Board of Education, to provide entertainments on the home front and provide employment for artists during wartime. Its success strengthened the case for public subsidy for the theatre and after World War II it became the ▷ Arts Council of Great Britain.

Censorship
Systematic censorship has never been an important restriction on English writing except in times of war; but English writers have certainly not always been entirely free.

Until 1640 the monarch exercised undefined powers by the Royal Prerogative. Early in her reign, Elizabeth I ordered dramatists not to meddle with politics and in the reign of Charles I the term Crop-ears was used for opponents of the king who lost their ears as a penalty for criticizing the political or religious authorities. Moreover, printing was monopolized by the Stationer's Company, whose charter might be withdrawn by the Crown, so that the monopoly would cease.

In the Civil War, Parliament was in control of London, and issued an edict that the publication of any book had to be licensed. The edict provoked John Milton's *Areopagitica*, an appeal for freedom of expression. Its influence was not immediate; after the Restoration of the Monarchy, Parliament issued a similar edict in the Licensing Act of 1663. The Act was only for a period, however, and in 1696 it was not renewed. The lapsing of the Licensing Act was the starting point of British freedom of the press except for emergency edicts in times of war in the 20th century, although in the early 19th century the government attempted a form of indirect censorship by imposing a tax on periodicals which restricted their sale amongst the poor. Nonetheless there are still laws extant which restrict freedom of political expression beyond certain limits.

Also serious are the English laws of libel and of obscene libel. The first exists to punish attacks on private reputation, and the second concerns the defence of sexual morals. The restrictions are serious restraints on opinion because they are vaguely defined, so that it is difficult for a publisher or writer to know when they are being infringed. Moreover, prohibition under obscenity law is frequently reversed, *eg* ▷ D. H. Lawrence's ▷ *The Rainbow* was suppressed for obscenity, but by 1965 it was a prescribed text for study in schools. One of the most celebrated challenges to public morality was the test which Penguin Books' publication of D. H. Lawrence's ▷ *Lady Chatterley's Lover* gave to the 1959 Obscene Publications Act; the 1960 'Trial of Lady Chatterley' altered the way in which the Act could be interpreted, and after it the censorship of writing on sexual grounds became much more difficult. Organizations such as Mary Whitehouse's National Viewers and Listeners Association have thus channelled their pro-censorship energies into images of violence and sexual explicitness on television and in films. The 1984 Video Recordings Act in effect raised the British Board of Film Classification 'from an industrial advisory body to legally empowered censors' (Mandy Merck).

Censorship in the theatre has been a special case since the 18th century. Henry Fielding's comedies attacking the Prime Minister, Robert Walpole, led in 1737 to the restriction of London theatres to two 'patented' ones – Covent Garden and Drury Lane – and the Court official, the Lord Chamberlain, had to license plays. In 1843 the Theatres Act removed the restriction on the theatres and defined the Lord Chamberlain's powers to the restraint of indecency. The Lord Chamberlain's censorship came to an end in 1968.

Since 1979 there has been a gradual return to the censorship of literature and this has been extended to cover the media. The Official Secrets Act is in the process of being rewritten so as to prevent both former Crown servants from revealing information – especially in autobiographies – as well as the media from printing or broadcasting, sometimes in dramatic form, any of this material. A directive was issued in November 1988 to prevent the broadcasting of statements from people of named organizations; again this may have an effect on drama. Also in 1988, the government emended the 1986 Local Government Act to forbid any Local Authority promoting homosexuality through educational means, printed material or support of gay writers. The Broadcasting Standards Council was established in 1988 in order to monitor taste and decency in the media. Finally, a non-governmental form of censorship may be found in the effects of the concentration of ownership in publishing houses and the press, which severely limit the range of writing that is commercially encouraged.

Two organizations attempt to alert people to the extent and dangers of these new censorship laws: the Campaign for Press and Broadcasting Freedom and the Writers' Guild of Great Britain.

Bib: Findlater, R., *Banned: A Review of Theatrical Censorship in Britain*; Barker, M., *The Video Nasties: Freedom and Censorship in the Media*; Chester and Dickey (eds.), *Feminism and Censorship.*

Chekhov, Anton Pavlovich (1860–1904)
Russian dramatist and short-story writer. In his last four plays (*The Seagull, Uncle Vanya, Three Sisters, The Cherry Orchard*) he evolved a dramatic form and idiom of dialogue which were highly original and had a great influence on 20th-century drama. His originality lay in his combination of faithfulness to the surface of life with poetic evocation of underlying experience. This he achieved partly by exploiting the character of human conversation when it seems to be engaged in communication, but is actually concerned with the incommunicable. This leads on to the non-communicating dialogue in the work of playwrights such as Beckett and Pinter, when the characters on the stage alternately baffle and enlighten the audience by the undercurrents implicit in their words. The realism of Chekhov's stories is similarly subtle and original; they have similar faithfulness to surface combined with delicate artistic pattern, giving significance to seeming irrelevance and slightness of incident. An outstanding exponent of the method in English is the New Zealand writer ▷ Katherine Mansfield.

Bib: Magarshack, D., *The Plays of Anton Chekhov*; Styan, J. L., *Chekhov in Performance.*

Cheshire Cheese, The
A tavern off Fleet Street in London, and a favourite resort of Ben Jonson, and, after it was rebuilt, of Samuel Johnson and of ▷ Yeats, who liked to claim it as a haunt. It still exists.

Chesterton, G. K. (Gilbert Keith) (1874–1936)
An extremely versatile writer of essays, stories, novels, poems; Chesterton is best described as a polemicist, since polemics entered into everything he wrote, whether it was detective stories (the Father Brown series; 1911, 1914, 1926, 1927), fantasy (*The Man who was Thursday*, 1908), comic verse, or religious studies such as *St Francis of Assisi* (1923) or *St Thomas Aquinas* (1933). He wrote against life-denial, whether manifested in the denial of humanity in the Victorian political economy, or the sceptical withdrawal into ▷ aestheticism of the 1890s. His basis of attack was a conviction that life is to be enjoyed with all the faculties; he also had the belief that such fullness of life required a religion large enough to comprehend all the spiritual and moral potentialities in man, and he found this religion in Roman Catholicism. He was not received into the Catholic Church until 1922, but from *The Napoleon of Notting Hill* (1904) – a fantasy about a war between London boroughs – he shows the romantic medievalism which for him was a large part of the appeal of Catholicism. The period of his greatest influence was probably between 1900 and 1914, when he belonged to a group of vigorous witty polemicists, including ▷ George Bernard Shaw, ▷ H. G. Wells, ▷ Hilaire Belloc. He was from the first an ally of the Catholic Belloc against the agnostic socialists, Wells and Shaw. He had in common with both his antagonists a genius for vivid particularity strongly reminiscent of the Victorian novelist Charles Dickens; with Shaw he shared a delight in witty and disturbing paradox, which he used as Shaw did, to startle his readers out of the acceptance of platitudes into genuine thinking. In spite of his homely, zestful humanity, one notices nowadays a journalistic superficiality about Chesterton's work, as though he felt that his audience demanded entertainment as the indispensable reward for receiving

enlightenment, and this may account for the neglect of his work since his death.

Politically, with Belloc, he preached an alternative to socialism in Distributism, a vision of a society of small proprietors. His critical work perhaps survives better than his other work; it included studies of Browning (1903), Dickens (1906), Thackeray (1909), ▷ Chaucer (1932), and *The Victorian Age in Literature* (1913). He is otherwise perhaps best read in selection, for instance in *Selected Stories* (ed. K. Amis) and *G. K. Chesterton: A Selection from his Non-fictional Prose* (selected by W. H. Auden).

▷ Catholicism in English literature; Detective fiction.

Bib: Belloc, H., *The Place of Chesterton in English Letters*; Canovan, H., *Chesterton, Radical Populist*; Hollis, C., *The Mind of Chesterton*.

Children's books

Until the 19th century, children were not regarded as beings with their own kind of experience and values, and therefore did not have books written specifically for their entertainment. The literature available to them included popular versions of old romances, such as *Bevis of Hampton*, and magical folk-tales, such as *Jack the Giant-Killer*, which appeared in chapbooks. Children also read such works as John Bunyan's *Pilgrim's Progress*, Daniel Defoe's *Robinson Crusoe* (1719), and Jonathan Swift's *Gulliver's Travels* (1726); Perrault's collection of French ▷ fairy-tales appeared in English as *Mother Goose's Fairy Tales* in 1729.

During the ▷ Romantic period it was recognized that childhood experience was a world of its own and, influenced, in many cases, by Rousseau's ideas on education, books began to be written especially to appeal to children. Such works as Thomas Day's *Merton and Sandford* (1783–9), Maria Edgeworth's *Moral Tales* (1801) and Mrs Sherwood's *The Fairchild Family* (1818) usually had a serious moral tone, but showed an understanding of a child's mind that was lacking from Anne and Jane Taylor's cautionary tales in verse (later to be parodied by ▷ Hilaire Belloc in *The Bad Child's Book of Beasts* etc.).

It was not until the Victorian period that writers began extensively to try to please children, without attempting to improve them at the same time. Edward Lear's *Book of Nonsense* (1846) and Lewis Carroll's *Alice* books combine fantasy with humour. Romance and magic had a strong appeal to the Victorians, and fairy stories from all over the world were presented in versions for children. The collection of the brothers Grimm had appeared in 1824 as *German Popular Stories* and Hans Christian Andersen's original compositions were translated into English in 1846. Andrew Lang's *Fairy Books* were published later in the century. Adventure stories for boys, such as Captain Frederick Marryat's *Masterman Ready* (1841) and Robert Louis Stevenson's *Treasure Island* (1883) became a flourishing genre, but the tradition of moral improvement persisted in such books as Charles Kingsley's *Water Babies* (1863). Children's literature is a field to which women writers have made a notable contribution; in the latter half of the 19th century enduring classics were written by Mrs Molesworth (*The Tapestry Room*, 1879), Louisa May Alcott (*Little Women*, 1868), Anna Sewell (*Black Beauty*, 1877) and E. Nesbit (*The Story of the Treasure-Seekers*, 1899, etc.).

Animals have loomed large in children's books, ▷ Beatrix Potter's *Peter Rabbit* appeared in 1902 (doing much to establish the book where text and illustrations were of equal importance), Kenneth Grahame's *The Wind in the Willows* in 1908, the first of Hugh Lofting's *Dr Dolittle* books in 1920, ▷ A. A. Milne's *Winnie the Pooh* in 1926 and the first of Alison Uttley's *Little Grey Rabbit* books in 1929. Charges of anthropomorphism seem to have had little effect on the popularity of these books, and another writer whose lack of critical acclaim has hardly diminished her sales is ▷ Enid Blyton. Recently, allegations of racism and sexism have been laid against old favourites, and there have been efforts to bring children's literature into touch with 20th-century problems, such as single-parent families and racial prejudice. As well as writers (*eg* Noel Streatfield and ▷ Nina Bawden) who have concerned themselves with stories about everyday life, there have been others who have continued the tradition of magical fantasy. ▷ Tolkien's *The Hobbit*, Philippa Pierce's *Tom's Midnight Garden*, ▷ C. S. Lewis's *Tales of Narnia*, Ursula Le Guin's stories about *Earthsea* and the work of Alan Garner all fall into this category. In a rather different field, Rosemary Sutcliff has won recognition for the careful research underlying her historical novels. Mention should also be made of Ladybird books, which, in addition to their fiction publications, have done much to introduce children to a wide variety of topics, from music to magnetism. Following Robert Louis Stevenson's *A Child's Garden of Verses* (1885), children's verse has been written by Belloc, ▷ De La Mare, A. A. Milne, ▷ Ted Hughes and ▷ Charles Causley.

Bib: Rose, J. *The Case of Peter Pan, Or, the Impossibility of Children's Fiction*; Styles, M., Bearne, E., and Watson, V. (eds.), *After Alice: Exploring Children's Literature.*

Christie, Agatha (1890–1976)

▷ Detective fiction writer (who also wrote romantic novels as Mary Westmacott), Agatha Christie is one of the most well known, and certainly the most widely translated, of British writers this century. Her large range of intricate but formulaic novels gained her a vast readership, and they have been widely filmed, televised and staged (*The Mousetrap*, 1952, is the longest-running stage play, still showing in London's West End). Even though she continued to write from the 1920s until her death, most of her work evidences a nostalgia for the pre-war England of the prosperous classes with which she is aptly identified, the setting for novels populated by abnormal, criminal psyches (crime is never, for Christie, socially justifiable) and brilliant, sexless sleuths (Hercule Poirot and Miss Marple being the most famous). Her books include: *The Mysterious Affair at Styles: A Detective Story* (1920); *The Murder of Roger Ackroyd* (1926); *Murder on the Orient Express* (1934); *Death on the Nile* (1937); *Ten Little Niggers* (1939); *Sparkling Cyanide* (1945); *Ordeal by Innocence* (1958) and *Endless Night* (1967).

Bib: Keating, H. (ed.), *Christie: The First Lady of Crime*; Sanders, D. and Lovallo, L. (eds.), *The Agatha Christie Companion*; Shaw, M. and Vanacker, S., *Reflecting on Miss Marple.*

Church of England

The history of the Church of England is closely bound up with the political and social history of England. In the Middle Ages the Church of England was a division of the Catholic Church of western Europe. It became independent in 1534, when Henry VIII caused Parliament to pass the Act of Supremacy which declared him to be the 'Supreme Head of the English Church and Clergy'. This action was political rather than religious; Henry was conservative in his religious beliefs, and reaffirmed the traditional Catholic doctrines by his Act of the Six Articles (1539). However, a Protestant party, influenced by the German reformer Martin Luther, had long been growing in England and was favoured by the Archbishop of Canterbury, Thomas Cranmer. Under the boy King Edward VI, the Protestants seized power, and Catholic doctrine was modified by Cranmer's two Books of Common Prayer. Under Mary I, however, England returned to Catholicism, but Mary too became unpopular owing to her persecution of Protestants, and her successor, Elizabeth I, attempted a compromise Settlement, by means of which she hoped to keep in the Church of England both the Catholics and the extremer Protestants. She succeeded, in so far as her Settlement prevented religious conflict breaking into civil war during her reign.

The Roman Catholics were and remained a small minority, but during the first half of the 17th century the extreme Protestants (now known as Puritans) grew in strength, especially in London and in the south and east. Under the Protectorship of the Puritan Oliver Cromwell, the Church of England ceased to exist as a state religious organization, but in 1660 the monarchy and the Church of England were restored, and Puritans were excluded from the Church, from political rights and from attendance at the universities of Oxford and Cambridge. From this time, the Puritans (increasingly called Dissenters or Nonconformists) set up their own Churches. Within the Church, religious differences remained and were the basis of the newly emerging political parties, the Whigs being more in sympathy with the Puritans and the Tories being closer to, though never identified with, the Roman Catholics.

During the 18th century the apathy into which the Church of England had fallen was shaken by the religious revival led by John Wesley, who worked mainly among the poorer classes. Although Wesley was forced to form a separate Methodist Church, his example inspired the Evangelical Movement within the Church of England, which by the 19th century was an important force towards social reform. A different sort of revival was led by a group of Anglicans at Oxford University, of whom John Henry Newman was the most active. The resulting Oxford (or Tractarian) Movement affirmed the spiritual independence of the Church and its continuity with the medieval Catholic Church. Newman eventually became a Roman Catholic, and the Oxford Movement lost in him its main inspiration. He left behind him, however, divisions of opinion within the Church that exist today: the High Church is composed of Anglicans who are essentially Catholic in belief, though they reject the authority of the Pope; they can be said to be descendants from

Henry VIII's Reformation. The Low Church feels itself to be Protestant, and can be said to favour the Reformation of Edward VI. A third group, prominent in the mid-19th century but not to be distinguished now, was the Broad Church; it developed from the Evangelical Movement and was especially active in social and political reform. These have all existed under the common organization of the Church.

Today, the Church of England is the state Church, under the Crown, only in England; in Scotland and Wales, the Commonwealth, and the U.S.A., members of churches originally derived from the Church of England are known as Episcopalians. Recently one of the key debates taking place within the Church concerns the possible ordination of women.

Churchill, Caryl (b 1938)
British feminist (▷ Feminism) dramatist who has produced some of her best work in collaboration with Joint Stock Theatre Company. *Light Shining in Buckinghamshire* (1976) explored the betrayal of leveller ideals during the English Civil War. *Cloud Nine* (1978) used an imperialist context to examine sexuality. Analysis of sexual stereotyping within a clear political context is characteristic of Churchill plays, especially her recent ebullient comedy about stock market swindlers, *Serious Money* (1987). Other plays include: *Owners* (1972); *Vinegar Tom* (1976); *Top Girls* (1982); *Fen* (1982); *Softcops* (1984); *A Mouthful of Birds* (1986; with David Lan).

▷ Royal Court Theatre.

Bib: Keyssar, H., *Feminist Theatre*; Wandor, M., *Carry on Understudies*.

Cixous, Hélène (b 1937)
French writer. Hélène Cixous's work has been most influential when it has actively attempted to challenge the categories of writing, and her work encompasses poetry and poetic prose, ▷ feminist theory, philosophy and ▷ psychoanalysis. She is a key player in the French feminist ▷ *écriture féminine* movement, and has written some 40 influential texts (only a few of which have been translated into English), beginning with her PhD thesis on ▷ James Joyce (published in English as *The Exile of James Joyce or the Art of Replacement* in 1972), and including *The Newly Born Woman* (with Catherine Clément), the seminal essay on women and writing 'The Laugh of the Medusa' (*'Le Rire de la Meduse'*) (published in English in 1976), dramas and fiction (including *Portrait de Dora*, Cixous's vindication of ▷ Freud's famous patient, the central figure in one of his most important case histories and latter-day feminist heroine), and literary-critical works (*To Live the Orange* is a celebration of the work of Brazilian writer Clarice Lispector). Cixous is Professor of Literature at the experimental University of Paris – VIII which she co-founded in 1968, and director of the *Centre d'Études Féminine*.

Bib: Marks, E. and de Coutivron, I. (eds.), *New French Feminisms*; Conley, V. A., *Hélène Cixous: Writing the Feminine*; Sellers, S. (ed.), *Writing Differences: Readings from the Seminar of Hélène Cixous*; Wilcox, H. et al, *The Body and the Text*; Moi, T. *Sexual/Textual Politics*.

Classic, Classics, Classical
These words are apt to cause confusion. The term 'classic' has been used to denote a work about whose value it is assumed there can be no argument, *eg Portrait of a Lady* is a classic. The word particularly implies a changeless and immutable quality; it has sometimes been used to deny the need for reassessment, reinterpretation and change. Because only a few works can be classics, it may be argued that the term is synonymous with the best. This is not necessarily the case, especially with regard to changes in literary taste and a constantly moving canon of texts.

'Classics' is the study of ancient Greek and Latin literature. 'Classic' is used as an adjective as well as a noun, *eg* ▷ Henry James wrote several classic novels. 'Classical' is mainly used as the adjective for 'classics', *eg* classical scholarship.

Classical mythology
Ancient Greek mythology can be divided between the 'Divine Myths' and the 'Heroic Myths'.

The divine myths are known in differing versions from the works of various Greek poets, of whom the most notable are Homer and Hesiod. Hesiod explained the origin of the world in terms of a marriage between Earth (Ge or Gaea) and Sky (Uranus). Their children were the 12 Titans: Oceanus, Crius, Iapetus, Theia, Rhea, Mnemosyne, Phoebe, Tethys, Themis, Coeus, Hyperion, and Cronos. Cronos overthrew his father, and he and Rhea (or Cybele) became the parents of the 'Olympian gods', so called from their association with the sacred mountain Olympus. The Olympians, in their turn, overthrew Cronos and the other Titans.

The chief Olympians were Zeus and his queen Hera. The other gods and goddesses were the offspring of either, but as Zeus was usually at war with Hera, they were not the joint parents. They seem to have been seen as male and female aspects of the sky; their quarrels were the causes of bad weather and cosmic disturbances. The principal offspring of Zeus were Apollo, Artemis, Athene, Aphrodite (sometimes represented as a daughter of Uranus out of the sea), Dionysus, Hermes, and Ares. Zeus had three sisters, Hestia, Demeter (the corn goddess) and Hera (also his wife), and two brothers, Poseidon who ruled the sea, and Hades who ruled the underworld. In the 3rd century BC the Olympian gods were adopted by the Romans, who used the Latin names more commonly known to later European writers. Uranus, Apollo, and some others remained the same. Gaea became Tellus; Cronos = Saturn; Zeus = Jupiter (or Jove); Hera = Juno; Athene = Minerva; Artemis = Diana; Hermes = Mercury; Ares = Mars; Hephaestus = Vulcan; Aphrodite = Venus (and her son Eros = Cupid); Demeter = Ceres; Poseidon = Neptune. There were numerous minor deities such as nymphs and satyrs in both Greek and Roman pantheons.

The Olympian deities mingled with men, and rivalled one another in deciding human destinies. They concerned themselves particularly with the destinies of the heroes, *ie* those men, sometimes partly divine by parentage, who were remarkable for the kinds of excellence which are especially valued in early societies, such as strength (Heracles), or cunning (Odysseus). Each region of Greece had its native heroes, though the greatest heroes were famous in legend all over Greece. The most famous of all was Heracles (in Latin, Hercules), who originated in Thebes. Other leading examples of the hero are: Theseus (Athens); Sisyphus and Bellerophon (Corinth); Perseus (Argolis); the Dioscuri, *ie* Castor and Pollux (Laconia); ▷ Oedipus (Thebes); Achilles (Thessaly); Jason (Thessaly); Orpheus (Thrace). Like the Greek gods and goddesses, the Greek heroes were adopted by Roman legend, sometimes with a change of name. The minor hero of Greek legend, Aeneas, was raised to be the great ancestral hero of the Romans, and they had other heroes of their own, such as Romulus, the founder of Rome, and his brother Remus.

After the downfall of the Roman Empire of the West, classical deities and heroes achieved a kind of popular reality through the planets and zodiacal signs which are named after them, and which, according to astrologers, influence human fates. Thus in Chaucer's *The Knight's Tale*, Mars, Venus, Diana and Saturn occur, and owe their force in the poem as much to medieval astrology as to classical legend. Otherwise their survival has depended chiefly on their importance in the works of the classical poets, such as Homer, Hesiod, Virgil and ▷ Ovid, who have meant so much to European culture. In Britain, important poets translated and thus helped to 'naturalize' the Greek and Latin poems; *eg* Gavin Douglas in the 16th century and Dryden in the 17th century translated Virgil's *Aeneid*; Chapman in the 16th century and Pope in the 18th century translated Homer's epics. In the 16th and 17th centuries, poets used major and minor classical deities to adorn and elevate poems intended chiefly as gracious entertainment, and occasionally they added deities of their own invention.

While European culture was understood as a more or less distinct system of values, the poets used classical deities and heroes deliberately and objectively. In the 19th century, however, the deep disturbance of European beliefs and values caused European writers to use classical myth more subjectively, as symbols through which they tried to express their personal doubts, struggles and beliefs. Thus John Keats in his unfinished epic *Hyperion* tried to emulate Milton's great Christian epic, *Paradise Lost*, but instead of Christian myth he used the war of the Olympian gods and the Titans to embody his sense of the tragedy of human experience. Tennyson wrote dramatic monologues in which personifications of Greek heroes (*eg* Ulysses, Tithonus, Tiresias in eponymous poems) recounted the experiences associated with them in classical (or, in the case of Ulysses, medieval) legend, in such a way as to express the emotional conflicts of a man from the ▷ Victorian age like Tennyson himself. In the 20th century, writers have used figures from the classical myths differently again; they are introduced to establish the continuity of the emotions and attitudes characteristic of modern men and women with emotions and attitudes of those from the past. It is thus that ▷ T. S. Eliot uses Tiresias in his poem ▷ *The Waste Land*, and James Joyce uses the Odysseus myth in his novel ▷ *Ulysses*. In a comparable way, modern psychologists have used the Greek myths as symbolic expressions of basic psychological conflicts in human beings in all periods. ▷ Freud's theory of the Oedipus complex is the most famous of these reinterpretations.

Clerihew

A lightweight epigram, usually in four lines

of varying length, so called after its inventor, detective writer ▷ E. C(lerihew) Bentley. For example:

> *Alfred de Musset*
> *Called his cat 'pusset'.*
> *His accent was affected –*
> *That was to be expected.*

CND

The Campaign for Nuclear Disarmament, which was launched at a meeting of 5,000 people at the Central Hall, Westminster, in February 1958. Speakers included ▷ Bertrand Russell, ▷ J.B. Priestley and the historian A. J. P. Taylor. A non-party movement (it was not a national organization until 1966), its members rejected the nuclear deterrent on moral grounds and demanded unilateral nuclear disarmament by Britain. Public demonstrations included marches to the atomic research establishment at Aldermaston. After a period of diminished public sympathy in the late 1960s, CND was relaunched in 1980. Opposition to the basing of American Cruise missiles in Britain once again swelled its membership: 250,000 people attended a mass meeting in Hyde Park on 6 June 1982. With the end of the ▷ Cold War following the revolutions in Eastern Europe in 1989 and 1990, CND has fallen into decline; as the Soviet empire has withdrawn its armaments from former eastern bloc countries, so the U.S.A. is gradually withdrawing its nuclear weapons from NATO countries.

Coetzee, J. M. (b 1940)

South African novelist, translator and critic. Educated at the University of Cape Town, where he has taught literature and linguistics since 1972, having previously worked in computing in England and held an academic job at the State University of New York. Since 1984 he has been Professor of General Literature at Cape Town, and has held visiting professorships at various universities in the United States. His fiction includes *Dusklands* (two novellas, 1974); *In the Heart of the Country* (1977; published in the U.S.A. as *From the Heart of the Country*); *Waiting for the Barbarians* (1980); *Life and Times of Michael K* (1983) (Booker Prize winner); *Foe* (1986); *Age of Iron* (1990). Together with the novelist André Brink, he edited *A Land Apart: A South African Reader* (1986). His translations include: *A Posthumous Confession*, by Marcellus Emants (1976); *The Expedition to the Baobab Tree*, by Wilma Stockenstrom (1983). Critical writing: *White Writing: On the Culture of Letters in South Africa* (1988). His fiction frequently works through the self-conscious transformation of established genres, such as the 18th-century novel of travel and exploration (in *Foe*, which takes as its point of departure Daniel Defoe's *Robinson Crusoe*). Coetzee's most persistent concern has been the impact on the self of colonial power-structures; many of his protagonists are compromised by their privileged position within such structures.

Bib: Dovey, T., *The Novels of J. M. Coetzee: Lacanian Allegories*; Penner, A. R., *Countries of the Mind: The Fiction of J. M. Coetzee.*

Cold War, The

Loosely used to describe the power struggle that arose after the end of World War II between the communist and western democratic-capitalist nations. It had no specific beginning but was to be identified in the way each side perceived the other as a political and military threat and as the representative of an alien and menacing ideology. The Korean War (1949–53) intensified this opposition; its crisis came in 1961 when the Castro regime in Cuba allied itself unequivocally with the U.S.S.R. When it was discovered that Soviet missiles capable of destroying major U.S. targets were being installed on the island, an international crisis ensued in which nuclear war seemed to threaten. In the late 1980s, Gorbachev's work for conciliation and exchange between east and west has created the possibility of a more realistic and constructive understanding.

Following the 'revolutions' in the eastern bloc in the late 1980s and early 1990s, in which formerly communist countries pressed for economic change and an openness to capitalism, and particularly following the reunification of Germany in 1990, the Cold War was said to have ended. The Cold War has influenced the works of many recent writers, particularly ▷ John Le Carré and ▷ Graham Greene.

▷ Communism; Capitalism; CND.

Colonialism

Although it is known that colonies were established in early history, the term is now taken to refer to nationalistic appropriation of land dating from the Renaissance period in the west, and is usually understood as perpetrated on black or coloured non-Europeans in Asia, Africa, Australasia, the Americas or the Caribbean by the white western European powers. Colonialism does not have to imply formal annexation, however. Colonial status involves the imposition of decisions by one people upon another, where the economy or political structure has been brought under the overwhelming influence of another country. Western colonialism had its heyday from 1450 to 1900. It began in the Renaissance with the voyages of discovery; the new territories were annexed for their material resources and for the scope they offered to missionary efforts to extend the power of the Church. The last independent non-western territories were parcelled out in 1900. After World War I the growth of nationalism in Africa and Asia started to reverse the process. The establishment of the United Nations (1945), which declared colonial policy a matter of interest to the entire world, helped to spur the relinquishing of former colonies.

Works from ▷ Shakespeare's *The Tempest* to ▷ Joseph Conrad's ▷ *Heart of Darkness* demonstrate the struggle to determine the meaning of colonial power, though there was a strong tradition, founded on the imperialist myth of the Victorian era, of which ▷ Rudyard Kipling and ▷ Rider Haggard were the most famous exponents, that white intervention was made in the interests of the native inhabitants.

▷ Commonwealth literatures.

Bib: Memmi, A., *The Colonizer and the Colonized*; Sard, E., *Orientalism*; Spivack, G. C., *In Other Worlds*.

Commonwealth literatures

One of the most abiding consequences of British imperialism has been the legacy of the English language bequeathed to the former colonies of the Empire. It is a legacy that has at best proved a mixed blessing, but one which makes it possible to speak of a unity running through the literary production of countries as different from one another as Jamaica and New Zealand, as India and Canada. The writing of each of these countries has been strongly influenced by English cultural norms; at the same time the fact that English was the language of the colonizer has always made it a problematic medium for the Commonwealth writer. The St Lucian poet Derek Walcott (b 1930) encapsulates the essence of the problem in a poem entitled 'A Far Cry From Africa' which, while on one level dramatizing his own personal *angst* as a Caribbean person of mixed racial descent, responding to the Mau Mau uprising in Kenya in the 1950s, also addresses the sense of cultural schizophrenia he feels. He asks how, 'divided to the vein', he can 'choose/Between this Africa and the English tongue I love?'

This dilemma is present, to a greater or lesser degree, in virtually all Commonwealth writing in English, and texts from the New Literatures in English (a term which is often preferred to Commonwealth Literatures today, since it imposes fewer political constraints and does not imply that writers are read in the context of their national identification with an ex-colony) are frequently written in hybrid modes that demonstrate some kind of cross-cultural fusion between English and the value-systems of the local culture.

The nature of the local cultures varies considerably, but it is possible to identify two main types: those of the disrupted Third World society and the transplanted New World society. In the former category belong the primary oral ancestral cultures of Africa and the part-scribal, part-oral cultures of the Indian sub-continent, as well as a variety of myth-centred cultures in South-East Asia and Oceania and other parts of the globe. In all of these societies there has been a disruption of age-old traditions during the period of colonialism, and in the post-independence era an urge to reconstruct which has had to come to terms with the fact that it is impossible simply to turn back the clock but which nevertheless insists that the age-old traditions become a cornerstone in the process of rebuilding. Thus, in West Africa, writers like the Nigerians Wole Soyinka (b 1934) and ▷ Chinua Achebe (b 1930) have insisted that the artist has a crucial part to play in the process of reconstruction and have seen the author's role as a modern-day equivalent of that of the *griot*, or oral repository of the tribe's history; they have taken the view that he or she must be a spokesperson for the community, not an individualist in the western Romantic tradition of the artist, and Achebe has particularly stressed the importance of the artist's role as a teacher. In works like *A Dance of the Forests* (Soyinka; 1960) and *Arrow of God* (Achebe; 1964) these two writers, like many of their West African contemporaries, have re-examined the historical past of their societies and, without sentimentalizing it, implied that a dialogue between past and present is a *sine qua non* for progress in the future.

In the latter category, that of the transplanted New World society, belong the cultures of Canada, Australia and New Zealand, where in each case the majority population is of European origin and has had to adapt, transform or subvert Old World cultural forms and genres in order to make them relevant to very different landscapes and social situations. The Canadian writer ▷ Margaret Atwood (b 1939) dramatizes the problem of constructing an identity in a new land in a poem entitled 'Progressive Insanities of a Pioneer' (in *The Animals in That Country*; 1968) in which the settler finds himself 'a point/on a sheet of green paper/proclaiming himself the centre', but finding he has staked his plot 'in the middle of nowhere' is unable even to name the 'unstructured space' of his New World environment. Later, in her novel *Surfacing* (1972), Atwood offers a more positive approach to the same theme in a work which charts the spiritual odyssey of a contemporary Canadian woman who has constructed a false identity for herself as a result of having internalized a set of rationalist values that are particularly identified with the neo-imperialism of American patriarchal and technological society, but seen to be endemic in the modern world. Women and Canadians are represented as suffering from a common victim syndrome and needing to transform themselves by becoming 'creative non-victims'. The protagonist of *Surfacing* manages to achieve regeneration through reverting to an animal-like identity, regressing to a pre-linguistic mode of existence in which she sees herself as establishing contact with the gods of the original Amerindian inhabitants of Canada and the natural world of the country. Similarly, in ▷ Patrick White's *Voss* (1957) the hero's 19th-century exploration of the interior of Australia, an endeavour which is sharply contrasted with the complacent lives of the country's middle-class coastal dwellers, is only complete once he has died and his blood has seeped into the parched soil of the outback. In both novels the metamorphoses of identity and attitudes to the country that lie at the heart of the texts are complemented on a formal level by a complex metaphorical style that suggests linguistic transformation is crucial to the nationalistic quest. ▷ Peter Carey's writing offers a more nightmarish, postmodern vision of the contemporary Australian landscape, particularly in his collection of fragmentary short stories, *Exotic Pleasures* (1981).

Simply to label Canadian and Australasian cultures as 'transplanted' is, of course, finally simplistic, since it involves a perspective which confines itself to the majority population. In each case an indigenous population (Amerindians in Canada; Aborigines in Australia; and Maoris in New Zealand), which has been the victim of various kinds of brutalization and discrimination, continues to make a very important contribution to the national culture and in recent years has been doing so through the medium of English. For these groups the struggle for social justice and cultural survival has been – and is – the crucial cultural issue, as it is for the blacks of South Africa. It permeates the writing of Aborigines like Colin Johnson (b 1938), Kath Walker (b 1920), Kevin Gilbert (b 1933) and Jack Davis (b 1917), as well as the prize-winning novels of the Maori writers Witi Ihimaera (b 1944) and Keri Hulme (b 1947). Generally the criterion for Aboriginality has been self-definition and interestingly many writers who are only a small part Maori or Aborigine, like Keri Hulme and, in Australia, Archie Weller (b 1958), have chosen to identify with this aspect of their ancestry and have generally been accepted by the indigenous group in which they have chosen to locate themselves.

The notion of transplantation also comes to be of less value in the contemporary period, when the original phase of settlement is so far in the past that the sense of displacement has long ceased to operate for most of the country's inhabitants. Nevertheless, new waves of migrants (particularly southern European and South-East Asian immigrants into Australia, and middle European, Italian and East and West Indian immigrants into Canada) continue to experience numerous problems occasioned by transplantation. Yet, for the writers of these countries, the twin pulls of the overseas metropolis (the United States as much as Britain in the case of Canada) and the home country – internationalism and nationalism – have continued to be exercised in a variety of ways, not least through the dominance, until recently, of British and American publishing houses and the problem that local publication, when available, frequently meant a far more restricted readership. Place of publication has, of course, in many cases determined the range and nature of writers' references to local culture and their use of non-standard English linguistic forms.

The writing of one Commonwealth region, the West Indies, is the product of *both* disruption and transplantation; the region can be classified as *both* Third World *and* New World. The population of the contemporary Commonwealth Caribbean is almost entirely made up of descendants of peoples transplanted from the Old World (the original Carib and Arawak Indian inhabitants have been almost completely exterminated).

The most important population group, the descendants of the slaves who were brought from West Africa to work on the West Indian sugar plantations, underwent a very different experience of transplantation from Europeans who went to the Americas or Australasia, since they were forcibly transported and had their culture systematically destroyed in the New World. Family and tribal groups were generally split up on arrival and this led to the emergence of Creolized forms of English as the *lingua franca* through which the slaves communicated with one another and with their masters. So, while the influence of English culture, imposed through the colonial educational curriculum and a range of other institutions has been dominant until recently, the struggle to throw off this culture and replace it by local folk forms has been of a different kind to similar endeavours in other Anglophone New World societies.

Caribbean writing is characterized by a variety of rhetorical devices that take issue with the norms of English literature. Most prominent among these is a range of oral forms that illustrate the complex Creole language situation of the various Caribbean territories – in each case the spoken language is a continuum, with a variety of registers ranging from broad Creole at one extreme to something close to Standard English at the other. In recent years oral forms have come to be dominant in West Indian verse, with performers like the 'dub poets' ▷ Linton Kwesi Johnson (b 1952), Michael Smith (1954–83) and ▷ Jean Binta Breeze (b 1956) completely isolating themselves from the metrical forms of English poetry in favour of a verse which has its roots in the rhythms of reggae music and has parallels with the protesting affirmative ideology of Rastafarianism. Yet there are many other registers in which Caribbean oral poetry can operate, and in the work of poets like Edward Kamau Brathwaite (b 1930), Louise Bennett (b 1919) and Lorna Goodison (b 1947) one can frequently detect a number of different voices figuring in a single short poem to produce a mode of utterance that illustrates the polyphonic nature of Caribbean speech and the cultural diversity of the region.

Different Caribbean writers have taken a range of stands on the question of Caribbean aesthetics and while writers like Brathwaite have stressed the importance of the African legacy in the West Indies, others like Walcott and the Guyanese novelist Wilson Harris (b 1921) have put the emphasis on the mixed multi-cultural heritage of the region. Harris in particular, in a series of complex and hermetic novels, beginning with *Palace of the Peacock* (1960), which break all the rules of European classic ▷ realism, has argued for a cross-cultural vision of consciousness, which he sees as bringing about both psychic and social integration. Walcott take a similar view in arguing for a 'creative schizophrenia' and thus turning the fragmented cultural legacy occasioned by colonialism into a source of strength rather than divisiveness. It is a position which has analogues in each of the Commonwealth literatures.

The essence of contemporary Aboriginal writing has been seen to inhere in *bricolage* (a phrase coined by ▷ Claude Lévi-Strauss), using the bits and pieces of the various 'means at hand' in a flexible way to produce something new, and this model can be applied to the literary production of most of the Commonwealth countries. While all forms of discourse work in this way – traditional ideas of inspiration functioning in a vacuum have been seriously challenged in recent years – this view of how texts are originated has particular relevance for Commonwealth writing and oral forms, where cross-cultural connections abound and where English almost always functions in an ambiguous way. It is especially marked in the work of a complex, postmodernist writer like ▷ Salman Rushdie (b 1947) whose *Midnight's Children* (1981) draws on a vast range of Hindu, Islamic and Western, classical and modern, 'serious' and 'popular' traditions to produce a highly original collage. This takes on the qualities of a 'Bombay Talkie', the eclectic, decorum-confounding dominant film genre of India, a form that is frequently referred to in *Midnight's Children* and which provides a metaphor for the novel's structure. Yet *bricolage* is also a quality of Indian writing in English, such as the novels of ▷ R. K. Narayan (b 1907) and Nayantara Sahgal (b 1927) or the poetry of Nissim Ezekiel (b 1924) and Kamala Das (b 1954), that exhibits less technical virtuosity on the surface. In the work of each of these writers there is a fusion of traditional and Western elements (the novel itself is not an indigenous genre in India) which produces a hybrid mode of expression that exists at the interface of two or more cultures. Contemporary Indian writing in English is a paradox in that it is written in a tongue that is not the dominant spoken language anywhere in India (as a result Indian drama in English hardly exists) and yet it is perhaps the only modern Indian literature able to cross cultural boundaries and give a sense of pan-Indian identity. This situation is, however, only a particular manifestation of the complex cultural predicament of the various Commonwealth literatures in the post-Independence period. Despite their diversity, they have all had to respond to the alien cultural forms imposed during the period of colonialism and to mediate between these forms and modes of expression that have their origins in local or ancestral traditions.

Bib: Atwood, M., *Survival: A Thematic Guide to Canadian Literature*; Baugh, E. (ed.), *Critics on Caribbean Literature*; Goodwin, K., *A History of Australian Literature*; Gérard, A. (ed.), *European-Language Writing in Sub Saharan Africa* (2 vols.); Mukherjee, M., *The Twice-Born Fiction: Themes and Techniques of the Indian Novel in English.*

Communism

Communism may be interpreted in two ways: **1** the older, imprecise sense covering various philosophies of the common ownership of property; **2** the relatively precise interpretation understood by the Marx-Leninist Communist Parties throughout the world.

1 The older philosophies derive especially from the Greek philosopher Plato. His *Republic* proposes that society should be divided into classes according to differences of ability instead of differences of wealth and birth; the state is to provide for the needs of all, and thus to abolish rivalries and inequalities between rich and poor; children are to be educated by the state, and women are to have equal rights, opportunities and training with men. In England, one of the most famous disciples of Plato is Sir Thomas More in his *Utopia* (1516). More's prescriptions are similar to Plato's in many respects, but though he also requires equal opportunity and training for men, he goes against Plato in keeping the monogamous family intact, whereas Plato wanted a community of wives and children to be brought up by the state. Both Plato and More require for their schemes an all-powerful state in the charge of an intellectual aristocracy; what we should call 'enlightened totalitarianism'. With the growth of the power of the state in the 20th century, however, all forms of totalitarianism were regarded with abhorrence by liberal intellectuals, and so arose the 'anti-utopian' class of literature, for example ▷ Aldous Huxley's *Brave New World* (1932) and ▷ George Orwell's *Animal Farm* (1945) and *1984* (1948), vehemently satirizing totalitarian communism.

In practical experiment, the vows of poverty taken by members of orders of monks and friars and the communal ownership of property in such communities may have kept alight for people in general the ideal of the freedom of the spirit attainable by the renunciation of selfish material ambitions and competition. Protestant sectarian beliefs emphasizing the equality of souls led to such an abortive communistic enterprise as that of the Levellers in the Interregnum. In America, a number of experiments were undertaken by immigrant sects such as the Amana community, under the influence of the English socialist Robert Owen and the French socialists Fourier and Cabet, but few of them lasted long.

2 Modern so-called scientific communism, based mainly on ▷ Karl Marx and Lenin, differs from certain forms of modern socialism by affirming the necessity for revolutionary, as distinct from evolutionary, method, to be followed by a period of dictatorship. (Its death-knell may have been sounded by the recent wave of change throughout Eastern Europe.) Lenin attempted to implement the communist programme defined by Marx. Between the Revolution of 1917 and 1924, when he was killed, he tried to guide the newly inaugurated 'dictatorship of the proletariat' in Russia. Not all communism is revolutionary, however: the Italian communist party has adopted the parliamentary route to socialism. In the period 1989–91 communism was largely abandoned by the rapidly fragmenting, former Eastern bloc.

▷ Auden, Wystan Hugh; Spender, Stephen.

Compton-Burnett, Ivy (1884–1969)

Novelist. Her first novel, *Dolores* (1911) is distinguished from all her others by an approach to the method of novel-writing similar to that of the 19th century, in particular that of George Eliot, and a disposition to accept usual conceptions of moral retribution. From *Pastors and Masters* (1925) both the method and the moral vision change radically. The novels are narrated almost wholly through dialogue; the manner derives from Jane Austen, but with even less attempt to present visualized environments. In treating occurrences such as matricide, bigamy, betrayal and incest they show affinities with Greek tragic drama, while the novels of ▷ Samuel Butler are another important influence. The period is always 1890–1914; the setting, a prosperous household of the period; the characters include some who are arrogant to the point of evil, and are able, without retribution, to dominate those who are selfless or weak; the plots are melodramatic but never break up the surface of respectability. The dialogue is epigrammatic and pungent, with the consequence that the novels are all exceptionally concentrated structures. The effect is commonly of sardonic comedy with tragic conclusion, although the comic side tends to dominate.

After 1925 the novels are as follows: *Brothers and Sisters* (1929); *Men and Wives* (1931); *More Women than Men* (1933); *A House and its Head* (1935); *Daughters and Sons* (1937); *A Family and a Fortune* (1939); *Parents and Children* (1941); *Elders and Betters* (1944); *Manservant and Maidservant* (1947); *Two Worlds and Their Ways* (1949); *Darkness and Day* (1951); *The Present and the Past* (1953); *Mother and Son* (1955); *A Father and his Fate* (1957); *A Heritage and its History* (1959); *The Mighty and their Fall* (1961); *A God and His Gifts* (1963); *The Last and the First* (1971). Few distinguished novelists have shown such uniformity of treatment and lack of development throughout their career. Probably *A House and its Head* and *A Family and a Fortune* are her two outstanding achievements.
Bib: Hansford Johnson, P., *Ivy Compton-Burnett*; Liddell, R., *The Novels of Ivy Compton-Burnett*; Spurling, H., *Ivy When Young* and *Secrets of a Woman's Heart*.

Condensation
This term is used by ▷ Freud in *The Interpretation of Dreams* (1900) to describe the compression and selection that takes place during the process of dreaming. When subjected to analysis the details of the dream can be shown to relate to a series of deeper, more extensive psychic connections. Freud distinguishes between the 'manifest content' of the dream, which is what is remembered, and the 'latent content' which can only be arrived at retrospectively through the analytical business of interpretation. Interpretation seeks to reverse the process of condensation and to investigate 'the relation between the manifest content of dreams and the latent dream-thoughts' and to trace out 'the processes by which the latter have been changed into the former' (*The Interpretation of Dreams*). The term has also become part of the language of critical theory. Applied to a literary text it was first used to afford a partial explanation of the energies which bring the text into existence, or to give an account of the unconscious motivations of represented 'characters'. More recently, the analogy between the interpretation of dreams and of texts has been used to suggest the impossibility of arriving at an original 'core' of meaning, prior to ▷ displacement or condensation. Freud speaks of the dream's 'navel' – that knotted point of enigma which indicates that there is always something unresolved, unanalysed.

▷ Psychoanalytical criticism.

Conrad, Joseph (1857–1924)
Novelist. His name in full was Józef Teodor Konrad Korzeniowski. He knew hardly any English when he was 20; yet before he was 40 he had completed his first English novel, *Almayer's Folly* (1895), and ten years later he had published one of the masterpieces of the novel in Engish: ▷ *Nostromo* (1904). The background to Conrad as a novelist is complicated and important for understanding the richness of his art. 1 Early life. His father was a Polish patriot and man of letters, exiled from the Polish Ukraine by the Russian government, which then ruled it, for his political activity. His mother died when he was seven, and his father when he was 11, and his uncle subsequently became the main family influence in his life. 2 Life at sea. From the tales of sea life (in translation) by the English writer Captain Marryat, the American Fenimore Cooper, and the Frenchman Victor Hugo, he became fascinated by the sea and joined the crew of a French ship in 1874, and of an English one in 1878. By 1884 he was a British subject and had qualified as a master (ship's captain). In his voyages Conrad had visited the Mediterranean, South America, the Far East, and Central Africa. 3 Writing life. He began writing in about 1886 with at least as good an acquaintance with French language and literature as English. He brought to the English novel an admiration for the French ▷ realists Flaubert and Maupassant. He also had a knowledge of many peoples, and a profound feeling of the contrast between the tightly enclosed communities of ships' crews and the loose egocentric individualism characterizing land societies. In addition, he knew, from his childhood experience in Russian Poland and Russia itself, the tragic impingement of political pressures on personal life, in a way that was unusual in the West until after the outbreak of World War I in 1914. In his preoccupation with the exploration of moral issues he was in the English tradition, as F. R. Leavis acknowledges by including Conrad in his *Great Tradition*.

His major work is represented by the novels ▷ *Lord Jim* (1900), ▷ *Nostromo*, ▷ *The Secret*

Agent (1907) and *Under Western Eyes* (1911) and the novellas *The Nigger of the Narcissus* (1898); *Youth* (1902); ▷ *Heart of Darkness* (1902); *Typhoon* (1903) and *The Shadow Line* (1917). *Lord Jim* and *The Nigger of the Narcissus* are concerned with honour, courage and solidarity, ideals for which the merchant service provided a framework. *The Secret Agent* and *Under Western Eyes* deal with political extremism, the contrast between eastern and western Europe, and human folly, cruelty, fear and betrayal. *Nostromo*, set in an imaginary South American state, shares some of the themes of the other work, but is notable for its sense of history and the power of economic forces. *Heart of Darkness* is famous for its ambiguous and resonant portrayal of evil. Conrad's earlier novels, *Almayer's Folly* and *An Outcast of the Islands* (1896) have Far Eastern settings, and a less developed prose style. His later work includes *Chance* (1914), the first to bring him a big public; *Victory* (1915); *The Arrow of Gold* (1919); *The Rescue* (1920); *The Rover* (1932); and *Suspense*, which he was working on when he died. Conrad is one of the most important modern English novelists, both for his concerns and for his techniques. He addressed issues which have come to seem central to the 20th-century mind: the problem of identity; the terror of the unknown within and without; the difficulty of finding a secure moral base; political violence and economic oppression; isolation and existential dread. His technical innovations were particularly in the use of narrators, the disruption of narrative chronology and the employment of a powerful ▷ irony of tone.

His other works are: a number of volumes of short stories and essays, including *Tales of Unrest* (1898) and *Notes on Life and Letters* (1921). *The Mirror of the Sea* (1906) and *A Personal Record* (1912) are autobiographical. Conrad co-operated with ▷ Ford Madox Ford in the writing of two novels: *The Inheritors* (1901) and *Romance* (1903). The first three volumes of his *Collected Letters* were published in 1983, 1986 and 1988.

Bib: Baines, J., *Joseph Conrad: A Critical Biography*; Berthoud, J., *Joseph Conrad: the Major Phase*; Guerard, A. J., *Conrad the Novelist*; Najder, Z., *Joseph Conrad: A Chronicle*; Watt, I., *Conrad in the Nineteenth Century*; Hewitt, D., *Conrad: A Reassessment*.

Consciousness

In its most general sense consciousness is synonymous with 'awareness'. In a more specifically ▷ Freudian context it is associated with the individual's perception of reality. For Freud, of course, the impression which an individual has of his or her experience is partial, since awareness is controlled by the processes of the unconscious, which are never recognized in their true form. More recently 'consciousness' has been associated with the ▷ Enlightenment view of individualism, in which the individual is conceived of as being distinct from society, and is also held to be the centre and origin of meaning. Following from this, what distinguishes humanity is its alleged capacity for autonomy, and hence freedom of action. The ▷ Romantic equivalent of this philosophical position is that literature is the expression of the pre-existent 'self' of the writer, and that the greatest literature is that which manifests the writer's consciousness most fully. These views of consciousness should further be distinguished from the ▷ Marxist version, in which the self is 'produced' through 'material practices', by means of which social relations are generated. Theories of consciousness affect notions of the relationship between writer and reader, and it is in working out such relationships that the concept of 'consciousness' is important in current literary critical debate.

Contradiction

Used in literary criticism to identify the incoherences in a literary text. Derived from Hegel, Engels and ▷ Marx, contradiction, as applied to literature, implies that artistic representation is not the product of a unifying aesthetic impulse. Contradiction describes patterns of dominance and subordination and thus, in literary terms, points towards divisions within the work which challenge notions of aesthetic coherence.

Conversation poem

A reflective poem, originally in blank verse, in which the poet meditates aloud, ostensibly talking to a friend. It adopts a more intimate, introspective tone than its predecessor, the 18th-century verse epistle. The term is especially associated with Samuel Taylor Coleridge, who first used it. His *Eolian Harp* (1795), *This Lime-Tree Bower* (1800), *The Nightingale* (1798) and *Frost at Midnight* (1798) are often termed 'conversation poems'. Twentieth-century poets who have modified the form for their own purposes include ▷ W. H. Auden.

Cookson, Catherine (b 1906)

Romantic novelist. Cookson is one of the ▷ best-selling writers currently working in Britain, whose stories have much in common with classic Mills and Boon plots but which also deploy historical motifs and display richer characterization. Her native Northumberland, in which most of her novels are set, has become immortalized as 'Cookson Country' by the local tourist board, which at least is testament to the rich evocations of landscape and regional feeling which her primarily romantic fiction offers.

Her wide range of novels, all written since she was in her early forties, include: *Fanny McBride* (1977); *Pure as the Lily* (1978); *The Mallen Novels* (1979); *Tilly Trotter* (1980) and *Marriage and Mary Ann* (1984).
Bib: Radford, J. (ed.), *The Progress of Romance: The Politics of Popular Fiction*; Radway, J., *Reading the Romance*.

Cooper, William (b 1910)
Pen name of H. S. Hoff, novelist. Having already published four novels under his real name, Cooper came to prominence in 1950 with *Scenes from Provincial Life*, the story of an unconventional and sceptical schoolteacher living in a Midlands town around the outbreak of World War II. In reacting against the experimental tradition of the ▷ Bloomsbury Group and of ▷ modernism, Cooper's novel initiated the 1950s school of dissentient ▷ realism, which included such writers as ▷ John Braine, ▷ David Storey, ▷ Stan Barstow and ▷ John Wain. *Scenes from Metropolitan Life* (written in the 1950s but not published for legal reasons until 1982) and *Scenes from Married Life* (1961) complete a trilogy. Other novels include: *You Want the Right Frame of Reference* (1971), *Love on the Coast* (1973) and *Scenes from Later Life* (1983).

Coppard, A. E. (1878–1957)
Writer of short stories. He was largely self-educated, and began serving in a shop at the age of nine. Later he began writing while working as an accountant, and his literary interests were nourished when he obtained a post at Oxford where he met and made friends with the intelligentsia. The best of his stories are chiefly in the earlier volumes: *Adam and Eve and Pinch Me* (1921); *Clorinda Walks in Heaven* (1922); *Fishmonger's Fiddle* (1925); and *The Field of Mustard* (1926). Later volumes include: *Pink Furniture* (1930); *Tapster's Tapestry* (1938); *You Never Know Do You?* (1939); and *The Dark-Eyed Lady* (1947). He also wrote poems: *Collected Poems* (1928); *Easter Day* (1931); and *Cherry Ripe* (1935); and an autobiography, *It's Me, O Lord* (1957).

Coppard had a remarkably acute ear for the spoken word, and his best tales have the freshness and simplicity of aural folk-tales. Although his subject matter was often more sophisticated than this suggests, many of his finest stories are about the life of the countryside. He was influenced by ▷ Thomas Hardy's short stories, and he often shows a stoically resigned attitude to human destiny which is similar to Hardy's outlook, but he combined this with a remarkable talent for sharp comedy, again reminiscent of peasant folk-tales.

Copyright, The law of
The right of writers, artists and musicians to refuse reproduction of their works. The right is now established law in every civilized country. The first copyright law in England was passed under Queen Anne in 1709. Before this, it was possible for publishers to publish books without the author's permission, and without allowing him or her any profits from sale, a practice very common during the lifetime of ▷ Shakespeare. Until 1909, the laws of the United States did not adequately safeguard British authors against having their works 'pirated' there, *ie* published without their permission and without giving them suitable financial return.

Cornford, Frances (1886–1960)
Poet. Although Frances Cornford's poetic career spans the period of high ▷ modernism, she was essentially a ▷ Georgian poet, producing accessible, pastoral lyrics which often celebrate the life of and landscape around Cambridge, where she lived. She was a friend of many of the Georgians, especially ▷ Rubert Brooke, as well as being the mother of 1930s poet John Cornford and the grand-daughter of Charles Darwin. Her works include: *Poems* (1910); *Autumn Midnight* (1923); *Travelling Home* (1948); *Collected Poems* (1954); *On a Calm Shore* (1960).
Bib: Anderson, A., *A Bibliography of the Writings of Frances Cornford*; Delaney, P., *The Neo-Pagans*.

***Countess Kathleen, The* (1892)**
A verse play by ▷ W. B. Yeats. Its theme is a woman who sells her soul to the devil in order to save the poor from starvation. It marks the beginning of Yeats's career as a poetic dramatist, and was one of the plays used by the Irish Literary Theatre as a starting-point.

▷ Abbey Theatre.

Couplet
A pair of rhymed lines of verse of equal length. The commonest form is the so-called

heroic couplet of 10 syllables and five stressed in each line. It was first used in Chaucer's *Legend of Good Women*.

A thousand timës have I herd men telle
That ther is joye in heven, and peyne in
helle . . .

The heroic couplet had its most prolific period between 1660 and 1790. Blank verse was a derivative of the couplet.

The 8-syllable (octosyllabic) couplet gives a lighter, less dignified rhythm. It is less common after 1600 than before, but a notable later user of it is Jonathan Swift (*eg On the Death of Dr Swift*). Keats used it for 'The Eve of St Mark' (1819), and ▷ W. H. Auden for his *New Year Letter* (1941).

Couzyn, Jeni (b 1942)
Poet. Couzyn was born and educated in South Africa, which she left in 1965, and has since become a Canadian citizen, although she lives in Britain. Her volumes of verse include: *Flying* (1970); *Christmas in Africa* (1975); *Life By Drowning: Selected Poems* (1985). Couzyn edited the important 1985 ▷ anthology, *The Bloodaxe Book of Contemporary Women Poets*, and she also writes for children.

Covent Garden Theatres
In 1732 Edward Shepherd (1670–1747) planned the first Covent Garden Theatre, or Theatre Royal, on the site of the present Royal Opera House, to which the actor-manager John Rich transferred from Lincoln's Inn Fields. The present theatre opened in 1858. Although it is now famous for its internationally distinguished productions of opera it is not often realized that these are funded by the state. Before 1948 Covent Garden was a Mecca *palais de danse* with a two-month opera season. State funding for opera, with massively subsidized seats, was devised by J. M. Keynes as a means of raising the tone of British culture, and, as he hoped, of diffusing it more widely.

Coward, Sir Noël (1899–1973)
British stage and film actor, dramatist and director. He began his theatrical career at the age of 12 acting in a fantasy play called *The Goldfish*. As a dramatist he gained some notoriety with his early works, *The Young Idea* (1923), *The Vortex* (1924), *Fallen Angels* (1925) and *Sirocco* (1927), which was greeted with a riot. However his partnership with the promoter and theatre manager C. B. Cochran proved his ability to work creatively and successfully within the commercial theatre. His reputation rests mainly on the six comedies he wrote between 1923 and 1942: *Fallen Angels* (1925); *Hay Fever* (1925); *Bitter Sweet* (1929); *Private Lives* (1930); *Design for Living* (1932) and *Present Laughter* (1942).
Bib: Gray, F., *Noël Coward*; Kiernan, R. F., *Noël Coward*; Larh, J., *Coward the Playwright*.

Craig, Edward Gordon (1872–1966)
Son of actress Ellen Terry and designer E. W. Godwin, and one of the most influential of early 20th-century stage designers. He began his theatrical career working with Henry Irving at the Lyceum, though disillusionment with English theatre led him to spend much of his time on the continent. Most of his highly innovative designs were never actually put into practice, but of those that were his most famous were for a production of *Hamlet* at the Moscow Art Theatre, in 1912, and ▷ Ibsen's *The Pretenders* at the Royal Danish Theatre, Copenhagen, in 1926. His influential theories on the crucial role of the theatre designer and the importance of expressive, poetic movement are explored in his books, *The Art of the Theatre* (1905); *On the Art of the Theatre* (1911); *Towards a New Theatre* (1907); *The Marionette* (1918); *The Theatre Advancing* (1921); *Books and Theatres* (1925).
Bib: Craig, E., *Gordon Craig*; Innes, C., *Edward Gordon Craig*.

Critique
A term used in critical theory. Traditional conceptions of 'criticism' have privileged the acts of judgement and comparison but have often anchored them in the unspecified sensitivity of the reader. Criticism presupposes a direct relationship between reader and literary text; the reader responds to the stimulus of particular verbal forms which are evaluated according to their appeal to a universal human condition. The practice of 'critique', in a literary context, however, concerns itself not just with producing readings of primary texts and accounting for those social, cultural, or psychological motivations which are responsible for its appearance in a particular form, but also with appraising critical readings of those texts. Critique addresses itself to questions of why individual texts should be accorded importance at particular historical moments, and implicates 'criticism' in its more traditional guise as a process whereby meanings are constructed, as opposed to being passively discovered.

Cruelty, Theatre of

▷ Theatre of Cruelty.

Cuchulain

In Irish myth the hero of a cycle of prose legends called the Cuchulain or Ulster cycle (9th–13th centuries AD). In English, he is chiefly known by the poems and plays about him by ▷ W. B. Yeats. Yeats's work issued from his support of Irish nationalism, which revived interest in the Irish myths, and led to the publication of English versions of them.

▷ Irish literature in English.

Bib: Hull, E., *The Cuchullin Saga*.

Culler, Jonathan (b 1944)

Academic and critic whose works have done much to introduce English-speaking audiences to the works of ▷ structuralist and ▷ post-structuralist critics. His major studies include *Structuralist Poetics* (1975), *The Pursuit of Signs* (1981) and *On Deconstruction* (1983). He is Professor of English and Comparative Literature at Cornell University.

Cultural materialism

The Foreword to Jonathan Dollimore and Alan Sinfield's collection of essays *Political Shakespeare* (1985) acts as a manifesto for this new radical ▷ Marxist criticism. The authors themselves trace the origins of the theory to general dissatisfaction in the British academic world with the traditional essentialist ▷ humanism of existing criticism and the rise of numerous approaches (▷ Feminism, ▷ Structuralism, ▷ Psychoanalytic criticism) which challenged this premise. Apart from a debt to the political commitment to change, derived from Marxism, cultural materialism also draws upon ▷ Raymond Williams's cultural analysis which, as Dollimore and Sinfield put it, 'seeks to describe the whole system of significations by which a society or a section of it understands itself and its relations with the world'. Thus, cultural materialism rejects any notion of 'high culture', and sets material values in the place of the idealism of conventional criticism, looking instead, at texts in history. Cultural materialism also has links with ▷ new historicism (particularly the work of Stephen Greenblatt) in its emphasis upon the nature of subjectivity and the decentring of man, and with feminism, where the exploration of the gendered human subject is an overlapping interest.

▷ Post-structuralism; Marx, Karl; Shakespeare, William.

D

Dada
Artistic and literary movement. It arose in two distinct places at about the same time. One group was formed in Zurich in 1916 by three refugees, Tristan Tzara (1887–1968), Hans Arp (1887–1966) and Hugo Ball (1886–1927); another group was formed in New York in the years 1916–19 by Marcel Duchamp (1887–1968), Man Ray (1890–1976) and Francis Picabia (1879–1953). By 1920, both groups had united and made their headquarters in Paris where their journal was *Littérature* (1919–21). The Dada emphasis was on instinctual expression free from constraints and the consequent cultivation of destructiveness, randomness and incoherence; indeed, the very name 'Dada' (= hobbby horse) was a random selection from the dictionary. The movement lasted until the early 1920s. A number of its adherents joined the ▷ Surrealists, a movement which in part evolved out of Dada.

Daedalus
In Greek myth, an artist of wonderful powers. He made wings for himself and his son Icarus, and flew from Crete to Sicily to escape the wrath of King Minos, for whom he had built the labyrinth. The fact that he was an artist explains the use of a form of the name by ▷ James Joyce – Dedalus – in ▷ *Portrait of the Artist as a Young Man*, and ▷ *Ulysses*.

***Daisy Miller* (1879)**
A story by ▷ Henry James. It concerns the visit of an American girl to Europe, and is one of the stories in which James contrasts American freshness of impulse, moral integrity, and naïvety with the complexity and deviousness of the European mentality. The girl's innocence and candour is misinterpreted as moral turpitude by the Americans who are long settled in Europe, including the young man who acts as focal character for the narrative.

Dane, Clemence (1887–1965)
Playwright and novelist. Clemence Dane is the pseudonym of Winifred Ashton, a highly prolific playwright and novelist whose work was extremely successful in her lifetime, but who has to some extent been neglected by critical history. Her career was a long one – Dane published her first novel (which deals with power and lesbianism in a girls' public school), *Regiment of Women*, in 1917, and continued writing until her death – some of her later works were dramas for BBC television. She also wrote essays, and was awarded the CBE in 1953. Her plays include: *A Bill of Divorcement* (1921); *Naboth's Vineyard* (1925); *Manners* (1927); *The Saviours* (1942); and *Call Home the Heart* (1947). Her novels include *Enter Sir John* (1930); *The Moon is Feminine* (1938); and *He Brings Great News* (1939).

Daryush, Elizabeth (1887–1977)
Poet. Daryush was the daughter of poet ▷ Robert Seymour Bridges, and her writing is a continuation and expansion of his experiments in syllabic metre. She lived for some time in Persia, and syllabically translated some Persian poetry. Publications include: Daryush's own selection of her work, *Selected Poems, Verses I–VI* (1972) and the more recent *Collected Poems* (1976).

Davidson, John (1857–1909)
Poet. Best remembered for his ▷ ballads and songs, in particular *Thirty Bob a Week*, he also wrote plays, novels and philosophical works. A friend of ▷ W. B. Yeats and fellow member of the Rhymer's Club, a group of ▷ Nineties poets which met to read their poetry from 1890–94 at the ▷ Cheshire Cheese in Fleet Street. Davidson was also influenced by ▷ Nietzsche in his passionate atheism, exemplified by *God and Mammon* (1907), a trilogy of which only two parts were completed when Davidson committed suicide. He contributed to ▷ *The Yellow Book*, and was an important figure in the development of the 20th-century Scottish Renaissance (▷ Scottish literature).
Bib: Turnbull, A. (ed.), *Poems*; Lindsay, M. (ed.), *John Davidson: A Selection of his Poems* (Preface by ▷ T. S. Eliot).

Davie, Donald (b 1922)
Poet and literary critic. Donald Davie's rational, cool and technically pure poetry perhaps epitomizes the verse of the ▷ Movement; his critical work of 1952, *Purity of Diction in English Verse* was the Movement's bible. Davie was born in Barnsley, a place which recurs gloomily throughout his work, and has taught at universities in Britain and the U.S.A. His many publications include: *Brides of Reason* (1955); *The Forests of Lithuania* (1959); *Events and Wisdoms 1957–1963*; *Collected Poems 1950–70* (1972); *In the Stopping Train* (1977); *Under Briggflatts* (1989).

Davis, Jack (b 1917)
▷ Commonwealth literatures.

Day-Lewis, Cecil (1904–72)
Poet and critic. Day-Lewis was one of the small group of poets (with ▷ W. H. Auden and ▷ Stephen Spender) which made a considerable impact in the 1930s under the encouragement of ▷ T. S. Eliot and the political influence of ▷ Marx. His early poetry was often propagandistic, and, like many of his contemporaries, he wrote in support of the Republican cause in the Spanish Civil War (▷ Spanish influence on English literature), using with effect the ▷ sprung rhythm and alliteration of ▷ Gerard Manley Hopkins. World War II broke up the group and tempered Day-Lewis's political aims. His later work shows the versatility which caused him to be chosen as ▷ Poet Laureate in 1968. Works include *Collected Poems* (1954; reprinted 1970) and *Poems 1925–72* (ed. Parsons). Critical essays include *A Hope for Poetry* (1934), *The Poetic Image* (1946), *The Lyric Impulse* (1965). He also translated the poetry of Virgil and wrote ▷ detective fiction under the pen-name Nicholas Blake.

De Beauvoir, Simone (1908–86)
French novelist and one of the founding 'mothers' of 20th-century ▷ feminism, long associated with ▷ Sartre and the ▷ existentialist movement, whose views she promoted in a series of novels: *L'Invitée* (1943); *Le Sang des autres* (1944); *Les Mandarins* (1954). Her uncensored *Letters to Sartre* (1991) reveal the intensity and passion of their relationship. A play, *Les Bouches inutiles* was performed in 1945. She contributed greatly to the genre of autobiography (*Mémoires d'une jeune fille rangée* (1958); *La Force de l'âge* (1960); *La Force des choses* (1965); *Tout compte fait* (1974) (all translated). Her two-volume study of femininity and the condition of women, *The Second Sex* (*Le Deuxième sexe* 1949) is one of the most important feminist texts of this century, and her influence on subsequent thinkers is now eclipsing Sartre's. Contemporary feminist writers who have taken up her ideas in particular include Kate Millett (in *Sexual Politics*, 1970), ▷ Germaine Greer, Mary Ellman (in *Thinking About Women*, 1968) and Betty Friedan (*The Feminine Mystique*, 1963).
Bib: Moi, T., *Sexual/Textual Politics*; Moi, T., *French Feminist Thought: A Reader*.

Deconstruction
A concept used in critical theory. It has a long philosophical pedigree, but is usually associated with the work of the French philosopher ▷ Jacques Derrida. It is a strategy applied to writing generally, and to literature in particular, whereby systems of thought and concepts are dismantled in such a way as to expose the divisions which lie at the heart of meaning itself. If interpretation is a process designed to reduce a text to some sort of 'order', deconstruction seeks to undermine the basis upon which that order rests. Deconstruction challenges the notion that all forms of mental and linguistic activity are generated from within an autonomous 'centre', advancing the more disturbing proposition that such centres are themselves to be grasped textually only as rhetorical constructions.

▷ De Man, Paul; Difference; Post-structuralism; Grammatology.
Bib: Derrida., J., *Speech and Phenomena*; *Writing and Difference; Of Grammatology*; *Positions*; Norris, C., *Deconstruction: Theory and Practice*; Descombes, V., *Modern French Philosophy*.

Dedalus, Stephen
Principal character in ▷ James Joyce's novel ▷ *A Portrait of the Artist as a Young Man*; he is also a main character in Joyce's ▷ *Ulysses*. The surname derives from the mythical artist of ancient Greece, ▷ Daedalus.

Defamiliarization
In the context of critical theory this term has its origins in Russian ▷ Formalism and in the desire to distinguish between the Aristotelian view of writing as an image of reality and imaginative literature as a form of writing which deploys images rhetorically. The Russian term 'ostranenie' means literally, 'making strange', rendering unfamiliar that which has hitherto been regarded as familiar. It draws attention to the fact that 'reality' is never depicted in literature in an unprocessed, or unmediated way. Indeed, what literature exposes is the formal means whereby what is commonly taken to be reality itself is, in fact, a construction. In many ways, 'defamiliarization' is a form of ▷ deconstruction, although its objective is to replace one set of epistemological principles (those upon which ▷ capitalism as a particular kind of social formation rests), with other ways of organizing reality. By contrast, deconstruction has the effect of undermining all assumptions and certainties about what we know.

▷ Alienation effect; Brecht.

De la Mare, Walter (1873–1956)
Poet, novelist, writer of short stories. He was born in Kent, and educated at St Paul's Cathedral Choir School. From 1890 to 1908 he was a clerk in the offices of the Anglo-American Oil Company; he was then given a government ('Civil List') pension to enable him to devote himself to writing. Many of his poems and his stories were addressed to children. Books of verse of this sort were: *Songs of Childhood* (1902); *A Child's Day* (1912); *Peacock Pie* (1913). ▷ Children's stories: *The Three Mulla-mulgars* (1910); *The Riddle* (1923); *The Magic Jacket* (1943); *The Dutch Cheese* (1946). He had conspicuous talent for retelling traditional ▷ fairy-tales: *Told Again* (1927); and compiled two unusual anthologies: *Come Hither* (for children, 1923) and *Love* (for adults, 1943). His most remarkable prose fiction for adults is probably *On the Edge* (stories, 1926) and *Memoirs of a Midget* (novel, 1921). His books of verse for adults include: *The Listeners* (1912); *The Veil* (1921); *Memory and other poems* (1938); *The Burning-glass and other poems* (1945); *The Traveller* (1946); *Inward Companion* (1950); *Winged Chariot* (1951); *O Lovely England and other poems* (1953); *Collected Poems* (1979). See also ▷ W. H. Auden's collection, *A Choice of De la Mare's Verse* (1963).

His poems are conservative in technique, with the melody and delicacy of diction characteristic of the poetry of the late 19th and early 20th century, but are unusual in the quiet intensity with which they express evanescent, elusive and mysterious experience. His stories have a singular quietness of tone and are written in an unassuming style, conveying material which is on the borderline of conscious experience. De la Mare's unusual combination of intensity and innocence makes the borderline between his work for children and for adults an almost imperceptible one.
Bib: Mégroz, R. L., *De la Mare: A Biographical and Critical Study*; Reid, Forrest, *De la Mare: A Critical Study*.

Delaney, Shelagh (b 1939)
One of few female dramatists to make an impact during the 1950s. Her best-known play, *A Taste of Honey* (first performed in 1958), was written when she was only 17 and is about a young woman's relationship with her mother, negro lover and a homosexual art student. It was performed by ▷ Joan Littlewood's Theatre Workshop company, transferred to the West End, and was later filmed. Other plays include: *The Lion in Love* (1960); *The House That Jack Built* (1978); and for radio: *So Does the Nightingale* (1980); *Don't Worry About Matilda* (1983).

De Man, Paul (1919–83)
Arguably the most rigorous of the so-called Yale School of criticism, and by the time of his death had become the foremost exponent in the U.S.A. of Derridian deconstruction (▷ Jacques Derrida) in its most unsettling of forms. As Sterling Professor of Comparative Literature at Yale, he was responsible for the first major application of ▷ deconstruction to a variety of primary and critical texts, for example in his book *Blindness and Insight* (1971). His approach was extended in books such as *Allegories of Reading* (1979) and *The Rhetoric of Romanticism* (1984). De Man reflected on the whole of this process, and upon the resistance to certain sorts of theoretical enquiry in a collection of essays, *The Resistance to Theory* published posthumously in 1986. His reputation has suffered following the rediscovery of collaborationist pieces of journalism produced by de Man in the war years.
▷ Rhetoric.

Dennis, Nigel (b 1912)
Novelist. He is best known for *Cards of Identity* (1955), a satirical fantasy about the nature of individual and cultural identity, influenced by the ▷ existentialism of ▷ Jean-Paul Sartre. It reflects the atmosphere of British life in the early 1950s, but combines this with a self-referential concern with the nature of fiction. His other novels are: *Boys and Girls Come Out to Play* (1949); *A House in Order* (1966).

Depression, The
A 'depression' signifies the slowing of economic activity for a considerable period of time. High unemployment and poverty usually accompany economic depression. The most significant such period in Britain was the 1930s, which is currently called 'The Depression'. It gave rise to several novels documenting the plight of the working classes, the best known being Walter Greenwood's *Love on the Dole* (1933).

Derrida, Jacques (b 1930)
Although he is primarily a philosopher, the influence of Derrida's work on the study of literature has been immense. He is the originator of a mode of reading known as ▷ 'deconstruction', the major strand in what is now regarded as the general area of ▷ post-structuralism. His main works are *Speech and*

Phenomena (trans. 1973), *Of Grammatology* (trans. 1974), and *Writing and Difference* (trans. 1978). For Derrida, as for ▷ Saussure, language is composed of differences, that is, a series of non-identical elements which combine with each other to produce linguistic ▷ signs which are accorded meaning. Traditionally, this process is anchored to an organizing principle, a centre, but Derrida questions this concept and rejects the idea of a 'presence' in which authority resides, thereby lifting all restrictions upon the 'play' of differences. But, in addition to the idea that language is composed of 'differences', Derrida also deploys the term '*différance*' to indicate the continual postponement of 'presence' which is located in all signifiers (▷ sign). Thus, signs are produced through a relatively free play of linguistic elements (difference), but what they signify can never be fully present since meaning is constantly 'deferred' (*différance*). Derrida's influence has been greatest in the U.S.A. where after his visit to Johns Hopkins and his teaching at Yale, deconstruction has become the successor to American new criticism.

▷ Grammatology; De Man, Paul; Difference.

Desai, Anita (b 1937)
Indian novelist and short-story writer. Her novels offer a satirical view of social change in India since Independence, with a powerful sense of waste, limitation, self-deception and failure. *Where Shall We Go This Summer* (1975) and *Clear Light of Day* (1980) are particularly concerned with the problems of Indian women to whom westernization offers an apparent freedom. She uses visual detail and an impressionistic style in an attempt to convey a sense of the meaning underlying everyday behaviour and objects. Her other novels include: *Cry the Peacock* (1963); *Voices in the City* (1965); *Bye-Bye Blackbird* (1971); *Fire on the Mountain* (1977); and *In Custody* (1984). Story collection: *Games at Twilight* (1978). She has also written works for children, including *The Village by the Sea* (1982).

▷ Commonwealth literatures.

Detective fiction
This branch of literature is usually easy to distinguish from the much wider literature of crime and retribution in drama and in the novel. Unlike the latter, detective fiction seldom relies on the presentation of deep emotions or on subtle and profound character creation. Character, emotion, psychological analysis of states of mind, social reflections, will all be present as flavouring, and may even be conspicuous, but the indispensable elements are always a mysterious – but not necessarily horrible – crime, and a detective, who is commonly not a professional policeman, but who has highly developed powers of scientific deduction. It is essential that the surface details should be convincing, and that the author should keep no clues from the reader, who may thus have the satisfaction of competing with the detective at his game. In the detective story proper, as opposed to the crime novel, the criminal's identity is not revealed until the end, and provides the focus of attention. Precursors of the form are Wilkie Collins's novel *The Moonstone* (1868) and the stories of the American writer Edgar Allan Poe (1809–49), featuring the French detective Dupin. But the widespread popularity of detective fiction began with ▷ Arthur Conan Doyle's Sherlock Holmes stories, of which the first was *A Study in Scarlet* (1887). The staggering perspicuity of the amateur detective from Baker Street, and his superiority to the police and to his companion and foil, Dr Watson, won him a world-wide audience. Another early exponent of the detective short story was ▷ G. K. Chesterton, whose detective, Father Brown, is a modest and intuitive Roman Catholic priest who first appeared in *The Innocence of Father Brown* (1911). From the time of ▷ E. C. Bentley's classic work *Trent's Last Case* (1912) the full-length novel became the most popular form. After Conan Doyle, the dominant figure of detective fiction is ▷ Dorothy L. Sayers, whose aristocratic amateur detective, Lord Peter Wimsey, appears in works such as *Murder Must Advertise* (1933) and *The Nine Tailors* (1934); she also published a history of crime fiction in 1928 and wrote critical essays on the genre. Other prominent authors of detective fiction include ▷ Agatha Christie (the creator of Hercule Poirot and Miss Marple), Michael Innes (pseudonym of the novelist and critic J. I. M. Stewart), H. C. Bailey, ▷ P. D. James and H. R. F. Keating. The American school of tough detective fiction is exemplified by Raymond Chandler (1888–1959) and Dashiell Hammett (1894–1961).

▷ Allingham, Margery; Marsh, Ngaio.

Determination
A Marxist term used in critical theory, it is often confused with 'determinism' whereby a particular action or event is wholly caused by some external agency, and must therefore be assumed to be inevitable. In 'determination',

the traditional fatalistic implications of the term 'determinism' are softened considerably, to draw attention to those constraints and pressures which mould human action. Thus a distinction is to be made between a tendency which attributes all movement in the social formation to economic factors, and one which seeks to account structurally for the patterns of dominance and subordination (▷ contradictions) operating at any one moment in history. The concept of determination can also be used to ask questions about particular literary ▷ genres and their historical significance, as well as helping to account for particular elements of the rhetorical structures of texts. Determination helps in seeing texts as part of a larger social context rather than as isolated verbal constructs, and it helps also to raise a number of questions concerning the inter-relationship between literature and the ways in which it represents 'reality'.

Diachronic
▷ Synchronic.

Dialectic
Originally used to refer to the nature of logical argument, but in the 19th century this term underwent something of a re-evaluation, and came to be associated with the work of the German philosophers ▷ Kant and Hegel. 'Dialectic' referred to the process whereby the 'idea' (*thesis*) was self-divided, and its internal oppositions (*antithesis*) were resolved in a *synthesis* which opened the way to a higher truth. In ▷ Marxist thinking 'dialectic' refers to the ▷ contradictions present in any one phenomenon, and to their resolution through conflict. It is the nature of that opposition and that conflict which determines movement and change.

Diaries
As a form of literature in English, diaries begin to be significant in the 17th century. The spirit of criticism from the ▷ Renaissance and the stress on the individual conscience from the ▷ Reformation combined with the political and social turbulence of the 17th century to awaken people to a new awareness of personal experience and its possible interest for general readers. The private nature of the diary form also led to many women taking up this form of writing. Thus the art of the diary arose with the art of ▷ biography and ▷ autobiography. Diaries may first be divided into the two classes of those clearly meant to be strictly private and those written more or less with an eye to eventual publication. A further division may be made between those which are interesting chiefly as a record of the time in which the writer lived and those which are mainly a record of his personality.

The best known of the English diaries is that of Samuel Pepys (1633–1703), which was both purely private (written in code) and entirely unselfconscious, as well as an excellent record of the time. His contemporary, John Evelyn (1620–1706), is less famous partly because his diary is a more studied, self-conscious work. Jonathan Swift's *Journal to Stella* (covering the years 1710–13) is a personal revelation but unusual in that it was addressed to the woman Swift loved. The diary of the Quaker, George Fox (1624–91), is a record of his spiritual experience for the education of his followers. In the 18th and early 19th century the most famous is that of the novelist Fanny Burney (Madame D'Arblay, 1752–1840), considered as a record of the time ingenuously imbued with her own personality. The diary of the great religious reformer, John Wesley (1703–91), is comparable to that of Fox as a spiritual record, with a wider outlook on his time. In the 19th century the diaries of Thomas Creevey (1768–1838) and Charles Greville (1794–1865) are famous as records of public affairs, and that of Henry Crabb Robinson (1775–1867) for impressions of the leading writers who were his friends. In the 20th century the *Journal* of ▷ Katherine Mansfield is an intimate and vivid record of personal experience, and that of ▷ Virginia Woolf is an extremely interesting record of a writer's experience of artistic creation.

Dickens, Monica (b 1915)
Novelist, children's writer and journalist. Monica Dickens is best known as the author of the popular *Follyfoot* series of books written in the 1970s (and subsequently televised), but she only began writing for children in 1970, by which time she had already published a range of (often semi-autobiographical) novels, beginning with *One Pair of Hands* in 1939. The inspiration for Dickens's writing has often come from her working life, as a nurse (*One Pair of Feet*, 1942), as a journalist (*My Turn to Make the Tea*, 1951), with the Samaritans (*The Listeners*, 1970) and more generally in her life in the countryside (*The House at World's End*, 1970, and the *Follyfoot* books). Dickens was a columnist for the *Woman's Own* magazine from 1946 to 1965, and is the great-granddaughter of the ▷ Victorian novelist Charles Dickens. Other

works include: *Mariana* (1940); *The Fancy* (1943); *Flowers on the Grass* (1949); *The Winds of Heaven* (1955); *The Room Upstairs* (1966); *Follyfoot* (1971); *World's End in Winter* (1972); *Follyfoot Farm* (1973); *Stranger at Follyfoot* (1976); *The Ballad of Favour* (1985).

Didactic literature
Literature designed to teach, or to propound in direct terms a doctrine or system of ideas. In practice, it is not always easy to identify; so much literature is didactic in intention but not in form; sometimes writers renounce didactic intentions but in practice use didactic forms. The prevalence of didactic poetry in the 18th century arose from the especially high regard this century had for ancient Greek and Latin literature. The Romantic poets of the early 19th century reacted against the 18th-century Augustans (▷ Augustanism), and since then there has been a persistent prejudice against explicit didacticism. In fact much of Wordsworth (*eg The Excursion*, 1814) and of Shelley (*eg Queen Mab*, 1813) was highly didactic, though the undisguised passion to some extent conceals the fact. The 19th-century novelists, especially Dickens and George Eliot, used didactic digressions, but in the former such passages are especially of passionate social invective, and in the latter they are usually more integrated into the imaginative art than is apparent. In the 1930s there was a revival of verse didacticism, especially in the work of ▷ W. H. Auden, *eg New Year Letter* (1941). In general, the view now is that poets and even novelists may be didactic if they choose; in his essays on the novel, however, D. H. Lawrence argues against didactic writing, although his critics reply that he is one of the most didactic writers of the century. True didacticism, however, requires a body of assumptions commonly held by author and reader, as was true of the age of Pope, but is not so today.

Difference
A term introduced by ▷ Ferdinand de Saussure in his study of linguistics and used in literary theory. It is the means whereby value is established in any system of linguistic signs whether it be spoken or written. Saussure's *Course in General Linguistics* (1915) argues that in speech it is 'the phonetic contrasts' which permit us to distinguish between one word and another that constitute meaning. In writing the letters used to form words are arbitrary ▷ signs, and their values are therefore 'purely negative and differential' (Saussure). The result is that the written sign becomes important only in so far as it is different from other signs within the overall system of language. The notion of difference as a principle of opposition has been extended beyond the limits of Structuralist thinking laid down by Saussure. For example, the ▷ Marxist philosopher ▷ Mikhail Bakhtin in a critique of Saussurean ▷ Structuralism argued that 'the forms of signs are conditioned above all by the social organization of the participants involved and also by the immediate conditions of their interaction' (*Marxism and The Philosophy of Language*; 1930). Thus the clash of opposites through which meaning and value emerge is determined by the social positions of those who use the language. This means that secreted at the very heart of the form of the linguistic sign is a series of dialectical opposites whose interaction refracts the struggle taking place within the larger framework of society itself. For Bakhtin these oppositions can be defined in terms of the struggle between social classes, but the dialectical structure of these conflicts makes the notion of difference suitable for any situation which can be analysed in terms of binary opposites. For example, for ▷ feminism this would be an opposition between 'masculine' and 'feminine' as the basis upon which sexual identity is constructed. ▷ Jacques Derrida has adapted the term to form the neologism '*différance*', which denotes the deferral of meaning whereby no sign can ever be brought into direct alignment with the object that it purports to recall. This means that meaning is always *deferred*, and can never be final.

▷ Dialectic.

Discourse
A term used in critical theory. Especially in the writings of ▷ Michel Foucault, 'discourse' is the name given to the systems of linguistic representations through which power sustains itself. For Foucault discourse manifests itself only through concrete examples operating within specific areas of social and institutional practice. He argues that within individual discourses a series of mechanisms is used as a means of controlling desire and power, which facilitate 'classification . . . ordering [and] distribution' (Foucault). In this way a mastery is exerted over what appears to be the randomness of everyday reality. It is thus possible to investigate those discourses which have been used to master reality in the past *eg* discourses concerned with questions of 'sexuality', criminality and judicial systems of

punishment, or madness, as Foucault's own work demonstrates.

Bib: Foucault, M., *The Order of Things*; *Power/Knowledge: Selected Interviews and Other Writings* (ed. C. Gordon).

Displacement

In ▷ psychoanalysis, displacement (along with ▷ 'condensation') is associated by ▷ Freud with the mechanisms whereby the conscious mind processes the unconscious in dreams. 'Displacement' is a form of censorship which effectively distorts the ideas which act as the controlling forces of the dream (what Freud calls 'the latent dream-thoughts') and attaches them to other, more acceptable thoughts or ideas. This complex process is one which involves the omission or re-arrangement of detail, and modification of the dream thoughts. In order to reach the unconscious the 'manifest dream' must be interpreted as a symbolic expression of another text which lies beneath its surface and which is not readily accessible to the conscious mind. This whole mechanism rests on the assumption that psychic energy can attach itself to particular ideas, or objects (cathexis); those ideas or objects are related to the 'latent dream-thoughts', but derive their new-found significance by a process of association. Literature habitually invests objects and ideas with value, and psychic intensity, and the manner in which it does so can be read psychoanalytically as a manifestation of deeper, more disturbing activities going on in the mind of the writer, or – by analogy – in the 'unconscious' of the society of which the writer is a part.

Dissociation of Sensibility

A critical expression made famous by ▷ T. S. Eliot, and used in his essay *The Metaphysical Poets* (1921, included in his *Selected Essays*). He states: 'In the seventeenth century a dissociation of sensibility set in, from which we have never recovered; and this dissociation . . . was aggravated by the influence of the two most powerful poets of the century, Milton and Dryden.' Eliot's argument is that before 1660 poets, in particular the Metaphysical poets, were 'engaged in the task of trying to find the verbal equivalent for states of mind and feeling', and that after that date 'while the language became more refined, the feeling became more crude'. Poetry, henceforward, is put to more specialized purposes: 'Tennyson and Browning are poets, and they think; but they do not feel their thought as immediately as the odour of a rose. A thought to Donne was an experience; it modified his sensibility.' The implication behind the argument is that poets (with exceptions) ceased to bring all their faculties to bear upon their art: 'Racine or Donne looked into a good deal more than the heart. One must look into the cerebral cortex, the nervous system, and the digestive tracts.'

The theory has had great influence. Those who uphold it support it with the evidence provided by the rise of modern prose after 1660, and the gradual displacement of poetry from its centrality in literature thereafter; poetry either subjected itself to the rational discipline of prose (*eg* Pope), or, in the 19th century, it tended to cultivate areas of feeling to which this rational discipline was not relevant (*eg* Swinburne). However, the theory has been attacked for various reasons. Eliot himself felt that he had used the expression in too simplified a way (*Milton*, 1974, in *Poets and Poetry*), and that the causes of the process were more complicated than his earlier essay had implied. Other writers have suggested that such a dissociation did not happen; or that it happened in different ways at different periods; or that, if it did happen, no deterioration in imaginative writing can be attributed to it. See Frank Kermode, *Romantic Image* and F. W. Bateson in *Essays in Criticism*, vol. 1.

Divorce

Until 1857 divorce was possible only through Church courts which had kept their authority over matrimonial relations since before the Reformation, while losing it in nearly all other private affairs of laymen. Even after a marriage had been dissolved by a Church court, a special ('private') act of Parliament was necessary before the divorce was legalized. In consequence, divorces were rare and only occurred among the rich and influential. Adultery and cruelty were the accepted grounds, and the wife was commonly in an unfavourable position, so that no divorce was granted on account of a husband's adultery until 1801. The law of 1857 added desertion as a ground for divorce, and proceedings were taken out of the hands of the Church courts and put under the courts of the realm. Since 1938, unsoundness of mind may also be pleaded as a cause of divorce, and it has been further facilitated in other ways, perhaps the most important of which is the concept of 'marital breakdown'. This abolishes the idea of one of the partners being 'guilty' and the other, 'injured'.

▷ Marriage; Women, Status of.

Doolittle, Hilda
▷ H. D.

Douglas, Keith (1920–44)
Poet. Keith Douglas was born in Kent, and educated at Oxford University under the tutorship of poet ▷ Edward Blunden, before enlisting with the British Army when World War II broke out. He is the most famous English poet of that war, although he began publishing his work at the age of 16. His verse is precise, unsentimental and at times chilling, in its treatment of desire and sexuality as well as in its pervasive obsession with death and the relation of death to writing. Douglas was killed in Normandy, having also written about his involvement in the war in North Africa, his slim but intensely powerful corpus concluded at an early age. His work began to receive the acclaim it deserves only when ▷ Ted Hughes, a great admirer, edited and introduced a collection in 1964 (*Selected Poems*). See also the more recent *Complete Poems* (ed. Desmond Graham; 1978).

Doyle, Sir Arthur Conan (1859–1930)
Novelist; chiefly noted for his series of stories and novels about the amateur detective, Sherlock Holmes, a genius in minute deduction and acute observations. Holmes's friend, Dr Watson, is represented as the ordinary, ingenuous man, who needs to have everything pointed out to him and explained; and this offsets the ingenuity of the detective. The combination of acute detective and obtuse colleague has been imitated in many detective stories ever since. The Stories include: *A Study in Scarlet* (1887); *The Adventures of Sherlock Holmes* (1891); *The Memoirs of Sherlock Holmes* (1893); *The Hound of the Baskervilles* (1902); *The Return of Sherlock Holmes* (1905). Conan Doyle also wrote historical novels of merit; *eg Micah Clarke* (1888), *The White Company* (1891), and *Rodney Stone* (1896).
▷ Detective fiction.
Bib: Lamond, J., *Conan Doyle: A Memoir*; Conan Doyle, A., *The True Conan Doyle*; Carr, J. D., *The Life of Conan Doyle*; Roberts, S. C., *Holmes and Watson*; Pearsall, R., *Conan Doyle: A Biographical Solution*.

Drabble, Margaret (b 1939)
Novelist and short-story writer. Born in Sheffield and educated at Cambridge University. She achieved considerable popular success with her novels of the 1960s, which dealt with the personal dilemmas of intelligent and educated heroines. In *The Millstone* (1965) Rosamund struggles for independence, and achieves relative stability and a sense of moral responsibility through her love for her baby daughter, the result of a casual liaison. Drabble's later novels broaden their scope, subsuming feminist issues in a general concern for equality and justice, and addressing wider national and international issues. *The Needle's Eye* (1972) established her as a major writer by the moral intensity of its concern with social justice. *The Ice Age* (1977) is a sombre picture of the corrupt and sterile condition of Britain in the mid-1970s. Drabble sees herself as a social historian, and admires the novelist ▷ Arnold Bennett, a biography of whom she published in 1974. The literary allusion which has been a feature of all her work becomes more marked in the 1970s, and her narrative techniques become more adventurous, as in the three points of view, alterations of style and self-conscious authorial voice of *The Realms of Gold* (1975). The novelist ▷ A. S. Byatt is her sister. Her other novels are: *A Summer Bird-Cage* (1962); *The Garrick Year* (1964); *Jerusalem the Golden* (1967); *The Waterfall* (1969); *The Middle Ground* (1980); *The Radiant Way* (1987); *A Natural Curiosity* and *Gates of Ivory* (1991). Story collections: *Penguin Modern Stories 3* (with others) (1969); *Hassam's Tower* (1980), and she has also edited *The Oxford Companion to English Literature* (1984).
Bib: Creighton, J. V., *Margaret Drabble*.

Dramatic monologue
A poetic form in which the poet invents a character, or, more commonly, uses one from history or legend, and reflects on life from the character's standpoint. The dramatic monologue is a development from the conversation poem of Coleridge and Wordsworth, in which the poet reflects on life in his own person.

Tennyson was the first to use the form in the ▷ Victorian period, in *The Lotos-Eaters* (1833), *Ulysses* (1842) and *Tithonus* (pub. 1860). In these poems, he takes the standpoint of characters in Greek myth and the disguise enables him to express himself without inhibition, and particularly without involving himself in the responsibility of having to defend the attitudes that he is expressing. His most ambitious poem in this form is the monodrama *Maud* (1855).

However it was Robert Browning who used the form most profusely, and with whom it is most associated, *eg My Last Duchess* (1845); *Fra Lippo Lippi, Andrea del Sarto, The Bishop*

Orders His Tomb, Bishop Blougram's Apology, all in *Men and Women* (1855); *Mr Sludge the Medium* in *Dramatis Personae* (1864); and *The Ring and the Book* (1869). Browning used it differently from Tennyson: his characters are more detached from his own personality; the poems are attempts to explore a wide variety of attitudes to art and life. Still another use for the dramatic monologue is that to which Arthur Clough puts it in his poem *Dipsychus (Divided Mind*, 1850). This poem is in the form of a dialogue, but it is a dialogue between the two parts of a man's mind: that which tries to sustain moral principle, and that which is sceptical of principle, seeking only pleasure and material well-being.

A more searching irony was brought to the dramatic monologue by ▷ T. S. Eliot in *The Love Song of J. Alfred Prufrock* (1915) and *Gerontion* (1920). Since the 1930s a range of different developments have tended to make the dramatic monologue seem either false or outdated. The emphasis on authenticity of voice in poetry of the 1950s and 1960s, and the current tendency to foreground the author's ethnic origins in the language used (as in 'dub' poetry), have little use for a form to which indirectness is so intrinsic.

▷ Rudyard Kipling; Charlotte Mew.

Dubliners (1914)

A volume of short stories by ▷ James Joyce. Joyce later wrote: 'My intention was to write a chapter of the moral history of my country and I chose Dublin for the scene because that city seemed to me the centre of paralysis. I have tried to present it . . . under four of its aspects: childhood, adolescence, maturity and public life. The stories are arranged in this order.' He adds that he has used in them 'a style of scrupulous meanness', but, in fact, the apparent bare realism of the stories conceals subtle mimetic and symbolic effects which render the spiritual poverty and domestic tragedy of Dublin life through its characteristic colloquial idioms. The stories are based on Joyce's theory of the 'epiphanies', by which he meant that deep insights might be gained through incidents and circumstances which seem outwardly insignificant. Their effect is thus often through delicate implication, like the stories of ▷ Chekhov. However, some of them contain sharp humour, notably 'Grace', and more have very sensitive poignancy, especially the last and longest, 'The Dead'. This story, which moves from ironical satire to a highly poetic conclusion, is often regarded as a masterpiece; it was filmed in 1987 by John Huston.

Duffy, Maureen (b 1933)

Novelist, poet and dramatist. Her autobiographical first novel, *That's How it Was* (1962) is the account of a childhood of material insecurity and social isolation illuminated by a living relationship between mother and daughter. The themes of her fiction have been the outsider, the oppressions of poverty and class, the varieties of sexual experience and the power of love to transform and redeem. Her work reflects her socialism, lesbianism and commitment to animal rights. *The Microcosm* (1966) is a study of lesbian society using various modes of narration, including pastiche and ▷ stream of consciousness; it shows the distance between sexual creativity and ordinary life imposed by society. Duffy has lived in London for most of her adult life, and celebrated that city in *Capital* (1975). She employs colloquial language, and a laconic but vivid style. Her play *Rites*, a black farce set in a ladies public lavatory, was produced at the ▷ National Theatre in 1969. *Rites, Solo* (1970) and *Old Tyme* (1970) rework the Greek myths of the Bacchae, Narcissus and Uranus respectively in terms of modern sexual and public life. Her other plays are: *The Lay Off* (1962); *The Silk Room* (1966) and *A Nightingale in Bloomsbury Square* (1973). Other novels are: *The Single Eye* (1964); *The Paradox Players* (1967); *Wounds* (1969); *Love Child* (1971); *I Want to Go to Moscow* (1973); *Housespy* (1978); *Gor Saga* (1981); *Scarborough Fear* (as D. M. Layer, 1982); *Londoners: An Elegy* (1983); *Change* (1987). Poetry: *Collected Poems* (1985).

Du Maurier, Daphne (1907–89)

Novelist and short-story writer. Daphne Du Maurier began publishing in 1928, and her long career spanned and mastered a wide range of ▷ genres. She is a skilled writer of psychological suspense and supernatural tales, as well as the author of the classic romantic thriller, *Rebecca* (1938), which was filmed by Alfred Hitchcock in 1940, and has run to many editions in many different languages. Hitchcock also filmed Du Maurier's famous short story 'The Birds' in 1963, and the Hitchcock connection underlines what is perhaps most remarkable about Du Maurier's work: its concern with neo-Gothic motifs and the thin line which divides psychological obsession from supernatural possibilities. Du Maurier is also interested in exploring concepts of time in her fiction, both in the sense of how history is lived in the present (one of the concerns of her Cornish historical romances) and in concepts of non-linear time, and parallel time-scales, as the framework for her psychological thrillers. This last interest is best illustrated by the 1971 story *Don't Look Now*, which, again, was filmed, this time by Nicholas Roeg in 1973. Du Maurier's success as the originator of a number of classic modern horror films is important. She is also one of Cornwall's most famous inhabitants, and four famous Cornish historical romances, *Jamaica Inn* (1936), *Frenchman's Creek* (1941); *My Cousin Rachel* (1951) and *Rebecca* itself have become key props for the Cornish tourist industry. Du Maurier's passion for her county is also evident in her non-fictional writing, particularly *Vanishing Cornwall*.

Other works include: *The Loving Spirit* (1931); *The Apple Tree* (1952); *The Breaking Point* (1959); *The Birds and Other Stories* (1963); *The House on the Strand* (1969); *Echoes from the Macabre: Selected Stories* (1976); *The Blue Lenses and Other Stories* (1970). Autobiographical works include: *Growing Pains: The Shaping of a Writer* (1977) and *The Rebecca Notebook and Other Memories* (1980). **Bib**: Light, A., 'Rebecca' in *Feminist Review*, 1984; Radcliffe, E. J., *Gothic Novels of the 20th Century: An Annotated Bibliography*.

▷ Horror fiction; Detective fiction.

Dunn, Douglas (b 1942)
Poet. Dunn was born in Renfrewshire, Scotland, and educated in Scotland and Hull. His first volume, *Terry Street* (1969) showed him much under the influence of ▷ Philip Larkin in its documentation of everyday provincial life; his later volumes *St Kilda's Parliament* (1981) and *Elegies* (1985) show more varied subject matter, mediating on ▷ Celtic history and on his own Scottish ancestry and on the loss of loved ones. He has trained and worked as a librarian. His other poetry includes: *Backwaters* (1971); *Love or Nothing* (1974); *Barbarians* (1979); *Selected Poems* (1986).

▷ Scottish literature in English.

Dunn, Nell (b 1936)
Playwright and novelist. Dunn started work in the early 1960s as a key player in the British 'docudrama' movement (along with other writers and directors such as Ken Loach, ▷ David Mercer and Jeremy Sandford), which was a literary marriage of investigative journalism and naturalistic fiction. Dunn's first work, a series of short stories which observe ordinary working-class life in South London, *Up the Junction* (1963), brought her great fame in Britain, as did her early 1980s feminist play, *Steaming* (1981), about a group of women in a sauna, which was extremely successful. Her other works include: *Poor Cow* (1967); *Talking to Women* (1965); *I Want* (with Adrian Henri); *The Only Child* (1978).

Duration
One of the five categories in which ▷ Genette analyses narrative discourse, duration is concerned with the relationship between how long a fictional event would notionally last and how much of the text is devoted to telling of it (*eg* in ▷ Virginia Woolf's ▷ *To the Lighthouse*, the long first section of the novel tells the events of one day; the shorter second section tells the events of ten years). Duration, ▷ order and ▷ frequency are matters of temporal arrangement or 'tense'; the other two categories are ▷ mood and ▷ voice.

Durrell, Lawrence (1912–90)
Novelist and poet. He began writing before the war, and published an experimental novel, *The Black Book* (1938) in France which was partly the result of his fruitful and life-long friendship with American novelist Henry Miller. His present high international reputation is based in particular on the sequence *The Alexandria Quartet* comprising *Justine* (1957); *Balthazar* (1958); *Mountolive* (1958) and *Clea* (1960). *The Alexandria Quartet* has achieved fame partly through its lavishly exotic appeal, and partly through Durrell's experimental technique: a wide range of narrative forms are employed, and the same events are seen, and interpreted quite differently, by the different characters participating in them. *Tunc* (1968) and *Nunquam* (1970) together form *The Revolt of Aphrodite*, which explores the destruction of love and creativity by social pressures, embodied in the 'Firm', a vast and dehumanizing multi-national enterprise. Durrell followed up the success of *The Alexandria Quartet* with a five-volume novel, *The Avignon Quincunx*, which also used exotic settings and multiple narratives, and, combining elements of myth with philosophical speculation, satirized the values of western society. It is made up of the following volumes: *Monsieur; or, The Prince of Darkness* (1974); *Livia; or, Buried Alive* (1978); *Constance; or Solitary Practices* (1982); *Sebastian; or, Ruling Passions* (1983); *Quinx; or, The Ripper's Tale* (1985).

As the titles of his two major sequences suggest, the spirit of particular places was always of importance to Durrell; he said that in *The Alexandria Quartet* he 'tried to see people as a function of place'. He published many volumes of travel writing, particularly about the islands of the Mediterranean, including: *Prospero's Cell* (about Corcyra; 1945); *Reflections on a Marine Venus* (about Rhodes; 1953); *Bitter Lemons* (about Cyprus; 1957); *The Greek Islands* (1978). Durrell also published collections of short stories, including: *Sauve Qui Peut* (1966); *The Best of Antrobus* (1974); *Antrobus Complete* (1985); a number of plays, including: *Sappho* (1959); *Acto* (1961); *An Irish Faustus* (1963) and many volumes of poetry: *Collected Poems* (1960; revised 1968) and *Collected Poems 1931–74* (1980). But his greatest achievement was to express the indeterminate and multi-faceted nature of experience through the techniques of experimental fiction.

Bib: Fraser, G. S., *Lawrence Durrell: A Critical Study*; Friedman, A. W., *Lawrence Durrell and The Alexandria Quartet.*

E

Eagleton, Terry (b 1943)

One of the foremost ▷ Marxist critics writing in Britain today. Currently a Professor of English at Oxford, he has for some time been a leading force in Marxism's encounter with a range of intellectual movements from ▷ Structuralism onwards. His book *Criticism and Ideology* (1976) laid the foundation for the introduction into British literary criticism of the work of the French critic Pierre Macherey, and is a clear development of ▷ Louis Althusser's understanding of culture. In later works, such as *Walter Benjamin or Towards a Revolutionary Criticism* (1981), *The Rape of Clarissa* (1982), *The Function of Criticism* (1984), and *William Shakespeare* (1986), he has sought to develop a sophisticated ▷ materialist criticism which is prepared to engage with, but which refuses to be overawed by ▷ post-structuralism.

Eclecticism

In ancient Greece, a term for the kind of philosophy that did not follow any one school of thought (*eg* Platonism) but selected its doctrines from a number of schools. The term is now applied to thinkers, artists and writers who follow this principle in the formation of their thought or artistic methods.

Écriture féminine

A term usually reserved for a particular kind of critical writing by women, emanating from the radical ▷ feminism of contemporary critics such as Luce Irigaray, ▷ Hélène Cixous and ▷ Julia Kristeva. What unites this form of feminist criticism is the belief that there is an area of textual production that can be called 'feminine', that it exists beneath the surface of masculine discourse, and only occasionally comes to the fore in the form of disruptions of 'masculine' language. A further assumption is that woman is given a specific identity within the masculine structures of language and power, and that she must strive to challenge it. This particular brand of radical feminism takes the view that there is an 'essential' femininity that can be recovered, and that it is also possible to distinguish between a genuine feminine 'writing' and other forms of language.

Bib: Kristeva, J., *Desire in Language*; Moi, T. (ed.), *The Kristeva Reader*; Moi, T., *Sexual/Textual Politics*; Marks, E. and De Courtivon, I., *New French Feminisms*; Newton, J. and Rosenfelt, D., *Feminist Criticism and Social Change*; Greene, G. and Kahn, C. *Making the Difference: Feminist Literary Criticism*; Moi, T. (ed.), *The French Feminist Reader*; Wilcox, H. et al, *The Body and the Text: Hélène Cixous, Reading and Teaching*.

Edgar, David (b 1948)

Socialist playwright who has written for a number of ▷ fringe companies, including ▷ John McGrath's 7:84, and also had his work performed by the ▷ Royal Shakespeare Company and the ▷ National Theatre company. *Destiny* (1976) is an exposure of British fascism. This was followed by the documentary works *Mary Barnes* (1977) and *The Jail Diary of Albie Sachs* (1978). His adaptation of *Nicholas Nickleby* (1981) for the R.S.C. was much acclaimed and highly successful. More recent plays are *Maydays* (1983) and *Entertaining Strangers* (1985).

Bib: Bull, J., *New British Political Dramatists*; Chambers, C. and Prior, M., *Playwright's Progress*.

Education

The growth of national education: 1800–present day

The growth of state-funded education in Britain in the 19th century was slow. The state was reluctant to undertake national systems of education of any sort, and Britain was well behind the most advanced European countries, especially Prussia, in this respect. The principal reason for this slow development was the religious divisions of public opinion. Even today, 'Religious Instruction', taught non-denominationally, is often the only compulsory subject in state schools. The schools for the children of the mass of the people in the first part of the 19th century were controlled by rival Anglican and Dissenting movements. Since the Church of England was the established Church of the state, it claimed that it should have a monopoly of religious instruction in any state system, a claim that was strongly resisted by the Dissenters. Till 1870, the important advances towards nationwide education remained in private hands.

The most important of these advances, though it affected only a minority, was in the public school system, which had originated in the medieval system of grammar schools. Many of these had been closed in the middle of the 16th century, but others had been established in the later 16th and 17th centuries; in the 18th century they had again been allowed to decline. A few of them, however, had from early times achieved an importance above the rest; they had richer endowments, and drew their pupils from the nation at large and not merely from their immediate localities. These included Winchester (founded 1382), Eton (1440), Westminster (1560), Rugby (1567), and Harrow (1571). Their discipline was bad. By the early 19th century, the pupils were predominantly upper class. They produced some fine teachers and headmasters, but their educational standards varied extensively. However, in the 19th century, the character of these schools greatly changed, largely owing to the influence of one man – Thomas Arnold, headmaster of Rugby from 1828 to 1842. Arnold believed that his education should provide a boy with a training of the whole character, and not merely the mind, and so athletics became an essential element in public school education. Arnold's Rugby not only introduced new standards into the public schools, but it had two further important results. One was that it gave real significance to boarding school education; the boys lived at the school for three-quarters of the year, not, as before, merely because conditions of travel were difficult, but because the school could thereby educate the boy during his leisure as well as in the classroom, a consideration of importance when it was a question of educating his whole character, and when sport was an essential part of this character-training. The second result was that many new public schools were founded, so that until 1950 a public school education became the normal one, not only for upper-class boys but for the sons of professional men and the more prosperous businessmen as well. To some extent, the system was also extended to girls, but coeducational public schools, even today, are the exception rather than the rule.

There were special social and political reasons for this adoption of public school education by the middle classes. One was the continuing prestige of the English aristocracy. The middle-class businessman, especially if he had raised himself from a lower rank in society, wanted his son to be a 'gentleman', and by this time he could afford the high public school fees. But there was a more important reason. Britain, by 1850, was the centre of the largest overseas empire that the world had ever seen. This great empire required an unprecedented number of administrators, who had to be men of high moral quality and courage, as well as of good ability. The aristocracy could not provide them all from itself, and would have aroused social resentment had it tried; they came, therefore, from preponderantly middle-class backgrounds, and it was the public schools which gave them the education considered necessary to qualify them for the function. However, by giving the governing classes the recruits they needed, the public schools tended to prolong the complacent indifference of the state to its educational responsibilities. Since the public school tradition was almost entirely an Anglican one, the public schools also prolonged the opposition between the Dissenters and the Anglicans over education.

Education for other classes in the early to mid-19th century was less thorough. However, the ▷ Industrial Revolution had brought into being a new class of skilled worker: the 'mechanic' of the iron, steel and engineering industries. Such men needed brains for their skills, and their natural intelligence caused them to seek further education to advance their knowledge. This was provided by the growth of the voluntarily established Mechanics' Institutes, which began the movement of education in technology which has led to the enormous expansion of technical colleges under the control of local government authorities in the 20th century, especially since 1945.

Universal elementary education was introduced in 1870 by the provision of state schools wherever the Church schools were inadequate. In 1902, special Local Education Authorities were created with responsibility for both these types of school, and for secondary education as well. It was, however, not until the Education Act of 1944 that the state system was improved sufficiently for the more prosperous middle classes to consent to use it instead of the private system.

Yet even the Act of 1944 tended to perpetuate the cleavage between the classes. Education became compulsory between the ages of 5 and 14 (15 in 1947, and 16 in 1972), but at the age of 11, boys and girls were subjected to the '11+ (eleven plus) examination', dividing them into those who were sent to the Secondary Modern Schools (75% of the secondary school population) and the minority who were sent to the new state grammar schools. The secondary modern school child was expected to leave school at 15, but the grammar school child, though allowed to leave at the same age, was expected to continue to the age of 18. The system was clearly intended to provide an élite comparable to that of the public schools, but an élite based on real merit, and not on wealth. However, it was often criticized on the grounds that it favoured children who came from materially comfortable, well-educated backgrounds, since these advantages tend to accelerate the mental development of a child. Hence, under the 1964–70 Labour Government, the 11+ selection system was replaced by various forms of comprehensive schools, which do not require selection when children enter the school at 11, though it may divide them according to levels of ability ('streaming') after entry.

During the late 1970s and 1980s problems of lack of funding for schools and teachers, social pressures and consequent low teacher morale meant that comprehensive schools faced extremely difficult problems which were exacerbated by antagonistic government attitudes from 1979 onwards.

From September 1989 Conservative Government reforms introduced the 'national curriculum' for both primary and secondary schools, as well as reintroducing the notion of formally testing pupils at 11, as well as 16, and, for the first time, testing primary school children at the age of 7. From September 1989 schools could opt out of local authority control and receive direct funding from central government, becoming grant-maintained schools. Other developments in vocational education and City Technology Colleges still have to prove themselves.

▷ Adult education; Further education; EFL.

Education and the state

The main stages in the growth of state provision of education in Britain are as follows:

1 1833. The government began the practice of making an annual grant of £20,000 for the erection of school buildings. The grant was available to the National Society and the British and Foreign School Society only. The former was controlled by the Church of England and the latter by the Nonconformist (or Dissenting) religious denominations.

2 Forster's Act of 1870. This provided state education for all at the primary level, to the age of 11. In 1876 primary education became compulsory for all children.

3 Balfour's Act of 1902. This provided compulsory education up to the age of 14 and placed the secondary schools under the authority of the local government County Councils.

4 The Act of 1944. This paved the way for the raising of the school leaving age to 15 in 1947. Secondary schools were divided into three groups: grammar schools, attendance at which could extend to the age of 18, after which children might continue their education with state financial aid at universities or technical colleges; modern schools, which pupils normally left at 15, though further education might take place at technical colleges; a small number of technical schools, with emphasis on industrial or business training. Children were obliged to enter primary schools at the age of 5, and submitted to a test at the age of 11 to decide the secondary school best suited to their abilities.

This so-called '11+' examination soon came under heavy criticism and the local authorities often invented other expedients for arranging the secondary education of children. Much the most important of these was the spread of comprehensive schools, which are entered by children of all levels of ability without a preliminary test. The modern educational scene in Britain consequently exhibited much variety: grammar schools, modern schools and the 11+ test remained, but comprehensive schools increased widely in the 1960s with the encouragement of the Labour governments, and most grammar schools were amalgamated within this system. Today most children attend a comprehensive school, although private schooling is a popular alternative for those parents with sufficient financial resources.

The most significant intervention in education in recent years is the Education Reform Bill of November 1987. Its major proposals for primary and secondary schools were that schools be given the right to 'opt out' of local authority control and receive direct grant funding, subject to a simple majority vote, and the introduction of the national curriculum with three core subjects – English, maths, science – and seven foundation subjects. The main areas concerning higher education were that polytechnics were to be established as semi-independent corporations allowed to call themselves 'universities', that commissioners were to review university charters and to abolish academic tenure; and that a University Funding Council should replace the University Grants Committees.

Edwardian

A term descriptive of the political, social and cultural characteristics of the early years of the 20th century , roughly corresponding to the reign of King Edward VII (1901–1910). The period is often remembered nostalgically for its luxury and brilliance, soon to be darkened by the horror of World War I (1914–18) and obliterated by the relative austerity of the post-war years. This life of luxury, easy foreign travel, low taxation, etc. is also thought of as being relatively free from the close moral restraint commonly associated with the preceding ▷ Victorian period. It is sometimes remembered, however, that such brilliance was restricted to the upper class and the wealthier members of the middle class, and that life for four-fifths of the population was at best dull and at worst squalid and impoverished. This darker aspect of the time was responsible for the rise of the socialist ▷ Labour Party and the prominence of polemical writers, like ▷ George Bernard Shaw and ▷ H. G. Wells. Such writers attacked the social injustice and selfishness of the upper classes in an idiom designed to reach wide audiences. Another critic of the dominant materialism was the novelist ▷ E. M. Forster. ▷ Arnold Bennett was a more representative novelist: his novels were not polemical and convey a materialistic vigour and excitement which were important elements in the harsh but inspiring environments of the more prosperous provincial towns. Thus some aspect of materialism is generally associated with Edwardianism, whether it is being enjoyed, suffered or criticized. Politically, the period was one of disturbance and rapid development: trade unionism was militant, women fought for political rights (▷ Suffragette Movement), and the social conscience inspired legislation which was later to mature into the ▷ Welfare State of the 1940s.

EFL
Teaching English as a Foreign Language: a specialist skill and a profitable enterprise. It covers both the instruction of schoolchildren and their parents whose mother-tongue is not English but who live in Britain, which is a social necessity and prime task in a multi-racial society, as well as the work done in private language schools with older people not permanently resident in Britain. This is where the money lies. The number of these schools continues to increase: overseas the ▷ British Council has also expanded its teaching of English. Material relating to EFL teaching now takes up considerable space in many publishers' lists and is a major export.

▷ Adult education.

Elegy
An elegy is usually taken to be a poetic lament for one who has died, or at least a grave and reflective poem. In ancient Greek and Latin literature, however, an elegy was a poem written in a particular ▷ metre (line of six dactylic feet alternating with lines of five feet) and it had no necessary connection with death or gravity; the Latin poet Ovid used it for love poetry. Following his example, the English poet John Donne wrote a series of elegies with amorous or satirical themes. Most of the famous elegies in English, however, follow the narrower and more widely accepted definition: Milton's *Lycidas* is inspired by the death of his friend Edward King; Shelley's *Adonais* laments that of the poet Keats; Arnold's *Thyrsis*, that of his friend Clough. ▷ W. H. Auden's *In Memory of W. B. Yeats* is a famous 20th-century response to the death of Yeats. Contemporary poetry's interest in absence and bereavement has led to a renewed interest in the elegy, *eg* ▷ Douglas Dunn, *Elegies*. In 1992, Nigerian writer Ben Okri's volume of verse *An African Elegy* was published to considerable critical acclaim.

Eliot, T. S. (Thomas Stearns) (1888–1965)
Poet, critic, and dramatist. Born in St Louis, Missouri, he later settled in England, where his first important long poem – *The Love Song of J. Alfred Prufrock* – appeared in the magazine *Poetry* in 1915; his first book, *Prufrock and Other Observations* appeared in 1917. From 1917 to 1919 he was Assistant Editor of the magazine *The Egoist*. His most famous poem, ▷ *The Waste Land*, came out in 1922, in which year he established *The Criterion*, one of the most influential literary reviews of this century. In 1927 he became a naturalized British subject, and in the same year he demonstrated his conversion to Christianity by becoming a member of the Church of England. His remaining important volumes of poetry were *Ash Wednesday* (1930) and ▷ *Four Quartets* (1935–42). The total body of his verse is not large, but it is one of the most important collections of the century. His poetic influences were preponderantly the French 19th-century ▷ Symbolists (▷ Baudelaire, Mallarmé, Laforgue), and the early 17th-century dramatists (Middleton, Webster, Tourneur, the later ▷ Shakespeare) and their contemporaries the Metaphysical poets. The great sermon writers of the same period – John Donne, Jeremy Taylor, Bishop Andrewes – exercised a double influence on his style and his thought, and so did the great Italian medieval poet Dante. The contemporary who influenced him most and, in particular, greatly contributed to his early poetic development, was his fellow American ▷ Ezra Pound. Finally, the idealist philosophy of ▷ F. H. Bradley, whom Eliot studied as

a student at Harvard and Oxford, was an important formative influence on Eliot's mind; his early academic thesis on Bradley was published in 1963.

Eliot's importance as a critic is linked with his importance as a poet, inasmuch as his really influential criticism was concerned with a reassessment of the past in such a way as to lead up to his own poetic production. Thus *The Sacred Wood* (1920) came between his first two volumes of verse. The most important of these early essays were republished in *Selected Essays* (1932). His work as a critic of society and civilization, *After Strange Gods* (1933) and *Notes Towards a Definition of Culture* (1948), has been such as to produce less fruitful, more sectarian discussion than his best literary criticism.

Eliot also experimented with verse drama, *Murder in the Cathedral* (1935) and *The Cocktail Party* (1950) being the most commercially and artistically successful. In 1981 his 1939 collection for children, *Old Possum's Book of Practical Cats*, was turned into Andrew Lloyd Webber's hit musical *Cats*, thus reaching an enormous audience.

Eliot's non-dramatic poetry and his early criticism have had the effect in this century of reordering and renewing literary taste both in this country and in America. He was not alone, but he was outstanding, in reviving admiration for the Metaphysical poets, and reducing the relative status of the Spenserian and Miltonic strains in the English tradition. His poetry enlarged the range and form of poetic expression as a medium of the modern consciousness.

Bib: Hayward, J., *Selected Prose*; Matthiessen, F. O., *The Achievement of T. S. Eliot*; Kenner, H., *Invisible Poet*; Williamson, G., *A Reader's Guide*; Smith, G., *Eliot's Poetry and Plays*; Drew, E., *T. S. Eliot: The Design of his Poetry*; Gardner, H. L., *The Art of T. S. Eliot*; Moody, A. D., *Thomas Stearns Eliot, Poet*; Smith, C. H., *Eliot's Dramatic Theory and Practice*.

Ellis, Alice Thomas (b before 1939)
Novelist. Alice Thomas Ellis's work has much in common with that of ▷ Beryl Bainbridge, Patrice Chaplin and Caroline Blackwood (with whom Ellis wrote *Darling, You Shouldn't Have Gone to So Much Trouble* in 1980), who have all been collectively termed 'the Duckworth gang' for the similarity of their concerns and plot: most of their novels deal (with varying degrees of irony and biting wit) with modern women negotiating their own obsessions and a bizarre range of domestic situations, often stemming from sexual and romantic traumas. Thomas Ellis's works are psychologically astute black comedies of contemporary moral dilemmas, which map the terrain between modern sexual codes and (Ellis's strongly Catholic) religious background. She is married to the director of Duckworth publishers (hence 'the Duckworth gang'), and her works include: *The Sin Eater* (1977); *The 27th Kingdom* (1982) (which was nominated for the Booker Prize); *Unexplained Laughter* (1985); *Home Life* (1986); *Secrets of Strangers* (with Tom Pitt-Atkins, in 1986); *The Skeleton in the Cupboard* (1988); and *Pillars of Gold* (1992).

Ellis, Henry Havelock (1859–1939)
Psychologist, essayist and one of the founders of 'sexology'. Part of his work was scientific: *Man and Woman* (1894); *Studies in the Psychology of Sex* (1897–1910). Part of it was literary and expressed in reflective essays: *Little Essays in Love and Virtue* (1922); *Impressions and Comments* (1914–23); *The Dance of Life* (1923). In the latter work he exemplified the revival of the ▷ essay as a reflective form early in this century. He was a friend of the novelist ▷ Olive Schreiner.

Bib: Calder Marshall, A., *Life*; Collis, J. S., *An Artist of Life*.

Emecheta, Florence Onye Buchi (b 1944)
Novelist, short-story writer, radio and television playwright. Born near Lagos, Nigeria of Ibuza parents, she moved to England in 1962 and took a sociology degree at London University. She has worked in the Library Office at the British Museum and as a youth and community worker, and, since 1972, as a writer and lecturer. She has served on the Advisory Council to the British Home Secretary on race and equality, and on the Arts Council of Great Britain. In 1980–81 she was Senior Research Fellow in the Department of English and Literary Studies at the University of Calabar, Nigeria and she has held various visiting professorships in the United States. Her novels are: *In the Ditch* (1972); *Second Class Citizen* (1974); *The Bride Price* (1976); *The Slave Girl* (1977); *The Joys of Motherhood* (1979); *Nowhere to Play* (1980); *Destination Biafra* (1982); *Naira Power* (1982); *Double Yoke* (1982); *The Rape of Shari* (1983); *Adah's Story: A Novel* (1983); *A Kind of Marriage* (a novella, 1986; also as a teleplay, 1987); *Gwendolen* (1989). She has written several teleplays, including *Tanya: A Black Woman* and *The Juju Landlord*, and four works for children: *Titch the Cat* (1979);

Nowhere to Play (1980); *The Wrestling Match* (1980); *The Moonlight Bride* (1981); *Head Above Water* (1988) is an autobiography. Much of her work contains a strong ▷ autobiographical element and deals with the situation of women confronting oppression in both African and Western value-systems and social practices, while a number of her novels are historical, set in Nigeria before and after independence.

▷ Commonwealth literatures.

Empson, William (1906–84)
Critic and poet. Empson was born in Yorkshire and worked under ▷ I. A. Richards at Cambridge. His main critical works are: *Seven Types of Ambiguity* (1930), *Some Versions of Pastoral* (1935), *The Structure of Complex Words* (1951), and *Milton's God* (1961). Volumes of his verse include: *Poems* (1940) and *Collected Poems* (1955).

As a critic, he was very influential, especially through his analysis of the nature of language when it is used in imaginative writing, particularly poetry. His approach was influenced by the attitudes to language of 20th-century linguistic philosophers, especially ▷ Bertrand Russell and Wittgenstein, who concentrated on the tendency of language, by the ambiguities inherent in it, to confuse clear thought. Empson's teacher, Richards, in his *Principles of Literary Criticism* (1924), discussed the kinds of truth that are to be found in poetic statements, and how these truths differ from, without being less valuable than, the truths of philosophical and scientific statement. Empson's first book (*Seven Types*) discusses the way in which various kinds of semantic ambiguity can be used by poets, and shows the relevance of this study to the assessment of poems. It has become a major text in what came to be known as ▷ new criticism. His later books develop the psychological (particularly ▷ Freudian) and philosophical aspects of this approach. More recently post-structuralist and ▷ psychoanalytic critics have become interested in *Seven Types of Ambiguity*. Empson's poetry is difficult, academic – heavily annotated by him – and itself highly ambiguous. Although difficult and obscure, his poetry was greatly influential on the work of the ▷ Movement.

End-rhyme
Rhyme occurring in the usual position, *ie* at the end of a line; internal rhymes occur in the middle of a line, and head-rhymes are the correspondence of the beginnings of words, *ie* alliteration.

End-stopped lines
Lines of verse, especially blank verse, which end at the end of a sentence or at strongly marked pauses within the sentence. The opposite effect is produced by run-on lines, when the syntax makes the voice go on to the next line without pause.

▷ Enjambment.

English language
Historically, the language is categorized into three periods: Old English extending to the 12th century; Middle English, from the 12th to the 16th centuries; and Modern English.

Old English consisted of Anglo-Saxon and Jutish dialects, and was called English because the language of the Angles was the earliest discoverable in writing. Old English was strongly modified by Scandinavian elements in consequence of the Danish invasions, and Middle English by an extensive infusion of French vocabulary.

Middle English was divided into a variety of dialects; Langland, for instance, the author of *Piers Plowman*, wrote in the West Midland dialect; from the author or authors of *Sir Gawain and the Green Knight* and of *Pearl* wrote in a dialect from farther north, and Chaucer in the East Midland dialect. Because London was the chief city of England and the seat of the royal court, and because Caxton established his printing press there in the 15th century, East Midland became the forebear of Modern English. Since the 15th century English has not undergone important structural changes; social differences of speech as between the classes have been of greater importance, at least for literary purposes, than regional ones.

Exceptions to this statement have to be made, however, for the form of English spoken and written in southern Scotland, and for those regions of the British Isles where until comparatively recent times Celtic languages were predominant: north-west Scotland, Wales and Ireland. In Ireland especially, a variety of spoken language known as Hiberno English tends to follow the substratum of Irish Gaelic (▷ Irish literature in English). This non-standard idiom of English was exploited by Irish writers such as the dramatist ▷ J. M. Synge and the poet ▷ W. B. Yeats. Irish or Welsh writers may use standard English if they do not adhere to the surviving Celtic languages. In different ways Southern Scots is also important; it is a highly codified variety of non-standard English and has been unusual in that it has enjoyed a long-established written form

(▷ Scottish literature). The literature in Scots (known in the Middle Ages as Inglis and today sometimes as Lallans, *ie* Lowlands) is considerable, whether one thinks of the late medieval poets such as Dunbar, Douglas, or Henryson; an 18th-century poet such as Burns, or a 20th-century one like ▷ Hugh MacDiarmid. However, from the 17th century eminent Scottish writers took to writing in standard English, and this became universal amongst prose writers of the 18th century (Hume, Robertson, Adam Smith).

'The Queen's English' (or 'King's') is the term used for the language spoken by the educated classes in England; linguists, however, prefer the term 'Standard English'. The pronunciation most in use among educated people is known as 'Received Pronunciation'.

English vocabulary is basically Germanic, but it also contains a very large number of Latin words. French, of course, developed from Latin, and many of these Latin words entered English in their French form after the Norman Conquest in the 11th century. For about two and a half centuries the upper classes were French-speaking. Vestiges of this social difference survive in such distinctions as the word 'sheep' used for the live animal, and 'mutton' for the same animal when it is eaten at table; the English shepherds who cared for the sheep ate very little meat, whereas their Norman-French masters were chiefly concerned with the animal when it had been transformed into food. Even after the aristocracy became English-speaking in the 14th century, the adoption of French words continued to be frequent owing to the strong influence of French culture and ways of life on the English educated classes. Latin words, however, have also entered English independently of their French forms; the 'clerks', *ie* the literate class of the earlier Middle Ages, used Latin as a living language in their writings; they were churchmen, and Latin was the language of the Church all over Western Europe. In the 16th century, there was a new and different kind of influx from Latin owing to the fresh interest taken by scholars in ancient Latin culture.

The Latin contribution to the basically Germanic English vocabulary has resulted in a large number of Latin and Germanic synonyms, with important consequences for subtleties of English expression. The associations of Latin with the medieval Church and with ancient Roman literature cause the words of Latin origin to have suggestions of grandeur which the words of Germanic origin do not possess; thus we use 'serpent' in connection with religious and mythological ideas, *eg* the story of the Garden of Eden, but 'snake' will do in reference to the ordinary reptile. On the other hand, the Latinate word is emotionally less intimate than its Germanic synonym; when we wish to lessen the painfulness of death, we say that a man is 'deceased', instead of saying that he has 'died'. This kind of differentiation clearly carries important pragmatic consequences, yielding differences in tone and register. Thus, socially, it is often considered vulgar to use a synonym of French or Latin construction, as suggesting a disposition to speak stylishly rather than truly; many people consider it vulgar to use the French 'serviette' instead of the older 'napkin', the latter is also of French origin, but is more fully anglicized.

Some English writers, *eg* Milton and Samuel Johnson, and some periods of literature, especially the 18th century, are often singled out for their preference for the Latin part of the vocabulary, and in the 19th century the preference was sometimes regarded as a fault. Correspondingly, some literature is admired for its reliance on mainly German vocabulary, *eg* the ▷ ballads, and the poems of John Clare, and Christina Rossetti, but in this kind of judgement Latin and French words adopted long ago and grown fully familiar are allowed to have the same merit as words of Germanic descent. Language which shows sensitiveness to the value of contrasting Latinate and Germanic vocabulary is always allowed peculiar merit; such is the case with ▷ Shakespeare.

English has borrowed words from many other languages; the chief of these is ancient Greek which contributed extensively during the 16th-century ▷ Renaissance, and coloured the language similarly to the Latin contribution at the same time. Borrowings from other languages are more miscellaneous and less distinctive; the most distinctive are the modern borrowings from colloquial American diction.

English has not only borrowed more freely than most languages; it has been spread abroad more than any other world language. It is not only the first language of the larger parts of North America and Australasia, but it is spoken widely, sometimes as a first language in Africa and Asia (especially India), where it is a '*lingua franca*' in countries which have a variety of indigenous languages. This has complicated the study of literature in English; as the various territories of the former British Empire have acquired independence, so they have developed their own literatures, which although in the English language, have distinctive styles and directions (▷ Commonwealth literatures). Only a few 20th-century American writers, for instance, can be included in the truly English tradition; it is now necessary to talk of 'American literature'. It is similarly difficult to think of the Australian ▷ Patrick White or the West Indian ▷ V. S. Naipaul as English writers, in the sense of belonging to the English literary tradition.

In the 20th century the relationship between English language and literature has become theoretical, that is, based upon the developments in linguistic techniques as related to the *language* of literature. Today, the teaching of English language with literature is founded on the discipline of literary stylistics and rejects an impressionistic approach to literature, preferring to concentrate on the rigorous analysis of the language texts use. It is the theoretical framework, as for example with the works of ▷ Bakhtin, that forms the unifying basis for stylisticians, semioticians, literary theoreticians and linguists, as well as for the simple educational processes of teaching English language and literature. Since the introduction of the English Language 'A' level in the late 1980s, language studies are playing an increasingly important role in the English courses offered in higher education.

Bib: Carter, R. (ed.), *Language and Literature: An Introductory Reader in Stylistics*; Fowler, R., *Linguistic Criticism*; Carter, R., and Simpson, P. (eds.), *Language, Discourse and Literature: An Introductory Reader in Discourse Stylistics*.

Enjambment

A term describing the continuing of the sense from line to line in a poem, to the extent that it is unnatural in speaking the verse to make a pause at the line ending. The effect is that of 'run-on' lines.

▷ End-stopped lines.

Enlightenment

The term was originally borrowed into English in the 1860s from German (*Aufklärung*), to designate the spirit and aims of the French philosophers of the 18th century, such as Diderot and Voltaire. But as historical perspectives have changed the word has come to be used in a much wider sense, to denote the whole period following the ▷ Renaissance, during which scepticism and scientific rationalism came to dominate European thinking. Enlightenment grew out of Renaissance at different times in different countries. In Britain, the empiricism of Francis Bacon (1561–1626) and the secular pragmatism of Thomas Hobbes (1588–1679) mark its early stages. Its golden age began however with John Locke (1632–1704) in philosophy, and Sir Isaac Newton (1642–1727) in science, and it reached its height in the first half of the 18th century. Locke argued that 'Reason must be our last judge and guide in everything', and rejected medieval philosophy as superstition. Newton's theory of gravitation seemed to explain the mysteries of the solar system. The fact that Newton had also worked on optics was ingeniously alluded to in Alexander Pope's couplet: 'Nature, and Nature's Laws lay hid in Night./God said, *Let Newton be!* and All was *Light*'. More recently 'Enlightenment' has been given a yet wider historical application by the German philosophers Theodor Adorno and Max Horkheimer, whose book, *Dialectic of Enlightenment* (1944) sees the manipulative, calculating spirit of Enlightenment as the identifying characteristic of western civilization. They trace its manifestations from Odysseus's tricking of the primitive bumpkin Polyphemus, to the treatment of people as means rather than ends which characterizes both modern totalitarian politics and consumer capitalism. Recent ecological movements, which advocate a respect for nature, rather than an exploitation of it, continue the same dialectic.

▷ Augustanism.

Bib: Willey, B., *The Eighteenth-Century Background*; Redwood, J., *Reason, Ridicule and Religion: The Age of Enlightenment in England*.

Enright, D. J. (b 1920)

Poet, novelist and literary critic. Enright was an important figure in the ▷ Movement in the 1950s, and his poetry remains strongly humanistic and anti-romantic. His volumes of verse include: *The Laughing Hyena* (1953); *Bread Rather Than Blossoms* (1956); *Some Men Are Brothers* (1960); *Selected Poems* (1968); *Sad Ires* (1975); and *A Faust Book* (1979).

Epic

1 A narrative of heroic actions, often with a principal hero, usually mythical in its content, offering inspiration and ennoblement within a particular cultural or national tradition.

2 The word denotes qualities of heroism and grandeur, appropriate to epic but present in other literary or even non-literary forms.

Epics occur in almost all national cultures, and commonly give an account of national origins, or enshrine ancient, heroic myths central to the culture. For European culture at large, much the most influential epics are the *Iliad* and the *Odyssey* of Homer and the *Aeneid* by Virgil. ▷ C. S. Lewis in *Preface to Paradise Lost* makes a helpful distinction between primary and secondary epics: primary ones, such as Homer's, are composed for a society which is still fairly close to the conditions of society described in the narrative; secondary epics are based on the pattern of primary epics but written for a materially developed society more or less remote from the conditions described, *eg* Virgil's *Aeneid.* In English literature the Old English *Beowulf* may be counted as a primary epic. A number of attempts at secondary epic have been made since the 16th century, but John Milton's *Paradise Lost* is unique in its acknowledged greatness and its closeness to the Virgilian structure. Spenser's *The Faerie Queene* has many epic characteristics, but, in spite of the important classical influences upon it, the poem's structure is derived from the 'romantic epic' of the 16th-century Italian poets, Ariosto and Tasso; moreover, though allegory often plays a part in epics, the allegorical elements in *The Faerie Queene* are so pervasive as to present a different kind of imaginative vision from that normally found in them.

Many other works in English literature have epic qualities without being definable as epics. For example, Fielding described *Tom Jones* as a comic epic, and it is this as much as it is a novel: a series of adventures of which Tom is the hero, but of which the consequences are loss of dignity rather than enhancement of dignity. Melville's prose romance *Moby Dick* (1851) has true epic scale, seriousness of treatment and relevance to the human condition. ▷ James Joyce's ▷ *Ulysses* uses the *Odyssey* as the ground plan for a narrative about a day in the life of a Dublin citizen, and though the intention of this and of Joyce's succeeding work ▷ *Finnegans Wake* is in part comic, there is also in both books deep seriousness, such as derives from the authentic epic tradition. In fact, this tradition, in the last 300 years, has mingled with other literary forms, such as the romance, the comic romance (*eg Don Quixote*), and the novel, and it is in this mixed rather than in its original pure form that it has proved most productive.

Epigram

For the ancient Greeks the word meant 'inscription'. From this, the meaning extended to include very short poems notable for the terseness and elegance of their expression and the weight and wit of their meaning. Since the 17th century epigrams have become short and generally satirical in content; Pope was the greatest master of this style, and his poems include many epigrams. For 20th-century examples of the form, see in particular the work of Stevie Smith and Robert Graves.

▷ Aphorism.

Epiphany

A Church festival celebrating the showing ('epiphany' means manifestation) of the Christ child to the Magi, otherwise known as the three Wise Men or the Three Kings (*Matthew* II). The festival is 12 days after Christmas Day, so it is also called Twelfth Night. It concludes the season of Christmas festivities.

The novelist ▷ James Joyce began his career by writing what he called 'epiphanies', *ie* sketches in which the incident, though often in itself slight, manifests or reveals the inner truth of a character. This is the method he pursues in ▷ *Dubliners*. Other 'epiphanal' experiences might be ▷ Virginia Woolf's 'moments of being' or Wordsworth's 'Spots of Time'.

Episteme

The traditional meaning of the term 'epistemology' is 'the theory or science of the method or grounds of knowledge' (Oxford English Dictionary). In the work of the French philosopher ▷ Michel Foucault, 'episteme' has come to mean something more specific. He uses the term to describe 'the total set of relations that unite, at a given period, the discursive practices that give rise to epistemological figures, sciences, and possibly formalized systems' (*The Archaeology of Knowledge*; 1972). In short, the episteme is historicized as the basic unit used to describe the manner in which a society represents knowledge to itself. Foucault conceives of the episteme in dynamic rather than static terms, since knowledge is always a matter of the ways in which 'desire' and 'power' negotiate their way through the complex ▷ discourses of society. Foucault is at pains to point out, however, that the episteme does not establish a transcendental authority which guarantees the existence of scientific knowledge, but rather points towards the fact that different kinds of knowledge are inscribed in 'the processes of a historical practice'.

▷ Archaeology.

Erewhon (1872) and Erewhon Revisited (1901)
Satirical anti-utopias or dystopias by ▷ Samuel Butler. Sir Thomas More's *Utopia* is a description of an ideal country as different as possible from England. Erewhon (an anagram of 'Nowhere') represents a country many of whose characteristics are analogous to English ones, caricatured and satirized. Thus Butler satirizes ecclesiastical institutions through the Musical Banks and parental tyranny through the Birth Formulae; machinery has to be abolished before it takes over from human beings. In *Erewhon Revisited*, Higgs, the English discoverer of Erewhon, finds that his previous departure by balloon has been used by Professors Hanky and Panky to impose a new religion, according to which Higgs is worshipped as a child of the sun. Butler's method in these satires resembles Jonathan Swift's satirical technique in the Lilliput of *Gulliver's Travels*.

Essay, The
'Essay' derives from the French *essai* meaning 'experiment', 'attempt'. As a literary term it is used to cover an enormous range of composition, from school exercises to thorough scientific and philosophical works, the only quality in common being the implied desire of the writer to reserve to himself some freedom of treatment. But the essay is also a recognized literary form in a more defined sense: it is understood to be a fairly short prose composition, in style often familiarly conversational and in subject either self-revelatory or illustrative (more or less humorously) of social manners and types. The originator of the form was the great French writer Montaigne. In 1597 the first great English essayist, Francis Bacon, published his first collection of essays, which are impersonal and aphoristic, weightily sententious. However, it was Abraham Cowley who published the first essays in English closely corresponding to what is now understood by the form, and perhaps shows the first sign of its degeneracy: easiness of tone, which in Montaigne is a graciousness of manner introducing a serious and interesting personality, but which in less interesting writers may be an agreeable cover for saying nothing in particular.

In the early years of the 18th century Addison and Steele firmly established what is now known as the 'periodical essay' – a kind of higher journalism, intended often to please rather than instruct, but in their case to instruct through pleasure.

Dr Johnson in *The Rambler* and in his essays as 'The Idler' used the weighty, impressive style soon to be regarded as unsuitable for the medium. Oliver Goldsmith in *The Citizen of the World* (1762) perfected the graceful, witty manner which came to be considered ideal for it.

If the 18th century was what may be called the golden age of the English essay, the early 19th, in the work of Charles Lamb, William Hazlitt, Leigh Hunt and De Quincey, was perhaps its silver age. In these writers, social comment combines with a confessional, autobiographical element which had never been so prominent in the English essay before.

After 1830, the periodical essay in the tradition of Addison, Goldsmith, Hazlitt and Lamb dissolved into the morass of constantly increasing journalism; though they had emulators in the 20th century, the form was increasingly despised by serious writers, and the famous essayists of the later 19th century were the more specialized sort, such as Matthew Arnold and John Stuart Mill. Yet it is not true to say that the informal essay of serious literary interest has disappeared. In the later 19th and 20th centuries, essays of natural description of remarkable intensity were produced by Richard Jefferies and Edward Thomas. More important still is the use of the essay for unspecialized but serious social and cultural comment by – to take leading examples – ▷ D. H. Lawrence, ▷ George Orwell, and ▷ Aldous Huxley. With the growth in popularity of serious ▷ magazines and the extended articles in the Sunday newspapers, the essay is today having a considerable revival. These informal arguments and 'personality pieces', such as those by Bernard Levin in *The Times*, are very far, however, from the formal essay genre.

Essentialism
Philosophically, the notion of 'essence' refers to the proposition that the physical world embodies in it a range of fixed and timeless essences which precede existence. In Christianity this is exemplified in the division between the soul and body, where the latter is relegated to the realm of temporal existence. In ▷ materialist accounts essentialism has come to be associated with attempts to deny the primacy of history as a formative influence on human affairs and human personality. In also challenges the emphasis upon the autonomy of the individual as a theroretically 'free' agent who is the centre of meaning. Any questioning of the notion that essence

precedes existence deeply affects the issue of what is assumed to be the coherent nature of human identity. It also resists the attempt to reduce material reality to a set of mental images. To remove the human subject from the centre and to re-inscribe him or her in a series of complex historical relations is to challenge, at a theoretical level, human autonomy. It also suggests that those philosophical arguments which place the individual at the centre of meaning and authority are restrictive in that they propose a view of the world which masks the connection between knowledge and particular human interests.

▷ Existentialism.

Establishment
A term which has come into use since World War II to describe the institutions which by long tradition have prestige and authority in England. It probably originates in the official description of the Church of England as 'the Established Church' – *ie* the official state church, having the Queen at its head. The monarchy itself, and ▷ Parliament, are obviously part of the Establishment, and so is the government bureaucracy loosely known as 'Whitehall'. Beyond this nucleus, the constituents of the Establishment vary according to the point of view of any particular user of the term, but it nearly always includes the following items: the fashionable men's clubs in London, especially those with long-established intellectual or political prestige, such as the Athenaeum and the Carlton; the older members and leaders of the older political parties – the Conservatives and ▷ Liberals, and sometimes also the ▷ Labour Party; the 'ancient universities' of Oxford and Cambridge, and within them, certain colleges of special prestige, such as All Souls and Christ Church at Oxford and King's and Trinity at Cambridge; the ▷ public schools, especially the older and more fashionable ones, such as Winchester, Eton, Harrow, Westminster and Rugby; ▷ *The Times* newspaper, with its special prestige; and the officer corps of the fighting services, especially the Navy. Apart from these, the term may be made to include almost anyone or anything that has prestige from tradition or happens to occupy or constitute a position of authority.

The term 'Establishment' is generally used by those who are at least fairly young and by such as are opposed to, or at least critical of, the traditions of existing authority. The war left Britain with reduced importance in the world but without an urgent crisis to absorb social energies. The result was a feeling of restless discontent among the young, who felt – and to some extent still feel – the nation to have become static and dissatisfying. This mood produced the ▷ 'Angry young men' of the 1950s who dissented from the traditions of the nation as represented by the 'Establishment'. The playwright ▷ John Osborne and the novelists ▷ Kinglsey Amis and ▷ John Braine were prominent among these writers. In the 1980s the term has come to imply a political bias and one which is particularly Conservative.

Existentialism
A modern school of philosophy which has had great influence on European literature since World War II. The doctrines to which the term has been applied are in fact very various, but a number of common themes may be identified. The first is the primacy of the individual, and of individual choice, over systems and concepts which attempt to explain him or her. For instance, the ▷ essentialist notion that the human self is built on a pre-social 'essence' or core of selfhood. Existentialism argues, in ▷ Jean-Paul Sartre's words, that 'existence precedes essence': that is, that one's freely chosen individual path constitutes one's existential reality and self – the self, for the existentialist, is not *essentially* pre-ordained or God-given, but comes into being in the material world through social interactions. Sartre explores this in *Being and Nothingness*. The second is the absurdity of the universe; reality, it is claimed, always evades adequate explanation, and remains radically contingent and disordered. This absurdity causes anxiety, but also makes freedom possible, since our actions also cannot be causally explained or predicted. Neither the behaviour nor the nature of others can be understood by observation. Existentialism sees freedom of choice as the most important fact of human existence. According to Sartre, consciousness of our own freedom is the sign of 'authentic experience', as opposed to the 'bad faith' of believing oneself bound. Investigation of this freedom involves investigation of the nature of being, and this has caused existentialism to form two main streams, the first atheistic, which interprets individual existence as dependent on transcendent Being. The best-known leaders of existentialism have been the philosophers Martin Heidegger (1889–1976) and Karl Jaspers (1883–1969) in Germany, and Sartre (1905–80) and the philosopher and dramatist Gabriel Marcel (1889–1973) in

France. Marcel represents the religious stream whose progenitor was the 19th-century Danish thinker Sören Kierkegaard (1813–55).

Existentialism has had relatively little influence on British philosophy, because of the strong empirical tradition in Britain, although the novelist and philosopher ▷ Iris Murdoch has termed modern British empiricists existentialist in her essay *The Sovereignty of Good.* Correspondingly, existentialism has had a less powerful influence on literature than in France, where authors like Sartre, ▷ Simone de Beauvoir, and Albert Camus have expounded its doctrines in, for example, such works as Sartre's trilogy of novels, *Roads to Freedom* (1947–9) and his play *No Exit* (1944), or Camus's novel *The Outsider* (1942), or in de Beauvoir's series of autobiographies. Nevertheless, these doctrines have been important in two ways. First, they have directly influenced a number of experimental novelists with continental affinities, such as ▷ David Caute, ▷ Nigel Dennis, ▷ Andrew Sinclair, ▷ Colin Wilson and ▷ Christine Brooke-Rose. The most important writer in this category is ▷ Samuel Beckett in whose plays and novels the isolation and anxiety of the characters combine with an awareness of the issues of manipulation and choice implicit in the narrative and dramatic modes, to present existential dilemmas with unrivalled power. Second, existentialist doctrines have contributed much to the general ethos of ▷ postmodernism, and affected a number of major writers, prompting either admiration or resistance. Thus the postmodern concern with the nature of fictionality arises in part from the sense that neither individuals nor reality as a whole can be adequately conceptualized. The author's manipulation of his or her characters has provided a fruitful metaphor for the exploration of issues of freedom, as for example in the work of ▷ John Fowles, Iris Murdoch and ▷ Muriel Spark. Existentialism speaks powerfully to the sense of the 20th century as a chaotic and even catastrophic era, in which certainties have been lost and man is faced with the abyss of nothingness, or of his own capability for evil. It lays stress on extreme situations, which produce dread, arising from awareness of freedom of choice (according to Sartre) or awareness of original sin (according to Kierkegaard). Extremity and existential dread are important in the work of ▷ William Golding and ▷ Patrick White, and, earlier in the century, ▷ Joseph Conrad, who in this respect as in others anticipates the 20th-century *Zeitgeist.*

Expressionism

Expressionism was originally intended to define an artistic movement which flourished at the beginning of the 20th century in Europe, especially in Germany. The expressionist painters, such as Edvard Munch and Vasili Kandinsky, built upon the departure from realism of Vincent van Gogh and Henri Matisse, and developed towards the expression of feeling through colour and form. This often led to exaggeration and distortion, which induced unease in the viewing public. Similar haunting and irrational imagery were used in German expressionist cinema, such as Robert Wiene's *The Cabinet of Dr Caligari* (1919) and F. W. Murnau's *Nosferatu* (1922).

The origins of expressionism as a theatrical movement are to be found in the work of a number of German dramatists who wrote between 1907 and the early 1920s. These include Ernst Barlach, Reinhard Goering, Walter Hasenclever, Carl Hauptmann, Franz Kafka, Georg Kaiser, Oscar Kokoschka, Carl Sternheim and Ernst Toller. Even ▷ Brecht was influenced by the movement in his early days. Although their individual styles differ greatly the expressionist playwrights rejected the 'objective' approach of naturalism and developed a highly emotional and subjective form of dramatic expression which aimed to explore the 'essence' of human experience. In their view this could be revealed only by getting beyond the surface appearances of ordinary life and exploring man's subconscious desires and visions. The impulse for this was revolutionary, if politically unclear. ▷ Strindberg, Wedekind, ▷ Freud and ▷ Nietzsche were the idols of the movement. Bourgeois ideology was the enemy and the uniting vision ubiquitously advocated was the rebirth of man (with the emphasis very much on the male) in touch with his spirit and free from petty social restraints. The use of exaggerated gesture, disturbing sound, colour and movement was a vital part of the dramatists' technique of shocking the audience and conveying ecstatic or *Angst*-ridden states of being. Short disconnected scenes replaced carefully constructed plots and scenery was distorted and hallucinatory rather than realistic. Later dramatists, such as Eugene O'Neill, Elmer Rice and ▷ Sean O'Casey, have tended to borrow from the dramatic language of expressionism without necessarily sharing the fervour of their German predecessors.

F

Fabian Society

A large society of socialistic intellectuals, closely bound up with the British ▷ Labour Party. It was founded in 1884 and named after the Roman general Fabius Cunctator – 'Fabius the Delayer' – who in the 3rd century BC saved Rome from the Carthaginian army under Hannibal, by using a policy of attrition instead of open battle, *ie* he destroyed the army by small attacks on isolated sections of it, instead of risking total defeat by confronting Hannibal with the entire Roman army. The Fabian Society similarly advocated socialism by piecemeal action through parliamentary reform instead of risking disaster by total revolution; this policy has been summarized in the phrase 'the inevitability of gradualness'. The Fabians were among the principal influences leading to the foundation of the Labour Party in 1900. The years between 1884 and 1900 were those of its greatest distinction; they were led by ▷ George Bernard Shaw and Sidney and ▷ Beatrice Webb, and made their impact through the Fabian Essays on social and economic problems. They always advocated substantial thinking on solid evidence, in contrast to the more idealistic and 'utopian' socialism of such Victorian writers as William Morris. The diversification of socialist thought under the combined impact of theory emanating from France and political upheavals in Eastern Europe has perhaps made the Fabian framework anachronistic.

Fable

In its narrower, conventional definition, a fable is a short story, often but not necessarily about animals, illustrating a piece of popular wisdom, or explaining unscientifically a fact of nature. Animals are commonly used as characters because they are readily identified with simplified human qualities, as the fox with cunning, the lamb with meekness, the wolf with greed, the ass with stupidity. In primitive folklore, fables are worldwide. The tales in ▷ Rudyard Kipling's *Just So Stories* (1902) for children resemble the kind of primitive fable which seeks to explain facts of nature (such as how the leopard got its spots) without the aid of science. Sophisticated literatures favour the moral fable, the leading European tradition for which was established by the Greek fabulist Aesop. To this tradition belongs the medieval Latin and German beast satire of Reynard the Fox, from which is derived the best strict fable in English – Chaucer's *Nun's Priest's Tale* of the Cock and the Fox in the *Canterbury Tales*. Almost equally good are Robert Henryson's *Thirteen Morall Fabilis*. However, though fables are plentiful in English as in every literature, used illustratively and ornamentally amongst other matter, English literature is comparatively poor in strict fabulists. John Gay's *Fables* are usually regarded as pleasant minor works; John Dryden's *Fables Ancient and Modern* (1969) are mostly not fables, Rudyard Kipling's *Jungle Books* (1894, 5), like his *Just So Stories*, are children's classics. ▷ T. F. Powys' *Fables* (1929) are original and beautiful, and ▷ George Orwell's *Animal Farm* (1945) is very well known.

A broader interpretation of the term 'fable' allows a wider range of depiction: a tale which is a comment in metaphor on human nature, less directly figurative than allegory, and less roundabout in reaching its point than parable. In this broader meaning, English literature perhaps produced the greatest of all fables, Swift's *Gulliver's Travels*. But this broader interpretation admits an aspect of fable into almost any serious fiction; thus critics sometimes speak of a novelist's 'fable' in trying to express the underlying intention implicit in a novel. A modern view of this broader interpretation of the fable is expressed by ▷ William Golding in his essay 'Fable' in *The Hot Gates*, and its practice is exemplified in his own novels.

▷ Allegory.

Fainlight, Ruth (b 1931)

Poet and translator. Born in New York, Fainlight lives in Britain, although she is an American citizen. Her work is marked for its exploration of different poetic identities, and different possibilities for selfhood as a woman poet. Her volumes of poetry include: *Cages* (1966); *The Region's Violence* (1973); *Twenty One Poems* (1975); *Another Full Moon* (1976); *Sibyls and Others* (1980) and *Climates* (1983). She has also translated the Portuguese poet Sophia de Mello Breyner.

Fairbairns, Zoe (b 1948)

Novelist. Her novels are: *Live as Family* (1968); *Down: An Exploration* (1969); *Benefits* (1982); *Stand We At Last* (1983); *Here Today* (1984); *Closing* (1987). She uses a range of genres, such as ▷ science fiction (*Benefits*) or the crime thriller (*Here Today*; ▷ detective fiction) to explore the development of ▷ feminist consciousness. *Stand We At Last* recounts the lives of a succession of women from the middle of the 19th century up to the 1970s, and may be compared with *The Seven Ages* by ▷ Eva Figes in its project of rediscovering the unwritten history of women's experience.

Fairy-tales
Fairy-tales have often been seen as simple narratives to amuse children, but their more pervasive significance was noted as early as the 17th century when writers used the stories for a didactic purpose. In the 19th century there was an emphasis on the moral role and related psychological impact of the tales. The major development in the theoretic treatment of fairy-tales occurred, however, with ▷ Freud and ▷ Jung: the former saw the narratives as a way in which the subjects could work out their psychic problems, while the latter looked for universal and archetypal patterns. More recently the stories have been linked to a process of socialization as well as the imposition on girls of patriarchal value judgements. ▷ Angela Carter's feminist reworking of traditional fairy-tales attempted to counter this.

▷ Women, Status of.

Bib: Zipes, J., *Don't Bet on the Prince*.

Farce
A term used for comedy in which ▷ realism is sacrificed for the sake of extravagant humour. Its derivation is from stuffing used in cookery, and as a literary term it was applied to light and frivolous material introduced by actors into the medieval mystery plays. Normally it is now applied to lightweight comedies only.

Farrell, J. G. (James Gordon) (1935–79)
Novelist. His best work consists of carefully researched, and powerfully imagined historical novels. *The Siege of Krishnapur* (1973), a fictitious account of the Indian mutiny, won the Booker Prize; *The Singapore Grip* (1978) recounts the collapse of British power in Malaya, culminating in the Japanese capture of Singapore in 1942; *Troubles* (1970) is set in Ireland in 1919. These three novels, which form a kind of trilogy concerned with the long demise of the British Empire, represent an ambitious attempt at historical novel-writing. His career was ended by his early death on a fishing expedition in Ireland. Other novels are: *A Man From Elsewhere* (1963); *The Lung* (1965); *A Girl in the Head* (1967); *The Hill Station* (unfinished, 1981).

Fascism
The fasces, a bundle of rods bound round an axe, were the symbol of the civil power of ancient Rome. The symbol was adopted by Mussolini's Fascist Party which ruled Italy from 1922 to 1945. It was right-wing and anti-communist. The National Socialist Party in Germany (1933–45) and the Falangist Party that helped to bring Franco to power in Spain in 1938 were akin to the Italian Fascist Party, and to some extent modelled on it. This is also true of the smaller Fascist parties in other countries, though Oswald Mosley's British Union of Fascists was never politically significant. All such parties favoured strong nationalism, political dictatorship, the suppression of ▷ communism and socialism; under German influence, they were usually marked by racial prejudice.

English writers, especially between 1930 and 1945, were predominantly left-wing in sympathy, and used the term 'Fascist' in the sense of right-wing, despotic, reactionary, brutal, etc. and applied it to any person or body of people whose politics they disliked. This abusive use of 'Fascist', though tiresome and misleading, is not due merely to political prejudice: few political ideas of historical importance have been so closely associated with brutality as Fascism, and few have contributed so little of significance to political thinking. Nonetheless, Fascists' emphasis on leadership and (implicitly) on aristocracy of the sort that requires a trained élite and not hereditary privilege, appealed in varying degree to some leading British and American writers of the period 1920–40, such as ▷ W. B. Yeats and ▷ Ezra Pound. ▷ T. S. Eliot, ▷ Wyndham Lewis and ▷ D. H. Lawrence have also been accused of Fascist leanings. All these writers had right-wing tendencies because they reacted strongly against the simplifications of social theory resulting from the traditions of 19th-century liberalism and from ▷ Marxist Socialism; however, only Pound became deeply identified with Fascism.

Feinstein, Elaine (b 1930)
Poet, novelist and translator. Born in Lancashire and educated at Cambridge, Feinstein has taught literature at Essex University as well as working in publishing. Her poetry is written closely from personal situations, and is deeply experiential. Her volumes of verse include: *In a Green Eye* (1966) (her first collection); *The Magic Apple Tree* (1971); *The Celebrants* (1973); *Some Unease and Angels: Selected Poems* (1977) and *The Feast of Eurydice* (1980). She has also edited an edition of Marina Tsvetayeva's poetry, and her novels include *Children of the Rose* (1975) and *The Border* (1984).

Fell, Alison (b 1944)
Poet, journalist and fiction writer. Born in Dumfries, Fell has worked as a sculptor, with women's theatre and for the feminist journal *Spare Rib*, for whom she edited the fiction ▷ anthology, *Hard Feelings*. As well as her volume of poetry, *Kisses for Mayakovsy*, in 1981 she published a children's novel, and two novels.

Feminism
In literary criticism this term is used to describe a range of critical positions which argue that the distinction between 'masculine' and 'feminine' (▷ gender) is formative in the generation of all discursive practices. In its concern to bring to the fore the particular situation of women in society 'feminism' as a focus for the raising of consciousness has a long history, and can be taken to embrace an interest in all forms of women's writing throughout history. In its essentialist (▷ Essentialism) guise, feminism proposes a range of experiences peculiar to women, which are, by definition, denied to men, and which it seeks to emphasize in order to compensate for the oppressive nature of a society rooted in what it takes to be patriarchal authority. A more materialist (▷ Materialism) account would emphasize the extent to which gender difference is a cultural construction, and therefore amenable to change by concerted political action. Traditional materialist accounts, especially those of ▷ Marx, have placed the issue of 'class' above that of 'gender', but contemporary feminism regards the issue of 'gender' as frequently cutting across 'class' divisions, and raising fundamental questions about the social role of women in relations of production and exchange. In so far as all literature is 'gendered', then feminist literary criticism is concerned with the analysis of the social construction of 'femininity' and 'masculinity' in particular texts. One of its major objectives is to expose how hitherto 'masculine' criticism has sought to represent itself as a universal experience. Similarly, the focus is adjusted in order to enable literary works themselves to disclose the ways in which the experiences they communicate are determined by wider social assumptions about gender difference, which move beyond the formal boundaries of the text. To this extent feminism is necessarily the focus of an interdisciplinary approach to literature, psychology, sociology and philosophy.

Psychoanalytic feminism, for example, often overlaps with socialist feminism. It approaches the concept of gender as a problem rather than a given, and draws on ▷ Freud's emphasis on the instability of sexual identities. The fact that femininity – and masculinity – are never fully acquired, once and for all, suggests a relative openness allowing for changes in the ways they are distributed. Literature's disturbance and exploration of ways of thinking about sexual difference have proved a rich source for feminist critics. In the 1990s the multiplicity of feminist criticisms has led some women to welcome this as a ▷ utopian pluralism, while others fear that this pluralism is simply a reassertion of liberal values to the detriment of political activism.

▷ Women's movement.

Bib: de Beauvoir, S., *The Second Sex*; Greene, G. and Kahn, C. (eds.), *Making a Difference: Feminist Literary Criticism*; Millett, K., *Sexual Politics*; Spender, D., *Feminist Theorists*; Wollstonecraft, M., *Vindication of the Rights of Women*.

Fenton, James (b 1949)
Poet. Educated at Oxford, Fenton has worked as a journalist in Britain (as theatre critic for the *Sunday Times*) and abroad, including in Vietnam. His publications include: *Terminal Moraine* (1972); *A Vacant Possession* (1978); *A German Requiem* (1980); *The Memory of War* (1982).

Figes, Eva (b 1932)
Novelist and ▷ feminist writer. Born Eva Unger to a German Jewish family who escaped to England in 1939 after the imprisonment of her father by the Nazis. Educated at London University, she worked in publishing before writing her first novel *Equinox* (1966), a partly autobiographical and largely pessimistic account of a woman's search for meaning and human relationships. The influence of ▷ Virginia Woolf is apparent in her exploration of the inner world of the self and her lyrical sense of the flux of experience and the continuity of memories. *Days* (1974) and *The Seven Ages* (1986) seek to establish an unrecorded female history, linking many generations of women, while *Waking* (1981) is structured around seven waking moments of a woman or women. These ▷ modernist techniques combine with the influence of ▷ Samuel Beckett in *Winter Journey* (1967), which represents the inner world of an old man dying alone. Figes has a sense of herself as a European, and an awareness of the Holocaust which is a part of her family history, and draws on the work of one of the great European modernists,

Franz Kafka. *Konek Landing* (1969) is a Kafkaesque story of victims and executioners in a nameless country. Figes's work rejects the English realist tradition in favour of a ▷ postmodernist commitment to experiment, apparent especially in *B* (1972), a self-reflexive novel about the nature of creativity, and the problematic relations of reality and fiction. She has written short stories, radio plays, children's fiction, criticism, and a classic text of the feminist movement, *Patriarchal Attitudes: Women in Society* (1970). *Little Eden: A Child at War* (1978) is autobiography. Her other novels are: *Nelly's Version* (1977); *Light* (1983); *Ghosts* (1988).

Figures of speech

Alliteration The beginning of accented syllables near to each other with the same consonantal sound, as in many idiomatic phrases: 'safe and sound': 'thick and thin'; 'right as rain'. Alliteration is thus the opposite of ▷ rhyme, by which the similar sounds occur at the ends of the syllables: 'near and dear'; 'health and wealth'. Alliteration dominated the pattern of Old English poetry; after the Conquest, French influence caused rhyme to predominate. However, in the 14th century there seems to have been an 'alliterative revival', producing such important poems as *Piers Plowman* and *Sir Gawain and the Green Knight*. Alliterative verse was accentual, *ie* did not depend on the regular distribution of accented syllables in a line, but on the number of accented syllables in the lines.

After the 14th century, rhyme and the regular count of syllables became the normal pattern for English verse. Alliteration, however, continued to be used unsystematically by every poet.

Anacoluthon From the Greek: 'not following on'. Strictly speaking, this is not a figure of speech, but a grammatical term for a sentence which does not continue the syntactical pattern with which it starts. However, it may be used deliberately with the virtue of intensifying the force of a sentence *eg* by the sudden change from indirect to direct speech.

Anticlimax
▷ *Bathos* (below)

Antithesis A method of emphasis by the placing of opposed ideas or characteristics in direct contrast with each other.

Apostrophe A form of direct address often used by a narrator in the middle of his narrative as a means of emphasizing a moral lesson.

Assonance The rhyming of vowel sounds without the rhyming of consonants.

Bathos From the Greek: 'death'. The descent from the sublime to the ridiculous. This may be the result of incompetence in the writer, but Alexander Pope used it skilfully as a method of ridicule:

Here thou, great ANNA! whom three realms obey
Dost sometimes counsel take – and sometimes tea.
(*The Rape of the Lock*)

Pope wrote an essay *Bathos, the Art of Sinking in Poetry*, as a travesty of the essay by Longinus, *On the Sublime* (1st century AD). Longinus had great prestige as a critic in Pope's time.

Climax From the Greek: 'a ladder'. The climb from lower matters to higher, with the consequent satisfying of raised expectations.

Euphemism A mild or vague expression used to conceal a painful or disagreeable truth, *eg* 'he passed on' for 'he died'. It is sometimes used ironically.

Euphuism A highly artificial quality of style resembling that of John Lyly's *Euphues*.

Hyperbole Expression in extreme language so as to achieve intensity.

Innuendo A way of expressing dislike or criticism indirectly, or by a hint; an insinuation.

Irony From the Greek: 'dissimulation'. A form of expression by which the writer intends his meaning to be understood differently and less favourably, in contrast to his overt statement:

It is a truth universally acknowledged that a single man in possession of a good fortune must be in want of a wife.

This opening sentence of Jane Austen's *Pride and Prejudice* is to be understood as meaning that the appearance of such a young man in a neighbourhood inspires very strong wishes in the hearts of mothers of unmarried daughters, and that these wishes cause the mothers to behave as though the statement were indeed a fact.

Dramatic irony occurs when a character in a play makes a statement in innocent assurance of its truth, while the audience is well aware that he or she is deceived.

Litotes Emphatic expression through an ironical negative, *eg* 'She's no beauty', meaning that the woman is ugly.

Malapropism A comic misuse of language, usually by a person who is both pretentious and ignorant. The term derives from the character Mrs Malaprop in Sheridan's play *The Rivals* (1775). This comic device had in fact been used by earlier writers, such as ▷ Shakespeare in the portrayal of Dogberry in *Much Ado About Nothing.*

Meiosis Understatement, used as a deliberate method of emphasis by irony, *eg* 'Would you like to be rich?' – 'I should rather think so!'

Metaphor A figure of speech by which unlike objects are identified with each other for the purpose of emphasizing one or more aspects of resemblance between them. A simple example: 'the camel is the ship of the desert'.

Mixed metaphor is a confused image in which the successive parts are inconsistent, so that (usually) absurdity results: 'I smell a rat, I see it floating in the air, but I will nip it in the bud', *ie* 'I suspect an evil, and I can already see the beginnings of it, but I will take action to suppress it.' However mixed metaphor is sometimes used deliberately to express a state of confusion.

Dead metaphor is one in which the image has become so familiar that it is no longer thought of as figurative, *eg* the phrase 'to take steps', meaning 'to take action'.

Metonymy The naming of a person, institution or human characteristic by some object or attribute with which it is clearly associated, as when a king or queen may be referred to as 'the Crown':

Sceptre and Crown
Must tumble down,
And in the dust be equal made
With the poor crooked scythe and spade.
('The Levelling Dust', James Shirley)

Here 'Sceptre and Crown' refer to kings, and perhaps more broadly to the classes which control government, while 'scythe and spade' stand for the humble peasantry. Metonymy has taken on additional meanings since the advent of ▷ Structuralism. One of the originators of Russian ▷ Formalism, ▷ Roman Jakobson, draws a distinction between 'metaphor' – the linguistic relationship between two different objects on the grounds of their similarity – and 'metonymy' as a means of establishing a relationship between two objects in terms of their contiguity. Where metaphor is regarded as a major rhetorical device in *poetry*, metonymy is more usually associated with *prose.* The critic and novelist ▷ David Lodge takes up this distinction in his book *The Modes of Modern Writing* (1977), and suggests that 'metaphor' and 'metonymy' constitute a structurally significant binary opposition that enables the distinction to be made between poetry and drama on the one hand and prose on the other. Lodge emphasizes, however, that these terms are not mutually exclusive, but rather contribute to 'a theory of dominance of one quality over another'. Hence it is possible for a novel to contain 'poetic' effects and vice versa.

Oxymoron A figure of speech formed by the conjunction of contrasting terms; it derives from two Greek words meaning 'sharp and dull'.

Palindrome A word or sentence that reads the same backwards or forwards, *eg*

Lewd did I live; evil I
did dwel
(Phillips, 1706)

Paradox A statement that challenges the mind by appearing to be self-contradictory.

Pathetic fallacy A term invented by the critic John Ruskin (*Modern Painters*, Vol. III, Pt. iv, Ch. 12) to denote the tendency common especially among poets to ascribe human emotions or qualities to inanimate objects, *eg* 'an angry sea'. Ruskin describes it by dividing writers into four classes: those who do not use it merely because they are insensitive; superior writers in whom it is a mark of sensitivity; writers who are better still and do not need it because they 'feel strongly, think strongly, and see truly'; and writers of the best sort who use it because in some instances they 'see in a sort untruly, because what they see is inconceivably above them'. In general, he considers that the pathetic fallacy is justified when the feeling it expresses is a true one.

Personification A kind of metaphor, by which an abstraction or inanimate object is endowed with personality.

Play on words A use of a word with more than one meaning or of two words which sound the same in such a way that both meanings are called to mind. In its simplest form, as the modern pun, this is merely a joke. In the 16th and 17th centuries poets frequently played upon words seriously; this is especially true of ▷ Shakespeare and dramatists contemporary with him, and of the Metaphysical poets, such as John Donne and George Herbert.

This very serious use of puns or plays upon words decreased in the 18th century, when Samuel Johnson censured Shakespeare's fondness for puns (or, as Johnson called them, 'quibbles'). The reason for this disappearance of the serious 'play upon words' was the admiration of educated men for what Bishop Sprat in his *History of the Royal Society* (1667) called 'mathematical plainness of meaning', a criterion emulated by poets as well as by prose writers. In the 19th century, the play on words was revived by humorous writers and writers for children, such as Thomas Hood, Edward Lear and Lewis Carroll (▷ Children's books). Although their use of the pun was ostensibly comic, its effect in their writings is often unexpectedly poignant or even profound, especially in Carroll's 'Alice' books. Puns continued to be despised by the adult world of reason, but they could freely and revealingly be used in what was regarded as the childish world of nonsense and fantasy.

Modern poets and critics have recovered the older, serious use of the play on words. Ambiguity of meaning which in the 18th century was considered a vice of expression, is now seen as a quality of rich texture of expression, though of course 'good' and 'bad' types of ambiguity have to be distinguished. ▷ James Joyce used the technique with unprecedented elaboration in ▷ *Finnegans Wake*; ▷ William Empson revived the serious punning of Donne and Marvell in his poems, and investigated the whole problem in *Seven Types of Ambiguity* (1930). Just as admiration for mathematics and the physical sciences caused the decline of the play on words, so the revival of it has been partly due to the rise of another science, that of psychoanalysis, especially the school of ▷ Freud, with its emphasis on the interplay of conscious and unconscious meanings in the use of language.

Pun
▷ *Play on words* (above).

Rhyme A verbal music made through identity of sound in the final syllables of words. Several varieties of rhyme exist:

End-rhyme When the final syllables of lines of verse are rhymed.

Internal rhyme When one at least of the rhyming words is in mid-line; as in 'fair' and 'air' in the following couplet by Swinburne:

We have seen thee, O Love, thou art
fair; thou art goodly, O Love;
Thy wings make light in the air as wings
of a dove.

Masculine rhymes are single stressed syllables as in the examples already given.

Feminine rhymes are on two syllables, the second of which is unaccented. As in the following from Marlowe's *Passionate Shepherd*:

And I will make thee beds of roses
And a thousand fragrant posies;
A cap of flowers, and a kirtle
Embroider'd all with leaves of myrtle

Half-rhymes (pararhymes) are the rhyming of consonants but not of vowels (contrast ▷ *Assonance*). They are sometimes used as an equivalent for full rhymes, since consonants are more noticeable in rhyme music than vowels. Change in pronunciation sometimes has the effect of changing what was intended as full rhyme into half-rhyme, as in the following example from Pope:

Tis not enough, taste, judgement, learning,
join;
In all you speak, let truth and candour shine:

In the 18th century, 'join' was pronounced as 'jine'.

Simile Similar to metaphor, but in similes the comparison is made explicit by the use of a word such as 'like' or 'as'.

Syllepsis A figure of speech by which a word is used in a literal and a metaphorical sense at the same time, *eg* 'You have broken my heart and my best china vase'.

Synecdoche A figure of speech by which a part is used to express a whole, or a whole is used to express a part, *eg* 'fifty sail' is used for fifty ships, or the 'smiling year' is used for the spring. In practice, synecdoche is indistinguishable from metonymy (see above). Like metonymy this figure depends upon a relationship of contiguity, and is regarded as one side of the opposition between 'poetry' and 'non-poetry'. Both metonymy and synedoche operate by combining attributes of particular objects, therefore they are crucial rhetorical devices for the representation of reality, and are closely related to ▷ realism as a literary style in so far as they function referentially.

Transferred epithet The transference of an adjective from the noun to which it applies grammatically to some other word in the sentence, usually in such a way as to express the quality of an action or of behaviour, *eg* 'My host handed me a hospitable glass of wine', instead of 'My hospitable host handed me . . . .'

Zeugma A figure similar to syllepsis (see above); one word used with two others, to only one of which it is grammatically or logically applicable.

Finlay, Ian Hamilton (b 1925)
▷ Scottish poet and sculptor. Finlay works simultaneously in both words and the sculpture of physical objects, exploring the possibility of poetry as a form of visual art. His work is in certain ways representative of Concrete Poetry, the experimental movement which, since the 1960s, has sought to emphasize poetry's physical, typographical existence. Finlay has created a famous garden at Stonypath, Lanarkshire, which functions as a gallery for his work. His publications include: *The Dancers Inherit the Party* (1961); *Tea Leaves and Fishes* (1966); *Poems to Hear and See* (1971); *Heroic Emblems* (1978).

***Finnegans Wake* (1939)**
A novel by ▷ James Joyce. It is one of the most original experiments ever undertaken in the novel form, and the most difficult of his works to read. It purports to be one night in the life of a Dublin public-house keeper, H. C. Earwicker, and as he is asleep from the beginning to the end of the book, his experiences are all those of dream. The advantage of dream experience is that it is unrestricted by self-conscious logic, and operates by free association unrestrained by inhibitions. The basis of the 'story' is his relationships with his wife, Anna Livia Plurabelle, his daughter, Isobel, and his twin sons Shem and Shaun; it reaches out, however, into Irish and European myths as these are suggested to his sleeping consciousness by objects in his mean little house and neighbourhood. Joyce intends in fact to make Earwicker a type of 'Everyman'. The language is made by fusing together words so as to cause them – as in dreams – to suggest several levels of significance simultaneously; this is a device which had already been used playfully by Lewis Carroll in his poem 'Jabberwocky' in the dream story for children *Through the Looking-Glass* (1872). Joyce, however, in his desire to universalize Earwicker, freely combines words from foreign languages with English ones, so that Earwicker's mind becomes representatively European while remaining his own. The movement of the narrative is based on the ideas of the 18th-century Italian philosopher Vico, who believed that ages succeed each other – gods, heroes, men – and then recommence; this is followed out in Earwicker's successive identifications (as Adam, Humpty Dumpty, Christ, Cromwell, Noah, The Duke of Wellington, etc.), until at the end of the book the final sentence is completed by the first sentence at its beginning. The Christian pattern of fall and resurrection also contributes to the structure of the work. Another important influence on Joyce was the psychological ideas of ▷ Sigmund Freud on the mechanism of repression and the characteristics of dream association. Study necessitates the assistance of such a work as *A Reader's Guide to Finnegans Wake* by W. Y. Tindall.

Firbank, Ronald (1886–1926)
Writer of witty fantasies whose extravagant humour derives from the subtly calculated and highly wrought style. His best-known tales are probably *Vainglory* (1915); *Valmouth* (1919); *The Flower Beneath the Foot* (1923).

Fisher, Roy (b 1930)
Poet. Born in Birmingham, Fisher's work is realist in its evocation of the Midlands industrial landscape – this is especially true of his early work, which was generally unknown until the Oxford edition *Poems 1955–1980* (1981) appeared (most of his previous work had been published by the small presses, especially by Fulcrum). Fisher is a prolific poet, and his works include: *City* (1961); *The Memorial Fountain* (1966); *Collected Poems* (1969); *Matrix* (1971); *The Thing About Joe Sullivan* (1978); *A Furnace* (1986).

Flat and round characters
A categorization of characters, proposed by ▷ E. M. Forster in his influential study, ▷ *Aspects of the Novel*. Flat characters are 'constructed round a single idea or quality'; they are types or caricatures (such as Mrs Micawber in Dickens's *David Copperfield*). Round characters (such as Defoe's Moll Flanders) are 'capable of surprising [the reader] in a convincing way'. The idea of the flat character has passed into general use in the derogatory form of the 'two-dimensional character', but Forster himself recognized the virtues as well as the limitations of the flat character.

Focal character
The character within a narrative 'whose point of view orients the narrative perspective'

(▷ Genette). Where there is a focal character, his or her sense impressions and/or perceptions are what the narrative presents to the reader. The focal character is distinguished from the ▷ narrator, since the latter may be a different person. For example, there may be an impersonal, extradiegetic narrator, focalizing through a character in the third person, as in ▷ Henry James's ▷ *The Ambassadors*, or the narrator and focal character may be the same person, but at different points in time, as in ▷ Margaret Atwood's *Cat's Eye*.

▷ Narratology; Focalization.

Focalization

In ▷ narratology, focalization is an aspect of ▷ mood, and is adopted by ▷ Genette as a more precise term than 'point of view' to indicate the focus of a narrative. Internal focalization views events through the mind of a particular ▷ focal character, external focalization follows the experiences of a character without revealing his or her thoughts, while non-focalized narration is told by an impersonal narrator without restriction.

Ford, Ford Madox (Ford Hermann Hueffer) (1873–1939)

Novelist, critic, poet. His father was of German origin, and became music critic for ▷ *The Times*; his mother was daughter of the ▷ Pre-Raphaelite painter, Ford Madox Brown. Ford was first known as an aesthetic writer of fairy stories, but he became deeply interested in contemporary Fench writing and culture, and became a propagandist for the rigorous discipline of French art, exercising a strong personal influence on ▷ Joseph Conrad and ▷ Ezra Pound. He co-operated with Conrad on two novels, *The Inheritors* (1901) and *Romance* (1903). He was a prolific writer, but is now chiefly remembered for *The Good Soldier* (1915) and for the four novels known in Britain as *The Tietjens Tetralogy* (after the name of its hero), and in America as *Parade's End*: *Some Do Not* (1924), *No More Parades* (1925), *A Man Could Stand Up* (1926), and *Last Post* (1928). The tetralogy is regarded by some critics as the most memorable fiction about the war of 1914–18 (in which Ford served, although he was 40 on enlistment), and as the most remarkable account of the upheaval in English social values in the decade 1910–20. *The Good Soldier* is a subtle and ambiguous study of the cruelty, infidelity and madness below the respectable surface of the lives of two couples, and is notable for its use of an unreliable narrator.

Ford has an undoubted importance in literary history because of his personal influence. As a poet, he played a significant part in the founding of ▷ Imagism. In 1908–9 he was editor of the brilliant but short-lived *English Review*, to which ▷ Thomas Hardy, ▷ Henry James, ▷ H. G. Wells, Joseph Conrad and the Russian novelist Leo Tolstoy all contributed. He was also an early encourager of ▷ D. H. Lawrence. Brought up in the relatively narrow Pre-Raphaelite and ▷ aesthetic movements, in the 1900s he was a central figure among the writers who were thinking radically about problems of artistic form, especially in novel-writing. He regarded the 19th-century English novel as too much a product of the accident of genius, and, aligning himself with James and Conrad, was in opposition to H. G. Wells who preferred the title of journalist to that of artist. After World War I he moved to Paris and became part of a circle of expatriate writers, including ▷ James Joyce, Ernest Hemingway and Gertrude Stein. He also founded the *Transatlantic Review*.

After 1930 his imaginative writing was somewhat neglected but he is now recognized as an important figure of the ▷ modernist movement. Of present-day novelists, he has perhaps had most effect on ▷ Graham Greene. Apart from *The Tietjens Tetralogy* and *The Good Soldier*, novels selected for praise include the historical trilogy about Tudor England (*The Fifth Queen*, 1906; *Privy Seal*, 1907; *The Fifth Queen Crowned*, 1908). His *Collected Poems* were published in 1936.

Bib: Cassell, R. A. (ed.), *Ford Madox Ford: Modern Judgements*; Green, R., *Ford Madox Ford, Prose and Politics*; Meixner, J. A., *Ford Madox Ford's Novels: A Critical Study*; Mizener, A., *The Saddest Story* (biography); Ohmann, C., *Ford Madox Ford: From Apprentice to Craftsman*.

Formalism

School of literary thought which flourished in Russia after 1917. Its main exponents, particularly ▷ Roman Jakobson, focused on the differentiation between literary language and other forms of written expression. The insights of the Formalists have influenced later critics.

▷ Defamiliarization; Deconstruction.

Forster, E. M. (Edward Morgan) (1879–1970)

Novelist. His work is primarily in a realistic mode, and his ideas in the liberal tradition; indeed, much of his work is concerned with the legacy of Victorian middle-class liberalism.

He was educated at Tonbridge School (a public school whose ethos is characterized by Sawston in the first two novels) and then at King's College, Cambridge, of which he was later made an honorary fellow. Through contacts made at Cambridge he came to be associated with the ▷ Bloomsbury Group. He travelled in Europe, lived in Italy and Egypt, and spent some years in India, where he was for a time secretary to a rajah after World War I.

Forster's novels are: *Where Angels Fear to Tread* (1905); *The Longest Journey* (1907); *A Room with a View* (1908); ▷ *Howards End* (1910); ▷ *A Passage to India* (1924); and *Maurice* (1971). The last of these, which has a homosexual theme, was published posthumously, as was *The Life to Come* (1972), a collection of stories, many of which treat the same theme. His other two collections of short stories are: *The Celestial Omnibus* (1914) and *The Eternal Moment* (1928). These are mainly early work; they were published in a collected edition in 1947. His high reputation rests mainly on his fiction, but he has also written biographies and essays which are important for understanding his outlook as an imaginative writer. The biography of his friend Goldsworthy Lowes Dickinson (1934) is about a Cambridge scholar who was an important leader of liberal political opinion; that of his great-aunt, Marianne Thornton (1956), is enlightening about Forster's background. *The Hill of Devi* (1953) is an account of his experiences in India. The essays in *Abinger Harvest* (1936) and *Two Cheers for Democracy* (1951) include expressions of his opinions about politics, literature and society. ▷ *Aspects of the Novel* (1927) is one of the best-known critical works on the novel form. He co-operated with Eric Crozier on the libretto for Benjamin Britten's ▷ opera *Billy Budd* (1951).

Forster's dominant theme is the habitual conformity of people to unexamined social standards and conventions, and the ways in which this conformity blinds individuals to recognition of what is true in what is unexpected, to the proper uses of the intelligence, and to their own resources of spontaneous life. Spontaneous life and free intelligence also draw on traditions, and Forster shows how English traditions have on the one hand nourished complacency, hypocrisy, and insular philistinism, and on the other hand, humility, honesty, and sceptical curiosity. In several of the novels, and especially in *A Passage to India*, British culture is contrasted with a foreign tradition which has virtues that the British way of life is without. His style is consistently light and witty, strongly characterized by a use of irony. *A Passage to India* stands out from his work for the subtlety and resonance of its symbolism, and for its analysis of the paradoxes of ▷ colonialism.

Bib: Trilling, L., *E. M. Forster*; McConkey, J., *The Novels of Forster*; Bradbury, M. (ed.), *E. M. Forster: A Collection of Critical Essays*; Stone, W., *The Cave and the Mountain*; Furbank, P. N., *E. M. Forster: A Life* (2 vols).

Forster, Margaret (b 1938)
Novelist. Forster has produced a steady stream of writings since the early 1960s, as well as the screenplay (from her own novel) for one of the classic films of 'Swinging Sixties' London, *Georgy Girl* (1966, directed by Silvio Narizzano). Her works are broadly feminist, and often centre on a female protagonist or on relationships between women. Her other works include: *Dames' Delight* (1964); *The Bogeyman* (1966); *The Seduction of Mrs Pendlebury* (1974); *Mother Can You Hear Me?* (1979) and *Marital Rites* (1982). She has also written a biography of ▷ Victorian poet Elizabeth Barrett Browning, and published *Significant Sisters: The Grassroots of Active Feminism 1839–1939*.

Forsyte Saga, The
A sequence of novels constituting a study of ▷ Victorian and ▷ Edwardian society by ▷ John Galsworthy. They comprise: *The Man of Property* (1906); *The Indian Summer of a Forsyte* (1918); *In Chancery* (1920); *Awakening* (1920); *To Let* (1921). A television serialization of the work in 1967 was extremely popular.

Foucault, Michel (1926–84)
Along with ▷ Louis Althusser and ▷ Jacques Derrida, Foucault is one of the most influential of French philosophers whose work has been taken up by the practitioners of other disciplines. Foucault rejects the totalizing explanations of human development in favour of a more detailed analysis of how power functions within particular ▷ discourses. In *Madness and Civilization* (1965) he explored the historical opposition between 'madness' and 'civilization', applying ▷ Saussure's notion of differentials (▷ Difference) to the various ways in which society excludes the behaviour which threatens it. He later took this issue up in *Discipline and Punish* (1977), and *I Pierre Riviere* (1978). In *The Order of Things* (1971) and *The Archaeology*

of Knowledge (1972) he investigated the ways in which human knowledge is organized, and the transition from discourses which rely upon a notion of 'self-presence', to those which operate differentially to produce the kind of linguistic self-consciousness characteristic of ▷ postmodernism. In essays such as those translated in *Language, Counter-memory, Practice* (1977), he sought to clarify specific areas of opposition through which discourse is constructed. At the time of his death he had embarked on an investigation of the discourses of sexuality through the ages, and the three volumes of *The History of Sexuality* (1978–87) have now been published.

▷ Archaeology; Nietzsche.

***Four Quartets* (1935–42)**

Four poems written between 1935 and 1942 by ▷ T. S. Eliot, eventually published as a single work. They are contemplative, religious poems, each concerned with a distinct aspect of spiritual experience. Each has as its symbolic centre a place; each uses symbolically one of the four 'elements' of medieval physics; each has a structure analogous to the movements and the instruments of a musical quartet; the theme that unites the four is that of the human consciousness in relation to time and the concept of eternity. *Burnt Norton* (the element of air) centres on the rose garden of a ruined country house (Burnt Norton) in Gloucestershire and plays on the differences and relationships between the actual present, the past in memory, and speculation on what might have been. *East Coker* (earth) is based on a village in Somerset, whence the poet's ancestors derived, and it includes quotations from *The Governor* (1531) by Sir Thomas Elyot; the poem is concerned with man as part of the process of nature. *Dry Salvages* (water) is named after rocks off the coast of Massachusetts; the poem is concerned with racial time and memory, larger than the time of history and of the seasons, and embracing the more unconscious regions of the mind. ▷ *Little Gidding* (fire) derives its title from the religious community in the reign of Charles I, who is supposed to have visited it when broken by defeat at the battle of Naseby. Fire in this poem is used as destruction (with reference to the raids on London during World War II), purification, illumination, and as an emblem of Divine Love.

Four Quartets was Eliot's last major work in non-dramatic poetry; the remainder of his career was devoted to poetic drama.

▷ Gardner, Helen.

Bib: Drew, E., *T. S. Eliot: The Design of his Poetry*.

Fowles, John (b 1926)

Novelist. Born in Essex and educated at Oxford University. His novels are: *The Collector* (1963); *The Magus* (1965; revised edition 1977); *The French Lieutenant's Woman* (1969); *Daniel Martin* (1977); *Mantissa* (1982); *A Maggot* (1985). He is an experimental writer, interested in the nature of fiction and its interaction with history and reality, but he combines this with a skill in story-telling and an ability to create compelling characters and a vivid sense of social context. Several of his novels have been best-sellers, and three: *The Collector, The Magus* and *The French Lieutenant's Woman* have been filmed. His reception by the critics has tended to be more enthusiastic in the U.S.A. than in Britain. The recurrent concerns of his novels are the power of repressive convention and social conformity, the enigmatic nature of sexual relations, the desire to manipulate and control and the problem of individual freedom. The last of these concerns reflects the influence of ▷ existentialism.

The Collector, the story of the kidnapping of an attractive and wealthy girl by an introverted clerk, is in part a study of a pathological desire for possession, and in part a fable about social deprivation. It is in three parts, the first and last narrated by the man, and the second by the girl. Fowles's novels are highly allusive: *The Magus*, like *The Collector*, employs parallels with ▷ Shakespeare's *The Tempest*. It also draws on the literary archetype of the quest in its story of a young man who travels to a Greek island where he is lured by a series of magical illusions into a confrontation with existential uncertainty and freedom of choice. *The French Lieutenant's Woman* employs parody of 19th-century novelistic style, quotations from sociological reports, from Darwin, ▷ Marx, Arnold and Tennyson, and authorial interruptions. Fowles's belief in the fundamental uncertainty of existence is reflected in his use of open endings; in *The Magus* the future of the main characters is 'another mystery' and *The French Lieutenant's Woman* has a choice of endings. *Daniel Martin* is more realist than his earlier work, exploiting his descriptive skill in a range of settings: it has less of the element of mystery and a more clearly affirmative ending. He has also written a volume of short stories, *The Ebony Tower* (1974), and works of non-fiction, including: *Islands* (1978); *The Tree* (1979); *The Enigma of Stonehenge* (1980) and *Land* (1985).

Bib: Conradi, P., *John Fowles*; Loveday, S., *The Romances of John Fowles.*

Frame, Janet (b 1942)
New Zealand novelist and short-story writer. Her collection of stories, *The Lagoon* (1951), and her trilogy of novels *Owls Do Cry* (1957), *Faces in the Water* (1961) and *The Edge of the Alphabet* (1962) are about childhood innocence and the imagination, both threatened by bereavement and a repressive society. *Scented Gardens for the Blind* (1963) and *The Adaptable Man* (1965) explore the limitations and potentialities of language. Of her later work, *Intensive Care* (1970), written while Frame was in the U.S.A., draws on the horrors of the Vietnam War for a visionary satire on the place of war in the New Zealand consciousness. Her other novels are: *Living in the Maniototo* (1979); *A State of Siege* (1982); *The Carpathians* (1988). Other story collections: *You Are Now Entering the Human Heart* (1983). She has also written three volumes of autobiography, and the recent film, *An Angel at my Table*, was based on her life and books.

Fraser, Antonia (b 1932)
Novelist and historian. Antonia Fraser is a popular writer of historical ▷ biographies, who has done much to make the lives of famous figures in British history accessible to a wide audience. Her works are meticulously researched but have been criticized for lacking historical context and finally offering a selective reading of British history. She is now married to the dramatist ▷ Harold Pinter, with whom she continues to campaign vigorously for the arts in Great Britain. She has been a member of the ▷ Arts Council, and is a Fellow of the Royal Society of Literature. Her works include: *Mary Queen of Scots* (1969); *A History of Toys* (1966); *Cromwell, Our Chief of Men* (1973); *King Charles II* (1979); and *The Weaker Vessel: Woman's Lot in the 17th Century* (1984). Her fiction includes *Quiet as a Nun* (1977) and *The Wild Island: A Mystery* (1978).

Frayn, Michael (b 1933)
British dramatist and novelist. His first plays, *Jamie* (1968) and *Birthdays* (1969) were written for television. Since then he has acquired a reputation both as a leading comic writer for the stage, particularly with his production of *Noises Off* (1982), and an important translator of ▷ Chekhov's plays. Other plays include: *The Two of Us* (1970); *The Sandboy* (1971); *Alphabetical Order* (1975); *Donkeys' Years* (1976); *Clouds* (1976); *Liberty Hall* (1980); *Make and Break* (1980); *Benefactors* (1984). Translations: *The Cherry Orchard* (1978); *The Fruits of Enlightenment* (1979); *Three Sisters* (1983); *Number One* (1984); *Wild Honey* (1984); *The Seagull* (1986); *Uncle Vanya* (1988). Novels include: *The Tin Men* (1965); *The Russian Interpreter* (1966); *Towards the End of the Morning* (1967); *A Very Private Life* (1968); *Sweet Dreams* (1973).

Frazer, Sir James G. (1854–1941)
Anthropologist. His *Golden Bough* (1890–1915) is a vast study of ancient mythology; it has influenced 20th-century poetry such as ▷ T. S. Eliot's ▷ *The Waste Land* and late-Freudian psychoanalysis: ▷ Freud's work on civilization and society in the 1920s and 1930s had a strong engagement with Frazer. An abridged edition was published in 1922. Other publications include: *Totemism* (1887); *Adonis, Attis, Osiris, Studies in the History of Oriental Religion* (1906); *Totemism and Exogamy* (1910); *Folklore in the Old Testament* (1918). Frazer was a major influence on the development of 20th-century anthropology and psychology, and in addition edited works by Cowper and Addison.
Bib: Fraser, R. (ed.), *Sir James Frazer and the Literary Imagination.*

Free indirect discourse
A technique whereby a narrative reports the speech or thoughts of a character, referring to that character in the third person but adopting the character's own idiom. Free indirect discourse thus falls between direct speech (or thought), which quotes a character's words verbatim, and reported speech (or thought) which paraphrases the speech or thoughts of the character in the idiom of the ▷ narrator. When free indirect discourse is used there is often a productive ambiguity as to which judgements are attributable to the character and which to the narrator and/or ▷ implied author.

Free verse
A way of writing poetry without use of ▷ rhyme, ▷ stanza pattern, or ▷ metre. Free verse perhaps had French origins; at all events it is often referred to as *vers libre*. It was practised, especially in the first 30 years of this century, in an attempt to escape from the rather mechanical uses of rhyme and metre by the late ▷ Romantics, and has now become the established practice of many 20th-century poets. ▷ T. S. Eliot attacked the whole concept of free verse, declaring that it

could only be defined by negatives (*no* rhyme, etc.) and that a genuine form would have a positive definition (*Reflections on Vers Libre*; 1917); 'But the most interesting verse which has yet been written in our language has been done either by taking a very simple form, like the iambic pentameter, and constantly withdrawing from it, or taking no form at all, and constantly approximating to a very simple one.' Eliot himself was as bold as any of his contemporaries in rhythmic experimentation, but his methods are clearly one or other of the two which he here describes.
Bib: Hartman, C., *Free Verse*.

French literature
French literature has long had a vital influence on writing in English. In the late 19th and throughout the 20th century this relationship has been consolidated. The real shift in the fortunes of French poetry in England came in the mid-19th century with ▷ Baudelaire. Swinburne is the most immediate of his English conquests, with, next in line, those poets influenced by Swinburne, the ▷ Nineties poets, such as Ernest Dowson (1867–1900), and later Arthur Symons (1865–1945) who alternately regarded Baudelaire as deliciously decadent and frankly satanic. Baudelaire's authority is nonetheless most keenly felt as the breadth of his modernity becomes clearer. ▷ W. B. Yeats took that point, as did ▷ T. S. Eliot: 'Baudelaire is indeed the greatest exemplar in *modern* poetry in any language, for his verse and language is the nearest thing to a complete renovation that we have experienced' ('Baudelaire' in *Selected Essays*). Eliot uses Baudelaire potently in ▷ *The Waste Land* (1922). And while Eliot translated Saint-John Perse's (1887–1975) *Anabase* and no Baudelaire, his 1930 essay was occasioned by ▷ Christopher Isherwood's translation of Baudelaire's *Journaux Intimes* and it was Baudelaire again who was placed alongside the English Metaphysical poets as part of Eliot's canon. While the later Eliot moved away from these seminal influences, Baudelaire gave birth to two latter-day recorders of urban experience, poets F. S. Flint (1885–1960) and Richard Aldington (1892–1962). Baudelaire has been a pervasive presence in English poetry; even ▷ Philip Larkin, that arch-enemy of modernism, translated Baudelaire's 'Femmes Damnées' in a version published in 1978.

But Eliot, so sustaining of English literary critical values, could have his blind spots, and wilfully so. When in his 1948 essay 'From Poe to Valéry' he had occasion to reflect on some lines of descent in modern poetry, he ran along the ▷ Symbolist line but made no mention of the impact of ▷ Surrealism. Yet English Surrealism attracted its acolytes: Hugh Sykes Davis, Roland Penrose, ▷ David Gascoyne above all. It was Gascoyne who advertised the movement in England with *A Short Survey of Surrealism* (1935) and performed a valuable service in making its French exponents better known through translation.

Where English poetry since Eliot has become progressively more varied than its still-Mallarmé-haunted French counterpart, the other major genres have developed along a path away from French experimentation. This represents a reversal of the situation one hundred years ago. Throughout the 19th century, French and English prose entertained constant rapport, beginning with Stendhal whose *Chroniques pour l'Angleterre* were journalistic pieces aimed at a broad literate public. As a novelist, Stendhal beheads (*Le Rouge et Le Noir*) or cloisters away (*La Chartreuse de Parme*) those romantic heroes he had absorbed from a reading of Byron and English Romantics. By contrast, Balzac could stand for a more fully socialized version of the novelist's enterprise. If Stendhal is closer to the romance, Balzac is closer to epic; his individuals are bonded to large-scale social change and evolution, Empire to Restoration, aristocracy to bourgeoisie. The vigour or decay of the individual is analogous to the vigour or decay of the social unit. The individual is not part of, a token for, society and made or unmade by it. He or she absorbs society and seeks to act upon it according to his or her will. Balzac's characters are accordingly all larger than the ▷ realism of which they are taken to be the accredited representatives. As with Dickens's characters, their fictional representation is constantly extended beyond the terms set for ▷ mimesis alone.

Another version of the social story is followed in Flaubert. His task was, he said, to demoralize us; and he commences his career as a novelist by poisoning his romantic heroine, Emma Bovary. Flaubert progressively narrates the interwoven failures of individual and society, which are simultaneously a vitiation of historical and emotional plots (*L'Education sentimentale*) and the liquidation of character into cliché (*Bouvard et Pécuchet*). Flaubert's use of irony and his quasi-deconstructionist approach moves him closer to Stendhal than to Balzac, and it may be argued that no English novelist of the period exploited irony to so refined a degree as Standhal and Flaubert.

Despite Champfleury's (Jules Fleury, 1821–69) manifesto of 1857, realism was never a fixed body of doctrine consciously adhered to by all its supposed exponents. Nonetheless, it was as a realist that Flaubert was most admired in Britain, and the position of French realism was secured when Émile Zola experimented with veins of psychological determinism traced throughout several generations and several members of two families. Human beings in Zola may seem to be weasels fighting in a hole, yet as the advocate of ▷ naturalism (realism's more exact and scientific successor) Zola helped give impetus to British social and psychological realism explored by George Gissing and Arthur Morrison (1863–1945), ▷ George Moore and ▷ Arnold Bennett (the latter's *Journal* is based on the brothers Goncourt, also exponents of naturalism). Arguably, this vein proved consistently richer for the development of the English novel than the experimentation associated in France with the names of ▷ Proust and André Gide and reflected in the Anglo-Saxon world in the work of ▷ Henry James, ▷ Virginia Woolf and ▷ James Joyce. Unreliable protagonists narrating from a restricted angle of vision, disjointed temporal sequences, endings without full resolution – these became familiar devices in the first three decades of this century, but they had their counterparts principally in America rather than in Britain.

In France, this early opening up of the novel proved indispensable to the post-World War II developments – the overlapping of criticism and literature gravitating around the French ▷ Nouveau Roman (New Novel). The trajectory between the two points is admittedly not unilinear, and ▷ existentialist writing – which dominated the war years and through into the 1950s – projected a more traditional use of the novel (and for theatre) as dramatizing, faced with the absurd, the urgent choices of 'the human condition' (this was Montaigne's term before it became André Malraux's). The existentialist idiom caught a public mood and proved popular in Britain. If for existentialism the world existed to be acted upon and in, for the Nouveau Roman the world simply is. It cannot be colonized by mere human presence or behaviour nor is it open to shaping by intellectual speculation. In the circumstances, the unresponsiveness of things to words throws the attention back on to language itself. The caterpillar which the narrator insistently describes in ▷ Alain Robbe-Grillet's *La Jalousie* (1957) yields a plurality of meanings. Thus the Nouveau Roman anticipates and nurtures as well as illustrates ▷ Roland Barthes's encoded narratives, ▷ Mikhail Bakhtin's carnival, ▷ Jacques Lacan's dispossessed human subject, and ▷ post-structuralism's play of the signifier. As a movement, the Nouveau Roman was a formidable alliance of literature with psychology, philosophy, the human sciences in general.

One crucial result of this activity in France has been the revision of the literary canon: ▷ Marquis de Sade, ▷ Comte de Lautréamont and Mallarmé have long since taken their place alongside ▷ Samuel Beckett, Georges Bataille (1897–1962) and Maurice Blanchot (b 1907) to provide the instrumental forces of disruption which unsettle rather than confirm assumptions about the world (narrative or real). Thus current French objections to realism are not simply objections to a world view taken as paradigmatic for literature, they are equally objections to a type of critical view which sponsors such a world view as natural, co-extensive with the order of things. There is no immediate parallel in Britain for this overall reassessment in theory as well as literature. There are nonetheless equivalents and adaptations. In the novel, these include ▷ John Fowles's experiments, most notably in *The Magus* (1966) and *The French Lieutenant's Woman* (1969), William Boyd's (b 1952) splicing of Rousseau and cinema in *The New Confessions* (1987), Julian Barnes's (b 1946) witty and humorously ironical re-creation of Flaubert in *Flaubert's Parrot* (1984). All of these tend to question realism of character psychology, plot motivation and narrative expectation. Contemporary British ▷ feminism mirrors the coherence of the French position and its iconoclastic thrust, blending theoretical reflection with literary production. It has undoubtedly been stimulated by the work of ▷ Julia Kristeva and ▷ Hélène Cixous amongst others, and has drawn on the theoretical investigations of ▷ Jaques Lacan and ▷ Jacques Derrida.

French Revolution (1789–94)
The immediate effect of the French Revolution was to abolish the French monarchy, to reduce for ever the rigid class divisions of French society, and to begin wars (lasting till 1815) which for the time being extensively altered the map of Europe. Its lasting effect was to inspire the

European mind with the belief that change is historically inevitable and static order unnatural, and to imbue it with modern ideas of democracy, nationalism and equality at least of opportunity.

The impact of the Revolution on ▷ Romantic literature in Britain was profound. Wordsworth wrote later in *The Prelude* 'Bliss was it in that dawn to be alive', and William Blake wore a revolutionary cockade in the streets; Southey and Coleridge planned the ideal communist society, Pantisocracy; the philosophic novelist William Godwin published *Political Justice* and *Caleb Williams* to prove that reason was the only guide to conduct and society needed by man.
Bib: Everest, K., *Revolution in Writing: British Literary Responses to the French Revolution*.

Frequency
One of the five categories in which ▷ Genette analyses narrative discourse, frequency is concerned with the relationship between how many times a fictional event took place, and how many times it is narrated. Frequency, ▷ duration and ▷ order are matters of temporal arrangement or 'tense'; the other two categories are ▷ mood and ▷ voice.

Freud, Sigmund (1856–1939)
The founder of psychoanalysis, and one of the seminal figures of 20th-century thought. Born in Moravia, then part of the Austro-Hungarian Empire, he settled in Vienna. He began his career as a doctor specializing in the physiology of the nervous system and, after experimenting briefly with hypnosis, developed the technique of free association for the treatment of hysteria and neurosis. His work is based on a number of principles. The first is psychic determinism, the principle that all mental events, including dreams, fantasies, errors and neurotic symptoms, have meaning. The second is the primacy of the unconscious mind in mental life, the unconscious being regarded as a dynamic force drawing on the energy of instinctual drives, and as the location of desires which are repressed because they are socially unacceptable or a threat to the ego. The third is a developmental view of human life, which stresses the importance of infantile experience and accounts for personality in terms of the progressive channelling of an initially undifferentiated energy or libido. Important aspects of ▷ psychoanalytical theory and practice arising from these principles include the theory of infantile sexuality and its development, centred on the ▷ Oedipus complex, the techniques of free association and dream interpretation as means of analysing repressed material, and the beliefs that much behaviour is unconsciously motivated, that sexuality plays a major role in the personality, and that civilization has been created by the direction of libidinous impulses to symbolic ends (including the creation of art). Freud regarded neurotic and normal behaviour as differing in degree rather than kind.

Despite his scientific orientation, Freud's thought had affinities with that of the Romantic poets (▷ Romanticism), and several features of modern literature which show his influence also have Romantic antecedents. These include a particular interest in the quality and significance of childhood experience, a fascination with memory and with what is buried in the adult personality, and a concern with disturbed states of consciousness. Such features are found in the work of ▷ James Joyce and ▷ Virginia Woolf, as well as many later writers. The ▷ stream of consciousness technique and other experimental narrative techniques which abandon external realism in favour of the rendering of consciousness, of dreams or of fantasies, owe much to Freud's belief in the significance of these areas of experience, which had been relatively neglected by scientific thought. Furthermore, the technique of free association revealed a tendency of the mind, when rational constraints were lessened, to move towards points of psychic conflict, and this discovery helped to validate new means of structuring literary works, through association, symbol, and other forms of non-rationalistic patterning (for example in the work of ▷ T. S. Eliot). The view that the individual's unconscious life is as important as his or her public and social self is crucial to much 20th-century literature, a notable example being the work of ▷ D. H. Lawrence, which rests on the assumptions that human beings live through their unconscious, and that sexuality is central to the personality. The Freudian unconscious is in particular the realm of fantasy, and Freudian thought has encouraged the belief that fantasy is of profound significance in our lives, with considerable consequences for literary forms and modes.

Psychoanalysis has developed very considerably since Freud, and continues to interact with literary practice and theory. In the field of theory, those who have studied but radically revised Freud's ideas, such as ▷ Jacques Lacan and ▷ feminist theorists, have been especially important. In 1933–4

Freud analysed the poet ▷ H. D., who wrote an account of the process, *Tribute to Freud*.
Bib: Brown, J. A. C., *Freud and the Post-Freudians*; Freud, S., *Introductory Lectures on Psychoanalysis*.

Fringe theatre
A name which originates from unofficial theatre shows performed on the periphery of the Edinburgh Festival. The term is now used more generally and often refers to an alternative kind of theatre which provides a consciously oppositional entertainment to that on offer at mainstream establishment theatres. One of the typical fringe companies is ▷ John McGrath's 7:84 group which has always pursued a policy of touring plays and performing for working-class audiences away from conventional theatres (a policy which has been more successful in Scotland than in England). The term is useful in as much as it describes a general movement to a politically more radical kind of theatre since the late 1960s (which produced a number of dramatists, such as ▷ Howard Brenton, ▷ David Hare and ▷ David Edgar, who now tend to work within the theatre establishment). However, 'fringe' is now used to describe such a variety of theatrical activity that it no longer has a precise meaning. Other notable groups belonging, or who have belonged, to the political fringe are: Belt and Braces (founded in 1974); The Women's Theatre Group (1975); Gay Sweatshop (1975); Joint Stock Theatre Group (1974); Monstrous Regiment (1976).

Fry, Christopher (b 1907)
British dramatist whose first stage success was with *A Phoenix Too Frequent* (1946). *The Lady's Not For Burning*, first staged in 1948, starred ▷ John Gielgud and seemed to herald a return of verse drama to the stage. Other notable actors who played major roles in his plays include: ▷ Laurence Olivier in *Venus Observed* (1950), Paul Scofield in an adaptation of Anouilh's *Ring Round the Moon* (1950) and Edith Evans in *The Dark is Light Enough* (1954). His popularity on the commercial stage was short-lived and by the mid-1950s he was already out of favour. *Curtmantle* (1961) was performed by the ▷ Royal Shakespeare Company but was only a moderate success. His own particular brand of religious verse drama was, however, one of the few notable dramatic developments in the immediate post-war years. Film scripts include: *Barabbas* (1952); *Ben Hur* (1959); *La Bibbia* (1966).
Bib: Stanford, D., *Fry*.

Fuller, Roy (b 1912)
Poet and novelist. Fuller was born in Lancashire, and trained and worked as a solicitor. He began writing in the 1930s, and published two volumes of poetry whilst he was in the Royal Navy during World War II: *The Middle of a War* (1942) and *A Lost Season* (1944) (his first volume appeared in 1939). Subsequent texts have shown certain attributes of ▷ Movement irony, but with a broader technical and emotional scope, as well as a tendency to experiment with versification. His more recent publications include: *Counterparts* (1954); *Collected Poems* (1962) and *From the Joke Shop* (1975).

Furies, The
In Greek and Roman myth, the goddesses who pursued and punished evil-doers. The Romans called them *Furiae*; the Greeks *Erinyes* or, in propitiation, *Eumenides* (= the Friendly Ones). ▷ T. S. Eliot uses them in his play *Family Reunion* (1939); they are the objectifications of the hero's mysterious but overpowering sense of guilt. When he discovers the causes of the guilt in his family history, and is able to accept its burden, his 'furies' become 'friendly'.

Further education
Term used to refer to education undertaken after leaving school but a lower level than a degree course; usually of A level standard or below. There are 740 colleges of further education in England, nearly all under the control of local education authorities. Their courses are broadly vocational, in technical and commercial skills. A large proportion of students work only part-time, on day or block release or on evening courses. Two-thirds of the spending of these colleges goes on work-related studies. In the late 1980s, however, the involvement of employers in specifying how future workers should be educated has been officially encouraged: a privately funded body, the Business and Technician Education Council (BTEC), has been established to design syllabuses and validate courses offered at FE colleges; in 1986 the National Council for Vocational Qualifications (NCVQ) was set up by the government as a limited company to design and implement a new national framework for vocational qualifications.

▷ Adult education; Anti-industrialism; Capitalism.

G

Galsworthy, John (1867–1933)
Novelist and dramatist. As a novelist, his reputation was high in the first quarter of this century for his surveys of upper-class English life, especially the ▷ *Forsyte Saga* sequence (1906–21) and *A Modern Comedy* (*The White Monkey*, 1924; *The Silver Spoon*, 1926; *Swan Song*, 1928). After World War I, Galsworthy underwent severe criticism by novelists of the new generation as different as ▷ Virginia Woolf ('Modern Fiction' in *The Common Reader*; 1925) and ▷ D. H. Lawrence ('John Galsworthy', in *Phoenix*; 1927). These novelist-critics were writing in a period of rich experiment in rendering the inwardness of human experience and in testing and renewing humane values in the social context; to them, Galsworthy was artistically an obstructive conservative, severely limited to a vision of the outside of social phenomena and to a merely social definition of human beings. From such attacks, Galsworthy's reputation has never recovered among the intelligentsia; however, the popularity of a televised serial version of the *Forsyte Saga* in 1967 suggests that he may still be favoured by at least the older generation of the general public. His other novels are: *Jocelyn* (1898); *The Country House* (1907); *Fraternity* (1909); *The Patrician* (1911); *The Freelands* (1915); *Maid in Waiting* (1931); *Flowering Wilderness* (1932).

As a dramatist, Galsworthy was one of those in the first decade of the century who restored to the English theatre a substantiality of subject matter which had long been missing from it. His plays dramatized ethical problems arising from social issues. These too, however, have lost prestige, partly because of weaknesses similar to those that his novels are supposed to suffer from. Another criticism of the plays is that he brought to the theatre a novelist's vision rather than a dramatist's: during the last 50 years, British dramatists have believed that the drama requires an approach to the depiction of character and to the use of dialogue which is different to the vision of the novelist. Plays: *The Silver Box* (1906); *Joy* (1907); *Strife* (1909); *Justice* (1910); *The Pigeon* (1912); *The Eldest Son* (1912); *The Fugitive* (1913); *The Skin Game* (1920); *Loyalties* (1922); *The Forest* (1924).

▷ Realism.

Bib: Barker, D., *A Man of Principle*; Marrot, H. V., *The Life and Letters of John Galsworthy*; Fréchet, A., *John Galsworthy, A Reassessment*.

Gardner, Helen (1908–86)
Critic. Helen Gardner was perhaps one of the most formidable literary critics of the century, publishing a number of well-respected works which did much to promote the careful reading of many poets now firmly established in the literary canon. Gardner's position, in keeping with her generation, was in line with many of the ideas of ▷ 'new criticism', in believing that the written text is the sovereign expression of its author, whose meaning must be uncovered by close readings of the text. She was later to denigrate the proliferation of modern forms of critical theory (in her last work, *In Defence of the Imagination*, 1982), but she was one of the most influential critics of her generation. Her work on the Metaphysical poets and ▷ T. S. Eliot is particularly significant. Her texts include: *The Art of T. S. Eliot* (1949); *The Metaphysical Poets* (1957); *The Elegies and the Songs and Sonets of John Donne* (1965); *Literary Studies* (1967); *Religion and Literature* (1971).

Garner, Alan (b 1934)
Novelist and writer for children. Many of Garner's works are set in his home territory of Cheshire, and the south Manchester landmark Alderley Edge figures particularly prominently as the setting for a series of fantasy plots which mingle contemporary reality with an uncanny sense of the mythic past, which cause alternative values and belief systems to erupt into the present. Garner draws particularly on Celtic mythology and the beliefs of pre-Christian religions (especially in his first novels, *The Weirdstone of Brisingamen*, 1960, *Elidor*, 1965, and *The Owl Service*, 1967), and is also interested in the fictional possibilities of parallel time scales and relativity, which he explores in the more adult novel, *Red Shift* (1973). More recent works include *The Stone Book Quartet* (1976–8).

▷ Children's books.

Gascoyne, David (b 1916)
Poet and translator. Gascoyne was born in Salisbury, and published his first volume of verse when he was only 16 (*Roman Balcony*; 1932). His poetry is fairly unusual in being strongly influenced by that of French ▷ Surrealists, whom he has translated; at the age of 19 Gascoyne wrote *A Short Survey of Surrealism* (1935). His publications include: *Man's Life is this Meat* (1936); *Poems 1937–1942* (1943); *Collected Poems* (1965 and 1988); *The Sun at Midnight* (1970); and *Collected Verse Translations* (1970).

▷ French literature.

Gems, Pam (b 1925)
One of few female playwrights whose work has been performed by the ▷ Royal Shakespeare Company. She established her reputation relatively late in life, only becoming actively involved in the theatre when she was in her 40s. Although her plays deal specifically with female issues she distances herself from direct ▷ feminist polemic. A recurrent theme in her work is the need for women to discover their own identity in a world dominated and defined by men. Major works include: *Dead Fish* (later *Dusa, Fish, Stas and Vi*; 1976); *Queen Christina* (1977); *Piaf* (1978); *Loving Women* (1984); *Camille* (1985).
Bib: Keyssar, H., *Feminist Theatre*; Wandor, M., *Understudies*.

Gender
Originally used to distinguish between the categories of 'masculine' and 'feminine'. In modern ▷ feminist criticism it denotes something more than the different physical characteristics of both sexes. Feminist criticism regards 'masculinity' and 'femininity' as primary social constructions, supported by a range of cultural phenomena. The relationship between men and women is seen in material terms as a process of domination and subordination which functions objectively in material relations, but also subjectively in the ways in which men and women think of themselves. The concept of gender draws attention to the objective and subjective constructions of sexual difference, making possible an understanding of the mechanisms by which they operate, and offering the possibility of change.

There is a difference between the more sociological accounts and those – sometimes psychoanalytically based – which suggest there is something irreducible and specific in the nature of sexual difference. Here 'gender' is not one cultural label among others, but a firmly established basis for identity, as masculine or feminine (and not necessarily according to biological sex).

▷ *Écriture féminine*; Feminism.

Genette, Gérard (b 1930)
French critic. His book *Narrative Discourse* (1980, translated by Jane E. Lewin) provides one of the most systematic and thorough categorizations of forms and modes of narrative.

▷ Narratology.

Genre
In its use in the language of literary criticism the concept of 'genre' proposes that particular groups of texts can be seen as parts of a system of representations agreed between writer and reader. For example, a work such as Aristotle's ▷ *Poetics* isolates those characteristics which are to be found in a group of dramatic texts which are given the generic label ▷ 'tragedy'. The pleasure which an audience derives from watching a particular tragedy emanates in part from its fulfilling certain requirements stimulated by expectations arising from within the form itself. But each particular tragedy cannot be reduced simply to the sum of its generic parts. It is possible to distinguish between a tragedy by Sophocles, another by ▷ Shakespeare, or another by ▷ Edward Bond, yet at the same time to acknowledge that they all conform in certain respects to the narrative and dramatic rules laid down by the category 'tragedy'. Each example, therefore, repeats certain characteristics which have come to be recognized as indispensable features of the genre, but each one also exists in a relationship of difference from the general rule. The same kind of argument may be advanced in relation to particular sorts of poetry, or novel. The concept of genre helps to account for the particular pleasures which readers/spectators experience when confronted with a specific text. It also offers an insight into one of the many determining factors which contribute to the formation of the structure and coherence of any individual text.

Georgian Poetry
A series of verse ▷ anthologies of which five volumes appeared between 1912 and 1922. It was called 'Georgian' owing to the accession of George V (1910) and to imply a new start for English poetry, involving a degree of experiment and freshness of approach to the art. The poets represented in it included ▷ Rupert Brooke, W. H. Davies, ▷ Walter de la Mare, ▷ D. H. Lawrence, ▷ John Masefield and ▷ Robert Graves. However, the contemporary work of ▷ W. B. Yeats, ▷ Ezra Pound and ▷ T. S. Eliot, more original and more substantial than the work of the Georgian poets, quickly made their movement seem relatively unexciting. Since 1950 there has been some revival of interest in it. It was lyrical, colloquial, emancipated from some of the dead poetic convention left over from the decadent ▷ Romanticism of the previous century, but it lacked the strength and

boldness of thought which marked the work of Yeats, Eliot and Pound.

Bib: Vines, S., *Movements in Modern English Poetry and Prose*; Stead, C. K., *The New Poetic*; Ross, R. M., *The Georgean Revolt: The Rise and Fall of a Poetic Ideal 1910–1922*; Rogers, T. (ed.), *Georgian Poetry, 1911–1922: The Critical Heritage*; Reeves, J. (ed.), *Georgian Poetry*.

German influence on English literature
Unlike other European literatures, the literature of the German-speaking world did not begin to make itself felt in Britain until relatively recent times, partly because the great flowering of a literature written in the *modern* form of the German language did not take place until the second half of the 18th century. In the 20th century, however, the European character of modernism in literature, as of Romanticism before it, is impossible to mistake, and the German presence is particularly marked even if the complex and contradictory nature of modernism makes generalization hazardous. To study the poetry of Rainer Maria Rilke (1875–1926) and ▷ W. B. Yeats, for instance, is to be conscious of a broadly similar response to a common cultural situation rather than of indebtedness or influence. Deprived of belief in orthodox religion, both poets satisfied their need for a spiritual sense of existence by creating personal mythologies which display many striking parallels with each other. Rilke is unusual in being perhaps the only German writer to achieve recognition in England solely as a poet. This was certainly made possible by the Leishman, and Leishman–Spender translations, but ▷ Stephen Spender was not alone in his generation in being able to read German literature without the need for translations. ▷ Louis MacNeice himself was a co-translator of *Faust*, both ▷ W. H. Auden and ▷ Christopher Isherwood knew German, Auden translating Goethe's *Italienische Reise* and some works of ▷ Brecht. During the 1930s the rise of ▷ fascism in Germany brought about the exile of nearly every significant writer, and resistance to this evil united many writers of both countries in a sense of common purpose. In the theatre the leading German naturalist playwright Gerhart Hauptmann (1862–1946) may not have had the impact of the Scandinavian dramatists ▷ Ibsen and ▷ Strindberg but in intellectual left-wing circles at least he was read and admired. The presentation of industrial class conflict in *Die Weber (The Weavers*; 1892), where Hauptmann succeeds in creating a 'social' drama without individualized heroes, renewed interest in German theatre and in some ways foreshadowed the political commitment associated with the name of Brecht. Hauptmann is rarely performed in Britain now, but this is true of most German dramatists. German expressionist theatre (▷ Expressionism) swiftly found interest in Britain during the 1920s because of its radically experimental approach but only one work, G. Kaiser's (1878–1945) *Von morgens bis mitternachts (From Morning to Midnight;* 1916), achieved any success. The number of German plays one is likely to find regularly performed on the English stage now is relatively small in comparison to the presence of English works in German theatres. Goethe's *Faust* or Schiller's *Maria Stuart* are occasionally done, but one is far more likely to see the plays *Woyzeck* and *Dantons Tod* by Georg Büchner (1813–37). As in Germany, Büchner came to be valued only long after his premature death, but the vitality and continuing relevance of his plays and his justified reputation as an early forerunner of modern sensibility ensure continued interest in him. Frank Wedekind (1864–1918) has provided in his *Frühlings Erwachen (Spring's Awakening*; 1891) a masterpiece which has triumphantly survived translation, but it was one of Wedekind's admirers, Brecht, who has had the most extensive and long-lasting influence on the theatre of the English-speaking world. His opposition to Hitler and the commitment to peace which informs all his work have made him more acceptable in Britain than in America where his undisguised communist sympathies have told against him. The style of his so-called Epic theatre, particularly in its rejection of naturalism and its use of music, songs and verse, has been widely imitated even where – perhaps especially where – it has been detached from its original political thrust.

As might be expected, it is the modern novelists rather than the poets or dramatists who have reached the widest audiences. During the 19th century the figures of Walter Scott, William Thackeray and Charles Dickens exercised a profound influence on the development of ▷ realist fiction in Germany. Thomas Mann (1875–1955) was closest to this tradition in his novel of the decline of a bourgeois family, *Buddenbrooks* (1901), and for many years was held in high esteem, but, perhaps because his later fiction took a rather different and more philosophical direction, his reputation has waned in recent years. Hermann Hesse (1877–1962), after a period of considerable popularity, has suffered a similar fate, but the fascination of the Czech Franz Kafka (1883–1924) is undiminished. All his writings are fables of alienation and his name has become a byword for the bizarre and nightmarish. His unique vision is too personal for imitation, but it is hard to imagine how Joseph Heller's *Catch 22* (1961) and *Something Happened* (1974) could have been written without Kafka. A very different kind of fantastic realism characterizes the work of Günther Grass (b 1927) and, together with Heinrich Böll (b 1917), he stands out among the writers of the post-war generation as one whose work has spoken most immediately to his English-speaking contemporaries.

There can be little doubt that the profoundest influence on English literature and the literatures of most other countries in the 20th century stems not from the imaginative literature of Germany but from the philosophical. Probably this should not surprise us, since a philosophical tradition from which emerged in the 19th century the towering figures of Hegel, Schopenhauer and ▷ Nietzsche had already left its mark. In ▷ Karl Marx (1818–83) and ▷ Sigmund Freud (1856–1939), however, the German-speaking world produced two thinkers who have as decisively and permanently transformed the whole framework of terms within and by which we conceive society and the human mind as Darwin and Einstein have transformed our understanding of the physical world. This is no less true for a writer like Vladimir Nabokov (1899–1977), who dismisses Freud as the Viennese witch-doctor, than for ▷ D. M. Thomas. For the British there is, of course, a special poignancy in this, as both these radical thinkers were driven by political circumstances from their native countries and found refuge in Britain.

Goethe foresaw a time when, with the help of translations, national literatures would give way to a *Weltliteratur*. In the bookshops of what used to be the Federal Republic, where translations from English abound, one is inclined to feel that the day has arrived, but a visitor to a British bookshop in search of translations from the German is likely to reflect that here at least this consummation has still to come.

Gibbon, Lewis Grassic (1901–35)

Novelist. Lewis Grassic Gibbon is the pen-name of James Leslie Mitchell, a Scots writer whose most famous work, the trilogy of novels, *A Scots Quair (Sunset Song*, 1932, *Cloud Howe*, 1933, and *Grey Granite*, 1934) dramatizes working life in the early part of the 20th century in rural Scotland. Gibbon's work is characterized by his formally innovative combination of north-eastern Scottish dialogue and speech-rhythms, mixed with a burning belief in a rural form of socialism and feminism. Gibbon also wrote seven other novels under his own name, collaborated with poet ▷ Hugh MacDiarmid on *Scottish Scene, or, The Intelligent Man's Guide to Albyn* (1934), and, again under his own name, wrote three anthropological/archaeological texts. He died young, having produced a large body of wide-ranging work.

▷ Scottish literature in English.

Gibbons, Stella (1902–89)

Novelist. Gibbons's most famous work (perhaps more famous than its author), the novel *Cold Comfort Farm* (1932), was the first in a long series of astute, witty comedies of manners, a ▷ parody of both Lawrentian primitivism (▷ D. H. Lawrence) and rural fiction (popularized by writers such as Mary Webb, 1881–1927) which became a best-seller and has since been serialized for radio. Gibbons has also written short stories, poetry and many other novels; her works include *The Mountain Beast and Other Poems* (1930); *The Untidy Gnome* (1935); *Roaring Tower and Other Short Stories* (1937); *Nightingalewood* (1938); *Christmas at Cold Comfort Farm and Other Stories* (1940); *Westwood* (1946); *Conference at Cold Comfort Farm* (1949); *Collected Poems* (1951); *The Shadow of a Sorcerer* (1955); *The Pink Front Door* (1959); *The Charmers* (1965); *The Woods in Winter* (1970).

Gielgud, Sir John (b 1904)

English actor and director who first appeared on stage in 1921 at the Old Vic. He is most famous for his performances of leading roles in ▷ Shakespeare's plays, particularly during the 1930s and 40s. He began directing in 1932 with a production of *Romeo and Juliet* for the Oxford University Dramatic Society. His production of *Hamlet* at the New Theatre in 1934 ran for 155 performances and was a landmark in West End productions of Shakespeare. He has continued a distinguished acting career up to the present day. In 1991 he fulfilled his long-held ambition to put his performance of Prospero on film, in an innovative and experimental version of *The Tempest* by British director Peter Greenaway, *Prospero's Books*.

▷ Acting; Olivier, Laurence; Littlewood, Joan.
Bib: Gielgud, J., *Early Stages*; Gielgud, J., *Stage Directions*; Hayman, R., *John Gielgud*.

***Golden Bowl, The* (1904)**
A novel by ▷ Henry James. The theme is the relationship of four people: the American millionaire collector, Adam Verver; his daughter, Maggie; the Italian prince, Amerigo, whom Verver acquires as a husband for his daughter; and Charlotte Stant, whom Maggie acquires as a wife for her widowed father. To the grief of the father and the daughter Charlotte seduces the prince into becoming her lover; the story is about the defeat of Charlotte, and Maggie's recovery of the prince's affections.

The novel belongs to James's last phase, which some critics consider to be his best, and other consider to show an excessive obliquity of style. The language of the characters is charged with feeling and yet disciplined by their civilized restraint and their fear of degrading themselves and one another by damaging explicitness. It is a measure of their indirectness that the affair between the prince and Charlotte is never actually mentioned between the father and the daughter. Behind the conflict of personalities there is the theme of the clash between European and American kinds of values and consciousness; this theme is conspicuous in James's early novels, and he returned to it in his last period after a middle phase in which he was chiefly concerned with the European, and particularly the English, scene.

Golding, William (b 1911)
Novelist. His novels are: *Lord of the Flies* (1954; filmed 1963); *The Inheritors* (1955); *Pincher Martin* (1956); *Free Fall* (1959); *The Spire* (1964); *The Pyramid* (1967); *Darkness Visible* (1979); *Rites of Passage* (1980); *The Paper Men* (1984); *Close Quarters* (1987). *Sometime Never* (1956) and *The Scorpion God* (1971) are collections of novellas. He has also written a play, *The Brass Butterfly* (1958), and published two collections of essays, *The Hot Gates* (1965) and *A Moving Target* (1982).

The prestige which Golding has achieved since 1945 was acquired very quickly on the publication of his first book, *Lord of the Flies*. Its fame has no doubt been in part due to its pessimistic vision of human nature as inherently violent, reflecting the mood of the post-war and post-Hitler years; it also epitomizes mid-20th-century disillusionment with 19th-century optimism about human nature. Golding's father (see 'The Ladder and the Tree' in *The Hot Gates*) was a schoolmaster with radical convictions in politics, a belief that religion is outmoded superstition, and a strong faith in science. Golding's own work is strongly, but not explicitly, religious, in the Puritan tradition which emphasizes Original Sin. In 'Fable' (*The Hot Gates*) he explains how his first novel arose from his insights in the last war: 'Anyone who moved through those years without understanding that man produces evil as a bee produces honey, must have been blind or wrong in the head.' The book is also meant to counteract what may be called 'the desert island myth' in English literature, deriving from Daniel Defoe's *Robinson Crusoe*, and particularly evident in a famous book for boys, *The Coral Island* (1857) by R. M. Ballantyne. This myth nourished the belief that human beings in isolation from civilized restraints will sustain their humanity by innate virtues. Most of the boys in *Lord of the Flies* quickly degenerate into savages, and the process is made more horrifying by the convincing delineation of the characters: Golding, like his father, has been a schoolmaster. His later novels have shown variety of theme and treatment, but similar preoccupation with fundamental corruption and contradiction in human nature. They show, likewise, Golding's most conspicuous literary qualities: great inventiveness in realistic fantasy, and a disposition to use the novel form as fable. For instance, *The Inheritors* is ▷ science fiction about the remote human past: the elimination of innocent Neanderthal Man by the arrival of rapacious *homo sapiens* – a new version of the myth of the Fall. *Pincher Martin* is a dramatization of this rapacity in an individual, and a spectacular example of fantasy presented within the conventions of realism. *The Spire* shows comparable ingenuity used quite differently: it describes the building of the spire of Salisbury Cathedral and dramatizes the conflict between faith and reason. *Rites of Passage* employs a characteristic shift of perspective: the narrow viewpoint of the narrator, a snobbish young aristocrat on a voyage to Australia in the early 19th century, is undermined by his gradual understanding of the devastating experiences of an awkward but sincere clergyman.
Bib: Gregor, I., and Kinkead-Weekes, M., *William Golding: a Critical Study*; Johnston, A., *Of Earth and Darkness*; Medcalf, S., *William Golding*.

Gordimer, Nadine (b 1923)
South African novelist and short-story writer living in Johannesburg. She has won an international reputation and numerous prizes, including the Booker Prize for *The Conservationist* (1974). Much of her work is concerned with the situation of white middle-class liberals in South Africa, privileged by a system to which they are opposed, the relations of the private self to the political, and the failure of liberal compromise. Her work has become progressively bleaker and more disillusioned. In *A World of Strangers* (1958) she uses the perspective of an outsider coming to South Africa, while *The Conservationist* is written from the viewpoint of a rich and conservative capitalist, and employs symbolic elements in its treatment of the struggle for the control of the land. In 1991 she won the Nobel Prize for literature. Her other novels are: *The Lying Days* (1953); *Occasion for Loving* (1963); *The Late Bourgeois World* (1966); *A Guest of Honour* (1970); *Burger's Daughter* (1979); *July's People* (1981); *A Sport of Nature* (1987). Story collections include: *Selected Stories* (1975); *Some Monday For Sure* (1976); *A Soldier's Embrace* (1980); *Town and Country Lovers* (1980); *Something Out There* (1984); *Jump* (1991).
Bib: Heywood, C., *Nadine Gordimer*; Clingman, S., *The Novels of Nadine Gordimer: History from the Inside*.

Gosse, Edmund (1849–1928)
Critic, biographer and poet. He is especially known for his autobiography *Father and Son* (1907) – one of the classic works for interpreting the ▷ Victorian age. As a critic, he was one of the first to introduce the Norwegian dramatist ▷ Ibsen to the British public. He also wrote a number of studies of 17th-century literature and a life (1917) of his friend and contemporary, the poet Swinburne.

Graham, W. S. (William Sidney) (1918–86)
Poet. Graham was born in Scotland (▷ Scottish literature) into a working-class family and grew up on Clydeside where he trained and worked as an engineer. His early poetry was immediately associated with ▷ Dylan Thomas and the 'apocalyptic' poetry of the 1940s – Graham's first collection was characteristically energetic and vibrant. Much of his later life was spent around St Ives, in Cornwall, a situation that put him in contact with many of the important post-war British painters. Just as Cornwall's seascapes provided a rich source of metaphor and imagery for Graham's struggles with the opacity of language, so its equally craggy inhabitants fed his essentially Scottish wit, and later his talent for elegy. Along with ▷ David Gascoyne and ▷ George Barker, Graham wrote in a powerfully neo-Romantic style about problems of personal identity. Temporarily obscured from view by the achievements and tastes of the ▷ Movement, their poetry is among the strongest in English this century. Graham's most celebrated volume is *The Nightfishing* (1955); other works include *Malcolm Mooney's Land* (1970), *Collected Poems 1942–1977* (1979) and *Implements in their Places* (1977).
Bib: Lopez, T., *W. S. Graham*.

Grammatology
This term is used by the French philosopher ▷ Jacques Derrida to denote 'a general science of writing'. As a scientific practice, its objective is to disturb the traditional hierarchical relationship between 'speech' and 'writing' where the latter is regarded as an instrument of the former. Derrida's 'science of writing' is an attempt to deconstruct (▷ Deconstruction) the metaphysical assumptions upon which the hierarchical relationship between speech and writing is based. He takes to the limit the ▷ Saussurean notion of the arbitrariness of the linguistic ▷ sign, arguing against a natural relationship between the spoken word and what it signifies.

Granville-Barker, Harley (1877–1946)
Actor, producer, director, dramatist, dramatic critic. He began as an actor in 1891, but he achieved fame as a director (1904–21). He favoured the modern drama of ▷ Ibsen, ▷ Shaw and ▷ Galsworthy and did much to educate the public into accepting its often scandalizing themes drawn from contemporary social issues; in this he was much influenced by his close friendship with Shaw. However, his chief fame as a director was in his productions of ▷ Shakespeare. The previous generation of Shakespeare production, dominated by Henry Irving, had relied on the personalities of star actors, and Irving was continuing a tradition which went back to the 18th century. Granville-Barker concentrated on the production of the whole work, transferring the emphasis from the leading roles on to the speech and action of the entire cast. His own plays were in the Ibsen–Shaw tradition; the best known are *The Voysey Inheritance* (1905), *Waste* (which was forbidden by the censor) (1907), and *The Madras House* (1910).

In 1923 he became editor of *The Players' Shakespeare* for which he wrote prefaces to

individual plays. The series was discontinued, but the prefaces were published, and because they have Granville-Barker's unique stage experience as a basis, they now constitute the crown of his reputation. However he was also a lifelong publicist for the idea of a ▷ National Theatre, which was not to be established until 1976.
Bib: Purdom, C. B., *Harley Granville Barker, Man of the Theatre, Dramatist and Scholar*; Salmon, E., *Granville Barker: A Secret Life*; Kennedy, D., *Granville Barker and the Dream of Theatre*.

Graves, Robert (1895–1985)
Poet, critic, novelist. His poetry belongs to a distinctively English strain of lyrical verse which has been overshadowed by the more ambitious and more massive work of the Anglo-Irish ▷ W. B. Yeats and the American-born ▷ T. S. Eliot. Earlier representatives of this kind of verse were ▷ Thomas Hardy, ▷ Edward Thomas and the War poets such as ▷ Wilfred Owen, ▷ Siegfried Sassoon and ▷ Isaac Rosenberg. The development of Graves's work was decisively affected by his experiences as an officer in World War I, and understanding of it is helped by a reading of Owen and Sassoon. Such poetry was partly a means of preserving sanity in the face of extreme horror, partly a desire to awaken in the reader a distrust of attitudes imposed on him by convention, or adopted by himself to help him preserve his own illusions. Graves published his first poems during World War I, but he is not primarily one of the War poets; he extended the vision aroused by the war into the post-war world of human relations, especially those between the sexes, and into the impulses to self-deceive and to escape the realities of inner experience, especially by choosing to dull its image. He always wrote ▷ lyrics with skilful and precise rhythm and often poignant or pungent rhymes, and an austere yet lively, colloquial diction. A collected edition of his work was published in 1975.

As a critic he was at first a self-conscious ▷ modernist; *A Survey of Modernist Poetry* (1927), written with the poet Laura Riding, educated the public in new kinds of poetic expression by a pioneering critical interest in subtleties and ambiguities of language. His later criticism has been less influential; it includes *The Common Asphodel* (1949), *The Crowning Privilege* (1955).

Graves engaged extensively in historical and anthropological enquiry; this resulted in work on poetry and primitive religion, *eg The White Goddess* (1948), which aroused controversy but was taken up by some ▷ feminists in the 1960s and 70s, and in historical fiction of great popularity, *eg I, Claudius* and *Claudius the God* (1934). By far the most important of his prose works, however, is his ▷ autobiography recounting his experiences in World War I – *Good-bye to All That* (1929).
Bib: Seymour Smith, M., *Swifter than Reason*; Graves, R. P., *Robert Graves*.

Green, Henry (1905–73)
Pen-name of the novelist H. V. Yorke. His novels are: *Blindness* (1926); *Living* (1929); *Party-Going* (1930); *Caught* (1943); *Loving* (1945); *Back* (1946); *Concluding* (1948); *Nothing* (1950); *Doting* (1952). Of these, possibly the most distinguished are: *Living*, with an industrial working-class setting; *Loving*, about servants in an anachronistic great house in Ireland during World War II; *Concluding*, set in the future, about an institution for educating women civil servants; and *Party-Going*, a novel in which the events have only a few hours' duration and take place in a fog-bound London railway station. His style is condensed and poetically expressive; events are caught in movement, with a cinematic use of flash-backs to bring the past into relationship with the present. In his autobiography *Pack my Bag* he wrote: 'Prose should be a long intimacy between strangers with no direct appeal to what both may have known. It should slowly appeal to feelings unexpressed, it should in the end draw tears out of the stone.' Green is set aside from the ▷ modernist interest in the rendering of consciousness by a belief that the novelist should not attempt to portray the inner depths of characters, but should use their spoken words to capture the opaque and shifting surface of social relations. The later novels show increasing reliance on dialogue, following the example of the novels of ▷ Ivy Compton-Burnett. Green also professed admiration for the work of the French writer, Céline. He wrote no novels in the last 20 years of his life.
Bib: Stokes, E., *The Novels of Henry Green*; Russell, J., *Henry Green*; Bassoff, B., *Towards Loving*; Sarraute, N., in *The Age of Suspicion*; Mengham, R., *The Idiom of the Time*.

Greene, Henry Graham (1904–91)
Novelist. The son of a schoolmaster. He went to Balliol College, Oxford, and then became a journalist (1926–30) on ▷ *The Times*. He converted to Catholicism in 1926. His first novel, *The Man Within*, appeared in 1929. It

was followed by a steady succession of novels, of which the fourth, *Stamboul Train* (1932) made him well known. It was nonetheless one of the books he called 'entertainments', meaning that they were among his less serious works; this group also includes *A Gun for Sale* (1936), *The Confidential Agent* (1939), *The Ministry of Fear* (1943), and *Our Man in Havana* (1958). In 1934 he published *It's a Battlefield*, and in 1935 a volume of stories the title story of which, *The Basement Room*, was later adapted into the film, *The Fallen Idol* (1950). In 1935 came *England Made Me*. In the same year he travelled in Liberia, on which he based his travel book *Journey Without Maps* (1936). He then became film critic for the weekly journal ▷ *The Spectator* (of which he was made literary editor in 1940). His next novel, *Brighton Rock* (1938) was the first in which there was clear evidence of Catholicism. In the same year he was commissioned to visit Mexico and report on the religious persecution there; the result was another travel book, *The Lawless Roads* (1939) and one of his most famous novels, *The Power and the Glory* (1940). During World War II he worked for the Foreign Office, and again visited West Africa. After the war he became a publisher. Later fiction: *Nineteen Stories* (1947; including eight in *The Basement Room* volume); *The Heart of the Matter* (1948); *The Third Man* (1950; also made into a film); *The End of the Affair* (1951); *The Quiet American* (1955); *A Burnt-Out Case* (1961); *A Sense of Reality* (four stories, 1963); *The Comedians* (1966); *Travels with My Aunt* (1969); *A Sort of Life* (1971); *The Honorary Consul* (1973); *Lord Rochester's Monkey* (1974); *The Human Factor* (1978); *Dr Fischer of Geneva, or the Bomb Party* (1980); *Monsignior Quixote* (1982); *The Tenth Man* (1985); *The Captain and the Enemy* (1988).

He also wrote plays: *The Living Room* (1953); *The Potting Shed* (1957); *The Complaisant Lover* (1959); *The Return of A. J. Raffles* (1975); and books of critical essays, *The Lost Childhood* (1951) and *The Pleasure Dome* (film criticism, 1972). His *Collected Essays* were published in 1969 and his *Collected Plays* in 1985. His autobiographical works include *A Sort of Life* (1971), *Ways of Escape* (1981) and *Getting to Know the General* (1984).

Graham Greene's high reputation is partly due to his exploration of emotions that are particularly strong in the middle of the 20th century: the sense of guilt and frustration, impulses to violence and fear of it, pity, including self-pity. He had strong gifts for narrative and for the evocation of atmosphere, especially the atmosphere of squalid surroundings which convey deprivation and despair. His Catholicism counteracted the misery in his books by its implications of spiritual dignity remaining intact even amid degradation and abject suffering.

▷ Catholicism in English literature.

Bib: Allott, K., and Farris, M., *The Art of Graham Greene*; Lodge, D., *Graham Greene*; Pryce-Jones, D., *Graham Greene*; Sharrock, R., *Saints, Sinners and Comedians: the Novels of Graham Greene*; Smith, G., *The Achievement of Graham Greene*.

Greer, Germaine (b 1939)

Feminist theorist and critic. Germaine Greer is one of the most influential writers of her generation. Her groundbreaking feminist work of 1971, *The Female Eunuch*, was a brilliantly timed and characteristically outrageous critique of traditional images of femininity and women's role in Western society, as well as being a celebration of more radical female powers and talents hitherto suppressed and repressed. Greer is an incisive writer and considerable scholar, who nevertheless always exudes an intoxicating energy in her writing. She has had an enormously varied career, and is one of the foremost spokeswomen of British ▷ feminism (although she was born in Australia and continues to explore this identity in her more autobiographical writings). Greer has held university lecturing posts (at Warwick University in the early 1970s, and more recently in Cambridge and the U.S.A.), has written for the underground press (the cult journal *Oz* in the late 1960s), has edited a collection of 17th-century women's poetry (*Kissing the Rod*, 1988), has written on women's role in art history (*The Obstacle Race*, 1979), on fertility and maternity (*Sex and Destiny*, 1984), on Shakespeare (1986), and on the menopause (*The Change*, 1991).

Bib: Plante, D., *Three Difficult Women*.

Gregory, Lady (Augusta) (1852–1932)

Promoter of Irish drama, she founded the Irish Literary Theatre, with ▷ W. B. Yeats and Edward Martyn in 1898. This became the Irish National Theatre Society in 1902 and led to the establishment of the ▷ Abbey Theatre in Dublin. She wrote several plays for it and collaborated with Yeats in *The Pot of Broth* and *Cathleen ni Houlihan* (both 1902). Of her own plays the best known are *Spreading the News* (1904), *The Gaol Gate* (1906), *Hyacinth Halvey* (1906), *The Rising of the Moon* (1907) and *The Workhouse Ward* (1908). She also translated Molière into Irish idiom in *The Kiltartan Molière*.

▷ Irish literature in English.
Bib: Kohfeldt, M., *Lady Gregory: The Woman behind the Irish Renaissance.*

Grein, Jack Thomas (1862–1935)
Playwright, critic and manager who helped introduce the work of European playwrights to English audiences at the end of the 19th century. He founded the Independent Theatre Club in 1891, 'to give special performances of plays which have a literary and artistic rather than a commercial value'. The first production was ▷ Ibsen's *Ghosts* which met with a storm of abuse, and thereafter little of Ibsen's work was shown, although ▷ George Bernard Shaw's contribution to the controversy, *Widowers' Houses*, his first London production, was put on in 1892. Grein's dramatic criticism has been published in five volumes.
Bib: Orme, M., *J. T. Grein: the Story of a Pioneer.*

Griffiths, Trevor (b 1935)
British socialist playwright who began writing during the late 1960s. He has since written plays for television as well as the stage and collaborated with Warren Beatty on the script for the film *Reds*. His plays often dramatize a political debate between reformist and revolutionary standpoints. This is most obviously the case in *Occupations* (1970) and *The Party* (1973); it is also true of his comic work about club entertainers, *Comedians* (1975). He has expressed a preference for writing for television because of the wider audiences that can be reached than in the theatre.
Bib: Poole, M. and Wyver, J., *Powerplays: Trevor Griffiths in Television.*

Grotowski, Jerzy (b 1933)
Polish director who established the Laboratory Theatre in Wroclaw in the early 1960s, where he developed a training process for actors which emphasized the importance of physical as well as mental skills. His rejection of the expensive paraphernalia of traditional theatre in favour of what he called 'poor theatre' which relies more exclusively on the actor, has been a great inspiration for the British ▷ fringe theatre. He has also been an important influence on the work of the British director ▷ Peter Brook.
Bib: Grotowski, J., *Towards a Poor Theatre.*

Group Theatre
A private play society founded in 1933 and famous for its productions of the experimental poetic plays of ▷ Auden and ▷ Isherwood: *The Dog Beneath the Skin* (1936), *The Ascent of F6* (1937) and *On the Frontier* (1939). Other notable productions include ▷ T. S. Eliot's *Sweeney Agonistes* (1935) and ▷ Stephen Spender's *Trial of a Judge* (1938). Most of its productions were directed by Rupert Doone. Group Theatre was active, apart from an interim during the war years, until 1953.
Bib: Medley, R., *Drawn from Life: a Memoir of the 1930s Group Theatre*; Sidnell, M. J., *Dances of Death: the Group Theatre of London in the Thirties.*

Guardian, The
It was started in 1821 as a weekly paper, then called *The Manchester Guardian*, becoming daily in 1855. As the leading Liberal publication outside London, it ws edited from 1872 to 1929 by C. P. Scott. Its title was changed to *The Guardian* in 1959, and since 1961 it has been published from London. It is considered to be one of the more liberal papers of the 1980s and 1990s.

Gunn, Thom (b 1929)
Poet. Educated at Cambridge and Stanford University in California, Gunn now lives in San Francisco, although he is of British origin. His work was first associated with the ▷ Movement, but gradually it drew away from comparison with ▷ Philip Larkin or ▷ Kingsley Amis through its growing violent energy in the 1960s, although formally his precise, clear style is still akin to 1950s poetry. Gunn's work in the U.S.A. has drawn him close to American beat poets in rhythm and subject matter, motorbikes and rock music, and images of nihilism. He has experimented with syllabic, ▷ iambic and with ▷ free verse forms. His publications include: *Fighting Terms* (1954); *Poems* (1954); *The Sense of Movement* (1957) (which won the Somerset Maugham award); *Moly* (1971); *Jack Straw's Castle* (1976); *Selected Poems, 1950–1975* (1979); *The Passages of Joy* (1982); and *The Man with Night Sweats* (1992).

H

Haggard, Sir H. (Henry) Rider (1856–1925)
Son of a Norfolk squire, he spent several years in South Africa as a young man, writing books on its history and farming, but he is famous for his numerous adventure novels set in such exotic locations as Iceland, Mexico and ancient Egypt. They are characterized by gripping narrative and strange events, as well as evocative descriptions of landscape, wildlife and tribal society, particularly in Africa. He has had a world-wide readership and some of his stories have been filmed. *King Solomon's Mines* (1886) and *She* (1887) are the most famous novels. *The Days of My Life: an Autobiography* appeared in 1926.
Bib: Haggard, L. R., *The Cloak that I Left*; Ellis, P. B., *H. Rider Haggard: A Voice from the Infinite*; Higgins, D. S., *Rider Haggard: The Great Storyteller*.

Hall, Sir Peter (b 1930)
British director whose first major production was ▷ Samuel Beckett's ▷ *Waiting for Godot* at the Arts Theatre in 1955. From 1956 he directed at Stratford-on-Avon and became director of the theatre from 1960, when it became the Royal Shakespeare Theatre (▷ Royal Shakespeare Company). In 1972 he replaced ▷ Laurence Olivier as director of the ▷ National Theatre, from which he retired in 1988.
Bib: Hall, P., *Peter Hall's Diaries: the Stories of a Dramatic Battle*.

Hall, Radcliffe (1880–1943)
Novelist and poet. Writer of perhaps the most famous lesbian novel ever published (*The Well of Loneliness*, 1928), Radcliffe Hall began work as a poet with the publication of *'Twixt Earth and Stars* (1906), followed by *A Sheaf of Verses* in 1908, in which she started to represent and explore her lesbianism in the poems 'The Scar' and 'Ode to Sappho'. She won the Prix Femina and the James Tait Black Memorial Prize for the novel *Adam's Breed* in 1926, before the candid *Well of Loneliness* was tried and banned a year later, ensuring its author's notoriety. Because the novel partly represents the experience of lesbianism in the early 20th century as guilty and shameful, it has often been criticized by more recent lesbian writers for its less than positive portrayal of women in sexual relationships with other women. However, Radcliffe Hall's courage in publishing it, and the openness of the way she lived her writing life deserve recognition; Hall lived with women for much of her life. Her other works include: *Poems of the Past and Present* (1910); *The Forgotten Island* (1915); *The Forge* (1924); *The Unlit Lamp* (1924); *Miss Ogilvy Finds Herself* (1934); *The Sixth Beatitude* (1936).
Bib: Dickson, L., *Radcliffe Hall and the Well of Loneliness*; Franks, C. S., *Beyond 'The Well of Loneliness': The Fiction of Radcliffe Hall*; Troubridge; U. B., *The Life and Death of Radcliffe Hall*.
▷ Homosexuality; Feminism.

Hammett, Dashiell (1894–1961)
▷ Detective fiction.

Hampton, Christopher (b 1946)
British dramatist, another product of the ▷ Royal Court theatre where he was the first resident dramatist (1968–70), while also working there as literary manager. His most recent play is the much acclaimed adaptation, *Les Liaisons Dangereuses* (1985), performed by the ▷ Royal Shakespeare Company, a dramatization of a novel by Choderlos de Laclos about sexual combat and power in France just prior to the revolution of 1789. This was rewritten by Hampton for the screenplay of Stephen Frears's very successful 1988 film, *Dangerous Liaisons*. Typically of Hampton, the play does not deal explicitly with politics, though it provides a witty and vivid insight into a world of decadence and ruthlessness on the brink of collapse. Other works include: *Total Eclipse* (1968); *The Philanthropist* (1970); *Savages* (1973); *Treats* (1976); *Tales from the Vienna Woods* (1977); *Don Juan Comes Back From the War* (1978); *Tales from Hollywood* (1983). Hampton has been described as a modern classicist, not least for his translations of plays by ▷ Chekhov, ▷ Ibsen and Molière: *Uncle Vanya* (1971); *Hedda Gabler* (1971); *A Doll's House* (1971); *The Wild Duck* (1980); *Ghosts* (1983); *Don Juan* (1972); *Tartuffe* (1984).

Hardy, Thomas (1840–1928)
Novelist and poet, and former architect. He was the son of a village stonemason in Dorset; thus he was close to the country life by his origins, and he never lost feeling for it. As he grew up, he underwent the painful loss of faith so common among intellectuals in England in the second half of the 19th century; this led him to a tragic philosophy that human beings are the victims of indifferent forces. At

the same time he witnessed the steady weakening from within and erosion from without of the part of rural England with which he was so much identified. This region is the six south-western counties of England, approximately coterminous with the 6th-century Saxon kingdom of Wessex, by which name he calls them in his 'Novels of Character and Environment'. These novels are by far his best known: *Under the Greenwood Tree* (1872); *Far from the Madding Crowd* (1874); *The Return of the Native* (1878); *The Mayor of Casterbridge* (1886); *The Woodlanders* (1887); ▷ *Tess of the D'Urbervilles* (1891); ▷ *Jude the Obscure* (1895). Two volumes of stories are *Wessex Tales* (1888) and *Life's Little Ironies* (1894). Hardy's originality was his discernment of the intimate relationship of character and environment, and his characters nearly always became less convincing when this relationship loses closeness, *ie* in his socially higher, more sophisticated characters. This may account for the fact that the other two groups of his novels have much less prestige. He called them 'Romances and Fantasies' (*A Pair of Blue Eyes*, 1873; *The Trumpet-Major*, 1880; *Two on a Tower*, 1882; *A Group of Noble Dames*, 1891; *The Well-Beloved*, 1897) and 'Novels of Ingenuity' (*Desperate Remedies*, 1871; *The Hand of Ethelberta*, 1876; *A Laodicean*, 1881).

Hardy's poetry is as distinguished as his novels; indeed he regarded himself as primarily a poet. Though he wrote poetry from the beginning of his career, his best verse was chiefly the fruit of his later years when he had abandoned novels. It is in some respects very traditional – ballads such as *The Trampwoman's Tragedy* and tuneful, rhyming lyrics. But though traditional – in touch with folk song and ▷ ballad – Hardy was never conventional. His diction is distinctive; he experimented constantly with form and stresses, and the singing rhythms subtly respond to the movement of his intense feelings; the consequent poignance and sincerity has brought him the admiration of poets since 1945, who seem especially sensitive to dishonesty of feeling. His ▷ lyrics have the peculiarity that they nearly always centre on incident, in a way that gives them dramatic sharpness. Amongst the most admired are some that he wrote to his dead first wife, included in *Satires of Circumstance* (1914).

Bib: Hardy, E., *Life*; Brown, D., *Thomas Hardy*; Stewart, J. I. M., *Thomas Hardy: A Critical Biography*; Gittings, R., *Young Thomas Hardy*; *The Older Hardy*; Millgate, M., *Thomas Hardy: A Biography*; *Thomas Hardy, His Career as a Novelist*; Bayley, J., *An Essay on Hardy*; Goode, J., *Thomas Hardy*; Butler, L. (ed.), *Alternative Hardy*.

Hare, David (b *1947*)
British left-wing dramatist who established his reputation during the 1970s as a writer for ▷ fringe companies. Since then he has chosen to work from within the establishment as a writer and director at the ▷ National Theatre. Major stage plays include: *Brassneck* (1973), a collaboration with ▷ Howard Brenton; *Teeth 'n' Smiles* (1975); *Fanshen* (1975); *Plenty* (1978); *A Map of the World* (1983); *Pravda* (1985), another collaboration with Howard Brenton; *The Secret Rapture* (1988). Television plays: *Licking Hitler* (1978); *Saigon: Year of the Cat* (1983). Films: *Wetherby* (1985), *Plenty* (1985), *Strapless* (1990).

Bib: Bull, J., *New British Political Dramatists*; Chambers, C. and Prior, M., *Playwrights' Progress*.

Harris, Wilson (b 1921)
Guyanese novelist and short-story writer. The landscape and history of Guyana play an important part in his work, which is concerned with such issues as the legacy of the colonial past and the destruction and re-creation of individual and collective identity. His novels are visionary, experimental, anti-realist explorations of consciousness, employing multiple and fragmentary narrative structures, and symbolic correspondences between inner and outer landscapes. The later novels use a wider range of geographical settings, including England, Mexico and South America. His volumes of short stories, *The Sleepers of Roraima* (1970) and *The Age of the Rainmakers* (1971) locate a redemptive power in Amerindian myth. His novels are: *The Guyana Quartet: Palace of the Peacock* (1960); *The Far Journey of Oudu* (1961); *The Whole Armour* (1962) and *The Secret Ladder* (1963); *Heartland* (1964); *The Eye of the Scarecrow* (1965); *The Waiting Room* (1967); *Tutamari* (1968); *Ascent to Omai* (1970); *Black Marsden* (1972); *Companions of the Day and Night* (1975); *Da Silva da Silva's Cultivated Wilderness, and the Genesis of the Clowns* (1977); *The Tree of the Sun* (1978); *The Angel at the Gate* (1982); *Carnival* (1985); *The Infinite Rehearsal* (1987).

▷ Commonwealth literatures.

Bib: Gilkes, M., *Wilson Harris and the Caribbean Novel.*

Harrison, Tony (b 1937)
Poet. His early volumes, *The Loiners* (1970) and *The School of Eloquence* (1978), established his recurrent subject matter – becoming distanced through education from his working-class, northern upbringing. This intensely felt sense of loss and belonging is still being explored in *V* (1985). Other volumes of poetry include: *Newcastle is Peru* (1974); *Bow Down* (1974); *Continuous* (1982); and *The Common Chorus* (1992). He has also translated Aeschylus's *Oresteia* and French drama for the theatre; see *Dramatic Verse 1973–1985* (1985).

Hartley, L. P. (Leslie Poles) (1895–1972)
Novelist. His novels and stories are: *Night Fears* (1924); *Simonetta Perkins* (1925); *The Killing Bottle* (1932); a trilogy – *The Shrimp and the Anemone* (1944), *The Sixth Heaven* (1946) and *Eustace and Hilda* (1947); *The Travelling Grave* (1948); *The Boat* (1949); *My Fellow Devils* (1951); *The Go-Between* (1953); *The White Wand* (1954); *A Perfect Woman* (1955); *The Hireling* (1957); *Facial Justice* (1960); *Two for the River* (1961); *The Brickfield* (1964); *The Betrayal* (1966); *Poor Clare* (1968); *The Love Adept* (1968); *My Sister's Keeper* (1970); *The Harness Room* (1971); *The Collections* (1972); *The Will and the Way* (1973). His reputation rests chiefly on the trilogy (especially *The Shrimp and the Anemone*) and *The Go-Between*. These both contain very sensitive child studies, and relate the influence of childhood experiences on the development of the adult. Hartley was in the tradition of ▷ Henry James, whom he resembles in his presentation of delicate but crucial personal inter-relationships; the influence of ▷ Sigmund Freud intervened to give Hartley a different kind of psychological depth, more concerned with the recovery of the self buried in the forgotten experiences of the past than with the self buried under the false assumptions of society.
Bib: Bien, P., *Hartley*; Mulkeen, A., *Wild Thyme, Winter Lightning.*

Hauptmann, Gerhart (1862–1946)
German dramatist and exponent of a 'naturalistic' style of writing in early plays like *The Weavers* (1892), a play based on factual events relating to social struggle and revolt in the Silesian weaving industry. Much of the play is written in the Silesian dialect. *The Thieves' Comedy* (1904) was shown by ▷ Harley Granville Barker as part of his Court Theatre repertory.
Bib: Sinden, M., *Gerhart Hauptmann: The Prose Plays.*

H. D. (Hilda Doolittle) (1886–1961)
Poet. H. D. was born in Bethlehem, Pennsylvania, educated at Bryn Mawr, where she was a contemporary of American poet Marianne Moore, and moved to Britain in 1911. She was an important figure in the ▷ Imagist group, signing her first poems, published in Harriet Monroe's *Poetry* in 1913, 'H. D. Imagiste'. She was a close associate of ▷ Ezra Pound, to whom she was briefly engaged in 1907. The 'Hellenic hardness' of her work epitomized Imagism. She married fellow writer Richard Aldington in 1913, becoming part of the network sometimes known as the 'Other ▷ Bloomsbury' which was dominated by ▷ D. H. Lawrence, who is characterized in H. D.'s novel *Bid Me To Live* (published 1960). From 1916 she co-edited, with ▷ T. S. Eliot, *The Egoist*, Dora Marsden's originally ▷ feminist journal which had published amongst other texts ▷ James Joyce's ▷ *Portrait of the Artist as a Young Man* in serial form in 1914–15. In 1917 H. D. separated from Aldington, gave birth to her daughter Perdita, and began to travel with her friend ▷ Bryher (Winifred Ellerman), with whom she spent much of the rest of her life. Her first collection, *Sea Garden*, was published in 1916, followed by *Hymen* (1921), *Heliodora and Other Poems* (1924), and *Red Roses for Bronze* (1929). The trilogy, *The Walls Do Not Fall* (1944–6) and *Helen in Egypt* (1961), perhaps H. D.'s most important works, have only recently received the critical attention they deserve. Her poetry is intense, difficult, and infused with her passion for classical Greek culture. Although primarily known as a poet, H. D. wrote novels, and having undergone psychoanalysis with ▷ Freud in Vienna 1933–4, published an account of the process. *Tribute to Freud* is important both as a poetic and visionary text and as a key text in debates about psychoanalysis and feminism.
Bib: Duplessis, R. B., *H. D. The Career of That Struggle*; Buck, C., *H. D. and Freud: Bisexuality and a Feminine Discourse.*

Head, Bessie Emery (1937–86)
African novelist and short-story writer. Born in South Africa in a mental hospital, where

her Scottish mother had been confined as a result of her relationship with her Zulu father, she was brought up by a foster family until the age of 13, then attended a mission school in Durban and trained as a teacher. She taught in South Africa, worked as a journalist for *Drum* magazine and became involved in African nationalist circles, but in 1963 went into exile in Botswana, where she worked, with other political refugees, in a village garden co-operative in Serowe, commemorated in her book *Serowe: Village of the Rain Wind* (1981), which is built around interviews. She took Botswana citizenship in 1979. Her first three novels contain a considerable element of autobiography, most notably *A Question of Power* (1974), which is based directly on her own experience of mental breakdown, but also *When Rain Clouds Gather* (1969), about a Botswana agrarian community, and *Maru* (1971), which deals with racial prejudice through the story of an orphaned Masarwa woman, teaching in a Botswana village where her people are regarded as outcasts. *The Collector of Treasures and Other Botswana Village Tales* (1977) is a volume of short stories, while *A Bewitched Crossroad: An African Saga* (1984) is a history of the Bamangwato tribe. *Tales of Tenderness and Power*, published posthumously in 1989, is a collection of stories, personal observations and legends, while *A Woman Alone*, published posthumously in 1990, consists of ▷ autobiographical fragments.

▷ Commonwealth literatures.

Bib: Vigne, R. (ed.), *A Gesture of Belonging: Letter from Bessie Head 1965–1979*.

Heaney, Seamus Justin (b 1939)
Poet. His early nature poetry, drawing on his upbringing as a farmer's son, is found in *Death of a Naturalist* (1966) and *Door into the Dark* (1969), and shows the influence of ▷ Ted Hughes. The political situation in Northern Ireland begins to be explored in *North* (1975) and *Field Work* (1979), from the standpoint of Heaney's ▷ Catholic background. The strongly individualistic, meditative and solitary vein that marks the distance between his own outlook and that of sectarianism continues to be apparent in subsequent collections: *Station Island* (1984), *The Haw Lantern* (1987), and *Seeing Things* (1991).

▷ Irish literature in English.

Bib: Morrison, B., *Seamus Heaney*; Curtis, T. (ed.), *The Art of Seamus Heaney*; Corcoran, N., *Seamus Heaney*.

***Heart of Darkness* (1902)**
A ▷ novella by ▷ Joseph Conrad. It is narrated by Marlow, an officer in the Merchant Navy who also appears in Conrad's other works ▷ *Lord Jim*, *Youth* and *Chance*. Sitting on board a ship anchored in the lower reaches of the River Thames, he tells a group of friends the story of his journey up the Congo River in Africa, in the employment of a Belgian trading company. This supposedly benevolent organization is in fact ruthlessly enslaving the Africans and stripping the area of ivory, and what Marlow sees on his arrival in Africa disgusts him. At the company's Central Station he hears much about Kurtz, their most successful agent, who is apparently lying ill at the Inner Station up river. Marlow's attempts to set out to reach him are delayed by the machinations of the manager and other agents, who are jealous of Kurtz's success. When the steamer which Marlow is to captain is finally repaired and the party sets off, Marlow experiences a powerful sense of dread as the boat carries them deeper into the primitive world of the jungle, but this is combined with a strong desire to meet Kurtz. After being attacked by natives from the bank, they reach the Inner Station, where an eccentric young Russian adventurer who idolizes Kurtz tells Marlow of his power over the local inhabitants, and the fluency and fascination of his ideas. But Kurtz's hut is surrounded by heads on poles, and it becomes apparent that, in addition to writing a report on the 'Suppression of Savage Customs', ending with the words 'exterminate all the brutes!', he has become compulsively addicted to unspecified barbaric practices, presumably involving human sacrifice. He has also acquired an African mistress. Marlow tries to get Kurtz away down river, but he dies, his last words being 'The horror! The horror!' Back in Europe, Marlow tells Kurtz's fiancée that he died with her name on his lips.

The story has come to be regarded as a classic of 20th-century literature, and its ambiguity has made it the subject of numerous interpretations.

***Heartbreak House* (1917)**
A play by ▷ George Bernard Shaw. It is set in an English country house, and ends with the outbreak of World War I. The guests are intellectuals, and the mood is one of disillusionment reminiscent of plays of ▷ Chekhov, *eg The Cherry Orchard*. But Shaw typically exploits the conventional

theatre of the later 19th century, introducing love rivalries which invite expectation of passionate climaxes, but end in calculated anti-climaxes. The Preface discusses the role of the English country house – either hunting or intellectual – in the English scene; the play brings out the frustration and disillusionment which burden the latter.

Hegemony
Originally used to denote political domination. In its more modern meaning and in its use in literary criticism it has come to refer to that process of political control whereby the interests of a dominant class in society are shared by those subordinated to it. Hegemony depends upon the consent of subordinate classes to their social positions, but the constraints within which that consent operates, and the ways in which it is experienced, are determined by the dominant class. This concept also offers ways of understanding the different kinds of social and personal relationships represented in literary texts. Along with a number of other concepts, it opens the way for an analysis of the different forms of negotiation that take place within texts, and between text and reader, and serves to emphasize the social context of experience, ▷ consciousness and human interaction.

Herbert, James (b 1943)
Britain's best-selling ▷ horror novelist, Herbert rose to notoriety in the 1970s as a purveyor of unabashed visceral gore set in grimy, modern urban surroundings. His first novel *The Rats* (1974) was a huge paperback hit, earning Herbert the title 'King of the Nasties'; described by the author as a metaphor for urban collapse in which 'the rats are the establishment', the novel set new standards of gruesome violence for popular horror fiction. Although subsequent works such as *The Fog*, *Lair* and *Domain* have continued this penchant for dismemberment, Herbert has also explored more subtle territory; *Fluke* (1977) is a satirical reincarnation fantasy notable for its restrained tone, while *Shrine* (1983) takes a bold swipe at organized religion and fraudulent 'miracles'. Having worked as an advertising art director before turning to writing, Herbert is unique in retaining total control of his book covers, which he designs himself. Works include: *The Survivor* (1976); *The Spear* (1978); *The Dark* (1980); *The Jonah* (1981); *Domain* (1984); *Moon* (1985); *The Magic Cottage* (1987).

Heritage culture
A term coined to identify the growth and funding, with government backing of institutions devoted to the preservation and representation of Britain's past. This includes, besides the National Trust and English Heritage (The Historic Buildings and Ancient Monuments Commission), such periodicals as *This England* and *Heritage, The British Review*, *Heritage Outlook* and *Historic House*. Large sums of money are involved, with serious political implications. The first National Heritage Act was passed in 1980, the year after Margaret Thatcher came to power. It provides both for the preservation of that range of property which it defines as 'the heritage', and also seeks to ensure its display. It eases the means whereby property can be transferred to the state in lieu of various taxes and indemnifies museums which could not otherwise afford to insure the objects they send out on loan. It also established the National Heritage Memorial Fund, out of the remains of The National Land Fund, a sum realized from the sale of surplus war materials and intended to be used as a memorial to the dead of World War II. The National Heritage Act of 1983 set up English Heritage, a body designed to promote the display of England's history through reanimations aimed at a mass tourist market. Heritage culture, in its many variations, aims to control our idea of the national past, making it more palatable and distinctly nostalgic.
▷ Postmodernism.
Bib: Wright, P., *On Living in an Old Country*.

Hermeneutics
Used in literary criticism to denote the science of interpretation as opposed to commentary. Hermeneutics is concerned primarily with the question of determining meaning, and is based upon the presupposition of a transcendental notion of understanding, and a conception of truth as being in some sense beyond language. Hermeneutics also postulates that there is one truth, and is therefore opposed on principle to the notion of 'pluralism' that is associated with ▷ deconstruction and materialist readings.

Heyer, Georgette (1902–74)
Novelist. Georgette Heyer was a phenomenally prolific and popular writer of detective stories and historical romances, the latter populated with a mixture of fictional characters and real historical figures, and often set in the Regency period. Whilst her

writing has traditionally been criticized for its predictably escapist plots, recent feminist work on romantic fiction has emphasized its interest as fantasy and the important role that her books play in many women's lives. Her works include: *The Black Moth* (1921); *Simon the Coldheart* (1925); *The Barren Court* (1930); *The Convenient Marriage* (1934); *Regency Buck* (1935); *Royal Escape* (1937); *Beau Wyndham* (1941); *Arabella* (1949); *Bath Tangle* (1955); *April Lady* (1957); *Freedom* (1965); *Lady of Quality* (1972).
Bib: Radway, J., *Reading the Romance*.
▷ Detective fiction; romantic fiction.

Hill, Geoffrey (b 1932)
Poet. His first two volumes, *For the Unfallen* (1959) and *King Log* (1968), established the characteristics of his poetry: intense moral seriousness, intellectual complexity and a concern with mythical and historical subjects, most notably with the victims of war or persecution. *Mercian Hymns* (1971), a remarkable sequence of prose poems, added elements of humour and ▷ autobiography; *Tenebrae* (1978) is dominated by the relation of divine and human love, while *The Mystery of the Charity of Charles Peguy* (1978) is a single extended meditation on the life of the French poet. Hill's work shows many continuities with the Modernists, especially ▷ T. S. Eliot, and testifies to the influence of a wide range of European and American thinkers and poets. *The Lords of Limit* (1984); *Collected Poems* (1985).
Bib: Robinson, P. (ed.), *Geoffrey Hill: Essays on his Work*; Sherry, V., *The Uncommon Tongue*.

Hill, Susan (b 1942)
Novelist, short-story writer and radio dramatist. Since graduating from London University, she has worked as a literary journalist and broadcaster. Her novels are sensitive, formal and conventionally structured, and tend to explore loss, isolation and grief. *In The Springtime of the Year* (1974) recounts the gradual adjustment to bereavement of a young widow. She has written effectively of the experience of children (*I'm The King of The Castle*; 1970) and the elderly (*Gentlemen and Ladies*; 1968). Two of her novels deal with intense male friendships; these are *The Bird of Night* (1972) and, probably her best-known work, *Strange Meeting* (1971). The latter takes its title from a poem by ▷ Wilfred Owen, and is set in the trenches of Flanders during World War I. Other novels: *The Enclosure* (1961); *Do Me A Favour* (1963); *A Change for the Better* (1969); *The Woman in Black: A Ghost Story* (1983). Story collections are: *The Albatross* (1971); *The Custodian* (1972); *A Bit of Singing and Dancing* (1973).

Hogarth Press, The
Publishing house. Started by ▷ Virginia Woolf and her husband Leonard, at their home, Hogarth House, Richmond, the Hogarth Press moved to Tavistock Square in 1924 and became an allied company of Chatto and Windus in 1947. John Lehmann became a partner in 1938. In the early years of its existence the press published work by, among others, Virginia Woolf, ▷ T. S. Eliot and ▷ Katherine Mansfield, as well as translations of the work of European novelists and poets.

Holden, Molly (1927–1981)
Poet. Born in Swindon and educated in London, Molly Holden's gentle and understated poetry is now beginning to receive greater attention, but being essentially at odds with more radical poetic trends, this rather fragile 'nature poetry' (which draws on the influences of ▷ Thomas Hardy and ▷ Edward Thomas) has hitherto brought it a limited readership. She has also written three novels for children. She was a long-term sufferer of multiple sclerosis, of which she died in 1981. Her poetic works include: *A Hill Like a Horse* (1963); *The Bright Cloud* (1964); *Make Me Grieve* (1968); *Air and Chill Earth* (1971); *The Country Over* (1975); and the posthumous *New and Selected Poems* (1986).

Holtby, Winifred (1898–1935)
Novelist and journalist. Winifred Holtby's short career was extremely prolific. She is best known as the writer of *South Riding* (1936), a study of life and rural politics in her native Yorkshire, but Holtby's career is much more varied than this suggests. She was a farmer's daughter whose first book of poetry was published when she was only 13 (*My Garden and Other Poems*). She then went on to study at Oxford (where she met and befriended ▷ Vera Brittain), worked as a nurse in the First World War, and wrote the first full-length critical study of ▷ Virginia Woolf (1932). She also lectured, and had a distinguished journalistic career (writing for, amongst others, the *Manchester* ▷ *Guardian* and the *News Chronicle*). Her other works include: *Anderby Wold* (1923); *The Land of*

Green Ginger (1927); *Poor Caroline* (1931); *Mandoa! Mandoa!* (1933); *Women and a Changing Civilisation* (1934); *Letters to a Friend* (1937).
Bib: Brittain, V., *Testament of Friendship*; Handley-Taylor, G., *Winifred Holtby: A Concise and Selected Bibliography with Some Letters*.

Homosexuality
Accorded a marginal place in literary representation, and when it has been shown, usually hedged about with implications of the exotic, the abnormal or at least the exceptional. When ▷ Radcliffe Hall published her plea for the recognition and acceptance of lesbianism, *The Well of Loneliness* (1928) – even though it had a sympathetic preface from the sexologist ▷ Havelock Ellis, testifying to its scientific accuracy – the book was condemned as obscene and banned. This is in line with official attempts to promote heterosexual activity within marriage as the healthy norm. In the 1950s and 1960s aversion therapy was used in an effort to impose or restore this norm in homosexuals. The Kinsey Reports on *Sexual Behaviour in the Human Male* (1948) and *Female* (1953), however, showed that what had been defined as deviant behaviour was far more widespread than had been believed, thus challenging the 'naturalness' of heterosexuality. Homosexual behaviour in certain circumstances defined as private was decriminalized, but not until ten years after the Wolfenden report recommended it. Meanwhile novelistic discussions of homosexuality tended to promote toleration. It is mostly in works from outside England, by Jean Genet (*Our Lady of the Flowers*), William Burroughs (*The Naked Lunch*) or James Baldwin (*Giovanni's Room*), for example, that one has a more vital vision. Recent scholarship is identifying gay and lesbian communities as potentially important centres of innovation; see Shari Benstock, *Women of the Left Bank*, an account of women writers in Paris in the early years of this century, which identifies a close connection between the writers' political experience as homosexuals and their readiness to experiment with representation.
▷ Censorship.

Hopkins, Gerard Manley (1844–89)
Poet: He was converted to Roman ▷ Catholicism in 1866, and entered the Jesuit Order in 1868. He then gave up poetry, but resumed writing in 1875 with *The Wreck of the Deutschland*, his first important poem. Although Hopkins is a ▷ Victorian poet, so unusual were his poems that they were not published in his own lifetime; after his death they passd to his friend, ▷ Robert Bridges, who delayed their publication until 1918, and even then Hopkins's fame did not become widespread until the second edition of 1930. The date of his publication, the interest he shared with modern poets in the relationship between poetry and experience and his technical innovation and intense style, have caused him to be thought of as belonging more to the 20th century than to the 19th. His ▷ 'sprung rhythm' is a technical term meaning the combination of the usual regularity of stress patterns with freely varying numbers of syllables in each line. This was not new, but was contrary to the practice that had predominated in English poetry since Edmund Spenser, which required a uniform pattern of syllabic counts as of stresses. In Hopkins's poetry, the rhythm of the verse could more easily combine with the flow and varying emphasis of spoken language, so that the two kinds of expressiveness unite. A kindred sort of concentration is obtained by his practice – natural to the spoken language but uncommon in writing – of inventing compound words, especially adjectives, *eg* 'dappled-with-damson west' for a sunset, 'lovely-asunder starlight' for stars scattered over the sky. John Keats was a strong influence upon him (as upon so many of the later Victorians) and Hopkins shared Keats's gift for evoking in words the physical response suitable to the thing they express. This was the more conspicuous in Hopkins because of his intense interest (for which he found support in the 13th-century philosopher Duns Scotus) in the qualities which give any object its individual reality, distinguishing it from other objects of the same class. For these qualities he invented the term 'inscape'. He also invented 'instress' for the force of these qualities on the mind. This intensity of response to the reality and beauty of objects was akin to the intensity of his feeling about the relationship between God and man. All Hopkins's poetry is religious, and in quality recalls the early 17th-century devotional poets, John Donne and George Herbert; in his 'terrible sonnets', for instance, Hopkins engages in direct dialogue with God as does Donne in his *Holy Sonnets*, or Herbert in a lyric such as *The Collar*. Thus Hopkins unites the rhythmical freedom of the Middle

Ages, the religious intensity of the early 17th century, the response to nature of the early 19th, and he anticipated the 20th century in challenging conventional encumbrances in poetic form.

Bib: Gardner, W. A., *Life*; Hartman, G. H. (ed.), *Hopkins*; Bottrall, M. (ed.), *Gerard Manley Hopkins: Poems*; Bergonzi, B., *Gerard Manley Hopkins*; Roberts, G. (ed.), *Gerard Manley Hopkins: The Critical Heritage*; Oug, W. J., *Hopkins, the Self and God*; Weyland, N. (ed.), *Immortal Diamond: Studies in Gerard Manley Hopkins*.

Horror fiction

Although horror fiction has undergone astonishing changes since the earliest of 'Gothic' novels (Horace Walpole's *The Castle of Oranto*, 1764, M. G. Lewis's *The Castle Spectre*, 1798, Anne Radcliffe's *The Mysteries of Adolpho*, 1794, M. G. Lewis's *The Monk*, 1796) the themes of transgression with which the genre deals have remained largely unchanged. Returning obsessively to taboo subjects (death, sex, incest, decay, bodily corruption, psychosis) horror novels have been described both by critics and champions as an 'undergrowth of literature' whose function is to speak the unspeakable. In his critical work, *Supernatural Horror in Literature*, H. P. Lovecraft declares: 'The oldest and strongest emotion of mankind is fear, and the oldest and strongest kind of fear is of the unknown. These facts few psychologists will dispute, and their admittedness must establish for all time the genuineness and dignity of the weirdly horrible tales.' Sixty years later leading contemporary horror novelist Stephen King writes: 'Horror appeals to us because it says, in a symbolic way, things we would be afraid to say ... It offers us a chance to exercise (not exorcise) ... emotions which society demands we keep closely in hand' (*Danse Macabre*, 1981). Similarly, British horror novelist Ramsey Campbell has described the genre as 'the branch of literature most often concerned with going too far. It is the least escapist form of fantasy. It shows us sights we would ordinarily look away from or reminds us of insights we might prefer not to admit we have.'

Whilst much early Gothic fiction is rooted in American literature (Edgar Allan Poe is frequently cited as the godfather of modern Gothic), Britain has produced a number of key texts. Bram Stoker's *Dracula* (1897) set the tone for future tales of vampirism, while Mary Shelley's *Frankenstein* (1818) has become the genre's single most reworked (and indeed abused) text, both on page and later screen. Of the longevity of these horror icons David Punter writes: '*Frankenstein* and *Dracula* are still granted fresh embodiments [because of] both their own imagistic flexibility and ... the essential continuity under capitalism of the anxieties about class and gender warfare from which they sprang.' The question of whether classic horror fiction alludes to contemporary rather than timeless fears has been of central import in recent years. Following a slump in the 1960s, horror fiction was revitalized in 1971 by the extraordinary success of ▷ William Peter Blatty's occult chiller *The Exorcist*. Described by the author as 'a 350 page thankyou note to the Jesuits' for his education, *The Exorcist* rekindled modern popular religious debate, but its success was attributed by some to a contemporary fear of adolescent rebellion which the novel appeared to reflect. In the wake of Blatty's success, American short-story writer ▷ Stephen King published his first novel *Carrie*, which also dealt with aggressive adolescence. In Britain, ▷ James Herbert rapidly became the leading light of modern pulp horror fiction, producing viscerally gory tales set against a backdrop of modern urban decay. 'The rats are the establishment,' explained Herbert of the subtexts of his first best-seller *The Rats*. Although Herbert's later work became more discreet, he opened the flood-gates for a slew of writers specializing in sensationally violent fantasy; most notable is Shaun Hutson (*Spawn, Slugs, Assassin*), a connoisseur of outlandish mutilation with a recurrent sexual bent, while Guy N. Smith (*Crabs, The Sucking Pit, Crabs on the Rampage*) deserves mention for his prolific output. In the early 1980s, ▷ Clive Barker and ▷ Ramsey Campbell rose to the forefront of the British 'new wave' of horror writers. Challenging the 'innate conservatisms and prejudices of the field'. Barker and Campbell forged a new brand of horror which sought to demystify taboo subjects rather than merely revel in them. In America, Stephen King's popularity remains unchallenged, but he is outstripped in terms of invention by Peter Straub, author of *Ghost Story* (1979), and with whom King collaborated on *The Talisman* (1984). Current upcoming authors include K. W. Jeter, Kim Newman, Thomas Ligotti, Michael Marshall Smith, Nicholas Royle, Ian R. MacLeod, D. F. Lewis and Joel Lane. Recent short-story collections are: *Best New Horror*

(Steven Jones and Ramsey Campbell, eds.) and *Dark Voices* (edited by Sutton, D. and Jones, S.).
Bib: King, S., *Danse Macabre* (1981); Newman, K., and Jones, S., *Horror: 100 Best Books* (1988); Sullivan, J., (ed.), *The Penguin Encyclopaedia of Horror and the Supernatural.*

Housman, A. E. (1859–1936)
A classical scholar who published two small volumes of ▷ lyrics of enormous popularity: *The Shropshire Lad* (1896) and *Last Poems* (1922). They are very pessimistic but have an immediate musical appeal, and several have in fact been set to music by a number of composers, *eg* Vaughan Williams. His lecture *The Name and Nature of Poetry*, in which he described poetic creation as an essentially physical experience, also achieved considerable fame in his own age.
Bib: Housman, L., *AEH: Some Poems, Some Letters and a Personal Memoir*; Richards, G., *Housman 1879–1936*; Watson, G. L., *Housman: a divided life*; Graves, R. P., *A. E. Housman: the Scholar-Poet.*

***Howards End* (1910)**
A novel by ▷ E. M. Forster. The theme is the relationship between the Schlegel family (Margaret, Helen, and their brother Tibby) who live on an unearned income and are liberal, enlightened, and cultivated, and the Wilcoxes, who work in the commercial world which the Schlegels are inclined to despise but from which they draw their income. The Wilcoxes are snobbish, prejudiced, insensitive, and philistine; in fact they have much in common with the middle classes as described by Matthew Arnold in his critique of English culture – *Culture and Anarchy* (1869). Mrs Wilcox, however, who has bought her husband the old house, Howards End, belongs to the older, aristocratic continuity of English culture; never understood by her husband and children, on her death she bequeaths the house unexpectedly to Margaret Schlegel. Margaret comes into the inheritance at the end of the book, but only after she has married and subdued to her values Mrs Wilcox's former husband. Meanwhile Helen, moved by sympathy and indignation, has become pregnant by Leonard Bast, a poor bank-clerk who has been the victim of both the Schlegel and the Wilcox social illusions and mishandling. Bast dies after being beaten by one of the Wilcox sons, and Helen and her child come to live at Howards End with Margaret and Mr Wilcox. The house remains a tentative symbol of hope for the future of English society. The novel as a whole explores the impact of early ▷ feminist ideas, and ▷ anti-industrialism. The Merchant Ivory film *Howards End*, with a screenplay by Ruth Prawer Jhabvala, was released to critical acclaim in 1992.

Hughes, Richard (1900–76)
Novelist, dramatist and poet. He published four novels: *A High Wind in Jamaica* (1929); *In Hazard* (1938); *The Fox in the Attic* (1961) and *The Wooden Shepherdess* (1971). He was educated at Charterhouse School, and at Oxford University, where he met ▷ W. B. Yeats, ▷ A. E. Coppard, T. E. Lawrence and ▷ Robert Graves. As an undergraduate he wrote a one-act play, *The Sister's Tragedy*, which was staged in 1922 and enthusiastically received, and a volume of poems entitled *Gipsy Night* (1922). In 1924 he wrote the first original radio play, *Danger* and a stage play, *A Comedy of Good and Evil.* Born in Surrey but of Welsh descent, he adopted Wales as his home, but travelled extensively around the world. His travels are reflected in his book of short stories, *In the Lap of Atlas: Stories of Morocco* (1979), as well as in his first two novels, which are set mainly at sea and are intense studies of moral issues in the context of human crisis. *A High Wind in Jamaica*, his best-known work, is the story of a group of children captured by pirates. It deals with violence, the relation of innocence and evil, and the fallibility of human justice, and takes an unsentimental view of childhood. *In Hazard* describes in great detail the events on board a cargo ship at sea during a hurricane, and has affinities with the work of ▷ Joseph Conrad. After an administrative post in the Admiralty during World War II, Hughes worked as a book reviewer and teacher. His last two novels are part of a projected historical sequence entitled *The Human Predicament*, recounting the events leading up to World War II. Other publications include: *The Man Born to be Hanged* (1923) (stage play); *A Moment of Time* (1926) (short stories); *The Spider's Palace* (1931) and *Don't Blame Me* (1940) (short stories for children); *Confessio Juvenis* (1926) (collected poems).
Bib: Thomas, P., *Richard Hughes.*

Hughes, Ted (b 1930)
One of the liveliest poets writing in Britain since 1945. His works include: *The Hawk*

in the Rain (1957); *Lupercal* (1960); two volumes of verse for children – *Meet My Folks* (1961) and *Earth Owl and Other Moon People* (1963); *Wodwo* (1967); *Crow* (1970); *Poems* (1971); *Eat Crow* (1971); *Prometheus on his Crag* (1973); *Spring Summer Autumn Winter* (1974); *Cavebirds* (1975); *Gaudete* (1977); *Remains of Elmet* (1979); *Moortown* (1979); *River* (1983); *Season Songs* (1985); *Flowers and Insects* (1986); and *Shakespeare and the Goddess of Complete Being* (1992). His rather violent poetry appeared when English verse was dominated by the poets of the ▷ Movement (▷ Larkin); in contrast with these restrained, disillusioned, ironic and often urban poems, Hughes's work explored and celebrated violence and the life of the unconscious, and he was a key member of the 'new poetry' group (included in A. Alvarez's important anthology of that name published in 1962). Hughes is remarkable for his evocation of natural life, in particular of animals, presented as alien and opposed to the civilized human consciousness, and for that reason, as in the poetry and prose of ▷ D. H. Lawrence, peculiarly close to sub-rational instinct in the self. Hughes married the poet ▷ Sylvia Plath in 1956. On the death of ▷ John Betjeman in 1984 Hughes was made ▷ Poet Laureate.
Bib: Sagar, K., *The Art of Ted Hughes*; *Gifford, T. and Roberts, N., Ted Hughes: a Critical Study*.

Hulme, Keri (b 1947)
▷ Commonwealth literatures.

Hulme, Thomas Ernest (1883–1917)
Poet and essayist. His attacks on 19th-century Romanticism and the verbosity that often expressed it were an important influence on the theory and practice of ▷ Imagism as a poetry of concentration and verbal compression. His writings in support of a modern classicism that should be austere and authoritarian were also important for ▷ T. S. Eliot and ▷ Wyndham Lewis. His output as a poet was tiny: *The Complete Poetical Works* were published as an addendum to the *Ripostes* of ▷ Ezra Pound in 1912, but his essays and ▷ translations of writers like the French vitalist philosopher Henri Bergson were of immense significance in the development of ▷ modernism. See *Speculations* (ed. H. Read; 1924); *Further Speculations* (ed. S. Hynes; 1955).
Bib: Kermode, F., in *Romantic Image*; Roberts, M., *T. E. Hulme*.

Humanism
The word has two distinct uses: **1** the intellectually liberating movements in western Europe in the 15th and 16th centuries, associated with new attitudes to ancient Greek and Latin literature; **2** a modern movement for the advancement of humanity without reliance on supernatural religious beliefs.

1 Humanism in its first sense had its beginnings in Italy as early as the 14th century, when its pioneer was the poet and scholar Petrarch (1304–74), and reached its height (greatly stimulated by the recovery of lost manuscripts after the fall of Constantinople in 1453) throughout Western Europe in the 16th century, when it first reached England. Its outstanding characteristic was a new kind of critical power, and some of the important consequences of humanism were these: the rediscovery of many ancient Greek and Latin works; the establishment of new standards in Greek and Latin scholarship; the assumption, which was to dominate English education until the present century, that a thorough basis in at least Latin literature was indispensable to the civilized man; the beginnings of what we nowadays regard as 'scientific thinking'; the introduction of the term ▷ Middle Ages for the period between the fall of the Roman Empire of the West (5th century AD) and the ▷ Renaissance, meaning by it a period of partial and inferior civilization. In the 17th and 18th centuries, humanism hardened into neo-classicism.

2 Modern humanism assumes that man's command of scientific knowledge has rendered religion largely redundant. Its central principle is that 'man is the measure of all things', and elsewhere in Europe it is sometimes called 'hominism' (Lat. *homo* = man).

'Humanism' is also used as a general expression for any philosophy that proposes the full development of human potentiality. In this sense, 'Christian humanism', since the 16th century, has stood for the marriage of the humanist value attached to a conception of humanity based on reason with the Christian value based on Divine Revelation. 'Liberal humanism' values the dignity of the individual and their inalienable right to justice, liberty, freedom of thought and the pursuit of happiness; its weakness lies in its concentration on the single subject and its failure to recognize the power of institutions in determining the conditions of life.

Huxley, Aldous (1894–1963)
Novelist and essayist. His novels are 'novels of ideas', involving conversations which disclose viewpoints rather than establish characters, and having a polemical rather than an imaginative theme. An early practitioner of the form was Thomas Love Peacock, and it is his novels that Huxley's earlier ones recall: *Crome Yellow* (1921); *Antic Hay* (1923); *Those Barren Leaves* (1925). *Point Counter Point* (1928) is his best-known novel and is an attempt to convey a social image of the age with more imaginative depth and substance, but his polemical and inquisitorial mind was better suited to *Brave New World* (1932), in which a future society is presented so as to bring out the tendencies working in contemporary civilization and to show their disastrous consequences. Fastidious, abhorring what he saw to be the probable obliteration of human culture by 20th-century addiction to technology, but sceptical of religious solutions – he was the grandson of the great 19th-century agnostic biologist Thomas Huxley – he turned in the 1930s to Eastern religions such as Buddhism for spiritual support. This is shown in *Eyeless in Gaza* (1936). This and his last books – *After Many a Summer* (1939), *Ape and Essence* (1948), *Brave New World Revisited* (1958) – return to the discursive form of his earlier work. His novels and his essays (Collected Edition; 1959) are all concerned with how to resist the debasement of 'mass culture' and to sustain the identity of the human spirit without the aid of faith in supernatural religion of the Christian kind.
Bib: Bowering, P., *Aldous Huxley*; Ferns, C. S., *Aldous Huxley, Novelist*; Woodcock, G. *Dawn and the Darkest Hour*.

Ibsen, Henrik (1828–1906)
Norwegian dramatist; his working life (1850–1900) began in a period when the art of the theatre had fallen low everywhere in Europe, and perhaps lowest of all in Britain. By the end of the century Ibsen's example had revived interest in the drama everywhere and had profoundly influenced a number of other important dramatists, such as ▷ Strindberg in Sweden, ▷ Chekhov in Russia, and ▷ Shaw in Britain. Ibsen began by writing romantic and historical dramas. Then, in self-imposed exile, he wrote his great poetic dramas, *Brand* (1866) and *Peer Gynt* (1867). About 10 years later he started on the prose dramas, the sequence of which continued to 1900. The first group of these treated social problems with startling boldness: *Pillars of Society* (1877); *A Doll's House* (1879); *Ghosts* (1881); *An Enemy of the People* (1882). After this, his work became increasingly psychological, anticipating the 20th century in the handling of inner conflicts, self-deceptions, and frustrations: *The Wild Duck* (1884); *Rosmersholm* (1886); *The Lady from the Sea* (1888); *Hedda Gabler* (1890). So far these plays had been extremely realistic, but the psychological phase showed a new and interesting dramatic use of symbols. In the last group of plays the symbolism takes precedence over the realism: *The Master Builder* (1892); *Little Eyolf* (1894); *John Gabriel Borkman* (1896), and *When We Dead Awaken* (1900). It was the social realist phase which most influenced Shaw, and it was Shaw who was the most eloquent introducer of Ibsen's art to the British public, particularly in his book *Quintessence of Ibsenism* (1891). The English dramatic revival of 1890–1914 (as distinct from the Anglo-Irish one by ▷ Yeats and ▷ Synge happening at the same time) thus consisted predominantly of realist plays dealing with social problems, by such writers as Shaw, ▷ Galsworthy, ▷ Granville-Barker. The psychological and symbolical phases of Ibsen's work have had, together with the writing of Chekhov and Strindberg, greater influence since 1920.
Bib: Beyer, E., *Ibsen: The Man and his Work* (trans. Wells, M.); Meyer, M., *Henrik Ibsen: A Biography*, 3 vols.; Williams, R., *Drama from Ibsen to Brecht*.

Idealism
In philosophy, any form of thought which finds reality not in the mind of the perceiver (the subject), nor in the thing experienced (the object) but in the idea in which they meet. In its earliest form idealism was developed by Socrates and his disciple Plato. Their influence was important in the 16th-century Europe of the ▷ Renaissance, *eg* on Edmund Spenser. A modern idealist, ▷ F. H. Bradley, had as strong an influence on the poet ▷ T. S. Eliot.

In ordinary usage, idealism means the ability to conceive perfection as a standard by which ordinary behaviour and achievement were to be judged. This view is really an inheritance from Plato, who believed that earthly realities were imperfect derivatives of heavenly perfections. To 'idealize' a thing or person is to present the image of what ought to be, rather than what experience knows in ordinary life. In imaginative art we have come to consider this as a fault, but to a 16th-century critic such as Sir Philip Sidney poetry existed for just such a purpose. This is not, however, the kind of influence which Bradley had on Eliot; Bradley maintained that no reality existed outside the spirit, and he influenced Eliot towards interpreting the phenomena and dilemmas of his age in religious terms.

In modern critical theory idealism is associated with the anti-materialist impulse to denigrate history and social context. The meaning of this term is complicated by its history within the discipline of philosophy, and by its common usage as a description of human behaviour not susceptible to the 'realistic' impulses of self-interest. The term is sometimes used in critical theory to denote the primacy of thought, and to indicate a particular kind of relationship between writer and text where it is a sequence of ideas that acts as the deep structure for events and relationships.

Ideology
This term is defined by ▷ Karl Marx and Friedrich Engels (1800–95) in *The German Ideology* as 'false consciousness'. A further meaning, which ▷ Raymond Williams traces to the usage initiated by Napoleon Bonaparte, denotes a fanatical commitment to a particular set of ideas, and this has remained a dominant meaning in the sphere of modern right-wing politics, especially in relation to the question of dogmatism. The term has come to the fore again in the ▷ post-structural Marxism of ▷ Louis Althusser, where it is distinguished from 'science'. Ideology here is defined as the means whereby, at the level of ideas, every social group produces and reproduces the conditions of its own existence. Althusser

argues that 'Ideology is a "representation" of the imaginary relationship of individuals to their real conditions of existence' (*Lenin and Philosophy*; 1971). In order to ensure that political power remains the preserve of a dominant class, individual 'subjects' are assigned particular positions in society. A full range of social institutions, such as the Church, the family and the education system, are the means through which a particular hierarchy of values is disseminated. The point to emphasize, however, is that ideology disguises the real material relations between the different social classes, and this knowledge can only be retrieved through a theoretically aware analysis of the inter-relationships that prevail within society at any one time. A ruling class sustains itself in power, partly by coercion (repressive apparatuses), but also by negotiation with other subordinate classes (▷ hegemony; Althusser's ideological state of apparatuses).

Social change occurs when the ideology of the dominant class is no longer able to contain the contradictions existing in real social relations. The function of literary texts in this process is complex. In one sense they reproduce ideology, but also they may offer a critique of it by 'distancing' themselves from the ideology with which they are historically implicated. Since all language is by definition 'ideological', in so far as it is motivated by particular sorts of social relationship, the language of a literary text can very often be implicated in an ideology of which it is not aware. The text's implication in ideology can only be excavated through a critical process which seeks to uncover the assumptions upon which it is based.

▷ Archaeology.

Bib: Althusser, L., *For Marx*; Thompson, J. B., *Studies in the Theory of Ideology*.

Imaginary

When used in contemporary literary theory, this term originates in ▷ Jacques Lacan's re-reading of ▷ Freud, where it refers generally to the perceived or *imagined* world of which the infant sees itself as the centre. In other words, this is the first opportunity that the child has to construct a coherent identity for itself. But in Lacan's view this image is a myth; it is an imaginary subjectivity that allows the ego to speak of itself as 'I', but which represses those fragmentary energies which constitute the unconscious. ▷ Louis Althusser uses the term 'imaginary', which he takes from Lacan, in a very different way, while retaining the concept of a constellation of forces which contribute to the formation of the human subject. In Althusser the subject *mis*recognizes his or her place in the social order through an ideology which posits as 'natural' a fixed relationship between social classes. What is at issue for both Lacan and Althusser is the way in which individual human subjects are constituted by an order which extends beyond the images through which that order is represented to them. In Lacan's psychoanalytical theory the realm of the 'imaginary' is contained within that of the ▷ 'symbolic order', and it is the function of psychoanalysis to uncover the 'real' relations which exist beneath this series of representations. In Althusser, the 'mirror' phase can be equated with 'ideology' in that this is the means through which individual human subjects *misrecognize* themselves and their position in the social order.

▷ Psychoanalytical criticism.

Imagism

A poetic movement founded by a group led by ▷ Ezra Pound in 1912; it published four anthologies – *Des Imagistes*, 1914; *Some Imagists*, 1915–16–17. The inspiration came from the ideas of ▷ T. E. Hulme (1886–1917) who was an anti-romantic, believing that words were being used by poets to obscure emotions instead of to clarify them. The kind of poet he had in mind was the Victorian Algernon Swinburne. The Imagist credo may be summarized as:

1 Use the language of common speech, but use it exactly.
2 Create new rhythms for new moods.
3 Allow complete freedom in subject.
4 Present an image, but avoid vagueness.
5 Produce poetry that is hard and clear.
6 Concentration is the essence of poetry.

Pound was an American, though he was then living in England; Imagism was an Anglo-American movement, with an English periodical, *The Egoist* (started 1914), and an American one, *Poetry* (from 1912). Pound was himself the most distinguished of the Imagists, though he separated from the movement in 1914. Notable contributors to the anthologies included ▷ D. H. Lawrence, ▷ James Joyce and ▷ H. D. The movement was more organized and distinct in its aims than most English literary movements.

▷ Vorticism.

Bib: Jones, P. (ed.), *Imagist Poetry*.

Imperialism

A desire to build up an empire, that is, to dominate politically and assimilate other countries. It has a long history, from Rome to the present day, although the main period of imperialism began with the 17th-century conquests of the Americas and reached its height in the 1880s and 90s. The British Empire has this century developed into the Commonwealth, but a more ingenious form of imperialism can be seen in the pervasive economic and political influence of the U.S.S.R. in the East and the U.S.A. in the West, at least until recently.

▷ Commonwealth literatures; Kipling, Rudyard.

Implied author

The notional possessor of the set of attitudes and beliefs implied by the totality of a text; distinguished from the 'real' or biographical author. The distinction is necessary because a text may imply a set of beliefs (and perhaps a personality) which the author does not, in life, possess, and because different texts by the same author often imply different values.

Intertextuality

A term first introduced into critical theory by the French ▷ psychoanalytical writer ▷ Julia Kristeva, relating specifically to the use she makes of the work of ▷ Mikhail Bakhtin. The concept of intertextuality implies that literary texts are composed of dialectically opposed utterances, and that it is the function of the critic to identify these different strands and to account for their oppositions within the text itself. Kristeva notes that Bakhtin's '"dialogism" does not strive towards transcendence ... but rather towards harmony, all the while implying an idea of rupture (of opposition and analogy) as a modality of transformation' (*Desire and Language*; trans. 1980). Similarly, no text can be entirely free of other texts. No work is written or read in isolation, it is located, in Kristeva's words, 'within the totality of previous ... texts'. This is a second important aspect of intertextuality.

▷ Feminism.

Ireland

A brief sketch of the confused and tormented history of this country must concentrate on its relations with England, and this account may conveniently be divided into phases.

1150–1600 – Period of Disorder

Henry II was the first English king to be acknowledged sovereign of Ireland, but at no time before 1600 did the English succeed in establishing an efficient central government. In the 12th century Ireland consisted of warring Celtic kingdoms, with a Norse settlement along the east coast. The conquest was not undertaken by Henry but by his Anglo-Norman nobility, notably Richard Strongbow, Earl of Pembroke in alliance with the Irish king of Leinster. By 1500 Ireland was ruled by a mixed English and Irish aristocracy, the former regarded as English by the Irish and as Irish by the English. English law and speech were secure only in a narrow region known as the Pale, centred on the capital city of Dublin. The first real crisis in relations between England and Ireland arose in the 16th century, when the Irish refused to receive the English Protestant Reformation. Fierce wars against Spanish armies which landed in Ireland with a view to invading England were followed by fierce suppression under Elizabeth I, for instance under the governorship of Lord Grey de Wilton. The poet Edmund Spenser was appointed his secretary (1580) and given a grant of land in the province of Munster as part of a plan to settle the country with Protestant overlords; his castle was burnt down in 1598, a year before his death. Spenser's singularly stern view of Justice in *The Faerie Queene* (Artegall, Bk. V) is a reflection of his Irish experiences. By 1600 Ireland was a nation of mixed English and Celtic people, with an English-speaking aristocracy, and firm identification with the Roman Catholic faith. The problem as England saw it in the next two centuries was how to subdue the country to effective Protestant rule.

1600–1800 – Irish Protestant Ascendancy

The policy of settling Protestants in Ireland was notably successful in one of the four provinces under James I (1603–25) when Ulster became the Anglo-Scottish Protestant fortress which it has remained to this day. Oliver Cromwell was savage in subjection of Catholic Ireland to his authority, and by extensive confiscations increased the class of Protestant landlords. In the 18th century, penal laws further disabled Catholic landholders, refused political rights to Catholics, and barred them from most professions and from education. The only Irish university (founded by Elizabeth in 1591), Dublin, was a Protestant one. However, towards the end of the 18th century, partly owing to the Irish patriotism of Anglo-Irish Protestants (including the satirist Jonathan Swift and the philosopher Berkeley), the penal laws were reduced in severity, and in 1782 an Irish constitution was promulgated, by which the Irish Protestants were given political rights and limited powers in an Irish Parliament freed from Privy Council control. The experiment was a failure, and in 1801 Ireland was united politically and in all other respects with England and Scotland, Irish Protestants receiving for the first time representation in the English Parliament.

1801–1921 – The Union

The 19th century was the age of steady emancipation of Irish Catholics and mounting Irish patriotism. The population at the beginning of the century was four and a half million, fewer than one and a half million being of English or Scottish Protestant descent. The Anglo-Irish were the social leaders of the country; the Scots were a middle class of businessmen and farmers; the native Irish were largely peasants. In 1829 Catholic Emancipation removed all the important restrictions on Catholics, notably the political ones. Henceforward there was a growing party of Irish Catholics in the English House of Commons, in the last quarter of the century known as the Home Rule Party from its intention to win national independence for Ireland. In the middle of the century reform was concentrated on land matters; this was the more necessary for the misery of the Irish peasantry whose sufferings were increased by the severe famines of the 1840s, leading to deaths on a massive scale and to massive emigration to the U.S.A. In 1841 the population was over eight million, and it is now about three million; Ireland is thus one of the very few countries in the world whose population has actually diminished in the last 100 years. Attempts to obtain Home Rule through the English Parliament failed. A brief rebellion in 1916 was put down, but a severe one in 1919–21 resulted in independence within the Commonwealth. It was led by the Sinn Fein party, and the great bitterness of the fighting arose in part from their fanaticism and the brutality of the English auxiliary police (called 'Black and Tans' from their uniform) sent to suppress the rebels.

The Irish Free State

This state was formed in 1922 and included the three provinces of Munster, Leinster, Connaught, and three counties of Ulster. The remaining six counties of Ulster, being mainly Protestant and Anglo-Scottish in population, have separate status as Northern Ireland with representation in the English Parliament. The Irish Free State took the name of Eire (Ireland) in 1937, and is no longer a member of the Commonwealth. It is a republic with a president and two houses of parliament, the Dáil and the Seanad. The first official language is nominally Gaelic, but it is a minority language, since English has long been the majority language.

▷ English language.

Irish literature in English

Ireland – England's first and closest colony – presents a recent history of literary movement and concerns that is very differently paced from that of its colonist. From 1171 the year of Ireland's conquest by Henry II, until the latter years of the 19th century, the history of Irish literature in English is, largely speaking, part of the general history of English literature. Since the Irish Literary Revival began in the 1880s, however, the existence and the memory of a literature in Ireland's original tongue, Gaelic, has interacted with the country's adopted vernacular at every level: in the detail of syntax; in the choice – or rejection – of subject matter; and in each writer's wrestle with identity.

Throughout the 18th and 19th centuries – and into the 20th – writers from Anglo-Irish Ireland made a rich and vigorous contribution to English literature: Jonathan Swift, William Congreve, Oliver Goldsmith, Sheridan, Oscar Wilde and ▷ George Bernard Shaw are amongst the better known. Their writings were not primarily concerned with the matter of Ireland or their author's own Irishness. Those who did write of Ireland, like Dion Boucicault (1820–90), who is held by many to be the inventor of the 'stage Irishman', and Thomas Moore (1779–1852), the purveyor to the drawing-rooms of London of an Ireland sugared by sentiment and exile, capitalized on what looks with hindsight like caricature. All these writers of the Anglo-Irish Ascendancy, coming from their background of landed privilege, seemed to be unaware of the still surviving Gaelic tradition of native Irish literature, with its long ancestry and close connections with mainland Europe – a tradition eloquently evoked in Daniel Corkery's *Hidden Ireland* of 1924, and recently made available anew in Seán Ó Tuama and Thomas Kinsella's 1981 anthology *An Duanaire: Poems of the Dispossessed.*

Moreover, during this pre-Revival period only a handful of creative writers mirrored the growing interest that folklorists like T. Crofton Croker (1798–1849), travellers (again, many of them from Europe) and diarists were taking in Irish peasant life outside the 'Pale'. Maria Edgeworth (1767–1849) and William Carleton (1794–1869) stand almost alone in the seriousness with which they looked at their native land and its inhabitants. Edgeworth's *Castle Rackrent* (1800) and Carleton's *Traits and Stories of the Irish Peasantry* (1830–3) are isolated landmarks; and Carleton, an adopted member of Ascendancy culture who was born a Catholic peasant, has been read in recent years with renewed interest and recognition.

In the decades that followed the devastation of native Gaelic culture by the famine and mass emigration of the 1840s, a new sense of Ireland's nationhood began, paradoxically, to emerge. The poets and dramatists of the Literary Revival of the 1880s and 1890s regarded Standish O'Grady (1846–1928) as its prime mover. His two-volume history of Ireland – *The Heroic Period* (1878) and *Cuchullin and His Contemporaries* (1880) – sent them back with a new authority to the ancient matter of Ireland. And it was on this material, and on a new attention to the distinctive English actually spoken in Ireland, that the renaissance of Irish letters was founded. Its chief authors – the most notable being ▷ W. B. Yeats (1865–1939), ▷ J. M. Synge (1871–1909) and ▷ Lady Gregory (1852–1932) – were still, to begin with, the sons and the daughters of the Ascendancy, but before long they were joined in their work of forging the soul of the soon-to-be-independent nation by writers who sprang from the native and Catholic population. A common task was perceived.

The history of Irish literature in English is closely linked, then, to the political history of the nation that (except for the six counties in its north-east corner) won its independence from British rule in 1921, and declared its Republican status when leaving the Commonwealth in 1949 (▷ Ireland). The first battle in the war of independence had, after all, been led by a poet, Padraig Pearse (1879–1916), and inspired partially at least by his romantic ideas of blood-sacrifice:

All changed, changed utterly.
A terrible beauty is born.
(Yeats, 'Easter 1916')

Irish writers since the Revival have had to reconsider and redefine ideas of continuity and cultural identity that are quite different from those that face English writers in the post-colonial period, though there are affinities with the experience of the other Celtic nations of Britain – the Welsh (▷ Welsh literature) and the Scots (▷ Scottish literature).

In the hundred-odd years since the poet and translator Douglas Hyde (1860–1949) gave a lecture to the newly formed National Literary Society in Dublin entitled 'The Necessity of De-Anglicising Ireland' (1892), Irish writers have had continually to ask themselves and each other quite how, and to what extent, de-Anglicization is to be carried out – and who they are when they have done it. Questions of national identity cross over with questions of personal identity in this distinctive version of the 20th-century artist's problematic relation to society.

Ireland's writers began by looking to their country's heroic past and its idealized idea of the west, the non-anglicized land of saints, scholars and a noble peasantry; but they also looked, from the very start, to the literatures of Europe, and cast a cold and realist eye at their own urban and rural present. ▷ James Joyce (1882–1941) taught himself enough Norwegian as a schoolboy to write a letter to his hero, ▷ Ibsen, who was already a profound influence on the playwrights of Dublin's ▷ Abbey Theatre; George Egerton (Mary Dunne, 1859–1945) translated Knut Hamsun's *Hunger* and wrote about the 'New Woman' in her novel *Keynotes* (1893) before the old century ended. Kate O'Brien (1897–1974) and Maura Laverty (1907–66) found inspiration and objectivity by living for a time in Spain, Ireland's old ally. For many Irish writers – Joyce, ▷ Samuel Beckett (1906–89) and Francis Stuart (b 1902) are early examples, followed later to Paris by the poets Denis Devlin (1908–59) and Brian Coffey (b 1905) – this looking outside Ireland necessarily became a longer physical exile; the required distance from which to practise their art – or indeed to have it published and read. For during the first half-century of independence, the Irish state's narrow, inward-looking patriotism and the tight grip of a reactionary Catholic clerisy directly impoverished cultural life within Ireland: ▷ censorship meant that most works of serious literature by Irish men and women were banned in their own country.

Those who stayed, returned, or at least kept a foothold in the place, were able to refine and multiply the means of reclaiming or repairing an Irish heritage. They worked from an intimate knowledge of place, like Patrick Kavanagh (1904–67), who immortalized his townland of Mucker in *The Great Hunger* (1942) and *Tarry Flynn* (1948); others, like Austin Clarke (1896–1974) and later Thomas Kinsella (b 1928), worked from a more scholarly knowledge of the Gaelic-language heritage than was available to the Revivalists. By the mid-20th century poets in particular were recognizing the impossibility of bridging the gap to the past, and were finding that the fractured state of Irish culture itself offered a fruitful area of exploration for the isolated and disillusioned artist/commentator. Flann O'Brien (Brian O'Nolan, 1911–66) created a comic and fantastic Gaelic/modernist world in his novel *At Swim-Two-Birds* (1939) as his response to this artistic dilemma.

It tended to be the novelists and short-story writers who recorded the day-to-day reality of life in the young state. ▷ Sean O'Faolain (b 1900) and ▷ Frank O'Connor (Michael O'Donovan, 1903–66) demonstrated, in their short stories of the Troubles and after, not just a consummate art, but a seminal understanding of the why and how of that wished-for 'de-Anglicization'. Written from the fringes, but courageously central in their concerns, the novels and short stories of the Aran Islander ▷ Liam O'Flaherty (1897–1984) are eloquent accounts of the dignity and constraints of life in the no longer idealized rural west; and Patrick McGill's *Children of the Dead End* (1914) is a classic account of the reality of land-hunger and migratory labouring.

At home and abroad, then, Irish writers were grappling with the question of identity, and a body of remarkable writing was being assembled into a tradition of its own. But the achievements of three writers in particular placed a burden of success on subsequent generations. In poetry, the novel and drama, the work of Yeats, Joyce and Synge proved difficult to build on directly. Over the years a pattern can be discerned in which Ireland's vigorous – but even in the 1980s essentially naturalistic – tradition of fiction has more in common with the elegiac and story-telling parts of Yeats's *œuvre* than with Joyce's modernism. Conversely, poets have found in ▷ *Ulysses*' concern with the here and now of life as it is lived – and lived in the city – a more usable language than Yeats's lovely rhetoric or Synge's Gaelic-shadowed experimentalism. It is, perhaps, in drama that writers have found least constraint from the work of their predecessors. Over the years ▷ Sean O'Casey (1880–1964), Samuel Beckett, ▷ Brendan Behan (1923–64), and Brian Friel (b 1929) have each developed their own idiosyncratic dramatic structure and voice.

During this first century of a consciously Irish literature in English, Gaelic has continued to be the linguistic bedrock of Irish writers. Whether through translations that are creative works in their own right, from Hyde's *Love Songs of Connacht* (1893) to Kinsella's *The Tain* (1969) and ▷ Seamus Heaney's *Sweeney Astray* (1983), or by regarding all periods of Gaelic literature as a nourishing tradition alongside other literatures, Irish poets have constantly enriched their work in English. A few have decided to write only in Gaelic – two notable poets being Seán Ó Ríordiáin (1917–77) and Nuala Ní Dhomhnaill (b 1952) – but such writers are nevertheless an essential part of the English-language writing scene, both in their professional friendships and in creative translation by their peers. One excellent poet, Michael Hartnett (b 1941), publicly dedicated himself in 1975 to writing wholly in Irish; he has recently reverted to writing in both languages.

One half-century into the new state, a rather less easily accommodated bedrock issue surfaced: the rekindling of violent conflict on a large scale in the Six Counties in 1968. To the chagrin of some writers south of the Border, the work of many poets and playwrights of the North has been received with far more interest and critical acclaim in recent years than has been granted to writing from the South. For a time, all the artistic as well as the political action has seemed to be north of the Border. While the unprecedented prosperity of the 1960s and 70s inclined the South to a certain complacency, in the North it has seemed to both sides 'as though the whole of Anglo-Irish history has been boiled down and its dregs thrown out, leaving their poisonous concentrate on these six counties' (the final sentence of David Thomson's *Woodbrook*; 1974).

With fitting reluctance, and in very different styles, the writers of the North have taken on this new artistic burden. The fortuitous presence of the catalytic English poet and critic Philip Hobsbaum in Belfast in the mid-1960s prepared the ground for a second Irish renaissance. The 'Group' he fostered contained most of the male poets who have become well known, the youngest of whom is ▷ Paul Muldoon (b 1951). The most impressive to date is Seamus Heaney, who has in his *œuvre* explored all the different and conflicting themes and preoccupations of Irish writing, and used his part-time chosen exile in the U.S.A. to enlarge his and Ireland's understanding of poetic possibility.

The North has also produced one of the most exciting women poets of Ireland, Medbh McGuckian (b 1951); she, and Eavan Boland (b 1944) in the South, are the most visible of a new generation of women poets of real distinction. In the field of the novel, Irish women have managed, as women have in English generally, to make a substantial contribution; but the pressures of a conservative and patriarchal society have been less kind to women poets. As Irish women free themselves from the extremes of traditional roles, all the expected fields of women's writings are growing rapidly, and making strong connections with writing in England and the U.S.A. Particularly notable are ▷ Edna O'Brien (b 1930), Julia O'Faolain (b 1932), Jennifer Johnston (b 1930) and the promising Deidre Madden (b 1961).

The great expansion in Irish publishing over the last 20 years, especially of contemporary work, augurs well for the continuing vigour of all areas of Irish literature in English, and in Gaelic too. Another hopeful sign is the Republic's decision not to tax artists' earnings. In recent years writers of all nations, including Seamus Heaney, have moved to voluntary exile in the Republic.

Bib: *Macmillan Dictionary of Irish Literature*; Heaney, S., *Preoccupations: Selected Prose 1968–1978*; Kee, R., *The Green Flag: A History of Irish Nationalism*; Garratt, R., *Modern Irish Poetry: Tradition and Continuity from Yeats to Heaney*; Worth, K., *The Irish Drama of Europe from Yeats to Beckett*; Kinsella, T., (trans.), *The Tain*; Brown, T., *Northern Voices: Poets from Ulster*; O'Connor, U., *Celtic Dawn*.

Isherwood, Christopher (1904–86)
Novelist and dramatist. Born in Cheshire and educated at Repton School (where he met ▷ Edward Upward), and Cambridge and London universities. At preparatory school he met ▷ W. H. Auden, with whom he later collaborated on three plays, *The Dog Beneath the Skin* (1935); *The Ascent of F6* (1936) and *On the Frontier* (1938). These are primarily political and psychological parables. Isherwood's first two novels, *All The Conspirators* (1928) and *The Memorial* (1932), employ ▷ modernist styles and techniques. His experience of teaching English in Berlin from 1930 to 1933 is reflected in *Mr Norris Changes Trains* (1935) and *Goodbye to Berlin* (1939), which employ a more realistic mode. The latter is a series of linked tales recording the atmosphere and characters of a decadent Berlin in the last days of the Weimar Republic; the narrator is characterized by a certain passivity and detachment, summarized in his claim: 'I am a camera with its shutter open ...' The section entitled 'Sally Bowles' was dramatized in 1951 as *I am a Camera* and turned into a stage musical in 1968 as *Cabaret*, which was also successfully filmed by Bob Fosse in 1972 as a vehicle for Liza Minnelli. Isherwood visited China in 1933 with Auden, and together they wrote *Journey to a War* (1939). In 1939 they both emigrated to the U.S.A., where Isherwood became naturalized in 1946. All his major work is written in the first person, and his American novels draw extensively on his own development as a theme. They are: *Prater Violet* (1945), *The World in the Evening* (1954), *Down There On A Visit* (1962), *A Single Man* (1964) and *A Meeting By the River* (1967). He also wrote numerous screenplays, and several autobiographical and travel pieces, including *Lions and Shadows* (1938), *Christopher and his Kind* (1976) and *The Condor and the Cows: a South American Travel Diary* (1950). He translated works relating to the mystical Hindu philosophy of Vendanta, a philosophy which is advocated in *A Meeting By the River*.

Bib: King, F., *Christopher Isherwood*; Summers, C. J., *Christopher Isherwood*.

Ishiguro, Kazuo (b 1954)
Novelist and short-story writer. Born in Nagasaki, Japan, he has lived in Britain since 1960, where he studied at the universities of Kent and East Anglia (▷ Bradbury, Malcolm). He has worked as a grouse-beater at Balmoral Castle and as a community and social worker in Scotland and London. He now lives in Guildford, Surrey. His work was included in *Introduction 7: Stories by New Writers, 1981*. His first two novels, *A Pale View of Hills* (1982) and *An Artist of*

the Floating World (1986) explore post-war Japanese cultural displacement through the thoughts and memories of individuals: a Japanese woman living in England, stirred to retrospection by her daughter's suicide; a painter, once employed by the pre-war Imperial regime, living in a provincial Japanese town. In *The Remains of the Day* (1989), which won the Booker Prize, an English butler on a tour of Britain reassesses the lost opportunities of his life. His work has been widely praised for its delicacy of style and subtlety of psychological insight.

Italian influence on English literature
Apart from the influence of Italian literature, Italy as a country was particularly important to England in the 16th and early 17th centuries. The English attitude to Italy was complicated – a mixture of admiration, envy, intense interest and disapproval amounting to abhorrence. The Italian cities were for Englishmen the centres and summits of civilization, and such centres in most periods are supposed to represent not only what is most advanced in thought and behaviour, but also what is most extravagant and corrupt.

However, after 1650 Italy by no means lost its fascination for the English, but it was Italy as a storehouse of the past, rather than a challenging present, that drew Englishmen. In the 18th century the English invented a sort of tourism; what was called the 'Grand Tour' formed part of the education of upper-class young men and Italy was one of its principal objectives. They were drawn to the architectural and sculptural remains of the old Roman Empire, the framework of their literary education in Latin literature. In the second half of the 19th century the art critic John Ruskin and the Pre-Raphaelite painters and poets turned their interest to the Italian Middle Ages.

Twentieth century Italian writing has had a powerful impact on British work. At the beginning of the 20th century Giosuè Carducci's (1835–1907) classical, apolitical and solemn poetry won him the Nobel Prize of 1906, but the decadent school was soon to produce two important names in Italian literature: Gabriele D'annunzio (1863–1938) and Luigi Pirandello (1867–1936). D'annunzio's *The Child of Pleasure* (1890) in the novel and *Praises* (1904) in poetry influenced the aesthetic, ▷ Symbolist and Pre-Raphaelite schools in England. Pirandello's international reputation is well known; from the production of *Six Characters in Search of an Author* (1921) his strikingly original tone and characters became immensely influential in drama. The reputation of Italian authors in other countries has continued in the 20th century, often rivalling the golden age of medieval Italianate influence. The works of Italo Calvino (1923–85), Primo Levi (1919–87) and Umberto Eco (b 1932) are published in English almost as soon as in the original Italian. Levi's autobiographical accounts of his experiences in Auschwitz, as for example in *The Periodic Table* (1975), Eco's theoretical works and his best-seller *The Name of the Rose* (1981), and Calvino's neo-realism trilogy *Our Ancestors* (1952–9) have an international readership. Other 20th-century Italian writers of note are the novelist Alberto Moravia (b 1907) (the pen-name of Alberto Pincherle), who, like Calvino, writes neo-realistic works concerned with socio-political issues, as for example, *Two Women* (1957); Giorgio Bassani (b 1916), a confessional novelist aware of the torments of evil and morality, as in his work *The Garden of the Finzi-Contini* (1962); and finally the poet Eugenio Montale (1896–1981), the most renowned Italian poet of the 20th century and winner of the 1976 Nobel Prize; his most famous work is *Cuttle-fish Bones* (1925).

Jacobson, Dan (b 1929)
Novelist, ▷ short-story writer and critic. Born in South Africa, he moved permanently to England in 1954, and is now Professor of English Literature at University College, London. His novels are: *The Trap* (1955); *A Dance in the Sun* (1956); *The Price of Diamonds* (1957); *The Evidence of Love* (1960); *The Beginners* (1966); *The Rape of Tamar* (1970); *The Wonder Worker* (1973); *The Confessions of Joseph Baiz* (1977). His story collections include: *A Long Way From London* (1958); *The Zulu and the Zeide* (1959); *Beggar My Neighbour* (1964); *Through the Wilderness* (1968); *A Way of Life* (1971); *Inklings: Selected Stories* (1973); *Hidden in the Heart* (1991); and *The God-Fearer* (1992). Up to and including *The Beginners*, the story of three generations of an immigrant Jewish family, the novels are set in South Africa, and are largely naturalistic in style. *The Rape of Tamar*, which inspired the play *Yonadab* by ▷ Peter Shaffer, is a more experimental work, much concerned with the ambiguities of narration. It has an Old Testament setting, and a self-conscious, and highly characterized narrator. *The Confessions of Joseph Baiz* is the fictional autobiography of a man who can love only those whom he has betrayed, and is set in an imaginary totalitarian country, somewhat resembling South Africa. Recurrent concerns of Jacobson's novels and stories include power, religion, guilt and betrayal, and his work is characterized by its inventiveness and wit. His non-fiction includes: *The Story of the Stories: The Chosen People and its God* (1982); *Time and Time Again: Autobiographies* (1985); *Adult Pleasures: Essays on Writers and Readers* (1988).

Jakobson, Roman (1896–1982)
Born in Moscow, where he was educated. He worked in Czechoslovakia for almost 20 years, between 1920 and 1939, and after the German invasion he escaped to Scandinavia, before going to the U.S.A. where he taught in a number of universities, and became Professor of Russian Literature at the Massachusetts Institute of Technology. During his formative years he was heavily influenced by a number of avante-garde movements in the Arts, but in his own work he laid specific emphasis upon the formulation of a 'poetics' which took into account the findings of ▷ Structuralism, and the work of the Russian ▷ formalists. He was an active member of the Society for the Study of Poetic Language (OPOYAZ) which was founded in St Petersburg in 1916, and in 1926 he founded the Prague Linguistic Circle. His wife Krystyna Pomorska notes, in a recent collection of his writings, that poetry and visual art became for Jakobson the fundamental spheres for observing how verbal phenomena work and for studying how to approach them (Roman Jakobson, *Language and Literature* 1987).
Bib: Hawkes, T., *Structuralism and Semiotics*; Jakobson,R., *Language and Literature* and *Verbal Art, Verbal Sign, Verbal Time*; Bennett, T., *Formalism and Marxism*; Erlich, V., *Russian Formalism: History-Doctrine.*

James, Henry (1843–1916)
Novelist. Born in New York; his father was an original writer on philosophy and theology, and his brother, William James, became one of the most distinguished philosophers and psychologists of his day. His education was divided between America and Europe. Europe drew him strongly, and he finally settled in Europe in 1875 after a series of long visits. He was naturalized British in 1915. Towards both continents, however, he had mixed emotions. As to America, he belonged to the eastern seaboard, New England, which had its own well-established traditions originating in English Puritanism, and he was out of sympathy with the American ardour for commercial enterprise and westward expansion. As to Europe, he was fascinated by the richness of its ancient societies and culture, but he brought an American, and especially a New England, eye to the corruption which such advanced development generated. The conflict was fruitful for his development as an artist, and it was not the only one; he was also aware of the contrast between the contemplativeness of his father's mind and the practical adventurousness characteristic of his brother's outlook and of Americans in general. And in his close study of the art of the novel, he felt the difference between the intense interest in form of the French tradition and the deeper moral interest to be found in the English tradition.

In the first period of his work, his theme is preponderantly the clash between the European and the American outlooks: *Roderick Hudson* (1875); *The American* (1877); *The Europeans* (1878); *Daisy Miller* (1879); *The Portrait of a Lady* (1881). To this period also belong two novels about American life: *Washington Square* (1881); *The Bostonians* (1886); and two restricted to English life, *The Tragic Muse* (1890); *The Princess Casamassima* (1886). His second period shows a much more concentrated and difficult style of treatment, and it concerns English society only: *The*

Spoils of Poynton and *What Maisie Knew* (1897); ▷ *The Awkward Age* (1899). Between his first and second periods (1889–95) he experimented in drama; this was his least successful episode, but the experiment helped him to develop a dramatic technique in the writing of his novels. He wrote 12 plays in all. In his last period, the most intensive and subtle in style, James returned to the theme of the contrast of American and European values: ▷ *The Wings of a Dove* (1902); ▷ *The Ambassadors* (1903); ▷ *The Golden Bowl* (1904). On his death he left unfinished *The Ivory Tower* and *The Sense of the Past*. Some of his best fiction is to be found among his short stories, and he was particularly fond of the ▷ 'novella' form – between a story and a usual novel in length; *The Europeans* and *Washington Square* come into this class, and so does his well-known ghost story, ▷ *The Turn of the Screw* (1898) (▷ horror fiction).

In his criticism, James is important as the first distinguished writer in English to give the novel and its form concentrated critical attention. His essays have been collected under the title *The House of Fiction* (1957), edited by Leon Edel. He also wrote books of travel, the most notable of which is *The American Scene* (1907), and autobiographical pieces – *A Small Boy and Others* (1913); *Notes of a Son and a Brother* (1914) and *Terminations* (1917). (The last is also the title of a story published in 1895.)

Bib: Edel, L., *Henry James*; Matthiessen, F. O., *Henry James: The Major Phase*; Anderson, Q., *The American Henry James*; Leavis, F. R., in *The Great Tradition*; Dupee, F. W., *Henry James*; Bewley, M., in *The Complex Fate* and in *The Eccentric Design*; Wilson, E., in *The Triple Thinkers*; Krook, D., *The Ordeal of Consciousness in James*; Gard, R., (ed.), *James: The Critical Heritage*; Tanner, T., *Henry James*; Berland, A., *Culture and Conduct in the Novels of Henry James*.

James, P. D. (b 1920)

Writer of crime stories and ▷ detective fiction. P. D. James's skilful and subtle detective novels have made her into one of Britain's most popular writers, not simply for the dexterity with which she handles her suspense plots, but for the complex characterization and social context of her writing. Like the great women crime writers of the previous generation (▷ Agatha Christie, ▷ Dorothy L. Sayers, ▷ Margory Allingham and ▷ Ngaio Marsh), James has a central sleuth who figures in many of her novels – Adam Dalgleish of Scotland Yard, who first appeared in *Cover Her Face* (1962). Her other works include: *A Mind to Murder* (1963); *Unnatural Causes* (1967); *An Unsuitable Job for a Woman* (1972); *The Black Tower* (1975); *Innocent Blood* (1980); and *A Taste for Death* (1986).

Jellicoe, Ann (b 1927)

One of few women to break into the theatre business as a writer and director during the 1950s and 60s. She was a ▷ Royal Court writer and a member of the Theatre Writers' Group organized there between 1958 and 1960, which also included ▷ John Arden, ▷ Edward Bond and ▷ Arnold Wesker. Her early plays include *The Sport of My Mad Mother* (1958), about teddy-boy violence, and *The Knack* (1961), about sexual competition. The written text of both these plays only gives a slight impression of their effect in performance since she writes in a non-literary style with clear ideas for direction in mind. Later plays such as *Shelley* (1965) and *The Giveaway* (1969) are less unconventional. More recently she has become renowned for her productions of community plays in which she has drawn on the talents of large numbers of people from single communities, bringing together professionals and amateurs, adults and schoolchildren. An example of such work is *Entertaining Strangers* written by ▷ David Edgar and originally performed in Dorset (later re-written by him for a ▷ National Theatre production in 1987).

Bib: Jellicoe, A., *Community Plays: How to Put Them On*.

Jennings, Elizabeth (b 1926)

Poet. Published her first collection, *Poems*, in 1953, and was initially associated with the ▷ Movement, although the mystical quality of her work (Jennings is a ▷ Catholic) makes this categorization problematic. She writes prolifically, generally using traditional verse techniques, but she has also experimented with ▷ free verse. Jennings has spent much of her life living and working in Oxford. Her second book, *A Way of Looking* (1955), won her the Somerset Maugham Award, and her most important collections to date are: *A Sense of the World* (1958); *Song for Birth and Death* (1961); *Recoveries* (1964); *The Mind Has Mountains* (1966); *Growing Points* (1975); *Moments of Grace* (1979); and *Celebrations and Elegies* (1982). *A Collected Works* and a *Selected Works* appeared in 1967 and 1979 respectively.

Jhabvala, Ruth Prawar (b 1927)
Novelist, short-story writer, and writer of screenplays. She was born in Germany of Polish parents who came to England as refugees in the year of her birth. She studied at London University and in 1951 married the Indian architect C. S. H. Jhabvala. From 1951 to 1975 she lived in India, and since then has lived in New York. Many of her novels are based on her own ambiguous position in India as a European with an Indian family. They explore the tensions of contemporary Indian society, such as the conflict of ancient and modern ideas and the interaction of westernized and non-westernized Indians. They are based on witty but sympathetic observation of social manners, largely in domestic settings. Some of the sharpest satire is reserved for the naïve and superficial enthusiasm of certain visiting Europeans, who are frequently exploited by a manipulative swami. *Heat and Dust* (1975) employs a double narrative consisting of the experiences of a contemporary English girl in India, and the love affair of her grandfather's first wife with an Indian prince in 1923. *In Search of Love and Beauty* (1983) reflects Jhabvala's change of home; it is a story of German Jewish émigrés in 1930s New York. Her other novels are: *To Whom She Will* (1955); *The Nature of Passion* (1956); *Esmond in India* (1958); *The Householder* (1960); *Get Ready For Battle* (1962); *A Backward Place* (1965); *A New Dominion* (1972); *Three Continents* (1988). Story collections are: *Like Birds, Like Fishes* (1963); *A Stronger Climate* (1968); *An Experience of India* (1971); *How I Became A Holy Mother* (1976). She has written a number of screenplays, some of which are based on her own works, as part of a highly successful film-making team with James Ivory as director and Ismail Merchant as producer: *The Householder* (1963); *Shakespeare Wallah* (with Ivory; 1965); *The Europeans* (1979) (based on the novel by ▷ Henry James); *Quartet* (1981) (based on the novel by ▷ Jean Rhys); *Heat and Dust* (1983); *The Bostonians* (1984) (based on the Henry James novel); *A Room with a View* (1986) and *Howards End* (1992) (based on the novels by ▷ E. M. Forster).

Johnson, B. S. (1933–73)
Novelist, poet and dramatist. His novels were highly experimental, taking as their main subject his own life as a novelist and the nature of the novel. He employed a whole range of ▷ postmodernist narrative devices for questioning the boundaries of fact and fiction. He claimed to write, not fiction, but 'truth in the form of a novel'. *Travelling People* (1963) uses a different viewpoint or narrative mode for each chapter, including a film scenario, letters and typographical effects. In *Alberto Angelo* (1964) the 'author' breaks into the narrative to discuss his own techniques, aims and sources. *The Unfortunates* (1969) is a loose-leaf novel of 27 sections, 25 of which can be read in any order. Johnson committed suicide at the age of 40, soon after completing *See the Old Lady Decently* (1975), which is based around the death of his mother in 1971, and incorporates family documents and photographs. His other novels are: *Trawl* (1966); *House Mother Normal* (1971); *Christie Malry's Own Double Entry* (1973). He also wrote plays, screenplays, television scripts and several collections of poems.

Johnson, Linton Kwesi (b 1952)
Poet and recording artist. Johnson was born in Jamaica and has lived in Britain since 1961; he read sociology at London University and is a Fellow at Warwick University. The most famous of the young Anglo-Jamaican poets to emerge since the mid-1970s (others include Benjamin Zephaniah and the older ▷ James Berry), influenced by reggae, dub and Rastafarian rhythms, his live performances and recordings with Virgin records have done much to open other forms of contemporary British poetry to a wide young audience. His three volumes of poetry have been extremely popular: *Voice of the Living and the Dead* (1974); *Dead Beat An' Blood* (1975); *Inglan is a Bitch* (1980).

▷ Commonwealth literatures.

Johnson, Pamela Hansford (1912–81)
Novelist. Perhaps her best-known work is the trilogy composed of *Too Dear for my Possessing* (1940), *An Avenue of Stone* (1947) and *A Summer to Decide* (1949). These extend from the late 1920s to the late 1940s, and combine observation of events and society with the study of intricate relationships arising from the attractions for each other of unlike characters. The formal quality reflects the influence of ▷ Marcel Proust, on whom Pamela Hansford Johnson composed a series of radio programmes, *Six Proust Reconstructions* (1958). Some of her later novels were more comic and satirical (*eg*, *Who is Here?*, 1962; *Night and Silence*, 1963; *Cork Street*, 1965 and *Next to the Hatter's*, 1965) but *An Error of Judgement* (1962) concerns the problem of apparently motiveless 'evil' in modern society and relates to her non-fictional investigation of the Moors Murder case (*On Iniquity* (1967)), which

traces the causes of contemporary forms of 'evil' to the so-called 'permissive society'. Pamela Hansford Johnson was married to the novelist ▷ C. P. Snow. Her other novels are: *The Survival of the Fittest* (1968); *The Honours Board* (1970); *The Holiday Friend* (1972); *The Good Listener* (1975); *The Good Husband* (1978); *A Bonfire* (1981).
Bib: Allen, W., in *Tradition and Dream*; Burgess, A., *The Novel Now*.

Jones, David Michael (1895–1974)
Poet and artist. His paintings, engravings and woodcuts are probably now better known than his writing, with the exception of *In Parenthesis* (1937), an account of his experiences in World War I that combines verse and prose. See also *The Anathemata* (1952), Jones's most important work, and *Epoch and Artist* (selected writings, 1959).

Jones, Henry Arthur (1851–1929)
Dramatist. He wrote some 60 plays, and is notable for beginning an English dramatic revival in the later years of the 19th century along with T. W. Robertson, ▷ Arthur Pinero and ▷ Shaw. For instance *Saints and Sinners* (1884) was not only a dramatic success, but aroused controversy by discussing religious issues in a study of middle-class provincial life. Other plays of comparable note: *The Middleman* (1889) and *Judah* (1890). His lectures and essays on drama were collected in *The Renascence of the English Drama* (1895).
Bib: Jones, A. D., *Life*; Archer, W., *The Old Drama and the New*; Cordell, R. A., *Henry Arthur Jones and the Modern Drama*.

Joseph, Jenny (b 1932)
Poet and prose writer. Joseph has been writing since 1961 (her first publication was *The Unlooked-for Season*, a volume of poetry). In 1974 she won the Cholmondely award for *Rose in the Afternoon*. Other volumes include: *The Thinking Heart* (1978) and *Beyond Descartes* (1983). She also writes for children.

Josipovici, Gabriel (b 1940)
Novelist, short-story writer and critic. Born in France, educated in Cairo, Cheltenham and at Oxford University, Josipovici is a lecturer and (since 1984) Professor of English at the University of Sussex. His novels are ambiguous and experimental works of ▷ postmodernist fiction, conveying a sense of fragmentation and uncertainty. *The Inventory* (1968), *Words* (1971) and *The Echo Chamber* (1980) are almost entirely in dialogue; *The Present* (1975) uses a present-tense narration and interweaves a number of stories: *Migrations* (1977) and *The Air We Breathe* (1981) are structured by the repetition of scenes and images. His other novels are: *Conversations in Another Room* (1984); *Contre-Jour* (1986); *In the Fertile Land* (1987). Story collections are: *Mobius the Stripper: Stories and Short Plays* (1974); *Four Stories* (1977). Plays include: *Evidence of Intimacy* (1972); *Echo* (1975); *Marathon* (1977); *A Moment* (1979); *Vergil Dying* (broadcast 1979). Criticism includes: *The Lessons of Modernism and Other Essays* (1977); *Writing and the Body* (1982); *The Book of God: An Essay on the Bible* (1988).

Journalism
The distinction between journalism and literature is not always clear, and before the rise of the modern newspaper with its mass circulation in the second half of the 19th century, the two forms of writing were even more difficult to distinguish than they are today. The most superficial but also the most observable difference has always been that journalism puts immediacy of interest before permanency of interest, and easy readability before considered qualities of style. But of course what is written for the attention of the hour may prove to be of permanent value; a good example is William Cobbett's *Rural Rides* in his weekly *Political Register* in the early 19th century.

The 'pamphlets' of writers such as Thomas Nashe and Thomas Dekker in the 1590s, and those on the controversial religious matters of the day such as the Marprelate pamphlets, are no doubt the earliest work with the stamp of journalism in English. However, the profession began to take shape with the wider reading public and the regular periodicals of the early 18th century. In that period we can see that it was the attitude to writing that made the difference – at least on the surface – between the journalist and the serious man of letters. Joseph Addison considered himself a serious man of letters, whereas Daniel Defoe, writing incessantly on matters of practical interest without concerning himself with subtleties and elegance of style, is more our idea of a journalist. The 18th century was inclined to disparage such writing as Grub Street, though this term included all kinds of inferior, merely imitative 'literature', that we would not accept as journalism. The trade of journalism taught Defoe the realism that went into his fiction. A good example of the combination of facts and fiction is his *A Journal of the Plague Year* (1722) which is both a fine example of journalistic reporting (from other people's accounts) and a fine achievement in imaginative realism.

Defoe in the 18th century and Cobbett in the 19th century both assumed that the main function of their writing was to *enlighten* their readers. In the 1890s, however, the 'popular press' arose in which the desire to entertain was as strong as the desire to inform, and profitability was a major concern. The distinction between the popular and serious press is still current. There has been a strong division in the 1980s especially between newspapers such as ▷ *The Times* and ▷ *The Guardian* and the tabloid press papers such as the *Sun* and the *Mirror*.

▷ Newspapers; Reviews and periodicals.

Joyce, James (1882–1941)
Novelist. He was Irish, and born at a time when Irish ▷ nationalism was moving into its fiercest, most desperate phase. Joyce was born into a ▷ Catholic family, was educated by the Jesuits, and seemed destined for the Catholic priesthood, yet he turned away from the priesthood, renounced Catholicism, and in 1904 left ▷ Ireland to live and work abroad for the rest of his life. But although he took no part in the movement for Irish liberation, he did not renounce Ireland; the setting for all his fiction is the capital city (and his home town) of Dublin. This and his own family relationships were always his centres, and from them he drew increasingly ambitious imaginative conceptions which eventually extended to the whole history of European culture.

His first important work was a volume of stories, ▷ *Dubliners*, published after long delay in 1914. The collection has artistic unity given to it by Joyce's intention 'to write a chapter of the moral history of my country . . . under four of its aspects: childhood, adolescence, maturity and public life'. The method combines an apparent objective realism with a subtle use of the symbolic and the mimesis of Dublin speech idiom and is based on Joyce's idea of 'epiphanies' – experiences, often apparently trivial, presenting to the observer deep and true insights. His first novel, ▷ *A Portrait of the Artist as a Young Man* (1916), is largely autobiographical and describes how, abandoning his religion and leaving his country, he discovered his artistic vocation. Its original method of narration causes the reader to share the hero's experience by having it presented to him with a verbal equipment which grows with the hero's development, from infancy to young manhood.

The next novel, ▷ *Ulysses* (1922), is still more original in the use of language. Its subject is apparently small – a single day in the life of three Dubliners – but Joyce's treatment of it makes it vast. The characters are made to correspond to the three main characters of Homer's *Odyssey*, and the 18 episodes are parallels to the episodes in that epic. The past is thus made to reflect forward on to the present, and the present back on to the past, revealing both with comic irony and endowing the apparently trivial present with tragic depth. In this book, modern man in the modern city is presented with unprecedented thoroughness and candour.

In his last book, ▷ *Finnegans Wake* (1939), Joyce attempts an image of modern 'Everyman' with all the forces of his experiences released – in other words it concerns one night of a character who, because he never fully wakes up, is not restricted by the inhibitions of normal daylight consciousness. To express this night consciousness Joyce uses a special dream language by which words are fused together to give instantaneous multiple allusiveness; the same technique had been used by the mid-19th-century children's writer Lewis Carroll in the poem called 'Jabberwocky' (*Through the Looking-Glass*; 1872). However, because Joyce wished to use the public-house keeper who is his hero as the representative of modern European man, he often fuses English words with those of other European languages, thus increasing the difficulty for the reader. Critics have pointed out that in *Finnegans Wake* the dream comes mainly through the ear; Joyce, like Milton with whose mastery of language his own has been compared, had poor sight, and his imagination worked especially through the sense of hearing.

He published three volumes of poetry, which show his sense of poignant verbal beauty: *Chamber Music* (1907); *Gas from a Burner* (1912); *Pomes Penyeach* (1927). His *Collected Poems* appeared in 1936. His single play, *Exiles* (1918), is interesting chiefly for showing his admiration for the Norwegian dramatist ▷ Ibsen. An early version of his *Portrait of the Artist* was published in 1944 (enlarged 1955) as *Stephen Hero*.

▷ Catholicism in English literature; Irish literature in English.

Bib: Ellmann, R., *James Joyce* (biography); *Ulysses on the Liffey* and *The Consciousness of Joyce*; Burgess, A., *Joysprick*; Peake, C. H., *James Joyce: the Citizen and the Artist*; Kenner,

H., *Joyce's Voices* and *Ulysses*; Tindall, W. Y., *A Reader's Guide to Finnegans Wake*; Joyce, S., *My Brother's Keeper*, Levin, H., *Joyce: a Critical Introduction*; Budgen, F., *James Joyce and the Making of Ulysses*; Gilbert, S., *James Joyce's Ulysses: a Study*; Denning, R. H. (ed.), *Joyce: The Critical Heritage*.

Jude the Obscure (1895)
The last novel by ▷ Thomas Hardy. In Hardy's words the theme is the 'deadly war ... between flesh and spirit' and the 'contrast between the ideal life a man wished to lead and the squalid real life he was fated to lead'. Jude Fawley is a village mason (like Hardy's father) who has intellectual aspirations. He is seduced into marriage by Arabella Donn; when she abandons him, he turns back to learning, but falls in love with Sue Bridehead, whose contradictory nature seeks freedom and yet frustrates her own desire. She runs away from her schoolmaster husband, Phillotson, who disgusts her, and joins with Jude in an illicit union. Their children die at the hands of Jude's only child by Arabella, who takes his own and their lives because he believes that he and they had no right to be born. Sue returns in remorse to Phillotson, while Jude is beguiled back by Arabella, who deserts him on his deathbed.

The setting and the four main characters are so representative that the novel is almost an allegory. Jude's native place is Marygreen, a run-down village which is a kind of emblem of decayed rural England. His ambition is to enter the university of Christminster, which is Oxford, but so named as a reminder by Hardy that the way of learning had once also been a goal of the spirit. Jude uproots himself from Marygreen but is unable to enter the university because of his social origins, though he lives in the town (where he meets Sue) and works there as a mason. Hardy's point is not so much the social one that the old universities of Oxford and Cambridge were all but closed to working-men; he is more concerned to show that the decay of spiritual goals in the England of his day matches the decay of the countryside. Sue Bridehead represents the 'new woman' of the day, emancipated in her own theory but not in body. Roughly speaking, Sue is all mind, Arabella all body, and Phillotson a kind of walking death – a man of the best intentions who is nonetheless helplessly destructive in consequence of his lack of both physical and spiritual vitality. The novel epitomizes Hardy's longing for spiritual values and his despair of them; its pessimism has strong poetic quality, and after completing it he gave himself entirely to poetry. Like many of Hardy's novels, *Jude the Obscure* is set in the recent past – about 20 years before the time of writing. Publication of the book caused an uproar; after its hostile reception Hardy wrote no further novels.

Jung, Carl (1875–1961)
Swiss psychiatrist. He was part of the group surrounding ▷ Sigmund Freud between 1907 and 1913, but because of disagreements with Freud, he left to form his own school of 'Analytical Psychology'. Jung attributed less importance to the sexual, and saw the unconscious as containing, not only repressed material, but also undeveloped aspects of the personality, which he divided into thinking, feeling, sensuous and intuitive aspects. The personal unconscious he held to be the reverse of the persona, or outer self, and to perform a compensatory function. Furthermore, beneath the personal unconscious lay the racial and collective unconscious, the repository of the beliefs and myths of civilizations, which at the deepest level were all united. Jung termed the themes and symbols which emerged from this collective unconscious, archetypes, and Jungian therapy uses dream interpretation to connect the patient with the healing power of these archetypes. Jung saw the libido as a non-sexual life force, and neuroses as imbalances in the personality. He made a comparative study of the myths, religions and philosophies of many cultures, and his thought has a religious and mystical tenor. He is also the originator of the terms 'introvert', 'extrovert' and 'complex'.

His influence on 20th-century literature results particularly from the importance he gave to myths and symbols as universal and creative modes of understanding. The creation, or reworking, of myths is a feature of the work of writers such as ▷ James Joyce (in ▷ *Ulysses*, about which Jung wrote an essay; 'Ulysses: A Monologue', 1932), ▷ T. S. Eliot, ▷ David Jones, ▷ Ted Hughes and ▷ Geoffrey Hill.

▷ Psychoanalytic criticism.

Bib: Jacobi, J., *The Psychology of C. G. Jung*; Wright, E., *Psychoanalytic Criticism*.

Keane, Molly (b 1904)
Novelist and playwright. Born into an upper-middle-class world of country life, Keane's witty novels are concerned with the narrow interests of the privileged and leisured Anglo-Irish community. Her career has had two phases: up to her mid-30s and then from the early 1980s onwards, punctuated by 20 years of non-production. Her works include: *Taking Chances* (1929); *Conversation Piece* (1932); *Devoted Ladies* (1934); *The Rising Tide* (1937); *Spring Meeting: A Comedy in Three Acts* (1938); *Loving Without Tears* (1951); *Good Behaviour* (1981) (which was shortlisted for the Booker Prize); and *Time After Time* (1983).

***Kim* (1901)**
A novel by ▷ Rudyard Kipling. Kim, whose real name is Kimball O'Hara, is the orphan son of an Irish soldier in India, and he spends his childhood as a waif in the city of Lahore. He meets a Tibetan holy man in search of a mystical river, and accompanies him on his journey. Kim falls in with his father's old regiment, and is adopted by them, eventually becoming an agent of the British secret service under the guidance of an Indian, Hurree Babu. In spite of the ingenuousness of Kipling's British chauvinism, conspicuous in the latter part of the book, the earlier part is an intimate and graphic picture of the humbler reaches of Indian life.

King, Stephen (b 1947)
American novelist. The biggest-selling horror novelist of all time, King began writing short stories for American magazines in 1966; his early work is collected in the anthology *Nightshift* (1978). His first novel *Carrie* (1975) tapped into the potent vein of paedophobia uncovered by ▷ William Peter Blatty's *The Exorcist* and was marketed as an '*Exorcist*-style' work. Unlike the many contemporary plagiarists of Blatty's best-seller, however, King flourished and developed a uniquely popular personal style, using corrupted symbols of cosy suburban Americana to explore the taboos of modern life, blending elements of archaic Gothic with a new style of horrific realism. In *Salem's Lot* (1975), King transposed the traditional vampire tale to a modern setting, creating a blackly satirical modern nightmare reminiscent of *Rosemary's Baby*. Similarly, *The Shining* (1977) updated the theme of the haunted house, drawing heavily upon Shirley Jackson's *The Haunting of Hill House*. King's 1981 critical work *Danse Macabre* has become the textbook of modern popular horror fiction and films. In 1977, he adopted the pseudonym Richard Bachman to escape the demands of his growing reputation, under which he wrote a number of novels including *The Running Man* (1982) and *Thinner* (1984). Although the popularity of King's prolific output has continued to increase (he has sold over 80 million books) the quality of his writing has been inconsistent. In the early 1980s, King's creative juices dried, and his output (which he describes as 'the literary equivalent of a Big Mac') became tedious and formulaic. Ironically, this bout of artistic sterility gave birth to *Misery* (1987), perhaps King's finest novel, wherein a writer of pulp romances attempts to escape his money-making legacy and find creative fulfilment, only to be imprisoned (literally) by the stifling demands of his Number One Fan.

A few of King's novels and short stories have been successfully adapted for the screen by renowned directors: Brian de Palma (*Carrie*), Stanley Kubrick (*The Shining*), David Cronenberg (*The Dead Zone*) and Rob Reiner (*Stand by Me*, *Misery*); many more have been destroyed in translation (*Children of the Corn*, *Firestarter*, *Graveyard Shift*, *Cujo*, *Christine*). King currently lives in Maine. Works include: *The Stand* (1978); *The Dead Zone* (1979); *Firestarter* (1980); *Cujo* (1981); *Different Seasons* (1982); *The Dark Tower* (1982); *Christine* (1983); *Cycle of the Werewolf* (1983); *Pet Sematary* (1983); *The Talisman* (1984, with Peter Straub); *The Eyes of the Dragon* (1984); *Skeleton Crew* (1985); *It* (1986); *The Dark Half* (1989); *Four Past Midnight* (1990); *Needful Things* (1991). As Richard Bachman: *Rage* (1977); *The Long Walk* (1979); *The Running Man* (1982); *Thinner* (1984).

Kipling, Rudyard (1865–1936)
Poet, short-story writer, novelist. He was born in India, educated in England, and returned to India at 17 as a journalist. In 1889 he came to England to live.

Kipling's poetry is striking for his success in using, vividly and musically, popular forms of speech, sometimes in the Browning tradition of the ▷ dramatic monologue, *eg McAndrew's Hymn*, or in the ▷ ballad tradition, *eg Barrack-Room Ballads* (1892). He was also able to write poetry appropriate to public occasions and capable of stirring the feelings of a large public, *eg* his famous *Recessional* (1897). His poetry is generally simple in its components but, when it rises above the level of doggerel, strong in its impact. It needs to be read in selection: *A Choice of Kipling's Verse* (ed. ▷ T. S. Eliot), with a very good introductory essay.

Kipling's stories brought him fame, and, partly under French influence, he gave close attention to perfecting the art of the ▷ short story. The volumes include *Plain Tales from the Hills* (1887), *Life's Handicap* (1891); *Many Inventions* (1893); *The Day's Work* (1898); *Traffics and Discoveries* (1904); *Actions and Reactions* (1909); *A Diversity of Creatures* (1917); *Debits and Credits* (1926) and *Limits and Renewals* (1932). The early stories in particular show Kipling's capacity to feel with the humble (common soldiers, Indian peasants) and the suffering. But he admired action, power, and efficiency; this side of his character brought out much of the best and worst in his writing. Some of his best stories show his enthusiasm for the triumphs of technology, and are about machines rather than people, *eg* in *The Day's Work*. On the other hand he was inclined to be crudely chauvinistic, and to show unpleasant arrogance towards peoples ruled by or hostile to Britain, though he also emphasized British responsibility for the welfare of the governed peoples. Yet again, he sometimes engaged in delicate if sentimental fantasy, as in *They* and *The Brushwood Boy* (1925); some of his later stories show a sensitive and sometimes morbid insight into abnormal states of mind, *eg Mary Postgate* (1917). The stories, like the poems, are best read in selection: *A Choice of Kipling's Prose* (ed. Somerset Maugham).

Kipling is not outstanding as a full-length novelist. His best novel is ▷ *Kim* (1901), based on his childhood in India; *Stalky and Co* (1899) is well known as a tale about an English public school, and is based on Kipling's own schooldays at the United Services College. *The Light that Failed* (1890) shows his more sensitive and sombre aspect. An autobiographical fragment, *Something of Myself*, was published in 1937.

Kipling's children's stories are minor classics of their kind: *The Jungle Books* (1894–5); *Just So Stories* (1902); *Puck of Pook's Hill* (1906). *Rewards and Fairies* (1910) is less celebrated.

▷ Children's books; Imperialism.

Bib: Birkenhead, Lord, *Rudyard Kipling* (biography); Page, N., *A Kipling Companion*; Carrington, C. E., *Life*; Dobree, B., *Kipling*; Orwell, G., in *Critical Essays*; Wilson, E., in *The Wound and the Bow*; Green, R. L. (ed.), *Kipling: The Critical Heritage*; Oriel, H., *A Kipling Chronology*.

Kipps (1905)

A novel by ▷ H. G. Wells. It describes the social rise of a shop-assistant through an unexpected legacy, his engagement to a vulgarly snobbish young lady who has hitherto been out of his reach, and his painful acquisition of the false standards and cares which are forced upon him. He escapes the marriage by marrying suddenly a girl of his own former class, but he only escapes his worries when he loses his money. The book contains acute social observation and comedy in the Dickens tradition, though Wells's style is quite his own.

Koestler, Arthur (1905–83)

Novelist and philosopher. He was born in Hungary and educated at the University of Vienna. From 1932 to 1938 he was a member of the Communist Party (▷ Communism). He went to Spain as a correspondent during the Spanish Civil War, and was imprisoned by the Nationalists. Subsequently imprisoned in France during 1939–40, he joined the Foreign Legion before escaping to Britain in 1941. After World War II he became a British subject. From the 1930s to the 1950s his work was primarily concerned with political issues; his novel *Darkness At Noon* (1940) exposed Stalinist methods through the story of the imprisonment and execution of a former Bolshevik leader. From the 1950s onwards his writings were more concerned with the philosophical implications of scientific discoveries. His non-fiction trilogy, *The Sleepwalkers* (1959), *The Act of Creation* (1964) and *The Ghost in the Machine* (1967) considered the effect of science on man's idea of himself, and defended the concept of mind. A persistent feature of his work was a sense of horror at the barbarities of 20th-century Europe. Koestler, who had advocated the right to euthanasia, and who was suffering from leukaemia and Parkinson's disease, committed suicide together with his third wife, Cynthia Jefferies, in 1983. His other novels are: *The Gladiators* (1939); *Arrival and Departure* (1943); *Thieves in the Night* (1946); *The Age of Longing* (1951); *The Call Girls* (1972). Autobiographical writings include: *Arrow in the Blue* (1952); *The Invisible Writing* (1954). Other prose writings include: *The Yogi and the Commissar* (1945); *The Roots of Coincidence* (1972).

Bib: Hamilton, I., *Koestler: A Biography*; Pearson, S. A., *Arthur Koestler*.

Kristeva, Julia (b 1941)

French psychoanalyst, philosopher and linguistic theorist. Julia Kristeva was born and grew up in Bulgaria, and moved to Paris to study in 1966. She writes in French, and is now a naturalized French citizen, but she has often drawn on the language and psychology of exile in her work – in 1970 ▷ Roland

Barthes was one of the first theorists to respond enthusiastically to her work, calling her 'L'étrangère'. Kristeva's earlier work is more strongly concerned with ▷ semiotics and linguistic theory (*Séméiotiké*, 1969, outlines Kristeva's own brand of 'semanalysis'; see also *Desire in Language: A Semiotic Approach to Literature and Art*, 1980), and as her interest in psychoanalysis has burgeoned she has undertaken a series of studies of literature, poetics and abnormal psychology, and the relationship between language and the body (particularly *Powers of Horror*, 1982, *Tales of Love*, 1983, and *Black Sun* 1980). Her long-term interest in ▷ Symbolist and ▷ modernist writers continues to animate her work (Mallarmé and ▷ Lautréamont are the subject of *Revolution in Poetic Language* (1974), and Céline figures centrally in *Powers of Horror*), and she has also had a profound impact on the development of the so-called 'New French Feminist' movement (see essays and interviews with her in *New French Feminisms*, ed. E. Marks and I. de Courtivron, as well as *Desire in Language* and *About Chinese Women*, trans. 1977). Kristeva is a long-term member of the editorial board of the radical journal ▷ *Tel Quel*, and is a practising psychoanalyst (now called *L'Infini*).

▷ Feminism; Post-structuralism; Psychoanalytic criticism.

Bib: Moi, T. (ed.), *The Kristeva Reader*; Lechte, J., *Julia Kristeva*; Moi, T., *Sexual/ Textual Politics*.

L

Labour Party
Since 1923, one of the two main political parties in Britain, the other being the Conservative Party. The Labour Party was founded in 1900, and was called the Labour Representation Committee until 1906, when it took its present name. It claims to represent the interests of the working classes, and it favours state ownership of the means of production and distribution (state socialism) but it is not committed to complete socialization of the economy. The majority of its supporters are working-class, but it also has fairly extensive middle-class support among intellectuals.

It was under the Labour government of 1945–50 that the ▷ Welfare State was set up, and under Harold Wilson's Labour administration (1966–70) that important legal reforms were made, including the facilitating of birth control and divorce, the permitting of homosexuality and abortion, the abolition of hanging and theatre ▷ censorship.

Origins of the Labour Party:

1 The 19th-century working-class movements. The most important of these was the growth of trade unions, which began a process of confederation in 1866; it was in consequence of a resolution by the Trades Union Congress (TUC) in 1899 that the Party was founded. Earlier movements which contributed to the origins of the party were those of the socialist Robert Owen; the Chartist Movement which, though it failed in its objectives, educated the working class in political consciousness; the Philosophical Radicals or Utilitarians, led by John Stuart Mill, who appealed to intellectuals among the workers and elsewhere.

2 The Liberal Party. Throughout the 19th century the ▷ Liberals (formerly the Whigs) claimed to be the party of reform, although important social reforms were often initiated by Conservatives (Tories) such as Shaftesbury and Disraeli. It was in alliance with the Liberal Party that the workmen Members first entered Parliament in the last 20 years of the 19th century. The Liberals, however, received much support and money from employers of labour in the towns, so that a split caused by workers leaving the Liberal Party became inevitable.

3 The Nonconformists sects. The Protestant churches which refused conformity with the ▷ Church of England included Baptists, Congregationalists, Presbyterians, Quakers, Unitarians and Methodists, Most of their support was from the lower social classes, and, though they were predominantly non-political, they inevitably encouraged thoughtful discussion of political questions, especially social justice; they also assisted by helping to educate their members in social co-operation.

4 ▷ The Fabian Society. This was a society of socialist intellectuals, founded in 1884. It was led by some brilliant minds, including ▷ Bernard Shaw and ▷ Beatrice Webb, and became very influential.

5 ▷ Marx and the growth of Social Democracy in Europe. The European Social Democratic Federation was founded in 1881. However, although the British Labour Party has always had affinities with Social Democracy, in its origins it was not predominantly Marxist; its socialism derived more from earlier thinkers such as Owen.

6 The leadership of the Scottish Labour Movement – Keir Hardie. Scotland was not so bound by tradition to the existing political parties as England was, and the Scottish working class was on the whole better educated. The Scotsman Keir Hardie was one of the finest leaders of the British Labour Party at the time of the foundation of the party.

Lacan, Jacques (1901–81)
French psychoanalyst whose re-readings of ▷ Freud have become influential within the area of literary criticism. Lacan's *The Four Fundamental Concepts of Psychoanalysis* (trans. 1977), and his *Ecrits: A Selection* (trans. 1977) outline the nature of his revision of Freudian psychoanalytic method. A further selection of papers has appeared under the title of *Feminine Sexuality* (trans. 1982). It is to Lacan that we owe the terms ▷ 'imaginary' and ▷ 'symbolic order'. Similarly, it is to his investigation of the operations of the unconscious according to the model of language – 'the unconscious is structured like a language' – that we owe the notion of a 'split' human subject. For Lacan the 'imaginary' is associated with the pre-Oedipal (▷ Oedipus complex) and pre-linguistic relationship between mother and child where there appears to be no discrepancy between identity and its outward reflection. This is succeeded by the entry of the infant into the 'symbolic order', with its rules and prohibitions centred around the figure of the father (the phallus). The 'desire of the mother' is then repressed by the child's entry into language and the 'symbolic order'. The desire for 'imaginary' unity is also repressed to form the unconscious, which the interaction between analyst and patient aims

to unlock. Some of the fundamental divisions that Lacan has located in the 'subject' have proved highly adaptable for a range of ▷ materialist literary criticisms, including (more controversially) ▷ feminism.
Bib: Gallop, J., *Reading Lacan*; Clement, C., *The Lives and Legends of Jacques Lacan*; Wright, E., *Psychoanalytic Criticism*.

Lady Chatterley's Lover (1928)
▷ D. H. Lawrence's last novel. Constance Reid ('Connie') is the daughter of late-Victorian, highly cultured parents with advanced views. She marries Sir Clifford Chatterley in 1917, when he is on leave from the army; soon afterwards he is wounded, and permanently crippled from the waist down. Connie finds herself half alive, as though she has not been fully awakened; her dissatisfaction, however, does not proceed merely from her husband's disability, but from the impotence of civilization which the disability symbolizes. She is rescued from it by her husband's gamekeeper, Mellors, who fulfils her as a lover and as a human being. For Lawrence, the sexual relationship was potentially the profoundest human relationship: to treat it lightly was to trivialize the whole human being, and to regard it with shame was to repress essential human energies. He saw that 'advanced' young people took the former attitude, and that the older generation took the latter; he regarded both attitudes as leading symptoms of decadence in our civilization. He did not suppose that the sexual relationship could in itself constitute a renewal of civilization, but he considered that such a renewal depended on the revitalization of relationships, and that this revitalization could never take place without the recovery of a true and healthy sexual morality. 'I want men and women to be able to think sex, fully, completely, honestly and cleanly.' (*Apropos of Lady Chatterley's Lover*, 1930).

This aim led Lawrence to use unprecedentedly explicit language in conveying the love affair between Connie and Mellors, and the novel thus acquired unfortunate notoriety. In Britain, the full version was suppressed for immorality, but an expurgated version was published in 1928. An unabridged edition came out in Paris in 1929; the first British unabridged edition was published by Penguin Books in 1959. This led to an obscenity trial, the first test of the 1959 Obscene Publications Act, at which many distinguished authors and critics (including ▷ E. M. Forster) testified in defence of the novel. The acquittal of Penguin had important consequences for subsequent publishing. Lawrence's defence of the novel, *Apropos of Lady Chatterley's Lover*, is one of the finest of his essays.

▷ Censorship and English literature.

Lamming George (b 1927)
Barbadian novelist. After teaching in Trinidad he moved to Britain in 1950. His novels are concerned with the West Indian identity, both individual and collective, and the aftermath of colonialism and slavery. *The Emigrants* (1954) is a bleak portrayal of identity sought and lost among black emigrants to England in the 1950s; *Season of Adventure* (1960) represents the awakening to a new and more liberal consciousness of the daughter of a West Indian police officer; *Water with Berries* (1971) uses parallels with the colonial symbolism of ▷ Shakespeare's *The Tempest* to represent the historical consequences of colonialism through the personal crises of three West Indian artists living in London. His other novels are: *In the Castle of my Skin* (1953); *Of Age and Innocence* (1958); *Natives of my Person* (1972); *The Pleasures of Exile* (1984).
Bib: Paquet, S. P., *The Novels of George Lamming*.

Langue
This term appears throughout ▷ Ferdinand de Saussure's *Course in General Linguistics* (1915) to denote the system of ▷ signs which makes up any language structure. According to Saussure, individual utterances (▷ parole) are constructed out of elements which have no existence 'prior to the linguistic system, but only conceptual and phonetic differences arising out of that system'. This observation is fundamental to ▷ Structuralism, which is concerned with the positioning of particular elements within a nonvariable structure. 'Langue' is the term used to denote the linguistic structure itself, that is the rules which lie behind particular linguistic events.

Larkin, Philip (1922–85)
Poet. He was the most eminent of the group known as the 'New Lines' poets (from an anthology of that name, 1956 ed. by Robert Conquest) otherwise called the ▷ Movement. Many of them held posts in universities, and their work is characterized by thoughtfulness, irony, self-doubt, humility, and the search for completely honest feeling. These qualities are in accord with the imaginative temper of ▷ Thomas Hardy's poetry; Larkin,

who greatly admired Hardy, has also been compared to ▷ W. H. Auden, though his political conservatism and concern to proclaim the pathos and humour of everyday experience rather than address the 'academic' reader represent a turning away from the technical radicalism of writers like Auden and ▷ T. S. Eliot. Publications: *The North Ship* (1945); *The Less Deceived* (1955); *The Whitsun Weddings* (1964); *High Windows* (1974); Editor *Oxford Books of Twentieth Century English Verse* (1973). Larkin also wrote two novels, *Jill* (1946) and *A Girl in Winter* (1947); see also his book of essays *Required Writing* (1983). Larkin was also known for his passion for jazz music; see *All What Jazz?: A Record Diary 1961–1968* (1970).
Bib: Thwaite, A. (ed.), *Larkin at Sixty*; Motion, A., *Philip Larkin*.

Laurence, Margaret (1926–87)
Canadian novelist and short-story writer. She wrote a series of novels and short stories centred on Manawaka, Manitoba, a fictional small town on the Canadian prairies: *The Stone Angel* (1964); *A Jest of God* (1966); *The Fire Dwellers* (1969); *A Bird in the House* (stories; 1970); *The Diviners* (1974). These works explore the social history of Canada, through the lives of several generations of women, dealing with themes such as the claustrophobia of small town life, the force of social inhibitions, the quest for identity and the importance of a sense of the past. Laurence's earlier work reflects the seven years which she spent in Somalia and Ghana between 1950 and 1957. *A Tree For Poverty* (1954) is a translation of Somali oral poetry and prose; *This Side Jordan* (1960) is a novel about racial tension in the Gold Coast (now Ghana); *The Tomorrow Tamer* (1963) is a collection of stories; *The Prophet's Camel Bell* (1963) is a travel narrative; *Long Drums and Cannons; Nigerian Dramatists and Novelists 1952–66* (1968) is literary criticism.

▷ Commonwealth literatures.
Bib: Thomas, C., *Laurence*.

Lautréamont, Comte de (pseudonym of Isidore-Lucien Ducasse) (1846–70)
French writer of lyrical prose pieces which appeared under the title *Les Chants de Maldoror* in 1868, with a slightly expanded posthumous version in 1890. The hero, Maldoror, is a demonic figure and his world is one of delirium and nightmare interspersed with blasphemy and eroticism. The hallucinatory quality of this work attracted the interest of the Surrealists (▷ Surrealism), who claimed Lautréamont as one of their own and promoted his work. Their interest has been carried forward into contemporary French criticism, especially in the work of ▷ Julia Kristeva.

Lawrence, D. H. (David Herbert) (1885–1930)
Novelist, poet, critic. The son of a coal-miner, he passed through University College, Nottingham, and for a time worked as a teacher. He eloped to Italy with Frieda Weekley, the German wife of a Nottingham professor, in 1912, and married her in 1914. His hatred of World War I, together with the German origins of his wife, caused them unhappiness in 1914–18; after the war they travelled about the world, visiting especially Australia, Mexico and the U.S.A. Lawrence died of tuberculosis at Vence in France in 1930. His reputation has grown gradually, and he is likely always to remain a controversial figure.

Lawrence's life, art, criticism, poetry, and teaching were all so closely related that it is unusually difficult to distinguish one aspect of his achievement from all the others. Misunderstandings about his supposed obsession with sexuality and the needless legal action for obscenity in connection with two of his novels (▷ *The Rainbow* and ▷ *Lady Chatterley's Lover*) initially distorted judgement of his work, but he is now firmly established as a major ▷ modernist novelist. On the other hand, he has been the subject of irrelevant hero-worship which is equally distorting, and which he would have repudiated. He was a deeply religious – though not a Christian – writer who believed that modern man is perverting his nature by the wilful divorce of his consciousness from his spontaneous feelings. He has been accused of social prejudice. It is true that he was keenly critical of society; but he was the first major English novelist to have truly working-class origins, and this, together with his wide range of friendships with men and women of all classes, gave him unusual perceptiveness into the contradictions of English society. His attitude to women has been severely criticized (see K. Millett, *Sexual Politics*; 1970), as have the general political implications of his ideas (see J. Carey 'D. H. Lawrence's Doctrine' in S. Spender (ed.), *D. H. Lawrence: Novelist, Poet, Prophet*; 1973).

Novels: *The White Peacock* (1911); *The Trespasser* (1912); ▷ Sons and Lovers (1913), an autobiographical novel, was his first distinguished work, and it was followed by what are generally regarded as his two masterpieces, ▷ *The Rainbow* (1915) and ▷ *Women in Love* (1921); *The Lost Girl* (1920); *Aaron's Rod* (1922); *Kangaroo* (1923) about Australia; *The Plumed Serpent* (1926) about Mexico; *Lady Chatterley's Lover* (1928), banned except for an expurgated edition until 1959. The unfinished *Mr Noon* was published in 1984. He also wrote several volumes of short stories and novellas which include much of his best fiction. Among the best known of these are *St Mawr, The Daughters of the Vicar, The Horse Dealer's Daughter, The Captain's Doll, The Prussian Officer, The Virgin and the Gipsy*.

One of Lawrence's most distinguishing features as an artist in fiction is his use of natural surroundings and animals realistically and yet symbolically, to express states of experience which elude direct description. This 'poetic' element in his fiction is reflected in much of his verse; some of this is in rhymed, metrical stanzas, but a great deal of it is free of verse conventions and close to the more condensed passages of his prose. Lawrence began writing poetry at the time when ▷ Imagism was seeking more concrete expression, and he contributed to Imagist anthologies. Some critics (*eg* A. Alvarez, *The Shaping Spirit*) are inclined to see his poetry as among the most important produced in the century, deserving to be set alongside the work of ▷ T. S. Eliot and ▷ W. B. Yeats.

Lawrence's descriptive, didactic, and critical prose is also important. His psychological essays, *Psychoanalysis and the Unconscious* (1921) and *Fantasia of the Unconscious* (1922) are imaginative, not scientific works, and contribute to the understanding of his creative mind. His descriptive volumes, *Sea and Sardinia* (1921), *Morning in Mexico* (1927), show his outstanding powers of presenting scenes with sensuous immediacy, and his characteristic concentration of all his interest – moral and social, as well as aesthetic – on to natural environment. The same concentration is to be seen in his critical and didactic writing; he brought moral, aesthetic, and social judgements into play together. Much of his best critical writing is contained in the posthumous volumes *Phoenix* I and II; the *Study of Thomas Hardy* is of particular importance for the understanding of Lawrence's own work. His letters are being published in seven volumes (vols 1–3, 1979–84). He was an excellent letter-writer: *Letters* (ed. Aldous Huxley).

Lawrence wrote eight plays including: *The Widowing of Mrs Holroyd* (1920); *Touch and Go* (1920); *David* (1927); *A Collier's Friday Night* (1965); *The Daughter in Law* (1967); *The Fight for Barbara* (1967). These have never received the attention accorded the rest of his work.
Bib: Leavis, F. R., *D. H. Lawrence, Novelist*; E. T., *D. H. Lawrence, a Personal Record*; Lawrence, F., *Not I, but the Wind*; Moore, H. T., *The Intelligent Heart*; Nehls, E., (ed.) *Lawrence: a Composite Biography*; Spilka, M., *The Love Ethic of D. H. Lawrence*; Draper, R. P., *Lawrence: The Critical Heritage*; Hough, G. G., *The Dark Sun*; Kermode, F., *Lawrence*; Burgess, A., *Flame into Being*; Sagar, K., *The Life of D. H. Lawrence* and *D. H. Lawrence: Life Into Art*; Macleod, S., *Lawrence's Men and Women*; Smith, A. (ed.), *D. H. Lawrence and Women*.

Lawrence. T. E. (Thomas Edward) (1888–1935)
Soldier and author, T. E. Lawrence is more popularly known as 'Lawrence of Arabia'. This title was inspired by his guerilla leadership activities in Arabia during World War I, of which he subsequently gave an epic and heroic account in the classic *Seven Pillars of Wisdom* (1926) – a shortened version of this book was later published as *Revolt in the Desert* (1927).

In many ways Lawrence epitomizes the image of the 'boy's own hero'; organizing in 1916 the Arab revolt against the Turks and developing imaginative and risky guerilla tactics, he was offered, but refused, both the Victoria Cross and a knighthood. After the war he went on to enlist in the ranks of the R.A.F. under two pseudonyms. His diaries for this period were published in 1955 as *The Mint*.

Lawrence was also something of an archaeologist and translator; in 1932 he published a translation of Homer's *Odyssey*. In 1962 the film director David Lean turned Lawrence's life and work with the Arab freedom movement into the cinema classic *Lawrence of Arabia*.

Leavis, Frank Raymond (1895–1978)
Critic. From 1932 till 1953 he edited ▷ *Scrutiny*, a literary review with high critical standards, and pervaded by his personality. It maintained that the values of a society in all its activities derive from its culture, and that central to British culture is English literature; that a literature can be sustained only by discriminating readers, and therefore by a body of highly trained critics working together, especially in the collaborative circumstances of a university (*Education*

and the University; 1943). The need for the testing of judgements by collaborative discussion is important in Leavis's view of criticism. Unfortunately, collaboration may become uncritical discipleship, and this was one of the two unfortunate consequences of the exceptional force of Leavis's personality. The other unfortunate consequence was the hostility which this force of personality aroused in many critics who were not among his collaborators and followers. He maintained that true critical discernment can be achieved only by a total response of the mind – intellectual, imaginative and moral; thus a critical judgement reflects not only the work of literature being judged, but the worth of the personality that makes the judgement, so that Leavis's censure of critics with whom he strongly disagreed was sometimes extraordinarily vehement, as in his *Two Cultures?: The Significance of C. P. Snow* (1962). However this vehemence was a price he paid for his determination to sustain a living tradition of literature not only by assessing contemporary writers with the utmost rigour, but also by reassessing the writers of the past, distinguishing those he thought had a vital relevance for the modern sensibility from those that stood as mere monuments in academic museums. Such evaluative treatments caused him to be widely regarded as a destructive critic; his attack on the three-centuries-long prestige of Milton (*Revaluation* 1936 and *The Common Pursuit* 1952) gave particular offence.

Leavis's intense concern with the relationship between the kind of sensibility nourished by a literary culture and the quality of a society as a whole has a historical background that extends to the beginning of the 19th century. It first appears in Wordsworth's *Preface to the Lyrical Ballads* (1800), is to be felt in the writings of the 19th-century philosopher John Stuart Mill (see *Mill on Bentham and Coleridge*, ed. by Leavis, 1950), and is explicit in Matthew Arnold's writings, especially *Culture and Anarchy* (1869). Later the theme is taken up by the novelists, *eg* in Gissing's *New Grub Street* and, both in his novels and in his criticism, by ▷ D. H. Lawrence. The outstanding importance of novels in connection with the theme caused Leavis to be foremost a critic of the novel; perhaps his most important single book is *The Great Tradition: George Eliot, Henry James, Joseph Conrad* (1948), but this should be read in conjunction with his books on Lawrence and (with ▷ Q. D. Leavis) on *Dickens the Novelist* (1970). Although still influential, Leavis must now be considered together with more contemporary literary theory, such as ▷ post-structuralism, which has tended to challenge radically and contradict vehemently his criticism.

▷ New criticism.

Leavis, Q. D. (1906–81)
Literary critic. Q. D. Leavis was educated at Cambridge in the 1920s (she was a student of ▷ I. A. Richards), and became a central figure in what came to be known as 'Cambridge criticism', the 'traditional' form of moral criticism (as distinct from Richards's ▷ new criticism), which is more readily associated with her husband, ▷ F. R. Leavis. As one of the founders of the journal ▷ *Scrutiny* and writer of the influential *Fiction and the Reading Public* (1932), Q. D. Leavis helped to establish English literature as a discipline in its own right. *Fiction and the Reading Public* is primarily a sociological and psychological account of popular reading patterns, which consolidates her more fundamental celebration of great literary classics as the primary source of the essential humane values which she promoted. Leavis's work is thus often read as the direct descendant of the cultural criticism of ▷ Victorian critic Matthew Arnold, but it is also important for its psychological dimension, and, in her essays, for a serious interest in the work of women writers, which is not generally seen as characteristic of her *Scrutiny* contemporaries. In tandem with bringing up a family, she also wrote *Dickens the Novelist* (1970) with her husband, and a wide range of essays, which are collected in three volumes as *Collected Essays* (1983).

Le Carré, John (David John Moore Cornwell) (b 1931)
Le Carré is one of the most intriguing of Cold War novelists, managing to write challenging and sophisticated work for a popular audience. Le Carre's work is grim, bitter and unromantic, and his characters are brilliantly bleak psychological cases of individuals (often secret service workers) in morally compromised situations. His reputation was established with his third novel, *The Spy Who Came in from the Cold* in 1963, in which Le Carré's most famous character, George Smiley, appears. Although most of his works – including *Call for the Dead* (1961); *The Looking-Glass War* (1965); *A Small Town in Germany* (1968); *Tinker, Tailor, Soldier, Spy* (1974); *The Honorable Schoolboy* (1977); *Smiley's People* (1980) and

The Perfect Spy (1986) – are concerned with espionage, in *The Naive and Sentimental Lover* (1971) and *The Little Drummer Girl* (1983), he turned to the Middle East and explored the Palestinian situation. Le Carré's work is eminently filmable, and many of his works have been translated into feature films or television dramas. In 1990 a film was made of Le Carré's 'glasnost' novel *The Russia House* (1988); scripted by ▷ Tom Stoppard, it was the first Hollywood film to be made on location in the Soviet Union.
Bib: Barley, Tony: *Taking Sides: The Fiction of John Le Carré.*

Lehmann, Rosamund (1901–90)
Novelist and short-story writer. The poet and critic John Lehmann was her brother. Her novels depict the experience of educated and sensitive women, focusing in particular on infatuation, betrayal and the contrast between the relative safety of childhood and the disillusionment of adolescence and adulthood. They make considerable use of memories and impressions, rendered in a lyrical prose style. She was initially associated with ▷ Virginia Woolf and ▷ Elizabeth Bowen for her rendering of the consciousness of women, but her work is generally regarded as narrower in scope. Her novels are: *Dusty Answer* (1927); *A Note in Music* (1930); *Invitation to the Waltz* (1932); *The Weather in the Streets* (1936); *The Ballad and the Source* (1944); *The Echoing Grove* (1953); *A Sea-Grape Tree* (1976). Story collection: *The Gipsy's Baby* (1946). She has also written her autobiography, *The Swan in the Evening* (1967).

Lessing, Doris (b 1919)
Novelist and short-story writer. Born in Persia (now Iran) and brought up in Southern Rhodesia (now Zimbabwe), she settled in London in 1949. Her writing spans an exceptionally wide range of genres, settings and narrative techniques, but is unified by certain persistent concerns: the analysis of contemporary culture and of social process; a sense of 20th-century history as catastrophic and an attempt to link this to personal unhappiness; a mystical and sometimes utopian emphasis on higher states of consciousness; an intense anger at social injustice; an interest in radical revisions of the self and of personal and sexual relations.

Her first novel, *The Grass is Singing* (1950), is the story of a relationship between a white woman and a black man in Rhodesia, and was followed by the *Children of Violence* series, a *Bildungsroman* about a young Rhodesian girl in revolt against the establishment, ending in England with a vision of future chaos and a tentative hope for a utopian future. The series consists of: *Martha Quest* (1952); *A Proper Marriage* (1954); *A Ripple from the Storm* (1958); *Landlocked* (1965); *The Four Gated City* (1969). *The Golden Notebook* (1962) exemplifies the element of ▷ post-modernist experiment in Lessing's work, in its use of multiple narratives and its concern with fiction and the reconstruction of the self, but it also addresses social issues of the 1960s: the crisis in radical politics, women's liberation, the value of psychoanalysis. During the 1970s Lessing started to write ▷ science fiction, and has remained a fierce exponent of its value as a literary form. Her series *Canopus in Argus: Archives* comprises: *Shikasta* (1979); *The Marriages Between Zones Three, Four and Five* (1980); *The Sirian Experiments* (1981); *The Making of the Representative for Planet 8* (1982); *The Sentimental Agents* (1983). These novels attempt to set human history and human relationships in the context of a battle between good and evil in the universe and an evolutionary quest for a higher state of being. Lessing has continued to show her inventiveness and flexibility with *The Diary of Jane Somers* (1984), a critique of society's treatment of the old, *The Good Terrorist* (1985), a study of the making of a terrorist, and *The Fifth Child* (1988), which uses elements of the horror story genre to explore problems in liberal ideals. Her other novels are: *Briefing for a Descent into Hell* (1971); *The Summer Before Dark* (1972); *Memoirs of a Survivor* (1974). Story collections include: *This Was the Old Chief's Country* (1951); *Five: Short Novels* (1953); *The Habit of Loving* (1957); *A Man and Two Women* (1963); *African Stories* (1964); *Winter in July* (1966); *The Black Madonna* (1966); *The Story of a Non-Marrying Man* (1972).

Her other works include: *Going Home* (1957), a study of Southern Rhodesia; *In Pursuit of the English* (1960), a study of England in 1960; *A Small Personal Voice: Essays, Reviews, Interviews* (1974). *The Making of the Representative for Planet 8* has been turned into an opera, with music by Philip Glass (1988).
Bib: Sage, L., *Doris Lessing*; Sprague, C., and Tiger, V. (eds.), *Critical Essays on Doris Lessing.*

***Lesson of the Master, The* (1892)**
A story by ▷ Henry James. Its theme is the barrier set up against the true artist by supposedly cultivated society, which

can understand nothing about the artist's dedication and can therefore only hinder him by its unintelligent praise based on false standards.

Letter-writing
This is clearly an important branch of literature even when the interest of the letters is essentially historical or ▷ biographical. Letters may also be, by intention or by consequence of genius, works of intrinsic literary value. The 18th century (the age of the epistolary novel) was more than any other the period when letter-writing was cultivated as an art. Earlier than the 18th century, postal services were not sufficiently organized to encourage regular letter-writing, and the art of familiar prose was inadequately cultivated; by the mid-19th century, communications had improved enough to make frequent and full letter-writing redundant. By then letters had intrinsic, literary interest chiefly by virtue of the writer's talent for literary expression in other modes of writing, added to the accident that they found letters a congenial means of communication. The letters of the poet ▷ Gerard Manley Hopkins and the novelist ▷ D. H. Lawrence are examples. In the first 30 years of the 19th century the Romantic habit of introspection resulted in a quantity of extremely interesting letters. Many 20th-century writers have had large collections of their letters published; ▷ Virginia Woolf wrote a copious amount, and ▷ Sylvia Plath's *Letters Home* (written to her mother) is a famous later anthology.

Levertov, Denise (b 1923)
Poet and prose writer. Levertov was born and grew up in Britain but has lived in the U.S.A. since 1948. Her first publication was *The Double Image* (1946), and her work was also included in Kenneth Rexroth's *The New British Poets* (1948). Her most recent work is published in Britain by Bloodaxe, and she also features in the important *Bloodaxe Book of Contemporary Women Poets* (1985). Her volumes of verse include: *Collected Earlier Poems 1940–1960*; *Poems 1960–1967*; *To Stay Alive* (1971); *Life in the Forest* (1978); *Candles in Babylon* (1982); *Selected Poems* (1985); *Oblique Prayers* (1985). Her volumes of prose essays include: *The Poet in the World* (1973) and *Light up the Cave* (1982).

Lewis, C. S. (Clive Staples) (1898–1963)
Novelist, critic, poet and writer on religion. Born in Belfast, Lewis served in France during World War I. From 1925 until 1954 he was a Fellow of Magdalen College, Oxford and tutor in English, and from 1954 was Professor of Medieval and Renaissance Literature at Cambridge. His fiction reflects an interest in fantasy, myth and fairy-tale with an underlying Christian message. He wrote a ▷ science fiction trilogy: *Out of the Silent Planet* (1938); *Perelandra* (1943) (as *Voyage to Venus*, 1953); *That Hideous Strength* (1945). *The Lion, The Witch, and The Wardrobe* (1950) was the first of seven fantasy stories for children. His popular theological works include: *The Problem of Pain* (1940); *Miracles* (1947) and *The Screwtape Letters* (1942), which takes the form of letters from an experienced devil to a novice devil. *A Grief Observed* (1961) is a powerful autobiographical work, an account of his grief at the death of his wife. He also wrote such classics of literary history as *The Allegory of Love* (1936) and *A Preface to Paradise Lost* (1942).

▷ Children's books.

Lewis, Percy Wyndham (1882–1957)
Painter, novelist, critic and polemical journalist. Before 1914 he was leader of the ▷ Vorticist movement in painting, which, drawing on the French Cubist movement and the Italian Futurist movement, advocated dynamic, semi-abstract representation of angular, precise and rhythmical forms. Lewis carried over this predilection for vigour and energy into literature, taking a boldly independent attitude to modern culture, rather like that of the poet ▷ Ezra Pound with whom he edited the review *Blast* (1914–15), and asserted the right and the power of the intellect to take command in the cultural crisis. He was opposed to domination by political ideology (though he wrote favourably of Hitler in 1931), by psychological cults and by the bureaucratic and welfare state; he made it his principal aim to expose the confusion of mind which he considered to be overwhelming 20th-century man, and the hollowness of humanity which he believed to be the consequence of encroaching mechanization. He had something in common with his friend ▷ T. S. Eliot (see ▷ *The Waste Land*) but never became a Christian; with ▷ D. H. Lawrence (see ▷ *St Mawr*) whose mysticism he nevertheless despised; with ▷ James Joyce, though he was strongly opposed to his subjective ▷ stream of consciousness technique; with ▷ F. R. Leavis and the other ▷ *Scrutiny* critics, who, however, rejected him as brutally negative. He prided himself on his very distinctive style of expression, which is energetic and

concentrates on presenting the externals of human nature with icy clarity.

His outstanding writings are probably his novels and stories: *Tarr* (1918); *The Wild Body* (stories; 1927); *The Apes of God* (1930 – a satire); *Snooty Baronet* (1932); *The Revenge for Love* (1937 – considered by some critics to be his best novel); *The Vulgar Streak* (1941); *Rotting Hill* (stories; 1951); *Self Condemned* (1954); and the four-part fable *The Human Age – The Childermass* (1928), *Monstre Gai* (1955), *Malign Fiesta* (1955), to have been completed by *The Trial of Man* which he did not live to finish.

His ideas are expounded in his philosophical work *Time and Western Man* (1927) and his autobiographies *Blasting and Bombardiering* (1937) and *Rude Assignment* (1950). He wrote notable literary criticism in *The Lion and the Fox: the Role of Hero in the Plays of Shakespeare* (1927), *Men without Art* (1934) and *The Writer and the Absolute* (1952).

Bib: Grigson, G., *A Master of Our Time*; Kenner, H., *Wyndham Lewis*; Meyers, J., *The Enemy*; Materer, T., *Wyndham Lewis: the Novelist*; Meyers, J. (ed.), *Wyndham Lewis: a Revaluation*; Jameson, F., *Fables of Aggression: Wyndham Lewis, the Modernist as Fascist*.

Liberal Democratic Party

Originally the Liberal Party, this political group was the successor of the former Whig Party; the change of name came about gradually after 1830 owing to a change in the composition of the party's supporters. In its political sense, the word 'Liberal' was an importation from Spain and France. After the end of the Napoleonic Wars (1815) it was first applied to what were considered to be extreme or even revolutionary reformers. However, by the end of the 1830s, the Whigs were increasingly calling themselves Liberals, and it became the accepted name for the party by the 1860s. Until 1923 the Liberals and the Conservatives were the principal political parties in Britain. The differences between them changed from decade to decade, but the Liberals were always more representative of town and industrial interests, and more inclined to strive for reform, whereas the Conservatives stood more for the countryside and sought stability. The disastrous decline of Liberal strength since 1923 has been due to a realignment of social interests.

In the 1970s the Liberal Party regained some strength. The general disillusionment with the polarized party system of Conservative and Labour also produced another political group in the Parliamentary arena. In 1981 a number of MPs broke away from the Labour Party and formed the Social Democratic Party, which was intended to 'break the mould' of British politics. The growing power of the Conservative government in the 1980s and the lack of proportional representation, however, sapped the energies of the centrist groups, and in 1988 the two parties merged to form the Social and Liberal Democrats. They are now known as the Liberal Democrats.

Little Gidding

A small religious community founded by the Anglican theologian Nicholas Ferrar (1592–1637) at a manor house in Huntingdonshire in 1625. It was dispersed, and the buildings were destroyed, by Parliamentary soldiers at the end of the Civil War (1646).

Charles I visited the community in 1633 and according to tradition he came again after his final defeat at the battle of Naseby (1645). The community is the starting point of one of ▷ T. S. Eliot's poems which takes its title from it (in ▷ *Four Quartets*), and an account of it comes into the historical novel *John Inglesant* (1881) by J. H. Shorthouse.

Littlewood, Joan (b 1914)

British director and founder of the Theatre Union in the 1930s with her husband Ewan MacColl. The company reformed after the war as Theatre Workshop, based firstly in Manchester and, from 1953, in East London at the Theatre Royal, Stratford East. Littlewood developed a method of working with actors which encouraged collaboration and improvisation. Her two most famous productions were ▷ Brendan Behan's *The Hostage* and *Oh, What a Lovely War*, the latter accredited to Theatre Workshop, Charles Chilton and the members of the original cast. Her aim was to provide a 'fun palace' for working-class audiences, though commercial pressures meant that the company had to rely heavily on West End transfers for survival, which destroyed her attempts to create a genuine ensemble.

Bib: Goorney, H., *The Theatre Workshop Story*.

Lodge, David (b 1935)

Novelist and critic, born in London and educated at London University. Since 1976 he has been Professor of Modern English Literature at the University of Birmingham. His novels are: *The Picturegoers* (1906); *Ginger,*

You're Barmy (1962); *The British Museum is Falling Down* (1965); *Out of the Shelter* (1970); *Changing Places* (1975); *How Far Can You Go?* (1980); *Small World* (1984); *Nice Work* (1988); *Paradise News* (1991). His earlier novels are views of English society in a light, realistic mode, but *The British Museum is Falling Down* introduces extensive use of parody and a farcical element. He is best known for *Changing Places* and *Small World*, inventive, humorous tales of academic life, full of jokes, puns, allusions, parodies and reflexive comments on the nature of narrative which reflect his interest in critical theory. They have affinities with the campus novels of ▷ Malcolm Bradbury. *Out of the Shelter* is a ▷ *Bildungsroman*, and *How Far Can You Go?* explores the personal struggles of a group of Catholics from the 1950s to the 1970s, concentrating in particular on the issue of contraception. Criticism includes: *Language of Fiction* (1966); *The Novelist at the Crossroads* (1971); *The Modes of Modern Writing* (1977); *Working With Structuralism* (1981).

Look Back in Anger (1956)
A play by ▷ John Osborne, first performed at the ▷ Royal Court theatre where it immediately made a major impact. The plot and dramatic structure are fairly conventional: Jimmy Porter, from a working-class background, lives in cramped conditions with his upper-middle-class wife Alison. Alison's friend persuades her to leave Jimmy only to fall for him herself. When Alison has a miscarriage her friend obligingly makes way for her to return to her former husband. The story and subsidiary characters are really a vehicle for Jimmy's tirades against the class-ridden nature of British society in the post-war period. For many amongst the original audiences Jimmy was a kind of modern Hamlet figure, even though a modern audience would be more likely to focus on the sexist manner in which he hectors and bullies his wife. Nonetheless, the fact is that the play captured a particular mood of disillusionment in the period and established the Royal Court as a venue for drama of social protest.

▷ Angry young men.

Lord Jim (1900)
A novel by ▷ Joseph Conrad. It is narrated by Marlow, an officer in the Merchant Navy who also appears in Conrad's other works, ▷ *Heart of Darkness, Chance* and *Youth*. The first 35 chapters we are to suppose recounted to companions after dinner; the rest is in the form of a letter and written narrative subsequently posted to one of these friends. Jim is a young sailor, the son of an English country parson, who dreams of being a hero. He becomes chief mate of the *Patna*, a decrepit ship with second-rate officers, carrying pilgrims from Singapore to Jeddah. When the ship seems about to sink he loses his nerve and, at the last moment, jumps into a small boat with the other officers. When they reach land they discover that the *Patna* has stayed afloat and been towed to safety. The other officers disappear, but Jim stays to face disgrace at the official enquiry. He meets Marlow, to whom he tells his story, and subsequently, persecuted by his sense of lost honour, Jim takes up humble employment as a water clerk in various Eastern ports (it is thus that Marlow introduces him to us at the start of the novel). Through the intervention of Marlow, Jim is sent by Stein, a benevolent trader, to a remote trading post in the jungle called Patusan. There, in alliance with a local chief called Doramin, who is Stein's friend, Jim defeats in battle the forces of Sherif Ali, a half-caste Arab bandit leader, and becomes a venerated figure. However, when a party of European adventurers led by the scoundrelly Gentleman Brown appears in Patusan, the memory of his past dishonour fatally weakens Jim's resolve. He asks Doramin to let them go free, pledging his own life for their good behaviour. They massacre a party of the villagers, including Doramin's son, and Jim allows himself to be shot by Doramin.

Lowry, Malcolm (1909–57)
Novelist. He was educated in England, but spent most of his later life in Mexico, the United States, and British Columbia. His first novel, *Ultramarine*, was published in 1933. His reputation chiefly rests on his second novel, *Under the Volcano* (1947). The central character, Geoffrey Firmin, is British Consul in a Mexican city situated under two volcanoes, just as in ancient times the Underworld, Tartarus, was supposed to be situated beneath the Sicilian volcano, Etna. Firmin is an alcoholic who has rejected the love of his wife and his friends and taken to drink as escape from the inhumanity of the modern world (the events take place in 1938) and his own sense of guilt and failure. The novel is highly allusive and symbolic, with metaphysical and mythical overtones, and the narrative is partly ▷ stream of consciousness. It shows the influence of ▷ Joseph Conrad and ▷ James Joyce and it has been described as the most distinguished work of fiction

produced by an English novelist since 1945. A number of works were published posthumously, including: two novels entitled *Dark as the Grave Wherein My Friend is Laid* (1968) and *October Ferry to Gabriola* (1970), which were put together from Lowry's drafts by his widow; *Selected Poems* (1962) and a volume of short stories, *Hear Us, O Lord, from Heaven Thy Dwelling Place* (1961).
Bib: Woodcock, G., *Lowry: the Man and His Work*; Day, D., *Lowry, a Biography*; Cross, R. K., *Malcolm Lowry: a Preface to His Fiction*.

M

MacCaig, Norman (b 1910)
Poet. A Scottish writer, educated at Edinburgh University, and often compared to fellow Scot ▷ Hugh MacDiarmid, MacCaig uses mainly traditional poetic forms for his witty verse, although he has also been drawn towards ▷ free verse. His publications include: *Far Cry* (1943); *Riding Lights* (1955); *A Common Gate* (1960); *Surroundings* (1967); *Selected Poems* (1971); *Tree of Strings* (1977); *The Equal Skies* (1980); *A World of Difference* (1983); *Voice-Over* (1988).
▷ Scottish literature in English.

MacDiarmid, Hugh (Christopher Murray Grieve) (1892–1978)
Poet and critic. A ▷ Marxist, and a leading Scottish nationalist. His outstanding contribution has been the revival of the Lowland Scottish branch of English (once called Inglis, now for literary purposes, Lallans, and still the medium of speech) as a poetic medium. The language had a distinguished literary phase about 1500, and reached another peak in the work of Robert Burns in the 18th century, but thereafter was overwhelmed by southern English. In the earlier and greater period, Scots poetry was part of the wide European tradition; Burns's excellence drew from the surviving vigour of Lowland Scots culture. MacDiarmid's success has arisen from his ability to follow the example of Burns in far less promising conditions, and to resist southern English modes by his awareness of the wider context of Europe. His best-known poem in Lallans is *A Drunk Man Looks at the Thistle*. He has also written in southern English. *Complete Poems 1920–1976*, ed. M. Grieve and W. R. Aitken.
▷ Scottish literature in English.
Bib: Glen, D., *Hugh MacDiarmid and the Scottish Renaissance*.

Mackenzie, Compton (1883–1972)
Novelist. Son of a British actor-manager and an American actress. A very prolific writer of great popularity; his best-known novels are probably *Sinister Street* (1913–14) and *The Four Winds of Love* – a sequence composed of *The East Wind* (1937); *The South Wind* (1937); *The West Wind* (1940); *West to North* (1940); *The North Wind* (1944–5). When he began writing, ▷ Henry James regarded him as one of the most promising of younger novelists, and ▷ Ford Madox Ford thought highly of *Sinister Street*. However, serious critics have rarely given him extensive attention.
Bib: Dooley, D. T., *Mackenzie*.

MacNeice, Louis (1907–63)
Poet. He was born in Northern Ireland, the son of an Anglican clergyman who became a bishop. During the 1930s he was associated by the reading public with a group of left-wing poets led by ▷ W. H. Auden. They were certainly his friends, but, although he had socialist sympathies, he never committed himself politically; in politics, as in religion, he was ▷ agnostic. He excelled in witty, sensuous verse of rhythmical versatility and with a strong element of caustic pessimism. He also wrote criticism, notably *The Poetry of W. B. Yeats* (1941), numerous plays for radio, and translated the *Agamemnon* of Aeschylus (1936) and Goethe's *Faust* (1951). He collaborated with Auden in *Letters from Iceland* (1937). *Collected Poems*, ed. E. R. Dodds (1979).
Bib: Fraser, G. S., in *Vision and Rhetoric*; Thwaite, A., *Essays on Contemporary English Poetry*.

Magazine
Originally meaning 'storehouse', the word has also denoted, since the 18th century, a periodical containing miscellaneous material, *eg* the *Gentleman's Magazine* (founded 1731): 'a Monthly Collection to store up, as in a Magazine, the most remarkable pieces on the subjects above-mentioned' (from the introduction to the first number). In the 18th and early 19th century magazines only differed from other serious periodicals (*eg* the *Edinburgh Review* and the *Quarterly*) in having greater variety of content and being open to imaginative writing. Distinguished magazines of this kind include *Blackwood's* and the second *London Magazine* (1820–29). Later in the 19th century, magazines became predominantly popular periodicals devoted principally to fiction. Since World War II magazines have often been seen as synonymous with reading matter specifically directed at women; examples are *Vogue*, *Cosmopolitan*, and the feminist magazines *Spare Rib* and *Everywoman*. Whilst literary magazines have declined in popularity, one of the current best-selling magazines in Britain is the T.V. listings publication, *Radio Times*. See *Wellesley Index to Periodicals*.
▷ Reviews and periodicals.

Magic realism
A term applied in literature primarily to Latin American novelists such as Jorge Luis Borges (1899–1987), Gabriel García Márquez (b 1928) and Alejo Carpentier (b 1904), whose work combines a realistic manner with strong elements of the bizarre, supernatural

and fantastic. This technique has influenced novelists such as ▷ John Fowles, ▷ Angela Carter and ▷ Salman Rushdie.

▷ Spanish influence on English literature.

Mahon, Derek (b 1941)
Poet. Mahon was born in Belfast and educated at Dublin, and has lectured at the universities of Sussex and Ulster. Along with fellow poets James Simmons, ▷ Paul Muldoon, ▷ Seamus Heaney and Michael Longley, he is an important figure in the Northern Irish renaissance in contemporary poetry. See *Night Crossing* (1968); *Beyond Howth* (1970); *Lives* (1972); *The Snow Party* (1975); *Light Music* (1977); *Poems 1962–1978* (1979).

▷ Irish literature in English.

Mallock, W. H. (1849–1923)
A ▷ Catholic controversialist now best known for his satirical novel *The New Republic*, portraying leading members of the Victorian intelligentsia, including John Ruskin, Matthew Arnold, Walter Pater and Thomas Huxley. He wrote a number of books on social questions against socialism. His *Memoirs of Life and Literature* was published in 1920.
Bib: Adams, A. B., *The Novels of W. H. Mallock*; Wolf, R. L., *Gains and Losses: Novels of Faith and Doubt in Victorian England.*

Manning, Olivia (1915–80)
Novelist and short-story writer. Her major work is *The Balkan Trilogy* set in Romania, Greece and Egypt during the early stages of World War II, and which consists of: *The Great Fortune* (1960); *The Spoilt City* (1962) and *Friends and Heroes* (1965). It is told primarily through the consciousness of a newly married Englishwoman, and builds up a strong sense of place and of history through the portrayal of a wide range of characters and the accumulation of details of daily experience. The story is continued in *The Levant Trilogy*: *The Danger Tree* (1977); *The Battle Lost and Won* (1978); *The Sum of Things* (1980). Other novels: *The Wind Changes* (1937); *Artist Among the Missing* (1949); *School for Love* (1951); *A Different Face* (1953); *The Doves of Venus* (1955); *The Rain Forest* (1974). Story collections: *Growing Up* (1948); *My Husband Cartwright* (1956); *A Romantic Hero* (1967).

Mansfield, Katherine (1888–1923)
Short-story writer. Born (Katherine Mansfield Beauchamp) in Wellington, New Zealand; married the critic ▷ John Middleton Murry in 1913. Her story collections are: *In a German Pension* (1911); *Je Ne Parle Pas Français* (1918); *Bliss* (1920); *The Garden Party* (1922); *The Dove's Nest* (1923); *Something Childish* (1924); *The Aloe* (1930); *Collected Stories* (1945). Her *Journal* (1927, enlarged edition 1934) and *Letters* (1928) were edited by Murry. The stories resemble in their form those of the Russian writer ▷ Chekhov, and ▷ James Joyce's ▷ *Dubliners*; they do not have a distinct plot with a definite beginning and ending and a self-sufficient action, conveying instead an impression of continuity with ordinary life, and depending for their unity on delicate balance of detail and feeling. She contributed to the development of the ▷ stream of consciousness technique, and to the ▷ modernist use of multiple viewpoints.
Bib: Alpers, A., *The Life of Katherine Mansfield*; Hanson, C., and Gurr, A., *Katherine Mansfield.*

Marriage
According to Laurence Stone, in England marriage only gradually acquired its function of regulating sexual chastity in wedlock: up to the 11th century polygamy and concubinage were widespread and divorce was casual. Even after that time divorce by mutual consent followed by remarriage was still widely practised. In the 13th century, however, the Church developed its control, asserting the principles of monogamy, defining and outlawing incest, punishing fornication and adultery and ensuring the exclusion of bastards from property inheritance. In 1439 weddings in church were declared a sacrament and after 1563 in the Roman Catholic Church the presence of a priest was required to make the contract valid. In this way, what had been a private contract between two families concerning property exchange – Claude Lévi-Strauss was the first to point out in 1948 women's universal role in such transactions between men – became regulated. In 1753 Lord Hardwicke's Marriage Act ensured that weddings had to take place in church, duly registered and signed; verbal spousals would not be legally binding. No one under 21 could marry without parental consent and there were heavy penalties for clergymen who defied these injunctions. After this, the Civil Marriage Act of 1836 was passed to regulate all marriages solemnized other than in accordance with the rites of the Church of England. Divorce, with the option of remarriage, was not available except by private Act of Parliament, which only the

rich could afford: there were only 131 cases between 1670 and 1799. The poor used a ritualized wife-sale (as in ▷ Thomas Hardy's *The Mayor of Casterbridge* – the last recorded example was in 1887) or desertion. In 1857 the Matrimonial Causes Act introduced civil divorce for adultery: again only the rich could afford it and only men could do the divorcing. Wives were not permitted to divorce their husbands for adultery until 1923. In 1937 three additional grounds for divorce were introduced, cruelty, desertion and insanity. Further liberalization of the divorce laws took place in the 1960s: recognition of the concept of marital breakdown has allowed a less punitive and accusatory procedure.

▷ Divorce; Women, status of.

Marsh, Ngaio (1899–1982)
Detective novelist. Her works include: *A Man Lay Dead* (1934); *Enter a Murderer* (1935); *Death in Ecstasy* (1936); *Death at the Bar* (1940); *Died in the Wool* (1945); *Opening Night* (1951); *Singing in the Shrouds* (1958); *Hand in Glove* (1962); *Black Beech and Honeydew* (1965); *A Clutch of Constables* (1968); *Tied up in Tinsel* (1972); *Last Ditch* (1977); *Photo Finish* (1980). Ngaio Marsh is frequently bracketed with her three female ▷ detective-writing contemporaries (▷ Margerey Allingham, ▷ Agatha Christie, ▷ Dorothy L. Sayers) who together comprise the formidable bedrock of classic inter-war crime writing. Although she was born, educated and lived in New Zealand (her name is Maori), Marsh's novels are nevertheless often set in the English country house, or in the theatre, which she loved and dedicated much of her working life to: she was a successful director, and the action of her last novel (*Light Thickens*, 1982) take place in the middle of a production of *Macbeth*. Marsh's 'serial detective' is Roderick Alleyn, a character of some complexity whose role is nevertheless always set out as a function of plot and narrative mystery, for Marsh the primary factors in detective writing.

Martian poetry
The name of the so-called 'Martian' school of poetry derives from the second collection of ▷ Craig Raine, *A Martian Sends a Postcard Home* (1979). Everyday objects are described in an unusual, often highly striking manner, as if being seen for the first time by an alien visiting earth. The poet attempts to write from a position of innocence, radically outside of the society he or she observes, reading things from a position of exile, or as an anthropologist. The ordinary or commonsense world is twisted, often by an outrageous use of simile (▷ Figures of speech):

Rain is when the earth is television.
It has the property of making colours darker.
(Raine, 'A Martian Sends a Postcard Home')

Much contemporary poetry makes use of 'Martian eye' techniques, but the chief poets of the school are Raine and Christopher Reid (b 1949).

Marx, Karl (1818–83)
Born in Trier of German-Jewish parentage, and attended university in Berlin and Bonn where he first encountered Hegelian dialectic. He met Friedrich Engels (1820–95) in Paris in 1844, and in 1848, the Year of Revolutions, they published *The Communist Manifesto* together. In that year Marx returned to Germany and took part in the unsuccessful revolution there before fleeing to Britain where he was to remain until his death in 1883. In 1867 he published *Capital*, the voluminous work for which he is best known. Marx is justly renowned for his adaptation of the Hegelian dialectic for a materialist account of social formations, which is based upon an analysis of the opposition between different social classes. He is, arguably, the most prolific thinker and social commentator of the 19th century whose work has had far-reaching effects on subsequent generations of scholars, philosophers, politicians and analysts of human culture. In the political ferment of the 1960s, and especially in France, his work has been subject to a series of extraordinarily productive re-readings, especially by philosophers such as ▷ Louis Althusser, which continue to affect the understanding of all aspects of cultural life. In Britain Marx's work is what lies behind a very powerful literary and historical tradition of commentary and analysis, and has informed much work in the areas of sociology, and the study of the mass media. *Capital* and a range of earlier texts have come to form the basis of the materialist analysis of culture.

▷ New historicism.

Bib: Blumenberg, W., *Karl Marx*; Mehring, F., *Karl Marx: The Story of his Life*; McLellan, D., *Karl Marx: His Life and Thought*; Eagleton, T., *Marxism and Literary Criticism*; Bennett, T., *Formalism and Marxism*.

Masefield, John (1878–1967)
Poet and novelist. He went to sea in 1893, and published his first volume of poems,

Salt-Water Ballads in 1902. He was a prolific poet; the first edition of his *Collected Poems* came out in 1923, and the collection increased steadily until 1964. His work has immediate appeal, and is strongest in narrative verse: *The Everlasting Mercy* (1911); *The Widow in the Bye Street* (1912); *Dauber* (1913); *The Daffodil Fields* (1913); *Reynard the Fox* (1919). He was chosen as ▷ Poet Laureate in 1930. His novels have romantic charm, *eg Sard Harker* (1924); *Odtaa* (1926). *The Midnight Folk* (1927) is a classic of children's literature.

▷ Children's books.

Bib: Babington Smith, C., *John Masefield, a Life*; Spark, M., *John Masefield*.

Materialism
The philosophical theory that only physical matter is real and that all phenomena and processes can be explained by reference to it. Related to this is the doctrine that political and social change is triggered by change in the material and economic basis of society.

▷ Marx, Karl.

Matura, Mustapha (b 1939)
Trinidadian dramatist. One of the few black playwrights as yet to have made a major impact beyond the ▷ fringe world of community theatre. His plays deal with both personal and institutional forms of racism. Matura has been an important influence on new black British playwrights such as Tunde Ikoli and Hanif Kureishi. Major works: *Nice* (1973); *Welcome Home Jacko* (1981); *Play Mas*, *Independence* and *Meetings* (1982); *Trinidad Sisters* (1988).

▷ Commonwealth literatures.

Maugham, William Somerset (1874–1965)
Novelist, short-story writer and dramatist. Educated at King's School, Canterbury, and Heidelberg University; he then studied medicine in London. His first novel, *Liza of Lambeth* (1897) shows the influence of Zola, an example of the growing importance of French influence on English fiction at the end of the 19th century. His semi-autobiographical novel *Of Human Bondage (*1915) made his name. Other novels include: *The Hero* (1901); *The Moon and Sixpence* (1919); *The Painted Veil* (1925); *The Casuarina Tree* (1926); *Cakes and Ale* (1930). The professional accomplishment of his novels gave him a wide foreign public, and after 1930 his reputation abroad was greater than at home, though interest in him revived here towards his 80th birthday. He celebrated his 80th year by the special republication of *Cakes and Ale*, a novel which satirizes the English propensity for admiring the 'Grand Old Men' among their writers. Some of his best fiction is in his short stories, in volumes such as *The Trembling of a Leaf* (1921), *The Mixture as Before* (1940). His plays were successful, but have lost interest now. They include: *Our Betters* (1917); *Caesar's Wife* (1919); *East of Suez* (1922); *The Constant Wife* (1926); *The Letter* (1927); *The Breadwinner* (1930); *Sheppey* (1933).

Bib: Maugham, R., *Somerset and All the Maughams*; Morgan, T., *Somerset Maugham*; Brander, L., *Somerset Maugham: A Guide*.

McEwan, Ian (b 1948)
Novelist and short-story writer. His first collection of stories, *First Love, Last Rites* (1975) gained immediate notoriety for its erotic, perverse and macabre concerns, which also figure in *In Between the Sheets* (1978). His first novel, *The Cement Garden* (1978) is a story of adolescent guilt, while *The Comfort of Strangers* (1981) is a dream-like narrative set in Venice and ending in violence. His recent work includes *The Child in Time* (1987) and *The Innocent* (1990). He has also written a television play, *The Imitation Game* (1981) and a screenplay, *The Ploughman's Lunch* (1983).

McGrath, John (b 1935)
One of the foremost writers of the political ▷ fringe during the 1970s and 80s. In 1971 he founded the 7:84 company (the name is based on a statistic which revealed that 7 per cent of the population owned 84 per cent of the country's wealth). The company was divided into two, between Scotland and England, in 1973. One of McGrath's most successful works was the popular entertainment *The Cheviot, the Stag and the Black, Black Oil* (1973), written for 7:84 Scotland. In this he compared the plundering of Scottish oil assets with the Highland Clearances. He has consistently insisted on disassociating himself from the theatre establishment and once said he would 'rather have a bad night in Bootle' than write a play for the ▷ National Theatre. His radical ideas about the politics of entertainment are recorded in his book, *A Good Night Out* (1981). Other plays are: *The Game's a Bogey* (1974); *Fish in the Sea* (1977); *Little Red Hen* (1977); *Yobbo Nowt* (1978); *Joe's Drum* (1979); *Blood Red Roses* (1981); *Swings and Roundabouts* (1981).

McKerrow, R. B. (Ronald Brownlees) (1872–1940)
Editor and bibliographer who was co-founder of the Malone Society (1906), dedicated to the study and editing of early and often neglected English drama. He wrote the seminal *An Introduction to Bibliography for Literary Students* (1927). He was one of the driving forces behind the 'New Bibliography' and is the author of the important *Prolegomena* (1939) for an Oxford edition of ▷ Shakespeare's works. This latter, which aimed at discovering an editorial methodology from ten selected texts, has proved an important milestone on the road to the new and revisionary Oxford University Press Shakespeare edited by Gary Taylor and Stanley Wells.

Mercer, David (1928–80)
British dramatist renowned for his television work as much as his stage plays, some of which have been performed by the ▷ Royal Shakespeare Company. He was one of the first to write serious plays for television dealing with the working class. Mercer's treatment of this subject has been accused of being excessively nostalgic and only his middle-class, not his working-class, characters are generally given any intellectual depth. Social alienation and madness are commonly the fate of those who move away from their class origins. Although he wrote from a Marxist perspective (▷ Marx, Karl) there is little optimism about the modern world in his plays. Television plays include: *The Generations* (1961–3); *Morgan, A Suitable Case for Treatment* (1962); *For Tea on Sunday* (1963); *In Two Minds* (1967); *On the Eve of Publication* (1968); *The Cellar and the Almond Tree* (1970); *Emma's Time* (1970). Stage plays include: *Ride a Cock Horse* (1965); *Belcher's Luck* (1966); *After Haggarty* (1970); *Duck Song* (1974); *Cousin Vladimir* (1978); *The Monster of Karlovy Vary* (1979); *Then and Now* (1979).
Bib: Trussler, S. (ed.), *New Theatre Voices of the Seventies*.

Metafiction
This term is applied to fictional writing which questions the relationship between reality and fiction through deliberately and self-consciously drawing attention to its own status as a linguistic construct. Examples would include ▷ John Fowles's *The French Lieutenant's Woman*.

Metalanguage
A term coined by the linguist L. Hjelmslev to describe a language which refers to *another language* rather than to non-linguistic objects, situations or events. In the words of ▷ Roland Barthes it is 'a second language in which one speaks about the first' (*Mythologies*). In this sense, metalanguage can be used as a means of reflecting on language itself.
▷ Metafiction.

Metre
From the Greek word meaning 'measure'. In poetry, metre is the measure of the rhythm of a line of verse, when the line is rhythmically systematic, *ie* can be divided into units of 'metrical feet'. The names for these feet all derive from ancient Greek verse. The commonest feet in use in English are as follows:

∪ /   ∪ /   ∪ /
Iambus *eg* the words 'again', 'revenge',
∪ /
'delight'.
∪ / ∪ / ∪ / ∪
'Iambics march from short to
/
long.'

/ ∪   / ∪   / ∪
Trochee *eg* the words 'never', 'happy',
/ ∪
'heartless'.
/ ∪ / ∪ / ∪
'Trochee trips from long to
/
short.'

∪ ∪ /   ∪ ∪ /
Anapest *eg* the words 'entertain',
∪ ∪ /   ∪ ∪ /
'supersede', 'engineer'.
∪ ∪ / ∪ ∪ / ∪
'With a leap and a bound the
∪ / ∪ ∪ /
swift anapaests throng.'

/ /   / /
Spondee *eg* the words 'maintain',
/ /   / /
'heartbreak', 'wineglass'
/ / / / /
'Slow spondee stalks, strong
/
foot . . .'

/ ∪ ∪   / ∪ ∪
Dactyl *eg* the words 'melody',
/ ∪ ∪   / ∪ ∪
'happiness', 'sorrowful'.
/ ∪ ∪
'. . . yet ill able
/ ∪ ∪ / ∪ ∪ /
'Ever to come up with dactyl
∪ / ∪ ∪
trisyllable.'

The illustrative lines are taken from Coleridge's mnemonic rhyme 'Metrical Feet' (the dactyl example in particular being a joke).

It is important to remember three points when analysing ('scanning') English verse:

1 Despite Coleridge's use of 'long' and 'short' for iambic and trochaic feet, these words are inappropriate to English metrical feet, which are composed of accented and unaccented syllables (two accented ones in the case of the spondee) irrespective of their length.

2 Except in the case of the iambus, it is unusual to find lines of verse composed entirely of the same foot; this is especially true of the spondee and the dactyl.

3 It is unwise to think of metre at all when reading a great deal of English verse. Old and Middle English alliterative verse was not metrical. In the late 19th and 20th centuries, many poets used inconsistent metrical forms, depending more on the natural rhythms of the English speaking voice (▷ Gerard Manley Hopkins).

Verse lines have names according to the number of feet they contain; much the commonest English line is the iambic ▷ pentameter (five feet). The hexameter has six feet, and is called an Alexandrine when it is iambic. Other lengths:

monometer = one foot;
dimeter = two feet;
trimeter = three feet;
tetrameter = four feet;
heptameter = seven feet;
octameter = eight feet.

▷ Free verse; Sonnet.

Mew, Charlotte (1869–1928)
Poet. Mew lived in London in the shadow of her oppressive family, and having had little educational advantages, published her first poems in ▷ *The Yellow Book*. Her small corpus of poetry was very well received by ▷ Thomas Hardy, ▷ John Masefield, Harold Monro and ▷ Walter de la Mare, whose influence secured her a civil list pension in 1923. Her most famous poem, 'The Farmer's Bride' (1916), deals with a difficult marital relationship, and is characteristic of the strength of her work in analysing suffering and loss. 'Madelaine in Church', a ▷ dramatic monologue, is perhaps Mew's most powerful text. She committed suicide after the death of her sister. The best recent edition of her work is the 1982 Virago collection, *Collected Poems and Prose*.

Middle Ages, The
A term used by historians to cover the period between the fall of the Roman Empire of the West (end of the 5th century) and the beginning of the ▷ Renaissance, conventionally dated from the extinction of the Roman Empire of the East (Byzantine Empire) in 1453.

In English history, however, it is common to think of the Middle Ages as extending from the Norman Conquest of 1066 until the end of the Wars of the Roses and the accession of Henry VII (first of the House of Tudor) in 1485. The period from the 5th to the 11th centuries is called loosely the Old English period. The term Middle Ages was first used by John Donne in a sermon in 1621.

▷ English language.

Middleton, Christopher (b 1926)
Poet, literary critic and translator. Middleton was born in Cornwall, educated at Cambridge and became a university lecturer in Germany, England and then America. He teaches German studies, and his work is influenced by German and French literature, although it is notoriously eclectic, drawing also on English ▷ Victorian poets, ▷ Dada and ▷ Spanish poetry. Middleton's work is both technically precise and extremely difficult – it employs highly disruptive techniques, disturbing conventional syntax and rhythm and in this lies its obscurity. His texts include: *Torse 3: Poems 1949–1961* (1962); *Our Flowers & Nice Bones* (1970); *The Lonely Suppers of W. V. Balloon* (1975); *Pataxanadu* (1976).

Milne, A. A. (Alan Alexander) (1882–1956)
Novelist, dramatist, children's writer. He was for many years assistant editor of *Punch*, and he became widely popular as the author of light comedies and novels. His earliest play is *Wurzel-Flummery* (1917) and his best known *Mr Pim Passes By* (1919). However he achieved fame by four ▷ children's books, centring on his son, Christopher Robin. Two of these are verse: *When We Were Very Young* (1924) and *Now We Are Six* (1927). The other two are prose stories, with Christopher Robin's teddy bear Winnie the Pooh as hero: *Winnie the Pooh* (1926); *The House at Pooh Corner* (1928). They have been translated into many languages; *Winnie the Pooh*, rather to its advantage, into Latin.

Mimesis
In Plato's *Republic* 'mimesis' is used to designate 'imitation', but in a derogatory way. The term is given a rigorous, positive meaning in Aristotle's ▷ *Poetics* where it is used to describe a process of selection and representation appropriate to tragedy: 'the imitation of an action'. Literary criticism

from Sir Philip Sidney onwards has wrestled with the problem of the imitative function of literary texts, but after ▷ Structuralism with its questioning of the referential function of all language, the term has taken on a new and problematic dimension. Mimesis has frequently been associated with the term ▷ 'realism', and with the capacity of language to reflect reality. At particular historical moments, *eg* the ▷ Renaissance, or the present time, when reality itself appears to be in question, then the capacity of language to represent reality is brought to the fore. The issue becomes even more complex when we realize that 'reality' may be something other than our experience of it. The debate has been carried on most vigorously at a theoretical level in the exchanges earlier this century between the Hungarian critic Georg Lukács, and the dramatist ▷ Bertolt Brecht. The nub of the debate between these two ▷ Marxist thinkers was how best to represent 'the deeper causal complexes of society' (Brecht). Brecht rejected the view propounded by Lukács that the novel was the literary form which pre-eminently represented social process, arguing that realism was a major political, philosophical and practical issue and should not be dealt with by literature alone. Such a view rejected the metaphysical implications which lay behind the Aristotelian notion of mimesis, in favour of a more historical analysis which saw literature as part of the process of social change.

Mo, Timothy (b 1953)
Novelist. Born in Hong Kong of an English mother and a Cantonese father and educated at St John's College, Oxford. He has worked as a journalist. His first novel was *The Monkey King* (1978), a lively story of family and business intrigue, set in Hong Kong and New Territories on the Chinese Mainland. *Sour Sweet* (1982) is the touching story of a Chinese family, first-generation immigrants in London, whose initial isolation is mitigated when they open a take-away, leading to comic cross-cultural confusions, until the father accidentally becomes involved in the world of the Triad gangs in Soho (the subject of a parallel narrative in the novel). *An Insular Possession* (1986) blends history and fiction in its account of conflicts between Britain and China over the opium trade in the 1830s and 1840s, as does *The Redundancy of Courage* (1991), which concerns an initially uncommitted Chinese hotel-proprietor who becomes involved in the resistance movement, after the American-backed Indonesian invasion of East Timor in 1975.

▷ Commonwealth literatures.

Modernism
Twentieth-century English literature may be divided into two phases: modernism and ▷ postmodernism. In both phases, changes in literary technique and subject matter are closely linked with comparable transformations in music, art and architecture. Modernism and postmodernism were also inspired by, and contributed to, social changes, and developments in philosophy, psychology, anthropology and science. Since the term 'modernism' was first used earlier in the 20th century, its meaning has developed and been revised. It now is agreed to mean the influential international movement in literature, drama, art, music and architecture which began in the latter years of the 19th century and flourished until at least the 1920s. Modernism was felt to be a reaction to ▷ realism and ▷ naturalism, undermining the representationalism (▷ mimesis) associated with those movements.In fiction the ▷ stream of consciousness novel was a prime example of modernism. In critical terms, modernist writing challenged the approaches of students and critics alike and so contributed to the development later in the century of new approaches to literature and reading. Literary modernism in England started during the first decade of the century, but World War I played a major part in its development, contributing especially to the sense of radical newness, of the apocalyptic and of destruction and desolation. The prolonged and massive slaughter of the war put paid to the Victorian sense of progress. In poetry, it was ▷ T. S. Eliot and ▷ Ezra Pound who were the leading spirits of modernism, Eliot through his poetry and his criticism; Pound to some extent in his poetry, but even more through his role as man of letters, theorist, starter of movements and champion of artists and writers. Reacting against the ▷ Romantics, and against the conventions of Edwardian poetry, these writers introduced ▷ free verse, fragmentary and innovative structures and allusive and eclectic modes of thought. The best-known example of these developments is Eliot's ▷ *The Waste Land* (1922). Powerful accounts of the experience of war are found in the work of the ▷ War poets, in particular ▷ Isaac Rosenberg, ▷ Wilfred Owen, ▷ Siegfried Sassoon, ▷ Edmund Blunden, Ivor Gurney and Charles Sorley, and later in David Jones's

In Parenthesis (1937). Some of the War poets had also been associated with the ▷ Georgian Poets, whose work appeared in Edward Marsh's five anthologies of 1912–22 and who, in technical terms, represented a relatively traditional strain in poetry. Three poets are best considered independently of movements (which are anyway somewhat arbitrary and temporary phenomena): ▷ W. B. Yeats, ▷ Thomas Hardy and ▷ Gerard Manley Hopkins. Yeats, the greatest of modern Irish poets, followed a unique line of development, from the aestheticism of his early work to the eloquent symbolic power of his major poetry of the 1920s and 30s. Hardy, though born in 1840, did not publish his poetry until 1898 (it appeared in eight volumes between 1898 and 1928). His idiosyncratic diction and metrical experiment were to influence, among others, ▷ Philip Larkin. Hopkins had died in 1889, but his lyrical and visionary work had appeared only in anthologies prior to 1918. Other poets who published major work before 1930 included ▷ D. H. Lawrence, ▷ Robert Graves and the Scottish poets ▷ Hugh MacDiarmid and ▷ Edwin Muir.

In the novel the modernist period is dominated by six major figures: ▷ Henry James, ▷ Joseph Conrad, ▷ James Joyce, ▷ Virginia Woolf, ▷ D. H. Lawrence and ▷ E. M. Forster. Each made a distinctive contribution to the modernist transformation of fiction. James's work is notable for a fine moral sense, a complex style, and subtle studies of human consciousness (▷ *The Ambassadors*; 1903); Conrad's for narrative experiment, irony, sense of history and tragic moral vision (▷ *Nostromo*; 1904); Joyce's for linguistic exuberance, broad humanity and structural richness (▷ *Ulysses*; 1922); Woolf's for the representation of the texture of consciousness and for symbolic and poetic qualities (▷ *To The Lighthouse*; 1927); Lawrence's for the exploration of the unconscious and a unique and unrelenting vision of human nature and history (▷ *The Rainbow*; 1915); Forster's for a blend of liberalism with human insight and symbolic power (▷ *A Passage to India*; 1924). Other writers who made significant contributions to modernism include ▷ Ford Madox Ford and ▷ Dorothy Richardson. Alternative modes of fiction were the popular, realistic, relatively conventional works of ▷ Arnold Bennett and ▷ John Galsworthy, the ▷ science fiction and social realism of ▷ H. G. Wells, and the tragicomic satire of ▷ Evelyn Waugh, ▷ Wyndham Lewis and ▷ Aldous Huxley.

In the theatre the early decades of the century were dominated by ▷ George Bernard Shaw, who created a drama of ideas which questioned prevailing assumptions and expounded his socialist views. The concern with contemporary social and moral problems in Shaw's work reflected the influence of the Norwegian dramatist ▷ Henrik Ibsen. In Ireland the ▷ Abbey Theatre, Dublin, became the centre of an Irish dramatic revival. In the first decade of the century the theatre staged ▷ J. M. Synge's poetic dramas of Irish peasant life, and in the 1920s the more naturalistic and overtly political tragicomedies of ▷ Sean O'Casey. In the 1930s, and again in the 1950s, ▷ T. S. Eliot attempted to revive verse drama in English, while ▷ W. H. Auden and ▷ Christopher Isherwood co-operated on plays which, while mixing verse and prose, owed something to the early expressionist work of the German dramatist ▷ Bertolt Brecht.

In the 1930s political concerns predominated in both fiction and poetry. A group of poets led by W. H. Auden employed the ideas of ▷ Marx and ▷ Freud and dealt directly with contemporary social issues such as unemployment, class conflict and the approach of war, as well as exploring psychological states. The main members of this group were ▷ Stephen Spender, ▷ Cecil Day-Lewis and ▷ Louis MacNeice. In the 1940s the Welsh poet ▷ Dylan Thomas achieved considerable popularity with his lyrical and rhetorical style of poetry. Novelists of importance who emerged during the 1930s and 40s included ▷ Graham Greene, ▷ George Orwell, Christopher Isherwood, ▷ Elizabeth Bowen, ▷ Joyce Cary and ▷ C. P. Snow.

Since 1945 two tendencies have been evident in English literature. One of these is identifiable with postmodernism considered as a phase of western culture, and is characterized by a continuing interest in experimental techniques, the influence of philosophy and literary theory (in particular ▷ existentialism, ▷ structuralism and ▷ post-structuralism) and a creative interchange with continental, American, Latin American and other literatures. The second tendency is a reaction against aesthetic and philosophical radicalism in favour of the reassertion of more traditional modes: this tendency has an English and anti-cosmopolitan streak. This division does not necessarily entail a polarization into opposed camps; both tendencies are sometimes found in the work of the same writer.

The reassertion of traditional modes was especially evident in the 1950s. The group of poets who became known as the ▷ Movement favoured clarity, irony, scepticism and a no-nonsense tone: these included ▷ Philip Larkin, ▷ Donald Davie and ▷ John Wain. Just as the Movement was a reaction against the influence of Symbolism, of Ezra Pound and of Yeats, so the modernist novel provoked a comparable reaction. The value of the realistic and satirical novel was reasserted by the work of the so-called ▷ 'angry young men', (such as ▷ John Osborne, ▷ John Braine, ▷ Alan Sillitoe and ▷ Kingsley Amis) who expressed a mood of alienation and revolt. Both these movements are, however, partly journalistic inventions, and of less importance than the individual bodies of work which emerged from them: Philip Larkin's sceptical, poignant and witty poetry; Kingsley Amis's entertaining and often acrimonious tales of English life. In the satirical and realistic vein, ▷ Angus Wilson is one of the most considerable post-war novelists, while ▷ Iris Murdoch, another writer who emerged in the 1950s, combines intricate tragicomic plots with philosophical and artistic concerns. Murdoch's sense of life as a battle of good and evil is shared by ▷ William Golding, ▷ Muriel Spark and ▷ Anthony Burgess; these writers blend elements of realistic narrative with post-modernist techniques such as intertextuality (sustained allusion to another literary work) and devices which draw attention to the contingency of narrative and its interpretation. In the novel, postmodernism has taken the form of a foregrounding of fictionality which undermines the mimetic illusion, or a multiplication of perspectives which emphasizes uncertainty and subjectivity. Such features are found particularly in the work of ▷ John Fowles, ▷ Lawrence Durrell, ▷ Bryan S. Johnson and ▷ Salman Rushdie. Rushdie also employs the mode of ▷ magic realism, developed primarily by Latin American novelists like Gabriel García Márquez (b 1928). The prose writings of ▷ Samuel Beckett have a Joycean linguistic playfulness, but their experimentalism is dominated by a relentless and progressive minimalism. Other notable areas of development in the post-war novel have been the feminist novel, ▷ science fiction, the fantasy novel, and ▷ horror fiction.

During the 1960s a number of major poetic talents emerged: ▷ Ted Hughes, ▷ Sylvia Plath, ▷ Charles Tomlinson, ▷ Geoffrey Hill and ▷ Seamus Heaney. All of these poets except Heaney were included in the anthology *The New Poetry* (1962). In the polemical introduction, Al Alvarez championed the cause of poetry which, absorbing the implications of psychoanalysis and World War II, abandoned the gentility of the Movement. Hughes's poetry of extremity, physicality, anthropomorphism and the creation of myth rapidly gained him popularity and a place on the school syllabus. Plath, like Eliot and Pound, came to England from the U.S.A.; she is best known for her powerfully sensuous and symbolic explorations of disturbed states of mind, which associate her with fellow Americans such as Robert Lowell and John Berryman. Charles Tomlinson and Geoffrey Hill are poets with smaller, but devoted followings. Tomlinson is very much a cosmopolitan poet, influenced by American and continental models, and by the painting of Cézanne; his poems render the process and significance of visual perception with an unerring subtlety. Hill's work combines religious and historical subject matter and an almost overpowering sense of tradition with an intensely physical imagination and a postmodernist scepticism about the ability of language to engage with reality. Heaney's work, with its sensuous precision, its involvement with Irish political issues and its deeply personal yet highly accessible concerns, has made him one of the most popular and admired of contemporary poets, pre-eminent among a flourishing group of Ulster poets, including ▷ Paul Muldoon, John Montague, ▷ Derek Mahon and Michael Longley.

The power of English drama to confront contemporary experience was revived in the 1950s by a new generation of dramatists who employed colloquial speech with an expressive and symbolic power which showed the influence of the leaders of modern European drama: ▷ Ibsen, ▷ Strindberg, ▷ Chekhov and Brecht. Foremost among them was Samuel Beckett, whose play *Waiting for Godot* (first published in Britain in 1955) initiated a new era with its existentialist preoccupations and anti-realist techniques. The ▷ Theatre of the Absurd of Beckett and Eugene Ionesco influenced the work of another of this generation, ▷ Harold Pinter, whose plays explore the ambiguities and failures of everyday communication through terse, minimalist dialogue and significant silences. Blending realism and sinister fantasy, they suggest the fear and violence underlying mundane experience. The dramatists of the 1950s reacted against the upper-middle-class milieu of the work of ▷ Noël Coward and ▷ Terence Rattigan. In the work of ▷ John Osborne and ▷ Arnold Wesker this took the form of so-called 'kitchen-sink drama', which deals with working-class life and social conflict. Since 1950 it has been the drama, more than any other form of English literature, which has directly addressed public issues and exhibited political commitment, frequently of a radical nature. These features were evident in the 1950s and 60s in the work of Wesker, ▷ John Arden and ▷ Edward Bond, and more recently in that of ▷ Howard Brenton, ▷ Howard Barker, ▷ Trevor Griffiths and ▷ David Edgar. Many of the dramatists mentioned here have been brought to public notice by the productions of the English Stage Company, whose home at the ▷ Royal Court Theatre in London has been a centre for innovatory drama since 1956. Another important development has been the success of ▷ fringe theatre in exploiting the dramatic potential of small, open performing spaces. Feminist drama has flourished, prominent exponents being ▷ Ann Jellicoe, ▷ Nell Dunn, ▷ Shelagh Delaney and ▷ Caryl Churchill. Three of the most popular of contemporary dramatists are ▷ Peter Shaffer, ▷ Alan Ayckbourn and ▷ Tom Stoppard. Shaffer's work has a wide range, embracing comedy, studies of obsession and creativity, and historical epic. Ayckbourn and Stoppard both make use of humour; Ayckbourn in farces of middle-class life, pervaded by a lurking desperation; Stoppard in witty, playful, parodic and allusive dramas which explore political and metaphysical issues.

Across the range of literary forms an increasing contribution is being made by writers from India, Africa, Australia, New Zealand, Canada, and the West Indies (▷ Commonwealth literatures). A primary characteristic of postmodernism as an era is the diversity and rapid circulation of culture, evident not only in the multi-cultural nature of contemporary literature in English, but also in the success of ▷ fringe theatre and small poetry presses and in the sheer range of styles and modes of literature currently available to a large public. But theories of postmodernism also suggest that cultural artefacts function increasingly as commodities, and this emphasizes the extent to which such diversity is dependent upon economic forces and political decision-making, and in these respects the future of literature is highly unpredictable.

▷ Postmodernism; Deconstruction; Symbolism; Aestheticism.

Mood
One of the five categories in which ▷ Genette analyses narrative discourse, mood is described by him as 'the regulation of narrative information' through the control of 'distance' and 'perspective'. The analysis of mood in a novel therefore includes the question of ▷ focalization.

▷ Narratology.

Moore, G. E. (1873–1958)
Philosopher. He lectured on philosophy at Cambridge from 1911 to 1925, when he became Professor. His principal book is *Principia Ethica* (1903); he also wrote *Ethics* (1912) and *Philosophical Studies* (1922). His philosophy was that of the 'New Realism', in opposition to the ▷ idealism of ▷ F. H. Bradley whose work was in the tradition of Hegel. Where the Idealists tended to a poetic conception of truth and ethics, rhetorically expressed and appealing to the emotions as much as to the reason, Moore appealed to the reason only, basing his arguments on common sense, and holding it to be the function of philosophy to clarify statements and arrive at fully intelligible definitions. At the same time, he argued that all experience is to be enjoyed, and that the richest possessions are aesthetic experience and personal friendship. He consequently had two kinds of influence, philosophical and literary. Philosophically, he was one of the starting points for ▷ Bertrand Russell and the Logical Positivists such as A. J. Ayer, but in literary circles he had considerable personal influence on the ▷ Bloomsbury Group, centred on the novelist ▷ Virginia Woolf and her husband Leonard. The Bloomsbury Group owed its cohesiveness to a cult of personal relations such as Moore advocated, and some of its members regarded the state of mind of perfect aesthetic appreciation as one of the aims of life.
Bib: Schilpp, P. A., *The Philosophy of Moore*; Johnstone, J. K. *The Bloomsbury Group*.

Moore, George (1852–1933)
Irish novelist. He combined an ▷ aestheticism in tune with the aesthetic movement at the end of the 19th century, and the Celtic revivalism that went with a part of it, with a ▷ naturalism which showed the influence of late 19th-century French literature, especially from the novelist Zola. His most famous novels are: *A Mummer's Wife* (1885); *Esther Waters* (1894); *Evelyn Innes* (1898); *Sister Theresa* (1901); *The Brook Kerith* (1916); *Héloise and Abélard* (1921). He was equally well known for his autobiographical studies: *Confessions of a Young Man* (1888); *Avowals* (1919, 1926); *Hail and Farewell* (1911–14) and *Conversations in Ebury Street* (1924). His

carefully worked style was more admired in his own day than it is now.

▷ Celtic Twilight.

Bib: Korg, J., in *Victoria Fiction* (ed. L. Stevenson); Brown, M. J., *Moore: a Reconsideration*; Sechler, R. P., *George Moore: 'a Disciple of Walter Pater'*; Yeats, W. B., in *Dramatis Personae*; Hough, G., in *Image and Experience*.

Morrison, Blake (b 1950)

Poet and critic. Morrison is a prominent figure in contemporary British poetry, perhaps more as a critic than a poet, and he has taught at London University and the Open University, as well as writing on poetry and fiction for *The Observer* and the *Times Literary Supplement*. He has published critical studies of ▷ the Movement and of ▷ Seamus Heaney, and is co-editor (with ▷ Andrew Motion) of *The Penguin Book of Contemporary British Poetry* (1982). His poetic works include *Dark Glasses* (1984) and *The Ballad of the Yorkshire Ripper* (1987).

Motion, Andrew (b 1952)

Poet and critic. Motion is a prolific young writer, who has also worked as a lecturer in English (at the University of Hull), and has edited the *Poetry Review*. His publications include (poetry): *The Pleasure Steamers* (1978); *Independence* (1981); *Secret Narratives* (1983); *Dangerous Play* (1984) and *Natural Causes* (1987); and (criticism): *The Poetry of Edward Thomas* (1978) and *Philip Larkin* (1982). Motion is currently working on the official biography of ▷ Larkin, who died in 1985.

Movement, The

One of the most important 'movements' in post-war British poetry, *the* Movement was really made into a coherent poetic body with the publication of three important anthologies: ▷ D. J. Enright's *Poets of the 1950s* (1955), Robert Conquest's *New Lines* and G. S. Frazer's *Poetry Now* (both 1956). As with any poetic school all of the prominent members of the Movement can ultimately be linked only through a tenuous range of connections, and indeed by 1957 its cohering impulse was dissolving. Some of its major figures are generally understood to be ▷ Kingsley Amis, Conquest and Enright, ▷ Donald Davie, ▷ Thom Gunn, ▷ Elizabeth Jennings, ▷ Philip Larkin and ▷ John Wain. The work which is covered by this umbrella term is sardonic, lucid and self-consciously ironic. Opposed to the romantic and apocalyptic tone of much 1940s poetry, especially that of ▷ Dylan Thomas and ▷ W. S. Graham, Movement poetry is meticulously crafted and witty, controlled and commonsensical.

Bib: Morrison, B., *The Movement*.

***Mrs Dalloway* (1925)**

A novel by ▷ Virginia Woolf. Set in London, it is the story of one day in the life of Clarissa Dalloway, the wife of Richard Dalloway, a Member of Parliament (the Dalloways appeared in Woolf's earlier novel, *The Voyage Out*). Clarissa spends the day preparing for a party she is to give that evening, a party which provides the culmination of the novel. The ▷ stream of consciousness narrative represents the thoughts of Clarissa and a range of other characters with whom she is acquainted or connected by chance occurrences of the day. Throughout the novel memories of the past are blended with present sensations, and the narrative builds up a highly poetic evocation of the atmosphere of London and of the interaction of different lives. The principal characters, apart from the Dalloways, are: their daughter Elizabeth and her embittered and envious tutor, Miss Kilman; Peter Walsh, with whom Clarissa was in love during her youth; Sally Seton, Clarissa's girlhood friend; and Lady Bruton, a society hostess. In contrast to this group, whose lives are linked, are Septimus Warren Smith and his wife Rezia; Septimus is in a highly disturbed state after his experiences during World War I and the news of his suicide intrudes on Clarissa's party, brought by Sir William Bradshaw, a manipulative psychiatrist whom Septimus has consulted. The novel ends with the affirmation of life with an awareness of loss and death.

Muir, Edwin (1887–1959)

Autobiographer, critic, poet, and novelist. He spent his childhood on a farm in the Orkney Islands, from which his father was compelled by economic hardship to move to Glasgow. For several years Muir struggled to earn his living in Glasgow as a clerk in various businesses; he became interested in socialism, and started writing. In 1919 he married, moved to London, and became a journalist. Thereafter, he travelled widely in Europe, and held a number of teaching posts. In 1940 he produced the first version of his autobiography, *The Story and the Fable*, expanded, revised and republished as *Autobiography* in 1954. The experiences of his own lifetime afforded him deep insight – social, cultural, spiritual. He had moved from a pre-industrial society in Orkney to 20th-century industrialism at its grimmest in Glasgow. He was deeply aware of the Scottish roots of his culture, and was liberated from their limitations partly through ▷ German literature and thought – ▷ Nietzsche, Heine, Hölderlin; in the 1930s he and his wife Willa translated Kafka. Experience of psychoanalysis liberated the deeper levels of his imagination, and led him, through illumination about the relationship of man to his natural environment, to strong and unusually lucid religious feeling. His *Autobiography* is a modern classic.

His birthplace, Orkney, has had some measure of detachment from the history of the rest of Scotland, and it is partly this that enabled him to show some of the most penetrating perceptions about modern Scottish culture in *Scottish Journey* (1935) and *Scott and Scotland* (1936). His critical works include: *Latitudes* (1924); *Transition* (1926); *The Structure of the Novel* (1928); *The Present Age* (1939); *Essays on Literature and Society* (1949).

Poetry: *First Poems* (1925); *Journeys and Places* (1925); *Chorus of the Newly Dead* (1926); *Variations on a Time Theme* (1934); *The Narrow Place* (1943); *The Voyage* (1946); *The Labyrinth* (1949); *Prometheus* (1954); *One Foot in Eden* (1956); *Collected Poems 1921–1958* (1960). He came to writing poetry late, through urgency of personal feeling rather than a professionally poetic concern with the medium. Nonetheless his later volumes embody some of his most moving insights, *eg* 'The Combat' from *The Labyrinth*.

His novels are: *The Marionette* (1927); *The Three Brothers* (1931); *Poor Tom* (1932). Biography: *John Knox* (1929).

▷ Autobiography; Scottish literature in English.

Bib: Knight, R., *Edwin Muir; an Introduction to His Work*; Butter, E., *Edwin Muir, Man and Poet*.

Muldoon, Paul (b 1951)
Poet. Born in County Armagh and educated at Queen's University, Belfast, Muldoon is one of the younger generation of poets to emerge from Northern Ireland in the last two decades (see also ▷ Seamus Heaney and ▷ Derek Mahon). He works for the B.B.C. His publications include: *Names and Addresses* (1978); *New Weather* (1973); *Mules* (1977) and *Why Brownlee Left* (1980).

▷ Irish literature in English.

Murdoch, Iris (b 1919)
Novelist and philosopher. Her novels are: *Under the Net* (1954); *Flight from the Enchanter* (1955); *The Sandcastle* (1957); *The Bell* (1958); *Bruno's Dream* (1960); *A Severed Head* (1961; dramatized 1963); *An Unofficial Rose* (1962); *The Unicorn* (1963); *The Italian Girl* (1964; dramatized 1967); *The Red and the Green* (1965); *The Time of the Angels* (1966); *The Nice and the Good* (1968); *A Fairly Honourable Defeat* (1970); *An Accidental Man* (1971); *The Black Prince* (1973); *The Sacred and Profane Love Machine* (1974); *A Word Child* (1975); *Henry and Cato* (1976); *The Sea, The Sea* (1978); *Nuns and Soldiers* (1980); *The Philosopher's Pupil* (1983); *The Good Apprentice* (1985); *The Book and the Brotherhood* (1987).

Iris Murdoch is one of the most prolific and the most popular of serious contemporary novelists. Born in Dublin and educated at Somerville College, Oxford and Newnham College, Cambridge, she has lectured in philosophy. Her husband is the critic John Bayley. Her profession as a philosopher is reflected in many aspects of her fiction. She has written a study of the work of Jean-Paul Sartre (*Sartre, Romantic Rationalist*, 1953) and her interest in, and dissent from, Sartre's ▷ existentialism is evident in her first two novels, which treat existential issues of identity and freedom. These concerns have persisted in her work, but *The Bell* and *The Time of the Angels* introduce religious themes, and since *The Nice and the Good* many of her novels have directly addressed ethical questions. *The Good Apprentice*, for example, explores the idea of a character who, without explicit religious faith, sets out to be good. Although her works are novels of ideas, they combine this with exciting and sometimes macabre plots, elements of the grotesque and supernatural and touches of social comedy. They are highly structured, both by the use of symbolism, and by the patterning of shifting personal relationships.

Her plays include: *The Three Arrows* (1970); *The Servants and the Snow* (1973); *Art and Eros* (1980). Other works are: *The Sovereignty of Good* (1970); *The Fire and the Sun: Why Plato Banished the Artists* (1977); *Acastos: Two Platonic Dialogues* (1986).

Bib: Byatt, A. S., *Iris Murdoch*; Conradi, P., *Iris Murdoch: the Saint and the Artist*; Johnson, D., *Iris Murdoch*; Todd, R., *Iris Murdoch*.

Murry, John Middleton (1889–1957)
Critic. His own struggles to achieve personal integration, his close relationship with ▷ D. H. Lawrence, and his marriage to ▷ Katherine

Mansfield, led him to write about a number of writers relating their personal lives to their art: *Dostoevsky* (1916), *Keats and Shakespeare* (1925), *Studies in Keats (*1930), *William Blake* (1933), *Shakespeare* (1936), *Jonathan Swift* (1954). He is perhaps best known for his controversial study of D. H. Lawrence, *Son of Woman* (1931) (▷ Carswell, Catherine), and for *The Problem of Style* (1922). He was editor of the *Athenaeum* from 1919 to 1921, and published the work of a number of major writers, including ▷ T. S. Eliot and ▷ Virginia Woolf.
Bib: Lea, F. A., *The Life of John Middleton Murry*.

Myers, Leopold Hamilton (1881–1944)
Novelist. His father, F. W. H. Myers (1843–1901) was a characteristic product of the 19th-century ▷ agnosticism so prominent among the educated classes; his reaction against it took the form of attempts to prove the existence of the soul by scientific experiment; he was one of the founders of the Society for Psychical Research. The son's concern with the spiritual life took the form of seeking answers to the question 'Why do men choose to live?' His chief opponents in his pursuit of the answer were not scientific rationalists in the tradition of T. H. Huxley, (1825–95) but aesthetes of the Bloomsbury tradition, who left moral experience to look after itself while they cultivated enjoyment of 'states of mind'. He also regarded the great influence on English writing of the French novelist ▷ Marcel Proust (1871–1922) as pernicious, because Proust likewise esteemed experience aesthetically and not morally. Myers considered that this led to the trivializing of life, and his novels dramatize the opposition between those who interpret experience through moral discrimination and those who vulgarize it by regarding it as a means to aesthetic experience only; from the latter evil arises. He regarded civilized society as corrupted by its moral indifference.

His first novel, *The Orissers* (1922) presents the issue in bare terms, but his principal work was the sequence of novels about 16th-century India, published together as *The Near and the Far* in 1943. Myers chose the remote setting of India under the Emperor Akbar because he wanted to escape from the secondary preoccupations of daily life in modern England, and to treat moral and spiritual issues with the large scope which the India of that date, with its multiplying religions and philosophies, afforded him. Evil is represented in the novel through Akbar's son Prince Daniyal, intelligent, artistic, but morally nihilistic, and rival of his merely stupid brother Salim for succession to the throne. Good is expressed through the character of the Guru (teacher) of the last section (*The Pool of Vishnu*): 'All communion', he says, 'is through the Centre. When the relation of man and man is not through the Centre it corrupts and destroys itself.' In his later years he became a ▷ Communist. He committed suicide in 1944. Other novels include: *The Clio* (1925); *Strange Glory* (1936).

▷ Bloomsbury Group.
Bib: Bantock, G. H., *L. H. Myers: A Critical Study*.

N

Naipaul, V. S. (Vidiadhar Surajprasad) (b 1932)
Trinidadian novelist of Indian descent. Educated at Queens Royal College, Port of Spain, Trinidad, and Oxford University, he settled in England in 1950. His brother was the novelist Shiva Naipaul (1945–85). V. S. Naipaul is the most admired of contemporary Caribbean novelists writing in English and has won many literary awards. His work is concerned with personal and political freedom, the function of the writer and the nature of sexuality, and is characterized by fastidiousness, clarity, subtlety, and a detached irony of tone. His earlier novels, *The Mystic Masseur* (1957), *The Suffrage of Elvira* (1958) and *Miguel Street* (1959) convey both the vitality and the desolation of Trinidadian life. *The Mimic Men* (1967) is a satirical examination of the economic power structure of an imaginary West Indian island. *A House for Mr Biswas* (1961), often regarded as his masterpiece, tells the tragicomic story of the search for independence and identity of a Brahmin Indian living in Trinidad. His other novels are: *Companion (*1963); *In A Free State* (1971); *Guerillas* (1975); *A Bend in the River* (1979). Naipaul has also produced criticism, journalism, autobiography and travel writing, including: *The Middle Passage* (1962); *An Area of Darkness* (1964); *A Congo Diary* (1980); *Finding the Centre* (1984).

▷ Commonwealth literatures.

Bib: Hamner, R. D. (ed.), *Critical Perspectives on V. S. Naipaul.*

Narayan, R. K. (Rasipuran Krishnaswami) (b 1906)
Indian novelist and short-story writer. His novels are: *Swami and Friends* (1935); *The Bachelor of Arts* (1937); *The Dark Room* (1938); *The English Teacher* (1945); *Mr Sampath* (1949); *The Financial Expert* (1952); *Waiting for the Mahatma* (1955); *The Guide* (1958); *The Man Eater of Malgudi* (1961); *The Vendor of Sweets* (1967); *The Painter of Signs* (1976); *A Tiger for Malgudi* (1983); *Talkative Man* (1986). His novels are set in the imaginary southern Indian community of Malgudi, based on the town of Mysore, which he uses to epitomize Indian culture from the days of the Raj to the present. The early novels show the continuing influence of British culture, in particular on the education system, and contain elements of ▷ autobiography. His work attains a new seriousness with *The English Teacher*, which is based on his own marriage and the early death of his wife. His mature work deals with spirituality and with human weakness, corruption failure and lack of fulfilment in an ironic and sceptical manner, supported by the vivid realization of the life of the town. *The Guide*, the story of a con man who becomes a saint, is one of his outstanding works, while *A Tiger for Malgudi* represents an excursion into a fantasy mode; drawing on the Hindu doctrine of reincarnation, it has a tiger as its hero and narrator. Story collections are: *Malgudi Days* (1943); *Dodu* (1943); *Cyclone* (1944); *An Astrologer's Day* (1947); *Lawley Road* (1956); *A House and Two Goats* (1970); *Old and New* (1981); *Malgudi Days* (1982) (not the same as the 1943 volume); *Under The Banyan Tree* (1985). Narayan has also written travel literature, memoirs, essays and versions of the Indian epics *The Ramayana* and *The Mahabharata*.

▷ Commonwealth literatures.

Bib: Walsh, W., *R. K. Narayan: a Critical Appreciation.*

Narratology
The systematic study of the structures, forms and modalities of narrative, including questions of temporal arrangement or tense (▷ order, ▷ duration, ▷ frequency), ▷ mood (the manner of narration and point of view, including ▷ focalization), and ▷ voice (the identity and relationship to the action of the ▷ narrator and narratee). Early considerations of narratological questions are found in ▷ Henry James's Prefaces (1907–09) and ▷ E. M. Forster's book ▷ *Aspects of the Novel* (1927). Wayne Booth's *The Rhetoric of Fiction* (1961) inaugurated a more wide-ranging and systematic approach, while the influence of ▷ Structuralism produced the rigorous analysis of categories of narrative typified by ▷ Gérard Genette's *Narrative Discourse* (1980). There is a more accessible summary of this approach in Shlomith Rimmon-Kenan, *Narrative Fiction: Contemporary Poetics* (1983).

Narrator
A fictional person or consciousness who narrates all or part of a text. A narrator may be a character within a story, who then tells a story, such as Marlow in ▷ Conrad's ▷ *Heart of Darkness*; this is known as an intradiegetic narrator. Alternatively, a narrator may be extradiegetic, that is, outside the story that he or she narrates, like the narrator of Fielding's *Tom Jones* (who has a strong personality, but does not participate in the story as such), or like the largely impersonal and uncharacterized narrator of ▷ Henry James's ▷ *The Ambassadors*. Such extradiegetic narrators are different from the ▷ implied

author since they may be ▷ unreliable narrators.

Nationalism

The emotion or the doctrine according to which human egotism and its passions are expanded so as to become identical with the nation state. As a widespread phenomenon it is usually dated from the American War of Independence (1775–83) and from the ▷ French Revolution and the wars that followed it. This makes it an especially 19th- and 20th-century phenomenon, which it undoubtedly is, but on the other hand intense national self-consciousness existed among the older European nations before, though without the fanaticism which has been characteristic of it since 1790.

Nationalistic feelings have been exploited by various fascist and totalitarian movements in the 20th century, and were strongly deployed by the Nazi Party in Hitler's Germany up to and during World War II. More positively, nationalism has also been a potent aspect of various revolutionary movements in colonial countries who have sought and gained independence during this century. Writers in ▷ Commonwealth countries often discusss these implications of nationalism, and, from the other side, those writers involved in anti-fascist campaigns (for instance, 1930s poets such as ▷ W. H. Auden and ▷ Stephen Spender) have explored the negative ramifications of nationalism.

National Theatre, The

The idea of a national theatre in London had existed since the 18th century. Serious efforts to create such an institution began early this century with the publication in 1903 of *The National Theatre: A Scheme and Estimates*, by William Archer and ▷ Harley Granville-Barker. Enthusiastic lobbying of governments continued after World War I and by 1938 a fund of £150,000 had been raised. However, it was not until 1962 that a National Theatre Board was established. This body created a National Theatre company led by ▷ Sir Laurence Olivier, which was based at the ▷ Old Vic whilst a new theatre was built for it on the South Bank at Waterloo. This was finally completed in 1976; the theatre has three auditoria: the Lyttelton, Olivier and Cottesloe theatres, providing a proscenium stage, an open stage and a workshop studio. The first general director was ▷ Sir Peter Hall, who was replaced by Richard Eyre in 1988. Current associate directors are Bill Bryden, Howard Davies, William Dudley and Peter Gill. The company policy is to present a diverse repertoire, embracing classic, new and neglected plays from the whole of world drama and to give audiences a choice of at least six different productions at any one time.
Bib: Elsom, J. and Tomalin, N., *The History of the National Theatre*.

Naturalism

In literature, a school of thought especially associated with the novelist Émile Zola. It was a development of ▷ realism. The Naturalists believed that imaginative literature (especially the novel) should be based on scientific knowledge, and that imaginative writers should be scientifically objective and exploratory in their approach to their work. This meant that environment should be exactly treated, and that character should be related to physiological heredity. Influential in France and Germany, the movement counts for little in Britain; the novelists George Gissing and ▷ Arnold Bennett show traces of its influence in the treatment of environment in relation to character.

▷ French literature.

New criticism

This term is given to a movement which developed in the late 1940s in the U.S.A., and which dedicated itself to opposing the kind of criticism that is associated with ▷ Romanticism, and 19th-century realism. The 'practical criticism' of ▷ I. A. Richards was an influential stimulus to this movement in which emphasis was placed upon the self-contained nature of the literary text. In the work of 'new' critics such as Cleanth Brooks, W. K. Wimsatt, John Crowe Ransom, Allen Tate, and R. P. Blackmur, concern with the 'intention' of the writer was replaced by close reading of particular texts, and depended upon the assumption that any literary work was self-contained. New criticism placed a particular emphasis upon poetry, and asserted, in the words of Archibald MacLeish, that the individual poem 'must not mean but be'.

New historicism

A theoretical movement which developed in America in the 1980s, partly as a reaction against the ahistorical approaches of ▷ new criticism and the unselfconscious historicism of earlier critics. New historicism draws upon ▷ Marxist criticism in its emphasis upon political and social context and rejection of individual aspiration and universalism, but at the same time it insists that historical context can never be recovered objectively.

New historicists do not assume that literature reflects reality and that these 'reflections' enable the reader to recover without distortion the past presented in the texts. Rather, they look for an interplay between text and society, which can never be presented neutrally. Moreover, readers must be aware of their *own* historical context: we read texts from the perspective of our own age and can never perfectly re-create history.

▷ Cultural materialism; Marx, Karl; Poetics.
Bib: Greenblatt, S., *Renaissance Self-fashioning*; Howard, J. E. and O'Connor, M. F., *Shakespeare Reproduced*; Tennenhouse, L., *Power on Display*; Veeser, H. A., *The New Historicism*.

Newspapers
Periodicals resembling newspapers began in a small way in the reign of James I; in the decades of the Civil War and the Interregnum they increased in number owing to the need of either side to engage in propaganda. From 1695 this form of press ▷ censorship was abandoned; newspapers and weekly periodicals began to flourish.

The first English daily, the *Daily Courant*, a mere news-sheet, began in 1702, but in the earlier part of the 18th century papers more nearly resembling what we now know as the weekly reviews were of greater importance, and leading writers conducted them, *eg* Daniel Defoe's *The Review* (thrice weekly – 1704–13); Steele's *Tatler* (thrice weekly – started 1709); Steele and Addison's *Spectator* (daily – started 1711); and the *Examiner* (started 1710), to which the chief contributor was Jonathan Swift. Samuel Johnson's *Rambler* (1750) was of the same kind. Of these men, only Defoe resembled fairly closely what we nowadays regard as a journalist as distinct from a man of letters.

The first attempt to reach a mass circulation was made through this kind of periodical by William Cobbett with his *Weekly Political Register* (started 1802), and in 1808 Leigh Hunt's weekly *Examiner*, directed to a more educated public though with less remarkable literary merit, began to rival Cobbett's paper as a medium of radical comment and criticism.

Of daily papers founded in the 18th century, the *Morning Post* (started 1772) survived until 1936, and ▷ *The Times* (started 1785) is today the daily with the greatest prestige, though it has a comparatively small circulation. Other important dailies with a shorter life were the *Morning Chronicle* (1769–1862), and the *Morning Herald* (1780–1869). Both reached peak circulations of about 6,000. To reach the very large circulations of today, newspapers had to await the abolition of the stamp duty – a tax on newspapers – in 1855. The Stamp Tax was started in 1712. It was a method of restricting circulations by raising the prices of newspapers. The government of the day resented criticism of its policies but did not dare revive the Licensing Act, the lapsing of which in 1695 was really the start of the British freedom of the press. The abolition of the tax, together with the advent of cheap paper and a nationwide potential public thanks to universal literacy, led to a new kind of newspaper at the end of the 19th century. Alfred and Harold Harmsworth, later Lord Northcliffe and Lord Rothermere, founded the *Daily Mail* in 1869; by 1901 it was selling a million copies. Other popular newspapers followed it with steadily increasing circulations.

Several unfortunate consequences have followed this development:

1 Much ▷ journalism has degenerated into mere commerce, so that news is regarded as what is most saleable, *ie* what appeals most readily to the baser and more easily roused human appetites.

2 Newspapers, in order to keep their prices down, have come to rely on advertising revenue, which is attracted chiefly to those with very large circulations so that some with smaller circulations have been eliminated.

3 The British newspapers have divided rather sharply into the serious ones with a large influence but a small circulation, and the popular ones or tabloids, which often achieve their large circulations by irresponsible appeals to the baser public tastes. Finally, modern newspapers, as great capitalistic enterprises, tend to be right wing politically, so that left-wing opinion is underrepresented in the daily press. However, British newspapers are jealous of their independence: they are quick to resist any tendency by the government to check their freedom of expression. Since the war, the Press Council has been established for the purpose of limiting the abuse of this freedom by, for instance, the infringement of personal privacy; however, its powers are limited to public rebuke, and it has no power to penalize or censor newspapers.

The 20th-century weekly reviews have seldom been able to compete with the daily papers in the size of their circulations. However, the strong tradition of weekly journalism inherited from the 18th and 19th centuries ensure that the 'weeklies' have large influence among the intelligentsia. The oldest of the influential weeklies is the *Spectator* which has no connection with Addison's periodical, but was founded in 1828. It is conservative and is counterbalanced by ▷ *The New Statesman and Society* on the left. The most authoritative literary periodical in Britain is *The Times Literary Supplement*, a weekly, which is published by *The Times* newspaper.

New Statesman and Society, The
The leading left-wing weekly periodical of the intelligentsia. It was founded in 1913; its Conservative counterpart is ▷ *The Spectator*. In politics it has always followed a general line of ▷ Fabian socialism.

New Theatre, The
The present Albery Theatre in St Martin's Lane was known as the New Theatre from its opening in 1903 to 1973.

Nichols, Grace (b 1950)
Poet and novelist. Born in Guyana, and educated at the University of Guyana, Nichols came to live in Britain in 1977. Her publications include a biting attack on colonialism in *I is a Long Memoried Woman* (1983) (which won the Commonwealth Poetry Prize), and the playfully ironic *The Fat Black Woman's Poems* (1984). She also writes ▷ children's books.

▷ Commonwealth literatures.

Nichols, Peter (b 1927)
British dramatist whose first major success was with *A Day in the Death of Joe Egg* in 1967, a serious comedy about the struggles of a family with a spastic child. This was first seen at the Glasgow Citizen's Theatre and later transferred to London. In 1969 *The National Health* was produced at the ▷ National Theatre. Again Nichols used comedy to dramatize a serious subject, in this case terminal illness and undignified death. His more recent plays are: *Passion Play* (1980); *Poppy*, a musical, (1982); *A Piece of My Mind* (1986).

Nietzsche, Friedrich Wilhelm (1844–1900)
German philosopher. He challenged the concepts of 'the good, the true, and the beautiful' as, in their existing form of abstract values, a decadent system at the mercy of the common man's will to level distinctions of all kinds. He set his hope on the will to power of a new race of men who would assert their own spiritual identities. Among his more famous works are a book on the philosopher Schopenhauer and the composer Wagner, whom he regarded as his own teachers: *Unzeitgemässe Betrachtungen* ('Thoughts out of Season'; 1876); *Die Fröhliche Wissenschaft* ('The Joyful Wisdom'; 1882); *Also sprach Zarathustra* ('Thus spake Zarathustra'; 1891).

Critic Walter Kaufmann has argued for Nietzsche's position as one of the important progenitors of ▷ existentialism, and he had a considerable influence on some of the major English writers in the first quarter of this century. His ideas inspired ▷ George Bernard Shaw in the latter's belief in the Superman-hero as the spearhead of progress, *eg* his conception of Joan of Arc in his play *Saint Joan*, and ▷ D. H. Lawrence wrote in Nietzsche's spirit in his affirmation of spontaneous living from deep sources of energy in the individual – human 'disquality' (see ▷ *Women in Love*, ch. 8) as opposed to democratic egalitarianism, although Lawrence also criticized (his conception of) Nietzsche's notion of Will to Power. Nietzsche also had a strong influence on the development of ▷ Freudian psychoanalysis, and this is indicative of the contradictory responses he has provoked in his readers: Lawrence was a vehement critic of Freud, and Freudian psychoanalysis is incompatible with existentialism, yet Nietzsche is said to have influenced all three. The Irish poet ▷ W. B. Yeats also affirmed a natural aristocracy of the human spirit, and saw in Nietzsche a continuation of the message of the poet William Blake (1757–1827), who preached the transcendance of the human 'identity' over the 'self', which is defined and limited by the material environment. In recent criticism Nietzsche's work has been re-evaluated by ▷ post-structuralist theory, especially with regard to his discussion of metaphor and metonymy and the privileging of a rhetorical reading of philosophical texts.

Nietzsche is also an important figure in the development of ▷ deconstruction, and (although deeply critical of the whole notion of 'influence'), has strongly influenced the writing of Georges Bataille, ▷ Michel Foucault and ▷ Jacques Derrida.

▷ German Influence on English Literature.

Bib: Deleuze, G., *Nietzsche and Philosophy*; Descombes, V., *Modern French Philosophy*; Kaufmann, W., *Nietzsche: Philosopher, Psychologist, Antichrist*.

Nineteenth Century, The
A monthly review founded in 1877 by J. T. Knowles, its first editor. It was renamed *The*

Nineteenth Century and After in 1900, and *The Twentieth Century* in 1950. It was distinguished for bringing together leading antagonists of opposing views. Contributors included Ruskin, Gladstone, T. H. Huxley, ▷ Beatrice Webb, William Morris, Ouida and ▷ Oscar Wilde.

Nineties Poets
The group of poets centred around the Rhymer's Club in the 1890s, including Lionel Johnson (1867–1902), Ernest Dowson (1867–1900) and Arthur Symons (1865–1945). The Rhymer's Club met at the Cheshire Cheese café in Fleet Street, immortalized by ▷ W. B. Yeats in *The Trembling of the Veil* and 'The Grey Rock', and published two volumes of its members' verse in 1891 and 1894. Nineties poetry was part of the *fin-de-siècle* ▷ Aesthetic movement. Strongly influenced by French (▷ French literature) culture and particularly French ▷ Symbolist poetry, it was also a development of the work and ideas of Algernon Swinburne, Walter Pater and the Pre-Raphaelite Brotherhood. The confessional and decadent quality of their work, together with the incidence of untimely death in their lives, led Yeats to label them 'The Tragic Generation' in his *Autobiographies*. They were important in their influence on poets like Yeats and ▷ Ezra Pound. Much of their work was published in the journals ▷ *The Yellow Book* and *The Savoy* (which Symons edited).
Bib: Stanford, D., *Poets of the Nineties*; Thornton, R. K. R., *Poetry of the 'Nineties*.

Noh plays
A kind of drama practised in Japan since the 15th century. It is highly formal, austere, and ritualistic, making a great part of its effect through ▷ symbolism. Its artistic economy and symbolism have greatly interested some Western writers in the 20th century – see the book, *Noh, or Accomplishment* by Fenollosa and ▷ Pound. The poet ▷ W. B. Yeats imitated the form in some of his experiments to revive the verse drama, *eg At the Hawk's Well* (1917).

Nonsense literature
This covers several kinds of literature, which have in common that they all in some way deliberately defy logic or common sense, or both. In English folk literature, many ▷ nursery rhymes come into the category. The most important kind, however, is undoubtedly in ▷ children's literature, especially the poems of Edward Lear and the *Alice* stories by Lewis Carroll, both of which are to be taken seriously as literature. Both writers are ▷ Victorian and this perhaps accounts for their imaginative depth; they wrote in a period of intense mental restlessness before the time of ▷ Freud and thus they gave themselves wholly to their fantasies, undisturbed by the idea that they might be betraying secrets of their own nature. Modern writers, *eg* ▷ James Joyce in his ▷ *Finnegans Wake*, will as fearlessly reveal their depths, but it will not be to children. Another reason why nonsense literature reached its peak in the Victorian period is perhaps that this was almost the earliest period when intelligent minds considered that children were worth writing for merely in order to amuse them, and not to elevate their minds. Twentieth-century writers in plenty have thought children worth amusing but the child-public is now a recognized one, whereas Lear and Carroll wrote for a few young friends; they were thus as much concerned with their own interest and amusement as with that of their audience.

***Nostromo* (1904)**
A novel by ▷ Joseph Conrad. The setting is an imaginary South American state called Costaguana, intended to be typical of that continent; all the events occur in or near Sulaco, capital city of the Occidental Province in Costaguana. At the beginning of the novel, Costaguana is ruled by a brutal and corrupt dictator after a short period of enlightened and liberal rule. The Occidental Province, however, remains a refuge of enlightenment and comparative prosperity, thanks partly to its geographical isolation from the rest of the country, and mainly to the existence of a large silver mine, run by an Englishman, Charles Gould, who secures the financial support of an American millionaire. In outline, the story is the history of how the Occidental Republic establishes its independence of the rest of the country, but at the same time loses the ideals which inspired it in the struggle.

Each of five main characters serves as a focus for a strand of narrative:

1 Charles Gould (nicknamed 'King of Sulaco'), in his struggles to save the mine from ruin by the corrupt government, becomes the centre of the party of freedom and justice; but he becomes increasingly dehumanized by his preoccupations, and estranged from his wife, whose values of humaneness and compassion are betrayed, despite the eventual triumph of her husband's party.

2 Captain Mitchell, the Harbourmaster, is another Englishman; stupid, but honest and courageous, he is unable to see beneath the

surface of events, and is used by Conrad to record these deceptive appearances.

3 Gian'Battista Fidanza, the Italian chief of the dockworkers, is universally known as 'Nostromo' ('Our Man'). He has a romantic pride in the devotion of his men, and in the knowledge that Mitchell, Gould, and their associates have complete confidence in his integrity. His spiritual downfall, unknown to any but himself, is due to his desire to preserve the appearance of integrity while yielding to secret dishonesty.

4 Martin Decoud is the journalist of the Sulacan revolution; he is totally French by education and culture, though not by descent. He is cynically entertained by the spectacle of Costaguaneran politics, but romantically attached to Antonia Avellanos, daughter of José, a Sulacan scholar and liberal politician. He dies of the physical isolation brought upon him by circumstances, since his highly cultivated consciousness is incapable of sustaining a sense of his own reality when the spectacle of events and the woman he loves are removed from him.

5 Dr Monygham is an Irishman, embittered by his self-contempt arising from his betrayal, under torture, of his political associates. His humanity is preserved by his devotion to Mrs Gould, who is for him the uncontaminated embodiment of what is good in human nature.

These are only the chief characters, and they do not exhaust the novel's large cast. They are united by the theme of individual isolation even in co-operation with one another, and by a discrete pattern of symbols, of which the chief is the silver of the mine. This operates at first as an instrument of liberation, and later as a force of corruption; all the time it is a symbol of the illusiveness of human idealism. The novel depicts the pervasive and debasing effects of 'material interests' (primarily the economic power of U.S. business). The narrative structure is highly complex, and uses shifts of chronology and retrospective narration to combine a detailed account of 17 days of crisis with a sense of the broad sweep of historical events.

***Nouveau roman* (new novel)**

A French literary movement originating in the late 1950s and associated principally with Nathalie Sarraute (b 1902), Claude Simon (b 1913), Michel Butor (b 1926), Robert Pinget (b 1919) and Alain Robbe-Grillet (b 1922). Their common concern was a challenge to narrative assumptions based on strictures of the orderly unfolding of plot and life-like characters moving in a recognizable universe. These assumptions, however widely held, suppose that literature is mimetic, that it imitates life. The *nouveau roman* set out to challenge the illusion of reference (that the novel 'refers' to life) insofar as reference is tied to representation. It held that the so-called naturalness of narrative was a set of artifices to which we had become accustomed and that narrative order and significance were an illusion fostered by the omniscient author. For the 'new' novelists, representation is not an *a priori* given; it is produced. Drawing on the work of André Gide and ▷ Marcel Proust, notably Gide's *mise en abyme* technique, the *nouveau roman* will therefore expose its own means of production and raise the problem of its own narrative existence. Correspondingly, the role of the reader is also revised. He or she is called upon to co-author the text, to act not as a passive recipient of information, but as an active producer of meanings. Indeed, given the fragmentary or elliptical nature of *nouveau roman* narrative presentation, the reader's active endeavours are an inevitability. The author is thus not the final guarantor of meaning and the reader's search for meaning is often thematized as an (impossible) attempt to solve an enigma (the *nouveau roman* frequently adopts the detective story format).

The impact of the *nouveau roman* was greatly magnified by the fact that the practice of novel writing was accompanied by thorough-going critical reflection on that practice. The novelists themselves were also heavily engaged in theory and frequently worked alongside professional academic theoreticians or were allied to magazines such as ▷ *Tel Quel*. Of the original group of new novelists, Robbe-Grillet and Simon are still strong practitioners. While the mainstream of the English novel has been little affected, the techniques of the *nouveau roman* have influenced writers such as ▷ Christine Brooke-Rose and ▷ Brigid Brophy. In the 1970s there emerged the new new novel (*nouveau nouveau roman*), centring on the novelist and theorist Philippe Sollers (b 1936) and displaying many of the traits of ▷ deconstructive and ▷ post-structuralist principles.

Bib: Robbe-Grillet, A., *Pour un Nouveau Roman* (Towards a new novel).

Nouveaux Philosophes, Les

A title coined by the magazine *Les Nouvelles littéraires* in June 1976 to describe a group of writers among whom the most prominent are André Glucksmann (*Les Maîtres penseurs*, 1977; reviewed by Michel Foucault) and

Bernard-Henri Lévy (*La Barbarie à visage humain*, 1977; *L'Idéologie française*, 1981). The group combined certain traits of Foucault and ▷ Jacques Lacan (often simplified and distorted) with right-wing views – hostility to ▷ Marxism, vague spiritual yearning and finding the source of all value in the individual. As a group, their influence was at its height in the late 1970s and is now played out (it was in any case media-promoted), but Glucksmann and Lévy are still well known.

Novella
A long short story or short novel, such as ▷ Joseph Conrad's ▷ *Heart of Darkness* (1902), ▷ Henry James's *The Aspern Papers* (1888), or ▷ D. H. Lawrence's *The Virgin and the Gipsy* (1930).

Nuclear power
After World War II there was enormous enthusiasm for the utilizing of nuclear energy, the turning of swords into ploughshares, and Britain and the U.S.A. rapidly became involved in this, with the ancillary aim of creating the correct materials for their bombs. The use of nuclear energy was expected to be cheap and clean; the reality is less clear. Costs are hard to determine, being inextricably connected with weapon programmes and also with the governments' wish to promote a new technology. Little thought was given until quite late in the development of nuclear power about how to dispose of the waste products: far from being clean it produces extremely hazardous by-products. The shortage of conventional fuel in the mid-1970s led to rapid building programmes in many parts of the world, not least in the U.S.A., and although the technology attempted to meet every contingency, it was, almost inevitably, flawed. After a well-publicized accident in the U.S.A. at Three-Mile Island in 1979 (in which no one was seriously hurt and little if any radioactive material escaped) the American programme of nuclear building was doomed: the incident revealed that despite all the care, accidents could still happen. Other countries did not respond to the incident with the same decisiveness and outside the U.S.A. the building of nuclear power plants continued, even in countries where there is no reason to believe safety standards will be high. In 1986 a reactor in Chernobyl in the U.S.S.R. exploded, releasing vast amounts of radioactivity into the atmosphere and causing certain produce to be unsafe for human consumption as far away as Britain. Although it was possible to point to special failings in the Soviet designs and operating procedures, it nevertheless incurred widespread doubts about nuclear power throughout the world. It was also instrumental in revealing hitherto suppressed facts: it was learned that the British nuclear programme had had a serious fire and release of nuclear radiation in the 1950s but at that time official secrecy had hidden from the public the true scale and seriousness of the event.

The threat of nuclear war and the guilt associated with the capacity to produce such destruction have been powerful influences on imaginative writing since 1945. Fear, too, of a governmental secrecy which jeopardizes the lives of its citizens and of the world in the interests of power politics, as well as fantasies of life after the Bomb, are common themes. See Nevil Shute's *On The Beach* (1957), Russell Hoban's *Riddley Walker* (1980) and the films *Silkwood* (1983) and *Defence of the Realm* (1985).

Since the end of the Cold War, however, the threat of nuclear war has diminished, with both sides signing disarmament treaties, although less developed countries who have recently gained the capacity to deploy nuclear weapons are increasingly the focus of concern for anti-nuclear campaigners.

▷ CND.

Nursery rhymes
A body of folk verse, some of it very ancient, some of it being concealed comment on political events, some of it apparently never having had any meaning.

O

Objective correlative
An expression first used by the critic and poet ▷ T. S. Eliot, in his essay on ▷ Shakespeare's play, *Hamlet* (1919). Eliot describes Shakespeare's play as an artistic failure because it 'is full of some stuff that the writer could not drag to life, contemplate, or manipulate into art'. He goes on: 'The only way of expressing emotion in the form of art is by finding an "objective correlative"; in other words, a set of objects, a situation, a chain of events which shall be the formula of that *particular* emotion; such that when the external facts . . . are given, the emotion is immediately evoked'. He then instances the sleep-walking scene in *Macbeth* as a successful 'objective correlative', and adds: 'The artistic "inevitability" lies in this complete adequacy of the external (*ie* the event on the stage is witnessed by the audience) to the emotion; and this is precisely what is deficient in *Hamlet*.'

Eliot's adverse judgement of *Hamlet* has not been widely accepted, but the term 'objective correlative' has passed into critical currency.

O'Brien, Edna (b 1932)
Novelist and short-story writer, born in County Clare, Ireland. Novels include: *The Country Girls* (1960); *The Lonely Girl* (1962) (as *Girl With Green Eyes*, 1964); *Girls in Their Married Bliss* (1964); *August is a Wicked Month* (1965); *Casualties of Peace* (1967); *A Pagan Place* (1970); *Night* (1972); *Johnny I Hardly Knew You* (1977); *The High Road* (1988). Her novels are concerned primarily with women's experience of loss, guilt and self-division; they are characterized by a certain lyricism and nostalgia, combined with a detached humour which has become more bitter as her work has developed.

Her first three novels form a trilogy about the lives of two contrasted women, and use a realistic mode which is replaced by internal monologues in some of her later work. Her style is very effective in the short-story form: *The Love Object* (1968); *A Scandalous Woman* (1974); *Mrs Reinhardt* (1978); *Returning* (1982); *A Fanatic Heart: Selected Stories* (1984). She has also written plays, screenplays and T.V. plays.

Observer, The
A ▷ newspaper published only on Sundays, started in 1792. It is central in its politics, and aims to appeal to the thoughtful, better-educated public.

O'Casey, Sean (1880–1964)
Irish dramatist best known for his three plays about tenement life in Dublin around the time of Irish independence in 1921. These were first performed at the ▷ Abbey Theatre: *The Shadow of a Gunman* (1923), *Juno and the Paycock* (1924) and *The Plough and the Stars* (1926). The last of these was greeted with a riot on its opening night. His next play, *The Silver Tassie* (1928), was an anti-heroic piece which experimented with expressionistic techniques. The play was rejected for performance at the Abbey by ▷ W. B. Yeats. After this O'Casey lived in England in self-imposed exile until his death. With *The Star Turns Red* (1940), *Purple Dust* (1940), *Red Roses for Me* (1943), *Oak Leaves and Lavender* (1947), *Cock-a-Doodle Dandy* (1949) and *The Bishop's Bonfire* (1961), he continued experimenting with non-naturalistic theatrical devices. These later plays deserve greater recognition than they have been given to date.

▷ Irish literature.

Bib: Kosok, H., *O'Casey the Dramatist*; Krause, D., *Sean O'Casey: The Man and His Work*.

O'Connor, Frank (pen-name of Michael O'Donovan) (1903–66)
Irish writer, especially famous for his short stories. He was born in Cork, received little education, and for some time worked as a librarian in Cork and Dublin. He was encouraged to write by the Irish poet AE (George Russell), and his publisher, Harold Macmillan (later the English Conservative Party leader) influenced him in deciding for a literary career. He participated in the Irish Rebellion after World War I. His first volume of short stories, *Guests of the Nation*, was published in 1931. Other volumes are: *Bone of Contention* (1936), *Three Tales* (1941), *Crab Apple Jelly* (1944), *The Common Chord* (1948), *Traveller's Samples* (1951), *My Oedipus Complex* (1963). His translation of poetry and legends from the Irish are also famous: *A Golden Treasury of Irish Poetry* (1967). He wrote two novels which have less repute than his short stories: *The Saint and Mary Kate* (1932) and *Dutch Interior* (1966). His critical works include one of the best studies of the art of the short story, *The Lonely Voice*, and a study of the novel, *The Mirror in the Roadway*. He also published two volumes of an uncompleted autobiography, *An Only Child* and *My Father's Son*. From 1952 he taught in an American university.

O'Connor's stories are remarkable for their insight, comedy, pathos and compassion.

His field was the lower ranges of Irish society, which he understood profoundly, and which he universalized by his generous intelligence and sympathies in a way that recalls Chekhov's treatment of Russian life. **Bib**: Sheehy, Maurice (ed.), *Michael/Frank*.

Oedipus complex

In ▷ Freudian psychoanalysis Sophocles's story of Oedipus who killed his father and married his mother, is used as a model of the way in which human desires and feelings are structured during the passage from infancy to adulthood. The triangular relationship modelled on Sophocles' text can be used to explain relationships within the family which is the model of socialization available to the child. In order for successful socialization to occur, the child must emerge from the position of desiring an incestuous relationship with individual parents – for which in the case of the male, the penalty would be castration – and to transfer the affections for the mother on to another. The difficulties which this sometimes causes are illustrated in novels such as ▷ D. H. Lawrence's ▷ *Sons and Lovers* where Paul Morell is faced with having to transfer his affections for his mother onto other women. The Oedipus complex, and the model of triangulated desire upon which it is built, must be overcome in order for individual gendered human subjects to take their place in a world of which they are not the centre. This process of 'decentring' is explained by ▷ Jacques Lacan as an acceptance of the repression of desire imposed upon the subject by the father, an acceptance of a 'symbolic castration'. This raises a number of difficulties in the case of the gendered *female* subject who can never break free of the castration complex imposed upon her by a phallocentric ▷ symbolic order. Basically the Oedipus complex is used to account for a particular hierarchy of relationships within the family unit. It is a process through which the male is expected to pass in order to reach mature adulthood, and it seeks to offer an explanation of the ways in which authority operates as a system of constraints and laws.

▷ Psychoanalytic criticism.

Bib: Laplanche, J. and Pontalis, J. P., *The Language of Psychoanalysis*.

O'Faolain, Sean (b 1900)

Irish novelist and writer of short stories. He was born in Dublin and attended the National University of Ireland and Harvard University in the U.S.A. He participated in the Irish Rebellion following World War I, and later lived in England as a teacher. His novels include *A Nest of Simple Folk* (1933) and *Bird Alone* (1936). His first volume of stories, *Midsummer Night Madness* (1932), vividly reflects the atmosphere of the Irish disturbances. A collected edition of the stories was published in 1958, and in 1966 he published a further volume, *The Heat of the Sun*. Among his other writings are two biographies which are studies of Irish leaders, one on Daniel O'Connell entitled *King of the Beggars* (1938), and *The Great O'Neill* (1942). His critical work includes *The Short Story* (1948). His autobiography *Vive Moi!* appeared in 1965. He was made Director of the Arts Council of Ireland in 1957.

O'Flaherty, Liam (1897–1984)

Irish novelist and writer of short stories. Born in the Aran Islands he was educated for the Roman Catholic priesthood, but did not enter it. He fought in World War I, and settled in England in 1922. His first volume of stories, *Spring Sowing*, was published in 1926; it contains stories of Irish peasant life and wild nature. At his best, his stories have the intensity of fine lyric poetry, and he is peculiarly gifted at representing the exhilaration and poignancy of life directly exposed to natural forces. Other volumes of stories include: *The Mountain Tavern* (1929), *The Wild Swan* (1932), *Two Lovely Beasts* (1948). His novels include *The Informer* (1925 – made into a film in 1935) and the historical *Famine* (1937). His autobiography is entitled *Shame the Devil* (1934).

Oisin

Also known as Ossian. In 1760–63, James Macpherson published a series of blank verse epics which he attributed to Ossian and claimed to have translated from the Gaelic. His version had an immense success and a wide influence; however, Macpherson was later proved not to have translated the poems, but to have synthesized them from a number of genuine Celtic legends, in which the hero Oisin occurs. Dr Johnson was among the earliest sceptics; when asked whether he thought any man 'of the modern age' could have written the poems, he replied: 'Yes, Sir, many men, many women, and many children.'

▷ W. B. Yeats wrote a narrative poem *The Wanderings of Oisin* (1889), the earliest of his attempts to create a new literature out of Celtic mythology. In the ancient legends Oisin bridged the gap between the heroic pagan age and Irish Christianity;

his longevity was due to a long sojourn in Fairyland.

▷ Celtic Twilight; Irish Literature in English.

Old Vic Theatre, The
Situated in Waterloo Road, this is one of London's most famous theatres. Built in 1816–18, during the 19th century it drew on the local working-class population for its audiences, with productions of popular melodramas. In 1880 it was converted into a temperance amusement-hall. From 1881 to 1883 it was managed by the ▷ Shakespearean actor and director William Poel. Under the management of Lillian Baylis, from 1912 to 1937, it became famous for its popular productions of Shakespeare's plays financed on a shoe-string budget. Her great achievement was to attract some of the best actors and directors of the time when they could have earned far greater salaries working in the West End. The theatre was damaged during World War II but reopened in 1950 and continued the tradition of performing Shakespeare plays along with other classics. Between 1963 and 1976 it served as the home for the ▷ National Theatre company before the new National Theatre was built. It has now been restored and re-established as a venue for neglected classics.
Bib: Roberts, P., *The Old Vic Story.*

Olivier, Laurence (1907–89)
Actor and producer, knighted in 1947, and created a life peer in 1970. He established his reputation at the ▷ Old Vic Theatre during the 1930s, especially with his performance of *Hamlet* in 1937. The range and success of his career on stage and in films mark him as the leading English actor of this century. In 1961 he was appointed director of the Chichester Festival Theatre and made the first director of the ▷ National Theatre.
Bib: Gourlay, L. (ed.), *Olivier*; Olivier, L. *Confessions of an Actor.*

Open University
The Open University was established in 1969, began teaching in 1971 and is now based at Milton Keynes. Its aim to provide degree courses for those students who do not have formal qualifications, who are not of a standard, and who do not have the opportunity or the finance to enter for full-time university degrees. The courses are based at home and the teaching is done mainly through television and radio. Its popularity continues to increase.

Order
One of the five categories in which ▷ Genette analyses narrative discourse, order is concerned with the relationship between the chronological order of fictional events and their order in the narrative (*eg* 'flashbacks'). Order, ▷ duration and ▷ frequency are matters of temporal arrangement or 'tense'; the other two categories are ▷ mood and ▷ voice.

▷ Narratology.

***Orlando* (1928)**
A fantasy by ▷ Virginia Woolf in which the evolution of poetic genius is traced through the Sackville family and their country mansion of Knole from Thomas Sackville (1536–1608) to the poet Victoria Sackville-West (1892–1962). This is done through an immortal character Orlando, who changes sex from a man into a woman in the 17th century, after growing to male adulthood in Elizabethan times. She then discovers that life as a woman in the 18th and 19th centuries offers different and limited freedoms. The book is a parodic combination of historical novel and biographical fantasy which explores the themes of androgyny and women's creativity. It is thus perhaps the closest Woolf gets in her fiction to an exploration of the ideas she outlines in *A Room of One's Own* (1931) and *Three Guineas* (1938).

Orton, Joe (1933–67)
British dramatist renowned for his black humour, witty and savage verbal dialogue in the tradition of ▷ Oscar Wilde, and iconoclastic attacks on social conventions. He was murdered by his homosexual partner when his career had barely begun. His first play, *Entertaining Mr Sloane* (1964), is a comedy about suburban sex. In this, as in his other plays, much of the humour is derived from the disparity between what characters say and what they actually mean or do. This was followed by two farces, *Loot* (1966) and *What the Butler Saw* (produced in 1969); the former about money, death and police corruption and the latter about sex and institutionalized corruption. Other plays are: *The Ruffian on the Stair* (staged 1966), *The Erpingham Camp* (staged 1967) and *Funeral Games* (staged 1970). In 1987 Stephen Frears directed a film adaptation (by Alan Bennett) of Lahr's biography of Orton, *Prick Up Your Ears.*
Bib: Bigsby, C. W. W., *Joe Orton*; Lahr, J., *Prick Up Your Ears.*

Orwell, George (pseudonym of Eric Blair) (1903–50)
Novelist, journalist and critic. Born into a poor but proud middle-class family, he was sent to a private school, from where he won a scholarship to Eton. His snobbish upbringing, and the uneasiness he felt in living with boys richer than himself, gave him a distaste for middle-class values and, in relation to the working classes, a sense of guilt which was intensified by the large unemployment of the 1930s. He served in the Burma Police (1922–7), and then resigned from dislike of what he interpreted as ▷ imperialist oppression – *Burmese Days* (1934). He then tried to appease his sense of social guilt by living for 18 months in the utmost destitution – *Down and Out in London and Paris* (1933). At the height of the economic ▷ depression in the 1930s, he was commissioned by a left-wing publisher, Gollancz, to make a personal investigation of conditions in the north of England – *The Road to Wigan Pier* (1937). By the time of its publication, Orwell was fighting for the Republicans in Spain, where he was wounded in the throat – *Homage to Catalonia* (1938). He came to regard himself as an independent and democratic socialist. During World War II, he was rejected for the army on medical grounds, and worked for the Indian service of the B.B.C. In 1945 he published his masterpiece, the fable *Animal Farm* a satire on Stalinism. After the war he wrote his most famous work, *1984* (1949), a vision of a world ruled by dictatorships of the Stalinist style, taken to an extreme in which private life and private thought are all but eradicated by surveillance, propaganda, and the systematic perversion of language.

His other novels are: *A Clergyman's Daughter* (1935); *Keep the Aspidistra Flying* (1936); *Coming Up For Air* (1939). Among his best works are his social and literary critical essays: *Inside the Whale* (1940); *The Lion and the Unicorn* (1941 – subtitled *Socialism and the English Genius*); *Critical Essays* (1946); *Shooting an Elephant* (1950). Recurrent themes in his work are the effect of poverty on the spirit, the difficulty of reconciling public demands with private desires and conscience, and the danger of corrupted language. He was literary editor of *Tribune* 1943–5. His *Collected Essays, Journalism and Letters* were published in 1968 (ed. S. Orwell and I. Angus).
Bib: Woodcock, G., *The Crystal Spirit*; Williams, R., *Orwell*; Crick, B., *George Orwell, a Life*; Meyers, J., *George Orwell: The Critical Heritage*.

Osborne, John (b 1929)
Dramatist. He is widely thought of as the leader of the dramatic revival which started in the 1950s, through the great popular success of *Look Back in Anger* (1956), which found an infectious contemporary idiom for the frustration of the younger British generation since World War II, and for their rejection of the traditional values of 'the Establishment'. The play gave currency for a decade to the term ▷ 'the angry young men'. His later plays include: *The Entertainer* (1957); *Epitaph for George Dillon* (1958); *The World of Paul Slickey* (1959); *Luther* (1961); *The Blood of the Bambergs* (1962); *Under Plain Cover* (1962); *Inadmissible Evidence* (1965); *A Patriot for Me* (1965); *A Bond Honoured* (1966); *Time Present* (1967); *West of Suez* (1972); *A Sense of Detachment* (1972); *A Place Calling Itself Detachment* (1972); *The Picture of Dorian Gray* (1973); *Watch It Come Down* (1975); *The End of Me Old Cigar* (1975). For television: *A Better Class of Person* (1985); *God Rot Tunbridge Wells* (1985). Osborne has published two volumes of autobiography: *A Better Class of Person* (1981) and *Almost a Gentleman* (1991).
Bib: Allsop, K., *The Angry Decade*; Banham, M. *Osborne*; Trussler, S., *The Plays of Osborne*.

Owen, Wilfred (1893–1918)
The best known of the so-called 'War poets' of World War I: *Poems* (1920). He served as an infantry officer, was awarded a decoration for bravery, and was killed a week before the armistice. Before the war he was already writing mildly sensuous poetry influenced by John Keats; for some time during the war he continued to write in this late-Romantic tradition. But he then adapted his technique so as to express the intensity of the suffering of the Western Front, deliberately introducing elements of discordance and harshness into his style especially by the use of 'para-rhyme', *ie* the repetition of consonants but changing the vowels, as in the words 'hall'-'hell'. The best known of his poems is *Strange Meeting* – a dream about an encounter with an enemy soldier who is, humanly, a friend, in surroundings which are both those of the war and of hell. Owen's poems were used by the composer Benjamin Britten in one of his major musical compositions, *War Requiem*.
▷ War poets.
Bib: Owen, H., *Life*; critical study by D. S. R. Welland; Hibberd, D., *Owen the Poet*.

Oxford Groups (Buchmanism)
A religious movement in Britain during the 1930s, inspired and led by the American

evangelist Frank Buchman. It was organized in small groups, whose members met to discuss their problems under Divine Guidance received in answer to prayer, a procedure similar to that employed by the 18th-century Methodists and the 17th-century Quakers. Opponents alleged that Divine Guidance was unduly right wing; the movement was concerned about the spread of ▷ atheism through ▷ Communist cells throughout Europe. It was largely despised by intellectuals, but had wide influence especially among the upper classes. Since World War II the movement has been reformed under the title MRA – Moral Rearmament. MRA seems to have many of the same characteristics as the Groups, but to be more international in scope. To left-wing intellectuals, both the Groups and MRA have represented a kind of ▷ 'Fascism'.

P

Pankhurst, Sylvia (1882–1960)
Poet and political writer. Sylvia Pankhurst's extraordinary career as a political activist, first for women's suffrage and later in wider socialist causes (for women in London's East End, and for Ethiopian independence) has overshadowed her equally extraordinary writing. She produced strong biographical and historical accounts of the suffrage movement (for example, the definitive biography of her mother, the *Life of Emmeline Pankhurst*, 1935, and *The Suffrage Movement*, 1931), and published two volumes of passionate, radical poetry in her lifetime: *Writ on a Cold Slate* (1922) and a translation of the Romanian poems of M. Eminescu *Poems* (1931).

▷ Feminism.

Bib: Castle, B., *Sylvia and Christabel Pankhurst* (1987); Pankhurst, R. K. P. *Sylvia Pankhurst: Artist and Crusader* (1979); Romero, P. W. E., *Sylvia Pankhurst: Portrait of a Radical* (1987).

Pantomime
Originally, in ancient Rome, a representation by masked actors, using gestures and dance, of religious or warlike episodes. One actor played many parts, male and female, with changes of mask and costume. It was often accompanied by music. It was used for episodes in medieval religious drama, and as the 16th-century Italian *commedia dell 'arte* it became a form of popular drama that spread all over Europe together with a number of traditional characters such as Harlequin and the Clown. In the 18th century it established itself in England. Nowadays the children's pantomimes performed in Britain after Christmas are usually musical plays representing traditional folk-tales (*Puss in Boots, Dick Whittington*, etc.) in a vulgarized form, but sometimes introducing traditional characters from the *commedia dell 'arte*. Certain conventions are peculiar to it: the hero of the story or 'principal boy' is always performed by an actress, and a comic character known as the 'pantomime dame' is performed by an actor, a gender-reversal which is a direct inheritance of the 'world-turned-upside-down' ▷ carnivalesque mode.

Parliament
The name of the supreme law-making body of Great Britain and Northern Ireland. It has two parts – the House of Commons, whose members are elected, and the House of Lords, the majority of whose members still sit by hereditary right. 'House' in these expressions does not refer to a building, but is equivalent to 'assembly'; the Lords and Commons meet in different chambers of the same building, officially called the Palace of Westminster but colloquially known as the Houses of Parliament.

Scotland had her own Parliament until the Union of Parliaments in 1707, since when she has sent representatives to Westminster; Ireland sent members from 1801, when her own parliament was abolished; Wales never had her own parliament but has sent members to Westminster since union in 1535. In 1922, Irish representation at Westminster was reduced to Ulster, or Northern Ireland, since the rest of the country became an independent republic. With the growing calls for more regional power and devolution, this situation, particularly in Scotland, is likely to change.

Since the 17th century, the Commons has been unquestionably the more important House; since the Parliament Act (1911) the legal powers of the House of Lords have been severely reduced, by that law and by later legislation.

Parody
A literary form which constitutes a comic imitation of a serious work, or of a serious literary form. Thus Fielding's *Joseph Andrews* is partly a parody of Richardson's *Pamela*, and Pope's *Rape of the Lock* is a parody of grand epic in the style of Homer and Virgil. It is difficult to draw a line between parody and ▷ burlesque; the latter is more obviously comic in its style of imitation. ▷ Stella Gibbons' *Cold Comfort Farm* is one example of 20th-century parody (of the primitivism of writers such as D. H. Lawrence); less famous short examples can be found in *The Faber Book of Parodies*.

Parole
In the work of ▷ Ferdinand de Saussure, the founder of ▷ Structuralism, this is usually translated as 'speech' or 'speech act'. It refers to a particular instance of speech. '*Parole*' is to be distinguished from ▷ '*langue*' (language) which is the linguistic system which underpins every utterance (*parole*). Speakers of a language (*langue*) avail themselves of parts of that system and reactivate it each time they engage in speech (*parole*).

▷ Sign.

Parties, Political
The English political scene has been dominated by political parties since the mid-17th century. It was not till the 19th century that political parties became highly organized,

and though there have seldom been more than two important ones, these have not always been the same. Nonetheless, there has been a continuity in the history of parties sufficient to give a long history to political loyalties. The principal phases of party development are summarized as follows:

1640–1660: the Civil War and Interregnum. ▷ Parliament, especially the House of Commons, successfully led a rebellion against the king, and established a republic. The division was partly religious (Puritan against Anglican), and partly economic (the commercially progressive south and east against the more traditional north and west).

In the period from 1660 onwards, the ▷ Tories were strong upholders of the monarchy and of the Church of England; the Whigs, without opposing the continuance of either as institutions, laid emphasis on the rights of Parliament. After a decline in power from 1714 to 1760, the Tory Party had a revival in its fortunes, and the 19th century saw politics divided again into a debate between the Tories and the Whigs, increasingly known as the ▷ Liberals. The period 1832–1918, however, saw the evolution of the modern parties: Liberals, Conservatives and, finally, ▷ Labour. The parties became more self-conscious and closely organized; Whigs came to call themselves Liberals, and Tories changed their name to Conservatives. Until 1840, the division was between the agricultural interest (Conservative) and the industrial interest (Liberal), and the old religious divisions survived, so that the Conservatives were the guardians of the Church of England, and the more decidedly Protestant sects – now called Nonconformists – voted Liberal. In the second half of the 19th century the upper classes of both towns and countryside tended to vote Conservative, and the Liberals depended increasingly on the urban working-class vote. However, the Liberals, by their traditions, could never become a predominantly working-class party; hence the Labour Party was founded in 1900. After World War I, social discontents caused the Labour Party to succeed the Liberal Party as one of the two largest in the country. Since 1923, the Liberals have been reduced to a small though not insignificant Parliamentary body and have adopted the new name of Liberal Democratic Party. The Labour Party, on the other hand, owes as much to the great 19th-century Liberal traditions as to the doctrinaire socialism of ▷ Marx. In the 1980s, due to a reworking of constituency boundaries and the trend towards right-wing politics, the Conservative Party achieved an almost unassailable position. Moreover, the divisions in the opposition parties added to the overwhelming success of the Tory Party, and consequently the 1980s became known as the decade of Thatcherism, after the long-serving (and first woman) Conservative Prime Minister Margaret Thatcher, who held power from 1979 to 1990.

***Passage to India, A* (1924)**
A novel by ▷ E. M. Forster. It had originally been planned ten years earlier, and its picture of India belongs partly to that period. The scene is the city of Chandrapore on the banks of the Ganges, and India is under British rule. The background characters consist mainly of the British officials and their wives, and the local Indian intelligentsia. The main characters are as follows: Aziz, a Muslim Indian doctor; Godbole, a Hindu professor; Fielding, the headmaster of the Government College; Ronald Heaslop, another of the British officials; and two visitors from Britain, Mrs Moore, the mother of Heaslop by her first marriage, and Adela Quested, who is engaged to him. Both women have strong liberal principles, and make friends easily with Fielding, the only liberal in the resident British colony. Fielding is also a friend of Aziz, and a colleague of Godbole. Aziz issues an impulsive invitation to the British visitors to visit the local Marabar Caves; these have a strong significance for the Hindus, although Godbole, when he is asked about them, is unable to explain it. The climax of the book occurs when this visit takes place. Heat, discomfort, and the caves themselves cause Mrs Moore and Adela to suffer traumatic experiences. Mrs Moore loses all her faith and idealism; Adela has an attack of hysteria which temporarily convinces her that Aziz has attempted to rape her. This supposed rape brings the already strained relations between the British and the Indians to a crisis, but the crisis is resolved (not without disgracing the more reactionary British officials) by Adela's return to sanity in the witness-box. Mrs Moore, although she is now vague and disillusioned, is in touch with a new kind of truthfulness which helps Adela's restoration. Only Mrs Moore and Godbole understand the true nature of Adela's experience in the caves, and they understand it from opposite, though complementary, points of view.

The novel has psychological, political, and religious dimensions, and it is the last of these that is the most important. The Christianity, or the sceptical liberalism, of the more enlightened of the British is shown to be adequate for normal relationships and practical affairs, but they have become too shallow for the interpretation of deeper human experience; Aziz's Muslim faith is stronger, but it is more an aesthetic and cultural tradition than a binding spiritual faith. Godbole's Hinduism, on the other hand, is profound and intelligent, though it is no guide to the daily conduct of affairs. This religious dimension is presented by constant symbolism, ranging in character from unobtrusive (though often important) details, to the conspicuous and suggestive image of the caves themselves. *A Passage to India* is usually regarded as Forster's masterpiece, and is certainly one of the finest English novels of the 20th century. In 1984 the novel was adapted by British director David Lean into an epic film.

▷ Imperialism.

Peake, Mervyn (1911–68)
Novelist, dramatist, poet and painter. Peake was born in China, but his family returned to England in 1923, where he subsequently trained as an artist. He is best known for his trilogy *Gormenghast*, a fantasy epic set in a grotesque world, consisting of *Titus Groan* (1946), *Gormenghast* (1950) and *Titus Alone* (1959). In form it is a ▷ *Bildungsroman* with multiple subplots, and it is distinguished by a rich vocabulary and by the effects of Peake's strong visual imagination. Peake's work met a mixed critical reception, but gained a considerable cult following, aided by the increasing popularity of fantasy fiction associated with the work of ▷ J. R. R. Tolkien.
Bib: Gilmore, M., *A World Away: a Memoir of Mervyn Peake*; Batchelor, J., *Mervyn Peake: A Biographical and Critical Exploration.*

***Peter Pan* (1904)**
A children's play by ▷ J. M. Barrie, originally called *Peter Pan, or the Boy who wouldn't grow up*. It became, and remains, extremely popular for its whimsical charm and its ingenious use of some traditional features of children's romances, such as Red Indians, the pirate Captain Hook who lives in fear of a crocodile which has already consumed one of his hands, and the fairy Tinkerbell.

▷ Children's books.

Phillips, Caryl (b 1958)
Novelist, playwright, travel writer. Born in St Kitts, West Indies, brought up in Leeds, England, and educated at Oxford, he has been writer-in-residence at the Factory Community Centre, London, at the Literary Criterion Centre, Mysore, India and at the University of Stockholm, Sweden. Plays: *Strange Fruit* (1981); *Where There is Darkness* (1982); *The Shelter* (1984); *The Wasted Years* (1985); *Playing Away* (1987). Novels: *The Final Passage* (1985); *A State of Independence* (1986); *Higher Ground* (1989); *Cambridge* (1991). Travel writing: *The European Tribe* (1987).

▷ Commonwealth literatures.

Pinero, Sir Arthur Wing (1855–1934)
Dramatist. His earliest plays were farces, but in 1889 *The Profligate* showed a great advance in seriousness over earlier plays in the century, when the English theatre had been practically bankrupt of contemporary drama of interest. At about this time, largely owing to the influence of ▷ Ibsen, drama was being revised radically in Europe. Pinero's *The Second Mrs Tanqueray* (1893) was at the time of its production a conspicuous contribution to the new movement; it was translated into French, German and Italian, and attracted the leading European actress of the age, Eleonora Duse. Pinero followed this success with other plays which sustained his reputation in Britain at least, such as *Trelawny of the 'Wells'* (1898) and *The Gay Lord Quex* (1899). He was, in fact, a prolific writer, publishing 39 plays between 1891 and 1930.

His plays are now seldom produced and little studied: in wit and dramatic ingenuity he was soon excelled by ▷ George Bernard Shaw. Like Tom Robertson before him, his brilliance was like that of a candle in the dark: he was conspicuous in contrast to the dullness that preceded him.
Bib: Dunkel, W. D., *Life*; Boas, F. S., *From Richardson to Pinero*; Lazenby, W., *Pinero.*

Pinter, Harold (b 1930)
British dramatist. Major works are: *The Room* (1957); *The Birthday Party* (1958); *The Dumb Waiter* (1957); *A Slight Ache* (radio 1958, stage 1961); *A Night Out* (1960); *The Caretaker* (1960); *The Homecoming* (1964); *Old Times* (1971); *No Man's Land* (1975); *Betrayal* (1978); *A Kind of Alaska* (1982); *Mountain Language* (1988).

His distinctiveness among contemporary dramatists, among whom he is perhaps the most remarkable, arises from his use of dialogue. Words are used less for communication than for justification by the speaker's self to himself, and as weapons against others who exist not for

relationship but in order that each may find assurance that he exists himself. The characters live in constant mistrust and fear, requiring refuge and assurance from their physical environment, and expecting mysterious invasions. When strong emotion actually brings about relationship through words, however inarticulately, the effect is dramatically poignant. Pinter's characters have been compared to ▷ Samuel Beckett's, but the resemblance is probably superficial; Beckett's characters exist in dissolving relationships, whereas Pinter's require social bonds. The idiom, however, of both dramatists derives in part from dramatists working at the end of the 19th century – the Swedish ▷ Strindberg, the Russian ▷ Chekhov, and the Belgian Maerterlinck.
Bib: Esslin, M., *The Theatre of the Absurd* and *Pinter: A Study of his Plays*; Taylor, J. R., *Anger and After*, Quigley, A. E., *The Pinter Problem*; Bull, J., *Stage Right: The Recovery for the Mainstream.*

Pitter, Ruth (1897–1992)
Poet. Pitter's long writing career began with the publication of *First Poems* in 1920, and developed through traditional routes: her poetry is accessible, simple and anti- ▷ modernistic. She has also written on gardening. In 1955 she became the first women to win the Queen's Gold Medal for Poetry. Her works include: *Persephone in Hades* (1931); *A Mad Lady's Garland* (1934); *The Rude Potato* (1941); *On Cats* (1947); *Still By Choice* (1966); *Poems 1926–1966* and *End of Drought* (1975).
Bib: Gilbert, R., *Four Living Poets*; Russell, A. (ed.), *Ruth Pitter: Homage to a Poet*; Watkin, E. I. *Poets and Mystics*.

Plath, Sylvia (1932–63)
Poet and novelist. She was brought up in the U.S.A.; her father, who died when she was nine, was of Prussian origin and her mother Austrian. Her university education was at Smith College, Massachusetts, and Newnham College, Cambridge. She married the English poet ▷ Ted Hughes in 1956. For a time she taught at Smith College, but in 1959 she settled in England. In 1960 she published her first volume of poetry, *The Colossus*, and in 1963 her only novel, *The Bell Jar*, under the pen-name of Victoria Lucas. Her reputation was established on the posthumous publication of her book of poetry, *Ariel* (1965). This volume aroused more interest in Britain than any other since ▷ Dylan Thomas's *Deaths and Entrances* (1946). The poems combine bold imagery and original rhythms with strenuous artistic control; their themes concern states of mind in extremity. In a commentary recorded for the ▷ British Council, she declared: 'One should be able to control and manipulate experiences, even the most terrifying . . . with an informed and intelligent mind.' Plath committed suicide in 1963. Other important posthumous publications are *Crossing the Water* (1971) and *Winter Trees* (1972); Plath also wrote a radio play, *Three Women*, broadcast in 1962. *Collected Poems* (ed. Ted Hughes; 1981); *Letters Home* (1978).
Bib: Alvarez, A., in *Beyond All This Fiddle* and *The Savage God*; Uroff, M. D., *Sylvia Plath and Ted Hughes*; Rose, J., *The Haunting of Sylvia Plath*; *The Art of Sylvia Plath: A Symposium* (ed. Charles Newman) contains a bibliography.

***Playboy of the Western World, The* (1907)**
A play by ▷ John Millington Synge. The scene is a remote part of rural Ireland. The hero, Christy Mahon, arrives at a village inn in flight from the law, since he believes himself to have killed his tyrannical father. Instead of being handed over to the police or regarded with abhorrence, he is treated with admiration, and the innkeeper's daughter, Pegeen Mike, falls in love with him. He is at first a miserable youth with no belief in himself, but the universal admiration and Pegeen's love build up his confidence, until he behaves like a true hero. This fiction is destroyed momentarily when his father, who has merely been injured, suddenly appears on the scene. The assault on the father is then suddenly removed from fiction into fact, and the village, including Pegeen, turn against Christy. However, Christy turns into yet a third type of person; he defies the village, through sheer desperation at the idea of sinking back into subservience to his father, and makes his departure in the bullying style which has always been his father's character. The play is thus a mixture of ironic comedy, poetic tragedy, and exuberant farce.

The language is that of the superstitious Irish peasantry, musical and imaginative in its idiom, and though the dialogue is prose, it reaches an intensity that is unique in drama in the English language since the days of ▷ Shakespeare. Irish nationalist opinion was deeply angered by Synge's refusal to idealize the Irish character, and its early performances at ▷ W. B. Yeats's ▷ Abbey Theatre in Dublin caused riots.

▷ Irish literature in English.

***Plays Pleasant and Unpleasant* (1898)**
A collection of seven plays by ▷ George Bernard Shaw. The four 'pleasant' plays are comedies with serious themes (the character of the true soldier, what constitutes moral strength, the nature of greatness, etc.) but nothing likely to dismay or shock the conventional moral sense of the audiences of the day. These are: ▷ *Arms and the Man, Candida, The Man of Destiny, You Never Can Tell.* The three 'unpleasant' plays dealt with social topics (sexual morality and the ownership of slum property) such as were generally felt to be unsuitable for presentation in the theatre. These are: *Widower's Houses, The Philanderer, Mrs Warren's Profession.*

Poel, William (1852–1934)
Actor, director and ▷ Shakespeare scholar. He founded the Elizabethan Stage Society in 1894. Poel's influential productions of the plays of Shakespeare and his contemporaries rejected the traditional techniques of stage realism dominant at the end of the 19th century. Characteristic of his productions was an attempt to recreate Elizabethan stage conditions by performing on a bare apron stage. He also pursued a policy, not always successfully, of restoring full uncut texts for production. Though it is now accepted that he overstressed the notion of the 'bare' Elizabethan stage, he was, with ▷ Harley Granville Barker, a great influence on the development of Shakespeare productions in this century.

▷ Old Vic Theatre.

Bib: Speaight, R., *William Poel and the Elizabethan Revival.*

Poet Laureate
The laurel, also known as the bay (*Laurus nobilis*), was sacred to Apollo, the god most associated with the arts. The Greeks honoured Olympic victors and triumphant generals, by crowning them with a wreath of laurel leaves. In the 15th century the universities of Oxford and Cambridge gave the title 'laureate', meaning worthy of laurels, to various poets including John Skelton, and it was later given to court poets like Ben Jonson. In 1668 the title gained its modern status when John Dryden was granted a stipend as a member of the royal household charged with writing court odes and celebrating state occasions in verse. Since the time of Dryden the laureateship has been awarded to a few poets of lasting worth and to many of mediocre talent, chosen for reasons of fashion or political acceptability. The list is as follows: Thomas Shadwell, Nahum Tate, Nicholas Rowe, Laurence Eusden, Colley Cibber, William Whitehead, Thomas Warton, Henry James Pye, Robert Southey, William Wordsworth, Alfred Tennyson, Alfred Austin, ▷ Robert Bridges, ▷ John Masefield, ▷ Cecil Day-Lewis, ▷ John Betjeman and ▷ Ted Hughes. Poets who were offered the laureateship but declined it include Thomas Gray, Sir Walter Scott, Samuel Rogers, William Morris and ▷ Philip Larkin. Wordsworth was the first Poet Laureate to make his acceptance of the office conditional on his not being obliged to honour official occasions with specially composed poems, though some later laureates have continued the practice, notably Tennyson, Betjeman and Hughes.

Poetics
In Aristotle's ▷ *Poetics* the rules of 'tragedy' are abstracted from a collection of specific instances to form a theoretical model. The function of 'poetics', therefore, has always been to organize formally details of poetic structures, and to this extent it is both prescriptive and descriptive. This Aristotelian usage persists, though in considerably extended form, in the titles of works of critical theory, such as Jonathan Culler's *Structuralist Poetics* (1975). The theoretical works also address the issue of an organized system of analytical methods, as well as aesthetics of artistic construction. More recently, for example in the work of ▷ new historicist critics such as Stephen Greenblatt, the phrase 'cultural poetics' is used to designate an investigation into 'how the boundaries were marked between cultural practices understood to be art forms and other, contiguous, forms of expression' (*Shakespearean Negotiations*; 1988). Such investigations seek to explain how particular aspects of general cultural life are given artistic expression. Whereas Aristotle's *Poetics* can be said to have a ▷ formalist bent, one of the ways in which the term has come to be used today locates the formal aspects of literary texts within a social context.

Poetics
A treatise on poetry by the Greek philosopher Aristotle. He had already written a dialogue *On the Poets*, which has only survived in fragments, and a treatise on rhetoric; knowledge of both is to some extent assumed in the *Poetics*. The *Poetics* is considered to have been an unpublished work, resembling notes for lectures addressed to students rather than a full worked-up treatise for

the general public, like the *Rhetoric*. This accounts for its fragmentary character. Thus Aristotle distinguishes Tragedy, Epic and Comedy as the chief kinds of poetry, but Comedy is practically omitted from fuller discussion. Lyric, though it is referred to, is not included among the chief kinds, either because Aristotle considered it to be part of music or because he considered it to be taken up into Tragedy. The main part of the work is therefore concerned with Tragedy and Epic – the former more extensively than the latter. Aristotle's method is essentially descriptive rather than prescriptive; that is to say, he is more concerned with what had been done by acknowledged masters such as Homer and Sophocles, than with what ought to be done according to so-called 'rules'.

Nonetheless, the *Poetics* became the most authoritatively influential of all critical works. Its dominance in European critical thought from the 16th to the 18th centuries was partly due to its influence on the most widely read of the Roman critics, Horace, and partly because it was rediscovered at the end of the 15th century when the ▷ Renaissance was at its height, and the spirit of the Greek and Latin writers was felt to be civilization itself. Critics such as the 16th-century Italian Scaliger took what are mere hints in Aristotle and erected them into important rules of art, such as the 'neo-Aristotelian' ▷ unities of time and place. In England, the important critics, such as Dryden and Jonson, regarded Aristotle and neo-Aristotelianism with strong respect rather than total reverence, but the complete submission of minor critics such as Thomas Rymer is exemplified by his obtuse treatment of Shakespeare's *Othello* in the essay *Short View of Tragedy* (1692). Neo-Aristotelianism was set aside by the Romantics, who cultivated literary virtues which are different from Aristotelian shapeliness and order, but the influence of the *Poetics* is still evident in Wordsworth's Preface to the *Lyrical Ballads*.

Today the *Poetics* remains one of the most outstanding works of European thought. Critics still use Aristotle's terminology in classifying poetic forms; his theory of art as imitation (different from Plato's) is still the starting-point of much aesthetic discussion; such terms as 'harmatia', for the element in human nature which makes it vulnerable to tragedy, 'peripeteia' for the reversal of fortunes common in tragic narrative, and 'katharsis' for the effect of tragedy on the mind of the audience, have been useful for a long time. It continues to be widely studied as one of the earliest works of literary critical theory.

Pornography
This is generally understood to mean representations or literature which is intended to produce sexual excitement. There is, however, a considerable degree of dispute about pornography and it has become the subject of legal cases and public campaigns. The most notorious of these must be the trial concerning ▷ D. H. Lawrence's ▷ *Lady Chatterley's Lover* in 1960. On the right-wing are those moralists who wish to police public standards and ban all sexual material, arguing that it depraves and corrupts. Some ▷ feminists also attack pornography on the grounds that it is male violence against women; they have particularly broad categories, including advertising. The liberal viewpoint, summed up by the Williams Committee of 1979, draws a distinction between public and private pornography, and if it is not hurting anyone will not interfere legally. Other feminists have worked to offer alternative erotic representations in literature, photography and art which will be appealing to women.

▷ Censorship.

Bib: Dworkin, A., *Pornography: Men Possessing Women*; Kappeller, S., *Pornography of Representation*; Special *Screen* edition on Pornography (1982); Lawrence, D. H., 'Pornography and Obscenity' in *Phoenix*.

Porter, Peter (b 1929)
Poet. Born in Brisbane, Australia, Porter has lived in Britain since 1951. His work is most famous as an acutely satirical, witty analysis of the decadence of post-war society, and was included in A. Alvarez's 1960 ▷ anthology *The New Poetry*. His work includes: *Once Bitten, Twice Bitten* (1961); *Poems Ancient and Modern* (1964); *A Porter Folio* (1969); *The Last of England* (1970); *Living in a Calm Country* (1976) and *English Subtitles* (1981).

***Portrait of a Lady, The* (1881)**
A novel by ▷ Henry James. The heroine, Isabel Archer, is brought from America to England by her aunt, Mrs Touchett, the wife of a retired American banker. Isabel has the candour and freedom conspicuous among American girls of the period; she also has beauty, intelligence, and a spirit of adventure and responsiveness to life. She refuses offers of marriage from both Lord Warburton, a 'prince' of the English aristocracy, and Caspar Goodwood, a 'prince' of American

industry. In the meantime her cousin, Ralph Touchett, has fallen in love with her, but he is slowly dying of consumption and dare not become her suitor. Instead, he tries to play the 'fairy godmother' by persuading his father to leave her the money which would have been due to himself. His action has two unfortunate results: it awakens Isabel's New England Puritan conscience through the sense of responsibility which the possession of wealth entails, and it attracts the rapacious Madame Merle, whose guilty secret is that she is looking for a rich stepmother for her daughter by her former lover, Gilbert Osmond. Osmond (like Madame Merle herself) is an artistic but cold-blooded and totally self-centred expatriate American. Isabel in her humility is easily made to feel her own cultural inferiority to the exquisite exterior qualities of Osmond, whom she sees as the prince she has been looking for – a man deprived of noble potentialities by the unjust circumstance of his poverty. She marries him, only to discover his hollowness, and that her marriage is imprisonment in the ogre's castle.

The novel, sometimes regarded as James's masterpiece, shows his conception of the relationship of the American and European consciousness; the Americans have integrity, the will to live, and good will towards humanity, but they lack richness of tradition and are restricted by the limitations of the New England Puritan inhibitions; the Europeans (especially some of the American expatriates) have rich cultural awareness but this commonly corrupts their integrity, and instead of good will they have immense rapacity. On the other hand the best kind of American expatriate (Ralph Touchett) combines the best of both worlds.

Portrait of the Artist as a Young Man, A (1916)

An autobiographical novel by ▷ James Joyce. The theme is the life of a middle-class Irish boy, Stephen Dedalus, from his infancy in the strongly Catholic, intensely nationalistic environment of Dublin in the 1880s to his departure from Ireland some 20 years later. In his boyhood he sees his elders bitterly divided in consequence of the Church's rejection of Parnell, the nationalist leader, owing to the scandal of his private life. As he grows up he is repelled by the pettiness, treacheries and vindictiveness of Irish nationalism, and for a time is drawn towards the rich spirituality of the Catholic tradition. The Irish Catholic Church, however, also suffered from provincialism and narrowness, and a moment of revelation on the seashore shows him that the largeness of an artistic vocation will alone suffice for him to harmonize the spiritual and fleshly sides of his nature, and enable him to rise above the vulgarity of his environment; but the choice brings with it the decision to leave Ireland.

The originality of the novel consists in its presentation of the hero's experience from within his own consciousness. The language gradually expands from the fragmentary diction of an infant on the first page through the connected but limited range of expression characteristic of a schoolboy to the sophistication of a fully articulate university student.

▷ Irish literature in English.

Postmodernism

The break away from 19th-century values is often classified as ▷ modernism and carries the connotations of transgression and rebellion. However, the last 30 years have seen a change in this attitude towards focusing upon a series of unresolvable philosophical and social debates, such as race, gender and class. Rather than challenging and destroying cultural definitions, as does modernism, postmodernism resists the very idea of boundaries. It regards distinctions as undesirable and even impossible, so that an almost ▷ Utopian world, free from all constraints, becomes possible. Postmodernism remains a controversial term, but may be linked to a transformation of European culture at the end of World War II. This war produced the death camps and the atomic bomb, and thus generated a new sense of man's propensity to evil, of the destructive potential of scientific knowledge, and of the perils of political totalitarianism. The end of Empire and the post-war changes in the world economy and power-structure involved new relationships between Britain and other cultures.

It must be realized, though, that post-modernism has many interpretations and that no single definition is adequate. Different disciplines have participated in the postmodernist movement in varying ways, for example, in architecture traditional limits have become indistinguishable, so that what is commonly on the outside of a building is placed within, and vice versa. In literature, writers adopt a self-consious ▷ intertextuality sometimes verging on pastiche, which denies the formal propriety of authorship and genre. In commercial terms postmodernism may be seen as part of the growth of consumer

▷ capitalism into a multi-national and technological identity.

Its all-embracing nature thus makes postmodernism as relevant to street events as to the avant-garde, and as such is one of the major focal points in the emergence of interdisciplinary and cultural studies.

Bib: Jameson, F., *Post-modernism and Consumer Society*; Lyotard, J.-F., *The Post-modern Condition*.

Post-structuralism

At first glance, the term post-structuralism seems to imply that the post-structuralists came after the structuralists and that post-structuralism was the heir of ▷ structuralism. In practice, however, there is not a clear-cut division between structuralism and post-structuralism. Although the two have different focuses of interest and preoccupations, many of their concerns bind them together. Structuralism encompasses approaches to criticism which use linguistic models to enable critics to focus not on the inherent meaning of a work but on the structures which *produce* or generate meaning. Post-structuralism focuses on the ways in which the texts themselves subvert this enterprise. Leading post-structuralists include ▷ Derrida, ▷ Lacan, J. Hillis Miller and ▷ Paul de Man.

▷ Deconstruction; Feminism; Reception Theory.

Bib: Culler, J., *On Deconstruction*.

Potter, Beatrix (1866–1943)

Writer for children. One of the most famous and widely translated writers of children's stories, Potter's anthropomorphic tales of animal adventures have been famously praised by ▷ Graham Greene for their lack of sentimentality. Beginning with *The Tale of Peter Rabbit* (1901) (published and printed – as well as, of course, illustrated – by Potter herself), her simple stories have become classics of ▷ children's writing. Potter was also an accomplished naturalist, artist (illustrating all her own work), and (later) sheep farmer. Her numerous works hardly need listing; they include: *The Tale of Squirrel Nutkin* (1903); *The Tailor of Gloucester* (1903); *The Tale of Jemima Puddle-Duck* (1908); *The Tale of Mr Tod* (1912). See also *The Journals of Beatrix Potter* (1966) and *Dear Ivy, Dear June: Letters from Beatrix Potter* (1977).

Bib: Godden, R., *The Tale of the Tales*; Greene, G., 'Beatrix Potter' in *Collected Essays*; Linder. L., *The History of the Writings of Beatrix Potter*; Taylor, J., *Beatrix Potter: Artist, Storyteller, Countrywoman*.

Pound, Ezra (1885–1972)

American poet. He came to Europe in 1907, and made London his home during the period 1908–20. His influence on English poetry during this period, especially on that of his fellow American, ▷ T. S. Eliot, was very great. English poets had become insular, and they tended (with some exceptions) to occupy themselves with a marginal field of experience left over to them by the novelists, abstaining from the issues that were central to the destiny of their thoroughly industrialized society. They also restricted themselves to a limited diction, consecrated as 'poetic', with an obvious emotional appeal. The recent British poets who interested Pound were Robert Browning for his direct and 'unpoetic' address to the reader, and the Irish poet ▷ W. B. Yeats, for his austere seriousness and energy. In his campaign to reform diction he became the leader of the ▷ Imagist Movement, though he later abandoned it; this phase is illustrated by his *Ripostes* (1912) and *Lustra* (1916). It also drew him to Chinese poetry, from which he made excellent English verse, although his are not such accurate translations as those of his contemporary Arthur Waley.

In his campaign to free English poetry from insularity, Pound accepted the concept, which he shared with some other American writers (*eg* ▷ Henry James and T. S. Eliot), that European culture is a whole, not segmented into national cultures. Thus he offered fresh insights into ▷ French and ▷ Italian poetry back to the ▷ Middle Ages (see his critical essays, *Make It New*) and into the Latin classics. In his poetry he used the diction of everyday speech with a subtle ear for its rhythms. Like Eliot, he abandoned the logical continuity of prose in favour of a juxtaposition of ideas and images whose continuity appears through their psychological association. Also like Eliot, he used quotation frequently, thereby relating his treatment of his themes with the treatment accorded by past poets to similar themes, and thus illuminating the fundamental alterations in outlook and assumption brought about in the course of history. This technique of quotation is conspicuous in Eliot's poem ▷ *The Waste Land*, which Pound heavily revised. A comparable poem by Pound is *Hugh Selwyn Mauberley* (1920), which heralded his departure from Britain by offering an assessment of the state of culture there at the time. He moved to Paris, and in 1924 to Italy, where he became increasingly sympathetic to ▷ Fascism, partly in consequence of his strongly held and eccentric economic theories (see his *ABC of Economics*).

From this time onwards, his poetry output consisted almost entirely in working on his extended poem ▷ the *Cantos*, which was not finished at his death. The *Pisan Cantos* (1948) are the most famous section, recording his incarceration in Pisa by the American forces at the end of World War II, while waiting to stand trial for treason. Found unfit to plead at his trial in 1948, he was committed to St Elizabeth's Hospital, Washington D.C., from where he was released in 1958, spending the rest of his life in Italy. See also his *Literary Essays* (ed. T. S. Eliot), and *The Translations of Ezra Pound* (ed. H. Kenner).
Bib: Kenner, H., *The Poetry of Ezra Pound* and *The Pound Era*; David, D., *Ezra Pound: Poet as Sculptor*; Bush, R., *The Genesis of Ezra Pound's 'Cantos'*.

Powell, Anthony (b 1905)
Novelist. He writes sophisticated comedy of upper-class life in England since 1920; his approach may be compared with the different treatment of the same society by ▷ Aldous Huxley, ▷ Evelyn Waugh, and by ▷ D. H. Lawrence in *St Mawr*. Early novels are: *Afternoon Men* (1931); *Venusberg* (1932); *From A View to a Death* (1933); *Agents and Patients* (1936); *What's Become of Waring* (1939).

In 1948 he produced a study of John Aubrey, the 17th-century anecdotal biographer, author of *Brief Lives*. He then began his major work which, it has been suggested, owes something to Aubrey as it clearly does to the sequence *A la recherche du temps perdu* by the French novelist ▷ Marcel Proust. Powell's sequence of novels is called *A Dance to the Music of Time*. The narrator, whose personality is kept in detachment but not eliminated, is an upper-class young man with whose life various circles of friends intertwine in a kind of dance, and in a way that is only conceivable in the upper levels of any society. The characters make a pattern of contrasts, the most serious and interesting being that of the man of distinction – Stringham – who evokes the high style of an Elizabethan courtier such as Ralegh, but who is in the wordly sense a failure, and Widmerpool, the man of grotesque and crude manners and feeling, who is yet a worldly success owing to his insensibility and the force of his ambition. *A Dance to the Music of Time* consists of: *A Question of Upbringing* (1951); *A Buyer's Market* (1952); *The Acceptance World* (1955); *At Lady Molly's* (1957); *Casanova's Chinese Restaurant* (1960); *The Kindly Ones* (1962); *The Valley of Bones* (1964); *The Soldier's Art* (1966); *The Military Philosophers* (1968); *Books Do Furnish a Room* (1971); *Temporary Kings* (1973); *Hearing Secret Harmonies* (1975). The sequence begins in 1921 at the narrator's public school; it ends after the war with the death of Widmerpool in circumstances of sinister pathos. Powell has followed up his novel sequence with a sequence of memoirs entitled *To Keep the Ball Rolling: Infants of the Spring* (1978); *Messengers of Day* (1978); *Faces in My Time* (1980); *The Strangers All Are Gone* (1982). Other novels: *O, How the Wheel Becomes It!* (1983); *The Fisher King* (1986).
Bib: Bergonzi, B., *Anthony Powell*; Spurling, H., *Invitation to the Dance*; Tucker, J., *The Novels of Anthony Powell*.

Powys, John Cowper (1872–1963)
Novelist, poet and essayist. Principal novels are: *Wolf Solent* (1929); *A Glastonbury Romance* (1932); *Weymouth Sands* (1934); *Maiden Castle* (1936); *Owen Glendower* (1940); *Porius* (1951). Works of criticism and thought: *Visions and Revisions* (1915; revised 1935); *Psychoanalysis and Morality* (1923); *The Religion of a Sceptic* (1925); *The Meaning of Culture* (1929); *In Defence of Sensuality* (1930); *The Art of Happiness* (1935); *The Pleasures of Literature* (1938). One of his most famous books is his *Autobiography* (1934), developed from his contribution to the *Confessions of Two Brothers* (1916) written with Llewelyn Powys.

Like his brother, ▷ T. F. Powys, his fiction is influenced by his background in the English West Country, but his prose is contrasted with his brother's by its expansiveness and diffuseness. His writing combines a strongly physical sensationalism with a fascination for the intangible and mysterious reaches of human experience. He is concerned with the transformation of ordinary life by a contemplative intensity which generates a mythical sense of the individual's relation to his natural environment. His work shows the influence of ▷ Thomas Hardy, with whom he was acquainted, although Powys is more clearly identified with ▷ modernist forms than Hardy. Critics are divided as to whether Powys is an overrated or an underrated novelist.
Bib: Graves, R. P., *The Brothers Powys*; Cavaliero, G., *John Cowper Powys, Novelist*; Churchill, R. C., *The Powys Brothers*.

Powys, Theodore Francis (1875–1953)
Novelist and short-story writer; brother of ▷ John Cowper Powys. His novels and fables are set in the rural south-west of England;

the characters are presented with a simplicity and poetry resembling the style of the Old Testament of the Bible, but the individuality of the expression is too distinct for the resemblance to be obvious, and the tone is naïve on the surface but sophisticated in its pagan, often cynical implications. At its best, *eg* in *Mr Weston's Good Wine* (1927) and *Fables* (1929), Powys's art rose to exquisite tragic poetry; at its worst it descended to brutality and cruelty. His fiction is a very late and unusual example in English of a writer using purely rural traditions and environment; the tragic pessimism, less humane and more sophisticated than ▷ Thomas Hardy's, is perhaps a reflection of the disappearing vitality of that way of life. Some other works: *Mark Only* (1924); *Mr Tasker's Gods* (1925); *Kindness in a Corner* (1930). *Fables* was republished as *No Painted Plumage* in 1934.
Bib: Coombes, H., *T. F. Powys*; Hunter, W., *The Novels and Stories of T. F. Powys*.

Press Council, The
A body established by the British Government to maintain good and responsible standards of ▷ journalism. When newspapers seem to abuse their powers by interfering with private life and liberty, complaints may be made to the Council which can then, if it thinks the abuse is genuine, administer a public rebuke to the newspaper concerned. It has no powers of censorship.

Priestley, J. B. (John Boynton) (1894–1984)
British novelist and playwright, whose first success was with *Dangerous Corner* in 1932, a thriller dealing with the theme of time. This was followed by two other 'time' plays, *Time and the Conways* and *I Have Been Here Before*, in 1937. He is notable for experimenting with a variety of dramatic subjects and styles from the popular thrillers such as those mentioned above and *An Inspector Calls* (1945), to conventional comedies like *Laburnum Grove* (1933) and *When We are Married* (1938), the ▷ Chekhovian *Eden End* (1934) and the expressionistic *Johnson over Jordan* (1939). One of his later works was a dramatization with ▷ Iris Murdoch of her novel, *A Severed Head* (1963).
Bib: Evans, G. L., *Priestley the Dramatist*.

Pritchett, V. S. (Victor Sawdon) (b 1900)
Novelist, short-story writer, critic and travel writer. He left school at 15 to work in the leather trade, and also worked in the photographic trade in Paris before becoming a journalist. Since 1926 he has been a regular critic for the ▷ *New Statesman*, and since 1946 a director. He is best known for his short stories, which are economical and understated, employing colloquial dialogue. His work is primarily in a ▷ realist mode, and consists of ironic observation of society and human eccentricity. Story collections are: *Collected Stories* (1982); *More Collected Stories* (1983). His novels are: *Clare Drummer* (1929); *Shirley Sanz* (1932); *Nothing Like Leather* (1935); *Dead Man Leading* (1937); *Mr Beluncle* (1951). Criticism includes: *The Living Novel* (1946); *Balzac: A Biography* (1973); *The Myth Makers: Essays on European, Russian and South American Novelists* (1979).

Proust, Marcel (1871–1922)
French writer. Early in his career, he was the author of critical works, *Les Plaisirs et les jours* (1896; translations from Ruskin), *Pastiches et mélanges* (1919) and two posthumously published works *Contre Sainte-Beuve* (1981), and the incomplete novel *Jean Santeuil* (1952). Proust is nonetheless known for one book, his major work, *A la recherche du temps perdu*. It runs to 3,000 printed pages and was originally published in eight parts between 1913 and 1927. The novel was first translated by C. K. Scott-Moncrieff under the title *Remembrance of Things Past*, but a recent and much improved version has been completed by Terence Kilmartin.

A la recherche is the story of an artistic vocation, the attempt to write a novel which is similar to (though not the same as) that which the reader has before him. The novel itself is full of artist-figures, and the narrator's own endeavours to perceive pattern in disorder and fragmentation centre crucially on a discovery, a discovery about time and memory. The attempt to resurrect and recapture time past through voluntary memory cannot but fail, for voluntary memory is sifted for its relevancies. The past can consequently only be reached by involuntary memory, itself triggered by the most apparently innocuous and circumstantial of objects: a madeleine dipped in tea, a starched napkin, an uneven paving-stone. These objects are associated with forgotten events in the past, and those instants when the bond between past and present is recovered and the past reborn are 'privileged moments' (*moments privilégiés*). The novel jettisons a unilinear plot, while the central focus for narration is restricted to that of Marcel (not to be confused with Proust himself); impressions and sensations are fed through his consciousness which evolves over time and constitutes a devolved, perceptually limited human subject. Proust's portrayal of social and above all sexual relations, moreover, intensifies the sense of a self unable to know others, until the narrator realizes that only art gives access to others, since only in art is there the 'real residue' of the personality.

Proust's novel aroused two kinds of reactions. His minuteness in rendering human consciousness, for example, recalls both ▷ Henry James and ▷ James Joyce. His perception that the insignificance of an incident at the time of experiencing it contrasts with the importance it may come to have in the memory anticipates ▷ Virginia Woolf. The design by which relationships amplify through a lifetime into a pattern evocative of musical composition was emulated by ▷ Anthony Powell in *A Dance to the Music of Time*. On the other hand, other 20th-century novelists, such as ▷ D. H. Lawrence and ▷ L. H. Myers, have rejected Proust on the grounds that his principles are merely aesthetic.

Psychoanalytic criticism

Psychoanalytic and literary criticism both seek to interpret their respective objects of enquiry, and both involve the analysis of language. In its early manifestations psychoanalytical criticism (*eg* Ernest Jones's *Hamlet and Oedipus*; 1949) sought to apply the methods of psychoanalysis to particular texts, in order to uncover their 'unconscious'. Jones's claim was to reveal the causes of Hamlet's behaviour beginning from the assumption that 'current response is always compounded partly of a response to the actual situation and partly of past responses to older situations that are unconsciously felt to be similar'. The French psychoanalyst ▷ Jacques Lacan's re-reading of ▷ Freud has sought to render problematical this relationship between patient and analyst, and, by implication, between text and reader. Lacan's description of the unconscious as being structured 'like a language' raises fundamental questions for the authoritative role usually ascribed to the literary critic. To this extent the 'unconscious' of the literary text is brought into confrontation with the unconscious of the critic.

Many of the terms taken from psychology which are associated with Lacan's reading of Freud have been incorporated into the language of literary criticism; for example, the decentred subject of psychoanalysis, ▷ condensation, ▷ displacement, the realm of the ▷ 'imaginary', the ▷ symbolic order, all refer in some way to textual mechanisms.

Bib: Laplanche, J. and Pontalis, J-B., *The Language of Psychoanalysis*; Lacan, J., *The Four Fundamental Concepts of Psychoanalysis*; Wright, E., *Psychoanalytical Criticism*.

Punch

A weekly comic periodical, founded in 1841. Thomas Hood and W. M. Thackeray were early members of its staff, and it employed a number of distinguished illustrators in the 19th century including Leech, Tenniel, Keene, and du Maurier. From 1849 for a century it kept the same cover picture – of Punch of the puppet-shows. It was at first a radical paper, but as it became more and more an upper-class 'institution', so in politics, tone and taste it began to represent an influential but increasingly narrow section of the upper middle class. It has published the work of many famous cartoonists, including, in recent years, Ronald Searle, Michael Heath, Bill Tidy and Gerald Scarfe. The magazine ceased publication in 1992 due to financial difficulties.

***Pygmalion* (1912)**

A play by ▷ George Bernard Shaw. The theme is the transformation of Eliza, an impoverished, illiterate and wretchedly neglected London girl, into the image of a fashionable lady who can make an imposing appearance at an ambassador's reception. The transformation is contrived by the phonetician Higgins, who undertakes it as a scientific experiment; he resembles the sculptor Pygmalion in bringing into existence a being of great beauty, but, like Pygmalion's statue, Eliza possesses no life, in this case because Higgins has invested no feelings in her, merely using her as an instrument of his research. The play has always had great success, though it is one of the least convincing of Shaw's plays: the real transformation of Eliza could not have been made by changing Eliza's speech sounds, and Shaw falls a victim to the same fallacy that he exposes in Higgins, inasmuch as he, too, fails to understand the true nature of his own creation. The plot was later used as the basis for the musical *My Fair Lady*, first staged in 1956.

Pym, Barbara (1913–80)

Novelist. Educated at Oxford University, she served with the W.R.N.S. during World War II, and subsequently worked at the International African Institute in London. Between 1950 and 1961 she published six novels; there then followed 16 years during which she could not find a publisher. After praise from Lord David Cecil and the poet ▷ Philip Larkin in 1977 her work received renewed attention, and she published a further three novels. Since then her work has enjoyed considerable popularity. Her novels are sensitive, shrewd, ironical portraits of English middle-class life, with a particular focus on the lives of women; the social contexts are frequently academic and clerical. She is often said to write in the tradition of Jane Austen. A further three novels were published posthumously. Her novels are: *Some Tame Gazelle* (1950); *Excellent Women* (1952); *Jane and Prudence* (1953); *Less Than Angels* (1955); *A Glass of Blessings* (1958); *No Fond Return of Love* (1961); *Quartet in Autumn* (1977); *The Sweet Dove Died* (1978); *A Few Green Leaves* (1980); *An Unsuitable Attachment* (1982); *Crampton Hodnet* (1985); *An Academic Question* (1986).

Bib: Benet, D., *The Life and Work of Barbara Pym*.

Rainbow, The (1915)
A novel by ▷ D. H. Lawrence. It is set in Lawrence's own background, the English Midlands; the subject is three generations of the Brangwen family extending from the middle of the last century to the early years of the present one.

The Brangwens are a family of farmers and have for generations lived on their own land which, by the time at which the novel begins, is near an encroaching industrial area. The men of the family are depicted as concentrating their minds earthwards, on their work and surroundings; the women have tended to look outwards to society, and to emulate their social superiors. Tom Brangwen, the first of the main characters, is sent to a grammar school by his ambitious mother; the experience both frustrates him and arouses him. His awakened need for what is strange and mysterious attracts him to Lydia Lensky, an aristocratic but impoverished Polish exile, a widow, and the mother of a small daughter. They marry and although their marriage meets difficulties it becomes a happy one. Lydia and Tom remain ignorant of much in each other's nature, but Lydia finds confidence in Tom's established way of life, while he finds enlargement precisely in what, for him, is mysterious in his wife. Tom's stepdaughter, Anna, is attracted to his nephew, Will Brangwen, who has had an urban upbringing and has a strong artistic imagination and profound religious instincts inherited from his forefathers. This marriage is much less happy. Anna is suspicious and jealous of her husband's religious spirit, and since he himself cannot relate it to a way of life, she succeeds in destroying it. In doing so, she unintentionally transforms him from an original artist into a mere craftsman in the William Morris style. They are united in a passionate night-time sensuality, but have no daytime union. Their daughter, Ursula, belongs to the first generation of modern women: she sets out to be a teacher, and after an intense struggle in one of the characteristically inhuman English board schools, she succeeds in affirming her independence. But her love affair with Skrebensky, a thoroughly Anglicized descendant of another Polish exile, ends in frustration. She inherits from her mother a capacity for passion which expresses her full nature, whereas his nature is divided between a dead conformity to society and a sensuality which is incapable of real passion. Ursula tries to compromise by suppressing her instincts, but a concluding scene, in which she is exposed at night to the menace of restless horses, on to which she projects her disturbed emotions, shows that she is wrong in attempting this solution. The story of Ursula and her sister Gudrun is continued in ▷ *Women in Love*, originally conceived as part of the same novel. The title of the novel refers to its central symbol of a rainbow, or arch. This symbol signifies an ideal which modifies with time, from the stability of an achieved relationship in the first generation to the transcendant hope of a collective rebirth at the end of the novel.

The novel was for a time suppressed on grounds of immorality, but is now regarded as one of Lawrence's greatest achievements.

Raine, Craig (b 1944)
Poet. His first two collections, *The Onion, Memory* (1978) and *A Martian Sends a Postcard Home* (1979), established a vogue for ▷ 'Martian' poetry in this country. *Rich* (1984) shows him extending his work into areas such as prose ▷ autobiography. He has also written an opera libretto and work for the theatre.

Raine, Kathleen (b 1908)
Poet and critic. Raine has been prolifically publishing poetry since the 1930s; in 1943 *Stone and Flower: Poems 1935–43* appeared. In 1956 *Collected Poems* appeared, followed by *The Hollow Hill* (1964). The 1981 *Collected Poems, 1935–80* gathered together much of her important work. Raine is also well known as a scholar of William Blake, and has also written on ▷ Yeats and Coleridge. Recent collections include: *The Lost Country* (1971); *On A Deserted Shore* (1973); *The Oracle in the Heart* (1980), and *World Within a World* (1982), as well as three volumes of her ▷ autobiography. In 1991 she gave what she announced as her last public lecture, at Liverpool University.

Rationalism

1 In philosophy, the belief that reason, rather than sensation, is the only certain guide to knowledge.

2 In religion, the practice of seeking explanations which satisfy reason for what had been accepted as supernatural.

Rattigan, Sir Terence (1911–77)
British dramatist whose first stage success was with the light comedy *French Without Tears* (1936). This was followed by such plays as *Flare Path* (1942), *While the Sun Shines* (1943), and *Love in Idleness* (1944), the last

of these a modern treatment of Hamlet and Claudius. *The Winslow Boy*, a play about a father's struggle to defend his son on a charge of theft, won the Ellen Terry Award for the best play of the year in 1946. *The Browning Version* received the same award in 1948. *The Deep Blue Sea* (1952), a piece about passion and suicide, might have been more interesting had Rattigan been able to deal openly, in the play, with his own tragic homosexual love which inspired him to write it. But English repression is a subject which he knows and writes about well. Rattigan was well aware that his commercial success depended on the appeal of his plays to 'Aunt Edna', as he called the middle-brow members of his audience. His sound judgement of the market ensured continued success with *Separate Tables* (1955), *Variations on a Theme* (1958), *Ross*, a dramatization of the life of T. E. Lawrence (1960), *A Bequest to the Nation* (1970) and *Cause Célèbre* (1977).
Bib: Darlow, M. and Hodson, G., *Rattigan: The Man and His Work.*

Reader-response criticism
▷ Reception theory.

Realism
A term used in various senses, both in philosophy and in literary criticism. Three principal meanings, two of them philosophical and one literary, are particularly worth distinction.

1 In medieval philosophy, the realists were opposed to the nominalists. Realism here means that classes of things ('universals') have reality whereas individuals have not, or at least have less: *eg* individual birds take their reality from the classification 'bird'. The nominalists considered that only the individual bird has reality, and that the classification 'bird' is only a formulation in the mind.

2 Since the Middle Ages, realism has become opposed to ▷ idealism. Here realism means that reality exists apart from ideas about it in the mind, and idealism represents the view that we can know nothing that is not in our minds.

3 Literary realism is a 19th-century conception, related to 2 and coterminous with industrial capitalism. In general, it means the use of the imagination to represent things as common sense supposes they are. It does not apply only to 19th-century literature; Defoe is commonly called a realist because of his factual description and narration. Nineteenth-century realism in literature arose, however, from a reaction against 19th-century Romanticism, and it is related to naturalism; for a discussion of late 20th-century critiques of realism as a vehicle of ▷ ideology, see Catherine Belsey, *Critical Practice*. Realism is also used in modern literature in opposition to what is regarded as sentimentalism – the disposition to represent feelings (*eg* the various forms of love) as nicer than we know them to be; an illogical extension of this use of the term is sometimes to apply it to literature that represents experience as nastier than we know it to be. Finally, realism in literature is sometimes related to nominalism, *ie* the realist writer is he who represents individuals rather than types; in this sense, modern literary realism is the opposite of the realism of medieval philosophy.

Reception theory
This movement is associated pre-eminently with the German contemporary literary theorists Wolfgang Iser and Hans-Robert Jauss, and is often linked with reader-response criticism. Reception theory emphasizes the reader's consumption of the literary text over and above the question of the sum total of rhetorical devices which contribute to its structure as a piece of literature. The work of reception (*Rezeptionästhetik*) causes the reader constantly to rethink the canonical value of texts, since it involves noting the history of a text's reception as well as the current value which it may possess for the critic. In so far as reception theory concerns itself with larger historical questions, it emphasizes histories of response which help to account for the reception of particular texts in the present. The approach to 'history' outlined here is pragmatic, and the emphasis is laid firmly on the matter of the interaction between text and reader and on the way cultural context is required to make sense of literature.
Bib: Holub, R., *Reception Theory*; Fish, S., *Is there a text in this class?*

Redgrove, Peter (b 1932)
Poet and novelist. Redgrove is a prolific writer whose work straddles many forms – he has worked as a scientific journalist, and has written many novels, poems, plays (he won the Italia prize in 1981) and non-fiction (including *The Wise Wound* with poet ▷ Penelope Shuttle, with whom he lives in Cornwall). His poetic work was originally associated with that of the Group, the 'school' of post-Movement (▷ Movement) poets which included his contemporaries at Cambridge in the late 1950s, ▷ Ted Hughes and ▷ Sylvia Plath. Redgrove is now also a lay psychoanalyst.

His poetry publications include: *The Collector* (1960); *The Force* (1966); *Sons of my Skin* (1975); *The Weddings at Nether Powers* (1979); *The Applebroadcast* (1981) and *The Man Named East* (1985).

Renaissance in England, The
'Renaissance' (or 'Renascence') derives from Latin 'renascentia' = 'rebirth'. The word was first used by Italian scholars in the mid-16th century to express the rediscovery of ancient Roman and Greek culture, which was now studied for its own sake and not used merely to enhance the authority of the Church. Modern scholars are more inclined to use the term to express a great variety of interdependent changes which Europe underwent politically, economically and culturally between 1450 (although the starting-points were much earlier) and 1600. The religious outcome of these changes is expressed through the terms Reformation and Counter-reformation, a sequence of events which were closely bound up with the Renaissance.

In England, the Renaissance is usually thought of as beginning with the accession of the House of Tudor to the throne in 1485. Politically, this marks the end of the period of civil war amongst the old feudal aristocracy (the Wars of the Roses) in the mid-15th century, and the establishment of something like a modern, efficient, centralized state; technically, the date is close to that of the introduction of printing into England – an invention without which the great cultural changes of the Renaissance could not have occurred. Culturally, the first important period in England was the reign of the second Tudor monarch, Henry VIII. This was the period of the English ▷ humanists More, Grocyn, Linacre and the poet Sir Thomas Wyatt.

Several distinctive features characterize the English Renaissance. The first is the lateness of its impact: Italian, French, German, Dutch and Spanish scholars had already worked on the ancient Greek and Latin writers, and had produced works of their own inspired by the classics; in consequence, English culture was revitalized not so much directly by the classics as by contemporary Europeans under the influence of the classics (▷ translation). Castiglione's *The Courtier*, Machiavelli's *The Prince*, Ariosto's *Orlando*, were as important in the English Renaissance as Virgil's *Aeneid* or the plays of Seneca, and it was characteristic that North translated Plutarch's *Lives* not from the original Greek but from a French version. Such an influx of foreign influences, both contemporary and ancient, might have overwhelmed the native English literary tradition but for two more distinctive features: England as an insular country followed a course of social and political history which was to a great extent independent of the course of history elsewhere in Europe, for example in the peculiarity of the English Reformation, and this assisted the country in preserving its cultural independence; and owing to the example of the works of the 14th-century poet Chaucer, the native literature was sufficiently vigorous and experienced in assimilating foreign influences without being subjected by them. A fourth characteristic of English Renaissance literature is that it is primarily artistic, rather than philosophical and scholarly, and a fifth is the coinciding of the Renaissance and the Reformation in England, in contrast to the rest of Europe where the Reformation (or, in countries that remained Roman Catholic, the Counter-reformation) succeeded the Renaissance.

The English Renaissance was largely literary, and achieved its finest expression in the so-called Elizabethan drama which began to excel only in the last decade of the 16th century and reached its height in the first 15 years of the 17th; its finest exponents are Christopher Marlowe, Ben Jonson and ▷ William Shakespeare. Non-dramatic poetry was also extremely rich, and reached its peak in the same period in the work of Edmund Spenser, Philip Sidney, Shakespeare and John Donne, but it is typical of the lateness of the Renaissance in England that its most ambitious product, John Milton's epic *Paradise Lost*, was published as late as 1667. Native English prose shaped itself more slowly than poetry; More wrote his *Utopia* in Latin, which was the vehicle of some other writers including Francis Bacon (in much of his work) owing to its advantages (for international circulation) over English, at a time when the latter was little learned in other countries. Nonetheless English prose developed with vigour in native English writers such as Roger Ascham, Thomas North, Richard Hooker, in the English works of Francis Bacon, and in the translators of the ▷ Bible.

Renault, Mary (1905–83)
Writer of popular historical novels. Renault was born and educated in England, working as a nurse during World War II, after which she emigrated with her life-long partner Julie Mullard to South Africa, where she was an active anti-apartheid campaigner until her death in Cape Town. Most of Renault's

highly successful novels deal with the classical world, and, in their exploration of the transition from matriarchal social systems and religion to more modern partriarchy, they show the influence of ▷ Robert Graves's *The White Goddess*. All of Renault's novels are distinguished by the meticulous research and accuracy of historical details which underpin them. Her best-known books are the Alexander trilogy (which covers the life of Alexander the Great: *Fire from Heaven*, 1970, *The Persian Boy* 1972, and *Funeral Games* 1981), and two novels narrated by Theseus (*The King Must Die*, 1958, and *The Bull from the Sea*, 1962). Her other works include: *Purposes of Love* (1939); *The Charioteer* (1953); *The Last of the Wine* (1956); *The Mask of Apollo* (1966); *The Praise Singer* (1978).
Bib: Dick, B. F., *The Hellenism of Mary Renault*; Wolf, P., *Mary Renault*.

Reviews and periodicals
The English periodical press arose gradually from the controversial religious and political pamphleteering of the late 16th and 17th centuries. It became established as a recognized institution early in the 18th century, and it was also in the 18th century that the review, which expresses opinion, became distinguished from the newspaper, which gives priority to information on current events. The great age for the periodical press was, however, 1800–1914; this was the period when the quarterlies and the monthlies had their widest influence, and the weeklies their largest circulation proportionately to the size of the reading public. Since 1914, the influence of the quarterlies and monthlies has declined; the weeklies have remained important, but they have had to compete on the one side with the tendency of newspapers to include a large amount of material originally restricted to reviews, and on the other with the medium of broadcasting. Modern review publications include the *T.L.S.* (▷ *The Times*) and the *New York Review of Books*.

Rhetoric
Rhetoric in the medieval period was a formal skill of considerable importance. It was taken to mean the effective presentation of ideas with a set of rules or style, and was founded in the classical tradition of Aristotle and Cicero. It was taught in monastic schools as part of the *trivium*, Rhetoric, Logic and Grammar, which used as its basic text Geoffrey de Vinsauf's *Poetria Nova* (1200). Rhetoric not only formed patterns in which texts should be written, but it also governed how the works should be received and allocated them to particular categories, *eg* epic, debate or sermon. The system of rhetoric was paramount to the operation of literature in the medieval period.

Similarly, almost all of the practice or theory of writing in the ▷ Renaissance period was touched by what became known as the 'Art of Rhetoric'. Rhetorical theory formed an important part of the educational syllabus at the universities, and almost every major writer of the 16th and 17th centuries would have undergone some training in rhetoric. Rhetoric was learned first through reading the classical textbooks on rhetoric, in particular the works of Quintilian (especially the *Institutio Oratore*) and Cicero. Secondly, practical rhetorical exercises were performed by the student in which a particular topic was debated. In these debates, the student was expected to be able to organize an argument according to set formulae, producing examples with which to sustain the analysis which themselves would be derived from a suitable store of words, images, fables and metaphors discovered in reading classical texts.

But the production of arguments was only one part of the rhetoricians' skills. Rhetoric also involved the classification of language – in particular the classification and analysis of ▷ figures of speech. Further, it was understood as an enabling tool by which ▷ discourse could be reproduced. In essence, therefore, it offered a system for producing both speech and writing. This system can be considered under five distinct parts: **1** 'invention', which signifies the discovery of arguments applicable to a given case; **2** 'arrangement' or 'disposition', which governed the ordering of the arguments to be used; **3** 'style' or the actual choice of words and units of expression; **4** the important area of 'memory', which helped the rhetorician develop skills in recalling the order and substance of the argument being deployed; **5** 'delivery', which was applicable mainly to spoken discourse and which governed such details as the appropriate facial expressions or gestures which might be used.

Whilst rhetoric was understood as a way of facilitating the classification of the various parts of an argument it was also a powerful tool in the analysis of discourse and it can thus be understood as a form of literary criticism. It was, however, in its abiding influence on stylistic forms that it was of most importance to the Renaissance writer. Numerous textbooks on rhetoric were published throughout the 16th century in

England. Perhaps the most important were: Leonard Cox, *The Art or Craft of Rhetoric* (1624); Richard Sherry *A Treatise of Schemes and Tropes* (1550); Thomas Wilson, *Art of Rhetoric* (1553); Henry Peacham, *The Garden of Eloquence* (1577); and Abraham Fraunce, *Arcadian Rhetoric* (1584). But many other texts were written with the art of rhetoric either governing the structure or informing the language. Sir Philip Sidney's *An Apologie for Poetrie*, for example, is structured according to rhetorical principles of organization.

Recent developments in critical theory have sought to re-emphasize rhetoric as a form of critical practice, particularly in relation to the *effects* that any verbal construction may have on those to whom it is addressed. In this respect rhetoric is closely associated with some of the larger issues which surface in relation to the theory of 'discourse'. The recent emphasis upon the *structure* of discourse draws attention away from language as a means of *classifying* to one of examining the way discourses are constructed in order to achieve certain effects. Here the emphasis would be on the different *ways* in which particular figures are presented in language, and what that presentation may involve. This form of rhetorical analysis has been undertaken by ▷ Jacques Derrida in volumes such as *Of Grammatology* (1974), by ▷ Paul de Man in his *Blindness and Insight* (1971), by ▷ Terry Eagleton in *Criticism and Ideology* (1976), and in a whole range of texts by ▷ Michel Foucault.

Rhys, Jean (1894–1979)
Adopted name of novelist, born Jean Williams on the West Indian island of Dominica. Brought up speaking both English and the Dominican French dialect, she lived in Europe from the age of 16, moving between London, Vienna and Paris before finally settling in Devon. *The Left Bank* (1927), a series of sketches of Bohemian life in Paris, was followed by four novels which tell the stories of isolated, poor, victimized women, adrift in London or Paris, in a laconic, lucid style which combines the tragic and the absurd. These are: *Postures* (1928) (in the U.S.A. as *Quartet*; 1929); *After Leaving Mr Mackenzie* (1931); *Voyage in the Dark* (1934) and *Good Morning Midnight* (1939). After a considerable period of critical neglect, *Wide Sargasso Sea* (1966) reawakened widespread interest in her work, especially among ▷ feminists. It recounts the early life of the first Mrs Rochester from Charlotte Brontë's *Jane Eyre*, rendering the alienation and suffering of an isolated consciousness with great power. Set mostly in the West Indies, it is richer in imagery and symbolism than her earlier work, combining lyricism and psychological insight with an exploration of political, racial and sexual oppression. She has written two books of short stories: *Tigers Are Better Looking* (1968) and *Sleep It Off Lady* (1976). *Quartet* was made into a film (with a screenplay by ▷ Ruth Prawer Jhabvala) by the director James Ivory in 1981.
Bib: Stanley, T. F., *Jean Rhys: A Critical Study*.

Richards, I. A. (1893–1979)
Critic. His approach to poetry was philosophic, linguistic and psychological. One of his important insights was that we are inevitably influenced by some kind of 'poetry', even if it is only that of bad films and magazine covers, or advertisements. In *Principles of Literary Criticism* (1924) and *Science and Poetry* (1926) he discusses what kind of truth is the subject matter of poetry, the place of poetry in the context of the rest of life, and what is the nature of critical judgements of poetry. He worked to his conclusion on Benthamite (Utilitarian) lines, of asking what is 'the use' of poetry, but his conclusion was not far from that of Matthew Arnold, that poetry's function in the modern world is that formerly provided by religion – to provide a 'touchstone' of value, and hence, if only indirectly, a guide to living (see Arnold's 'Study of Poetry', in *Essays in Criticism*, 2nd Series, 1888). This view resembles the judgements of other writers of the 1920s and 30s, such as ▷ Pound, ▷ Wyndham Lewis, ▷ Eliot, ▷ Leavis, though each of them arrives at his judgement by a different approach. Richards's *Practical Criticism* (1929) is a teaching manual for the study of poetry with the aim of training students to judge poems presented anonymously, without being influenced by the author's reputation; its ideas have been extensively followed in English and American schools and universities. Much of his later work was purely linguistic, *eg Basic English and its Uses* (1943). Other works: *The Meaning of Meaning* (with Ogden, 1923); *Coleridge on Imagination* (1934); *The Philosophy of Rhetoric* (1936); *Speculative Instruments* (1955); *Goodbye Earth and Other Poems* (1959); *The Screens* (1961).

▷ New criticism.
Bib: Hyman, S., *The Armed Vision*.

Richardson, Dorothy (1873–1957)
Novelist. Born in Abingdon, Berkshire, she worked as a governess from the age of 17,

before moving to London where she became an intimate of ▷ H. G. Wells and part of a circle of socialists and intellectuals. She took up journalism, and for the rest of her life earned a meagre living by this means, while dedicating herself to her long novel, *Pilgrimage*, which consists of the following volumes: *Pointed Roofs* (1915); *Backwater* (1916); *Honeycomb* (1917); *The Tunnel* (1919); *Interim* (1919); *Deadlock* (1921); *Revolving Lights* (1923); *The Trap* (1925); *Oberland* (1927); *Dawn's Left Hand* (1931); *Clear Horizon* (1935); *Dimple Hill* (1938); *March Moonlight* (1967). It is a semi-autobiographical work, recounting the life of the heroine, Miriam Henderson, through concentration on her continuous subjective experience of the present moment. Richardson, together with ▷ Virginia Woolf and ▷ James Joyce, was responsible for the development of the ▷ stream of consciousness technique (though she disliked this term) which was an important aspect of the ▷ modernist revolution in narrative.
Bib: Rosenberg, J., *Dorothy Richardson: the Genius They Forgot.*

Richardson, Henry Handel (1870–1946)
Pseudonym of Australian novelist and short-story writer Ethel Florence Lindesay Richardson Robertson. She studied music in Leipzig from 1887 to 1890, lived in Strasbourg 1895–1903, and in England from 1903. Her trilogy *The Fortunes of Richard Mahony* uses elements of her father's life, and is the sombre tale of an emigrant doctor's rise to riches and unexpected loss of fortune. It consists of *Australia Felix* (1917); *The Way Home* (1925); *Ultima Thule* (1929). Her work shows the influence of Goethe and the German Romantic tradition. Her other novels are: *Maurice Guest* (1908); *The Getting of Wisdom* (1910); *The Young Cosima* (1939). Story collections include: *The End of Childhood and Other Stories* (1934).
Bib: McLeod, K., *Henry Handel Richardson: A Critical Study.*

Riley, Joan (b 1958)
Novelist. Born in Jamaica, and educated at the universities of Sussex and London, she teaches black history and culture and works for a drugs advisory agency. Her novels are: *The Unbelonging* (1985); *Waiting in the Twilight* (1987); *Romance* (1988). Her work is concerned with the hardships, and the search for a sense of meaning and identity, of people born in Jamaica and living in Britain.
▷ Commonwealth literatures.

Roberts, Michèle (b 1949)
Poet, short-story writer and novelist. Roberts is a prolific writer, has appeared widely on television, radio and in anthologies, and regularly gives readings of her work. She was very influential on the development and recognition of contemporary poetry in her capacity as poetry editor of the London listings magazine *City Limits*, a post now held by younger poet and critic, Briar Wood. Her recent publications include *The Mirror of the Mother* (1986), a volume of poetry, *The Book of Mrs Noah* (1987) and *In the Red Kitchen* (1990).

Romanticism
Two phases in the development of this concept need to be distinguished:
1 *'Romantick' taste* (c 1650–c 1789) The adjective 'romantic' came into use in the mid-17th century, at the point when the romance form, which had dominated secular literature during the Middle Ages and the ▷ Renaissance, fell from prominence. As ▷ Enlightenment philosophy and neo-classical taste developed, the romance form was subjected to self-conscious analysis and criticism. In its early stages the word took various forms: 'romancy', 'romancical', 'romantique', 'romantick'. Its meaning, 'like a romance', carried a number of different connotations, related to the various features of romance: the archaic rituals of chivalry, magic, superstition, improbable adventures, idealistic love, and wild scenery. Samuel Pepys used the word in 1667: 'These things are almost romantique, and yet true'. And the *Oxford English Dictionary* cites a 1659 reference to 'An old house in a romancey place'.

During the 18th century romantic wildness was disapproved of by the more puritanical, rational and enlightened reader. Some thinkers, however, such as the third Earl of Shaftesbury, self-consciously boasted of their emotional idealism and enthusiasm for wild scenery. Also most readers enjoyed the 'romantick' alternatives to neo-classicism indulged in at times by the poets and prose writers. Sometimes poets employed imitations of ornamental, medieval or 'Gothic' forms, such as the Spenserian stanza and the ▷ ballad, though romantic sensibility could also be expressed in the heroic ▷ couplet. Alexander Pope's *Eloisa to Abelard* and *Elegy to the Memory of an Unfortunate Lady*, James Thomson's *Castle of Indolence*, Thomas Gray's translations of Norse and Welsh ballads and his ode, *The Bard*, and James Macpherson's Ossian, illustrate the range of romantic taste in the 18th century. The subjects of these works – passionate love, religious enthusiasm, laziness, medieval history, suicide – lie outside the mainstream of ▷ Augustanism, and they all share (with different degrees of seriousness) a sense of daring literary excess.

2 *The Romantic Movement* (1789–1824) The six great poets of what is now generally called the Romantic Movement, are in many ways extremely diverse. William Blake, the pioneer of the group, was broadly speaking a fundamentalist Christian, who felt that William Wordsworth's pantheistic 'natural piety' made him 'a Heathen Philosopher at Enmity against all true Poetry'. Lord Byron emulated the wit and urbanity of Alexander Pope, whereas John Keats was contemptuous of neo-classical couplet writers who 'sway'd about upon a rocking horse,/And thought it Pegasus'. Percy Bysshe Shelley was an atheist, Samuel Taylor Coleridge became an apologist for the Church of England. However, despite their differences, these poets show essential similarities in their response to the same historical situation, and do form a coherent group. It will be best to begin by describing their characteristics, leaving the label, 'Romanticism', to be explained afterwards.

The ▷ French Revolution dispelled the literary self-consciousness of the period of Sensibility. On the political level, the bourgeois complacency of the earlier period was suddenly lost. Even conservative writers at this time, such as Edmund Burke and Sir Walter Scott, were forced to find new arguments in favour of the *status quo*, based on appeals to ancient tradition and emotional prejudice, rather than the authority of Reason and the natural order. The major poets were less inhibited. Blake was morally indignant about the institutions of State and Church. Wordsworth and Coleridge began their careers as fervent proponents of social revolution, while the second-generation Romantics, Byron, Shelley, and (less prominently) Keats, remained true to the original revolutionary spirit through the succeeding period of reaction. The Romantics rejected the rigid social and literary hierarchy of the 18th century. Where Pope in the *Essay on Man* condescendingly conceded 'the poor Indian' his Natural Religion, Wordsworth feels profoundly shamed by that of the lowly leech gatherer in *Resolution and Independence*. The feelings of the individual take precedence over Reason and social convention, and particularly in the works of Wordsworth, outcasts, the very young, the very old, the poor and the mad, are seriously attended to. In the work of both Blake and Wordsworth youth becomes the fountain of wisdom rather than age. In a similar way dreams take on a new significance as the key to the unconscious depths of our being. Coleridge in his *Biographia Literaria*, gives a new, more complex meaning to the key Romantic term 'imagination'.

Fundamental to Romanticism is a new attitude towards the role of man in nature. The writers of the Enlightenment period, the Earl of Rochester, John Dryden and Pope had shared with the ancients a certainty as to what nature was, and a confidence about their place in it. For them *human* nature was an integral part, even the greatest glory, of 'Nature', and (like gravity) obeyed 'Nature's laws'. In the early stages of Enlightenment it seemed easy to reconcile the new exploitative science and technology with a traditional piety about God's creation. But by the end of the century a crisis had developed. Enlightenment had finally robbed nature of its authentic, primitive awesomeness. More practically its manipulative exploitation by man seemed in danger of destroying nature itself. William Cowper expressed this new mood of diffidence and alienation in his aphorism: 'God made the country, and man made the town', while Shelley declared more boldly that 'man, having enslaved the elements, remains himself a slave'. Newton's light had reduced nature to a manipulable material system. It had become either a useful recreation facility (Wordsworth wrote a guidebook to the picturesque Lakes), or – in atavistic reaction – a mystical substitute for religion. Shelley's proposed answer to the crisis of Enlightenment, like that of all the Romantic poets, was to cultivate the 'imagination' and 'the poetical faculty'.

Nature thus ceases to be an objective intellectual concept for the Romantics, and becomes instead an elusive metaphor. The brisk clarity of Pope's: 'First follow *Nature* . . . which is still the same', is replaced by the anxious emotive rhetoric of Wordsworth's: 'And I have felt/A sense sublime/Of something far more deeply interfused'. Nature is often approached indirectly – seen from afar, or not *seen* at all: 'I cannot see what flowers are at my feet,/Nor what soft incense hangs upon the boughs,/But, in embalmed darkness, guess each sweet' (*Ode to a Nightingale*, stanza V). The relation between the poet and nature becomes ambiguous and insecure: 'I see, not feel, how beautiful they are!' (*Dejection: An Ode*, stanza II); 'Whither is fled the visionary gleam?'/Where is it now, the glory and the dream?' (*Ode: Intimations of Immortality*, ll. 56–7); 'The wilderness has a mysterious tongue/Which teaches awful doubt' (Shelley, *Mont Blanc*, II. 76–7). From being the middle term in the Great Chain, 'The glory, jest, and riddle of the world!' (*Essay on Man*, II, l. 17), or – less buoyantly but equally definitively – a 'reas'ning *Engine*' inevitably destined for the dirt (Rochester, *Satyr on Reason*, ll. 29–30), the human being has become a dubious subjectivism, constantly redefining his or her identity.

The Romantic poets continued to employ the 'romantick' forms of the earlier period: Spenserian stanzas, ballad, and irregular ▷ ode. They cultivated medievalism and imitated Elizabethan and Jacobean playwrights. They also revived the neglected ▷ sonnet form. However, their designation 'Romantic Poets' derives less from their development of previous romantic taste, than from the growing popularity of German aesthetic categories in England. In the late 18th century Goethe and Schiller had developed the contrast between romantic (emotional, inspirational) art, and classical (serene, balanced) art, into a theoretical opposition between aesthetic absolutes, and the German critic Schlegel and the French essayist Mme de Staël had popularized this distinction. At first, observers in England saw this debate as a strictly foreign phenomenon. Byron in a letter of 1820 remarked 'I perceive that in Germany as well as in Italy, there is a great struggle about what they call *Classical* and *Romantic*', and he went on to hope that such disputes would not spread to England. However, such a polarity does seem to underlie some of Keats's work. His *Hyperion*, and his *Ode on a Grecian Urn* (written after he had seen the Parthenon or 'Elgin' marbles in London), can be seen as 'classical', while his *Eve of St Agnes* and *Ode to a Nightingale* are 'romantic'.

The abstract noun 'Romanticism' did not come into use in England until the mid-19th century; early citations in the *Oxford English Dictionary* are in reference to the music of Liszt, and in the phrase 'German Romanticism'. By the time readers began to see these six English poets as forming a single 'movement' it seemed natural to simplify their work in accordance with this categorization. Romanticism thus stands as an emotional reaction against the rational classicism of 18th century Augustanism. It is important to remember that all these terms embody large simplifications. If they are used without a sense of the historical complexities which lie behind them, they can distort the literature to which they refer, rather than illuminate it. Traces of Romanticism are to be found in key 20th-century works, and the Romantic movement has had a profound impact on modern work. The poet ▷ W. B. Yeats, for instance, has been called 'The Last Romantic', and writers whose work has emphasized passionate or vitalist experiences (such as novelist ▷ D. H. Lawrence or poet ▷ Dylan Thomas) have often been aligned with the concerns of Romanticism rather than with those of contemporary modernists.

Bib: Abrams, M. H., *The Mirror and the Lamp*: Praz, M., *The Romantic Agony*; Ford, B. (ed.), *New Pelican Guide to English Literature, Vol. 5: From Blake to Byron*; Bloom, H., *The Visionary Company*; Watson, J. R., *English Poetry of the Romantic Period: 1789–1830*; Butler, M., *Rebels and Reactionaries: English Literature and its Background: 1760–1830*; McGann, J., *The Romantic Ideology*; Mellor, A.K., *Romanticism and Feminism*.

Rosenberg, Isaac (1890–1918)

Poet. He was born in Bristol, and educated at an elementary school in London. He then became apprenticed to an engraver, and entered the Slade School of Art in 1911. He joined the army in 1915, serving as a private soldier, and was killed in action. He was the most original of all the 'War poets'. His work is full of rhythmic energy, less sombre than ▷ Wilfred Owen's, and bolder in imagery. Owen reacted with indignation and compassion against the war; in the Preface to his poems he wrote: 'Above all I am not concerned with Poetry. My subject is War, and the pity of War. The Poetry is in the pity.' Rosenberg wrote in a letter (1916): 'I will not leave a corner of my consciousness covered up but saturate myself with the strange and extraordinary new conditions of this life, and it will all refine itself into poetry later on.' Works include: *Night and Day* (1912); *Youth* (1915); *Poems* (ed. G. Bottomley, with a Memoir by L. Binyon; 1922). *Collected Poems* (ed. G. Bottomley and D. Harding, 1937). Rosenberg's definitive *Collected Works* appeared in 1979.

▷ War poets.

Bib: Cohen, J., *Journey to the Trenches: The Life of Isaac Rosenberg*; Liddiard, J., *Isaac Rosenberg: The Half-Used Life*.

Royal Court Theatre

A theatre of this name has existed in Sloane Square since 1871. The first outstanding period of its history was between 1904 and

1907 when, under the management of J. E. Vedrenne and ▷ Harley Granville Barker, the work of new writers such as ▷ Shaw and ▷ Galsworthy was presented, as well as works by Euripides, ▷ Ibsen, Hauptmann and Maeterlinck. Since 1956, when ▷ John Osborne's ▷ *Look Back In Anger* was performed by George Devine's company, the English Stage Company, the theatre has consistently supported the work of new writers, helping to establish, amongst others, the reputations of John Osborne, ▷ John Arden, ▷ Edward Bond, ▷ Christopher Hampton, ▷ Caryl Churchill, Bill Gaskill, Peter Gill and Max Stafford-Clark.
Bib: Browne, T., *Playwright's Theatre*; MacCarthy, D., *The Court Theatre*; Roberts, P., *The Royal Court Theatre 1965–1972*.

Royal Shakespeare Company
The resident company at the Royal Shakespeare Theatre (formerly the Memorial Theatre) in Stratford-upon-Avon since 1960. The first general director was ▷ Peter Hall who was replaced by Trevor Nunn in 1968. Recent directors for the company include Bill Alexander, John Barton, Terry Hands, Barry Kyle and Adrian Noble. Although the company mainly produces ▷ Shakespeare's plays, there is a policy of showing the work of his contemporaries and encouraging new modern writers. The company now has a second theatre in Stratford, The Swan, which contains a scaled-down imitation of an Elizabethan stage. It also has two theatres for large- and small-scale productions in the Barbican Centre in London.
Bib: Beaumann, S., *The R.S.C., A History of Ten Decades*; Chambers, C., *Other Spaces: New Theatre and the R.S.C.*

Rudkin, David (1936)
British dramatist whose first major play, *Afore Night Come* (1962) explored mysterious dark forces affecting apparently ordinary life in the modern British countryside. This, and later plays, have been performed by the ▷ Royal Shakespeare Company. For some years Rudkin turned his back on the stage and worked for television, his two best-known plays during this time being *Children Playing* (1967) and *Blodwen Home from Rachel's Wedding* (1969). *Cries from Casement as His Bones Are Brought to Dublin* (1973) and *Ashes* (1975) marked his return to the stage with dramatizations of events in Northern Ireland (a subject often avoided by modern British dramatists). Rudkin is clear about the political purpose behind his work: 'I believe the dramatist's function in a society to be to transmute the idiosyncracies of personal life experience into metaphors of public, political value to mankind.' Other plays include: *The Sons of Light* (1977); *The Triumph of Death* (1981); a translation of *Peer Gynt* (1983); *The Saxon Shore* (1986).

Rushdie, Salman (b 1947)
Novelist. Born in Bombay and educated at Cambridge University, his second novel, *Midnight's Children* (1981) won the Booker Prize and became a best-seller. It is a voluminous work, ranging in time from World War I to 1977, and combining a realistic portrayal of poverty and suffering with magic, fantasy, farce, symbolism and ▷ allegory in a manner which associates it with ▷ magic realism. Its many narrative strategies compete with, and undermine, each other, and serve to question the relation of history to fiction; in this respect Rushdie is a ▷ postmodernist writer. In particular, narrative multiplicity functions in his work as a form of resistance to the unitary nature of ▷ imperialist ideology and political control. He is an inventive, self-conscious and versatile writer, with a flamboyant and indulgent style. His other novels are: *Grimus* (1975); *Shame* (1983), and ▷ *The Satanic Verses* (1988) which aroused worldwide controversy and criticism from Muslims for its alleged blasphemy. Following the death sentence imposed upon Rushdie by the Ayatollah Khomeini, Rushdie went into hiding in 1989, and produced his children's book (▷ children's books), *Haroun and the Sea of Dreams* in 1990. Travel writing: *The Jaguar Smile: A Nicaraguan Journey* (1987).

Russell, Bertrand Arthur William, Lord (1872–1970)
Philosopher. Russell's important work on mathematical philosophy and logic is one of the foundations of 20th-century Anglo-Saxon philosophy. His most influential texts are *The Principles of Mathematics* (1903); *Principia Mathematica* (1910–13, written in collaboration with his Cambridge tutor, A. N. Whitehead); *The Problems of Philosophy* (1912); his epistemological works *Mysticism and Logic* (1918), *Analysis of Mind* (1921) and *Human Knowledge* (1948); and the accessible *History of Western Philosophy* (1945). As this indicates, Russell's working life was long and illustrious; he was a fringe member of the ▷ Bloomsbury Group (writing on aesthetics, and a famous sparring-partner for ▷ D. H. Lawrence). Later in life Russell was a founder member

of ▷ CND. He was married to writer Dora Russell.

Russian Formalism
▷ Formalism.

Russian influence on English literature
The international importance of Russian literature belongs chiefly to its achievements in the 19th century. Until the middle of the 19th century, the influence was chiefly from Britain upon Russia: Laurence Sterne, Walter Scott, Lord Byron and, later, Charles Dickens all made an important impression on Russian writers. Since about 1850, however, the balance of influence has been in the opposite direction, although Russian literature has chiefly been known in translation, which has limited extensive public knowledge to prose works, especially the novels. These have been widely read, especially in the famous translations by Constance Garnett, who translated Tolstoy, Dostoevski, Turgenev, ▷ Chekhov and Gogol in the decades before and after 1900.

Tolstoy and Turgenev were the first Russian novelists to receive wide acclaim in Britain and Tolstoy is still considered by many the supreme novelist. His reputation in Britain owed much to Matthew Arnold, whose essay in praise of Tolstoy appeared in 1887, and is included in *Essays in Criticism, Second Series*, 1888. His tribute is the more noticeable because he otherwise ignored novelists in his criticism, and it made its mark because he was the most influential critic of his day. However, other critics contributed their admiration for the Russians in the last quarter of the 19th century. This interest was awakened by the feeling that the Russians, besides the French, were the only nation to produce a range of major novelists comparable to those writing in English and that, unlike the French, they shared with the British and Americans a moral concern with human nature in society. There was also the feeling that the Russian novelists went beyond the British and Americans, excelling in their rendering of religious experience, though the full force of this was not felt until Constance Garnett produced her translation of Dostoevski's *Brothers Karamazov* in 1912.

In America, interest in Russian writing seems to have gone deeper, because of a feeling that these two great continental nations shared comparable experiences in the disorderly variety of their rapid growth. It was not merely this, however, that made the great Anglo-American novelist ▷ Henry James a lifelong admirer of Turgenev. Turgenev was already well known in England from the middle of the century when he became the friend of George Eliot. These two novelists were the predominant influences on James's own work. He admired both for the depth of their moral insights but he admired Turgenev for what he saw as his superior artistic strictness in handling the elusive novel form. Turgenev thus combined for James the virtues of the French novelists with those of the English novelist he most admired. Gilbert Phelps, in *The Russian Novel in English Fiction* (1956), traces Turgenev's influence in some of the detail of James's novels and suggests his further influence on George Gissing, George Moore, Arnold Bennett, ▷ John Galsworthy and ▷ Joseph Conrad. Conrad is the most doubtful instance of these writers showing the Russian influence; as a Pole, he felt antagonistic to Russia and he did not know Russian, and yet it is impossible not to think of both Turgenev and Dostoevski when reading ▷ *Under Western Eyes*.

Chekhov's influence on the short story and on the drama seems evident, although it may be that the distinctive development of the ▷ short story in English (for instance in ▷ James Joyce's ▷ *Dubliners* and in ▷ Katherine Mansfield) is as much an example of parallel development in the form as owing to Chekhov's initiation. In the drama, Chekhov's original handling of human speech as a medium has been developed in the works of ▷ Samuel Beckett and ▷ Harold Pinter.

The prestige of Russian literature in the mid-20th century remains very high in Britain, especially Boris Pasternak's *Doctor Zhivago* (1957) and the works of Alexander Solzhenitsyn. What is admired is the rendering of human experience and suffering on an heroic scale, and the courage and vitality of literary productivity in the face of adverse and repressive conditions. In the 1980s, however, with the more liberal regime in Russia, more, frequently dissident, literature has become available to the West, for example the poetry of Irina Ratoslinskaya.

In late 1991 and early 1992, the Soviet Union began to break up as ▷ communism ceased to be a dominant and cohering political force in Eastern Europe. Writing in Russian will thus cease to be identified with the U.S.S.R. in its old form.

Sackville-West, Hon. Victoria Mary ('Vita') (1892–1962)
Poet, novelist, travel writer. Born at Knole, Kent, to one of the oldest families in England, she married Harold Nicolson and travelled with him during his diplomatic career before settling at Sissinghurst Castle, Kent in 1930. From 1918 until 1921 her relationship with Violet Keppel (later Violet Trefusis) was of great importance in her life. In 1922 she met ▷ Virginia Woolf and began a correspondence, and a friendship that inspired Woolf's novel, *Orlando* (1928). Her earlier novels were: *Heritage* (1919); *The Dragon in Shallow Waters* (1921); *Challenge* (1923); *Grey Wethers* (1923); *Seducers in Ecuador* (1924). Her next three novels were best-sellers: *The Edwardians* (1930); *All Passion Spent* (1931); *Family History* (1932). *Thirty Clocks Strike the Hour* (1932) was a collection of short stories, while her remaining four novels were: *The Dark Island* (1934); *Grand Canyon* (1942); *The Easter Party* (1953); *No Signposts in the Sea* (1962). Her fiction evokes a social world in realistic detail and, while largely traditional in form, explores themes such as duality within the gender identity of the individual and the assertion of women's rights. Her volumes of poetry were: *Constantinople* (1915); *Poems of West and East* (1917); *Selected Poems* (1941); *Collected Poems* (1933). *The Land* (1926), which belongs to the pastoral genre, *Solitude* (1938) and *The Garden* (1946) were all long poems. Her other works include a family history, entitled *Knole and the Sackvilles* (1922), travel books on Persia, gardening books and biography.
Bib: Watson, S. R., *V. Sackville-West*; Nicolson, N., *Portrait of a Marriage*; Nicolson, N. and Trautman, J., (eds.), *The Letters of Virginia Woolf, Vol. III 1923–1928*; De Salvo, L. and Leaska, M. A., *The Letters of Vita Sackville-West to Virginia Woolf*; MacKnight, N. (ed.), *Dearest Andrew: Letters from Vita Sackville-West to Andrew Reiber, 1951–1962*; Leaska, M. A. and Phillips, J., *The Letters of Violet Trefusis to Vita Sackville-West*; Glendinning, V., *Vita: The Life of Vita Sackville-West*; Raitt, S., *Vita and Virginia.*

Sade, Donatien Alphonse, Marquis de (1740–1814)
French novelist and philosopher. His belief that the destructive impulses of human beings are a natural yet uncontrollable source of pleasure, counterblasted the doctrine of Rousseau, according to whom man undistorted by social forces was naturally good. Sade's ideas profoundly influenced the dark side of ▷ Romanticism but, with the exception of Swinburne, were less pervasive in England. Sade has recently received renewed attention in France (*eg* ▷ Roland Barthes, *Sade, Fourier, Loyola*; 1971), where he has fed into a ▷ Nietzschean strain of literary and theoretical thinking.

Saintsbury, George Edward Bateman (1845–1933)
Literary historian and critic. His works include: *A Short History of French Literature* (1882); *A Short History of English Literature* (1898); *A History of Criticism* (1900–4); *A History of English Prosody* (1906–21); *The History of English Criticism* (1911); *A History of the French Novel* (1917–19). He also wrote studies of Dryden, Walter Scott, and Matthew Arnold. His treatment of literary study was historical; that is to say, principles of evaluation or critical theory were for him secondary to coherent narration.

Sansom, William (1912–76)
Short-story writer, novelist and travel writer. He served in the London Fire Brigade in World War II, an experience which gave rise to *Fireman Flower* (1944), a volume of short stories, which was the form in which he was most successful. His work covers a wide range of subject matter and styles, from documentary realism to macabre fantasy. In *The Body* (1949) the mental stability of the first-person narrator gradually disintegrates as a result of obsessive jealousy.
Bib: Michel-Michot, P., *Sansom: A Critical Assessment.*

Sargeson, Frank (b 1903)
New Zealand novelist, short-story writer and dramatist. His stories tend to deal with a small group of characters and to be narrated from within the consciousness of one of them, often a character with limited powers of self-expression, like the narrator of the ▷ novella *That Summer* (1946). His novels are more various in tone, but render the sense of a claustrophobic and somewhat Puritan New Zealand society by means of irony, comedy and a skilful rendering of idiom. His novels are: *I Saw In My Dream* (1949); *I For One . . .* (1954); *Memoirs of a Peon* (1965); *The Hangover* (1967); *Joy of the Worm* (1969); *Sunset Village* (1976). Story collection: *Collected Short Stories* (1965).
Bib: Copland, R. A., *Frank Sargeson.*

Sartre, Jean-Paul (1905–80)
French writer. His areas of activity and influence covered philosophy, the novel,

drama, literary criticism and political commitment. He was the major exponent of atheistic existentialism in France and made an early impact with his novels *La Nausée* (1938) and *Les Chemins de la liberté*, a projected tetralogy of which only three volumes were published: *L'Âge de raison* (1945), *Le Sursis* (1945) and *La Mort dans l'âme* (1949). In *La Nausée*, the central character, Roquentin, discovers that far from being central to the nature of things, man is metaphysically superfluous (*de trop*) in the universe. *Les Chemins de la liberté* are set at the outbreak of World War II and portray the urgent necessity of commitment, especially in the form of political action, to secure personal and collective freedom. The same themes run through Sartre's drama, which is more accessible than the fiction and has proved more enduringly popular (*Les Mouches*, 1943, a version of the Orestes story; *Huis Clos* 1945; *Les Mains sales*, 1948). The philosophical background to existentialism was expounded in *L'Être et le néant (*1943) and *Critique de la raison dialectique* (1960).

Sartre also wrote a number of existentialist-oriented biographies, of ▷ Baudelaire, of Jean Genet (1910–86) and of Flaubert. His volums of *Situations* contain mainly essays on politics, literature and society and in 1945 he founded the important literary and political review, *Les Temps modernes*. In 1964 he published his autobiography, *Les Mots*, which seeks to expose the ideology of the autobiographical genre and views with irony his years of childhood under his grandfather Charles Schweitzer (Sartre was the cousin of Albert Schweitzer (1875–1965)). In the same year, Sartre was awarded and refused the Nobel Prize for Literature. His work greatly influenced the ▷ feminism of ▷ Simone de Beauvoir, with whom he shared a lifelong relationship.

Bib: Barnes, H., *Sartre*; Meszaros, J., *The Work of Sartre;* Murdoch, I., *Sartre: Romantic Rationalist*; Stern, A., *Sartre*; Macquarrie, J., *Existentialism*; Descombes, V., *Modern French Philosophy*.

Sassoon, Siegfried (1886–1967)

Poet and autobiographer. His *Memoirs of a Fox-Hunting Man* (1928) and *Memoirs of an Infantry Officer* (1930) are accounts of his life as a country gentleman before World War I, and of his experiences during it. He also became famous for his savagely satirical poems written during his military service, his first and most famous volume of anti-war poems being *Counter-Attack* (1918). He was a friend of ▷ Wilfred Owen, and influenced Owen's writing. The two volumes of memoirs were put together as *The Complete Memoirs of George Sherston* (1937), which includes an additional section, *Sherston's Progress*. His poems, including volumes published since World War I, are in a collected edition (1961).

▷ War poets.

***Satanic Verses, The* (1988)**

Novel by ▷ Salman Rushdie which received mixed reviews on its publication in 1988. Controversy erupted when Muslims protested that the book was blasphemous. Copies were burned in Bradford and demonstrations took place there and elsewhere in Britain, Pakistan and the U.S.A. In Iran mass demonstrations against the author, book and publisher caused international tension to rise. The Ayatollah Khomeini passed a death sentence on Rushdie, who went into hiding. The novel returned to the ▷ best-seller lists in the wake of the controversy, which raised many issues of freedom of speech and expression, and the freedom to publish.

Satire

A form of attack through mockery; it may exist in any literary medium, but is often regarded as a medium in itself. The origins of the word help to explain the manifestations of satire. It derives from the Latin 'satura' = a vessel filled with the earliest agricultural produce of the year, used in seasonal festivals to celebrate harvest; a secondary meaning is 'miscellany of entertainment', implying merry-making at such festivals, probably including verbal warfare. This primitive humour gave rise to a highly cultivated form of literary attack in the poetry of Horace, Persius (1st century AD) and Juvenal. Thus from ancient Roman culture two ideas of satire have come down to us: the first expresses a basic instinct for comedy through mockery in human beings, and was not invented by the Romans; the second is a self-conscious medium, implying standards of civilized and moral rightness in the mind of the poet and hence a desire on his or her part to instruct readers so as to reform their moral failings and absurdities. The two kinds of satire are inter-related, so that it is not possible to distinguish them sharply. Moreover, it is not easy to distinguish strict satire in either of its original forms from other kinds of comedy.

1 Strict satire, *ie* satire emulating the Roman poets. This was one of the outcomes of ▷ Renaissance cultivation of ancient Latin literature. Between 1590 and 1625

several poets wrote deliberate satires with Juvenal, Persius and Horace in mind; the most important of these were John Donne and Ben Jonson. The great age of the strict satire was the 18th century, notably in the work of Alexander Pope who emulated the relatively genial satire of Horace, and Samuel Johnson, who emulated the sombre style of Juvenal. Satire of this sort makes its object of attack the social forms and corruptions of the time, and its distinctive medium is the heroic couplet.

2 Comedy of Humours and Comedy of Manners. These are the most easily distinguishable forms of dramatic satire. The former is associated chiefly with Ben Jonson, and has its roots in the older Morality drama, which was only intermittently satirical. The 'humours' in Jonson's conception are the obsessions and manias to which the nature of human beings invites them to abandon themselves; they have a close relation to the medieval Seven Deadly Sins, such as lust, avarice and gluttony. The Comedy of Manners belongs to the period 1660–1800, and, especially, to the first 40 years of it. Its most notable exponents are William Congreve at the end of the 17th century and Sheridan at the end of the 18th. This comedy is less concerned with basic human dispositions and more with transient social ones; rational social behaviour is the standard in the mind of the dramatist. Both these forms of satire were taken over by novelists; the 18th-century novelist Henry Fielding began as a writer of dramatic comedies of manners, but Dickens in the 19th century writes more distinctly in the tradition of the comedy of humours, with a strong addition of social stagnation. Satire in the theatre has, since the 1960s, been replaced by television satire, with radical programmes such as *Beyond the Fringe* and more recently, *Spitting Image*.

3 Satire of ▷ parody and ▷ irony. This includes the most skilful and powerful satire in the language; its most productive period is between 1660 and 1750. Parody at its most powerful implies the writer's complete respect for the serious form which he is using in a comic way; thus in this period (which included the very serious ▷ epic *Paradise Lost*) the prestige of the epic form was still high, and Dryden and Pope used their appreciation of epic to make ironic contrast between the grandeur of its style and the pettiness, meanness and destructiveness of their chosen subject.

Irony does not necessarily use parody, but even when it does not, it operates in a similar way, by addressing the reader in terms which he has learnt to receive as acceptable at their face value, and then shocking him into recognition that something quite unacceptable is the real subject.

4 Novelistic satire. Much satire in novels from the 18th to the 20th century cannot be summed up under comedy of manners. The novels of Peacock, for example, establish a tradition of comic discussions mocking at contemporary trends of thought; Peacock's example was partly followed by Meredith and ▷ Aldous Huxley. Another variant is the 'anti-utopia', using an imaginary country to satirize actual tendencies in contemporary Britain. The most notable examples of this are ▷ *Erewhon* by ▷ Samuel Butler and *Brave New World* by ▷ Aldous Huxley. Apart from these examples, it is difficult to find a novelist who does not use satire at least intermittently, usually as social comment. Eminent examples are: Fielding, Jane Austen, Thackeray, Dickens, ▷ Wells, ▷ Wyndham Lewis, ▷ Forster, and more recently ▷ Angus Wilson, ▷ Evelyn Waugh, ▷ George Orwell, and the 'campus novels' of ▷ Kingsley Amis and ▷ David Lodge.

Saussure, Ferdinand de (1857–1913)
Swiss linguist, generally regarded as the founder of ▷ Structuralism. Saussure's *Course in General Linguistics* was published two years after his death, in 1915, and represents a reconstruction of the three series of lectures which he gave at the University of Geneva during the years 1906–7, 1908–9, and 1910–11. It was Saussure who pioneered the distinction between ▷ 'langue' and ▷ 'parole', and who sought to define the operations of language according to the principles of combination and ▷ difference. Although ▷ deconstruction has done much to undermine the Structuralist base of Saussure's thinking, the concept of 'difference' as a determining principle in establishing meaning ('signification') remains one of the key concepts in modern critical theory. Moreover, Saussure's work provided the foundation for the methodological analysis of ▷ sign systems (▷ semiotics), and the types of linguistic investigation which he undertook have been successfully appropriated by literary critics, as well as by social anthropologists such as Claude Lévi-Strauss (b 1908).

Schreiner, Olive (Emilie Albertina) (1855–1920)
Daughter of a Methodist missionary of German descent and an English mother, Olive Schreiner was born in Basutoland, the sixth

of 12 children. Self-educated, she became governess to a Boer family at the age of 15 and began to write. She came to England in 1881 to seek a publisher and in 1884 met ▷ Havelock Ellis with whom she developed a close friendship. Ten years later she returned to South Africa and married the politician Samuel Cron Cronwright who became her literary assistant and later literary executor. They took trips to England and travelled around Africa together. Her first and most acclaimed work is *The Story of an African Farm* (1883), which was published under the pseudonym Ralph Iron. Its unorthodox religious views and ▷ feminist standpoint caused a considerable stir. She wrote most after her return to South Africa: *Trooper Peter Halket of Mashonaland* (1897), *From Man to Man* (1926) and *Undine* (1929), all with feminist themes, and short stories, *Dreams* (1891), *Real Life* (1893) and *Stories, Dreams and Allegories* (1920). She also wrote *Woman and Labour* (1911). See also: *Letters* (1924).
Bib: Schreiner, S. C. C., *The Life of Olive Schreiner*; First, R. and Scott, A., *Olive Schreiner*.

Science fiction
The term 'science fiction' was coined in the mid-19th century, though it was 'reinvented' and given wider currency in the late 1920s by the American magazine editor Hugo Gernsback, who popularized the stories deriving from, pre-eminently, ▷ H. G. Wells and Jules Verne. To Gernsback a science fiction story was 'a charming romance intermingled with scientific fact and prophetic vision' (editorial, *Amazing Stories*, 1926). Wells had called what would now be dubbed his science fiction 'scientific romances', and the relation between romance, particularly Gothic romance, and science fiction has often been remarked on by definers of the form. ▷ Kingsley Amis in *New Maps of Hell* (1960), a work which did much to encourage serious critical attention to this branch of popular literature, allows for a broadening of the speculative base of science fiction through reference to sciences, or 'pseudo-sciences', like sociology, psychology, anthropology, theology and linguistics.

Darko Suvin (*Metamorphoses of Science Fiction*, 1979) remarks that 'cognition' would be a more appropriate word than science in defining this literary genre, and his emphasis on estrangement, or alienation, provides a useful direction for the discussion of science fiction in terms of recent critical theory, which has given new life to the Russian ▷ Formalist assertion that literature 'defamiliarizes' conventional assumptions. Science fiction, which is a product of and response to an era of rapid scientific and technological development, has often been concerned to promote new ways of seeing appropriate to, for example, the human consequences of industrialization, the implications of Darwinian evolutionary theory, Einstein's theory of relativity, and the second law of thermodynamics concerning the ultimate entropy of a closed system like the universe. Though the popularity of science fiction may result from the withdrawal of much modern mainstream fiction from traditional forms of storytelling, its concerns as speculative, defamiliarizing literature set it apart from the conventions of classic realism with its emphasis on, for example, characterization. Critics hostile to the science fiction genre have complained that its presentation of human character compares unfavourably with that of realist fiction, whereas others have argued that this represents a response to a world dehumanized by technology, or a radically different viewpoint for asking the question 'What constitutes the human?'

Mary Shelley's *Frankenstein, Or The Modern Prometheus* (1817) is centrally concerned with this question of defining the human through its treatment of artificially created life and offers the polar opposites of the human as idealist romantic hero and as mere mechanism. This duality is figured in a wide range of subsequent science fiction, most obviously in the genre's obsession with robots and other forms of artificial life and intelligence. In constructing a nameless 'other', Frankenstein's creation or 'monster', *Frankenstein* deals with another obsessively pursued theme of science fiction – confrontation with the alien. Mary Shelley's text, in its repeated patterns of dualism, of attempted completion of incomplete individuals, suggests the possibility, dear to much recent science fiction, that Earth is the alien planet and 'otherness' is the repressed in the human psyche or in human society.

Frankenstein may be regarded as a significant root work of science fiction, but it was the scientific romances of ▷ H. G. Wells which established the genre in the 1890s. Many of these share with *Frankenstein* an unsettling pessimism deriving from a perception of the destructive and alienating uses to which technological development might be put, while much American science fiction, at least in the period before World War II, suggested an optimistic faith in the possibilities of scientific and technological development, springing, perhaps, from a culture defining itself through reference to an expanding frontier. Wells established an influential British tradition of bleaker Darwinism, emanating from an imperial culture already in decline.

Wells's *The Time Machine* (1895) provides a model for a range of subsequent science fiction. It introduces, in almost comic pseudo-scientific discourse, a technological means of travel through time; it facilitates sociological criticism and prediction through the use of utopian and dystopian discourses; it treats the themes of confrontation with the alien, of the last man on earth, of the entropic death of the world; it provides new contexts for old myths; and it defamiliarizes the cosy certitudes of the late Victorian male world in which it starts. *The War of the Worlds* (1898), repeatedly adapted and imitated in the 20th century, may be regarded as the genesis of the bulk of science fiction treatments of interplanetary war or invasion by the alien. *Mr Blettsworthy on Rampole Island* (1928), which employs the traditional device of the dream as a means of transport in place of a time-machine, involves an inversion of dream and reality of a kind familiar in a wide range of science fiction. *The Shape of Things to Come* (1933), widely known through the Alexander Korda film version, represents a more optimistic element in Wells's science fiction in that it suggests the possibility of redemption through an enlightened, technologically oriented élite; yet images of global disorder and collapse are, perhaps, most vividly projected in this text.

Mark Rose, in *Alien Encounters: Anatomy of Science Fiction* (1981), approaches the definition of science fiction through its phases of development. Thus the scientific romances of such as Wells transform earlier kinds of romance, like the Gothic, and fill a gap left by the predominance of realistic fiction. Later phases manifest a generic self-consciousness, in that science fiction texts come to be based on an explicit form. Rose provides the example of ▷ C. S. Lewis, whose science fiction output is in part a response to the fiction of Wells. The settings of Lewis's space trilogy, *Out of the Silent Planet* (1943), *Perelandra* (1943) and *That Hideous Strength* (1945), are respectively Mars, Venus and Earth, but Lewis's preference for angels rather than space-ships as a means of interplanetary travel has led to some questioning of their status as science fiction. The trilogy evinces an attachment to supernatural Christianity rather than to science, in opposition to the element of pessimistic materialism in Wells; but some variant of such mysticism is not uncommon in the genre. For example, Lewis's near-contemporary, Olaf Stapledon, in works like *Last and First Men* (1930), *Last Man in London* (1932) and *Star-Maker* (1937), projected what he called 'myths' of future history on a scale that goes beyond Wells's scientific romances.

▷ Aldous Huxley acknowledged that his *Brave New World* (1932) started out as a parody of H. G. Wells's *Men Like Gods*, and it has become, in the words of Brian Aldiss (b 1925) (*Billion Year Spree*, 1973) 'arguably the Western World's most famous science fiction novel'. The status accorded this satirical dystopian text, like that enjoyed by the still controversial *1984* (1949) by ▷ George Orwell, may result from the fact that, in the context of the author's novel output outside the field of science fiction, it can be regarded as somehow 'mainstream' fiction. Both of these works have been regarded as more 'serious' than most science fiction, though this may be based on questionable assumptions about instrinsic literary merit.

A number of British writers were regular contributors to the pre-World War II American science fiction magazine which did much to create a persistent downmarket image for the genre in the popular imagination. The first magazine devoted entirely to science fiction was Hugo Gernsback's *Amazing Stories* (published from 1926), which made an effort to appear respectably scientific and educational in a market which often relied upon lurid presentation. It was followed by such titles as *Science Wonder Stories, Wonder Stories* and *Astounding Stories* in the late 1920s and early 1930s. Besides Wells, British contributors included John Russell Fearn, Eric Frank Russell and John Beynon Harris. Fearn, whose work appeared in *Amazing Stories* first in 1933, produced a staggering quantity of novels and short stories under no less than 25 pseudonyms as well as editing two British science fiction magazines. Russell, whose output was modest compared to Fearn's, began publishing in *Astounding Stories* in 1937 and went on to contribute to British magazines like *Tales of Wonder* and *Fantasy*. Harris is better known as ▷ John Wyndham, though he also wrote as John Beynon, J. B. Harris and Johnson Harris. He published short stories and novels from 1930 on, though his reputation rests on the novels he produced as John Wyndham from 1951, the year in which *The Day of the Triffids* was published.

'Exiles on Asperus' (in *Wonder Stories Quarterly*, 1933) by John Beynon Harris demonstrates how Wyndham was not temperamentally drawn to the 'space-opera' conventions of the American magazines or to their attachment to science fiction 'gadget' stories. He was happier, and more successful, developing the Wellsian tradition of science fiction in novels centring on an imagined disaster arising from the upsetting of the natural and social orders generally through the agency of technology. His catastrophe stories, including *The Day of the Triffids*, *The Kraken Wakes* (1953), and *The Midwich Cuckoos* (1957), belong to a class of British science fiction stretching from Wells to the present, including New Wave scientific fiction which in some ways represented a reaction against Wyndham's formulae. *The Day of the Triffids* makes use of traditional science fiction theme of the Last Man/Last Woman, a new Adam and Eve faced with the arduous complexities of an unfamiliar world. The treatment evokes a characteristically English romantic nostalgia, reminiscent of Richard Jefferies's vision of the ruined capital in *After London* (1885). The remaking of a new world out of the scraps of the old in *The Day of the Triffids* also suggests a debt to Daniel Defoe's *Robinson Crusoe* (1719), but Wyndham's novel is predominantly Wellsian, though it retains a safe, genteel quality not so typical of Wells.

Arthur C. Clarke (b 1917), one of the most celebrated science fiction writers of the 20th century, combines meticulous attention to the scientific and technological aspects of the genre, in the tradition of Jules Verne, with a lyrically didactic commitment to the benign evolutionary potential of technology that owes much to the impact of Clarke's early reading of Stapledon. Both were powerfully expressed in Stanley Kubrick's film *2001* (1968), for which Clarke wrote the screenplay. The kind of wondering transcendence conveyed at the end of that film is characteristic of Clarke's work, encountered in, for example, one of his most popular novels, *Childhood's End* (1953); while *The Deep Range* (1957) develops into a lesson in respect for the non-human creatures of the earth as the prospect of contact with the beings from other worlds approaches.

The first novel of Brian Aldiss, *Non-Stop* (1958), gave an indication of the exhilarating variety which has proved a feature of his subsequent fictional output. *Hothouse* (1962) and *Greybeard* (1964) treat the well-established theme of imagined catastrophe, but combine a playful abundance of exotic science fiction invention with romantic nostalgia. A Swiftian satirical mode characterizes *The Dark Light Years* (1964), while the alienating detachment of *Report on Probability A* (1968) draws the techniques of the French ▷ *nouveau roman* into the orbit of science fiction. *Frankenstein Unbound* (1973) and *Moreau's Other Island* (1980) reinvent seminal science fiction texts for a new context, while the abundance of Aldiss's Helliconia trilogy (1982–5) defies brief categorization. The epilogue to the third volume, *Helliconia Winter* (1985), a translated extract from Lucretius, *De Rerum Natura*, might be applied to Aldiss's *œuvre*: 'Everything must pass through successive phases. Nothing remains forever what it was.'

Aldiss's commitment to science fiction, his urge to experiment and enjoy, and to extend the possibilities of the genre, gave him a respected place in the so-called New Wave science fiction writing associated with the magazine *New Worlds* under the editorship of Michael Moorcock (b 1939) from 1964. Until then *New Worlds* had been edited by E. J. Carnell, who was also responsible for *Science Fantasy*. Carnell's magazine published a wide range of British science fiction, including the work of such prolific authors as Kenneth Bulmer, who employed 15 pen-names in addition to his own name, and John Brunner, who began publishing science fiction at the age of 17. The scale of Brunner's output may have resulted in his work being critically underrated, though his dystopian novels *Stand on Zanzibar* (1968), *The Jagged Orbit* (1969), and *The Sheep Look Up* (1972) achieved critical acclaim. Like Brunner, Moorcock is a prolific author who started young; he was editing *Tarzan Adventures* at the age of 17. His 'sword and sorcery' fantasies embody the apocalyptic theme which runs through much of his later science fiction, in which he reconstructs the past as well as imagining the future; this kind of reconstruction may be seen as a way of deconstructing the present. Works like *War Lord of the Air* (1971) and *The Land Leviathan* (1974) present a past manufactured from a range of literary reference to, for example, Verne, Wells and ▷ Joseph Conrad, and demonstrate Moorcock's attachment to the concept of the 'multiverse', which proposes a variety of separate realities which can sometimes interact. His fondness for series of novels and a modernist tendency to fragment his narratives are particularly evident in his Jerry Cornelius novels, including *The Final Programme* (1969), *A Cure for Cancer* (1971), *The English Assassin* (1972) and *The Condition of Muzak* (1977).

New Worlds under Moorcock represented

a spirited reaction against the continuing influence of American pulp science fiction, and a number of American authors were attracted to its programme. But it was a British author ▷ J. G. Ballard (b 1930) who was championed most consistently by the magazine. The Conradian tone of much of Ballard's science fiction contrasts with the racier products of some *New Worlds* writers, influenced by the current 'rock' culture; he has never been much interested in the traditional science fiction fare of space travel and the distant future, preferring to focus on something challengingly closer to the present, defamiliarizing the familiar earth into the alien planet, and insisting that the outward thrust of science fiction be matched by an inward journey. The estranging, detritus-strewn landscapes of much of his fiction indicate Ballard's fascination with surrealist art, though his *Empire of the Sun* (1983), a novel drawing on his boyhood experience of World War II in the Far East, reveals a source closer to home for his images of collapse and desolation. Ballard's catastrophe novels, like *The Drowned World* (1962), *The Drought* (1965) and *The Crystal World* (1966), bear some relation to the disaster stories of John Wyndham and John Christopher, though there is little in the way of romantic nostalgia in his treatment of 'biospheric' disasters. What might be seen as his post-imperial pessimism has not generally endeared Ballard to an American audience. His experimental 'condensed' novels, which first began appearing in *New Worlds*, were published together in *The Atrocity Exhibition* (1970) and, again, did not find favour in the U.S.A. The disturbing presentation of perverse urban nightmares in *Crash!* (1973), *Concrete Island* (1974) and *High Rise* (1975) bring the concept of the science fiction catastrophe even closer to our own time, as if the irreversible disaster had already occurred in our culture.

▷ Doris Lessing, who turned to science fiction in the early 1970s when her reputation as a mainstream novelist was already established, is also drawn towards visions of the decline and breakdown of society. The last volume of the 'Children of Violence' novels, *The Four-Gated City* (1969), ultimately projects into the future, but from the publication of *Briefing for a Descent into Hell* (1971) Lessing has shown a firm commitment to the exploratory, speculative potential of science fiction, with particular reference to questions of gender and the theme of spiritual awakening. The evocations of collapse and depletion in Lessing's science fiction, which, in the 1980s, turns to space fiction on the grand galactic scale, are set against the possibility of a utopian alternative, and its emphasis is more mystical than scientific. In *Briefing* and *Memoirs* the alternative might amount to no more than dreams; but in *Shikasta* (1979) utopian society is destroyed by a malign galactic empire, while in *The Marriages between Zones Three, Four and Five* (1980) it is confirmed that the project of utopian evolutionary development, through, for example, the use of psychic powers, lies within the province of women.

A number of ▷ Angela Carter's novels may be classed as science fiction, though, like Lessing, she tended not to focus primarily on science. *Heroes and Villains* (1970) is set in the familiar terrain of a post-catastrophe world and, using the structure of romantic fantasy, explores a variety of dualities, including fantasy/reality, beauty/barbarism, love/hate, male/female. Carter's particular skill, evident in *The Infernal Desire Machines of Dr Hoffman* (1972), *The Passion of New Eve* (1977) and *Nights at the Circus* (1983), lay in her exuberantly self-conscious, inventive storytelling in which romance, satire, horror and comedy interact exotically.

Ian Watson is also adept in exotic narrative, for example, *Whores of Babylon* (1988), but his reputation has been for intellectual, speculative brilliance. His texts, like Lessing's, have a tendency to the mystical and transcendent, and approach the possibility of such transcendence through the discourses of science, linguistics, mysticism and myth, as is impressively demonstrated by his first four novels: *The Embedding* (1973), *The Jonah Kit* (1976), *The Martian Inca* (1977) and *Alien Embassy* (1977).

Christopher Priest also built up during the 1970s a reputation as a thoughtful and inventive science fiction author through such works as *Inverted World* (1974) and *A Dream of Wessex* (1977).

The next new wave of science fiction is already upon us. Science fiction might be said to have begun with the work of a woman and, looked at one way, Mary Shelley's *Frankenstein* is a coded analysis of female experience. The women's movement of recent years, with a strong lead from the United States, has led to a powerful reaction against science fiction's traditional marginalization of women, and Lessing is not unique in turning to science fiction from a different novel tradition. Michèle Roberts, for example, adopts the dystopian mode in *The Book of Mrs Noah* (1973), while ▷ Zoë Fairbairns

uses science fiction's speculative resources to consider the issue of wages for housework in *Benefits* (1979). The Women's Press boasts a growing list of feminist science fiction, and one of the editors responsible for this, Sarah Lefanu, has written a study of feminism and science fiction, *In the Chinks of the World Machine* (1988). Commenting on the value of science fiction, Lefanu has said: 'It deals with the possibility of change, and allows the investigation of radical ideas'.
Bib: Aldiss, B., *Billion-Year Spree*; Kuhn, A., *Alien Zones*; Nicholls, P., *Encyclopaedia of Science Fiction*; and the journal, *Science Fiction Studies*.

Scott, Paul (1920–78)
Novelist. He served in India, Burma and Malaya during World War II and subsequently worked in publishing. His major achievement was *The Raj Quartet*, a tetralogy consisting of: *The Jewel in the Crown* (1966); *The Day of the Scorpion* (1968); *The Towers of Silence* (1971); *A Division of the Spoils* (1975). A portrait of Indian society at the time of Independence in 1947, it uses a range of narrative forms, including letters, journals, reports and memories. The story is built around the consequences of the rape of an English girl; consequences which serve to reveal corruption and racism in the Raj administration and the roots of the political unrest and intercommunal violence at the Partition of India. Scott was accorded little critical recognition until *Staying On* (1977), a gentle satire set after Independence, won the Booker Prize. His work is notable for its combination of complex narrative technique with historical accuracy. *The Raj Quartet* was televised as *The Jewel in the Crown* in 1984 and *Staying On* was adapted for television in 1981. Scott's earlier novels include *The Birds of Paradise* (1962).

Scottish literature in English
This belongs above all to the Lowlands; it is a distinctive branch of literature in the English language, the Lowland Scottish form of which had originally a close resemblance to that spoken in the north of England. Racially, linguistically and culturally, Lowland Scottish ties with England were close, despite the constant wars between the two countries between the late 13th and mid-16th centuries. In contrast, until the 18th-century destruction of Highland culture, the Lowlanders had little more than the political bond of a common sovereign with their Gaelic-speaking fellow countrymen of the north. While it is not true to say that Scottish literature is a branch of English literature, the two literatures have been closely related.

The 20th century has seen what is often described as the Scottish Renaissance, which suggests a revival in cultural production and political identity. There have been three waves in this redevelopment, the first, in the early part of this century, with a growth in nationalistic sentiment. In this period the work of Hugh MacDiarmid is most seminal, from his early Scottish propaganda in the *Scottish Chapbook* (started in 1922) to his most famous poem *A Drunk Man Looks at the Thistle* (1926) and later poetical works. MacDiarmid rejected the earlier nostalgic approach and placed Scottish literature firmly in the European ▷ modernist movement. Other important writers of the first wave include the poet ▷ Edwin Muir, and the novelists ▷ Lewis Grassic Gibbon (1901–35) and Neil M. Gunn (1891–1973). Muir adopts a mythopoeic discourse which Gibbon and Gunn take up as a sense of Celtic inheritance, although while Gibbon uses myth fatalistically, Gunn sees in it a possibility for Scottish self-regeneration. Like MacDiarmid, all actively reject nostalgia and evoke social and political themes.

The second wave which occurred during the 1940s and 1950s saw a continuation, but rejuvenation of the earlier themes. George Mackay Brown (b 1921), for example, takes up the mythic patterns, while Edwin Morgan's (b 1920) contemporary idiom, such as ▷ science fiction, and ▷ Ian Hamilton Finlay's concrete poems strongly assert their identification with European modernism.

The third period in the Scottish Renaissance is still happening and takes the broadest sense of national literary identity to its utmost limits. For example, 7:84, the dramatic company founded by ▷ John McGrath has an avowedly ▷ Brechtian and international socialist purpose, but at the same time is located unquestionably in a Scottish political scene – as with his *The Cheviot, the Stag and the Black, Black Oil* (1973) – and determinedly retains its ▷ fringe status. Novelists such as William McIlvanney (b 1936) similarly focus upon the political unrest and tension of modern urban life in Scotland. Like McIlvanney, the novelists ▷ Muriel Spark and Robin Jenkins (b 1912), the poets ▷ Douglas Dunn and Liz Lochhead (b 1947), and the dramatists Tom McGrath (b 1940) and John Byrne (b 1940), took advantage of the expansion of publishing in the 1980s to reach a wider and more international market. The 20th century has seen a reassertion of the national idiom in the Lallans (Lowland) renaissance, the most vigorous example of which is the work of Hugh MacDiarmid. This idiom can also be seen in the work of Henryson, Dunbar, Douglas and Burns; it is concrete, sardonic, realistic, harsh and physical.

Gaelic literature of the Highlands had what is said to be a 'golden age' in the later 18th century, just at the time when Gaelic culture was being destroyed by the English and the Lowland Scots for political reasons. The work in it (*eg* that of Alexander Macdonald, Dugald Buchanan) is little known outside the comparatively small number of Gaelic speakers in the Highlands, and does not belong to English literature.
Bib: Watson, R., *The Literature of Scotland.*

Scrutiny

A literary critical review published in Cambridge from 1932 to 1953; its principal editor was ▷ F. R. Leavis. *Scrutiny* was famous for its intellectual energy, the coherence of outlook among its contributors, and the urgency and purposefulness of its tone. This purposefulness was a response to a Leavisite analysis of the contemporary cultural scene which may be summarized as follows. The quality of Western (more particularly, British) civilization was deteriorating because of the influence upon it of commercial vulgarization. Such vulgarization could only end in the complete loss of those standards by which life in any organized society can be seen and felt to be valuable. The importance of a great literary tradition is that it constitutes a form of spiritual life that sustains high values and withstands vulgarization. However, such a tradition must itself be sustained by constant, sensitive and scrupulous critical activity carried on by alert and active intellects within the society. But the British literary tradition no longer possessed this kind of cultural leadership; the leading men of letters, on the contrary, with a few exceptions, regarded literature as an elegant pastime for a fashionable élite (such as the ▷ Bloomsbury Group) and they employed slack and inadequate standards in their judgements. *Scrutiny*, therefore, was intended to demonstrate the exacting standards which are required of criticism if a lively and effective literary tradition is to be sustained. The example to be followed was that of the review, *The Calendar of Modern Letters* (1925–27) edited by Edgell Rickword.

The strongest part of *Scrutiny's* critical attack was directed towards literary education. It sought to counteract the kind of academic inertia which tends to the passive acceptance of some literary reputations and the equally passive neglect of other writers. This policy led to an extensive re-evaluation of the writers of the past. In regard to poetry, this re-evaluation took the direction already pursued by ▷ T. S. Eliot (*Selected Essays*, 1932); in regard to the novel, the dominant influences were those of F. R. Leavis himself, and his wife ▷ Q. D. Leavis. *Scrutiny* had a pervasive influence in Britain and the U.S.A., especially among teachers at all levels of education.
Bib: Mulhern, F., *The Moment of Scrutiny*; Baldick, C., *The Social Mission of English Criticism.*

Secret Agent, The (1907)

A novel by ▷ Joseph Conrad. The subject is revolution and counter-revolution in western Europe; the scene is London; the 'secret agent' is Mr Verloc, of mixed nationality. He is employed by the embassy of an unnamed foreign power (Czarist Russia) to mix with anarchist conspirators who have taken refuge on British soil, and to report their activities. Between the embassy and the conspirators are the London police, represented by Chief Inspector Heat, whose work is to watch the anarchists but not to interfere with them until they commit crimes. The embassy wishes to force the British government and its police to suppress the anarchist colony, and uses Verloc to organize a bomb outrage (against Greenwich Observatory) so as to incriminate them. Verloc's seedy shop in Soho is a meeting place for the motley group of political fanatics, including Karl Yundt, a malevolent old terrorist, Ossipan, a scientific materialist who lives off women, Michaelis, a utopian Marxist, and the Professor, the most ruthless of the anarchists, who always carries with him a bomb to prevent arrest. The Professor is disquieted by the inability of the British masses to see politics in terms of violence; if violence were used by the government, the masses would believe that counter-violence was their only hope, and a revolutionary situation would exist in Britain. In addition to this political level, the novel has a psychological one: if either revolution or counter-revolution is to be accomplished successfully, the human instruments must be disinterested, but in fact both the revolutionaries and their opponents are dominated by self-regard. The only characters capable of full disinterest are those who are so wretched as to be incapable of reflecting on their own condition. Mrs Verloc's half-witted brother Stevie rises to one idea only: 'bad life for poor people'. He thus becomes the willing tool of Mr Verloc, who charges him with the task of placing the bomb. In the event, Stevie causes no damage to the Observatory but he is himself blown up. Mrs Verloc, who has married Mr Verloc solely to provide support for Stevie, though her husband supposes her entirely devoted to himself, murders him from rage and grief. She tries to flee the country with Ossipan and, when he deserts her, she throws herself overboard from a Channel ferry. In contrast to Winnie Verloc and Stevie, characters simplified by misery and elementary development, is the Assistant Commissioner of Police, who neither acts disinterestedly nor has any belief that he can, but lives by the awareness that self-knowledge is the only antidote to the poison of self-regard. He solves the mystery of the outrage, and thus frustrates the destructive folly of Mr Vladimir, the ambassador. The novel is distinguished by the use of a pervasive irony to expose the futility of political extremism, the strength of human illusions, and the suffering and chaos prevailing in a supposedly civilized society.

Selvon, Sam (b 1923)
Novelist, playwright (radio and theatre), screenwriter and short-story writer. Born in Trinidad, he served in the Royal Naval Reserve in the Caribbean during World War II, worked as a journalist for the Trinidad *Guardian* from 1946 until 1950, and then moved to London, working for three years as a civil servant in the Indian High Commission and then as a freelance writer, particularly for B.B.C. drama. Since 1978 he has lived in Canada. His novels are: *A Brighter Sun* (1952); *An Island is a World* (1955); *The Lonely Londoners* (1956); *Turn Again Tiger* (1958); *I Hear Thunder* (1963); *Housing Lark* (1965); *The Plains of Caroni* (1969); *Those Who Eat the Cascadura* (1972); *Moses Ascending* (1975); *Moses Migrating* (1983). *Ways of Sunlight* (1958) is a collection of short stories. His work is set in Trinidad and London, and many of his novels are concerned with the experience of cultural displacement, racism and the economic hardship of those moving to Britain from the West Indies, an experience treated with wit, humour and affirmation of growing confidence and assertion, as well as with indignation. Similar themes, and some of the same characters, appear in *Eldorado, West One*, a sequence of seven one-act plays (written 1969; published 1988). He has also written many radio plays, and *Switch* (1977), a play for the theatre. He was co-author of the film *Pressure* (1978) and has published a prose collection, *Foreday Morning: Selected Prose 1946–1986* (1989).

Semiology, semiotics
The term 'semiology' was used in ▷ Ferdinand de Saussure's *Course in General Linguistics* (published 1915) to describe 'a science of ▷ signs', whose objective is 'to investigate the nature of signs and the laws governing them'. The more current term, semiotics, was associated originally with the American philosopher C. S. Peirce. Peirce's tripartite division of signs into 'icon' (a sign possessing a similarity to its object), 'symbol' (a sign arbitrarily linked to the object), and 'index' (a sign physically associated with its object), has more recently been revised in Umberto Eco's *A Theory of Semiotics* (1976) where the emphasis throughout is upon the complex mechanisms and conventions which govern the production of signs.

Seth, Vikram (b 1952)
Poet, novelist, travel writer. Born in Calcutta, India, and educated at Corpus Christi College, Oxford, Stanford University and Nanjing University, China, he was trained as an economist. His volumes of poetry are *Mappings* (1980); *The Humble Administrator's Garden* (1985); *All You Who Sleep Tonight* (1990). *The Golden Gate* (1986) is a witty and accomplished novel, written in a form of sonnet borrowed from Pushkin's *Eugene Onegin*, and portrays the Californian life-style through the story of the relationships of a group of young professionals. Seth has also published *From Heaven Lake: Travels through Sinkiang and Tibet* (1983).

Shaffer, Peter (b 1926)
British dramatist who has established his reputation with a number of major successes: *The Royal Hunt of the Sun* (1964); *Black Comedy* (1965); *Equus* (1973); *Amadeus* (1974) and *Lettice and Lovage* (1987). The first is a spectacular play about the Spanish conquest of Peru; the second a short farce; the third an exploration of the disturbed psyche of a violent youth who puts out the eyes of a horse; *Amadeus* looks at the court composer Antonio Salieri's jealousy (and possible murder) of Mozart; *Lettice and Lovage* is a comedy written especially for the actress Maggie Smith.
Bib: Klein, D., *Peter Shaffer*.

Shakespeare, William (1564–1616) – biography and plays
Dramatist and poet. Although William Shakespeare lived and wrote four hundred

years ago, his work continues to have a profound influence, so much so that no guide to literature this century could afford to leave him out. He was baptized on 26 April 1564; his birth is commemorated on 23 April, which happens also to be St George's Day, the festival of the patron saint of England. His father, John Shakespeare, was a Stratford-on-Avon merchant who dealt in gloves and probably other goods; his grandfather, Richard Shakespeare, was a yeoman, *ie* small farmer, and his mother, Mary Arden, was the daughter of a local farmer who belonged to the local noble family of Arden, after whom the forest to the north of Stratford was named. John Shakespeare's affairs prospered at first, and in 1568 he was appointed to the highest office in the town – High Bailiff, equivalent to Mayor. A grammar school existed in Stratford, and since it was free to the sons of burgesses, it is generally assumed that William attended it. If he did, he probably received a good education in the Latin language; there is evidence that the sons of Stratford merchants were, or could be, well read and well educated. He married Anne Hathaway in 1582, and they had three children: Suzanna, born 1583, and the twin son and daughter, Hamnet and Judith, born 1585.

Thereafter Shakespeare's life is a blank, until we meet a reference to him in *A Groatsworth of Wit* (1592), an autobiographical pamphlet by the London playwright Robert Greene, who accuses him of plagiarism. By 1592, therefore, Shakespeare was already successfully embarked as a dramatist in London, but there is no clear evidence of when he went there. From 1592 to 1594 the London theatres were closed owing to epidemics of plague, and Shakespeare seems to have used the opportunity to make a reputation for himself as a narrative poet: his *Venus and Adonis* was published in 1593, and *The Rape of Lucrece* a year later. He continued to prosper as a dramatist, and in the winter of 1594 was a leading member of the Lord Chamberlain's Men with whom he remained for the rest of his career. In 1598, Francis Meres, in his literary commentary *Palladis Tamia, Wit's Treasury*, mentions Shakespeare as one of the leading writers of the time, lists 12 of his plays, and mentions his ▷ sonnets as circulating privately; they were published in 1609. The Lord Chamberlain's Men opened the Globe Theatre in 1598, and Shakespeare became a shareholder in it. After the accession of James I the company came under royal patronage, and were called the King's Men; this gave Shakespeare a status in the royal household. He is known to have been an actor as well as a playwright, but tradition associates him with small parts. He may have retired to New Place in Stratford in 1610, but he continued his connections with London, and purchased a house in Blackfriars in 1613. In the same year, the Globe Theatre was burnt down during a performance of the last play with which Shakespeare's name is associated, *Henry VIII. His will is dated less than a month from his death.*

Many legends and traditions have grown up about Shakespeare since near his own day, but they are untrustworthy. He was certainly one of the most successful English writers of his time; his income has been estimated at about £200 a year, considerable earnings for those days.

Scholars now largely agree on the order of composition of Shakespeare's plays, which are:

1590–91	*Henry VI, Parts II and III*
1591–92	*Henry V, Part I*
1592–93	*Richard III*
	The Comedy of Errors
1593–94	*Titus Andronicus*
	The Taming of the Shrew
	Two Gentlemen of Verona
1594–95	*Love's Labour's Lost*
	Romeo and Juliet
1595–96	*Richard II*
	A Midsummer Night's Dream
1596–97	*King John*
	The Merchant of Venice
1597–98	*Henry IV, Parts I and II*
1598–99	*Much Ado about Nothing*
	Henry V
1599–1600	*Julius Caesar*
	The Merry Wives of Windsor
	As You Like It
	Twelfth Night
1600–1	*Hamlet*
	Measure for Measure
1601–2	*Troilus and Cressida*
1602–3	*All's Well that Ends Well*
1604–5	*Othello*
	King Lear
1605–6	*Macbeth*
1606–7	*Antony and Cleopatra*
1607–8	*Coriolanus*
	Timon of Athens
1608–9	*Pericles*
1609–10	*Cymbeline*
1610–11	*The Winter's Tale*
1611–12	*The Tempest*

Shakespeare is now believed to have written

all of *Henry VIII* and to have collaborated with Fletcher on *Two Noble Kinsmen*.

Bib: Chambers, E.K., *William Shakespeare: A Study of Facts and Problems*, 2 vols., Schoenbaum, S., *Shakespeare's Lives; William Shakespeare: A Documentary Life*.

Shakespeare – criticism

As with any author of greatness, different ages have appreciated different aspects of Shakespeare. Twentieth-century criticism of Shakespeare has built up into a vast corpus, and changes in the productions of the Shakespeare critical industry show how criticism has itself developed through the century. However, in his own day, popular taste, according to Ben Jonson, particularly enjoyed *Titus Andronicus*, now regarded as one of the least interesting of his plays. John Dryden picked out *Richard II*; Samuel Johnson admired the comedies. It is possible to understand these preferences: *Titus* is the most bloodthirsty of all the plays, and suited the tastes of an age in which executions were popular spectacles. Dryden and Johnson both belonged to neo-classical periods. Johnson, like Dryden, was troubled by the differences in Shakespeare's tragedies from the formalism of ancient Greek and 17th-century tragedy which the spirit of their period encouraged them to admire, and Johnson's warm humanity caused him to respond to the plays which displayed wide human appeal while their mode permitted some licence of form. Both Johnson and Dryden rose superior to the limitations of their period in according Shakespeare such greatness. The inheritor of Johnson's mantle as the most perceptive critic of Shakespeare in the 19th century is S. T. Coleridge, whose seminal lectures on Shakespeare were inspired by German ▷ Romanticism. In his letter John Keats offers some of the most enduringly valuable comments on Shakespeare's works before A. C. Bradley published *Shakespearean Tragedy* in 1904, which was to prove the most influential text on Shakespeare for two generations.

If the 20th century has not produced a Johnson, or Coleridge or Bradley in Shakespeare studies, Wilson Knight (*The Imperial Theme, The Crown of Life*), ▷ Harley Granville-Barker (*Prefaces to Shakespeare*) and others such as D. A. Traversi (*An Approach to Shakespeare*) and H. C. Goddard (*The Meaning of Shakespeare*) have all contributed to our deeper understanding of the plays and poetry. Shakespeare's education has been closely scrutinized by T. W. Baldwin in two volumes, *Shakespeare's Smalle Latin and Lesse Greeke*, and Geoffrey Bullough's eight volumes on Shakespeare's sources, *Narrative and Dramatic Sources of Shakespeare*, are indispensable to Shakespearean critics. Increasingly the critical debate has been conducted in a number of specialized journals, particularly the long-established *Shakespeare Jahrbuch*, *Shakespeare Survey*, *Shakespeare Studies*, and *Shakespeare Quarterly*. A few books are outstanding in their focus on particular aspects of Shakespeare, such as C. L. Barber's influential essay on Shakespearean comedy and the rituals of English folklore and country customs, *Shakespeare's Festive Comedy*, and Northrop Frye's archetypal study of comedy and romance, *A Natural Perspective*. Howard Felperin's distinguished book on Shakespeare's last plays, *Shakespearean Romance*, and Janet Adelman's thought-provoking study of *Antony and Cleopatra* and its mythopoeic imagery in *The Common Liar*, both reflect the influence of Frye in their sober and formally predicated approaches.

Of a more radical bent is Jan Kott's famous essay on *King Lear* in *'King Lear*, or *Endgame*' (1964) which argued the case for Shakespeare as our contemporary, with his finger imaginatively on the pulse of a dark, modern human predicament. On the same lines, ▷ Peter Brook's famous production of *A Midsummer Night's Dream* in 1970 emancipated the play from its putative operatic and conformist frame and irretrievably altered our perception of it. By thus indicating the extent to which the theatre can influence interpretation of plays, Brook materially contributed to redirecting critical attention back to the stage.

Modern social and critical movements have made their impact felt in the field of Shakespeare studies: ▷ deconstruction, in the guise of a creative disintegration of the texts' organic status, and ▷ feminism provide the impetus for some of the most controversial writing on Shakespeare in the 1980s and 1990s, as do 'cultural materialism' and particularly 'new historicism'. The latter in particular seems set to command a wide audience in the works of Stephen Greenblatt and Louis Montrose, whose work combines the scholarly scruples of the older tradition with an acute sceptical and self-critical awareness of the historical and epistemological contexts of literary criticism in society.

Bib: Bradley, A. C., *Shakespearean Tragedy*; Barber, C. L., *Shakespeare's Festive Comedy*; Coleridge, S. T., *Shakespearean Criticism*; Dollimore, J., *Radical Tragedy*; Dryden,

J., *Essays*; Frye, N., *A Natural Perspective*; Greenblatt, S., *Renaissance Self-Fashioning*; Jardine, L., *Still Harping on Daughters*; Johnson, S., *On Shakespeare*.

Shaw, George Bernard (1856–1950)
Dramatist, critic, social thinker. His family belonged to the Irish Protestant gentry. His father was an unsuccessful businessman; his mother was a musician of talent. Apart from the musical education he received from her, he was practically self-educated. He came to London in 1876, and set to work as a novelist. The novel proved not to be his medium, but his efforts in the form were an apprenticeship for dramatic writing in which he excelled. He wrote five novels in all: the best known are *Cashel Byron's Profession* (pub. 1885–6) and *The Admirable Bashville* (pub. 1901). In 1884 he joined the newly formed socialist ▷ Fabian Society, of which he became a leading member; he edited *Fabian Essays* (1887) which was influential in forming socialist opinion in Britain. Between 1885 and 1898 he wrote much criticism for a number of papers; he was probably the most astute music and dramatic critic of his time.

His career as a dramatist began in 1892 and lasted substantially until 1939, though he wrote his last play when he was over 90. Through Joseph Archer, the translator, he had come to know the work of the Norwegian dramatist ▷ Henrik Ibsen and was profoundly impressed especially by Ibsen's plays of social criticism such as *A Doll's House*. In 1891 came his study *The Quintessence of Ibsenism*, and then he embarked on plays of social purpose on his own account. Shaw's art is, however, very different from Ibsen's; whereas for Ibsen the characters are always more important than the ideas in a play, and the characters engage in convincing talk, in Shaw's plays it is the ideas that really matter, and his characters don't talk – they make speeches. The speeches are composed in the operatic tradition of Mozart; Shaw once said that it was Mozart who taught him to write. As a dramatic critic and a student of Ibsen, he had learnt stagecraft thoroughly, and he knew how to achieve theatrical effect, to which his unique talent for wit, surprise, and paradox strongly contributed. In regard to ideas, he was concerned to shock his audiences out of their unthinking acceptance of social conventions, but he was careful (unlike Ibsen) never to scandalize them beyond their willingness to listen. Apart from socialism, his leading doctrine (derived partly from the French philosopher ▷ Bergson and partly from the German philosopher ▷ Nietzsche) was his belief in the 'Life Force' – that the progress of humanity depends in every generation on the evolution of geniuses, who comprise the spearheads of advance but inevitably arouse the hostility of their contemporaries. He was the first dramatist to realize that the reading public for plays was now larger than the theatre-going public; accordingly he published his own plays with long prefaces, which are commonly as famous as the plays themselves, and with elaborate stage directions intended not only for stage producers but for readers accustomed to the kind of detail provided by novels.

His most famous plays are probably: *Man and Superman* (1903); *Major Barbara* (1905); ▷ *Pygmalion* (1912); *Heartbreak House* (1917); *Back to Methuselah* (1921); *Saint Joan* (1924). Other plays: in ▷ *Plays Pleasant and Unpleasant* (1898) – *Widowers' Houses* (first staged 1892); *The Philanderer; Mrs Warren's Profession*; ▷ *Arms and the Man; Candida; The Man of Destiny; You Never Can Tell*. In *Plays for Puritans* (1901) – *The Devil's Disciple; Caesar and Cleopatra; Captain Brassbound's Conversion*. Other plays before 1914; *John Bull's Other Island; How He Lied to Her Husband; Press Cuttings; The Doctor's Dilemma; Getting Married; The Showing up of Blanco Posnet; Misalliance; Fanny's First Play; Androcles and the Lion; Overruled; Great Catherine*. After 1918: *The Apple Cart; In Good King Charles's Golden Days*.

Among Shaw's extensive political writings are his attack on the British government, *Common Sense about the War* (1914), and *The Intelligent Woman's Guide to Socialism and Capitalism* (1928).
Bib: Pearson, H., *Life*; Henderson, A., *Life*; Chesterton, G. K., *George Bernard Shaw*; Bentley, E., *George Bernard Shaw*; Meisel, M., *Shaw and the Nineteenth Century*; Morgan, M., *The Shavian Playground*.

Short story
This very early kind of fiction was first taken seriously in the 19th century as an independent literary form, making different demands on the writer and the reader from the demands of longer works of fiction such as the novel. Three writers originated this serious practice of the art of the short story: the American Edgar Allan Poe (1809–49); the Frenchman, Poe's disciple, Guy de Maupassant (1850–93); and the Russian ▷ Anton Chekhov. These writers evolved the qualities especially associated with the short story: close texture, unity of mood,

suggestive idiom, economy of means. Such qualities associate the short story with the short poem, and we find that in English the verse story anticipated the prose story in works such as the tales of George Crabbe and Arthur Hugh Clough's *Mari Magno* (1862). However, no relationship can be established between the verse of such writers and the prose of ▷ Rudyard Kipling, with Maupassant behind him, or that of ▷ Katherine Mansfield, who was strongly influenced by Anton Chekhov. These two wrote little else in prose except stories (Kipling wrote two novels), but the greatest masters of the short-story form – ▷ Henry James, ▷ Joseph Conrad, ▷ James Joyce, and ▷ D. H. Lawrence – were predominantly novelists. Their stories were perhaps formed less by the example of the foreign writers mentioned than by the structure of their own novels. These had a less distinctly marked plot line than those of earlier novelists, and yet a closer coherence; chapters from them can be extracted showing many of the essential qualities of short stories (*eg* 'Rabbit' in Lawrence's ▷ *Women in Love*, or the Christmas dinner in Joyce's ▷ *Portrait of the Artist*) in spite of their relationship to their respective novels as wholes. It seems therefore that the best stories of these writers were by-products of their novels, which by their structure suggested the evolution of stories as separate entities.

It is difficult to make a clear distinction between the short story and the *nouvelle* (▷ novella or long story); it is difficult also to say at what point a *nouvelle* stops short of being a novel; on the whole the *nouvelle* or 'long short story' seems to share with the short story as generally understood a unity of mood, which is not so likely to be found in a true novel, however short. All the masters of the short story who have been mentioned were also masters of the *nouvelle*, but not necessarily (*eg* Chekhov) of the novel form.

The period 1880–1930 was the flowering time of the short story in English; besides the English writers already mentioned, it included the early and best work of ▷ A. E. Coppard, who was one of the few English fiction-writers of any note (Katherine Mansfield being another) who have restricted themselves to the short-story form. Later short-story writers have been numerous, but they have mostly practised the art as an alternative and often subsidiary form to that of the novel. In Ireland, where the art of the novel has scarcely taken root, the art of the short story has flourished more distinctively. It begins with the stories of ▷ George Moore (*The Untilled Field*, 1903), but the Irish tradition becomes really outstanding in the first books of ▷ Liam O'Flaherty (*Spring Sowing*, 1926), ▷ Sean O'Faolain (*Midsummer Night Madness*, 1932), and ▷ Frank O'Connor (*Guests of the Nation*, 1931). In his book on the art of the short story, *The Lonely Voice* (1964), O'Connor offers an explanation as to why the short story should be the more natural form of fiction for Irish literary culture.

Since O'Connor, William Trevor has continued the Irish connection with the short story. Other contemporary writers who excel at the form include ▷ Peter Carey, whose early stories are collected in *Exotic Pleasures* (1980), and Ian McEwan, whose collections *First Love, Last Rites* (1975) and *In Between the Sheets* (1977) attracted great critical attention. ▷ Angus Wilson, ▷ Muriel Spark, ▷ Nadine Gordimer, ▷ Margaret Atwood, Desmond Hogan and Shena Mackay have also used the genre to interesting effect.

Bib: Bates, H. E., *The Modern Short Story*; O'Connor, F., *The Lonely Voice*; O'Faolain, S., *The Short Story*.

Shuttle, Penelope (b 1947)
Poet. Shuttle's forceful, strong verse has brought her considerable critical recognition, as has her 1978 book on feminine creativity and menstruation, *The Wise Wound* (written with her husband, ▷ Peter Redgrove). Her works include: *An Excusable Vengeance* (1967); *Wailing Monkey Embracing a Tree* (1973); *Photographs of Persephone* (1974); *The Dream* (1975); *Period* (1976); *Prognostica* (1980); *The Child Stealer* (1983).

Sign
This is the term used by ▷ Ferdinand de Saussure in his *Course in General Linguistics* (1915) to refer to any linguistic unit through which meaning is produced. In Saussure's theory, the *sign* is the combination of two discrete elements, the *signifier* (form which signifies) and the *signified* (idea signified). In the phrase 'A rose by any other name would smell as sweet', the word 'rose' is the signifier and the 'concept of a rose' is the signified.

Signifier and signified are distinct aspects of the sign, but exist only within it. One important aspect of Saussure's definition of the sign is that any particular combination of signifier and signified is *arbitrary*. So a 'rose' could be called a 'chrysanthemum' or a 'telephone', but would still be as aromatic. Saussure's perceptions have been extremely influential in the development of ways of discussing the processes through which meaning is achieved.

▷ Langue; Parole; Structuralism; Post-structuralism; Discourse; Barthes, Roland; Derrida, Jacques.

Signified

▷ Sign.

Signifier

▷ Sign.

Sillitoe, Alan (b 1928)

Novelist and poet. The son of a labourer in a cycle factory, he left school at 14 to work in a similar factory. His birthplace was the Midlands town of Nottingham, near which ▷ D. H. Lawrence also grew up. Sillitoe, like Lawrence, writes from the standpoint of one whose origins are outside London and the middle classes, and he is the best known of a group of post-war novelists from similar backgrounds, including ▷ Stan Barstow, ▷ John Braine and ▷ David Storey. The influence of Lawrence on these writers is inevitably strong, and especially so in the case of Sillitoe, but he presents a narrow spirit of social rebellion from which Lawrence is free. At present, his fame rests chiefly on his first novel, *Saturday Night and Sunday Morning* (1958), which has been filmed. The novel's hero, Arthur Seaton, has become a type-figure of the post-1945 industrial, Welfare State working man, born into an economic fabric against which his strong impulses rebel. More original and equally well known is the tale *The Loneliness of the Long-Distance Runner* (1959), a kind of fable of anarchic social rebellion. He has also written stories: *The Ragman's Daughter* (1963); *Guzman Go Home* (1968); *Men Women and Children* (1973); *Down to the Bone* (1976); *The Second Chance* (1980); and poems: *The Rats* (1960); *A Falling Out of Love* (1964); *Snow on the North Side of Lucifer* (1979); *Sun before Departure: Poems 1974 to 1982* (1984); *Tides and Stone Walls* (1986); and more novels: *The General* (1960), about the war in Malaya, in which Sillitoe served; *Key to the Door* (1961); *The Death of William Posters* (1965); *A Tree on Fire* (1967); *A Start in Life* (1970); *Travels in Nihilon* (1971); *Raw Material* (1972); *The Flame of Life* (1974); *The Widower's Son* (1976); *The Storyteller* (1979); *Her Victory* (1982); *The Last Flying Boat* (1983); *Down From the Hill* (1984); *Life Goes On* (1985); *Out of the Whirlpool* (a novella; 1987). In 1978 he published three plays: *This Foreign Field* (1970); *Pit Strike* (1977); *The Interview* (1978).

▷ Realism.

Bib: Atherton, S., *Allan Sillitoe: A Critical Assessment*.

Simpson, N. F. (Norman Frederick) (b 1919)

British dramatist sometimes classified as an absurdist writer, although his work is strongly influenced by a bizarre and zany humour in the English tradition of Lewis Carroll and the Goon Show. He wrote several short plays before his more famous *One Way Pendulum* in 1959, in which 500 weighing machines are taught to sing the Hallelujah Chorus. This was followed by a spy comedy, *The Cresta Run* (1965). Although he is not considered a major dramatist his work helped the development of drama away from conservative conventions during the 1950s and early 60s.

▷ Theatre of the Absurd.

Sinclair, Andrew (b 1935)

Novelist. Like ▷ David Caute, Sinclair is interested in ▷ postmodernist experimental narrative. *Gog* (1967), the epic journey through England of an alienated, semi-mythical character, blends realism and fantasy, and employs a variety of narrative forms, including critical essay, comic strip and film script. Sinclair's work has affinities with that of American writers such as Kurt Vonnegut. Other novels include: *Magog* (1972); *A Patriot for Hire* (1978).

Sitwell, Edith (1887–1964), Sir Osbert (1892–1969), Sir Sacheverell (1897–1988)

An eminent literary family, of whom Edith is best known as a poet, and her brothers (both of whom were also poets) as an autobiographer and a writer of travel books respectively.

Edith is the most celebrated of the three. Born of repressive and disapproving aristocratic parents, Edith's eccentric beauty and unconventionality set her apart. As an adolescent she encountered the work of Rimbaud, who influenced her greatly. Her first volume of poems was *The Mother and Other Poems* (1915). Her poetry is distinctive for her interest in elaborately contrived sound effects, experiments in rhythm, and startling imagery. Her sequence *Façade* (1923) is her most popular work; it was set to music by the composer William Walton. Osbert Sitwell indicates its character in his autobiography, *Laughter in the Next Room*: 'The idea of *Façade* first entered our minds as the result of certain technical experiments at which my sister had recently been working: experiments in obtaining through the medium

of words the rhythm of dance measures such as waltzes, polkas, foxtrots. These exercises were often experimental enquiries into the effect on rhythm, on speed, and on colour of the use of rhymes, assonances, dissonances, placed outwardly, at different places in the line, in most elaborate patterns'. The tone of *Façade* is light-hearted or satirical. From *The Sleeping Beauty* (1924) a more romantic tone predominated, and in 1929 *Gold Coast Customs* opened her most ambitious phase of philosophic verse with majestic themes. These include *Street Songs* (1942), *The Song of the Cold* (1945) and *The Shadow of Cain* (1947). Her prose works and criticism include a biography of Alexander Pope (1930). From 1916 to 1921 she edited *Wheels*, a magazine which represented a resistance to the ▷ Georgian poets.
Bib: Glendinning, V., *Edith Sitwell*; Pearson, J., *Façades*.

Smith, Stevie (Florence Margaret) (1902–71)
Poet and novelist. The 'unpoetic' life of Stevie Smith, who worked in an office and spent her life caring for her elderly aunt in a London suburb, is well known as the context for the production of her concise but anarchic poetry. Much of her work is animated by themes of sexual anxiety and an ambivalence towards Christianity which belies its popular image of comic whimsy. Of her novels, *Novel on Yellow Paper* (1936) is the most widely known. Several of her collections of witty, understated poems are accompanied by her own drawings. Works include: *Collected Poems* (1975); *Me Again: Uncollected Writings* (ed. Barbera, J. and McBrien, W.; 1983).

Snow, C. P. (Charles Percy) (1905–80)
Novelist; author of the sequence *Strangers and Brothers* comprising *Strangers and Brothers* (1940), *The Light and the Dark* (1947), *Time of Hope* (1949), *The Masters* (1951), *The New Men* (1954), *Homecomings* (1956); *The Conscience of the Rich* (1958), *The Affair* (1960), *Corridors of Power* (1964); *The Sleep of Reason* (1968); *Last Things* (1970).

He also played a large part in public affairs; he was created Baron (Life Peerage) in 1964, and served as a junior minister (Ministry of Technology) from 1964 till 1966. Trained as a scientist, he held strong views about the intellectual cleavage between men trained in the sciences and those trained in liberal studies in the modern world. His Rede Lecture at Cambridge, *The Two Cultures and the Scientific Revolution* (1959), became famous, partly because it provoked an exceptionally ferocious retort from the critic ▷ F. R. Leavis. Other novels include: *The Malcontents* (1972); *In Their Wisdom* (1974). He was married to the writer ▷ Pamela Hansford Johnson.
Bib: Cooper, W., *C. P. Snow*; Leavis, F. R., *Two Cultures? The Significance of C. P. Snow*.

Sonnet
A short poem of 14 lines, and a rhyme scheme restricted by one or other of a variety of principles. The most famous pattern is called the 'Petrarchan sonnet', from its masterly use by the Italian poet Petrarch. This divides naturally into an eight-line stanza (octave) rhyming *abba abba*, and a six-line stanza in which two or three rhymes may occur; the two stanzas provide also for contrast in attitude to the theme. The origin of the sonnet is unknown, but its earliest examples date from the 13th century in Europe, although it did not reach England until the 16th century. The immense popularity of the form perhaps derives from its combination of discipline, musicality and amplitude. The subject matter is commonly love, but after the 16th century it becomes, at least in England, much more varied.

The sonnet was an extremely popular form for Romantic and pre-Romantic poets, and in the 19th century it was used to great effect by Christina Rossetti, Dante Gabriel Rossetti, Elizabeth Barrett Browning (*Sonnets from the Portuguese*, 1847). ▷ G. M. Hopkins experimented very boldly in the form, and produced some of his best work in what he claimed to be sonnets, though they are often scarcely recognizable as such. Though in the earlier part of the 20th century the sonnet form appeared to have lost favour, in the later part of this century there has been a revival of interest in the form. The most notable example of this re-awakening of interest is perhaps the two 'sonnet sequences' by John Berryman (1938–68) published in 1952 and 1967; other important 20th-century sonnet writers are ▷ W. H. Auden and ▷ Tony Harrison.

***Sons and Lovers* (1913)**
The first of ▷ D. H. Lawrence's major novels. It is based on his own early life in the Midlands coal-mining village of Eastwood (Nottinghamshire), on his relationship with his mother and with his father who was a mineworker, and on those with his early women friends.

Eastwood is called Bestwood in the novel; the character who corresponds to Lawrence himself is Paul Morel. The strongest relationship is the close tie between Mrs Morel and Paul, who has two brothers and a sister. Mrs Morel comes of a proud, Dissenting middle-class family. She inherits the uncompromising traditions of English Dissent, and, though her family has been impoverished, she has an inherent aristocracy of temperament derived from her family tradition of high standards. The father, Walter Morel, a miner, is a contrast to his wife, both in his background (he is the grandson of a French refugee and an English barmaid) and in his easy-going, pleasure-loving, spontaneous temperament. The marriage is an unhappy one: Mrs Morel's strictness and truthfulness are outraged by her husband's slackness and deceitfulness. In the war between them, the children take the side of the mother.

The closeness between Mrs Morel and Paul develops after the death of her eldest son, William, and Paul's own serious illness. He goes to work in a Nottingham factory, but he has his mother's intellectual seriousness and artistic sensitivity, and has ambitions to become an artist. Mrs Morel invests in him all her pride of life and the hopes and passions that her marriage has disappointed. She finds a rival in Miriam Leivers, the shy and intensely serious daughter of a local farmer, and bitterly opposes her friendship with Paul. He is affected by his mother's opposition, and at the same time he resents what he considers to be Miriam's excessive spirituality and her emotional demands upon him, since he believes these to be a barrier to the sensual release for which he craves. He reacts against Miriam by engaging in a sensual love affair with Clara Dawes, a married woman who has quarrelled with her husband. This relationship is not opposed by Mrs Morel, since it is a physical one and does not compete with her own emotional possessiveness. Paul, on the other hand, finds that Clara affords him no more release than Miriam had done; he is unconsciously subjected, all the time, to his mother. The mother's protracted illness and death, and Paul's fight with Baxter Dawes, Clara's husband, are complementary climaxes of the novel. Both together constitute his release, although the death leaves him with a sense of complete dereliction: he has to face the choice of willing himself to live or surrendering to his own desire for death.

The book was early regarded as a vivid presentation of the working of the ▷ Oedipus complex. Lawrence was not acquainted with ▷ Freud's theories when he started work on the novel in 1910, but had come into contact with them before completing the final version in 1912. It is in its own right a major novel, but it certainly constitutes Lawrence's attempt to release himself from the problems of his own early development. He later declared that his study of his father had been unfair and one-sided. Jessie Chambers, the woman on whom Miriam was based, wrote a study of Lawrence as a young man as a reply to her characterization as Miriam; this was published as *D. H. Lawrence, A Personal Record* by E. T. (1935).

Spanish influence on English Literature
The earliest translation of a Spanish masterpiece into any language was that of Cervantes' *Don Quixote* (1605–15) by Thomas Shelton in 1612 (Part I) and 1620 (Part II). Of all Spanish texts, *Don Quixote* was to have the most profound influence on English literature: in the 17th century Francis Beaumont's *The Knight of the Burning Pestle* (1607) and Samuel Butler's *Hudibras* (1663) utilize the comic elements of the novel, while Philip Massinger's *The Renegado* (1624) combines material from *Don Quixote* together with Cervantes' play, *Los Baños de Argel* (1615). In the 18th century Henry Fielding's *Don Quixote in England* (1734) and Laurence Sterne's *Tristram Shandy* (1760–7), and in the 19th century the novels of Walter Scott and Charles Dickens perpetuate English indebtedness to Cervantes.

The 16th and 17th centuries in Spain are known as the Golden Age, which paralleled in quality, but greatly exceeded in abundance of texts, the creativity of the Elizabethan and Jacobean ages in England. The plays of Pedro Calderón de la Barca (1600–81) have often been compared to those of ▷ Shakespeare, for example by Shelley, who learned Spanish in order to read Calderón's dramas and partially translated into English Calderón's famous religious drama, *El mágico prodigioso (The Wonder-Working Magician*, 1637). Shelley also admired *La cisma de Inglaterra (The Schism of England*, perf. 1627), a play dealing with the same subject as Shakespeare's *Henry VIII*.

The 17th-century translations of James Mabbe further facilitated Spanish literary influence in England; works translated by Mabbe include Cervantes' *Novelas ejemplares* (1613; *Exemplary Novels*, trans. 1640); the late medieval novelesque play *La Celestina* (c 1499) by Fernando de Rojas (c 1465–1541); and Mateo Alemán's (1547–?1614) picaresque novel, *Guzmán de Alfarache* (trans. 1622). The latter text, with *Don Quixote*, formed part of the broader, generic development of the picaresque novel in Spain, England and elsewhere in Europe, while *La Celestina* was one of the earliest medieval texts to be translated into English. The tradition of translating Iberian masterpieces into English continues through to the 20th century: Joan Martorell's novel, *Tirant lo Blanc* (1490), was translated in 1984 by D. H. Rosenthal.

Translation has inevitably played an important role in the interrelationship between Spanish and English literatures, but occasionally the two cultures actually converge, as in the English poetry of the Spanish Romantic poet and intellectual, Joseph Blanco White (1775–1841) whose sonnet, 'To Night', appears in *The Oxford Book of English Verse 1250–1918* (ed. A. Quiller-Couch). In the 20th century, Spanish texts in English have become more readily available, for example, the works of Federico García Lorca (1898–1936), especially his dramas *Blood Wedding* (perf. 1933) and *The House of Bernada Alba* (perf. 1945), enjoy regular revivals in Britain. His socialist sympathies, together with an almost openly acknowledged homosexuality, ran parallel to, although surprisingly did not influence, the English poets such as ▷ W. H. Auden and ▷ Stephen Spender who were involved in the Spanish Civil War. Lorca's work has had far greater impact on post-war American fiction than on English literature. Perhaps fittingly, in recent years it is Latin American literature which has had the most pronounced effect on English writing and on the reading public in England. The ▷ 'magic realism' novels of Gabriel García Márquez (b 1928), such as *Cien Años de Soledad (One Hundred Years of Solitude*, 1967), and the novels, essays and criticism of Carlos Fuentes (b 1928), such as *Terra Nostra* (1975), are now internationally famous in English as well as Spanish.

Spark, Muriel (b 1918)
Before becoming a novelist, Spark was a poet (*Collected Poems*, 1967). Her first novel was *The Comforters* (1957), which she has described as 'a novel about writing a novel', *ie* an experiment in, and exploration of what it means to write fiction. At about the same time she became a convert to Roman Catholicism, and her novels since have tended to take a parabolic form (characteristic of other contemporary novelists, *eg* ▷ Iris Murdoch, ▷ William Golding) combining overt, often wittily satirical ▷ realism with implications of an extra-realist, spiritual dimension. One of her best-known works is *The Prime of Miss Jean Brodie* (1961), the story of the influence over a group of schoolgirls of a progressive spinster schoolteacher in Edinburgh. It is characteristic of Spark's work in its combination of the comic and the sinister, and the skilful use of anticipations of later events. Her three ▷ novellas, *The Public Image* (1968); *The Driver's Seat* (1970) and *Not to Disturb* (1971) exemplify the economy, precision and hardness of her work; they invite little sympathy for their characters, but rather convey a strong sense of pattern and fate underlying an apparent contingency of events. Her other novels are: *Robinson* (1958); *Memempto Mori* (1959); *The Ballad of Peckham Rye* (1960); *The Bachelors* (1960); *The Girls of Slender Means* (1963); *The Mandelbaum Gate* (1965); *The Hothouse by the East River* (1972); *The Abbess of Crewe* (1972); *The Takeover* (1976); *Territorial Rights* (1979); *Loitering with Intent* (1981); *The Only Problem* (1984); *A Far Cry From Kensington* (1988).

Other writings include a stage play *Doctors of Philosophy* (1962), radio plays collected in *Voices at Play* (1961), a further volume of poetry, *Going Up to Sotherby's* (1982) and short stories in *Collected Stories I (*1967); *The Stories of Muriel Spark* (1985).
Bib: Stanford, D., *Muriel Spark: A Biographical and Critical Study*; Stubbs, P., *Muriel Spark* (Writers and their Work series); Kemp, P., *Muriel Spark*; Bold, A., *Muriel Spark*.

Spectator, The
The name of two periodicals, the first appearing daily (1711–12 and 1714), and the second a weekly founded in 1828 and still continuing. The earlier is the more famous of the two, owing to the contributions of its famous editors, Addison and Steele; it had an important influence on the manners and culture of the time. The later *Spectator* has also had a distinguished history, however; it began as a radical journal, but is now the leading intellectual weekly periodical of the right.

▷ Reviews and periodicals.

Spender, Sir Stephen (b 1909)
Poet and critic. Son of a distinguished journalist, J. A. Spender, who was editor of the liberal *Westminster Gazette*. Educated at University College School, London, and University College, Oxford, where he became friendly with the poets ▷ W. H. Auden, ▷ C. Day-Lewis, and ▷ Louis MacNeice. The four, together with the novelist ▷ Christopher Isherwood, formed an influential group of left-wing writers in the 1930s. Spender was and is a passionately political poet, working

as a propagandist for the Republicans in the Spanish Civil War and, in *The Destructive Element* (1935), partly defending poetry's addressing of political subjects through a discussion of fellow poets ▷ W. B. Yeats and ▷ T. S. Eliot. As his career has progressed Spender's political orientation has changed; though briefly a member of the ▷ Communist Party, in 1950 he contributed to the anti-Communist collection of essays, *The God that Failed* (ed. R. H. S. Crossman). His volumes of verse include *Nine Entertainments* (1928), *Twenty Poems* (1930), *The Still Centre* (1939), *Ruins and Visions* (1942). As a critic he has written two studies of modern literature: *The Destructive Element* (1935) and *The Creative Element* (1953). His ▷ autobiographical writings include *World within World* (1951). In 1953 he became co-editor of *Encounter*, a monthly review of culture and world affairs. In 1969 he published a study of student politics: *The Year of the Young Rebels*. In 1970 he became Professor of English Language and Literature at University College, London. Later works include *Love–Hate Relations* (1974), *The Thirties and After* (1978), a critical study of T. S. Eliot and *Collected Poems 1928–85* (1985). Spender is also an important translator, particularly of ▷ German literature, and has collaborated with painter David Hockney in the 1982 account of their trip to China, *China Diary*. In 1988 he finally published his first novel, *The Temple*, the revised version of a novel concerning homosexuality first written more than 50 years previously.

Sprung rhythm
A term used by the poet ▷ Gerard Manley Hopkins to denote the method by which his verse is to be scanned. In his time most English verse was written in running rhythm, *ie* ▷ metres with regular stresses in the line:

Tonight the winds begin to rise
And roar from yonder dropping day
(Tennyson – *In Memoriam*)

Hopkins wished to free English verse from this rhythm, so as to bring verse into closer accord with common speech, to emancipate rhythm from the linear unit, and to achieve a freer range of emphasis. His theory of sprung rhythm (contained in the Preface to his *Poems*) is complicated, perhaps because he felt he had to justify himself to rather academic metricists like his friend ▷ Robert Bridges. In fact he was reviving the rhythm of Old English alliterative verse (he cites Langland's *Piers Plowman* as being in sprung rhythm) and in folk poetry including many ▷ ballads and ▷ nursery rhymes. In sprung rhythm the number of stresses in each line is regular, but they do not occur at regular intervals, nor do the lines have a uniform number of syllables. The rhythm also drives through the stanza, and is not basically linear. The following is an example:

Summer ends now; now, barbarous in beauty, the stooks rise
Around; up above, what wind-walks! what lovely behaviour
Of silk-sack clouds! has wilder, wilful wavier
Meal-drift moulded ever and melted across skies?
(Hopkins–*Hurrahing in Harvest*)

Stanislavsky, Konstantin (1863–1938)
Russian actor and director, and founder of the Moscow Art Theatre in 1898 with Nemirovich-Danchenko. He rejected the declamatory acting style of the Imperial Theatres and developed a rigorous actors' training which explored, among other things, character psychology and motivation. These ideas about acting can be studied in his published works: *My Life in Art*; *An Actor Prepares*; *Building a Character*, *Creating a Role*. He has been a great influence for the American Method and other naturalistic approaches to acting. However, he did not restrict his directing to naturalistic plays for which the so-called Stanislavskian approach was relevant.
Bib: Benedetti, J., *Stanislavski: An Introduction*; Magarshack, D., *Stanislavsky on the Art of the Stage*.

State funding
This is an important source of income for many of the 'arts' in Britain. Theatre, as for example the ▷ R.S.C., and opera, like the Royal Opera at Covent Garden, are subsidized by the state, while on a smaller scale local authorities provide grants for writers, bookshops and courses.
▷ Arts Council of Great Britain; Censorship.

Stead, Christina (1902–83)
Australian novelist. Educated at Sydney University Teachers' College, she moved

to Europe in 1928, and to the U.S.A. in 1935, travelling with the American political economist William James Blake, whom she married in 1952. She worked as a Hollywood screenwriter before moving to England and, in 1968, returning to Australia. Many of her novels are concerned with the experience of women, and in particular the quest for love. They are notable for their stylistic power, richness of observation, and vivid characterization, and contain an element of the fantastic. Her first works were collections of stories: *The Salzberg Tales* and *Seven Poor Men of Sydney*, both published in 1934. Of her novels, *House of All Nations* (1938) reflects her left-wing views in its account of a glittering, amoral world of financial speculation, while *The Man Who Loved Children* (1940), a novel of American family life, shows an interest in the causes of genius. In *For Love Alone* (1944) a girl escapes to Australia in search of love and freedom.

▷ Commonwealth literatures.

Stevenson, Anne (b 1933)
Poet. Stevenson was born in Britain, and now lives here, but was brought up and educated in the U.S.A. She has written critical texts as well as poetry, and has worked as a teacher. Her publications include: *Living in America* (1965); *Travelling Behind Glass: Selected Poems* (1974); *Enough of Green* (1977); *Minute by Glass Minute* (1982); *The Fiction-makers* (1985); *Selected Poems* (1986). Stevenson's controversially 'safe' biography of poet ▷ Sylvia Plath, *Bitter Fame: A Life of Sylvia Plath*, was published in 1989.

Stoppard, Tom (b 1937)
Czech-born British dramatist and something of an eclectic who has experimented with a variety of forms in his writing for stage and television. Characteristic of his plays is a heavy reliance on intellectual wit and allusion, which would appear to make his appeal rather esoteric, yet he has had several West End successes and is now established as a leading comic playwright. His major works include: *Rosencrantz and Guildenstern Are Dead* (1966); *The Real Inspector Hound* (1968); *Jumpers* (1972); *Travesties* (1974); *Dirty Linen* (1976); *Every Good Boy Deserves Favour* (1977); *Night and Day* (1978); *On the Razzle* (1981); *The Real Thing* (1982); *Rough Crossing* (1985); *Hapgood* (1987). Television plays include: *Professional Foul* (1977); *Squaring the Circle* (1984).
Bib: Bigsby, C. W. E., *Tom Stoppard*; Hunter, J., *Tom Stoppard's Plays*.

Storey, David (b 1933)
Novelist and dramatist. His novels include: *This Sporting Life* (1960); *Flight into Camden* (1961); *Radcliffe* (1963); *Pasmore* (1972); *A Temporary Life* (1973); *Saville* (1976); *A Prodigal Child* (1982); *Present Times* (1984).

Before he became a novelist and playwright Storey was an art student, and to pay for his studies in London he played at weekends in professional Rugby League football for a northern team. The son of a miner, Storey is the most interesting of a number of novelists in modern Britain who have in common that their social viewpoint is outside the middle class and centred geographically outside London; they include ▷ Alan Sillitoe, ▷ John Braine and ▷ Stan Barstow. Their obvious antecedent is ▷ D. H. Lawrence. Storey is distinguished from his contemporaries with a similar background by the absence of social belligerence and an ability to reach across from a provincial–industrial world denuded of art to a world of highly cultivated sensibility without playing false to the social experience that shaped him. His first novel, which has been filmed, is about his background world, in which sport is the principal cultural force; the next two are in different ways more ambitious and less successful, but their faults are interesting as the price paid for their serious experimental boldness. *Radcliffe* modifies 1950 ▷ realism with elements of the Gothic, allegorical and fantastic, while retaining a concern with class and social mobility; *Pasmore* continues this development by linking social instability to a personal crisis of identity. His plays often explore class antagonism and social dislocation. In *The Contractor* (1969) the process of manual work is presented dramatically as the action centres around the construction of a huge marquee on stage. This bold if somewhat sentimental gesture about the worth of work originally made a strong impression. Yet Storey's plays tend to avoid simplistic idealization of the working class or indeed any kind of simple obvious 'meaning'. The ▷ Chekhovian *Home* (1970) is set in a mental hospital, perhaps a metaphor for modern Britain, whose communication is painfully reserved. Much is hinted at but little is directly expressed. The later plays, *Mother's Day* (1976) and *Sisters* (1978) both have working-class settings and deal with what Storey termed the 'delusions, illusions and fantasies' of domestic life. Other plays include: *The Restoration of Arnold Middleton* (1966); *In Celebration* (1969); *The Changing Room* (1971); *The Farm* and *Cromwell* (both 1973): *Life Class* (1974); *Early Days* (1980).

Bib: Taylor, J. R., *David Storey*.

Strachey, (Giles) Lytton (1880–1932)
Biographer. His best-known works are *Eminent Victorians* (1918) – short biographical studies of Cardinal Manning, Florence Nightingale and General Gordon – and *Queen Victoria* (1921). He also wrote *Elizabeth and Essex* (1928), and criticism: *Landmarks in French Literature* (1912) and *Books and Characters* (1922). Strachey regarded most biographies of the 19th century as dull monuments to the subject, whereas he considered biography to be an art form, presenting the subject as a human being and showing him or her from unexpected aspects. Strachey was a prominent member of the ▷ Bloomsbury Group, living with diarist and painter ▷ Carrington.

▷ Biography.

Bib: Sanders, C. P., *Strachey: His Mind and Art*; Johnstone, J. K., *The Bloomsbury Group*; Holroyd, M., *Lytton Strachey*.

Stream of consciousness
A term which was used by William James in his *Principles of Psychology* but was first applied to literature in a 1918 review by May Sinclair of volumes of ▷ Dorothy Richardson's *Pilgrimage*. Since then it has been used for the narrative technique which attempts to render the consciousness of a character by representing as directly as possible the flow of feelings, thoughts and impressions. The term 'interior monologue' is also sometimes used. The classic exponents of the technique, apart from Richardson, are ▷ Virginia Woolf, ▷ James Joyce and the American novelist William Faulkner (1897–1962).

Strindberg, August (1849–1912)
Swedish dramatist and novelist. His father, a shipping agent, married his servant who had been his mistress during his first marriage. The unpromising circumstances of this parentage, intensified by his bad relations with his father, were the beginnings of a psychologically tormented life for Strindberg; he was married and divorced three times, and had a mental breakdown in 1895–6, described in *Inferno*, one of several autobiographical fragments and a vivid document. Intellectually he was immensely versatile: a student of Chinese, botany, chemistry, alchemy and painting. He had comparable literary versatility, and wrote radical journalism (1872–80), prose fiction (notably *The Red Room*, 1879), and his varied, original dramas. He is chiefly famous, at least outside Sweden, for the last. He wrote historical dramas (*Master Olof*, 1872; *Saga of the Folkungs*, *Gustavus Vasa*, *Eric XIV*, 1899) which show the influence of Shakespeare's history plays; tragedies influenced by Zola's ▷ Naturalism and the philosophy of ▷ Nietzsche; fantasies (*Easter*, 1900; *Dream Play*, 1902) under the influence of the Belgian dramatist, Maurice Maeterlinck (1862–1949); and, at the end of his career, highly symbolic dramas often called ▷ 'expressionist', of which the best known is *The Ghost Sonata* (1907). Two partly autobiographical works, *To Damascus* (1898) and *The Great Highway* (1909–12) can also be termed 'expressionist'.

Strindberg's dramatic inspiration was to epitomize human experience as the experience of conflict, and he sought to dramatize this conflict at its deepest and most intense. This shows most clearly in his naturalist phase, especially the two plays by which he is best known in Britain: *The Father* (1887) and *Lady Julia* (1888). To these may be added the double play *The Dance of Death* (1901), a Naturalist tragedy verging towards the expressionist symbolism of his later work. One of his strongest preoccupations at the time was the theme of conflict in relationships between women and men, since he considered women to be undergoing a fundamental change in their nature in their struggle for emancipation. He was aware of the possibilities of dramatic experiment on stage and enhanced the visual aspect of his plays. In dialogue he was also experimental, though not with such decisive success as his Russian contemporary, ▷ Anton Chekhov.

In Britain (in contrast to America), Strindberg did not have an influence comparable to that of ▷ Henrik Ibsen until after World War II. Since then, the outspokenness of such dramatists as ▷ John Osborne and ▷ John Arden, and the dialogue and stage experiments of ▷ Harold Pinter and ▷ Samuel Beckett, as well as new freedoms shown by many dramatists in the handling of stage sets and dramatic plots, all show his impact.

Bib: Lamm, M., *August Strindberg*.

Structuralism
A form of critical theory chiefly derived from the work of ▷ Ferdinand de Saussure and from Russian ▷ Formalism. Structuralism rejects the notion that the text expresses an author's meaning or that it reflects society and, instead, treats it as an independent unit which activates various objective relationships with other texts. Structuralism, then,

concentrates upon the relationship between cultural elements, especially those in binary oppositions, without which, it is claimed, meaning cannot exist.

▷ Post-structuralism.

Bib: Culler, J., *Structuralist Poetics*; Lodge, D., *Working with Structuralism*.

Subjectivity

In its use in the language of literary criticism this concept is not to be confused with the notion of 'individual response' with which it has customarily been associated. ▷ Louis Althusser and ▷ Jacques Lacan developed the notion of human beings as 'subjects', that is points at which all of those social, cultural, and psychic forces which contribute to the construction of the individual come together. Implicit in the concept of the 'subject' is the idea of the grammatical positioning of the personal pronoun in a sentence: the 'I' being referred to as 'the subject of discourse'. Also, implicit in the concept of 'subjectivity' is the notion of 'subjection', which raises fundamental questions about the ways in which the behaviour of individual 'subjects' is conditioned by external forces: the subject was originally defined as one who was 'subject to the law'. Within the boundaries of critical theory the 'subject" is never unified (except through the functioning of an ▷ ideology which is designed to efface contradiction), but is, in reality, split, or 'decentred'. This is part of a movement away from the kind of philosophical ▷ humanism which would place the individual at the centre of attention. It would attribute to him or her an autonomy of action as well as an authority arising out of the suggestion that he or she is the origin and source of all meaning. 'Subjectivity' is an indispensable category of analysis for ▷ feminism, ▷ psychoanalytic criticism and for the various kinds of ▷ materialist analysis of texts.

Sublimation

This term is used in ▷ Freudian psychoanalysis to describe the process whereby activities which have their origins in the unconscious, and which can be traced to primal issues of sexuality, are diverted and surface in other areas of human endeavour, as something else. This concept is of particular use to literary criticism, not only because it can provide an explanation of the mechanisms of artistic creation itself, but because it assists in the analysis of literary representations of human motives and actions. Implicit in sublimation is the notion of an unconscious whose operations, distorted as desires, rise to the level of the conscious.

Subversion

This is a term usually associated with the sphere of political action, but applied to literary texts it points towards the relationship between a particular text, or even a part of a text, and what is generally regarded as the prevailing order. Individual texts are capable of challenging dominant orthodoxies (*eg* ▷ James Joyce's ▷ *Ulysses* or ▷ D. H. Lawrence's *Lady Chatterley's Lover*), either at the level of literary form, or at the level of discernible content. Thus, they may be said to subvert expectations or dominant values. A more complex kind of subversion may take place within the boundaries of a particular text which otherwise would be accepted as conforming to prevailing values and attitudes. Where this happens, negotiation takes place (which can be analysed as part of the text's structure) whereby that which is dominant in the text seeks to contain and control those forces which could subvert it. Such a process is particularly evident in relation to sexual difference, where a potentially subversive 'femininity' is often seen to threaten the dominant masculine discourses which seek to contain it. Very often potentially subversive energies are only ever permitted to enter a text in marginalized forms, *eg* female promiscuity, as various forms of 'evil' all of which are shown to be a danger to the status quo. An acceptance of the judgements implied in these moral categories is usually a precondition of a reading which is complicit with its dominant discourses and structures. A more critical reading will seek to reinstate the text's 'subversive' elements in order to show precisely how certain values, and the literary structures which sustain them, are produced.

Suffragette Movement

Colloquial term for the Women's Suffrage Movement which pursued violent action to secure political rights for women before and during World War I. The suffrage movement has often been seen as the origin of the modern women's movement; it developed out of the campaigns led in the 1860s and 1870s by Josephine Butler against the notorious Contagious Diseases Acts. The origin of the Women's Suffrage Movement thus lies in the late 19th century. Specifically, the suffragettes wanted equal rights with men to have the vote (suffrage) in parliamentary elections and to be candidates for election. Among the famous leaders of the movement were Mrs Pankhurst and her two daughters, ▷ Sylvia and Christabel.

The movement ended in 1918 when votes were given to women at the age of 30; in 1928 they received equal rights with men.

▷ Women, Status of.

Bib: Tickner, L., *The Spectacle of Women*.

Surrealism

Inaugurated in Paris in 1924 by ▷ André Breton's first *Surrealist Manifesto* (two further manifestos were to follow in 1930 and 1934), its founding members included Louis Aragon (1897–1982), Robert Desnos (1900–45), Paul Eluard (1895–1952), Benjamin Péret (1899–1959) and Philippe Soupault (b 1897). The movement's ambition was a radical programme, extending beyond art and literature to embrace social and political reform. To advertise and propagate their aims, the Surrealists created a 'Bureau de recherches surréalistes' and a number of reviews: *Littérature* (1919), *La Révolution surréaliste* (1924), *Le Surréalisme au service de la Révolution* (1930) and *Minotaure* (1932). Purely within France, Surrealism's roots lay in Guillaume Apollinaire's (1880–1918) experiments with poem-objects and in the Cubist poetry of Pierre Reverdy (1889–1960). More broadly, as the first *Manifesto* made clear, it was especially indebted to Freudian (▷ Freud) theories of dreams and sought to overthrow rationalism in favour of unconscious mental states, so giving rise to an expanded sense of the psychic life. Such unconscious processes could best be liberated by activities such as 'automatic writing'. By this technique, a writer's faculty of conscious censorship is laid aside, allowing the chance encounter between two otherwise unrelated elements which might produce the surreal image and intimate the incursion of dream into reality.

Just as Surrealism travelled easily between forms of artistic production and ostensibly external forms such as psychology and philosophy, so its own artistic manifestations spanned poetry, prose and painting, though it is best known for and possibly most representatively manifested in the first and last of these. Max Ernst (1891–1976), René Magritte (1898–1967) and Joan Miró (1893–1983) helped establish the movement in art and Salvador Dali (1904–89) provided greater impetus still when he associated himself with Surrealism in 1929; his dream-like work was plainly inspired by Freud, while his surreal objects such as the lobster-telephone amuse and shock our sense of the everyday propriety of such objects. Louis Aragon, the foremost of Surrealism's several communists (Eluard was another), made an early contribution with his *Feu de joie* (1920) and *Le Mouvement perpétuel* (1925) as well as major novels. However, Aragon's commitment to communism from 1927 onwards finally led to his break with Surrealism in 1932, even though Breton's *Second Manifesto* of 1930 had called for the harmonization of Freud and ▷ Marx. World War II caused a hiatus in Surrealism's activities and despite the success of the various Surrealist Exhibitions (*eg* London, 1936; Paris 1938, 1947, 1959), by the 1950s the movement's force was to all intents and purposes spent.

The widespread influence of French Surrealism between the wars gave rise to two corresponding movements, Belgian Surrealism and English Surrealism.

Bib: Breton, A., *What is Surrealism?*; Howard, R., *The History of Surrealism*.

Swift, Graham (Colin) (b 1949)

Novelist and short-story writer. Born in London and educated at the universities of Cambridge and York, he worked as a part-time teacher of English in London colleges from 1974 to 1983. *Waterland* (1983) reflects on the significance of historical knowledge and the influence of the environment on human identity, through the tragicomic story of several generations of a Fenland family, interspersed with material about the history and geography of the area. His other fiction is: *The Sweet-Shop Owner* (1980); *Shuttlecock* (1981); *Learning to Swim and Other Stories* (1982); *Out of This World* (1988); *Ever After* (1992).

Symbolic order

A ▷ psychoanalytical term now frequently used in literary criticism. 'Symbolic' in this context refers initially to the notion that language itself is comprised of symbols which stand for things. But, the French psychoanalyst ▷ Jacques Lacan observes that: 'It is the world of words that creates the world of things', and in so doing introduces an 'order' into what would otherwise be disparate units. That process of ordering is motivated by a series of impulses and desires which are not usually available to the conscious mind. Thus, the symbolic order is that order of representations through whose organization the child enters into language and the social order as a gendered human 'subject'. In the case of ▷ Freudian psychoanalysis each symbol refers back to an Oedipal stage (▷ Oedipus complex) which the infant passes through on the way to maturity. In Lacan, the 'unconscious' is said to be structured like a language, already a system of representations through which the individual gendered subject realizes his or her identity. In some respect all literary texts traverse the realm of the symbolic order in that they represent and articulate those images through which reality is grasped discursively.

Symbolism

A name primarily associated with a school of French poets writing in the second half of the 19th century. The movement grew out of the work of ▷ Baudelaire (1821–67) and is above all associated with Paul Verlaine (1844–96), Arthur Rimbaud (1854–91) and Stephane Mallarmé (1842–98). In addition to Baudelaire, the American writer Edgar Allan Poe (1809–49) and the German music-dramatist Richard Wagner (1813–83) contributed to the shaping of Symbolism. It constituted a development from ▷ Romanticism in as much as it was poetry of the feelings as opposed to the reason, but it was a reaction against it in as much as it was more intellectual in its conception of the way poetry operates. This intellectualism did not imply that the content of poetry should be one of what is ordinarily called ideas: Mallarmé's affirmation was that 'Poetry is not made with ideas; it is made with words'. This looks forward to much 20th-century thought in all the arts, requiring that the artist should above all have respect for the medium in which he has chosen to work; it also anticipates ▷ T. S. Eliot's praise of the English 17th-century Metaphysical poets that 'they were, at best, engaged in the task of trying to find the verbal equivalent for states of mind and feeling'. Since 'states of mind and feeling' are ultimately mysterious and elusive, the Symbolists emphasized the suggestiveness of poetic language, but though this emphasis on suggestiveness makes much of their poetry obscure, their care for the organization and operation of language keeps it from vagueness, in the sense in which the poetry of their English contemporary, the late Romantic Algernon Swinburne, is very commonly vague. Swinburne is also much concerned with the poetic medium of words, but in such a way that his verse subdues the reader into a state of passive receptivity, whereas the French Symbolists evoke active participation; Swinburne relies for his effect on stimulating emotions already latent in the reader, whereas the Symbolists incite extension of these emotions. T. S. Eliot's essay on Swinburne (in *Selected Essays*) is a help in elucidating the distinction.

The French Symbolists are particularly important in English literature for their decisive influence on the two most important poets writing in English in the first half of the 20th century: T. S. Eliot and ▷ W. B. Yeats. Eliot's understand of them was much the more intimate and profound, but A. Symons's *The Symbolist Movement in Literature* (1899) acted on them both.

Bib: Wilson, E., *Axel's Castle*; Boura, C. M., *The Heritage of Symbolism*; Lehmann, A. G., *The Symbolist Aesthetic in France*.

Synchronic

Adjective used by ▷ Ferdinand de Saussure to describe the analysis of the meaning of a ▷ sign in relation to the other current elements of the language system ▷ langue. Saussure juxtaposes the synchronic study of language with the *diachronic* study of language which looks at the historical development of language. This is one of the important polarities in Saussure's theories.

▷ Parole.

Synge, John Millington (1871–1909)

Irish dramatist. He belonged to the Protestant Anglo-Irish segment of Irish society, but at the suggestion of ▷ W. B. Yeats in 1899, he devoted his career to interpreting Irish Celtic peasant life. From this proceeded his remarkable series of dramas which were the chief glory of the drama of the Irish literary renaissance, and of the ▷ Abbey Theatre in Dublin (under the direction of Yeats) through which this movement expressed itself. Part of the Irish dramatic endeavour was to revive poetic drama; Synge wrote in prose, but he exploited with great sensitivity the poetic suggestiveness of the rhythms, diction, and imagery of Irish peasant speech. At the same time he avoided the sentimentalities of late 19th-century romanticism and the falsifications which Irish nationalistic vanity required; the result was that his masterpiece, ▷ *The Playboy of the Western World* (1907) was received with rage and uproar. His other plays are: *The Shadow of the Glen* (1903); *Riders to the Sea* (1904); *The Well of the Saints* (1905); *The Tinker's Wedding* (1907), and his last play – drawn unlike the others from Irish myth – *Deirdre of the Sorrows*, published in 1910 after his death.

Synge also wrote descriptions of Irish peasant life in *The Aran Islands* (1907), *In Wicklow*, and *In County Kerry* (both published 1910).

▷ Irish literature in English.

Bib: Greene, D. H. and Stephens, E. M., *Life*; Price, F., *Synge and Anglo-Irish Drama*; Thornton, W., *J. M. Synge and the Western Mind*.

Tate Gallery, The
A public gallery for modern paintings and sculpture on the north bank of the Thames in London. It was established by a sugar-merchant, Sir Henry Tate, and opened in 1897. A 'Tate of the North' opened in Liverpool's Albert Dock in 1989; a 'Tate of the West', based on the work of the St Ives school of modern British painting, is set to open in 1993.

Tel Quel
A magazine, for many years the leading French avant-garde journal. Its name was taken from a work by Paul Valéry (1871–1945) and it was edited by Philippe Sollers (b 1936), novelist, theorist and husband of the feminist writer ▷ Julia Kristeva. In political terms, the magazine's sympathies were Marxist-Leninist-Maoist. It welcomed the student demonstrations of May 1968 with an issue entitled 'The Revolution, here and now' and its programme for a French 'Cultural Revolution' was backed by figures such as the composer Pierre Boulez (b 1925) and the novelist and theoretician Jean Ricardou (b 1932). *Tel Quel* provided a forum for left-wing intellectuals and gave rise to the *Tel Quel* group. Their joint publication, *Théorie d'ensemble* (1968), contained *inter alia* ▷ Jacques Derrida's essay '*La Différance*', ▷ Michel Foucault's piece '*Distance, aspect, origine*' (discussing Alain Robbe-Grillet and Sollers) and ▷ Roland Barthes's '*Drame, poème, roman*' (on Sollers). Alongside its support for radical political and theoretical positions, the magazine did much to promote the cause of a literary counter-orthodoxy, represented by ▷ Sade, ▷ Lautréamont, Georges Bataille and Robbe-Grillet.

In the late 1970s, *Tel Quel* began to lose its radical impetus. Sollers renounced his theoretical persuasions, sympathized with the right-wing group, ▷ Les Nouveaux Philosophes, and embraced ▷ Catholicism. From 1982, the magazine changed its name to *L'Infini* and found itself a new publisher.

Tennant, Emma (b 1937)
Novelist. Her work combines a ▷ feminist perspective with a ▷ postmodernist use of allusion, parody, and fantasy, and in these respects has some affinity with that of ▷ Angela Carter. *The Time of the Crack* (1973) and *The Last of the Country House Murders* (1974) are both set in the future; the former is an apocalyptic satire, while the latter is a black comedy which parodies country house detective fiction. *The Bad Sister* (1978) satirizes the divisive effect upon women of social roles and expectations: the heroine finds herself inhabited by a demented other self, and the book itself is split between a prosaic account of contemporary society and a realm of dreams and fantasy. The expression of feminist revolt through a disturbed mental state has antecedents in *The Golden Notebook* by ▷ Doris Lessing, and in the work of ▷ Virginia Woolf. Tennant's other novels are: *The Colour of Rain* (1964); *Hotel de Dream* (1976); *Wild Nights* (1979); *Alice Fell* (1980); *Queen of Stones* (1982); *Woman Beware Woman* (1983); *Black Marina* (1985); *The Adventures of Robina, by Herself* (1986); *The House of Hospitalities* (1987).

Theatre of Cruelty
A style of theatre developing out of the work of ▷ Antonin Artaud, introduced to English audiences in 1964 by a 'Theatre of Cruelty' season at the LAMDA Theatre arranged by ▷ Peter Brook and Charles Marowitz. These experiments were developed in Brook's productions of Peter Ulrich Weiss's *Marat/Sade* in 1964 and the improvised play *US* in 1966. Theatre of Cruelty aims to shock the audience out of its complacency and restricted conventional behaviour into an awareness of the primitive forces within human nature. To do this it requires a committedly non-rationalistic approach to acting.
Bib: Artaud, A., *The Theatre and its Double*; Styan, J. L., *The Dark Comedy*.

Theatre of the Absurd
A name given by the critic Martin Esslin to describe the work of a number of dramatists, including Ionesco, Genet, ▷ Beckett and ▷ Pinter. These and other authors do not belong to any 'school' as such but their plays often have in common the sense that human existence is without meaning. The idea is reflected in the form as well as the content of the plays, by the rejection of logical construction, and the creation of meaningless speeches and silences. Such devices helped to develop new forms of theatre during the 1950s and 60s no longer reliant on outmoded dramatic conventions.
Bib: Esslin, M., *The Theatre of the Absurd*.

Theatres
No special buildings were erected in England for dramatic performances until late in the 16th century. The first playhouse, known as The Theatre, was erected by James

Burbage in Shoreditch, outside the City of London, in 1576–7. It was followed by many others, including the Globe (1598) which is the most famous owing to its association with Shakespeare. None of these theatres survived the middle of the 17th century, but a contemporary sketch of one of them (the Swan) exists, and there is a detailed description in the contract for the Fortune (1600).

It was only after the Restoration of the monarchy in 1660 that the theatre began to assume its modern shape, with a proscenium arch dividing the audience from the stage, thus providing the greater scope for scenery and illusion. One of the earliest English theatres of this style was Drury Lane, which had already been a theatre in the reign of James I and was rebuilt in 1662. From this time the theatre became the special entertainment for the middle and upper classes, largely cut off from the mass of people, and it has, on the whole, remained that way.

The second half of the 19th century saw the widespread building of theatres, but there was no live taste for intelligent new plays until ▷ George Bernard Shaw, in the last decade of the 19th century, began to create one. In the 20th century there has been a sharp division between the commercial theatres which provide intellectually commonplace entertainment, and the theatres of the intelligentsia. Two companies of the latter kind have an official national status, ▷ The Royal Shakespeare Company and the ▷ National Theatre. The Royal Shakespeare Company produces Shakespeare's and other dramatists' plays at Stratford-on-Avon and, formerly, at the Aldwych theatre in London. Since 1982 the Royal Shakespeare Company have performed at their new base in the Barbican Centre near St Paul's, where they are spaciously accommodated in a London home of their own, similar to that of the National Theatre which, after opening at the Old Vic Theatre in 1963 transferred to a new site on the South Bank in Waterloo in 1976–77. Under the guidance of Trevor Nunn and Sir Peter Hall respectively, the two national companies have inventively produced the English repertoire from Shakespeare and his contemporary dramatists to classical and modern European and American drama. They have increasingly benefited from funding by the Arts Council whose key role in freeing the British theatre since World War II from the shackles of economic success at the expense of art cannot be underestimated. To the extent that both the great companies have enjoyed a certain artistic franchise, the gap between them and the more radical theatrical groupings has narrowed.

Of the latter the English Stage Company, founded in 1955 and housed for years in the Royal Court Theatre in London, is the most important. It pioneered new modes of dramatic expression and encouraged new dramatists by giving them a space for their writings. ▷ John Osborne's *Look Back in Anger* (1956) was launched at the Royal Court and went on to become a milestone in the history of modern British drama. The 1960s saw the blossoming in London and in Britain of ▷ fringe theatre which corresponded to the New York Off Broadway and Off-Off Broadway. It was associated with Americans such as Charles Marowitz and Jim Haynes, mostly working at different improvised venues in London. Their work, and that of many of the dramatists of the 1960s and 1970s, above all shows the influence of ▷ Brecht and ▷ Artaud. The theatrical scene in 1990s Britain is bleak, as resources are dwindling and funding bodies like the Arts Council are increasingly reluctant to underwrite commercially non-viable plays. The re-emergence in the metropolis of a new theatre of farce and social comedy is an indication that the age which was once hailed as that of the new radical Elizabethans is on the wane, as new norms of quietist conformism are endorsed in the theatre.

Thomas, D. M. (Donald Michael) (b 1935)
Novelist and poet. His best-known work is *The White Hotel* (1981), a fictional account of the life of one of ▷ Freud's patients, making extensive use of fantasy. It also contains poetry and a pastiche of a case study by Freud. His other works include *Ararat* (1983); *Swallow* (1984); *Selected Poems* (1983); *Flying in to Love* (1992).

Thomas, Dylan Marlais (1914–53)
Poet. He was born in the Welsh town of Swansea; much of his work shows the impression on his early life of grim Welsh religious puritanism contrasting with the equally Welsh characteristic of strong emotion combined with his own sensuality. His *18 Poems* (1934) and *Twenty-five Poems* (1936) bring together conflicting images in startling association, with pronounced and emotive verbal rhythms. The method has superficial resemblances to those of the 19th-century poet ▷ Gerard Manley Hopkins and the 17th-century Metaphysicals, but it presents

less access than they do for the analytical intellect. Thomas's theme is characteristically the relationship between the disorderliness of sexual impulses and the forces of growth in nature. *The Map of Love* (1939) is mixed prose and poetry; it includes one of his most remarkable poems, *After the Funeral*, in which the striking rhythm and images cohere round the figure of the woman for whose death the poem is an ▷ elegy. *Deaths and Entrances* (1946) contains most of Thomas's most famous work. The poems show the impression made on him by World War II (during which he remained a civilian) in *A Refusal to Mourn*, a more overt use of religious emotion in *The Conversation of Prayer*, and delight in natural environment (*eg Poem in October*, *Fern Hill*). These poems are often less obscure than earlier ones, but the method remains a strong attack on the emotions, achieved by the shock of the imagery and the sweep of the rhythm.

Thomas also wrote prose works – notably the stories entitled *Portrait of the Artist as a Young Dog* (1940) and the play *Under Milk Wood* published after his death (1954). The prose has no obscurity and exhibits, as the poems do not, Thomas's strong humour. The play shows a mastery of the medium of drama for sound broadcasting which remains unexcelled.

Thomas's wide fame derives especially from three qualities: his unashamed appeal to latent emotionalism in the common reader, on whom he made a direct impact perhaps greater than that of other modern poets except ▷ W. B. Yeats; his remarkable talent as a public reader of verse; his personality, which became a legend during his own lifetime, especially in America. On the other hand, his exuberance ran counter, before the war, to the intellectual fastidiousness of ▷ T. S. Eliot and the emotional scepticism of ▷ W. H. Auden, the two poets with the greatest prestige amongst the intelligentsia in England during the 1930s; again, he has been regarded with suspicion since 1945 by younger poets who have cultivated scrupulous honesty of feeling.

▷ Welsh literature in English.

Bib: Jones, T. H., critical study in *Writers and Critics* series; Fraser, G. S., in British Council *Writers and their Work* series; Holbrook, D., *Llaregyb Revisited*.

Thomas, Philip Edward (1878–1917)

Poet and essayist. He was educated at St Paul's School and Lincoln College, Oxford, and was killed at the battle of Arras during World War I. He made his living by writing a long series of prose works, beginning with *The Woodland Life* (1897) and including ▷ biography, criticism and essays on natural surroundings. The last are in a tradition that extends back through Richard Jefferies, about whom Thomas wrote a critical assessment (1909), to the poetry of William Wordsworth. It was not until 1914 that Thomas began to write poetry, under the influence of the American poet Robert Frost, whom he first met the year before. His poems are continuous with his prose studies of nature, but it is by the poems rather than the prose that his reputation has grown since his death. English 'nature poetry' at its best has never been merely descriptive, but has concerned the power of the natural environment to elicit the purest human responses, not only to the environment but to elemental human relationships, including the relationship of the poet with himself. Thomas's poems show integrity of responsiveness and sensitivity to the language of his day; they are without the weakening nostalgia and sensibility which showed the decadence of the nature poetry tradition in some of his contemporaries. After his death, his poetic achievement was at first overshadowed by the reaction against the decadence of his contemporaries. ▷ Ezra Pound and ▷ T. S. Eliot led public taste away from the whole tradition, in both its good and its bad aspects, in which Thomas wrote. However, *New Bearings in English Poetry* (1932) by ▷ F. R. Leavis contains an intelligent reassessment of his work. Since 1945, Thomas's austere honesty and delicacy of perception have caused his work to appeal strongly to English poets striving for the same virtues; with ▷ Thomas Hardy, he is seen as representative of distinctly English sensibilities in contrast to the partly alien sensibilities of Pound and ▷ W. B. Yeats.

Bib: Lives by Eckert, R. P., Moore, J., and Farjeon, E.; Thomas, H., *As It Was* and *World Without End*; Coombes, H., *Edward Thomas*; 'Hardy, De la Mare and Thomas' in *The Modern Age* (Pelican Guide); Leavis, F. R., *New Bearings in English Poetry*; Day Lewis, C., in *Essays by Divers Hands* (Transactions of the Royal Society of Literature Vol. XXVIII, 1956); Motion, A., *The Poetry of Edward Thomas*.

Thomas, R. S., (Ronald Stuart) (b 1913)

Poet. Since his first volume, *The Stones of the Field* (1946), he has maintained a regular and substantial output, including *Song at the Year's Turning* (1955), *Laboratories of the Spirit* (1975) and *Experimenting With an Amen* (1986). He is best known as a recorder of the rigorous beauty of the Welsh landscape, and of the duress of farming-community life there and the religious sensibility that evolves in such a context. In 1936 Thomas was ordained as a Church of Wales clergyman. *Selected Poems 1946–68* (1973), *Later Poems: a Selection* (1983), *Selected Prose* (revised ed. 1986).

▷ Welsh literature in English.

Bib: Dyson, A. E., *Riding the Echo: Yeats, Eliot and R. S. Thomas*; Phillips, D. Z., *R. S. Thomas*; Ward, J. P., *The Poetry of R. S. Thomas*.

Times, The

British newspaper. It was founded in 1785 as *The Daily Universal Register*, and took its present name in 1788. In the 19th century it took the lead in contriving new methods of collecting news (notably through the employment of foreign correspondents), and its succession of distinguished editors and contributors gave it an outstanding status among British newspapers. Though always in private ownership, it has always claimed to be an independent newspaper rather than a party one. The literary style of one of its staff writers caused it to be nicknamed 'The Thunderer' in the 19th century; the novelist Anthony Trollope consequently refers to it as *The Jupiter* in his novels, since this king of the gods was known as the Thunderer by the ancient Romans. *The Times* publishes *The Times Literary Supplement* and *The Sunday Times* weekly. Its outlook is traditional and often conservative in political terms.

▷ Newspapers.

Tiresias (Teiresias)

In Greek myth, a sage of Thebes whom the gods afflicted with blindness but then compensated with the gift of prophecy. In the most familiar form of the legend, he spent part of his life as a woman.

Tennyson's poem *Tiresias* is one of those ▷ dramatic monologues which are now among the most admired of his poems; here, Tiresias speaks with the voice of the lonely, timeless sage. He also occurs in Part III of ▷ T. S. Eliot's poem ▷ *The Waste Land*; here he is more the impartial witness of the crises of the human mind, and is described in a note as 'the most important personage in the poem, uniting all the rest'.

Toft, Eric John (b 1933)

Novelist and short-story writer. Born and brought up in Hanley, Stoke-on-Trent in the Potteries district of the English Midlands, he was educated at Hanley High School and Magdalen College, Oxford, and taught at Brighton College of Education. In a sequence of powerful realist novels, set primarily in the Potteries, he has created a story of change and development in English working-class life from 1917 to the present: *The Bargees* (1969); *The Wedge* (1972); *The Underground Tree* (1978); *The Dew* (1981). *The House of the Arousing* (1973), a volume of short stories, draws on the author's experience of travelling in Malaysia.

Tolkien, J. R. R. (John Ronald Reuel) (1892–1973)

Novelist, philologist and critic. From 1925 to 1945 he was Professor of Anglo-Saxon at Oxford University, and during the 1930s belonged to 'The Inklings', a literary society whose other members included ▷ C. S. Lewis. From 1945 to 1959 he was Merton Professor of English Language and Literature at Oxford. His large-scale fantasy of another world *The Lord of the Rings* (1954–6) has gained enormous popularity. His other novels are: *The Hobbit* (1937) and *The Silmarillion* (1977).

▷ Children's books.

Bib: Carpenter, H., *J. R. R. Tolkien: A Biography*; Carpenter, H., *The Inklings*.

Tolstoy, Count Leo Nikolaevitch (1828–1910)

Russian novelist, dramatist and moral philosopher. What are usually considered his two greatest novels, *War and Peace* (1865–9) and *Anna Karenina* (1875–7), have a spaciousness, profundity and balance of sanity which have caused them to be used as a standard by which the achievements of other novelists can be measured. Tolstoy occupied a powerful position in Russian society and the critical phase of history through which Russia was passing during his lifetime contributed significantly to the scale of his work.

He was early influenced by the thought of Jean-Jacques Rousseau and this, combined with his own direct experience of peasant life (although he himself came from the Russian landed gentry), developed in him a strong faith in spontaneous, simple living in contrast to the sophisticated, fashionable, educated society which he also knew well. From 1876, disillusioned by worldliness and inspired by the example of the peasants, he thought increasingly about the religious interpretation of experience, but his thinking turned him away from the Russian Orthodox Church to a religion of his own, pacifistic and on the side of self-abnegation; it did not admit the existence of life after death nor a personal God, his belief being that the kingdom of God is within man. Tolstoy's influence may be seen in the works of ▷ G. B. Shaw, ▷ E. M. Forster and ▷ D. H. Lawrence.

▷ Russian influence on English literature.

Tomlinson, Charles (b 1927)
Poet and literary critic. Tomlinson has been a university lecturer since 1956, and he also paints and translates. His work is precise and aspires to technical objectivity, influenced by both ▷ Donald Davie (who taught him at Cambridge and introduced Tomlinson's 1955 volume *The Necklace*), and by ▷ Imagists and American ▷ modernists, especially William Carlos Williams and Marianne Moore. He has experimented with ▷ free verse and rhythmic irregularities, and is constantly expanding his technical range. His later volumes include: *The Way of a World* (1969); *The Shaft* (1978); *Selected Poems 1951–1974* (1978); *The Flood* (1981).

Tonks, Rosemary (b 1932)
Poet and novelist. Rosemary Tonks was a poet of considerable innovation and originality, until her conversion to fundamentalist Christianity stopped her writing career short in the early 1970s. Her work is cosmopolitan, often parodic, and European in its influences and themes, drawing particularly on the concerns of French ▷ Symbolism and ▷ Surrealism (▷ French literature in England). Her works include: *Notes on Cafés and Bedrooms* (1963); *Opium Fogs* (1963); *Illiad of Broken Sentences* (1967); *Businessmen as Lovers* (1969); her last published work was *The Halt during the Chase* (1972).

***To the Lighthouse* (1927)**
A novel by ▷ Virginia Woolf. The setting is a house used for holidays by Mr and Mrs Ramsay. The household consists of themselves, their eight children, and a number of their friends, of whom the most important is the painter Lily Briscoe. The novel dispenses with plot and is organized into three parts, dominated by two symbols – the lighthouse out at sea, and Lily's painting of the house, with Mrs Ramsay sitting in the window with her son James. The parts are entitled 'The Window', 'Time Passes', and 'The Lighthouse'. The first part is dominated by Mrs Ramsay, who is intuitive, imaginative, and possesses a reassuring and vitalizing influence upon people and their emotions. The mysterious lighthouse flashing through the darkness is associated with her. In the interval represented by the second part of the novel, corresponding to the war years 1914–18, she dies, and the third part is dominated by Mr Ramsay who is intellectual, philosophical, and lonely. The lighthouse seen as a practical instrument, close at hand and by daylight, is associated with him. The middle section concerns the empty house, subject to the flux of time and its changes. Lily Briscoe, the artist, stands aloof from Mrs Ramsay's embracing influence and seeks to fix the constantly changing relationships of people and objects in a single composition; she completes the picture in the last sentence of the book, when the Ramsay son, James, achieves reconciliation with his father and with the lighthouse seen as fact. Mrs Ramsay, in her role as wife and mother, and Lily, single and an artist, represent alternative possibilities for a woman's way of life.

The story is told through the ▷ stream of consciousness technique – in the minds of the characters, especially James, Lily, and Mrs Ramsay. The novel, one of the most original of the many fictional experiments in the 1920s, is partly autobiographical, and based on Virginia Woolf's own family. Mr and Mrs Ramsay are her father and mother, Leslie Stephen and his second wife.

Tragedy
Tragedy as it is understood in Western Europe has its origins in the Greek dramas by the Athenian dramatists Aeschylus, Sophocles and Euripides, in the 6th–5th centuries BC. Essentially the spirit of this writing was that inevitable suffering overwhelms the characters, and yet the characters maintain their dignity in the face of this suffering, and prove their greatness (and the capacity of human beings for greatness) by doing so. Greek tragedy arose out of their religious interpretation of the nature of human destiny. When Christianity prevailed over Western Europe, a much more hopeful interpretation of human destiny dominated the thought of writers, and tragedy, in the Greek sense, became difficult to imagine and unnatural: if good men suffer in this world, they are rewarded in Heaven, and this is not tragic; wicked men who happen to suffer in this world may be damned in the next, but this is also not tragic because they are wicked. Hence medieval tragedy was on the whole reduced to the conception of the Wheel of Fortune – that chance in this world is apt to take men from prosperity to misfortune, whatever their spiritual merits.

In the late 16th century the tragic vision of

human experience was rediscovered by some English dramatists, notably by Marlowe and ▷ Shakespeare. In so far as it had a literary ancestry, this was not the tragedy of the ancient Greeks, which was scarcely known, but the comparatively debased imitation of it by the Roman poet Seneca, which helped to give rise to Elizabethan Revenge Tragedy or 'Tragedy of Blood'. More interesting was the growth of conceptions of human destiny which did not usurp the Christian conception, but existed side by side with it, as an alternative, or perhaps rather as a complementary, vision. Thus perhaps the first important English tragedy is Marlowe's *Doctor Faustus* in which the hero forgoes eternal happiness after death for the sake of earthly ecstasy; Marlowe sets in opposition the Christian doctrine of the soul and ▷ Renaissance delight in earthly experience. *Hamlet*, in which Shakespeare for the first time makes the task of revenge a genuine moral dilemma, is perhaps the next. The best-known achievements of English tragic drama are Shakespeare's five plays: *Othello*, *Macbeth*, *King Lear*, *Antony and Cleopatra* and *Coriolanus*. These cannot be summed up in a phrase, but they have in common that the hero's hope of some form of supreme earthly happiness collapses into terrible misery, brought about less by the hero's character than through the nature of earthly reality of which his character forms a part. Among Shakespeare's later contemporaries and his successors, several dramatists wrote distinguished plays in the tragic style *eg* Middleton's *The Changeling* and Webster's *The Duchess of Malfi* and *The White Devil*.

This period, from 1590 till about 1625, was the only one in English literature in which there were more than isolated examples of distinguished theatrical tragedy. The single important example of a work written in the Greek style is Milton's *Samson Agonistes*, but critics disagree as to whether it can be called truly dramatic. Numerous attempts were made to write tragedy in the Greek style, or in the neoclassical French style of Corneille and Racine, after 1660, but they lacked conviction; perhaps the best is Dryden's *All for Love*. Various attempts were made by 19th-century poets to revive the Shakespearean mode of tragedy. Of these, Shelley's *The Cenci* is the only noteworthy example, but even that was only a minor success.

Some of the plays of ▷ Synge and ▷ Yeats were genuinely remarkable and original tragedies, but their scale is unambitious. However, in the 1960s the work of such dramatists as ▷ Pinter, ▷ Osborne and ▷ Arden has revived dramatic tragedy in a more recognizable form.

Transference

This is the term used in ▷ Freudian psychoanalysis, along with others such as ▷ 'condensation' and ▷ 'displacement', to describe one of the mechanisms whereby unconscious desires enter into ▷ consciousness. It is given a more specific meaning in the relationship between analyst and patient (analysand) in psychoanalysis, as part of the process of removing those impediments to the recollection of repressed impulses on the part of the latter. Situations and emotions are relived during the treatment and these ultimately express the indestructibility of unconscious fantasies. In the structure of a literary work, repetitions of particular situations and events, and even the duplication of 'character', can be explained as kinds of transference of the 'unconscious fantasies' of the writer. In this way desires and feelings which in psychoanalysis occur in the life of the patient, are *transferred* on to the analyst/reader, producing a repetition or re-enactment of them. For example, in Shakespeare's *Hamlet* 'madness' is transferred from the hero on to Ophelia, and an analysis of that process situates the reader/spectator within a complex process of the construction of male/female subjectivity as a result. The issue can be complicated further if the writer 'Shakespeare' is taken to be the 'analysand' projecting unconscious desires and feelings through his 'characters' on to the 'analyst' (reader/spectator).

▷ Psychoanalytic criticism.

Transgression

As a term used in contemporary literary criticism, it is generally associated with the concept of ▷ 'subversion' in so far as it denotes the act of crossing accepted boundaries. Applied to literary texts it is usually taken to refer to any form of behaviour or representation which challenges the dominant values encoded within that text. A classic example of the process might be the introduction of the act of 'cross-dressing' in a number of ▷ Renaissance drama texts, and the resultant challenge which is posed to the issue of a stable sexual identity. Here, the practical constraints of the Elizabethan or Jacobean theatre, involving the impersonation of female roles by male actors, serve to highlight what in the world outside the theatre was becoming a controversial issue as the relative positions

of men and women in 17th-century society underwent re-evaluation.
Bib: Stallybrass, P. and White, A., *The Politics and Poetics of Transgression*; Dollimore, J., *Sexual Dissidence*.

Translation
The life of English literature has always issued from a combination of strong insular traditions and participation in wider European traditions. Translation has always been the principal means of assimilating European literatures into the English idiom, and it was particularly important before the 18th century, when the main streams of European cultural life were flowing through other languages. The aim of translators was then less to make an accurate rendering than to make the substance of foreign work thoroughly intelligible to the English spirit; the character of the translation thus proceeded as much from the mind of the translator as from the mind of the original writer. If the translator had a strong personality, the translation often became a distinguished work of English literature in its own right. Translators with less individuality often produced work of historical importance because of its contemporary influence on English writing.

Printing, the ▷ Renaissance, the rise of new educated classes, all helped to expand translation in the 16th century, which was the first major period for translation of classical writers.

Translations from the contemporary European languages were also numerous in the 16th and 17th centuries, and indicate the constant interest of English writers in foreign literatures.

Many of the translations made before 1660, especially those in prose, were marked by a super-abundance of words, characteristic of much English writing in the 16th and 17th centuries; the originals tended to be amplified rather than closely rendered. After the Restoration in 1660, writers attached importance to discipline and control, and to emulating these virtues as they were exemplified in the old Latin poets and in contemporary French writers of verse and prose.

Translation in the first 30 years of the 19th century, such as Cary's translation in blank verse of Dante's *Divine Comedy* (1805–12), Coleridge's version of Schiller's *Wallenstein* (1800), and Shelley's fragments of Goethe and Calderón (▷ Spanish influence on English literature), show the new kinds of influence on the Romantic writers. After 1830, translation became a kind of net for hauling in exotic writings, and its field became very wide, *eg* Fitzgerald's version of the Persian poem, *The Rubaiyat of Omar Kayyam* (1859), Richard Burton's *Arabian Nights* (1885–88), William Morris's translation of the Icelandic Sagas (beginning in 1869), Swinburne's version of Villon, as well as many new versions of the ancient Greek and Latin authors. Two vices of the period were a tendency to make foreign work express essentially English 19th-century sentiment (*eg* FitzGerald's *Rubaiyat*), and to use peculiarities of style under the mistaken impression that they gave authenticity to the work.

In the 20th century, translation has been cultivated with a new sense of its importance and difficulties. Among the most eminent of modern translations are ▷ Ezra Pound's *Cathay* (from the Chinese) and his version of the Old English *The Seafarer* (1912), and Willa and ▷ Edwin Muir's translations of Kafka (1930–49). In the 20th century translation has become more widespread, making texts in many languages readily available, and this has included critical as well as fictional works. However, while providing us with an international ▷ best-seller list, regularly including writers such as Umberto Eco (▷ Italian influence on English literature) and Gabriel García Márquez (▷ Spanish influence on English literature), there is a danger that a new saleable canon will be created and more marginal texts will remain trapped by linguistic barriers.

Travel literature
This large branch of English literature may be conveniently discussed under these headings: **1** fantasy purporting to be fact; **2** factual accounts; **3** travel experiences regarded as material for art.

1 *Literature of fantasy purporting to be fact*. As long as extensive travel was rarely undertaken, it was possible for writers to present accounts of fantasy journeys and to pass them off as fact without much fear of being accused of lying. Thus a 14th-century French writer wrote the *Travels of Sir John de Mandeville*, which is a work of fiction or compilation from narratives by other travellers, but purporting to be an account of genuine journeys written by Mandeville himself. The work was translated into English in 1377, became extremely popular, and was long regarded as genuine. Long after the extravagances of the story were seen to be falsehoods, Mandeville, a purely fictional English knight, was thought to be the genuine author.

2 *Literature of fact*. By the second half of the 16th century, the great Portuguese, Spanish and Italian explorers had discovered the Americas and greatly extended knowledge of eastern Asia. Liars could still find large, credulous audiences, but the facts were marvellous enough to require no distortion. Writers also began to feel strong motives for publishing truthful accounts. Thus Richard Hakluyt published his *Principal Navigations, Voyages and Discoveries of the English Nation* in 1589, partly for patriotic reasons. The English had been slow to start on exploratory enterprises, although by this time they were extremely active. Hakluyt, finding that the reputation of his nation stood low among foreigners in this field, wanted to demonstrate the reality of the English achievement, and at the same time to stimulate his fellow countrymen to further endeavours. His book is really a compilation of accounts by English explorers; an enlarged edition came out in 1598, and a still further enlarged edition was published under the title of *Hakluytus Posthumus, or Purchas his Pilgrims* by Samuel Purchas in 1625. The accounts vary from those by accomplished writers like Sir Walter Ralegh to others by writers with little or no experience of writing; they constitute an anthology of early English descriptive writing in which the writers are concerned with the truthfulness of their accounts rather than with entertaining or deceiving the reader.

The steady growth of English overseas trade kept alive a taste for accounts of great voyages throughout the 17th and 18th centuries. At the end of the 17th century Captain William Dampier published three books which included the imaginations of Defoe and Swift: *New Voyage Round the World* (1697), *Voyages and Descriptions* (1699), and *Voyage to New Holland* (1703). Dampier was an excellently direct and clear writer of his own books, but Lord George Anson's voyage round the world (1740–44) was written up from his journals by his chaplain, R. Waters, and depends on the singularly dramatic events for its force of interest. The last of these outstanding accounts of great voyages were the three undertaken by Captain James Cook, *A Voyage Round Cape Horn and the Cape of Good Hope* (1773), *A Voyage Towards the South Pole and Round the World* (1777), and *A Voyage to the Pacific Ocean* (1784). With the discovery of the coastlines of Australia and New Zealand, the main outlines of world geography became known, and the interest of both explorers and their readers passed to the mysteries of the great undiscovered interiors of the continents. With this change in subject matter, a change also came over the style of travel literature.

3 *Travel literature as material for art*. Mungo Park's *Travels in Central Africa* preserves the plain, unaffected style of 18th-century travel literature, but subsequent work, for instance that of Richard Burton, bears more of the stamp of the author's personal feelings and reactions. Partly, no doubt, this arose from the new importance attached to authorial personality due to ▷ Romanticism; also the contact with strange physical environments and peoples (in contrast to the emptiness and impersonality of the ocean) inevitably drew out authorial response. At all events, travel literature began to draw nearer to autobiography. Not only 'darkest Africa', but the Arabian peninsula fascinated writers. Burton was one of the first Englishmen to visit the holy city of Mecca, and wrote an account of it in *Pilgrimage to Al-Medinah and Mecca* (1855). Later Charles Doughty tried to restore the vividness of 16th-century language to 19th-century prose in his *Arabia Deserta* (1888), and ▷ T. E. Lawrence's *Seven Pillars of Wisdom* (1926), an account of the Arab struggle against the Turks in World War I, belongs to the same tradition of art made from travel in Arabia. Thus travel literature became a natural subsidiary form for the novelists; it is among the best writing of R. L. Stevenson and ▷ D. H. Lawrence. ▷ Joseph Conrad, who, as a sailor, was a professional traveller during the first part of his adult life, may be said to have completely assimilated the literature of travel into the art of the novel.

Increasing ease of travel since World War II has greatly increased the amount of travel writing. Eric Newby's *A Short Walk in the Hindu Kush* (1959) has become a classic. Other important contemporary travel writers include Bruce Chatwin (1940–89).

Travers, Ben (1886–1980)

British dramatist famous for his 'Aldwych farces', performed at the Aldwych Theatre by casts which included Mary Brough, Robertson Hare, Ralph Lynn, and Tom Walls. The first of these was *A Cuckoo in the Nest* (1925), followed by several others including *Rookery Nook* (1926), *Thark* (1927) and *Plunder* (1928). At the age of 89 he wrote the 'sex comedy' *The Bed Before Yesterday*, which was first performed in 1975, by which time Travers was able to deal explicitly with matters which he had previously only written about implicitly.
Bib: Smith, L., *Modern British Farce: a Selective Study*.

Tree, Sir Herbert Beerbohm (1853–1917)
English actor-manager famous for his productions at the Haymarket and Her Majesty's theatres, and for founding the Royal Academy of Dramatic Art. Productions at the Haymarket included ▷ Oscar Wilde's *A Woman of No Importance* (1893), ▷ Shakespeare's *The Merry Wives of Windsor* (1889) and *Hamlet* (1892). Most successful was an adaptation of a George du Maurier novel, *Trilby* (1895), the proceeds from which enabled him to build Her Majesty's. The repertoire at Her Majesty's was dominated by Shakespeare and historical verse drama. His Shakespeare productions were illustrative of the fashion of the period for spectacular 'romantic realism'. Detailed ostentatious sets, busy stage action and sometimes bizarre stage additions were all characteristic of these productions, disparagingly referred to by designer Gordon Craig as 'beautiful copies of Irving'. Tree combined the qualities of the showman and pioneer. The Shakespeare festivals at Her Majesty's from 1905 to 1913 matched those being given by actor-manager Frank Benson at Stratford. He also championed the cause of ▷ Ibsen, by running matinée performances of *An Enemy of the People*.
Bib: Bingham, M., *The Great Lover*.

Triolet
A graceful verse form of eight lines and two rhymes with a rhyme scheme *abaaabab*. It was invented in France in the 13th century, and was not used in England till the 17th century. Like other verse forms which have little merit beyond their gracefulness, it has seldom been used in English except by minor poets, and those chiefly of the late 19th and early 20th centuries.

Turnbull, Gael (b 1928)
Poet. Born in Edinburgh, Turnbull has long been a passionate champion of contemporary writing, especially visible since he set up the small but influential Migrant Press in the late 1950s. He has also been important in bringing ▷ Basil Bunting's work to prominence in Britain. His works include: *A Trampoline, Poems 1952–1964* (1968); *Scantlings* (1970); *A Gathering of Poems 1950–1980* (1983); and *A Winter Journey* (1987).

***Turn of the Screw, The* (1898)**
A ▷ novella by ▷ Henry James, published in *The Two Magics*. It is a ghost story, about a governess given sole charge of two children, Miles and Flora, in a country house named Bly. She comes to believe that she has to contend with the evil, ghostly influence of two dead servants, Peter Quint and Miss Jessell, over the children, who are ostensibly angelic but invisibly corrupted. Flora is taken away to London by the housekeeper, but Miles, when confronted by the governess with her belief, dies in her arms. The possibility that the governess is an hysteric who hallucinates the ghosts and herself manipulates the children provides a second layer of meaning. This layer is, however, absent in Benjamin Britten's opera of the same title. James's story, which he described as 'a trap for the unwary', is a masterpiece of ambiguity throughout.

Ulysses

A novel by ▷ James Joyce. It was first published in Paris in 1922, but was banned in England for its alleged obscenity until 1936. In a number of ways the book is an innovation in methods of presenting human experience through the novel form, and it is also the most ambitiously comprehensive attempt to do so, except perhaps for Joyce's next book, ▷ *Finnegans Wake* (1939). **1** It is an attempt to present a character more completely than ever before. The story shows in immense detail the life of a man during a single day of 24 hours. The man is Leopold Bloom, a Jew of Hungarian origin living in Dublin; the day is 16 June 1904. **2** To do this requires a method of conveying the process of thinking; Joyce's method has become known as the ▷ stream of consciousness technique, suggested to him by the work of a French novelist, Dujardin, and deployed by his contemporaries ▷ Dorothy Richardson and ▷ Virginia Woolf (▷ Henri Bergson). **3** At the same time as seeking to create imaginatively 'a whole individual', Joyce seeks to make this individual representative, by setting him against the background of the oldest extended portrait of a man in European literature. He does this by making Bloom analogous with Homer's Odysseus, and by dividing the book into episodes, each of which correspond to one in the *Odyssey*, though not in the same order. **4** Joyce varies the technique of written expressions so as to make his language as close an analogy as possible to the modes of modern human experience. Thus in the fierce drunken episode 15 (Circe), the method is dramatic dialogue; in the fatigued anti-climax of 17 (Ithaca), the questionnaire is used; in the final episode 18 (Penelope), the stream of consciousness is used to the full, without punctuation.

No human experience is complete without relationship; Bloom is a lonely man, with numerous casual acquaintanceships. However, two deeper relationships dominate his story: there is the physical relationship with his wife, Molly, whose fidelity he more than mistrusts, and a spiritual affinity with Stephen Dedalus, whom he does not meet till near the end, but who is a lonely young man unconsciously seeking a father, as Bloom is a lonely middle-aged man wanting a son. Molly is analogous to Penelope in the *Odyssey* and Stephen relates to Telemachus, the wife and son respectively of Odysseus.

In some respects Joyce is carrying the artistic devotion of the French novelists to an extreme: *Ulysses* is an elaborate formal construction of immense seriousness, showing a dedication to art for its own sake comparable to that of the novelist Flaubert; it is also a realistic exercise, carrying to extreme the Naturalism of Zola. It is also remarkable for its parodic comedy and ▷ carnivalesque sense of fun and its radical image of a 'world turned upside down', which is developed fully in *Finnegans Wake*. Finally, it is a vivid tribute to Joyce's Dublin, from which he had become self-exiled.

▷ Irish literature in English.

Under Western Eyes (1911)

A novel by ▷ Joseph Conrad. It is set in pre-revolutionary Russia and in Switzerland, and is told through the character of the English language teacher, who witnesses many of the events in Switzerland, and reconstructs those in Russia from the notebooks of the central character, Kyrilo Sidorovitch Razumov. Razumov is the illegitimate son of a Russian nobleman, and has been brought up in the household of a Russian priest. He is given to understand that if he behaves well, his real father will assist him in his career; accordingly he is studious at the university, and keeps himself rigorously isolated from student politics. His enigmatic silence on political subjects, however, is misinterpreted by the radical students as signifying that he is a strongly committed supporter of revolutionary activity; thus, when one of them, Victor Haldin, commits a political assassination and takes refuge with him, Razumov tries to disembarrass himself by betraying Haldin to the police. The police, however, will not allow him to return to his solitary studies; instead they send him to Switzerland, ostensibly as a revolutionary emissary, but actually to spy on the Russian revolutionaries in exile there. He finds them to be a circle composed partly of flamboyant or brutal self-seekers, such as Peter Ivanovitch, Madame de S., and Nikitin (nicknamed Necator, the killer). But there are also idealists of complete integrity, including Victor Haldin's sister, Nathalie Haldin. Nathalie is a pupil and friend of the English language teacher, who thus becomes involved in the story. She welcomes Razumov as a revolutionary hero, and the friend of her brother, for whose death he has in fact been responsible. Razumov is tormented by his guilt, his love and admiration for Nathalie, his horror and contempt of the debased elements among the revolutionaries, and the seeming impossibility of recovering his integrity and living otherwise than by false appearance. Eventually he confesses the truth to Nathalie and to the revolutionaries, and is reduced to total deafness by two blows from Nikitin Nathalie is appalled, but understands him. She has told her English friend: 'You belong to a people which has made a bargain with fate, and wouldn't like to be rude to it.' The Western (British and Swiss) attitude to politics and the individual is such that fateful choices such as the one forced on Razumov are not demanded. His drama 'under the Western eyes' of the English language teacher is the drama of a nation where the individual is not permitted to withdraw from political decision into private life. Razumov spends the rest of his days as a sick man in Russia, respected by the best of the revolutionary circle whom he has known in Switzerland, and cared for devotedly by one of them.

Unity Theatre
A left-wing amateur theatre group founded in London in 1936, with the aim of dramatizing current affairs such as the Spanish Civil War, the popular front against war and Fascism, and the problems of unemployment. The use of theatrical documentary and group composition was innovatory at the time. The company was influenced by European developments in the theatre, but more so by the Living Newspaper method developed in America, 'a method which makes a continual claim to observed truth, to verified fact, whilst at the same time ordering and shaping these facts dramatically so they are charged with emotion'. Notable productions were: Clifford Odets's *Waiting for Lefty* (1936); ▷ Brecht's *Senora Carrar's Rifles* (1938); *Busmen* (1938), a collectively written piece; and ▷ Sean O'Casey's *The Star Turns Red* (1940). A left-wing amateur company of the same name was formed in Glasgow in 1941.
Bib: Chambers, C., *The Story of Unity Theatre*.

Unreliable narrator
A ▷ narrator who cannot be relied upon to provide accurate information, so that the reader is obliged to try to deduce, from the possibly misleading account given by such a narrator, the true facts of the case. A narrator may be unreliable because of limited knowledge or understanding (*eg* the idiot Benjy in the first section of William Faulkner's *The Sound and the Fury*), because of being in a disturbed state of mind (*eg* the governess in one possible reading of ▷ *The Turn of the Screw* by ▷ Henry James), because of personal bias or dubious moral values (*eg* Dowell in ▷ Ford Madox Ford's *The Good Soldier*), or out of sheer wilfulness (*eg* the narrator of ▷ Peter Carey's *Illywhacker*). Unreliable narration tends to emphasize the subjective nature of truth and the technique often tends towards the implication that there is no such thing as an objective viewpoint.

Upward, Edward (b 1903)
Novelist. He was educated at Repton School and Cambridge University with ▷ Christopher Isherwood, with whom he invented a fantasy world, Mortmere, a setting for bizarre and anarchic stories which survive only in Upward's *The Railway Accident* (1969). *Journey to the Border* (1938) reflects Upward's commitment to ▷ Marxism; it ends with the neurotic protagonist rejecting his fantasies in favour of the 'real world' of the Worker's Movement. *In the Thirties* (1962), which ▷ Stephen Spender described as 'the most truthful picture of life in that decade', is the first part of a trilogy, *The Spiral Ascent*, which examines the conflict between private fulfilment and political activism. The trilogy concludes with *The Rotten Elements* (1969) and *No Home But the Struggle* (1977). Story collection: *The Night Walk* (1987).

Utopian literature
More's *Utopia* introduced into the English language the word 'utopian' = 'imaginary and ideal', and started a succession of 'utopias' in English literature. The idea of inventing an imaginary country to be used as a 'model' by which to judge earthly societies did not, however, originate with More, but with his master the Greek philosopher Plato, who did the same in his dialogues *Timaeus* and the *Republic*. *Utopia*'s most notable successors in the 17th century were Bacon's unfinished *New Atlantis* (1626), in which science is offered as the solution for humanity, and James Harington's *Oceana* (1656), which put forward political ideas that were to have a powerful influence in America. In the 20th century, ▷ H. G. Wells was, in his earlier days, a vigorous Utopian: *Anticipations* (1901), *A Modern Utopia* (1905), and *New Worlds for Old* (1908). Just before Wells, William Morris's *News from Nowhere* (1890) is a noteworthy socialistic utopia.

However, from the 18th century, much utopian literature is satirical, intended to give warning of vicious tendencies of society rather than to exemplify ideals. An example of this is Bernard de Mandeville's (1670–1733) *Fable of the Bees* (1714), about the downfall of an ideal society through the viciousness of its inhabitants; and Swift's *Gulliver's Travels* (1726) can be put in the same class. In the

19th century the best-known examples are Samuel Butler's ▷ *Erewhon* (1872) and *Erewhon Revisited* (1901). In the 20th century, fears for the future of mankind have predominated over the optimism about inevitable progress which was more typical of the 19th century, and this has led to a new kind of utopian writing, portraying our own society set in the future, showing our fears realized. For this kind of work, the term 'dystopia' has been invented. The first striking example was ▷ Aldous Huxley's *Brave New World* (1932), about the deadness of a civilization which has come to be dominated by scientific technology; ▷ E. M. Forster's tale *The Machine Stops* has a similar theme, and both are written in reaction against H. G. Wells's optimism about technology. ▷ George Orwell's *1984* is a nightmare about 20th-century political totalitarianism, the grimmer because Orwell brought the date of his anticipated society so close to the time of writing. A number of 20th-century women writers have explored utopian and dystopian worlds as a means of satirizing or criticizing sexual relations in the modern world, or as a way of exploring new possibilities for gender relations and identities. ▷ Doris Lessing's science fiction explores utopianism, whilst Marge Piercy's *Woman on the Edge of Time* juxtaposes an ideal future with the grim present. American feminist writer Charlotte Perkins Gilman's *Herland* (1916) is perhaps the most famous feminist utopia, whilst ▷ Margaret Atwood's *The Handmaid's Tale* explores a Christian fundamentalist dystopia.

▷ Science fiction.

Verfremdungseffekt
▷ Alienation effect.

Vers Libre
▷ Free Verse.

Victorian period
The period coinciding with the reign of Queen Victoria (1837–1901) is commonly divided into three:

1 *1837–1851: the Early Victorian period.* This was a time of struggle and growth; the age of the Chartist Movement and the Anti-Corn Law League, but also of the building of railways. The 'hungry forties' ended with the Great Exhibition in 1851, the culmination of the Industrial Revolution, which Britain achieved earlier than any other nation.

2 *1851–1870: the Mid-Victorian period.* Britain had passed the time of the worst popular discontents, and was at her height in wealth, power, and influence.

3 *1870–1901: the Late Victorian Period.* A less fortunate period, when other nations (especially Germany and the U.S.A.) were competing with Britain industrially. Britain had acquired much territory in consequence of her pursuit of trade; she now became imperialist in her jealousy and mistrust of other imperialist nations, and the period ended with the imperialist South African War (Boer War) of 1899–1901. Economically, Britain was becoming less the 'workshop of the world' than the world's banker. Domestically, partly in consequence of the second Parliamentary Reform Bill (enfranchising the town workers – 1867) and the Education Act (establishing a state system of education – 1870) it was a time of popular political and social movements which included the building up of trade unions and the formation of the ▷ Labour Party.

Culturally, the Victorian period was the age when change rather than stability came first to be accepted as normal in the nature of human outlook. Ancient foundations of religious belief were eroded, among intellectuals, by scientific advances, especially the biological discoveries of Darwin (▷ Agnosticism). The educated classes and their leaders sought to establish guiding values for living; it was the period of the 'Victorian Sage' – Carlyle, Mill, Arnold, Ruskin, and Tennyson – educating the social conscience. The relationship of the individual to himself, to other individuals, and to society at large is the study to which the novel is admirably adapted; the English novel developed in the works of Gaskell, Thackeray, Trollope, the Brontës, Dickens, George Eliot and ▷ Henry James into the art form of the age. Henry James is, however, an important transitional writer, whose works are frequently studied as examples of early ▷ modernism. Culturally and in many ways socially, the Victorian period saw the outset and display of the problems with which the 20th century has had to contend.

Voice
One of the five categories in which ▷ Genette analyses narrative discourse, voice is concerned with the way in which the act of narrating is 'implicated in the narrative'; the study of voice in a novel therefore attends to the identity and nature of the ▷ narrator and the real or implied audience or narratees.

Vorticism
Art movement which to some extent characterizes visual ▷ modernism in Britain, as one of the few discrete and self-conscious avant-garde movements in the British art world. To some extent Vorticism resembles the more famous European movements of futurism, cubism and expressionism, both in its celebration of German aesthetics and the principles of energy, speed, visual violence and dynamism, and in its close relationship with the literary world, particularly with the primarily poetic movement ▷ Imagism. Vorticism was furiously anti-Romantic and anti-representational, with the Vorticist 'mental emotional impulse' (in ▷ Percy Wyndham Lewis's famous words) 'let loose on a lot of blocks and lines', paralleling ▷ Ezra Pound's uncompromising series of poetic rules which would 'break the pentameter' and produce a genuinely new form of writing to unlock the dynamic energy at the heart of images and visual objects. Together, these creative ideas formed (again in Lewis's words) 'the Great English Vortex'. The Vorticists opposed the aesthetics of the ▷ Bloomsbury Group, their less dynamic contemporaries whose arts-and-crafts movement-inspired works strove for visual harmony and integrity; the Rebel Arts Centre was the Vorticist's answer to Bloomsbury's Omega Workshops. The Vorticist magazine-manifesto, *Blast*, which ran to two famous issues in 1914 and 1915, has recently been republished. Key figures in the movement also include painters and sculptors William Roberts, David Bomberg, Edward Wadsworth, Jacob Epstein, and Henri Gaudier-Brzeska.

W

Wain, John (b 1925)
Novelist, poet and critic. Prose fiction: *Hurry on Down* (1953); *Living in the Present* (1955); *The Contenders* (1958); *A Travelling Woman* (1959); *Nuncle and Other Stories* (1962); *The Young Visitors* (1965); *Death of the Hind Legs and Other Stories* (1966); *The Smaller Sky* (1967); *A Winter in the Hills* (1970); *The Life Guard* (1971); *The Pardoner's Tale* (1978), *Young Shoulders* (1982). Criticism: *Preliminary Essays* (1957); *Essays on Literature and Ideas* (1963); *The Living World of Shakespeare* (1964). His first novel showed him to be a leading member of the school of novelists who concern themselves with the changed surface and social texture of the post-war world. His novels are distinguished by unusual narrative force and economy, and his criticism by the clarity and forthrightness of his judgements. As a poet, Wain's work has been associated with that of the ▷ Movement and with later 'movements' of the 1960s, publishing *A Word Carved on a Sill* (1956); *Weep Before God* (1961); *Wildtrack* (1965); and *Feng* (1975).

***Waiting for Godot* (1953)**
A play by ▷ Samuel Beckett which could be categorized as a modern tragicomedy. The plot is utterly absurd, which is the point of the play, since it is implying that life itself is absurd (▷ Theatre of the Absurd). Two tramps, Estragon and Vladimir, wait for the mysterious Godot who never arrives. Their only visitors are Lucky and Pozzo, who are locked in a sadomasochistic bonding of master and servant from which there seems to be no escape. Despite its bleak view of life the play has great wit, drawing on the traditions of music hall and popular clowning. It was first performed in Britain in 1955 and is an undisputed landmark in British drama.

Warner, Rex (1905–86)
Novelist, poet and translator. He was educated at Oxford University, where he met ▷ W. H. Auden and ▷ Cecil Day-Lewis. His allegorical first novel, *The Wild Goose Chase* (1937), examines the political issues of the 1930s through a fantastic imaginary world and concludes with a ▷ communist ▷ Utopia. *The Professor* (1938) and *The Aerodrome* (1941) are similarly concerned with political power, and the conflict of love and personal integrity with totalitarianism. Warner's work is frequently compared with that of Kafka, but also shows the influence of classical literature, of which he made many translations. He also wrote several historical novels, including *The Young Caesar* (1958) and *Imperial Caesar* (1958), which are written in the form of supposed autobiography.

Warner, Sylvia Townsend (1893–1978)
Novelist, poet, short-story writer, musicologist and biographer. Born in Harrow, Middlesex, she worked in a munitions factory during World War I and in 1922 became one of the editors of the Oxford University Press *Tudor Church Music*. She lived in Dorset with the poet Valentine Ackland from 1932 until the latter's death in 1969; together they served as Red Cross Volunteers in Spain in 1930. Her novels are: *Lolly Willowes; or, The Loving Huntsman* (1926); *Mr Fortune's Maggot* (1927); *The True Heart* (1929); *Summer Will Show* (1936); *After the Death of Don Juan* (1938); *The Corner That Held Them* (1948); *The Flint Anchor* (1954). Her work is notable for its imaginative scope, including elements of the supernatural, mystical and historical and embracing fantasy, comedy and satire; the novels' settings include a South Sea Island, a medieval nunnery, the Paris of the 1848 revolution and the Essex marshes. She also published ten volumes of short stories, books on Somerset (1949) and on Jane Austen (1951), a biography of T. H. White (1967) and volumes of poetry, including: *The Espalier* (1925); *Time Importuned* (1928); *Opus 7* (1931, a long narrative poem); *Rainbow* (1932); *Whether a Dove or a Seagull* (1933, with Valentine Ackland); *Boxwood* (1957); *Two Poems* (1945); *King Duffus* (1968); *Azrael* (1978); *Twelve Poems* (1980). Her *Collected Poems* were published in 1982, edited by Claire Harman, and her *Letters* in 1982, edited by William Maxwell.
Bib: Harman, C., *Sylvia Townsend Warner: a biography*; Mulford, C., *The Narrow Place: Sylvia Townsend Warner and Valentine Ackland: Life, Letters and Politics 1930–1951*.

War poets
A group of poets who served in the army in World War I, and made poetry out of the experience. The three who are most commonly though of as 'war poets' are ▷ Wilfred Owen, ▷ Siegfried Sassoon and ▷ Isaac Rosenberg. ▷ Rupert Brooke, who wrote with feeling about the outbreak of war, died before he saw much action; his poetry does not in consequence reflect the shock and violence so evident in the other three. ▷ Edward Thomas was killed in action, but little of his poetry is about the war. ▷ Edmund Blunden and ▷ Robert Graves both survived to write memorable prose works about the

war, but their poetry was only indirectly affected by it.

The effect of the war on the verse of Owen, Sassoon and Rosenberg was to cause them to turn away from the rather tepid ▷ romanticism of much pre-war poetry, and to adapt their language to the new and terrible experiences. They thus played a significant part in the renewal of poetic language.

Waste Land, The (1922)
A poem by ▷ T. S. Eliot. It is 433 lines long, and is divided into five parts: I. *The Burial of the Dead*; II. *A Game of Chess*; III. *The Fire Sermon*; IV. *Death by Water*; V. *What the Thunder Said.* There is no logical continuity between the parts, or within each part except for the very short Part IV. The lines vary in length and rhythm and are usually unrhymed, but the poem is not written in ▷ 'free verse'. The author contributed his own (often cryptic) explanatory notes.

The theme is the decay and fragmentation of Western culture, conceived in terms of the loss of natural fertility. Despite the absence of logical continuity, *The Waste Land* possesses artistic coherence brought about by four closely related methods.

1 The use of symbols derived from two anthropologists: Jessie L. Weston (*From Ritual to Romance*) and ▷ James Frazer (*The Golden Bough*). These books relate to ancient myths about the alternation of fertility and barrenness. Although study of them undoubtedly helps the reader to understand the poem, it is not entirely necessary; Eliot intended the symbols to be imaginatively convincing, by their own force, to a sufficiently responsive reader.

2 The juxtaposition of passages with contrasting rhythms, diction, and imagery to accomplish 'a music of ideas . . . arranged not that they must tell us something, but that their effects in us may combine into a coherent whole of feeling and attitude'. (See ▷ I. A. Richards. Compare Eliot in *Shakespeare and the Stoicism of Seneca*: 'The poet who "thinks" is merely the poet who can express the emotional equivalent of thought.')

3 The use of past history in contrast to the present time, as a means of demonstrating the peculiarities of the present. This method is paralleled by ▷ James Joyce in ▷ *Ulysses* and ▷ Ezra Pound in his ▷ *Cantos*.

4 The use of literary quotation and parody in order to bring out the contrasts of past and present states of culture. At least 35 writers are quoted or parodied in *The Waste Land*.

The poem caused great controversy when it was published, and is often considered to mark the effective beginning of a distinctively 20th-century style of verse, although Eliot had already published verse in the new idiom with *The Love Song of J. Alfred Prufrock* (1915) and *Gerontion* (1920). *The Waste Land* is dedicated to Ezra Pound, whose extensive revisions of the poem can be seen in the facsimile of the original drafts edited by Valerie Eliot and published in 1971.

Bib: Williams, H., *T. S. Eliot: 'The Waste Land'*.

Waugh, Evelyn (1903–66)
Novelist. Born in London and educated at Hertford College, Oxford, he worked for a while as an assistant schoolmaster, an experience which provided the basis for his first novel, *Decline and Fall* (1928). His satires of the late 1920s and 1930s up to and including *Put Out More Flags* (1942), present the modern world as anarchic and chaotic, and are a blend of farce and tragedy. His technique included the extensive use of dialogue, and rapid changes of scene. Many of the early novels recount the picaresque and outrageous experiences of a naive central character, such as Paul Pennyfeather in *Decline and Fall*, and William Boot in *Scoop* (1938), a hilarious story of Western journalists in Africa. Waugh became a Catholic in 1930; this was initially reflected in his work only in a sense of the transience and emptiness of worldly concerns. But World War II, during which Waugh served with the Royal Marines in Crete and Yugoslavia, changed the character of his work; it became more explicitly Catholic, serious to the point of sombreness, and more three-dimensional in his portrayal of his characters. The first novel to show these qualities was *Brideshead Revisited* (1945). In 1961 he completed his most considerable work, a trilogy about the war entitled *Sword of Honour*. Among others of his novels that have achieved fame are *The Loved One* (1948), a satire on American commercialism, extending to the commercialization of death, and *The Ordeal of Gilbert Pinfold* (1957), a pseudo-autobiographical caricature of a 50-year-old Catholic novelist. His post-war work expresses a distaste for, and rejection of, modern civilization, and a pervasive sense of the vanity of human desires. All Waugh's work is marked by an exquisite sense of the ludicrous and a fine aptitude for exposing false attitudes. His comedy is closely dependent on the carefully calculated urbanity of his style. Other novels are: *Vile Bodies* (1930); *Black*

Mischief (1932); *A Handful of Dust* (1934); *Scott-King's Modern Europe* (1947); *Tactical Exercise* (1954); *Basil Seal Rides Again* (1963). Story collections are: *Mr Loveday's Little Outing* (1936); *Work Suspended* (1949).

Waugh also wrote travel books, selections from which have been collected under the title *When the Going Was Good* (1946), and biographies of the 19th-century poet and painter D. G. Rossetti (1928), and of the 16th-century Catholic martyr, Edmund Campion (1935).

▷ Catholicism in English literature.

Bib: Bradbury, M., *Evelyn Waugh* (Writers and Critics Series); Stannard, M., *Evelyn Waugh: the Critical Heritage*; Sykes, C., *Evelyn Waugh: a Biography*.

Waves, The *(1931)*

A novel by ▷ Virginia Woolf. It is the story of six characters, each of whom tells his or her own story in monologue, and reflects images of the others in his or her own mind. The monologues occur in groups, at different stages of their lives, and each group is preceded by a passage describing a time of day, from dawn to nightfall. It is a poetic, lyrical and highly patterned work, and presents human existence as an organic process, uniting individuals like waves in the sea. *The Waves* is the climax of Virginia Woolf's experiments in fictional form.

Way of All Flesh, The **(1903)**

A novel by ▷ Samuel Butler, written 1873–5 and published after his death, in 1903. It is one of the few purely satirical works of distinction of the ▷ Victorian period; the ▷ satire is directed against the Victorian cult of the family as the sacred and blessed nucleus of society, and the refuge from the harshness of the world. The arrogant, self-righteous, intolerant and stupid kind of Victorian parent is exemplified in the clergyman Theobald Pontifex, father of Ernest Pontifex. Victorian authoritarianism and repressiveness are also attacked in Theobald, seen as a religious humbug, and in Dr Skinner, headmaster of the public school that Ernest attends. The first 50 chapters of the book are autobiographical; Butler even includes actual letters in the text. The narrative is not told through Ernest (Butler as a boy) but in the first person through his friend the middle-aged Overton, who represents a more tolerant aspect of Butler; by this means, Butler conveys criticism of his intolerant younger self, in the person of Ernest. The book was much praised, especially by ▷ G. B. Shaw.

▷ Autobiography.

Webb, Beatrice (1858–1943)

Sociologist. She was the daughter of Richard Potter, a railway director and friend of the philosopher Herbert Spencer, who exercised a guiding influence over her education. Her mother was a product of the 19th-century Utilitarian school of thought. She early developed a strong social conscience, which led her to choose as her career the almost unprecedented one of 'social investigator'. Victorian sensitiveness to social abuses was strong amongst the intelligentsia, but she realized that constructive action was hampered by lack of exact information: 'The primary task is to observe and dissect facts.' In order to do so, she took bold steps for a Victorian girl of the prosperous middle class, such as disguising herself as a working girl and taking employment under a tailor in the East End of London. She and her husband were among the early members of the ▷ Fabian Society, and among the founders of the ▷ Labour Party. Her autobiographies *My Apprenticeship* (1926) and *Our Partnership* (1948) are in the tradition of John Stuart Mill's *Autobiography* (1873) in being essentially histories of the growth of opinions and ideas; *My Apprenticeship*, however, is very enlightening about social backgrounds in the 1880s, and a valuable addition to the Victorian novels, which, she said, were the only documents for the study of society available in her youth. She and her husband were among the founders of the weekly journal ▷ *New Statesman*, a leading left-wing journal.

Weldon, Fay (b 1931)

Novelist, dramatist and television screenwriter. Her novels include: *The Fat Woman's Joke* (1967); *Down Among the Women* (1971); *Female Friends* (1975); *Remember Me* (1976); *Words of Advice* (1977); *Praxis* (1978); *Little Sisters* (1978); *Puffball* (1980); *The President's Child* (1982); *The Life and Loves of a She-Devil* (1983); *The Shrapnel Academy* (1986); *The Rules of Life* (1987); *The Heart of the Country* (1987); *Leader of the Band* (1988). Story collections are: *Watching Me, Watching You* (1981); *Polaris* (1985). The ▷ feminism of her work is concentrated in the portrayal of the exploitation of women by men in domestic situations, and in relationships. Her tragicomic novels are powerful stories of pain, loss and betrayal, and their desperation is accentuated by the sense of a controlling social and biological pattern which negates the characters' attempts to make choices about their lives. The endings of her books, however, often hint at the emergence of a new and more liberated woman.

Welfare State

A term currently in use to describe the national system of social security brought into being by the ▷ Labour government of 1945–50 based on W. A. Beveridge's *Report on Social Insurance and Allied Services* (1942). The system depends on National Insurance payments which are obligatory for all adult members of the community apart from old-age pensioners and family dependants. It is also funded from general taxation. In return for these payments made weekly, the state grants financial assistance in the form of family allowances, payments during sickness and unemployment and to maintain those who have been permanently incapacitated by injury, and pensions for the old. Medical attention is partly free and partly assisted. State education, from the nursery school level for children under five to university level, is also frequently assumed in the concept of the Welfare State.

The Welfare State is thus the opposite of the *laissez faire* concept of the state which prevailed in the 19th century. According to the latter, the state was expected to allow society to develop freely according to 'natural' economic forces. Its function was merely to prevent interference with these in the shape of crime or insurrection. The *laissez faire* concept was never quite supreme; the state always assumed some responsibility for the very poor, for instance in the provision of workhouses. Nevertheless, *laissez faire* ideas prevailed to the extent that the state was assumed to have no basic responsibility for the individual material welfare of its citizens. The opposite 'Welfare' concept of the state's duties arose partly from the 19th-century religious thinking about society, and partly from the growth of socialist philosophies. The modern Welfare State is generally considered to have had its beginnings under the ▷ Liberal government of Campbell Bannerman and Asquith (1905–14); this introduced old-age pensions, some unemployment and health insurance, and other measures. In the 1980s *laissez faire* concepts of the state have been reasserted and responsibility for individual welfare repudiated as the market economy is encouraged.

Wells, H. G. (Herbert George) (1866–1946)

Novelist and journalist. He was brought up in the lower middle class, the son of a professional cricketer; in 1888 he took an excellent degree in science at London University. His social origins and his education explain much of his approach to life as a writer. The great novelist of the 19th-century lower middle classes is Dickens, and some of H. G. Wells's best fiction is about the same field of society; novels such as ▷ *Kipps* (1905) and *The History of Mr Polly* (1910) are of this sort, and they have the kind of vigorous humour and sharp visualization that is characteristic of early Dickens. On the other hand, rising into the educated class at a time of rapid scientific and technical progress, he ignored the values of traditional culture and art, and became fascinated with the prospects that science offered, for good as well as for ill. This side of him produced a different kind of writing: Wells was one of the inventors of ▷ science fiction. *The Time Machine* (1895), *The Invisible Man* (1897), *The War of the Worlds* (1898) and *The First Men in the Moon* (1901) are examples of his fantasies. But his social experience and his interest in technology also drew him to writing fictional-sociological studies in which he surveyed and analysed, often with the same Dickensian humour, the society of his time; *Tono-Bungay* (1908) is perhaps the best of these. Other examples are *Ann Veronica* (1909) about the problems connected with newly emancipated women, *The New Machiavelli* (1911) about socialist thinking – Wells had joined the ▷ Fabians in 1903 – and *Mr Britling Sees It Through* (1916) about World War I seen from the point of view of the 'Home Front'. But the interest in science also made him a ▷ utopian optimist, and this point of view caused him to write such didactic works as *A Modern Utopia* (1905) and *New Worlds For Old* (1908). There was always a great deal of naivety in Wells's optimism, and later in his life he paid the penalty by reacting into excessive gloom, in *Mind at the End of its Tether* (1945). He declared that *The Open Conspiracy* (1928) contained the essence of his philosophy. He was never a deep thinker, however; his work lives by the vitality of his humour and by the urgency with which he pressed his ideas. This urgency necessarily made him a popularizer, and his most notable work of popularization was *The Outline of History* (1920).

In some ways Wells resembles his contemporary, the dramatist ▷ George Bernard Shaw; both were socialists, both felt the urgency to enlighten mankind as quickly as possible, and both cared more that their works should have immediate effect than that they should be works of art – Wells told the novelist ▷ Henry James that he would rather be called a journalist than an artist. Possibly the most penetrating remark on Wells was that addressed to him by the novelist ▷ Joseph Conrad: 'You don't really care for people, but you think they can be improved; I do, but I know they can't.'

Bib: Mackenzie, N. and J., *The Time Traveller: Life of H. G. Wells*; Bergonzi, B., *The Early H. G. Wells* and *H. G. Wells: Twentieth-Century Views*; Parrinder, P. (ed.), *H. G. Wells: the Critical Heritage.*

Welsh literature in English

To define 'Anglo-Welsh' literature as that produced in English by Welsh writers is too simplistic. Writers' claims on Welsh ancestry vary enormously. Some even adopt Welshness as, for example, Raymond Garlick (b 1926), an Englishman who identified with Welsh political causes and became founder-editor of the literary magazine *Dock Leaves* (later *The Anglo-Welsh Review* 1957–88) and a critic and poet firmly within the Welsh context. Thus poet and novelist Glyn Jones's criterion of Anglo-Welshness – expressed in his critical work *The Dragon Has Two Tongues* as involvement in the Welsh situation – seems justifiable. So is George Herbert, brought up in the Marches and an influence on Henry Vaughan, acceptable? Does ▷ Gerard Manley Hopkins's three-year residence at St Bueno's seminary, during which he learnt Welsh, admit him? His assimilation of *cynghanedd* into English poetry transmitted Welsh metric to ▷ Dylan Thomas who could not speak Welsh. (*Cynghanedd* is a Welsh term indicating the technique of using internal rhymes with alliteration in a fixed metrical pattern.) For poet and critic Anthony Conran, W. H. Davies qualifies as Anglo-Welsh because his *New Poems* conforms to the thematic divisions of the *bardd gwlad*. Nevertheless, Conran concedes only two Anglo-Welsh poems to Edward Thomas, who is included on parentage, emotional attachment to Wales, and his belated influence on Anglo-Welsh poets. Richard Hughes and ▷ John Cowper Powys have received the accolade of critical studies in the *Writers of Wales* series through their eventually permanent residence in, and lifelong empathy for Wales. From Powys's Wessex came Jeremy Hooker (b 1941), whose 19 years in Wales made him a leading critic in the Anglo-Welsh field and temporarily changed his poetic direction. Thus a widely debatable area of Anglo-Welsh acceptability exists.

Historically, poetry is the dominant genre of Anglo-Welsh literature, prose a mainly 20th-century growth. The poetic origins can be traced to the 15th century, but excepting George Herbert, Henry Vaughan and John Dyer, all the major work belongs to the present century. What is significant, to cite Anthony Conran, is the 'seepage' from Welsh-language culture into English. For example, the traditional function of the Welsh-language poet was to commemorate the society he lived in whether, as earlier, in 'praise poems' for princes or, later, the local community. In the last-named instance, the *bardd gwlad*'s categories of poems included nature, love, beer, hunting songs, poems to individuals and moral poems. Some were in complex traditional metres, others in less exacting free metres, so form is an overriding concern. In serving his community, the Welsh poet is perceived as a craftsman, cultivating an objectivity that contrasts with English poetry from the Romantic revival onwards and particularly that of contemporary confessional egocentricity. The formal preoccupations of Welsh-language poetry assimilated by Anglo-Welsh practitioners over four centuries revealed affinities by the early 20th century with the English ▷ Georgians' objective descriptions of nature, in birds, flowers, landscapes, and of people and their working lives in an essentially rural setting. The legacy of this is Anglo-Welsh poetry's perseverance with tighter forms and greater objectivity than English contemporary poetry. Welsh-speaking Anglo-Welsh poets such as Glyn Jones (b 1905), Harri Webb (b 1920) and Anthony Conran (b 1931) have translated Welsh-language poems into English, often following the Welsh metric of the originals, such as *traethodl*, *cywydd*, or *englyn*, sometimes including the internal rhymes and alliterations of *cynghanedd*, and the accretion of comparisons known as *dyfalu*. As Welsh metric poses almost insurmountable technical problems when grafted on to the English language, any assimilation through the centuries has been gradual, and it is more the common thematic inheritance that unites Welsh and Anglo-Welsh poetry and differentiates the latter from English poetry. However, the growth of Anglo-Welsh literature is a concomitant of the historical process that weakened the influence of the Welsh language.

Anglo-Norman settlements of the Marches and South Wales were followed by Henry I's 12th-century Flemish settlement of South

Pembroke, subsequently augmented by English settlements in Gower and around Laugharne. Edwardian castles protected English merchants who were granted privileges within town walls, as at Caernafon and Conwy. Itinerant drovers and weavers soon forged linguistic links with England. The establishment of the Tudor dynasty brought Welsh influence into England, though Henry VIII's Acts of Union insisted on Welsh office-holders' proficiency in English, eventually producing an Anglicized squirearchy. Three centuries later, Victorian government policy further weakened the hold of the Welsh language by encouraging 'The Welsh Not', prohibiting Welsh-language conversation in schools. A piece of wood or slate with the letters 'WN' cut into it was hung round the neck of the last pupil caught speaking Welsh in class – whoever was left wearing it at the end of the school day would be punished. From the early 19th century, the increasing influx into the South Wales valleys not only drained the rural areas of the west and north but brought in labouring or technological expertise for pit-sinking, blast furnace, canal, tramroad, railway and docks construction. The ultimate figure of English-speaking immigrants in the South Wales valleys accounted for at least 40 per cent of the population, swamping the native Welsh speakers. The subsequent foundation of county schools from 1895 onwards provided secondary education in the medium of English. This explains why Glyn Jones, an early pupil at Merthyr's Cyfarthfa Castle Grammar School, though from a Welsh-speaking family, developed into an Anglo-Welsh writer. It was these socio-economic pressures that helped to create the 'first flowering' of Anglo-Welsh literature.

Many young provincial writers departed for London between the wars to find publishers who encouraged them to adapt their work for the metropolitan market. Caradoc Evans (1878–1945), according to the novelist and critic Professor Gwyn Jones the 'first distinctive ancestral voice' of Anglo-Welsh writing, produced the first London-published best-seller. In *My People* (1915) and subsequent short-story collections, Caradoc Evans invented grotesqueries of character and speech for his Cardi peasantry whose lust, greed and hypocrisy established a false Welsh stereotype that amused Londoners but gave unmitigated and lasting offence to the Welsh-speaking literary establishment. Notwithstanding, Caradoc Evan's commercial success encouraged a vein of fantasy among the 'first flowering' of Anglo-Welsh writers, Rhys Davies, Glyn Jones, and ▷ Dylan Thomas, which was continued in the post-war period by Gwyn Thomas. Moreover, the eccentric and grotesque provided a diversion from painfully harsh living conditions in decaying rural and unemployment-ravaged industrial communities. Beneath this surface, however, industrial realism encapsulates a political message – socialist in the 'first flowering', nationalist in the 'second flowering' in the 1960s. This idealism motivates an inevitably doomed nationalist military uprising in Glyn Jones's ▷ novella, *I Was Born in the Ystrad Valley*, as early as 1937. Communist political activism inspires Lewis Jones's *Cwmardy* (1937) and *We Live!* (1939), Jack Jones paints panoramic historical canvases behind his family epics in *Black Parade* (1935) and *Rhondda Roundabout* (1934), whereas Gwyn Jones employs a briefer time-scale in *Times Like These* (1936) where he examines the social and familial crises precipitated by the General Strike. However, it was Richard Llewellyn's *How Green Was My Valley* (1939) which became the popular stereotype of the Valley's industrial novel despite its inaccuracies and sentimentality, a far cry from Gwyn Thomas's rejected pre-war novel *Sorrow For Thy Sons* (eventually published in 1986, five years after his death). Gwyn Thomas's post-war hyperbolic wit, farcical situations and eccentric characters create a Valleys' world where laughter is the only antidote to poverty and unemployment. Meanwhile, short stories between the wars mediate between a poetic vision of Welsh-speaking Wales, Lawrentian-influenced in Rhys Davies and Geraint Goodwin, and the realistic depiction of industrial communities, infused with wit and humour. Only one poet identifies with the industrial milieu: Idris Davies, despite a ▷ Georgian vocabulary and the formal strait-jacket of the ▷ Housman quatrain, brings his strike-bound communities to life when he uses vernacular speech and escapes into free verse.

The two most original poets to appear in the 1930s were very different from Idris Davies in theme and technique. David Jones achieved the critical recognition due to him as a major poet only during the 1980s, shortly after his death. *In Parenthesis*, for example, encapsulated his experiences in World War I but appeared only two years before World War II. His juxtaposition of prose passages with poetry, all loaded with mythopoeic reference, represented an exciting new poetic dimension, though it received scant notice at the time. Very different was the critical reception for Dylan Thomas, who alienated himself from the Welsh concept of community-serving poet and escaped from Swansea to literary London as early as possible to promote his self-advertising poetic image. Nevertheless, his indisputable success and originality gave fresh impetus to Anglo-Welsh writing which found a mouthpiece in Keidrych Rhys's literary magazine *Wales*, published in three intermittent series between 1937 and 1960, and in Gwyn Jones's more academically respectable *Welsh Review*, published first in 1939 and then between 1944 and 1948. Unlike other Anglo-Welsh poets, Dylan Thomas flowered early because his poetry was self-created. Influenced by his work, some young poets published prematurely shortly after the war, including Leslie Norris and John Ormond, who then waited for 20 years for their individual, mature and successful voices to be heard. Inevitably, the war limited publishing so that the tragically brief war-time appearance of Alun Lewis's work was all the more remarkable.

In post-war years, attempts to revive *Wales* and the *Welsh Review* were short-lived through lack of funds, though *Dock Leaves* (founded 1949) survived in Tenby, thanks to Raymond Garlick and Roland Mathias. Despite the growing reputation of Vernon Watkins (1906–67) as a poetic visionary, Dylan Thomas's untimely self-destruction left a void that was eventually filled by ▷ R. S. Thomas (b 1913), whose major poetic status was rapidly endorsed by critics in England despite their disregard of most Anglo-Welsh literature. R. S. Thomas's concern for rural and urban poverty in Wales, reflected in his sympathy for the uncouth hill farmer, is revealed in firmly structured, emotionally restrained poems of arresting imagery. For him, nationalism would answer Wales's problems: God he listens for in answer to his own problems as priest-poet. Another major writer of nationalist stance is the novelist and poet Emyr Humphreys (b 1919). Humphreys, of North Walian orientation, examines conscience among the Welsh-speaking professional class, and impartially presents Nonconformity, while never seeking to depart from his fictive high seriousness or to indulge popular taste.

Meic Stephens (b 1938) was the prime mover behind the 'second flowering' which gathered momentum in the 1960s when nationalist ideas were superseding socialist politics. He founded *Poetry Wales* in 1965 with support from Harri Webb, thus providing a nationalist conscious poetic forum, fostering mutual interest between Wales's two languages, especially reinvigorating Anglo-Welsh poetry through John Ormond, Harri Webb, John Tripp, Raymond Garlick, Roland Mathias, Leslie Norris and Gillian Clarke. In 1967 he became Literature Director of the newly constituted Welsh Arts Council whose financial support for writers and publishers gave tremendous impetus to Welsh and Anglo-Welsh writing. An unfortunate effect, however, was that London publishers and reviewers disregarded Anglo-Welsh writing when it developed independently from metropolitan influences, leading to a critical undervaluing that still persists in England. In 1968 Meic Stephens led a move to create the English section of *Yr Academi Gymreig*, originally a literary society founded for Welsh-language writers only, but from then on providing invaluable encouragement to Anglo-Welsh writers. Concluding an exciting decade, Ned Thomas launched *Planet* in 1970, a magazine whose political thrust was left-wing and nationalist, and which also published literary material.

Recently, an updated view of Valleys society has informed the short stories and novels of Alun Richards (b 1929) and Ron Berry (b 1920). Alun Richards illuminates social tensions among the migratory professional classes, nuances between the Valleys and Cardiff, and Cardiff and London. His sensitive ear for dialogue contributed to the effectiveness of his work for the theatre (published in *Plays for Players*; 1975) and television. Ron Berry has explored Valleys sexual mores with lively humour. Closely associated with the border country of his upbringing, ▷ Raymond Williams's novels present the tensions of nationalism, social mobility, working-class solidarity and conflicting loyalties, though the political and socio-economic dimensions of his critical *œuvre* are more familiar. The novelists with Anglo-Welsh connections who have achieved most recent critical acclaim are Bernice Rubens, Alice Thomas Ellis, Stuart Evans and Peter Thomas, a newcomer as a novelist extending Gwyn Thomas's hyperbolic vision.

Anglo-Welsh literature has produced no playwright to emulate Emlyn Williams (1905–1988), though the recent emphasis has shifted from theatre via radio into television, as reflected in the careers of Gwyn Thomas, Alun Owen, Alun Richards and Elaine Morgan.

Although disappointment with the result of the referendum on devolution did not affect the republican nationalist views of some of the younger poets such as Nigel Jenkins and Mike Jenkins, a widening of poetic horizons has been taking place. Its trailblazer ▷ Dannie

Abse (b 1923) has exploited a series of fruitful tensions in his work which reflect contrasting life-styles: Cardiff/London; Welsh/Jewish; poetry/medicine. His sympathy for oppressed minorities reveals a humanitarianism and compassion haunted by the horror of the Holocaust. His range of themes ensures his international, as well as Anglo-Welsh, status. Another poet who has broadened his Anglo-Welsh context through exposure to the influence of American 'confessional' poets (such as Robert Lowell, ▷ Sylvia Plath, John Berryman and Anne Sexton), thereby producing many transatlantic poems, is Tony Curtis (b 1946) whose recent work invokes historical perspectives through condemnation of war and nuclear weapons. Peter Finch (b 1947) has experimented with concrete and multilingual, occasionally almost surreal, poetry. John Davies, Steve Griffiths, Robert Minhinnick, Mike Jenkins, Nigel Jenkins, Duncan Bush, Sheenagh Pugh and Chris Meredith are all acutely conscious of their present social reality while rejecting traditional Welsh stereotyping. Moving towards English influences, Oliver Reynolds (b 1957) has embraced the ▷ Martian 'new heartlessness', his poetic incisiveness deriving also from ▷ W. H. Auden. Hilary Llewellyn-Williams's rural, mythopoeic vision owes something to Gillian Clarke and Ruth Bidgood in that it is personal, familial and rooted in the Welsh landscape, its inhabitants and their history.

With a higher concentration of writers in Wales than anywhere in Britain, the vigorous growth of Anglo-Welsh literature is assured, particularly since, though it has retained its traditionally distinguishing characteristics, it has developed a more outward-looking stance. Happily, as this text proves, there are indications that the Anglo-Welsh literary movement may eventually receive its long overdue recognition from the English critical establishment.

Bib: Stephens, M. (ed.), *The Oxford Companion to the Literature of Wales*; Adams, S. and Hughes, G. R., *Essays in Welsh and Anglo-Welsh Literature*; Conran, A., *The Cost of Strangeness*; Garlick, R., *An Introduction to Anglo-Welsh Literature*; Hooker, J., *The Poetry of Place*; Jones, G., *The Dragon Has Two Tongues*; Jones, G. and Rowlands, R., *Profiles*; Mathias, R., *A Ride Through the Wood*; Mathias, R., *Anglo-Welsh Literature*; Curtis, T. (ed.), *Wales: the Imagined Nation*.

Wesker, Arnold (1932)
British dramatist, born in London's East End and son of a Russian Jewish tailor. After military service, he became a professional pastry cook, and then entered the London School of Film Technique. ▷ John Osborne's ▷ *Look Back in Anger* (1956) influenced him to concentrate on the theatre. In 1961, he became Director of Centre Forty-two, intended to break down such barriers to popular appreciation of the arts as commercialism and intellectual and social snobbery, or social fragmentation due to restricted ways of life and inarticulacy in the shaping of goals. These obstacles to communication in the mass of society are the subject matter of his plays which are pervaded by a search for cordial understanding and sympathy. His plays include: *Chicken Soup with Barley* (1958); *Roots* (1959); *The Kitchen* (1960); *I'm Talking about Jerusalem* (1960); *Chips with Everything* (1962); *The Four Seasons* (1966); *Their Very Own* and *Golden City* (1966); *The Friends* (1970); *The Old Ones* (1972); *The Wedding Feast* (1974); *The Merchant* (1976); *Love Letters on Blue Paper* (1977); *Caritas* (1981).

Wesker was one of the leaders of the post-war dramatic revival, together with ▷ John Osborne, ▷ Harold Pinter, and ▷ John Arden.

Bib: Taylor, J. R., *Anger and After*; Ribalow, H. U., *Arnold Wesker*; Leemig, G., *Arnold Wesker* (Writers and their Work series).

***What Maisie Knew* (1897)**
A novel by ▷ Henry James. Its theme is the survival of innocence in a world of adult corruption, the influence of adults on a child, and her influence on them.

Maisie Farange is a small girl whose parents have divorced each other with equal guilt on both sides. The parents are heartless and indifferent to their daughter, except as a weapon against each other and in their farcical, though not wholly vain, struggles to maintain acceptable social appearances. Maisie is passed from one to the other, and each employs a governess to take responsibility for her welfare. Both parents marry again, and eventually relinquish Maisie herself. By the end of the book Maisie finds herself torn between two prospective 'stepparents', each formerly married to her real parents, divorced from them, and about to marry each other, Maisie herself having been the occasion of their coming together. Her 'stepfather', Sir Claude, is charming and sweet-natured, but weak and self-indulgent; her 'stepmother', Mrs Beale, is genuinely fond of Maisie (as Sir Claude is) but is basically selfish and rapacious. In addition, the child has a simple-minded, plain and elderly governess, Mrs

Wix, who is herself in love with Sir Claude, and devoted to Maisie. The affection of none of them, however, is single-minded, as hers is for each one of them. The pathos of the novel arises from the warm responsiveness, deep need, and pure integrity of Maisie, from whose point of view all the events are seen. Its irony arises from the way in which the child's need for and dependence on adult care and love is transformed into responsibility for the adults themselves, who become dependent on her decisions. In the end these decisions lead her to choose life alone with Mrs Wix, who naïvely hopes to imbue her with a 'moral sense', unaware that beside Maisie's innocence her own idea of a moral sense represents modified corruption.

The novel is written in James's late, compressed and dramatic style, and is one of his masterpieces.

White, Patrick (1912–90)
Australian novelist, dramatist and poet. Born in London, educated in Australia, and at Cheltenham College and Cambridge University. He travelled widely in Europe and the U.S.A., served in the Royal Air Force during World War II, and then returned to live in Australia. His work combines an intense spirituality with social comedy and a distaste for human pretension and egotism. His first novel, *The Happy Valley* (1939), set in remote New South Wales, shows the influence of ▷ Joyce, while *The Living and the Dead* (1941) is primarily a condemnation of English society of the 1920s and 1930s. White established his reputation with *The Tree of Man* (1955) and *Voss* (1957). Both concern man's confrontation with the inhuman forces of nature in Australia, the former through the struggles of a young farmer, the latter through the journey among the Aborigines of a mid-19th-century German explorer. White's later works of fiction were two collections, each containing three short pieces: *Memoirs of Many in One* (1986) and *Three Uneasy Pieces* (1988). His other novels are: *The Aunt's Story* (1948); *Riders in the Chariot* (1961); *The Solid Mandala* (1966); *The Vivisector* (1970); *The Eye of the Storm* (1973); *A Fringe of Leaves* (1976); *The Twyborn Affair* (1979). Drama includes: *Return to Abyssinia* (1947); *Four Plays* (1965) (*The Ham Funeral*, 1961; *The Season at Sarsaparilla*, 1962; *A Cheery Soul*, 1963; *Night on Bald Mountain*, 1964); *Big Toys* (1977); *Signal Driver* (1983). Story collections are: *The Burnt Ones* (1964); *The Cockatoos* (1974). Verse: *The Ploughman and Other Poems* (1935).

▷ Commonwealth literatures.

Bib: Walsh, W., *Patrick White's Fiction*.

Whiting, John (1917–63)
British damatist and actor. Although his plays are now rarely performed, he is important as a pioneer of serious drama during the immediate post-war period. Plays include: *A Penny for a Song* (1951), *Saint's Day* (1951), *Marching Song* (1954) and *The Devils* (1961), based on ▷ Aldous Huxley's *The Devils of Loudon*. Both *A Penny for a Song* and *The Devils* were performed by the ▷ Royal Shakespeare Company.
Bib: Salmon, E., *The Dark Journey*.

Who's Who
An annual biographical dictionary of eminent contemporary men and women. First published in 1849.

▷ Biography.

Wickham, Anna (1884–1947)
Poet. Anna Wickham (pseudonym of Edith Harper) published her first volume of poetry in 1911 as *Songs of John Oland* (another of her pseudonyms), and whilst her writing career spanned the period of high modernism, her poetry is more characteristic of ▷ Edwardian and ▷ Georgian styles (so much so that it appeared in two important collections of the 1930s, *Edwardian Poetry* and *Neo-Georgian Poetry*, 1937). She committed suicide in 1947, and her published works include: *The Contemplative Quarry and the Man with a Hammer* (1921); *The Little Old House* (1921); *Thirty-Six New Poems* (1936), and the 1984 Virago Press publication of *The Writings of Anna Wickham: Free Woman and Poet* (ed. R. D. Smith).

Wilde, Oscar (Fingal O'Flahertie Wills) (1856–1900)
Dramatist, poet, novelist and essayist. He was the son of an eminent Irish surgeon and a literary mother. At Oxford University his style of life became notorious; he was a disciple of Walter Pater, the Oxford father of ▷ aestheticism, and he carried the doctrine as far as to conduct his life as an aesthetic disciple – a direct challenge to the prevailing outlook of the society of his time, which was inclined to regard overt aestheticism with suspicion or disdain. In 1888 Wilde produced a volume of children's fairy-tales very much in the melancholy and poetic style of the Danish writer Hans Christian Andersen – *The Happy Prince*. He followed this with two other volumes of stories, and then the novel, *The Picture of Dorian Gray* (1891), whose hero is

an embodiment of the aesthetic way of life. More commonly known were his comedies, *Lady Windermere's Fan* (1892), *A Woman of No Importance* (1893), *An Ideal Husband* (1895), and above all the witty *The Importance of Being Earnest* (1895). The plays are apparently light-hearted, but they contain strong elements of serious feeling in their attack on a society whose code is intolerant, but whose intolerance is hypocritical. In 1895, by a libel action against the Marquis of Queensberry, he exposed himself to a countercharge of immoral homosexual conduct, and spent two years in prison. In 1898 he published his *Ballad of Reading Gaol* about his prison experience, proving that he could write in the direct language of the ▷ ballad tradition, as well as in the artificial style of his *Collected Poems* (1892). His *De Profundis* (1905) is an eloquent statement of his grief after his downfall, but modern critics are equally as impressed by the intelligence of his social essays, such as *The Critic as Artist* (1891) and *The Soul of Man under Socialism* (1891). The paradox of Wilde is that, while for his contemporaries he represented degeneracy and weakness, there is plenty of evidence that he was a brave man of remarkable strength of character who made an emphatic protest against the vulgarity of his age and yet, artistically, was himself subject to vulgarity of an opposite kind.

▷ Homosexuality.

Bib: Critical studies by Roditi, E., Ransome, A.; Lives by Lemmonier, L.; Ervine, St. J.; Pearson, H.; Bentley, E. R., in *The Playwright as Thinker*; Beckson, K. (ed.), *The Critical Heritage*; Bird, A., *The Plays of Oscar Wilde*; Worth, K., *Oscar Wilde*; Ellmann, R., *Oscar Wilde*.

Williams, Raymond (1921–88)

The most influential of all radical thinkers in Britain in the 20th century. Williams's work spans literary criticism, cultural studies, media studies, communications and politics, and he also wrote plays and novels. He was, along with American critic Frederic Jameson, the most well-known ▷ Marxist critic writing in English. In *Culture and Society 1780–1950* (1958) and *The Long Revolution* (1961) he laid the foundation for a wide-ranging analysis of modern cultural forms, and can justly be accredited with the foundation of cultural studies as an interdisciplinary field of enquiry. In books such as *Modern Tragedy* (1966) and *Drama from Ibsen to Brecht* (1968), which was a revision of his earlier *Drama from Ibsen to Eliot* (1952), he challenged accepted ways of evaluating drama and dramatic forms, and in 1968 he was a guiding spirit behind the New Left's *Mayday Manifesto* (1968). For Williams writing was always and primarily a social activity, deeply implicated in politics. Through books such as *The Country and the City* (1973), *Marxism and Literature* (1977), *Politics and Letters* (1979), *Problems in Materialism and Culture* (1980), *Writing in Society, Towards 2000* (1983) and his *John Clare's Selected Poetry and Prose* (1986), he pursued these themes with an intellectual rigour which refused easy formulations. His was the intellectual force behind the current movement of cultural ▷ materialism, the British equivalent of American new historicism. Williams also wrote several novels, the most famous of which is the semi-autobiographical *Border Country* (1960).

Wilson, Angus (1913–91)

Novelist and short-story writer. Born in Durban, South Africa, Wilson was educated at Westminster School in London and at Merton College, Oxford. He worked for many years in the British Museum Reading Room, served in the Foreign Office during World War II, and, from 1963, taught English literature at the University of East Anglia. He was primarily a satirist (▷ satire), with a particularly sharp ear for the way in which hypocrisy, cruelty and smugness are betrayed in conversation. His first published works were short stories, *The Wrong Set* (1949) and *Such Darling Dodos* (1950), depicting English middle-class life around the time of World War II. His early work was traditional in form, inspired by his respect for the 19th-century English novel and a reaction against the dominance of post-Jamesian narrative techniques in the ▷ modernist novel. *Hemlock and After* (1952), *Anglo-Saxon Attitudes* (1956) and *The Middle Age of Mrs Eliot* (1958) deal with such issues as responsibility, guilt and the problem of loneliness. The surface is satirical, and at times highly comic, but, as the protagonist of *Anglo-Saxon Attitudes* comments, 'the ludicrous was too often only a thin covering for the serious and the tragic'. *The Old Men at the Zoo* (1961) represented a considerable change of mode: it is a bizarre fable concerning personal and political commitment, set in the London Zoo at a time of international crisis. From this point on Wilson's work became more experimental: *Late Call* (1964) makes use of pastiche, while *No Laughing Matter* (1967) reflects the influence of ▷ Virginia Woolf, employing multiple interior monologues, as well as parodic dramatic dialogue and

stories by one of the characters. It has a broad historical and social sweep, setting the story of a family between 1912 and 1967 in the context of British society as a whole. Like *Anglo-Saxon Attitudes* and *Late Call* it traces personal and public concerns back to the period immediately before World War I. *Setting the World on Fire* (1980) was another new departure in form; it is a complex and highly patterned work in which the myth of Phaeton is re-enacted in modern London. His other novels are: *As If By Magic* (1973). Story collections: *Death Dance* (1969); *Collected Stories* (1987). Travel writing: *Reflections in a Writer's Eye* (1986). Critical works include: *Émile Zola* (1952); *The World of Charles Dickens* (1970); *The Strange Ride of Rudyard Kipling* (1977).
Bib: Cox, C. B., *The Free Spirit*; Halio, J. L. (ed.), *Critical Essays on Angus Wilson*; Gardner, A., *Angus Wilson*; Faulkner, P., *Angus Wilson, Mimic and Moralist*.

Wilson, Colin (b 1931)
Novelist and critic. He is known primarily as the author of the ▷ existentialist work *The Outsider* (1956), which was much acclaimed at the time of its publication. He is the author of 15 novels, and over 50 works of non-fiction. His novels feature violence, sexuality and the idea of the outsider in society, and seek to acknowledge fictionality by using genres such as the detective story with a deliberate incongruity.

***Wings of the Dove, The* (1902)**
A novel by ▷ Henry James. The scene is principally London and Venice. Kate Croy and Merton Densher, a young journalist, are in love, but without the money to marry. Kate's rich aunt, Maud Lowder, takes into her circle Milly Theale, a lonely American girl of great single-mindedness, eagerness for life, and capacity for affection, and also a millionairess. Milly is travelling in Europe with Susan Stringham, an old friend of Mrs Lowder's. Mrs Stringham learns from Milly's doctor that the girl is suffering from a fatal illness, that her death cannot be long delayed, and that it can only be delayed at all if she achieves happiness. Mrs Stringham communicates this to Kate, who conceives a plot with a double purpose: Merton is to engage Milly's love, thus bringing her the happiness that she needs, and at the same time securing her money when she dies, so that Kate's own marriage to Merton can at last take palce. Milly's love for Merton is very real; because of it, however, she refuses another suitor, Lord Mark, who knows Kate's plot and in revenge betrays it to Milly. She dies, broken-hearted, but she leaves Merton her money. Merton and Kate, however, find that they are for ever separated by the shadow of the dead Milly between them.

The story is an example of James's 'international theme': in this case, the openness and integrity which he saw as strengths of the American personality are opposed to the selfishness and deviousness which he saw as part of the decadent aspect of European culture. It is written in the condensed, allusive style which is characteristic also of ▷ *The Ambassadors* and ▷ *The Golden Bowl*.

Winterson, Jeanette, (b 1959)
Novelist. Winterson's works have been praised for their originality of subject matter and form. Her first novel, the autobiographical *Oranges are Not the Only Fruit* (1985), is a witty account of her upbringing as the child of fundamentalist Christians and her development as a lesbian in a town in the north of England; it won the Whitbread Award for First Novel and was translated into an enormously popular television series. Her subsequent three novels have been rather more experimental and formally complex; these are *Boating for Beginners* (1986); *The Passion* (which won the John Llewelyn Rhys Prize in 1987); *Sexing the Cherry* (1989); and *Written On the Body* (1992).

Wodehouse, (Sir) P. G. (Pelham Grenville) (1881–1975)
Writer of humorous short stories and novels. Born in Guildford, Surrey and educated at Dulwich College, London, he was brought up partly by aunts in England, since his father was a judge in Hong Kong. Known always as P. G. Wodehouse, his most famous creations were the good-natured but disaster-prone young man about town, Bertie Wooster, and his ever-resourceful 'gentleman's gentleman' (manservant), Jeeves, first introduced in *The Man With Two Left Feet* (1917). The Jeeves and Wooster books include: *My Man Jeeves* (1919); *The Inimitable Jeeves* (1923); *Carry On Jeeves* (1925); *Right Ho, Jeeves* (1934); *The Code of the Woosters* (1938); *Jeeves in the Offing* (1960); *Stiff Upper Lip, Jeeves* (1963). Wodehouse depicted a range of other comic characters, evoking a charming escapist myth of the upper-class England of the 1920s. He also wrote school stories such as *Mike* (1909), sentimental romances such as *Love Among the Chickens* (1906), song lyrics and works for

the theatre and cinema. Despite a scandal when he broadcast from Germany during World War II, after having been captured, he remained immensely popular. He lived in Britain, France and the U.S.A., becoming an American citizen in 1945.
Bib: Donaldson, F., *P. G. Wodehouse*.

Women, Education of
In medieval convents, nuns often learned and received the same education as monks. Thereafter, women's intellectual education was not widely provided for until the later 19th century, though much would depend on their social rank, their parents, or their husbands. Thomas More in ▷ *Utopia* advocated equal education for both sexes; Jonathan Swift in the 'Land of the Houyhnhnms' (*Gulliver's Travels*) causes his enlightened horse to scorn the human habit of educating only half mankind, and yet allowing the other half (*ie* women) to bring up the children. On the other hand, in the 16th century the enthusiasm for education caused some highly born women to be very highly educated.

It is often difficult to interpret the evidence from the past as it is sometimes based on assumptions or fears about women's education that enlightened people do not now share.

Boarding schools for girls came into existence in the 17th century and became more numerous in the 18th, but either they were empty of real educational value or they were absurdly pretentious, like Miss Pinkerton's Academy described in W. M. Thackeray's *Vanity Fair* (1848); Mrs Malaprop in Sheridan's comedy *The Rivals* (1775) is a satire on half-educated upper-class women. Upper-class girls had governesses for general education, music masters, dancing masters, and teachers of 'deportment', *ie* in the bearing of the body; lower-class women were illiterate unless they learned to read and write at 'charity schools'.

The big change dates from the mid-19th century. Alfred Tennyson's *The Princess* (1850), for example advocates educational opportunities for women and the eponymous heroine actually founds a university for this purpose. Actual colleges were founded for the higher education of women (beginning with Queen's College, London, 1848), and schools (*eg* Cheltenham Ladies' College) comparable to the public schools for boys were founded. The women's colleges Girton (1869) and Newnham (1875) were founded in Cambridge, and others followed at Oxford. Societies were also founded for the advancing of women's education. All this in spite of warnings from medical men that cerebral development in the female must be at the cost of physiological, *ie* child-bearing, aptitude. Since the commencement of state education in 1870, the status of women teachers has been brought equal to that of men teachers, and since 1902 equal secondary education has been provided for both sexes.

***Women in Love* (1921)**
A novel by ▷ D. H. Lawrence. It continues the lives of the characters in ▷ *The Rainbow*. Ursula Brangwen is a schoolteacher, and her sister Gudrun is an artist. The other two main characters are Gerald Crich, a mine-owner and manager, and Rupert Birkin, a school-inspector. The main narrative is about the relationships of these four: the union of Rupert and Ursula after conflict, the union of Gerald and Gudrun ending in conflict and Gerald's death, the affinities and antagonisms between the sisters and between the men. The settings include Shortlands, the mansion of the mine-owning Crich family; Breadalby, the mansion of Lady Hermione Roddice, a meeting-place of the leading intellectuals of the day; the Café Pompadour in London, a centre for artists; and a winter resort in the Austrian Tyrol. The theme is human relationships in the modern world, where intelligence has become the prisoner of self-consciousness, and spontaneous life-forces are perverted into violence, notably in Gerald, Hermione, and the German sculptor Loerke. Symbolic episodes centred on animals and other natural imagery are used to present those forces of the consciousness that lie outside rational articulation, and personal relationships are so investigated as to illuminate crucial aspects of modern culture: the life of industry, the life of art, the use and misuse of reason, and what is intimate considered as the nucleus of what is public. Rupert Birkin is a projection of Lawrence himself, but he is objectified sufficiently to be exposed to criticism.

Women's Movement, The
The women's movement – under many names – is dedicated to the campaign for political and legal rights for women. It wishes to prevent discrimination on the grounds of gender and is, generally, a movement for social change.

There is no single source, although the history of women's quest for equality is a long one. The *Querelle des Femmes* in the medieval period, Aphra Behn and Mary Astell in the

17th century, and Mary Wollstonecraft in the Romantic Age all furthered women's rights. In the Victorian period ▷ feminism became linked with other social movements such as anti-slavery campaigners, evangelical groups and Quakers. The ▷ Suffragette Movement (1860–1930) united women and this solidarity was to re-emerge in the radicalization of the 1960s. The important works of this later stage in the women's movement are ▷ Simone de Beauvoir's *Le Deuxième Sexe* (1949), Kate Millett's *Sexual Politics* (1969) and ▷ Germaine Greer's *The Female Eunuch* (1970). The 1970s and 1980s have witnessed the second stage of the women's movement and seen its dismemberment into separate pressure groups – *eg* lesbianism, Third World – and its partial metamorphosis into post-feminism. This latter term has become popularized and takes for granted that women now have equality with men, but the mainstream of the women's movement denies this emphatically and perseveres with its campaign.

▷ Women, Status of.

Bib: Mitchell, J. and Oakley, A. (eds.), *What is Feminism?*, Eisenstein, H., *Contemporary Feminist Thought*.

Women, Status of

Unmarried women had few prospects in Britain until the second half of the 19th century. In the ▷ Middle Ages they could enter convents and become nuns, but when in 1536–9 Henry VIII closed the convents and the monasteries, no alternative opened to them. Widows like Chaucer's Wife of Bath in *The Canterbury Tales* might inherit a business (in her case that of a clothier) and run it efficiently, or like Mistress Quickly in Shakespeare's *Henry IV, Part II* they might run inns. The profession of acting was opened to women from the Restoration of the monarchy in 1660, and writing began to be a possible means of making money from the time of Aphra Behn. Later the increase of interest in education for girls led to extensive employment of governesses to teach the children in private families; such a position might be peaceful and pleasant, like Mrs Weston's experience in the Woodhouse family in Jane Austen's *Emma*, but it was at least as likely to be unpleasant, underpaid and despised, as the novelist Charlotte Brontë found. Nursing was also open to women, but nurses had no training and were commonly a low class of women like Betsey Prig and Mrs Gamp in Dickens's *Martin Chuzzlewit* until Florence Nightingale reformed the profession.

Wives and their property were entirely in the power of their husbands according to the law, though in practice they might take the management of both into their own hands. A Dutch observer (1575) stated that England was called the 'Paradise of married women' because they took their lives more easily than continental wives. Nonetheless, a middle-class wife worked hard, as her husband's assistant (probably his accountant) in his business, and as a mistress of baking, brewing, household management and amateur medicine.

The 19th century was the heroic age for women in Britain. No other nation before the 20th century has produced such a distinguished line of women writers as the novelists Jane Austen, Elizabeth Gaskell, Charlotte and Emily Brontë and George Eliot (Mary Ann Evans). In addition there was the prison reformer, Elizabeth Fry; the reformer of the nursing profession, Florence Nightingale; the explorer, Mary Kingsley; the sociologist, ▷ Beatrice Webb; pioneers in education, and the first women doctors. The Married Women's Property Act of 1882 for the first time gave wives rights to their own property which had hitherto been merged with their husbands'. Political rights came more slowly, and were preceded by an active and sometimes violent movement, led by the Suffragettes (▷ Suffragette Movement), who fought for them. Women over 30 were given the vote in 1918 as a consequence of their success in taking over men's work during World War I, but women over 21 (the age at which men were entitled to vote or stand for Parliament) had to wait until 1928. Now most professions are nominally open to women, including the law; a notable exception is the priesthood of the ▷ Church of England and some other religious denominations but there are signs of change even there.

The position of women at work is still generally subordinate to men: the success of a few women does not alter the fact that the average wage of women is about three-quarters that of men. Women are disproportionately under-represented in positions of security and power, for example in high-level management jobs or tenured university posts.

Woolf, Virginia (1882–1941)

Novelist and critic. She was the daughter of Leslie Stephen, the literary critic; after his death in 1904, the house in the Bloomsbury district of London which she shared with her sister Vanessa (later Vanessa Bell) became the centre of the ▷ Bloomsbury Group of intellectuals, one of whom, the socialist thinker Leonard Woolf, she married in 1912. Together they established the ▷ Hogarth Press which published much of the most memorable imaginative writing of the 1920s. She experienced recurrent bouts of mental illness and during one of these took her own life by drowning herself in the River Ouse, near her home at Rodmell, Sussex.

Her first two novels, *The Voyage Out* (1915) and *Night and Day* (1919), are basically ▷ realist in their technique, but in the next four – *Jacob's Room* (1922), ▷ *Mrs Dalloway* (1925), ▷ *To the Lighthouse* (1927) and ▷ *The Waves* (1931) – she became increasingly experimental and innovatory. Her attitude was formed by three influences: the negative one of dissatisfaction with the methods and outlook of the three novelists who, in the first 20 years of this century, dominated the contemporary public, ▷ H.G. Wells, ▷ Arnold Bennett, and ▷ John Galsworthy (see Woolf's essay 'Mr Bennett and Mrs Brown', 1923); the outlook of the Bloomsbury circle, with their strong emphasis on the value of personal relations and the cultivation of the sensibility; the sense of tragedy in the 19th-century Russian novelists, Tolstoy and Dostoievski, and the dramatist and short-story writer ▷ Chekhov. She sought to develop a technique of expression which would capture the essence of the sensibility – the experiencing self – and to do this, she reduced the plot-and-story element of novel-writing as far as she could and developed a ▷ stream of consciousness narrative to render inner experience. The last two of the four experimental novels mentioned are usually considered to be her most successful achievements, especially *To the Lighthouse*. In her later novels, *The Years* (1937) and *Between the Acts* (1941), she again used a more customary technique, though with stress on symbolism and bringing out the slight incident as possibly that which is most revelatory. She is now generally regarded as one of the greatest of the modernist innovators, and is also an important focus for feminist debate.

▷ *Orlando* (1928) is a composite work, ostensibly a biography of a poet (a tribute to ▷ Vita Sackville-West), but in part a brilliantly vivid historical novel (though her subject was her contemporary) and in part literary criticism. Her more formal literary criticism was published in two volumes, *The Common Reader* (1925) and *The Common Reader, 2nd Series* (1932). In these she expressed her philosophy of creative writing (for instance in the essay 'Modern Fiction', 1925) and her response to the writers and writings of the past that most interested her. She had a partly fictional way of re-creating the personalities of past writers which is sensitive and vivid. In her social and political attitude she was feminist, *ie* she was much concerned with the rights of women and especially of women writers. This is one of the basic themes of *Orlando* but it comes out most clearly in *A Room of One's Own* (1931). *Flush* (1933) is another experiment in fictional biography (of Elizabeth Barrett Browning's spaniel) and she wrote a straight biography of her friend the art critic Roger Fry (1940). Apart from *The Common Reader*, her volumes of essays and criticism include: *Three Guineas* (1938); *The Death of the Moth* (1942); *The Captain's Death Bed* (1950); *Granite and Rainbow* (1958). Her *Collected Essays* were published in 1966, her *Letters* between 1975 and 1980 and her diaries (*The Diary of Virginia Woolf*) between 1977 and 1984. *Moments of Being* (1976) is a selection of autobiographical writings. Her stories are collected in *A Haunted House* (1943).

Bib: Woolf, L., *Autobiography*; Bell, Q., *Virginia Woolf, A Biography*; Bowlby, R., *Virginia Woolf: Feminist Destinations*; Gordon, L., *Virginia Woolf: Writer's Life*; Clements, P., and Grundy, I. (eds.), *Virginia Woolf: New Critical Essays*; Marcus, J. (ed.), *New Feminist Essays on Virginia Woolf*; Naremore, J., *The World Without a Self*; Rosenthal, M., *Virginia Woolf*.

Y

Yeats, W. B. (William Butler) (1865–1939) Anglo-Irish poet. He was of Protestant family, a fact of importance in 19th-century Ireland where nationalism was so bound up with Roman Catholicism. His father was an eminent painter. He spent his boyhood between school in London and his mother's native county of Sligo, a wild and beautiful county in north-western Ireland which is a background to much of his poetry. His youth was passed during the upsurge of Irish political nationalism represented by the Home Rule movement led by Parnell. He shared the antagonism felt by English writers of Pre-Raphaelite background – notably William Morris – to the urban and industrial harshness and materialism of contemporary English culture. He sought a basis for resistance to it in Irish peasant folk traditions and ancient Celtic myth. His first work was on a theme from this mythology – *The Wanderings of Oisin*. Yeats was indeed fortunate in having such a cultural basis at hand for his anti-materialistic poetry, while his English contemporaries had further to look. His career divides naturally into four phases:

1 *1889–99*. During this period he was a leading member of the ▷ Aesthetic Movement in London, an outcome of Pre-Raphaelitism, but especially indebted to the Oxford scholar, Walter Pater. In its revolt against ▷ Victorian materialism, it tended to ▷ Catholicism and to mysticism. Its meeting-place was the Rhymers' Club, and its public voice the ▷ *Yellow Book*. Yeats shared its mystical sympathies, which in his case brought together Celtic and Indian mythology; these come out in his works of the period: prose – ▷ *The Celtic Twilight* (1893), *The Secret Rose, The Tables of the Law, The Adoration of the Magi* (1897); verse – *Crossways* (1889), *The Rose* (1893), *The Wind Among the Reeds* (1899); verse plays – *The Countess Cathleen* (1892) and *The Land of Heart's Desire* (1894).

2 *1899–1909*. Yeats, with the help of ▷ Lady Gregory, built up the Irish National Theatre, which found a home in the ▷ Abbey Theatre, Dublin. Until 1909, he was its manager, and he wrote plays for it, predominantly based on Irish myth. The period was disillusioning for him so far as his hopes for Irish culture went, but it was formative in his development as a major poet. He hoped to make the theatre the voice of a distinctively Irish modern culture, and at least he succeeded in creating one of the most interesting dramatic movements in contemporary Europe. In personal terms, the theatre business brought out new strength and realism in his character and in his writing; he was the first poet writing in English since the 17th century to seek intelligently and purposefully for an effective dramatic idiom and for new methods of dramatic production. His only volume of verse during these ten years was *In the Seven Woods* (1904); amongst his plays are *Cathleen ni Houlihan* (1902), *The King's Threshold* (1904), *Deirdre* (1907).

3 *1910–18 – the Period of Transition*. He had begun his career in the tradition of Spenser, Shelley and the Pre-Raphaelites, and he had always been interested in the mysticism of Blake, but he now became one of the poets, including ▷ Ezra Pound (whom he met at this time) and ▷ T.S. Eliot, drawn to the intellectually more vigorous tradition associated with the 17th-century Metaphysicals, especially Donne. He was no longer a ▷ romantic, at least in the decadent sense of a dreamer, but though his mood was harsher and he had lost some of his faith, he searched no less assiduously for symbols which could give meaning to history and life. At first he turned away from Ireland, but the Irish Rebellion of 1916 turned him back to the country which was after all the human context of his emotions. His books *The Green Helmet* (1910) and *Responsibilities* (1914) represent the new austerity of his poetry.

4 *1919–39*. It is in this period that Yeats grows into one of the most important poets of the 20th century, with the publication of *The Wild Swans at Coole* (1919), *Michael Robartes and the Dancer* (1921), *The Tower* (1928) and *The Winding Stair* (1933). This work is marked by strong rhythms, by stanza and rhyme patterns which enforce thought, by severe diction with few adjectives, and by a range of symbols each of which is a nucleus of meanings. The symbols are part of an elaborate theory of history (explained in the prose *A Vision*, 1925) derived from the Italian philosopher Vico (1668–1744) and the neo-Platonism of Plotinus (3rd century AD). Whatever the faultiness of the system considered apart from the poetry, it constituted for Yeats a mythology which he could use poetically to embody human experience widely and deeply. It is scarcely helpful to try to 'learn' this mythology in order to understand Yeats's poetry; it is elucidated by the poetry itself, if it is read in bulk. With these symbols (the tower, the moon, etc.) Yeats had a wide mythology of persons, some drawn from his own friends, some from history and myth, and some invented, *eg* Crazy Jane in *Words for Music Perhaps*. This, like *A Woman Young and Old, A Full Moon in March*

(1935) and *Last Poems* (1936–39), has more bitterness and less richness than the previous volumes of this period. Yeats continued to write plays and to improve his dramatic idiom, partly under the influence of the Japanese Noh drama; his best play is nearly his last – *Purgatory* (1939). After 1910, Yeats's prose is also distinguished, notably his *Autobiographies* (1915 and 1922), some of his critical essays, *eg Per Amica Silentia Lunae* (1918) and his essays on drama, *Plays and Controversies* (1923).

▷ Irish literature in English.

Bib: Hone, J. M., *Life*, Ellmann, R., *Yeats, the Man and the Masks*; *The Identity of Yeats*; Henn, T. R., *The Lonely Tower*; Stock, *W. B. Yeats*; Rudd, M., *Divided Image: a Study of Blake and Yeats*; Unterecker, J., *A Reader's Guide to Yeats*; Kermode, F., *Romantic Image*; Hall and Steinmann (eds.), a collection of essays; Leavis, F. R., *New Bearings in English Poetry*; Raine, K., *Yeats the Initiate*; Dorn, K., *Players and Painted Stage*; Ure, P., *Yeats the Playwright*; Smith, S., *W. B. Yeats*.

Yellow Book

An illustrated quarterly review, 1894–7. It was a main organ of the arts during the period, and though it was especially the voice of the ▷ Aesthetic Movement, it also published writers who did not belong to this movement, *eg* ▷ Henry James.

▷ Nineties Poets.

Chronology

This chronology gives a breakdown of important dates, both literary and historical. The literary dates are listed in the left hand column and the historical events in the right hand column. It begins with the late 19th century rather than the early 20th century to give the context of the earlier developments of and works by writers who were to become particularly influential on writing this century. The listing is necessarily selective.

1879
Browning: 'Dramatic Idylls'
Henry James: *Daisy Miller*
Meredith: *The Egoist*
1880
Browning: 'Dramatic Idylls' (second series)
Benjamin Disraeli: *Endymion*
Swinburne: *Songs of the Spring Tides*
1881
Hardy: *A Laodicean*
Henry James: *Portrait of a Lady*
Christina Rossetti: *A Pageant and Other Poems*
D. G. Rossetti: *Ballads and Sonnets*
1882
Matthew Arnold: *Irish Essays*
Swinburne: *Tristram of Lyonesse*
1883
Burton: trans. of *Arabian Nights Entertainments*
Stevenson: *Treasure Island*
1886
Henry James: *The Bostonians*
Stevenson: *Dr Jeckyll and Mr Hyde*
Kidnapped
1888
Matthew Arnold: *Essays in Criticism* (second series)
1889
Yeats: 'The Wanderings of Oisin'
1891
Gissing: *New Grub Street*
Hardy: *Tess of the D'Urbervilles*
William Morris: *News from Nowhere*
Shaw: *The Quintessence of Ibsenism*
Wilde: *The Picture of Dorian Gray*
1892
Wilde: *Lady Windermere's Fan*
Yeats: *The Countess Cathleen*
1893
Gissing: *The Odd Woman*
Wilde: *Salome*
1894
Kipling: *The Jungle Book*
William Morris: *The Wood beyond the World*
1895
Hardy: *Jude the Obscure*
H. G. Wells: *The Time Machine*
Wilde: *The Importance of Being Earnest*
Yeats: Poems
1897
Henry James: *What Maisie Knew*
H. G. Wells: *The Invisible Man*
Yeats: 'The Secret Rose'
1898
Conrad: *The Nigger of the Narcissus*
Hardy: *Wessex Poems*
Henry James: 'The Turn of the Screw'
Shaw: *Arms and the Man*
Mrs Warren's Profession
H. G. Wells: *The War of the Worlds*
Wilde: *Ballad of Reading Gaol*

1880
Liberal administration formed by Gladstone
1883
Karl Marx dies
1885
General Gordon dies at Khartoum
1886
Gladstone brings in Home Rule Bill for Ireland
Second reading of Home Rule Bill brings Liberal defeat
1887
The Golden Jubilee of Queen Victoria
1888
Local Government Act (establishes local councils)
1890
Parnell resigns as Irish Nationalist leader
1893
Jan. Independent Labour Party formed by Kier Hardie at Bradford conference
1898
19 May Gladstone dies

Literature	Events
1899	**1899**
Henry James: *The Awkward Age*	Boer War begins
John Cowper Powys: *Poems* (published)	
1900	**1900**
Conrad: *Lord Jim*	British Labour Party founded
Saintsbury: *History of Criticism*	Commonwealth of Australia proclaimed
1901	**1901**
Kipling: *Kim*	Queen Victoria dies and Edward VII accedes to the throne
Shaw: *The Devil's Disciple*	
1902	**1902**
Conrad: *Heart of Darkness*	Boer War ends
Hardy: *Poems of the Past and the Present*	Secondary schools established by Education Act for England and Wales
Henry James: *Wings of a Dove*	
Yeats: *Cathleen ni Houlihan*	
1903	**1903**
Henry James: *The Ambassadors*	Emmeline Pankhurst founds the Women's Social and Political Union
Shaw: *Man and Superman*	Orville and Wilbur Wright's first flight
1904	**1904**
Bradley: *Shakespearean Tragedy*	Entente Cordiale between Britain and France
Henry James: *The Golden Bowl*	
Yeats: *The King's Threshold*	
Stories of Red Hanrahan	
1905	**1905**
Shaw: *Major Barbara*	Unrest in Russia
Wilde: *De Profundis*	
1906	
Yeats: *Poetical Works* (two volumes – 1907)	
1907	
Conrad: *The Secret Agent*	
Nostromo	
1908	
Forster: *A Room with a View*	
	1909
	Institution of a system of old age pensions for all persons over 70 years of age
1910	**1910**
Forster: *Howard's End*	Death of Edward VII; accession of George V
	Commons resolution to reduce the life of Parliament from seven to five years with restrictions on the power of the Lords' veto
1911	**1911**
Rupert Brooke: Poems	Passage of the Copyright Act: copies of all British publications go to the British Museum and five other copyright libraries
Conrad: *Under Western Eyes*	National Insurance Bill introduced by Lloyd George
Lawrence: *The White Peacock*	Suffragette riots in London
1912	**1912**
R. Bridges: *Poetical Works*	Common's reject Women's Franchise Bill
Shaw: *Androcles and the Lion*	
1913	**1913**
Lawrence: *Sons and Lovers*	Commons pass Irish Home Rule Bill, rejected by the Lords
	Suffragette demonstrations in London
	'Cat and Mouse' Act
1914	**1914**
Joyce: *The Dubliners*	Germany declares war on Russia: start of the First World War
	Britain declares war on Germany
1915	**1915**
Buchan: *The Thirty-Nine Steps*	Second Battle of Ypres
F. Madox Ford: *The Good Soldier*	English and French forces land at Gallipoli
Lawrence: *The Rainbow*	
Somerset Maugham: *Of Human Bondage*	
Virginia Woolf: *The Voyage Out*	

1916
Joyce: *A Portrait of the Artist as a Young Man*
Shaw: *Pygmalion*
1917
T. S. Eliot: *Prufrock and Other Observations*
Henry James: *The Ivory Tower*
Shaw: *Heartbreak House*
Yeats: 'The Wild Swans at Coole'
1918
Rupert Brooke: *Collected Poems*
G. M. Hopkins: *Poems* (published)
Katherine Mansfield: 'Prelude'

1919
T. S. Eliot: Poems (published)
Hardy: *Collected Poems*
Sassoon: *The War Poems* (published)
1920
Katherine Mansfield 'Bliss'
Wilfred Owen: Poems
Pound: *Hugh Selwyn Mauberley*
1921
Lawrence: *Women in Love*
1922
T. S. Eliot: *The Waste Land*
Galsworthy: *The Forsyte Saga*
A. E. Housman: *Last Poems*
Aldous Huxley: *Mortal Coils*
Joyce: *Ulysses*
Yeats: *Later Poems*

1924
Forster: *A Passage to India*
Shaw: *St Joan*
Mary Webb: *Precious Bane*
1925
I. A. Richards: *Principles of Literary Criticism*
Virginia Woolf: *Mrs Dalloway*
1926
Lawrence: *The Plumed Serpent*
Sassoon: *Satirical Poems*
1927
R. Graves: Poems
Virginia Woolf: *To the Lighthouse*
1928
Lawrence: *Lady Chatterley's lover*
Selected Poems
Evelyn Waugh: *Decline and Fall*
Virginia Woolf: *Orlando*
Yeats: 'The Tower'
1929
R. Graves: *Good-bye to All That*
I. A. Richards: *Practical Criticism*

1930
Hardy: *Collected Poems*
Lawrence: *The Virgin and the Gypsy*
Masefield (becomes Poet Laureate – 1967)
Shaw: *The Apple Cart*
1931
Virginia Woolf: *The Waves*

1916
The Battle of Verdun
Lloyd George becomes Prime Minister
1917
Abdication of Czar Nicholas II
United States declares war on Germany
The October Revolution: Lenin leads Bolsheviks against Kerensky in Russia
1918
Second Battle of the Somme
Second Battle of the Marne
Execution of Nicholas II
Women over 30 given the vote
1919
Peace conference at Versailles adopts Covenant of the League of Nations
The Treaty of Versailles signed
1920
The League of Nations formed
The Government of the Ireland Act passed: providing for North and South to have their own Parliaments

1922
Proclamation of the Irish Free State
Mussolini joins Fascist government in Italy

1923
Establishment of the USSR
Equality in divorce proceedings given to women by the British Matrimonial Causes Act
1924
Ramsay MacDonald forms first Labour government

1925
British Unemployment Insurance Act

1926
May General Strike
Germany joins the League of Nations
1927
German financial and economic crisis
Rise of Stalin: expulsion of Trotsky
1928
Minimum voting age for women reduced to 21 from 30 years

1929
General Election victory for Labour Party
The Wall Street Crash: collapse of US Stock Exchange
1930
Gandhi begins his campaign of civil disobedience
Nazis win seats from moderates in German Elections

1931
The New Party formed by Oswald Mosley
National government formed by Ramsay MacDonald
Invergordon naval mutiny

1932
T. S. Eliot: *Sweeney Agonistes*
Aldous Huxley: *Brave New World*
F. R. Leavis: *New Bearings in English Poetry*
Evelyn Waugh: *Black Mischief*

1932
Hunger marches in Britain
Nazis gain majority in German parliament

1933
A. E. Housman: *The Name and Nature of Poetry*
Orwell: *Down and Out in Paris and London*
H. G. Wells: *The Shape of Things to Come*

1933
Adolf Hitler becomes Chancellor of Germany
Persecution of the Jews in Germany begins

1934
Evelyn Waugh: *A Handful of Dust*

1934
The British Union of Fascists addressed by Oswald Mosley
Adolf Hitler becomes Führer
Purge in the Russian Communist Party

1935
Auden (and Isherwood): *The Dog Beneath the Skin*
T. S. Eliot: *Murder in the Cathedral*
Empson: *Some Versions of Pastoral*
Spender: 'The Destructive Element'

1936
Aldous Huxley: *Eyeless in Gaza*
Dylan Thomas: *Twenty-five Poems*
Yeats: *Modern Poetry*

1936
Penguin Books founded
Accession of Edward VIII on death of George V
Spanish Civil War starts
The abdication of Edward VIII

1937
Orwell: *The Road to Wigan Pier*

1937
Irish Free State becomes Eire

1938
Auden (and Isherwood): *On the Frontier*
Beckett: *Murphy*
G. Greene: *Brighton Rock*
Macneice: *Modern Poetry*
Evelyn Waugh: *Scoop*
Yeats: *New Poems*

1938
Munich conference

1939
G. Granville Barker: 'Elegy on Spain'
T. S. Eliot: *The Family Reunion*
Isherwood: *Goodbye to Berlin*
Joyce: *Finnegans Wake*
Spender: 'The New Realism'
Poems for Spain

1939
Franco secures the surrender of Madrid: end of the Spanish Civil War
Britain and France declare war on Germany: start of the Second World War

1940
T. S. Eliot: 'East Coker'
G. Greene: *The Power and the Glory*
Dylan Thomas: *Portrait of the Artist as a Young Dog*

1940
National government formed, Churchill becomes Prime Minister
Evacuation of Dunkirk
Battle of Britain
Start of the Blitz: German night-time raids on London

1941
T. S. Eliot: 'Burnt Norton'
Virginia Woolf: *Between the Acts*

1941
Japanese bomb Pearl Harbour
United States declares war on Germany and Italy

1942
T. S. Eliot: 'Little Gidding'
Sassoon: *The Weald of Youth*
Spender: 'Ruins and Visions'

1943
T. S. Eliot: 'Four Quartets'
G. Greene: *The Ministry of Fear*
Kathleen Raine: *Stone and Flower: Poems* 1935–1943
Dylan Thomas: *New Poems*

1943
Germany surrenders at Stalingrad
Surrender of Italy

1944
Macneice: *Springboard: Poems* 1941–1944

1944
Butler's Education Act
'D-Day' landings on Normandy beaches

1945
Isherwood: *Prater Violet*
Larkin: 'The North Ship'
Orwell: *Animal Farm: A Fairy Story*
Evelyn Waugh: *Brideshead Revisited*

1946
Orwell: *Collected Essays*

1947
Larkin: *A Girl in Winter*
Lowry: *Under the Volcano*
Spender: *Poems of Dedication*

1948
G. Greene: *The Heart of the Matter*
F. R. Leavis: *The Great Tradition*
Pound: *Cantos 1–84*
Rattigan: *The Browning Version*
Evelyn Waugh: *The Loved One*

1949
T. S. Eliot: *The Cocktail Party*
Christopher Fry: *The Lady's Not for Burning*
Stevie Smith: *The Holiday*

1950
G. Greene: *The Third Man*
Doris Lessing: *The Grass is Singing*

1951
Larkin: *Poems*

1952
Beckett: *Waiting for Godot*
Doris Lessing: *Martha Quest*

1953
Orwell: *England, Your England*

1954
Kingsley Amis: *Lucky Jim*
Golding: *Lord of the Flies*
Thom Gunn: *Poems*
Dylan Thomas: *Under Milk Wood*

1955
Empson: *Collected Poems*
G. Greene: *The Quiet American*

1956
J. Osborne: *Look Back in Anger*

1957
Beckett: *Endgame*
Iris Murdoch: *The Sandcastle*
Patrick White: *Voss*

1945
The Yalta conference: meeting between Churchill, Roosevelt and Stalin
Mussolini dies
Death of Hitler
'VE' day
The Potsdam conference: meeting between Churchill and Atlee, Stalin and Truman
The United States drops atomic bombs on Hiroshima and Nagasaki
The surrender of Japan; end of Second World War
Labour win General Election

1946
United Nations General Assembly holds its first meeting
Arts Council founded
National Insurance comes into effect

1947
Nationalisation of the Coal Industry
Independence of India and Pakistan founded

1948
National Health Service founded
Nationalisation of British Railways
Berlin blockade and airlift
British Citizenship Act: Commonwealth citizens granted subject status
UN convention on Human Rights and Genocide

1949
Beginning of South African apartheid
North Atlantic Treaty signed by Britain, France, Belgium, Netherlands, Italy, Portugal, Denmark, Iceland, Norway, United States and Canada
Proclamation of the Republic of Eire
Proclamation of the Communist People's Republic of China

1950
Korean War begins

1951
The Festival of Britain
Conservatives win British General Election

1952
Death of George VI; accession of Elizabeth II
British atomic bomb announced
Mau Mau troubles in Kenya

1953
Death of Stalin
Coronation of Elizabeth II

1954
Nasser becomes Egyptian Premier

1955
West Germany admitted to NATO
Universal Copyright Convention

1956
Suez crisis
Russian invasion of Hungary

1957
The Common Market Founded when Treaty of Rome signed
The Wolfenden report on homosexuality and prostitution
Launch of Sputnik I
Independence of Ghana (formerly Gold Coast)

1958 G. Greene: *Our Man in Havana* C. Achebe: *Things Fall Apart* Alan Sillitoe: *Saturday Night and Sunday Morning*	**1958** The appearance of Beatniks
1959 John Arden: *Serjeant Musgrave's Dance* Beckett: *Krapp's Last Tape* Alan Sillitoe: *The Loneliness of the Long-Distance Runner* Muriel Spark: *Memento Mori* Wesker: *Roots* M. Horovitz founds *New Departures*	**1959** Obscene Publications Act
1960 Pinter: *The Birthday Party* *The Caretaker* *The Dumb Waiter*	**1960** 'Wind of Change' speech made by Macmillan Kennedy wins US Presidential election from Nixon
1961 G. Greene: *A Burnt-out Case* Thom Gunn: 'My Sad Captains' Ted Hughes: 'Meet My Folks!' Elizabeth Jennings: 'Song for a Birth or a Death' Iris Murdoch: *A Severed Head* John Osborne: *Luther* Muriel Spark: *The Prime of Miss Jean Brodie* V. S. Naipaul: *A House for Mr Biswas*	**1961** Yuri Gagarin becomes first man in space Britain applies for membership of the EEC East Germany closes the border between East and West Berlin The Berlin Wall Mass CND Rally in Trafalgar Square
1962 Anthony Burgess: *A Clockwork Orange* Margaret Drabble: *A Summer Bird-Cage* Ted Hughes (and Thom Gunn): *Selected Poems* Doris Lessing: *The Golden Notebook* David Storey: *This Sporting Life* Wesker: *Chips with Everything*	**1962** The United States blockades Cuba: the 'Cuban missile crisis'
1963 Nell Dunn: *Up the Junction* Iris Murdoch: *The Unicorn* C. P. Snow: *Corridors of Power*	**1963** The Beatles become popular Britain refused Common Market Entry The Profumo scandal: Profumo resigns The assassination of President Kennedy
1964 Bellow: *Herzog* Ann Jellicoe: *The Knack* Peter Schaffer: *The Royal Hunt of the Sun*	**1964** Harlem race riots in US Martin Luther King awarded Nobel peace prize Wilson forms Labour administration on resignation of Alec Douglas-Home Fighting in Vietnam
1965 John Fowles: *The Magus*	**1965** Edward Heath becomes Leader of the Conservative Party Death penalty abolished
1966 John Fowles: *The Magus* G. Greene: *The Comedians* Tom Stoppard: *Rosencrantz and Guildenstern are Dead*	**1966** Labour win British General Election Cultural Revolution in China
1967 Angela Carter: *The Magic Toyshop* Nell Dunn: *Poor Cow* Peter Nichols: *A Day in the Death of Joe Egg* Pinter: *The Tea Party and Other Plays* David Storey: *The Restoration of Arnold Middleton*	**1967** Legalization of homosexuality and abortion
1968 C. Day-Lewis (becomes Poet Laureate – 1972) Roy Fuller: *New Poems*	**1968** Assassinations of Bobby Kennedy and Martin Luther King Civil Rights Bill passed in the United States United Nations adopts Nuclear Non-proliferation treaty Richard M. Nixon elected President of the United States

1969
John Fowles: *The French Lieutenant's Woman*
G. Greene: *Travels with My Aunt*
Pound: *Cantos CX–CXVII* (published)
Booker Prize first awarded
1970
Ted Hughes: 'Crow'
Larkin: 'All What Jazz?'
1971
Edward Bond: *Lear*
Forster: *Maurice*
Thom Gunn: 'Moly'
Roger McGough: *After the Merrymaking*
Iris Murdoch: *An Accidental Man*
1972
John Betjeman becomes Poet Laureate
Margaret Drabble: *The Needle's Eye*
Ted Hughes: 'Crow' (enlarged edition)
Elizabeth Jennings: 'Relationships'
1973
Iris Murdoch: *The Black Prince*
1974
Auden: *Thank You Fog: Last Poems*
Beckett: *Not I*
Thom Gunn: 'Mandrakes'
'Song Book'
Doris Lessing: *The Memoirs of a Survivor*
1975
Bradbury: *The History Man*
Lodge: *Changing Places*
1976
New National Theatre completed
1977
National Poetry Centre dissolved
Tom Stoppard: *Professional Foul*
1978
David Hare: *Plenty*
Iris Murdoch: *The Sea, The Sea*
Emma Tennant: *The Bad Sister*
Fay Weldon: *Praxis*
1979
S. Heaney: *Field Walk*
C. Raine: *A Martian Sends a Postcard Home*
1980
Anthony Burgess: *Earthly Powers*
William Golding: *Rites of Passage*
1981
Edward Bond: *Restoration*
Salman Rushdie: *Midnight's Children*
1983
William Golding wins Nobel Prize for Literature
Fay Weldon: *The Life and Loves of a She-Devil*
1984
Kingsley Amis: *Stanley and the Women*
Anita Brookner: *Hôtel Du Lac*
Angela Carter: *Nights at the Circus*
Seamus Heaney: *Station Island*
Ted Hughes becomes Poet Laureate
D.H. Lawrence: *Mr Noon*
David Lodge: *Small World*
Craig Raine: *Rich*

1969
First American moon landings
1970
Lowering of the voting age in Britain to 18
Conservative win in British General Election
1971
Anti-Vietnam War demonstration in Washington
1972
Direct rule by British government in Northern Ireland
1973
Signing of Vietnam peace agreement
Britain joins the EEC
1974
Solzhenitsyn's expulsion from the USSR
General Election in Britain with no overall majority
Labour wins second General Election
The 'Watergate' scandal: Nixon resigns
1975
End of the Vietnam War
1979
Winter of discontent
Conservatives win General Election
1980
Soviet invasion of Afghanistan
American hostages in Iran
1981
Riots in London, Liverpool and Manchester
1982
The Falklands War
1983
Conservative victory in General Election
Anti-nuclear protests at Greenham Common
The Ballykelly Bombing
1984
Miner's strike

1985
Peter Ackroyd: *Hawksmoor*
Peter Carey: *Illywhacker*
Douglas Dunn: *Elegies*
David Hare: *Pravda*
Fay Weldon: *Polaris*

1985
Famine in Ethiopia – Live Aid concerts raise money for famine relief

1986
Kingsley Amis: *The Old Devils*
Margaret Atwood: *The Handmaid's Tale*
Wole Soyinka wins Nobel Prize for Literature

1986
Chernobyl nuclear power station explosion–radioactive cloud over much of Europe

1987
Peter Ackroyd: *Chatterton*
Caryl Churchill: *Serious Money*
Seamus Heaney: *The Haw Lantern*

1987
Conservative party wins third term of office
British government attempts to ban publication of Peter Wright's *Spycatcher*
'Black Monday' – British stock market crash

1988
Ayckbourn: *Henceforward*
Peter Carey: *Oscar and Lucinda*
Douglas Dunn: *Northlight*
David Lodge: *Nice Work*
Marina Warner: *The Lost Father*
Salman Rushdie: *Satanic Verses*

1988
Bicentenary of Australia

1989
Margaret Atwood: *Cat's Eye*
Peter Ackroyd: *First Light*
Anthony Burgess: *Any Old Iron*
Elizabeth Jennings: *Tributes*
Kazuo Ishiguro: *The Remains of the Day*
Martin Amis: *London Fields*
Ramsey Cambell: *Ancient Images*

1989
Russian troops complete withdrawal from Afghanistan
Controversy over *Satanic Verses* results in death threat to Salman Rushdie, who goes into hiding
Revolutions in Eastern Europe and beginnings of the break-up of the Warsaw Pact

1990
Peter Ackroyd: *Dickens*
A. S. Byatt: *Possession* (which wins the Booker Prize)
Nadine Gordimer: *My Son's Story*
John McGahern: *Amongst Women*
Brian Moore: *Lies of Silence*

1990
Nelson Mandela freed in South Africa and ANC unbanned
Iraq invades Kuwait
John Major replaces Margaret Thatcher as conservative Prime Minister of Britain
Revolutions in Eastern Europe continue
Reunification of Germany

1991
Fleur Adcock: *Time Zones*
Kingsley Amis: *Memoirs*
Martin Amis: *Time's Arrow*
Margaret Atwood: *Wilderness Tips*
Angela Carter: *Wise Children*
J. G. Ballard: *The Kindness of Women*
Bret Easton Ellis: *American Psycho*
Seamus Heaney: *Seeing Things*
Nadine Gordimer wins Nobel Prize for Literature and publishes *Jump*
Dan Jacobson: *Hidden in the Heart*
Caryl Phillips: *Cambridge*
Helen Zahavi: *Dirty Weekend*

1991
Gulf War
Attempted Coup in USSR; Mikhail Gorbachev resigns and Boris Yeltsin oversees break-up of Soviet Union. Soviet regions recognised as independent countries
British hostages Jackie Mann, John McCarthy and Terry Waite released

1992
Ramsey Cambell: *Waking Nightmares*
Angela Carter: *Expletives Deleted* (published posthumously)
Thom Gunn: *The Man with Night Sweats*
Tony Harrison: *The Common Chorus*
Ben Okri: *An African Elegy*
D. M. Thomas: *Flying into Love*
Barry Unsworth: *Sacred Hunger*

1992
Trade barriers within European Community lifted to form single market.
General Election in Britain results in fourth term of office for the Conservative party
Presidential Election in USA